W9-ATE-084

RUFUS KING

The Institute of Early American History and Culture is sponsored jointly by the College of William and Mary and Colonial Williamsburg, Incorporated.

RUFUS KING
From an engraving by William S. Leney
of a watercolor by Joseph S. Wood
Delaplaine's Repository, 1815

Library of Congress Catalog Card Number 68–15747
Printed by Heritage Printers, Inc.
Manufactured in the United States of America

RUFUS KING

AMERICAN FEDERALIST

by

ROBERT ERNST

Published for the
Institute of Early American History and (
at Williamsburg, Virginia, by
The University of North Carolina Press • (

To James Gore King
whose scholarly research
and reasoned judgments have
contributed much to the writing
of this book

PREFACE

THIS LIFE OF RUFUS KING SEEKS TO AVOID IMPRESSIONISM, QUESTIONABLE generalizations about the "life and times," and exaggeration of the man's importance. Though he was not in the same class with Hamilton or Jefferson, King was foremost in the second rank of political figures in the early years of the United States. Strangely enough, there never has been an adequate biography of him. The six-volume *Life and Correspondence of Rufus King* (New York, 1894–1900), edited by his grandson, Charles R. King, has frequently been used by scholars for source material illuminating the politics of the early national period, but few have read through these volumes. The old-fashioned and adulatory *Life and Correspondence* has been in effect a literary coffin, whose lid has been lifted almost exclusively by professional historians and graduate students. One other work, Edward H. Brush's *Rufus King and His Times* (New York, 1926), has been on college reading lists, but it is no biography—merely a sketch of 159 pages, deficient in scholarship, stilted in style, and ridiculously laudatory. The biographer's inattention to King may be partly explained by the relative paucity of personal material in the major collection of his papers at the New-York Historical Society, the compressed and often colorless style of his letters, and the conventionality and rectitude of his private life.

With the recent revival of interest in early American conservatism, scholars have turned their attention to various lesser, local figures, contributing to a fuller understanding of the Federalists than had been possible when interest was so largely focused on men like Hamilton, Jay, Gouverneur Morris, and H. G. Otis. Moreover, Page Smith's recent life of John Adams, the biographies of Hamilton by Broadus Mitchell and John C. Miller, and Clinton Rossiter's *Alex-*

ander Hamilton and the Constitution have been singularly revealing. Miller's *Federalist Era*, Shaw Livermore's *Twilight of Federalism*, and David H. Fischer's *Revolution of American Conservatism* are fine, up-to-date treatments. Among other works of merit are Manning J. Dauer's *Adams Federalists* and Stephen G. Kurtz's *Presidency of John Adams*. The publication of the Adams Papers and the recent editions of the papers of Hamilton, Jefferson, Madison, and Clay make all the more desirable a modern biography of King. In this book I have tried to meet the need by presenting as straightforward and detailed an account as is possible in a single volume. Abbreviations in quoted material have been spelled out in accordance with the expanded style for quotations.

I have had the good fortune to enjoy unlimited access to the letters and notebooks of Rufus King now possessed by his great-great-grandson, James Gore King of New York. Mr. King has generously shared with me his collection of related source materials and copies of letters and other documents. His scholarly researches into the family background and earlier career of Rufus King have saved me considerable time and expense, as have his accurate and lengthy transcriptions of voluminous documents in the Public Record Office in London. Through many conferences I have benefited from his knowledge and insights into the Revolutionary and early national periods of American history. His carefully detailed study, Rufus King, Young Statesman of Massachusetts, 1755–1789, is available in a three-volume typescript in the Harvard College Library.

Although it would be impossible to acknowledge personally the aid of all who have contributed to this book, I wish to thank, in addition to Mr. King, the staff of the New-York Historical Society, particularly its director, Dr. James J. Heslin, Messrs. Wilmer R. Leech and Arthur J. Breton, Miss Geraldine Beard, and Miss Rachel Minick, for their constant helpfulness. I am also grateful to the staff of the manuscript and rare book rooms of the New York Public Library; Miss Sylvia C. Hilton and Miss Helen Ruskell of the New York Society Library; Mr. John Alden, acting curator of rare books, Boston Public Library; Mr. Albert Blair of the National Archives; the staff of the manuscript division of the Library of Congress; Mr. Stephen T. Riley and staff of the Massachusetts Historical Society; the staff of the Harvard University Archives; the staff of the department of special collections of the Columbia University Libraries; Mrs. Ann Bowden, librarian of the Humanities Research Center,

University of Texas; Dr. Allan Nevins and Mrs. Helen S. Mangold of the Henry E. Huntington Library; Mrs. Alice P. Hook, formerly librarian of the Cincinnati Historical Society; Mr. Irving Brant, who kindly allowed me to use his notes on James Madison; Mr. John Pickering of Salem, Massachusetts, who permitted me to make notes of some Pickering family papers; Miss Mary A. Benjamin of New York City, who let me examine several King letters in her possession; Mr. S. L. de Vausney, vice-president and secretary of the Bank of New York, who guided me to the early manuscript records in the vault of that bank; Miss Helen Rose Cline, parish recorder of Trinity Church, New York City, for supplying me with extracts from the church's vestry minutes; and the Earl of Leicester and his librarian, Dr. W. O. Hassall of the Bodleian Library. In addition, I wish to acknowledge grants-in-aid from the Penrose Fund of the American Philosophical Society, the Henry E. Huntington Library, and Adelphi University, the latter in the form of a semester's reduced teaching schedule.

Permission to quote from manuscripts has been granted to me by the following institutions: the Cincinnati Historical Society, the William L. Clements Library at the University of Michigan, the Connecticut Historical Society (Hartford), the Columbia University Libraries, the Essex Institute (Salem, Mass.), the Forbes Library (Northampton, Mass.), the Historical Society of Pennsylvania (Philadelphia), the Henry E. Huntington Library (San Marino, Calif.), the Indiana University Libraries, the Maine Historical Society (Portland), the Massachusetts Historical Society (Boston), the Pierpont Morgan Library (New York), the New-York Historical Society, the New York Society Library, the Franklin D. Roosevelt Library (Hyde Park, N. Y.), the Library of the University of Texas, and the Yale University Library. I am grateful to the directors of these institutions.

Finally, I wish to acknowledge the wise suggestions and conscientious editing of James Morton Smith of the Institute of Early American History and Culture, and his associate editor, Miss Susan Lee Foard. I am also grateful for the assistance of their successors at the Institute, Stephen G. Kurtz and Marise Rogge.

ROBERT ERNST

CONTENTS

LIST OF ILLUSTRATIONS

RUFUS KING

CHAPTER I

PROLOGUE IN MAINE

IN 1804, NEARLY FORTY YEARS AFTER RUFUS KING HAD FIRST BECOME A student at Dummer School, he returned with his wife and two nieces to the small Massachusetts town of Byfield, not far from Newburyport, to pay a sentimental visit to the academy. Almost before his driver had halted in front of the home of Deacon Joseph Hale, King was out of his coach and into the house. He went immediately to the attic room which had served as a dormitory for Dummer boys and proudly showed his family his name, carved there years before.[1]

King was only twelve years old when in 1766 he left his home in Scarborough, Maine, for Dummer. His classmates came from all levels of New England society; some of them were destined for farming and seafaring, others for the counting house and the professions. Dummer was the first private school to be chartered in New England, and Samuel Moody, the headmaster, was a Harvard graduate who had been recommended for the position by the great evangelist, George Whitefield. As a teacher of Latin, Greek, and French, Master Moody set high standards of promptness, thoroughness, and accuracy. A large man with rugged features, he wore a long green flannel gown and a tasseled smoking-cap as he sat before his pupils in the gabled, one-room schoolhouse. Beside him lay his disciplinary aids—a rod, a long ruler, and an assortment of switches

1. B. J. Porter to William King, Sept. 18, 1804, William King Papers, Maine Historical Society, Portland, Me.

suited to victims of various ages. His strict demeanor relaxed at times, and he would smile, glance roguishly about, tell a funny story, and join in the laughter of his pupils. Then, at a tap of his finger he would quell the uproar and restore order. Moody sometimes played with the boys in their outdoor activities and sports, and if high tide occurred during study hours he might call a break and permit a swim in the Parker River.[2]

The country life in Byfield was nothing new for Rufus. He had been born at Dunstan Landing, a part of the Maine frontier village of Scarborough, three miles upstream from the mouth of the Scarborough River. The family home, one of the more imposing residences in Scarborough, was a mark of his father's standing in the community. The King "mansion" had two stories and an attic, with a kitchen wing extending from one end of the house. Nearby were a large barn and other outbuildings where the King children played with the farm animals and a pet deer. When they tired of their games there, the children could run in the pasture and woods, explore the tidal marshes of the Maine coast, or watch the harvesting of salt marsh hay.

Since the beginning of the century New Englanders had settled in this vicinity, lured by the fisheries and the lumber trade. The demand for Maine pine, the building of ships at the wharves, and the export of masts for the Royal Navy had given Dunstan Landing considerable importance. By the middle of the century it compared favorably with Falmouth (later Portland) and Kittery and attracted enterprising young men eager to advance their fortunes. Here Rufus's father Richard King had settled in 1748.

Richard was the son of John King, an English cutler and swordmaker who had emigrated to Boston late in the seventeenth century and married Mary Stowell of Newton, daughter of David Stowell, a weaver, and granddaughter of Samuel Stowell, a blacksmith and early settler of Hingham.[3]

2. James G. King, Rufus King, Young Statesman of Massachusetts, 1755–1789 (unpubl. Ph.D. diss., Harvard University, 1960), ch. 3; Nehemiah Cleaveland, *The First Century of Dummer Academy* (Boston, 1865), 20–27; John L. Ewell, *The Story of Byfield, a New England Parish* (Boston, 1904), 116. The 18th-century Scarborough is now West Scarboro.

3. Writ served on John King, Sept. 3, 1717, Records of the Court of Common Pleas of Suffolk County (Oct. 1717), Suffolk County Court House, Boston; undated statement of Aaron Porter, son-in-law of Richard King, Porter Papers, Craigie-Longfellow House, Cambridge, Mass.; Charles R. King, "Richard King," *Maine Historical and Genealogical Recorder*, I (1884), 152; George

Richard, the eldest of nine children, was born in 1718. Before he was twenty years old he became interested in the settlement of Maine; he and two uncles were among sixty participants in an unsuccessful plan to settle what later became Paris, Maine.[4] In the early 1740's this ambitious and energetic young man became a carpenter and housewright in Watertown, where he also served as a timber buyer for a Boston merchant. In 1745 Governor Shirley appointed him commissary of subsistence, with the rank of captain, on William Pepperrell's expedition that besieged and reduced the French fortress of Louisbourg.[5]

King gained status from his military appointment, and after a brief stay in Boston, moved to Maine. He bought land at Dunstan Landing and became known there as "Richard King of Scarboro, Gentleman."[6] To style oneself a gentleman in Scarborough must have seemed presumptuous to some of the local farmers and woodsmen, for Scarborough was a rustic town. Most of its people lived close to nature, fishing and trapping the abundant beaver in the nearby streams. In the forests bears and wolves roamed about, and hunters combined the pleasure of hunting with the duty of protecting their families.

The Indian menace was gradually abating as garrisons were built and manned. Newer settlements some distance from the coast were still the object of raids, but the Indians usually refrained from attacking the fortified coastal towns.[7]

Austin Morrison, Jr., King Families of New England (typescript in New York Public Library, New York, 1911), II, 155–56; Record Commissioners of the City of Boston, *Report . . . containing the Boston Marriages from 1700 to 1751* (Boston, 1898), 97; W. H. H. Stowell, *Stowell Genealogy . . .* (Rutland, Vt., 1922). Charles R. King, ed., *The Life and Correspondence of Rufus King*, 6 vols. (N. Y., 1894–1900), I, 1, states erroneously that Mary Stowell was the daughter of Benjamin Stowell.

4. William B. Lapham and S. P. Maxim, *The History of Paris, Maine . . .* (Paris, Me., 1884), 23–24, 56.

5. Henry Bond, *Family Memorials. Genealogies of the Families and Descendants of the Early Settlers of Watertown, Massachusetts* (Boston, 1855), 326–27; C. S. Ensign, Watertown . . . the South Side . . . (typescript, Historical Society of Watertown [Mass.], 1890); Middlesex County Deeds, XLV, 96, Middlesex County Court House, Cambridge, Mass.; William S. Southgate's sketch of Richard King [1852], Box A, Rufus King Papers, New-York Historical Society, N.Y.C.; King, ed., *King Correspondence*, I, 2; J. G. King, Rufus King, 3–4.

6. William S. Southgate, "History of Scarborough," Maine Hist. Soc., *Collections*, 3 (1853), 213.

7. *Ibid.*, 173–75; Dorothy S. Libbey, *Scarborough Becomes a Town* (Freeport, Me., 1955), 99.

Within a short time Richard King had become the most prominent merchant and citizen of Scarborough. He acquired his own sawmill and built himself a larger home. He constructed and bought ships, loading them with masts and lumber and sending them to England and the West Indies. At the warehouse near his home he opened a large store.[8] Less than a year after he came to Scarborough he was chosen as road surveyor; a few years later he was parish treasurer and foreman of a jury that laid out the road from Dunstan to Saco; and in 1755 he was chosen to the first of his four terms as selectman.[9]

In 1753, five years after moving to Scarborough, King married Isabella Bragdon, a daughter of Samuel Bragdon of York, Maine.[10] On March 24, 1755, Rufus was born. The couple had two other children, Mary, born November 1756, and Paulina, in March 1759. Seven months after the birth of Paulina, when Rufus was four and a half years old, Isabella King died. Mary Black, a first cousin of Mrs. King, hurried to Dunstan Landing to keep house for Richard King and his three small children. An ingenuous, warmhearted, strong-willed, and deeply religious woman, Mary Black cared for Rufus, Mary, and Paulina as if they were her own. In January 1762 she married Richard King, who was nearly twice her age, and during the next ten years bore him three boys and three girls. Richard's widowed mother also came to live in the household.

A dominating personality, Mary King lived by a strict Puritan morality tempered by kindness. In the King family, the Ten Commandments and the Sermon on the Mount governed all, and the

8. Augustus F. Moulton, *Grandfather Tales of Scarborough* (Augusta, Me., 1925), 17; J. G. King, Rufus King, 10; Southgate's sketch of Richard King, Box A, King Papers, N.-Y. Hist. Soc.

9. Southgate, "History of Scarborough," Maine Hist. Soc., *Colls.*, 3 (1853), 187–88; Scarborough Town Records, Town Clerk's Office, Scarborough, Maine. The town meeting chose King as selectman in 1755, 1758, 1759, and 1769, and as surveyor of highways in 1760. *Ibid.*; Libbey, *Scarborough*, 269.

10. The Bragdons had lived in York since its earliest settlement, and Isabella's great-great-grandfather, Arthur Bragington or Bragdon, Gentleman, had been a planter, constable, and "Marshal of the Province of Maine." Isabella's mother, Tabitha Banks, was descended from other early settlers of York, Richard Banks, John Alcock, and Capt. Richard Bonython from Cornwall, an early proprietor of Saco. Her sister, also named Tabitha, married Stephen Longfellow and became a great-grandmother of Henry Wadsworth Longfellow. York Deeds, VI, 74, York County Court House, Alfred, Me.; C. E. Banks, Bragdon Genealogy, New England Historic Genealogical Society, Boston; George Folsom, *History of Saco and Biddeford* . . . (Saco, Me., 1830), 116, 119; J. G. King, Rufus King, 7–8.

Golden Rule, as a granddaughter recalled, was "practised as a part of the economy, and was regarded as an imperious duty."[11] Strict observance of the Sabbath was never questioned by the Kings; church attendance was taken for granted, and Sunday was always a day of rest. For Mary, outward appearance and material wealth were no substitute for honor and goodness of character. She warned her children against gambling, vice, and libertinism. They were admonished to be charitable and helpful to the poor and to be worthy Christians in every way.[12]

Mary King's devotion to the family's welfare was matched by Richard King's kindness and love of children. According to family tradition, he frequently kept adults waiting at his general store while he served the children. The Kings owned a number of slaves as domestic servants, at least six at various times, and they were treated, a granddaughter remembered, as kindly as if they were members of the family. On one occasion Richard King and his Congregational pastor, the Reverend Richard Elvins, consented to a marriage between Junior, one of Elvins's slaves, and Hannah, a slave of King's, and bound themselves and their heirs "not to oblige said slaves to serve further Distant apart from Each other than the Bounds of the Parish."[13]

Richard King was a self-educated man. Of the thirty-seven books inventoried at his death, thirteen were law books or collections of statutes, reflecting the legal concerns of a prosperous landed merchant. Locke's *Essay Concerning Human Understanding*, a biography of Frederick the Great, and the philosophical letters of that enlightened ruler doubtless appealed to King's rational and political predilections. His interest in the classics is suggested by the names he gave two of his children, Rufus and Cyrus, and by his copy of Caesar's *Commentaries*. In addition, he owned a commentary on the Bible, several volumes of the *Spectator*, and practical reference works. Essentially a sober man of serious interest, he was nevertheless whimsical enough to write occasional bits of verse.[14]

King remained active in town affairs for many years and was en-

11. Dorcas King Leland, unpublished Sketch of my Grandmother King, written Jan. 14, 1848, owned by Arthur Lord, Newton, Mass. Copy owned by James G. King, N. Y. C.

12. *Ibid.*

13. Agreement dated Nov. 30, 1768, typescript of copy owned by Frederick Gore Richards, Newcastle, Me., in possession of James G. King, N. Y. C.

14. Richard King Papers, including inventory of Richard King's estate, June 13, 1775, Box A, Rufus King Papers, N.-Y. Hist. Soc.

trusted with increasing responsibility. He helped to set the boundary line between Scarborough and Falmouth (Portland) townships and shared executive duties as a selectman. Twice the town voted to pay his bills for expenses in supporting its poor. His interest in the youth of Scarborough was demonstrated by his vote for town support of a grammar school. The town meeting, which as elsewhere in New England controlled local government and was a sounding board on all important local matters, three times chose him as constable.[15]

Richard King prospered in these years, becoming one of Maine's most enterprising merchants. He sent out cargoes in his own ships and became a leading lumber exporter. Since many of the steady customers at his store had little or no ready cash, some paid him in land, and he thereby acquired some three thousand acres of Scarborough real estate, including several farms. When he died, he left more than five hundred acres (valued at £1,663), five yoke of oxen, about forty head of cattle, sixty-one sheep, and four pigs.[16]

King did not press his debtors and allowed the obligations of many customers to accumulate for years. Nevertheless his rapid rise to wealth and prominence aroused the jealousy of some. A list of long overdue taxes which he drew up in 1758 as parish treasurer did not add to his popularity, and many townsmen refused to pay their arrears. When in 1765 he declined to serve as constable, a certain John Stewart sought to have him fined for not serving. A fine was imposed, but King, knowing that legal grounds for the fine were lacking, refused either to serve or to pay the fine. The hostile and envious Stewart then denounced him and sought to influence others against him. A witness afterward swore that he "heard John Stuart [Stewart] tell Mr. King that he was poor when he came to Scarbo. and that he got his Estate by wronging the Poor, and now we have found you out, and your reign is but short."[17]

This was no idle threat. On the night of March 19, 1766, some disgruntled men, most of whom owed money to King, were incited by Stewart to take matters into their own hands and destroy the evi-

15. Scarborough Town Records, Scarborough.

16. King, ed., *King Correspondence*, I, 2; inventory of Richard King's estate, Box A, King Papers, N.-Y. Hist. Soc.

17. J. G. King, Rufus King, 12–13; Scarborough Town Records, Scarborough; statement of Benjamin Carter, in folder of testimony relating to the riot of 1766, Box A, Rufus King Papers, N.-Y. Hist. Soc. The list of overdue taxes, once owned by Richard King Hale, was copied by James G. King, N. Y. C., and this copy is in his possession.

dence of their indebtedness. Disguised as Indians and roaring drunk, they headed for King's homestead. Arriving an hour after midnight, they smashed windows, broke into the house, and terrorized the family and servants. Before invading the house, one rioter threw a hatchet through a window, narrowly missing King and his wife who, suddenly awakened, had rushed into the hall. Mrs. King, then seven months pregnant, all but collapsed from the shock, and the children were terror-stricken.[18]

After ransacking King's desk and burning his private papers, including deeds to land and other securities, the mob defaced the house, demolished furniture and kitchenware, and forced their way into King's store to destroy more papers there.[19] "The Terror, and Distress, the Distraction and Horror" of Richard King's family, wrote John Adams, who served as his attorney, "cannot be described by Words or painted upon Canvass. It is enough to move a Statue, to melt an Heart of Stone, to read the Story. A Mind susceptible of the Feelings of Humanity . . . must burn with Resentment and Indignation at such outragious Injuries. These private Mobs I do and will detest."[20]

Soon after the attack, King found a threatening note on his gate. Those who sought to arrest the rioters would have their homes and barns burnt and they themselves would be "cut in pieces and burnt to ashes." The constable and sheriff's officers were likewise threatened with death when armed ruffians swarmed about King's house while several county magistrates were meeting there. Only two rioters were taken; one escaped on his way to jail, and the other was released in the hope that he would testify against the others.[21]

The events of March 1766 were not an isolated episode in a fron-

18. Testimony and petitions relating to the riot of 1766, and Richard King to Silas Burbank, May 31, 1773, Box A, King Papers, N.-Y. Hist. Soc.; J. G. King, Rufus King, 13–14.

19. Southgate, "History of Scarborough," Maine Hist. Soc., *Colls.*, 3 (1853), 183; Records of the Cumberland County Court of Common Pleas, IV (1773–85), 29–33, Cumberland County Court House, Portland, Me.

20. Lyman H. Butterfield, ed., *Adams Family Correspondence*, 2 vols. (Cambridge, Mass., 1963), I, 131. The editor's notes (132–34) provide interesting details, including a portion of Adams's emotional harangue to the jury in 1774. See also L. Kinvin Wroth and Hiller B. Zobel, eds., *Legal Papers of John Adams*, 3 vols. (Cambridge, Mass., 1965), I, 136–40.

21. This paragraph is based on documents in Box A, King Papers, N.-Y. Hist. Soc., and Wroth and Zobel, eds., *Legal Papers of Adams*, I, 117–23. See also J. G. King, Rufus King, 16–17.

tier settlement. A year earlier the Stamp Act adopted by the British Parliament had evoked heated demonstrations in America. In many communities Sons of Liberty, emboldened by liquor, erected liberty poles, planted liberty trees, and held clamorous torchlight processions. Mobs of farmers, mechanics, shopkeepers, laborers, seamen, and the unemployed terrorized both seaport and inland towns, embarrassing those influential merchants who originally had encouraged them. The Scarborough rioters who attacked Richard King's home in 1766 called themselves Sons of Liberty. King was denounced as a supporter of the Stamp Act and as a prospective "stamp master" for the town, but the assault upon him seems to have stemmed more directly from the hostility of debtors who resented his social pretension and economic power. Some townspeople denied his claim that the parish owed him money, and, without specifying precisely, a few charged that he took advantage of the poor.[22] These accusations were never proven. That the town meeting elected King as "field driver" only five days after the riot indicates sympathy for him rather than enmity.[23]

Richard King discovered that justice did not come easily to a wealthy creditor. Realizing that local arrest warrants were useless, he obtained a summons from the clerk of the Superior Court in Boston. He gathered witnesses and paid the expenses of many while they attended the grand jury meeting at Falmouth. Fourteen of the alleged culprits were indicted. The ensuing trial dragged on for years, however, and King turned to other means of obtaining justice. He petitioned the Massachusetts House of Representatives and later the Governor and Council to devise means for bringing the offenders to justice and for protecting his family and property from continued threats of violence. Meanwhile the rioters roamed at large. They set fire to a house occupied by one of King's tenants, and on the night of May 14, 1767, burned King's well-stocked barn to the ground, echoing Mrs. King's distressed cries with yells in the nearby bushes. Years afterward, King's widow exaggerated for the benefit

22. Wroth and Zobel, eds., *Legal Papers of Adams*, I, 106–40, presents documents in the case of King *v.* Stewart, including several depositions. See especially 121–25, 129, and 131. In notes taken by John Adams as King's lawyer, the Stamp Act appears only twice: in a statement by counsel for the rioters that the province was in an uproar over stamped paper, and in an instance of hearsay testimony that King favored the Stamp Act. Microfilm of the Adams Papers, Pt. III, Reel 185, John Adams, Miscellany, Legal Papers, Massachusetts Historical Society, Boston.

23. Scarborough Town Records, Scarborough.

of her youngest son the calmness with which his father "could sit down composed and read, when his barn was in flames, and his property destroying by a set of vile wretches whom [as his debtors] he had fed and clothed."[24]

Young Rufus must have shared the tension of the King household. It is strange that no mention of these violent attacks occurs in his surviving writings. His youthful resiliency or a subconscious urge to forget may explain his reference, at the age of twenty, to a happy childhood.[25] His frightening experiences, however, may have fostered his deep-rooted concern as an adult for protection against turbulence and lawlessness.

A measure of security and respect for law was slowly restored in Scarborough. Many townspeople remained Richard King's friends, but for years a Stewart faction lingered on. This faction included some active members of Scarborough's Second Church at Dunstan, which the Kings also attended. Mrs. King refused to take Communion as long as the rioters were permitted to do so,[26] and Richard King was scandalized by the presence of those whom he considered false Christians:

> If mixt with those, vile Sons there are,
> Who Burn and Steal, and fallsly Sware,
> Or make their Gain by such fowl Deeds,
> Select them Lord, as vitious weeds;

24. J. G. King, Rufus King, 17–19, and documents in Box A, King Papers, N.-Y. Hist. Soc.; Mary Black King to Cyrus King, July 5, 1793, contemporary excerpt owned by Mrs. John H. Thomas, New Haven, Conn.

25. Rufus King to Samuel Sewall, July 25, 1775, Box 84, King Papers, N.-Y. Hist. Soc.

26. Southgate. "History of Scarborough," Maine Hist. Soc., *Colls.*, 3 (1853), 184–85; J. G. King, Rufus King, 20. King had influential friends in Falmouth, including Col. Samuel Waldo, Stephen Longfellow, Theophilus Bradbury, and Enoch Freeman, who exerted themselves on his behalf. Not until several years after the initial riot, however, did King obtain any indemnification. The Superior Court reversed the county court's verdict on one count and awarded King £200 damages, a bare tenth of what he had calculated as his loss. Undaunted, he persisted in his claim, retaining John Adams as his attorney in the summer of 1774. King died before the drawn-out proceedings came to an end, and it was left to Rufus King, acting as attorney for his stepmother, to win a further judgment in 1784 of £136. Records of the Cumberland County Court of Common Pleas, IV (1773-85), 29–33, County Court House, Portland. Records of the Superior Court of Judicature (1773–74), 92, Office of Clerk of the Supreme Judicial Court, Suffolk County Court House, Boston, Mass.; Cumberland County Minute Book, 1783–89, Supreme Judicial Court, Suffolk County Court House; Wroth and Zobel, eds., *Legal Papers of Adams*, I, 106–40.

Shall falls Confession Save the Soul,
Who still retains what he has Stole,
Or having don his Neighbor wrong,
Will God be pleased with his Song[?][27]

The last nine years of Richard King's life were full of uncertainty, embarrassment, and humiliation. As a conservative property-holder and a defender of Great Britain, he recoiled from the extremism and violence that increasingly characterized the relations between the colonies and the mother country. He had no sympathy for those who rejected British authority. During the period of the tea riots, he penned an argument opposing revolution against England. "Our only Safety," he wrote, "is in remaining firm to that Stock of which we are a Branch; and as a prudent man guards against a Pestilential Air when a plague is in the City, so should we guard against those falls [false] patriots . . . who advise us to resist, breake off, and prevent that grand circulation whereby we are become a great Plant, contributing to the Strength and Glory of the Stock, whose Branches cover . . . every Quarter of the Earth and with our own unighted force able to repell at least, if not Totally to concour [conquer] any unity of power that can be formed against us on Earth or Sea." Rome in her glory was small, he added, when compared with the British Empire. He was particularly distressed that "happy subjects" living under a mild and free government could think of calling in foreign aid. "Can we merely out of Frowardness because we are rebuked for spurning at the demand, and refusing to pay the threepence duty on Tea" think of exchanging "our fair Possessions for Servitude, our liberties for an Inquisition, and content ourselves to drag out the remainder of our Days in wooden Shoes? Great God prevent our madness! Why then this calling to arms?"[28]

Such ardent Loyalism on the part of Scarborough's leading citizen could not fail to arouse suspicion in the tense atmosphere of the 1770's. Anti-British feeling had risen to a feverish level in America, especially in New England after General Gage's entry into Boston in May 1774 and the closing of the port. Mobs had already begun to attack Tories. In this atmosphere, little pretext was needed for

27. By Richard King, Box A, King Papers, N.-Y. Hist. Soc. These particular stanzas are quoted in Butterfield, ed., *Adams Family Corr.*, I, 133.

28. Richard King, unpubl. paper on seeking foreign aid in the Revolutionary War, 1774–1775?, Box A, King Papers, N.-Y. Hist. Soc.

another assault upon Richard King. In June one of his ships, laden with lumber, sailed from Salem into Boston Harbor, its master having obtained official permission from the British to enter the closed port. The lumber was sold at a good price and used to build barracks for the royal troops in the city. Whether King was aware of the transaction or the ship's captain acted on his own initiative is uncertain.[29]

As the news spread that Richard King's lumber had been turned into barracks for the Redcoats, a company of volunteer militiamen marched from nearby Gorham to Scarborough to call him to account. They stopped at a Dunstan tavern, and after imbibing a liberal amount of liquor, they made one of King's neighbors kneel on a hogshead and recant his Toryism. Advancing upon King's house next, they forced him to mount a table where he read a prepared statement expressing his belief that the scattered people of the colonies could not hope to defeat England and that only for this reason had he kept aloof from the patriots. This infuriated the impatient soldiers who ordered King to kneel. "Erase that sentence," the captain commanded; "these soldiers can't endure the sentiment." King submitted, and the triumphant militia departed.[30]

To be forced to kneel in his own doorway before a band of vigilantes and to repudiate the cautious and conservative opinions of a lifetime was King's final humiliation. Now in his fifty-seventh year and in ill health, he brooded over this last assault on his dignity. He died nine months later, on March 27, 1775, three weeks before the "shot heard round the world."

29. Southgate, "History of Scarborough," Maine Hist. Soc., *Colls.*, 3 (1853), 190, asserts King's ignorance of the transaction, but according to Le Roy L. Hight, "A Scarborough Tory," *New England Magazine*, 20 (1899), 504, two of the ship captain's grandsons maintained that the captain had explained to them how King himself had made the trade.

30. J. G. King, Rufus King, 42–43; Southgate, "History of Scarborough," Maine Hist. Soc., *Colls.*, 3 (1853), 189–92.

CHAPTER II

YOUNG RUFUS KING

WHEN RICHARD KING DIED, RUFUS WAS IN HIS SECOND YEAR AT HARVARD College. After three or four years of grammar school studies in Scarborough with a young Harvard graduate, Samuel Eaton, and six years of classical training with Samuel Moody, Rufus had entered Harvard in the summer of 1773 at the age of eighteen. His stepmother had persuaded his father that there was something "more than common" about Rufus. When the boy left for Harvard, she accompanied him to Cambridge in her square-topped New England chaise.[1]

Harvard College comprised four handsome Georgian buildings and a small chapel. The main building, Harvard Hall, housed the commons and the kitchen, the library, a "musaeum," and lecture rooms where students could find Professor Winthrop tinkering with his "philosophical apparatus" or lecturing on science. Harvard Hall and three dormitories, Massachusetts, Stoughton, and Hollis, dominated a bare and unattractive playing field, Harvard Yard.

Of Rufus King's forty-eight classmates, at least eleven had been with him at Dummer. Authority over them was wielded by President Samuel Locke, who mysteriously resigned in December 1773 and

1. Mary Black King to Cyrus King, Oct. 29, 1792, owned by Miss Edith Douglass and Mrs. Mary Rackliffe, Newton Highlands, Mass.; unpublished sketch (*ca.* 1849) by Elizabeth Porter King of her father, Cyrus King, owned by Mrs. John H. Thomas, New Haven, Conn.; unpublished Sketch of my Grand Mother King, Jan. 14, 1848, by Dorcas King Leland, Bath, Maine, owned by Arthur H. Lord, Newton, Mass. Copy owned by James G. King, N. Y. C.

was succeeded by Samuel Langdon in October 1774.[2] The president and the professors were august and somewhat remote. Their residences east of the Yard could be seen through an orchard. But the tutors, who were unmarried, lived in the dormitories with the students. Rufus's class, like all freshman classes, endured not only the tutors' discipline but also sophomore "fagging," and they ran errands for upperclassmen between the library or buttery and the shops and taverns of Cambridge.[3]

In December, King and his fellow students shared the excitement kindled by the Boston Tea Party. When the Boston Port Act and other coercive laws went into effect on June 1, 1774, the city was occupied by the Redcoats. After the forced dissolution of the General Court, citizens held county conventions, prevented courts from meeting, and prepared for further resistance. The college suspended its festive commencement exercises in view of the "dark aspect" of public affairs. Rufus, who was on a two-week leave of absence from the college, may have been in Scarborough when his father was threatened at gun point by militiamen from Gorham. Whatever his feelings were about the persecution, it doubtless reinforced memories of his family's earlier trouble and nourished once again his aversion to violence.

It was during his student years in Cambridge that Rufus was attracted to the Anglican Church. Scarborough had no Anglican Church, but Christ Church in Cambridge was just across the Cambridge Common from the college. King's lifelong support of the Episcopal Church began there. To renounce the Congregational Church in which he had been brought up for the Anglican faith was an unusual step for a young man sympathetic to the patriot cause. His father may have persuaded him to do so, but it is more likely that the dignity and grandeur of the Church of England appealed to the impressionable youth who had not seen such things at home. In February 1775, Richard King requested of President Langdon that his son "be permitted to attend public Worship after

2. It was later revealed that a maidservant had become pregnant in Locke's house. Samuel Eliot Morison, *Three Centuries of Harvard, 1636–1936* (Cambridge, Mass., 1936), 100.

3. *Ibid.*, chs. 5, 6 *passim*; Winfred E. A. Bernhard, *Fisher Ames, Federalist and Statesman, 1758–1808* (Chapel Hill, 1965), ch. 2. Ames was in the class of 1774.

the manner of the Church of England." Rufus presented the request in person, and the faculty approved it on March 3.[4]

Just a month later, on April 4, young King learned that his father had died, and he hurried to join his sorrowing relatives. He took the loss of his "honor'd Father" with a calm sadness and resignation which reflected his awakened interest in religion. To his college friend, Samuel Sewall, he contrasted the carefree happiness of childhood with the difficulties of mature life. "Our happiness," he remarked, "in a great Measure depends upon Others; we depend upon each other almost for Life and every Enjoyment; and this being true, we can never enjoy Happiness uninterrupted; A *Brother* or a *Friend* must *die*. Trouble seems interwoven in our very Constitutions, and happiness compleat appears a Blessing not designed for Man in his feeble mortal state."[5] Now that Providence had enveloped Richard King in "her dark Abyss," his son accepted as just and right the "dark and intricate ways" of heaven: "I repine not for myself—Justice bears Sway in the ways of Heaven—my misfortunes can't make me so vain as to imagine that I cause *Changes* in the Course of Nature, but I look upon these Events as the constant Opperation of Providence—and laying Silence upon my Tongue, when thwarted in my Inclinations, I look with admiration towards the Cause."[6]

After recovering from the shock of his father's death, Rufus was anxious to learn how the change in his family's circumstances would affect his education. Fortunately, his sister Mary had in 1773 married Robert Southgate, a physician and lawyer at Scarborough, and the management of Richard King's estate devolved on him.[7] Rufus and his brother-in-law, who was thirteen years older, became warm friends. A careful and practical man, the loyal Southgate wrung from the estate enough to enable Rufus to complete his college education and to study law.[8]

While Rufus was still at Scarborough, the first shots of the Revolution were fired at Lexington Common and Concord Bridge. On

4. Harvard Faculty Records, IV, 3, Harvard University Archives, Cambridge, Mass.

5. Rufus King to Samuel Sewall, July 25, 1775, King Papers, N.-Y. Hist. Soc.

6. *Ibid.*

7. Moulton, *Grandfather Tales of Scarborough*, 71. Richard King died intestate. An inventory of his real and personal property at the time of his death is in the Rufus King Papers, Box A, N.-Y. Hist. Soc.

8. J. G. King, Rufus King, 48–49. While at college Rufus kept an account book, now owned by James G. King, N.Y.C.

May 1, the Committee of Safety sent the Harvard boys home, and the Provincial Congress took over the college buildings, using them to house Washington's militia.[9] Rufus encountered his first war experience while he was on a coasting vessel from Scarborough to Salem. Becalmed off Cape Ann, the coaster was boarded by British naval officers. They discovered that the captain had no clearance papers and ordered him to join a British vessel. After the officers left the ship, a timely breeze enabled the captain to disregard what King called "his Majesty's pilfering fleet on this station" and sail on to Salem.[10] Since the college had been suspended and its students dispersed, however, Rufus rode to Newburyport, where he remained for several months, studying again under his old schoolmaster Moody at nearby Byfield.[11]

At Newburyport King excitedly heard the news of British troop movements in the Boston area. Twenty-two transports had reached port during the week, bringing troops and five hundred horses. "I think the crisis has almost arrived," Rufus wrote his brother-in-law in June 1775. General Gage had released a "*most scandalously false*" account of the facts and had offered protection to "every one who shall be so wicked and so abandoned a villain as to desert his country's cause." With a great show of "pomp and pious sanctity," he had also decreed death and confiscation of property for those failing to comply with his "despicable request." Burning with resentment, King asserted that "America spurns the production of the petty tyrant, and treating it with deserved contempt, stands firm upon the pillars of liberty, immoveable as Heaven and determined as fate. One kindred spirit catches from man to man."[12] Soon after the battle of Bunker Hill, Rufus visited Cambridge and wrote Southgate a detailed report of the engagement.[13]

9. Morison, *Three Centuries of Harvard*, 147–48, 151.

10. King to Robert Southgate, May 18, 1775, owned by the estate of Rufus King Lennig. King, ed., *King Correspondence*, I, 17, quotes only one sentence: "Upon our passage we narrowly escaped Difficulties from some of the attendants upon the Ships of War."

11. William Coleman, "Rufus King," *Delaplaine's Repository of the Lives and Portraits of Distinguished American Characters* (Phila., 1815–16), 177. Coleman's belated statement is our sole authority, but he and King were close friends when it was made.

12. King to Robert Southgate, June 25, 1775, King, ed., *King Correspondence*, I, 7–8.

13. *Ibid.*, 8–10. This letter is undated but probably was written in June or July 1775.

In October the Harvard faculty and a number of students scattered since May gathered in Concord to resume their work, even though they had only a part of the college's library and none of its scientific apparatus there. By October 10, nearly a hundred boys had arrived and were boarding in taverns and private homes. King was there at least by November for his junior year.[14]

While at Concord Rufus showed a marked interest in history and public affairs. He borrowed from the college library Robertson's *History of Scotland*, Stacey's *History of Poland*, and Vertot's *Sweden*. He also took out Pye's *Moses*, a quarto volume of Bolingbroke, and issues of the *Annual Register* and *State Tryals*.[15]

He had been elected to the Speaking Club early in his sophomore year, and he developed an intense interest in oratory. Although the faculty frowned on this student diversion, the secrecy of the organization seems to have come primarily from a desire for exclusiveness. So secret was the club, in fact, that mere mention of its name meant expulsion. Its members met about every two weeks. They recited passages from classical and contemporary literature and from speeches on political issues. Rufus's performances included a recitation of the "Speech of Quintus to the Romans," participation with four others in "A Scene from the Robbinhood Club," and an oration, "A Piece of Whigism." On another occasion he was one of the "remarkers" who criticized the speakers. Although not a frequent orator at the club, he was evidently popular; in December 1775 he became deputy secretary of the society, and five months later he was elected president.[16]

As the weeks of deadlock continued, Rufus and his fellow students eagerly devoured the news of military preparations and shared the gossip about the British aristocracy in Boston. Though the son of a Loyalist, he sympathized with the patriots from the beginning, and hoped that "our troops" would recover from their Canadian failure and eventually capture Quebec.[17] After the British evacuated Boston and the American forces left their Cambridge barracks for New York, the college authorities arranged for an early return to Cam-

14. Harvard Faculty Records, IV, Harvard Univ. Archives.

15. Library Records, Harvard Univ. Archives.

16. Speaking Club Records, I, 69–100, *passim*, and 146, Harvard Univ. Archives.

17. King to Robert Southgate, Feb. 7, 17, 1776, King, ed., *King Correspondence*, I, 18–20.

bridge. It was there, three days before the Declaration of Independence, that Rufus King heard of Burgoyne's arrival "with 10,000 Foreigners" and of American efforts to raise recruits to resist them. He was tempted to join these volunteers. "In Camp there is a spacious field for ambition to play in," he wrote; "and the man who places 'death in one eye and honour in the other' will never fail of acquiring that distinction his soul thirsts for."[18] But Rufus had completed three years of college, and he determined to continue his education.

During the summer vacation King and a classmate, Jacob Herrick, remained in Cambridge and were entrusted with guarding the college buildings. They were each paid twenty shillings to act as "scarecrows."[19] Though regarded by the college authorities as responsible, King became less serious and more inclined to horseplay in his senior year. Only twice in his first three years of college were small fines assessed against him for infractions or property damage, but in his senior year he paid much more in fines than in all his other years combined. In the final quarter of that year his repair bill was more than £1, the highest in the college.[20] What was damaged is not known. He may well have held parties in his room since his orders for food and drink from the buttery were higher than before.[21]

King's lively conduct as a senior was tempered by serious reading. Although he retained a fondness for history and politics, his reading showed great variety and professional practicality. Of the books he borrowed from the library, *Don Quixote* was the only literary one, but four volumes of what was then called "philosophy," along with Rohault's *Physicks* and Long's *Astronomy*, indicated his interest in science. Vauban on *Fortification* and Hauxley's *Navigation* were natural wartime subjects, and Beccaria's *Essay on Crimes and Punishment* and the *Russian Code* revealed his leaning toward the law.[22]

Rufus had earlier shown a curiosity about legal cases, and the work of the great Italian jurist may have hastened his decision to become a lawyer. Shortly after reading Beccaria he announced that he was determined to study law. He did not know where or with whom, however. As long as he remained in college, his expenses were

18. King to Southgate, July 1, 1776, *ibid.*, 20–21.

19. Harvard Corporation Records, Bach. and Schol. (1750–78), II, 449, Harvard Univ. Archives.

20. Quarter Bill Book, 1770–84, Harvard Univ. Archives.

21. *Ibid.*

22. Library Records, Harvard Univ. Archives.

paid by his stepmother, by personal loans from Dr. Southgate, and by the proceeds from the sale of lumber from Richard King's estate. High prices, however, ate up his resources, and his finances were precarious.[23] He wrote Southgate, the administrator of his father's estate, about "doing something towards forwarding my plan. In short, I want to know how I am. I am in my own mind fixed; what my patrimony is, I know not."[24]

King graduated in 1777 at the head of his class[25] with distinction in mathematics, language, and oratory. Because of wartime hardships, continued fear of invasion, and the spread of smallpox, Harvard held no public commencement. At a private ceremony forty-one scholars received their degrees by a general diploma dated July 16.[26]

Immediately after graduation, Rufus moved to the bustling town of Newburyport to study law in the office of the brilliant and conservative Theophilus Parsons. King had known his father, the Reverend Moses Parsons, the minister at Byfield. Five years older than King, Theophilus Parsons had preceded him at both Dummer and Harvard and had gone on to legal studies with Theophilus Bradbury, an acquaintance of Rufus's father.[27] Parsons was admitted to the bar at Falmouth in 1774 and had only recently opened his law office in Newburyport.[28] King was one of his very first students.

23. Rufus King, account book, owned by James G. King. King's expenses for four years of college, including books and clothes, amounted to almost £325.

24. King to Robert Southgate, Nov. 17, 1776, King, ed., *King Correspondence*, I, 24.

25. *Harvard Quinquennial Catalogue* (1930), 197. According to E. V. Smith (pseud. of Euphemia V. Blake), *History of Newburyport* (Newburyport, 1854), 325, King graduated "with the first honors of the class of 1777, which was considered an excellent one. He was not only first in mathematics, the languages and oratory, but took the lead in every athletic sport, running, jumping, and swimming." There is no direct contemporary evidence of King's athletic prowess.

26. *Harvard Quinquennial Catalogue*, 197. King was one of 24 classmates later awarded the M.A. degree.

27. See Box A, King Papers, N.-Y. Hist. Soc., for evidence of Bradbury's legal work for Richard King.

28. John J. Currier, *History of Newburyport, Mass., 1764–1909*, 2 vols. (Newburyport, 1906–09), II, 262; see Zechariah Chafee, Jr., in *DAB* s.v. "Parsons, Theophilus, 1750–1813." Judge Edmund Trowbridge, a moderate Loyalist, resigned in 1775 from the Superior Court and removed his library to Moses Parsons's home in Byfield. There Theophilus Parsons studied with Trowbridge, *ibid.* It is possible that King himself studied with Trowbridge before moving to Newburyport. See Theophilus Parsons, [Jr.], ed., *Memoir of Theophilus Parsons* ... (Boston, 1859), 31.

During the summer of 1777, an episode in Scarborough helped King decide against returning to Maine. While visiting there in June, he bought a horse from Dr. Southgate. As he rode out of town he was accused of having stolen the animal from one Lyde, who had been banished from Falmouth as a Tory. King was angry that anyone should suspect him of theft or of possessing "even the horse a Tory ever rode upon," but consoled himself with the thought that people meant well, though he hoped that "they will not have cause to be so suspicious of every face."[29] The unfriendliness of the men who challenged him had deeper roots, however. On June 30 the selectmen of Scarborough included King and Southgate on a list of five men suspected of Toryism, and the town meeting voted to gather evidence in order to try the accused.[30]

King had been in Newburyport for barely a month when this somber news reached him. As the son of a Tory, he was naturally subject to the antagonism of wartime patriots who did not know him, and Southgate, as the son-in-law of Richard King, was another target of suspicion. Nevertheless, he had been a supporter of the American cause and was unprepared for the charge of Toryism. "I have no consciousness of having conducted myself in a manner unfriendly to my country: Nor did I conceive my Friends in Scarboro had," he wrote Southgate. "But it is the Spirit of the Times. An honest zeal, or rather the zeal of a man who means to conduct uprightly and well is sometimes detrimental; often injures the Cause it was meant to promote."[31]

Having settled in Newburyport, King could not be prosecuted as a resident of Scarborough. "Let the game go on; I am out of their power," he remarked, "and should the matter have been other ways circumstanced, I should have feared nothing from an honest unprejudiced jury. My heart tells me I have no grounds of fear."[32] Southgate, however, might face continued harassment at the hands of his Scarborough neighbors. After conferring with Parsons, King advised his brother-in-law to collect evidence of his patriotism such

29. King to Robert Southgate, June 26, 1777, King, ed., *King Correspondence*, I, 26.

30. Southgate, "History of Scarborough," Maine Hist. Soc., *Colls.*, 3 (1853), 198–99; Libbey, *Scarborough*, 130.

31. King to Robert Southgate, Aug. 21, 1777, King, ed., *King Correspondence*, I, 26–27. I have reversed the order of the words "myself conducted," which appear in the printed text.

32. *Ibid.*

as cheerfulness in paying taxes, irreproachable private remarks, and readiness to obey the law. Although Parsons generously offered to defend Southgate if he were brought to trial, both he and King correctly anticipated that the matter would be dropped for lack of evidence. In July a special town meeting at Scarborough reconsidered the earlier proceedings, and King, Southgate, and the other accused persons were restored to local favor.[33]

King adopted Newburyport as his home and remained there for seven years as a student, practicing attorney, and legislator. The prosperous and expanding town was an ideal place for the eager law student. A wartime construction boom was under way. The Marquis de Chastellux, traveling through in 1782, was impressed with the attractive buildings and likened the ornamental warehouses near the merchants' homes to the large greenhouses in France.[34] Ocean commerce had already produced great fortunes for the Hoopers, the Jacksons, and the Tracys. A marine society flourished, and the loaded wharves in a busy harbor were material evidence that lawyers would be useful in the prosecution of claims and the defense of property.

As a rather impecunious law student, King remained uneasy over the unhappy financial situation of his family in Scarborough and fretted over the melting down of his father's estate. He had hoped for his full share of the inheritance and was disappointed when he received only a single farm, in a partial division of the estate. Although it was the best of Richard King's farms and included 150 acres of land, it would bring little immediate income. He was unsure from day to day, paid dearly for his board, and was unable to buy the clothes he needed. He complained that he could not live in Newburyport for less than £90 per year. To avoid selling his newly acquired farmland, he continued to borrow considerable amounts in paper money and in lumber from Southgate on the security of the remainder of his inheritance.[35] Finally in June 1779 King traded his

33. Southgate, "History of Scarborough," Maine Hist. Soc., *Colls.*, 3 (1853), 199; Libbey, *Scarborough*, 198–99. Southgate fully supported the American cause and for some time had been making saltpetre for the militia. A physician, farmer, and expert well-builder, he acquired a practical legal knowledge and in 1784 began his many years' service as a judge of the Cumberland County Court.

34. Marquis de Chastellux, *Travels in North America in the Years 1780, 1781, and 1782*, ed. Howard C. Rice, Jr., 2 vols. (Chapel Hill, 1963), II, 492–93.

35. King to Robert Southgate, Aug. 24, Dec. 5, 1777, King, ed., *King Correspondence*, I, 27–29; J. G. King, Rufus King, 79–80. Years later, while in New

farm to Obed Emery of Biddeford for 450,000 feet of salable pine boards.[36] This small fortune in lumber, in addition to Southgate's aid, eased his financial worries considerably.

During the winter of 1777–78, Rufus joined a young men's club in Boston, riding down from Newburyport for its meetings. The club, composed of recent Harvard graduates, usually gathered in the studio of the painter John Trumbull at the corner of Court and Brattle Streets. In these rooms King joined Royall Tyler, Christopher Gore, William Eustis, Thomas Dawes, and Aaron Dexter in discussions of literature, politics, and the progress of the war—all drinking tea instead of wine, Trumbull recalled.[37] Dawes, Dexter, and Gore were, like King, former members of the Speaking Club at Harvard. Gore and Eustis were destined to be governors of Massachusetts, and Tyler, the future jurist, would write the first successful professionally produced American comedy, *The Contrast.* Tyler had a quick wit and a good nature.[38] With Trumbull and Gore, King maintained a warm and lifelong friendship. Twenty years later, when the three were United States officials in London, their families were very close.

King's visits to Boston were not always devoted to conversation and tea drinking at his club. On one occasion his conduct led to a bitter confrontation with the president and tutors of Harvard College. King, Tyler, and Samuel Sewall had spent an October evening in a Cambridge tavern drinking with some college seniors. When they left, according to the Harvard Faculty Records, "great Disorders ensued, such as horrid Prophanity, riotous and Tumultuous Noises, and breaking of Windows at College, and in its Vicinity . . .

York as a member of the Massachusetts delegation to the Confederation Congress, King asked Southgate to render a statement of his debt and offered to make an equitable settlement with him and with Aaron Porter, his other brother-in-law, who also had a claim on him. King offered to pay the debt in 1787; soon afterward, grateful for Southgate's steady assistance in time of need, King legally conveyed to him all his remaining interest in his father's estate. King, ed., *King Correspondence*, I, 5–6; Cumberland County Deeds, LXXIII, 160–62, Cumberland County Court House; J. G. King, Rufus King, 82–83.

36. Cumberland County Deeds, XX, 372–73, Cumberland County Court House.

37. John Trumbull, *Autobiography, Reminiscences and Letters . . . from 1756 to 1841* (N. Y., 1841), 50.

38. Frederick Tupper, "Royall Tyler, Man of Law and Man of Letters," Vermont Historical Society, *Proceedings* (1926–28), 68; Christopher Gore to King, May 28, 1786, King Papers, N.-Y. Hist. Soc.

to the Discredit and Scandal of this Society, and in direct Violation of Laws necessary to the good Order and well being of it." The exuberant alumni and several undergraduates were haled before a meeting of the faculty on the ground that they were amenable to the Harvard authorities for "irregular behavior within the precincts of the College."[39]

As they faced President Langdon and seven faculty members, the three drinking companions denied that the college had control over them. Sewall and Tyler criticized tutor Stephen Hall for reporting them to the faculty, although Tyler admitted that he had been drunk. That did not, however, confer on the college any jurisdiction over its alumni. Tyler spoke defiantly, the faculty thought, and King had "an Air of the greatest Insolence and Superciliousness" as he expressed "Surprize that the President should pretend to cite him, when the Charges against him were supported only or principally by . . . [Tyler], who confess'd that he was drunk at the time."[40] Prejudice against Tyler may have been justified. As an undergraduate, he and his roommate Christopher Gore had once angled for a live pig from their window over the front door. What they caught, though, was not a pig but a wig—"The biggest wig of Cambridge," that of President Langdon.[41] As for King, he was judged by the company he kept. Although the episode affronted the dignity of the president and tutors, the three proud and unintimidated graduates made the most of the college's lack of authority over its alumni.

In August 1778 King sought an opportunity to serve in the army as the war again spread north briefly. With college completed and his legal studies well launched, he volunteered for militia service. He took part in General John Sullivan's expedition aimed at recapturing Newport, Rhode Island, which the British had held since December 1776. After the evacuation of Philadelphia in June 1778, Newport and New York were the only important towns they held in the United States. The capture of Newport would mean the surrender of a large British force and an even greater symbolic victory for the Americans. On July 29 a strong French fleet under the command of the Comte d'Estaing arrived off Newport with four thousand French troops to cooperate with the commander at Providence,

39. Harvard Faculty Records, IV, 70, Harvard Univ. Archives.
40. *Ibid.*, 75.
41. Tupper, "Royall Tyler," Vt. Hist. Soc., *Proc.* (1926–28), 69.

General Sullivan. The New England volunteer militia, numbering about 7,500, joined Sullivan's force along with 1,500 Continentals dispatched by General Washington and commanded by Generals Greene, Lafayette, and Glover. To oppose them, Sir Robert Pigot, the British commander at Newport, had but 6,000 soldiers. A swift American and French success seemed assured.[42]

On August 15 the American army, with General John Glover's brigade on the left flank, advanced the length of the island of Rhode Island. Two days later the Americans erected fortifications outside Newport and began to entrench themselves. Rufus King was then appointed as an aide to General Glover, with the rank of major.[43]

Before the French troops landed, news came that a British fleet under Lord Howe was approaching, and d'Estaing sailed out to meet the challenge. As the fleets maneuvered for position, a great storm scattered them and prevented a battle. Heedless of the pleadings of Greene and Lafayette, d'Estaing sailed for Boston to refit, taking the four thousand French land forces with him. The disappointed and angry General Sullivan hoped for victory even without French help, but some three thousand of his volunteers drifted away in disgust to their homes and their harvests. As his superiority diminished, Sullivan retreated on the twenty-eighth to a strong position on Butts Hill at the northern end of the island. The British followed, and early the next day tried to storm the height. King, who was eating breakfast with General Glover and his staff in the General's headquarters in a house at the foot of Quaker Hill, luckily escaped injury in the opening cannonade. As the firing on the hill grew heavier, Glover ordered King to mount one of the horses saddled outside the door of the house and to observe and report. As soon as the young aide-de-camp quit the table, another officer, Henry Sherburne, took the vacant chair. Just then a spent cannon ball bounded through the window, rolled toward the table, and crushed Sherburne's foot. Afterward, King—who occasionally met Sherburne with his wooden leg—remarked that by right he himself should wear it.[44]

42. J. G. King, Rufus King, 90–91; George A. Billias, *General John Glover and his Marblehead Mariners* (N. Y., 1960), 163–73.

43. Essex Institute, *Historical Collections*, 5 (1863), 122; General Jonathan Titcomb's Orderly Books, August 1778, Massachusetts Archives, CCCXXVII, 37, Massachusetts State House, Boston. For a fuller account of King's war service in Rhode Island see J. G. King, Rufus King, ch. 11.

44. Trumbull, *Autobiography*, 53–54. This account may also be found in King, ed., *King Correspondence*, I, 12*n.*

General Glover's artillery and troops broke the British assault on the American position. Repulsed with heavy losses, the British were driven across the valley and up the opposite slopes of Quaker Hill and two adjoining hills. In this battle the hotly pursuing Americans captured a British battery and lost only 211 men, while the enemy lost almost four times as many.[45] In his report to the Continental Congress, General Sullivan singled out Glover's brigade for specific commendation: "The Enemy advanced on our left rear, but were repulsed by General Glover."[46]

The next day Sullivan learned that Sir Henry Clinton was moving up from New York with five thousand men to reinforce Pigot. The American general had no choice but to order a retreat, so on the night of the thirtieth the Americans crossed at Howland's Ferry to Tiverton on the mainland.[47] Newport remained in British hands for another year, until October 1779 when the emphasis of the war had shifted to the South.

After a short pause at Tiverton, Glover's brigade proceeded to Providence where on the evening of September 2 a near-mutiny flared among the volunteers, who were impatient to return home. The next day Glover reprimanded his men, ordered the rolls called twice a day, punished absentees, and requested all officers to sleep in camp.[48] Within a few days the volunteers were disbanded. On September 5, General Sullivan's headquarters at Providence terminated King's service, noting that he had served faithfully and had "merited the approbation of General Glover."[49]

Of Major King's service in that brief Rhode Island episode little is known. He served with a number of officers of whom at least three remained friends after the war: John Hancock, who commanded the Massachusetts militia; John Langdon, a colonel of the New Hampshire volunteers; and the Marquis de Lafayette, who although two years younger than King was a general in the Continental Army.

King's only surviving account of his part in the campaign is meager.

45. Essex Inst., *Hist. Colls.*, 5 (1863), 107, 121; C. W. Lippitt, "The Battle of Rhode Island," Newport Historical Society, *Bulletin*, 18 (1915), 11.

46. John Sullivan to Congress, Aug. 31, 1778, in Otis G. Hammond, ed., *Letters and Papers of Major-General John Sullivan, Continental Army* (New Hampshire Historical Society, *Collections*, 13–15 [1930–39]), II, 283.

47. Essex Inst., *Hist. Colls.*, 5 (1863), 107, 124.

48. *Ibid.*, 125–26.

49. *Ibid.*, 126.

"I enjoyed fine health upon the Island and the scene was not disagreeable to me," he remarked; "I saw and experienced enough to satisfy my curiosity."[50] That was all. He was not moved by military ambition, and whatever stirrings of martial glory he may have felt subsided after four weeks of military life. For him the Rhode Island episode was not the highroad to reputation but a byway among men under stress, a useful but temporary diversion from the main path of a legal career. So ended Rufus King's one brief venture as a soldier, and as the theater of war shifted from New England to the South, he turned again to the study of law.

50. King, ed., *King Correspondence*, I, 12. So far as is known, the original letter is not extant. The printed version is incomplete; it is, of course, possible that Charles R. King, the editor, excised significant details, but in this instance it does not seem likely.

CHAPTER III

NEWBURYPORT, THE LAW, AND THE GENERAL COURT

THEOPHILUS PARSONS, KING'S LEGAL MENTOR, WAS A GIFTED MAN, AND one of the most learned in New England. He was an avid reader of history, devoted to the study of government, but also fond of mathematics, literature and the classics. "He is in himself a law-library," observed one of his later students, John Quincy Adams, in 1787.[1] He had a tenacious memory and a disciplined mind, and his terse arguments were sometimes flavored with the spice of wit and sarcasm. A devout Christian and champion of the clergy, he was neither "allured by the dreams of Condorcet" nor tempted to substitute "reason for Deity."[2] His political conservatism made him a natural leader of those later dubbed the "Essex Junto." Physically he was tall and heavy-set; his hair was rapidly thinning, and at the age of thirty he covered his baldness with a wig.[3]

King, only five years younger, shared some of Parsons's traits of intellect and character. Both men had excellent memories, both were logical thinkers, both were temperamentally conservative, and both liked history and politics. Studying with Parsons in Newburyport,

1. [C. F. Adams, ed.], *Life in a New England Town: 1787, 1788. Diary of John Quincy Adams, while a student in the office of Theophilus Parsons at Newburyport* (Boston, 1903), 66.

2. Samuel L. Knapp, *Biographical Sketches of Eminent Lawyers, Statesmen, and Men of Letters* (Boston, 1821), 72.

3. *Ibid.*, 74.

King not only learned about law, but he also attended town meetings and rapidly acquired an understanding of Massachusetts politics.

In March 1778 the Massachusetts General Assembly submitted to the towns its draft of a new state constitution. That the legislature rather than a special convention framed it had already drawn some criticism, and now the document itself was under attack.[4] It contained neither a bill of rights nor a general guaranty of religious or civil liberty. Its proposed executive was too weak. The small towns were jealous of the slight increase in representation accorded the large towns in the General Court, and the larger towns, including Newburyport, feared that their greater populations would still be inadequately represented.

Spurred by Parsons, the Newburyport Town Meeting in March 1778 rejected the faulty plan of representation and took the initiative in calling for a county meeting to draft a protest.[5] Within three weeks, delegates of twelve Essex County towns convened in Ipswich; they adopted resolutions against the constitution and accepted a sixty-eight-page report written by Parsons showing the need for a bill of rights, stressing the wisdom of a separation of the powers of government, and arguing for some recognition of property in representation.[6] Presenting the case of the mercantile community of his county, Parsons emphasized liberty but called for limitations on democracy. The *Essex Result*, as the published report was popularly known, was instrumental in the voters' rejection of the constitution by a margin of five to one.[7]

A new and eventually successful draft of a state constitution was

4. For the text of the constitution of 1778 and objections to it see Robert J. Taylor, ed., *Massachusetts, Colony to Commonwealth, Documents on the Formation of its Constitution, 1775–1780* (Chapel Hill, 1961), ch. 4.

5. Harry A. Cushing, *History of the Transition from Provincial to Commonwealth Government in Massachusetts* (N. Y., 1896), 221; Parsons, ed., *Memoir of Parsons*, 47.

6. Parsons, ed., *Memoir of Parsons*, 51; see Chafee, in *DAB* s.v. "Parsons, Theophilus." Of the 28 delegates, 5 (including Parsons, Jonathan Jackson, and Tristram Dalton) represented Newburyport.

7. The *Essex Result* may be found in Parsons, ed., *Memoir of Parsons*, 358–402, and, abridged, in Taylor, ed., *Massachusetts, Colony to Commonwealth*, 73–89. The constitution was defeated by the voters, 9,972 to 2,083, Samuel Eliot Morison, "The Vote of Massachusetts on Summoning a Constitutional Convention, 1776–1916," Mass. Hist. Soc., *Proceedings*, 50 (1916–17), 244. For the relation of Newburyport to the *Essex Result*, see Benjamin W. Labaree, *Patriots and Partisans, the Merchants of Newburyport, 1764–1815* (Cambridge, Mass., 1962), 44–54.

the outcome of a convention held at Cambridge in the winter of 1779–80. Among Newburyport's five delegates were Parsons and Jonathan Jackson. Parsons insisted on a strong executive, a senate based on a property qualification, and the virtual establishment of Congregationalism as a state church.[8] He and Jackson were on a committee to draft the constitution, though in fact John Adams was its chief architect. Although Parsons was unhappy that the convention altered the committee's report and produced a more democratic instrument,[9] Newburyport voted unanimously to approve all of it except one article.[10]

Whether in the public forum of the town meeting or in the privacy of Parsons's office, Rufus King was exposed to the friendship of sophisticated politicians, to the art of persuasion, and to the mechanics of constitution-making. His rich experience with Parsons, his growing acquaintance with Newburyport's leading lawyers and merchants, and his first-hand knowledge of the birth of the new state constitution were shaping in the young law student the viewpoints that were to guide his public life. In the light of these advantages, he could hardly regret that he had not taken his legal training in England as he had once hoped to do.[11]

In July 1780, King ended his three-year apprenticeship with Parsons. At the end of its session in Salem that month, the Court of Common Pleas in Essex County admitted him to practice.[12] For three years he argued cases of trespass or small debts. By October

8. See Chafee in *DAB* s.v. "Parsons, Theophilus."

9. For Parsons's regrets, see his letter to Francis Dana, Aug. 3, 1780, in Taylor, ed., *Massachusetts, Colony to Commonwealth*, 159. Adams had been influenced by some of Parsons's ideas.

10. Newburyport Town Records, I, 326–28, Newburyport, Mass. The town meeting suggested a few amendments. There is no record of the 340 townsmen who approved the new constitution, but there is every reason to believe that King was among them.

11. About three months after leaving the army, King had inquired about an introduction to the Inns of Court or Chancery. He wished to know whether an American would be admitted during the course of the Revolution. "What," he asked, "would be the lightest expense at which a young Gentleman, wishing to make a decent appearance, could pass a year" there? King to ?, Dec. 20, 1778, King Papers, Boston Public Library, Boston, Mass.

12. Records of Court of Common Pleas, Essex County, VII (Mar. 1780–Sept. 1782), 14, Essex County Court House, Salem, Mass. King's keen understanding of the judicial history and arrangements of Massachusetts and the conflicting theories of the "rights of Englishmen" who had come to America is displayed in his letter to a Harvard friend, Joshua Coit, written Dec. 14, 1778, when Coit was studying law in New London, Conn., King Papers, N.-Y. Hist. Soc.

1781 he was a justice of the peace, and for a few years he presided over minor local disputes and witnessed recognizances in cases of assault and battery.[13] In June 1783, after completing the required three years of practice before the County Court, he was admitted to practice before the Supreme Judicial Court of Massachusetts. For several months thereafter he appeared in both state and county courts.[14]

In his first county cases, in April 1781, King acted in a number of suits as surety for several defendants who served notice of appeal from adverse decisions. The next year, among the dozen or more cases at the Ipswich session of the court was one in which he opposed his former teacher, representing the plaintiff while Parsons represented the defendant.[15] Of the cases in which he appeared at the Salem term in July 1782, he lost one to Parsons but won eleven others in a row. (Some he won by default, however, including two in which he himself was suing to collect small amounts due him in Maine.) To judge from the court docket books, he developed a thriving practice: his volume of business ranked with that of Parsons, William Wetmore, Samuel Sewall, Theophilus Bradbury, and John Tucker, the most active members of the Essex County bar.[16]

In what was apparently his first case before the Supreme Judicial Court, King was joint counsel with James Sullivan in opposition to Parsons. The bluff and hearty Sullivan had been a judge on the very bench before which he now appeared and had only recently resigned to resume his law practice. In this case, it was neither Sullivan nor Parsons but King whose argument impressed the court, the lawyers, and the audience.[17]

13. Newburyport Town Records, I, 377; Recognizance of Anthony Knap, Oct. 17, 1781, signed by King as "Just Peace" in Newburyport, E. A. Park, II, 18, Historical Manuscripts, Yale University Library, New Haven, Conn.; Recognizance of Timothy Newman, June 5, 1782, signed by Rufus King, "J. Peace," and entitled "Essex Memorandum," King Papers, Boston Pub. Lib. Both documents involve cases of assault and battery.

14. Records of Supreme Judicial Court of Massachusetts, 1783, Suffolk County Court House, Boston.

15. J. G. King, Rufus King, 127.

16. *Ibid.*, 128–29; Records of Court of Common Pleas, Essex County, VII (Mar. 1780–Sept. 1782), 42, Essex County Court House.

17. Thomas C. Amory, *Life of James Sullivan; With Selections from His Writings*, 2 vols. (Boston, 1859), I, *passim*; Knapp, *Biographical Sketches*, 291–313. William Coleman, a bystander, later recollected what appears to be this suit as King's first case at the bar, but it probably was his first at the state, not the county bar; *Delaplaine's Repository*, 178. See J. G. King, Rufus King, 131*n*.

A story, repeated in different versions long afterward, illustrates King's ability to fascinate an audience. In May 1783, delayed by court business in Plymouth, he mounted his horse on a Sunday morning for the long ride home to Newburyport. In Hanover Township he paused at a plain place of public worship, hitched his horse, and entered. Discovering that he was in a Quaker meeting, he sat quietly for some time; after seeing no outward sign of the movement of the Spirit among the assembled Friends, he stood up and spoke, much to the astonishment of all. What he said was appropriate and eloquent. Then, as suddenly as he had arrived, he withdrew and rode away. A few months later, when he rose to speak on the floor of the state legislature, the Quaker representative from Hanover exclaimed, "That is the man that spoke in our meeting-house."[18]

In a unique case, Murray *v.* Inhabitants of the First Parish of Gloucester, King not only displayed forensic skill but shared in establishing an important precedent. This case involved the interpretation of an article in the Massachusetts Bill of Rights that provided that taxpayers should support their local Congregational minister but also allowed persons of other Protestant sects to apply their money in support of their own minister. In 1780 a group of religious dissenters in Gloucester invited as their pastor the Reverend John Murray, the founder of American Universalism. These opponents of orthodox Calvinism were unincorporated and, having elected Murray as their spiritual leader, they refused to pay taxes to support the Congregationalist minister, Eli Forbes. In 1783 the town seized and sold at auction property belonging to certain of the Universalists to make up for these unpaid taxes.[19]

When the dissenting group sued for recovery, Rufus King, who as an Episcopalian was personally interested in the outcome of the case, served as Murray's counsel. The lawyers for the defense were Bradbury and Parsons, both Congregationalists. Parsons contended that the Universalist congregation, being unincorporated, was not a "religious society" within the meaning of the disputed article; moreover, since Murray had not been formally ordained, he could not be

18. George Lunt to Charles King, June 9, 1854, King, ed., *King Correspondence*, I, 13*n*.

19. John Murrray, *Life of Rev. John Murray, Preacher of Universal Salvation* (Boston, 1870), 324–30; Richard Eddy, *Universalism in Gloucester, Mass.* (Gloucester, Mass., 1892), 15, 19–24.

the required "teacher of piety, religion, and morality."[20] King countered this technical and narrow argument with a liberal interpretation of the exemption of independent congregations from the obligation to support the minister of the established church. Years later, Murray himself recalled King's eloquence in the face of a seemingly invincible phalanx of talent:

> Men characterized the oratory of that gentleman, as persuading, commanding, and like an irresistible torrent bearing down every obstacle. Many of the senior advocates seemed so to feel and acknowledge the superiority of Mr. King, as to surrender to him the right of closing causes of great importance; and a high law character declared that, had he a cause depending of the greatest intricacy and magnitude to be plead before the first tribunal in the world, he would prefer Mr. King as his advocate to any man he had ever heard speak.[21]

Despite King's forceful argumentation, the Essex County Court decided in favor of the defendants. King thereupon filed an appeal in the Supreme Judicial Court, but before the case could be argued he left the state to take his seat in Congress, and the appeal was carried on by James Sullivan and William Tudor.[22] Eventually a jury ruled in favor of Murray and the principle of exempting non-Congregational Protestants from sectarian taxation.[23]

By the middle of 1784 King seemed assured of success as a lawyer. He had won at least twenty of his thirty-five cases at the Newburyport term of the County Court in September and October 1783, and at the Salem term in December and the Ipswich term the next April he had won twenty-two of his thirty-one cases.[24] In the Supreme Judicial Court he won more cases as the months passed. His training had been exacting, and his courtroom experiences valuable. With an eye for detail and a retentive memory, he conscientiously prepared his briefs. He displayed a persuasive power in court, and his reputation was growing. He appeared sometimes as a colleague of Theophilus

20. Murray, *Life of Murray*, 331; Parsons, ed., *Memoir of Parsons*, 161.

21. Murray, *Life of Murray*, 331.

22. Essex Minute Book, Supreme Judicial Court, Suffolk County Court House, Boston; Murray originally had sought £80 in damages for money which the Congregational parishioners allegedly owed him and refused to pay.

23. Murray, *Life of Murray*, 331; James Sullivan to Rufus King, June 25, 1785, King Papers, N.-Y. Hist. Soc.; Amory, *Sullivan*, I, 183–84; Parsons, ed., *Memoir of Parsons*, 161–62.

24. J. G. King, Rufus King, 133–34.

Parsons and sometimes against him, but he was becoming Parsons's chief rival.[25] He associated with the leading attorneys in Massachusetts, including Bradbury, Sullivan, Wetmore, John Lowell, Perez Morton, and, of course, Parsons.

King became one of Newburyport's prominent citizens. He and Parsons drafted a by-law which ordained strict control over the size and amount of firewood sold to the poor by men who had been charging what the traffic would bear. In March 1783 the town meeting approved it. A year later he was chosen as one of the "visitors" who inspected the town's schools.[26] There is no record of the proceedings of the town meetings, but a young man as qualified and keenly interested as King could hardly have remained silent.

In 1782 and 1783 King was elected a warden at St. Paul's Episcopal Church.[27] It had a large congregation of tradespeople and their families, but also included a few of the richest merchants and their Negroes. Here in common worship, seamen, sailmakers, chandlers, coopers, and ropemakers, having scraped the tar and grease from their hands, sat under the same roof as the gentry, the men in their brilliant vests, blue coats and silver buttons, their wives in imported brocaded silk.[28] King had great respect and affection for the rector there, Edward Bass, who was later to become the first Episcopal Bishop of Massachusetts.[29]

Sometime before 1781, King joined the St. John's Lodge of the Society of Free and Accepted Masons. Each December 27 the brothers celebrated the feast of St. John the Evangelist, their patron saint, with the Reverend Mr. Bass preaching the sermon, and then adjourned for a convivial dinner at the General Wolfe Tavern.[30] John, Nathaniel, and Thomas Tracy, Stephen Hooper, John Swett, Captain Moses Brown, William Coffin, Joseph Marquand, and Parson

25. At the Falmouth (Portland) session of the Supreme Judicial Court in 1784, King prosecuted two suits on behalf of his stepmother against John Stewart (Stuart) *et al.*, growing out of the attacks on Richard King's home and property in 1766 and 1767. Both cases he won by default, securing £136 in damages and costs. *Ibid.*, 173–74.

26. Newburyport Town Records, I, 399, 401, 418; Currier, *History of Newburyport*, I, 313.

27. John J. Currier, *"Ould Newbury," Historical and Biographical Sketches* (Boston, 1896), 333.

28. William Lawrence, *Centennial Celebration of the Consecration of the Rt. Rev. Edward Bass, D. D., as the first Bishop of Mass.* (Boston, 1897), 17.

29. King to Daniel Kilham, Feb. 18, 1784, King-Kilham Correspondence, Columbia University Library, N.Y.C.

30. Currier, *History of Newburyport*, II, 119–20; J. G. King, Rufus King, 120.

Bass were among the members well known in Newburyport. King participated in eight meetings in 1782 and 1783, and several times he was *pro tempore* junior warden or treasurer, but after that he virtually ceased to attend.[31]

An eligible young bachelor with many friends, King moved easily in Newburyport society, attending the glittering parties given by such wealthy families as the Daltons, the Jacksons, the Greenleafs, and the Hoopers, and dances at the Tabernacle, or Assembly House, on Temple Street. He also liked to meet his close friends—Dr. Daniel Kilham, Dr. John Swett, Nat Carter, and Joseph Marquand—to talk politics, smoke his pipe, and drink a glass of Burgundy.[32]

In the spring of 1782, King's thoughts turned to romance. "The season of Love approaches fast," he observed to his friend Sewall. "I perceive the influence, but my pleasure depends much on the same principles as those of a much older man. I reflect on past seasons, the remembrance is pleasure; but there is a faint tincture of unhappiness arising from the regret *that they are past, and that I can never repete.* I have latterly thought that I would purchase pleasure by a sacrifice of some sentiments which are more artificial than natural."[33] The records do not show whether he followed this impulse.

During his years in Newburyport Rufus fell in love with Abigail Lee, daughter of a wealthy Marblehead merchant, Colonel Jeremiah Lee. Nabby, as she was called, was the sister-in-law of King's friend, Nathaniel Tracy.[34] Unfortunately she was suddenly diverted and swept off her feet by a young Irishman, with whom she had an affair. Although King consequently lost interest in Nabby as a possible wife, he remained fond of her, and in asking Kilham to lend her *The Sorrows of Werther*, avowed that he would always respect her "undissembled friendship"; if she reciprocated even a little, King wrote,

31. Records of St. John's Lodge, in the possession of the Lodge, Newburyport (The records previous to 1781 have been lost.); Smith, *History of Newburyport*, 373; Currier, *History of Newburyport*, II, 119.

32. King to Daniel Kilham, Mar. 8, 1785, King-Kilham Corr., Columbia Univ. Lib.; King, ed., *King Correspondence*, II, 601–16. Of his lady friends King's letters reveal no glimpse, except that he admired Mrs. Marquand, the former Rebecca Coffin. King was discreet and rarely committed gossip to paper. See King to ?, Dec. 20, 1778, King Papers, Boston Pub. Lib.

33. King to Samuel Sewall, Mar. 22, 1782, Free Library of Philadelphia.

34. J. G. King, Rufus King, 123–24; King to Daniel Kilham, Mar. 8, Apr. 26, Sept. 19, Oct. 10, 12, and Dec. 4, 1785, King-Kilham Corr., Columbia Univ. Lib. The pertinent passages are omitted in King, ed., *King Correspondence*, II, 604–08. The key to the girl's identity is provided in Elbridge Gerry to King, Mar. 24, 1785, owned by the heirs of Rufus King Lennig.

"I should believe myself possessed of merit, and without Vanıty, I should feel a very honorable pride."[35] During his long absences from town, he learned of her doings from Kilham and Elbridge Gerry. "Your little pet was here," Gerry reported from Marblehead in March 1784. "When she first came, she did not go out much, was sometimes seen at her window with loose attire and very pale and thin. . . . She was remarkably slim; there was no . . . suspicion in this quarter."[36] About a year later King learned that Nabby had given birth to a child, that the news was "hinted with delicacy" at Marblehead, and that the father had died of smallpox; Gerry wrote, "He drove the Nail of Misfortune into poor N— — —y and his death has clinched it."[37] To complete the tragedy, Abigail herself soon followed her seducer to the grave.[38]

In 1783, while he was courting Nabby, King entered state politics. On July 9, three months after the Continental Congress had ratified the provisional peace terms with Great Britain, a special town meeting elected King to the General Court. He was to complete the term of Jonathan Titcomb, one of Newburyport's three representatives, who had resigned to become a customs collector.[39] King was sworn in as a member of the House of Representatives on October 7 in the large west hall of the old State House in Boston.[40] At this time he had some acquaintance with Governor John Hancock, and he doubtless was eager to gain the friendship of the established leader in state politics.[41]

King was twenty-eight when he began his political career. Like

35. King to Kilham, Mar. 8, 1785, King-Kilham Corr., Columbia Univ. Lib. By this time King was in New York as a delegate to Congress.

36. Elbridge Gerry to King, Mar. 21, 1784, photostat from the Gerry Collection, Gerry Papers, Library of Congress.

37. Gerry to King, Mar. 28, 1785, letterbook owned by the heirs of Rufus King Lennig; Gerry to King, Apr. 28, 1785, photostat from the Gerry Collection, Gerry Papers, Lib. Cong.; Gerry to King, May 18, 1785, King Papers, N.-Y. Hist. Soc.

38. In 1785 or shortly afterward. See Thomas Amory Lee, "The Lee Family of Marblehead," Essex Inst., *Hist. Colls.*, 52 (1916), 339–42.

39. Newburyport Town Records, I, 409. King accepted on July 16, *ibid.*

40. Journal of Massachusetts House of Representatives (1783–1784), 219, Massachusetts State Library, Boston, Mass.

41. The Governor and his wife brought their five-year-old son John George Washington Hancock, and King's thirteen-year-old half-sister Betsy, in the Hancock barge to Point Shirley north of Boston for smallpox inoculations. Mrs. Hancock took care of the children. John Hancock to King, Sept. 30, 1783, King, ed., *King Correspondence*, I, 31–32.

Hancock, he was handsome and ambitious, with perhaps a trace of the haughtiness that characterized the Governor. He was five feet ten inches tall, with short dark hair, a ruddy complexion, a broad brow, piercing eyes, and a remarkable voice which, though penetrating, was described as "musical" or "high toned." He soon was regarded as one of the most eloquent and courteous debaters in the House of Representatives.[42]

Massachusetts in the postwar era was rife with fears and recriminations. Lawmakers were reluctant to waste the people's money on unnecessary expenses. High taxes, including a poll tax which gave the state at least one-third of its revenue, would have been an intolerable burden had the state not allowed a huge sum of arrears to accumulate.[43] As the state's debt was more than $7,000,000, any suggestion of spending was closely scrutinized. When the House of Representatives considered a public celebration of the ratification of the Peace of Paris, the penny-pinching calculations of budget-conscious legislators exasperated King. He observed caustically that "the spirit which governs very generally here is very pitiful and I fear will prove prejudicial."[44] Convinced that America's debts were trivial in relation to its human and material resources, he regretted that "there is a parsimony, which many in office call Republicanism, that casts an ill feature upon all public doings. This mistaken sentiment of political economy checks all government grants to the servants of government."[45] Able men were discouraged from seeking high offices, particularly federal positions, and as a result the state was "badly served."

For the peace celebration the General Court voted to hold a thanksgiving service after all and vaguely instructed Governor Han-

42. Richard E. Welch, Jr., "Rufus King of Newburyport: the Formative Years (1767–1788)," Essex Inst., *Hist. Colls.*, 96 (1960), 245.

43. Allan Nevins, *American States During and After the Revolution, 1775–1789* (N. Y., 1927), 500, 512, 516; Merrill Jensen, *The New Nation: a History of the United States during the Confederation, 1781–1789* (N. Y., 1950), 308–10; Jackson T. Main, *The Antifederalists, Critics of the Constitution, 1781–1788* (Chapel Hill, 1961), 58.

44. King to Daniel Kilham, Feb. 18, 1784, King-Kilham Corr., Columbia Univ. Lib.

45. *Ibid.* King learned that Louis XVI had offered to supply Harvard College with seeds and plants from his royal gardens. Although he hoped to see a botanical garden created at Cambridge, King doubted that the legislature would appropriate the money: "When justice is withheld from those who have ably and faithfully served the Public, little is to be expected from such a Government in favor of the Arts and Sciences"; *ibid.*

cock to order the firing of cannon and other "demonstrations of joy." Hancock asked for more explicit direction, but the House and Senate failed to agree, and the celebration had to be postponed. When the Governor sought an appropriation, the Senate was willing to let him determine the amount, but the House voted only £300.[46] King was appointed to a joint committee which recommended the cautious House proposal, though he no doubt dissented.[47] Insulted, Hancock, protested that the restriction to £300 implied a lack of confidence in him and asked to be excused from making the arrangements. King served on another joint committee which tactfully smoothed Hancock's ruffled feelings.[48]

After all this solemn niggling, the ceremonies were finally held on February 27, 1784. Bells rang and cannons boomed from morning to night. Major Davis's artillery company led a procession of dignitaries from the State House to the old South Meeting House for a church service, then back to the State House, where from the balcony the proclamation of ratification was read to a large crowd. The celebration continued at Faneuil Hall where an "elegant entertainment," including thirteen toasts accompanied by the discharge of cannon, was presented at public expense. In the evening Governor Hancock received high officials and other gentlemen at the Governor's House. Public buildings were illuminated, bonfires were lit on Dorchester Heights and at Roxbury, and a spectacular display of fireworks was set off on the Common.[49] Boston seems to have spent more than £300. Whether Hancock's private wealth supplemented the appropriation is not recorded.

The coming of peace did not abate the wartime hatred of Tories. As early as April 1783, the Boston Town Meeting resolved that Tories should never be allowed to return, and it successfully urged other towns to follow suit. Newspapers continued to print anti-Tory pieces charging that if the "haters of republicanism" were permitted to return to the Commonwealth, the result would be discord, anarchy, and confusion. Their conduct had been "one unwearied endeavor to subvert the liberties of American freemen, and to bring them to the

46. Jour. of Mass. House of Reps. (1783–84), 395–414, *passim*, Mass. State Lib.

47. *Ibid.*, 415.

48. *Ibid.*, 417, 419.

49. *Boston Gazette*, Mar. 1, 1784.

feet of a despotic, tyrannical monarch whose bloody reign has been marked by every species of cruelty . . . and wantonly crimsoned the fields with the gore of the innocent inhabitants."[50] Remembering the attacks on his father and the persistent intolerance of some Scarborough townspeople toward the King family, Rufus King winced at the vindictive spirit which pervaded the Bay State after the war. He noticed about him a toleration of "almost all opinions *excepting political*."[51]

In March 1784 the General Court repealed previous laws against the Tories but adopted a new one denying re-entry into Massachusetts to those who had borne arms against the United States or who had been named as traitors. An unproscribed Tory might return, but only with the governor's license, renewable at each session of the legislature, or an individual naturalization law.[52]

Those of republican and equalitarian leanings found a conspicuous object of suspicion in the Society of the Cincinnati. It had been formed by officers of the Continental Army shortly before they disbanded in 1783. Membership was limited to officers and was to be sustained through their eldest male descendants. The idea of an exclusive, perpetual military aristocracy was attacked as an affront to republican ideals. So unpopular were the Cincinnati that in February 1784 the General Court appointed a joint committee to consider measures to prevent harm from groups "formed to promote undue distinctions . . . and tending to establish an hereditary nobility." King served on this committee.[53] Although the record does not reveal his opinion at the time, he was probably influenced in the following year by his friend Elbridge Gerry, who sought the destruction of the "un-

50. *Ibid.*, Nov. 15, 1784. See also the letter from "an unshaken Whig," *ibid.*, Oct. 4, 1784, "Brutus" in the *Boston Evening-Post*, May 10, 1783, and "Messalla" in the Boston *Independent Chronicle*, Feb. 13, 1783. For advocacy of leniency toward Tories, see Boston *Massachusetts Centinel*, Apr. 28, 1784. For the postwar situation of the Loyalists see Jensen, *New Nation*, 265–81.

51. King to Daniel Kilham, Feb. 18, 1784, King-Kilham Corr., Columbia Univ. Lib. A portion of King's committee work in the legislature involved problems growing out of the confiscation of Tory estates and the return of Tory refugees. Jour. of Mass. House of Reps. (1783–84), 313–43, 352, 393, Mass. State Lib.

52. Jensen, *New Nation*, 269. As late as Apr. 4, 1785, a writer in the *Boston Gazette* criticized the General Court for failing to act on another bill against the Tories.

53. Jour. of Mass. House of Reps. (1783–84), 389, 420, Mass. State Lib.

constitutional Monster"; by 1786 King was against the Cincinnati and disgusted with their admirers.[54]

King sat on more than thirty working committees during his service in the legislature. In his first term he was on committees to make revenue collectors more accountable, to help settle a former state treasurer's accounts, to straighten out an ambiguity in a tax law, and to consider problems raised in the Governor's message (notably the British border encroachments in the Penobscot region of Maine). He was also among those selected to inquire into Harvard College's financial condition, to consider a change in the inheritance laws, and to investigate a standing committee's delay in laying before the General Court letters of the state's delegates to Congress.[55]

After Cornwallis's surrender in 1781 brought to an end the unifying experience of the Revolutionary War, Congress at Philadelphia was all the more plagued by economy-minded state governments. Dependent upon voluntary requisitions, and with most states already in arrears in their payments, the federal government was unable even to pay the interest on its debt. Its only hope lay in amending the Articles of Confederation, but that required the concurrence of all the states. A proposed amendment empowering Congress to collect a 5 per cent import duty for the purpose of paying off the foreign debt was frustrated when in November 1782 Rhode Island refused to agree to it.[56] The Rhode Island legislators, who declared the state's power of the purse to be "the most precious jewel of sovereignty," were fully aware that local tariff income relieved farmers of heavy land taxes.

On the day King first took his seat, the Massachusetts House of Representatives turned to a new tariff proposal based upon another congressional revenue plan. A 5 per cent impost was to go into effect for twenty-five years, and taxes were to be apportioned among the

54. Elbridge Gerry to Samuel Adams, Sept. 5, 30, 1785, Samuel Adams Papers, Bancroft Collection, N. Y. Pub. Lib.; King to Gerry, July 4, 1786, King Papers, N.-Y. Hist. Soc. King and Gerry were delegates to Congress when the latter informed Samuel Adams that the Massachusetts delegation would attempt to commit Congress to action which would "cripple, if not mortally wound, that unconstitutional Monster." Gerry to Adams, Sept. 30, 1785, Samuel Adams Papers, N. Y. Pub. Lib.

55. Jour. of Mass. House of Reps. (1783–84), 307, 311, 319, 322, Mass. State Lib. The debates were not reported in the sparse official record, and King's correspondence hardly mentioned his activity as a member of the House.

56. Like most of the other states, Massachusetts had acceded to the plan, but with reservations, including the requirement that her own officials collect the impost.

states according to population.[57] The prevailing method of apportionment, based on the value of improved land within each state, was impracticable if not impossible to administer, as the states had never made the necessary land evaluations. King favored apportioning taxation according to population, but he voted against compliance with the congressional plan.[58] He was a leader of the opposition. What he said at the time about the impost is not known, but long afterward he recollected his anti-federal stand: during the Revolution he had been convinced that France was becoming too influential in American councils, and that certain men and states were pro-French; therefore, the individual states ought not to augment the power of Congress but should keep it dependent upon the states, which thus would be able to exert more effective control over federal policy.[59] The fear of Gallic influence was still alive, and that prejudice in Rufus King was encouraged by men like the Adamses and Samuel Osgood.[60]

Evidently as a result of his forceful opposition to the impost, King was appointed to a joint committee to prepare a new bill. The committee recommended granting the impost on the condition that all the other states make similar grants. It is obvious that Rufus King had an important hand in thus crippling the impost plan which, even with this restriction, barely squeaked through by a vote of 72 to 65. Still not satisfied, he voted against it.[61]

57. *Journals of the Continental Congress, 1774–1789*, 34 vols. (Washington, 1904–37), XXIV, 256–61. For the general controversy over the impost, see Main, *Antifederalists*, ch. 4, esp. pp. 85–88 for the struggle in Massachusetts. See also E. James Ferguson, *The Power of the Purse: A History of American Public Finance, 1776–1790* (Chapel Hill, 1961), 174–76.

58. King, ed., *King Correspondence*, I, 15*n*, VI, 54. King was on a House committee to make the calculations needed for a decision on the question. Jour. of Mass. House of Reps. (1783–84), 229, Mass. State Lib.

59. *Ibid.*, 222, 224; Main, *Antifederalists*, 87; King, ed., *King Correspondence*, I. 15*n*. King and James Sullivan served together on many committees and developed a mutual affection despite their differences of opinion.

60. Samuel Osgood to John Adams, Dec. 7, 1783, Edmund C. Burnett, ed., *Letters of Members of the Continental Congress*, 8 vols. (Washington, 1921–36), VII, 378–88; Ralph L. Ketcham, "France and American Politics, 1763–1793," *Political Science Quarterly*, 78 (1963), 198–223. See especially 204–09, 211, 214. King's stepmother deeply distrusted the French. Mary Black King to Cyrus King, Sept. 2, 1793, contemporary excerpt owned by Mrs. John H. Thomas, New Haven, Conn.

61. Jour. of Mass. House of Reps. (1783–84), 225–26, 252, 259–60, Mass. State Lib. King's committee colleagues from the House supported the impost. The vote, on Oct. 17, was to engross the bill for return to the Senate; on Oct. 20 the House finally passed the bill to be enacted, by a close vote: 57 to 51. *Ibid.*, 267.

King's efforts to defeat or at least delay the enactment of a federal tariff were the work of a parochial northern New Englander. His legislative experience in the next few years would convince him that he had been wrong in 1783 and 1784. There was, however, much popular support for his early view that Massachusetts should resist pressures to deprive her of financial autonomy. In April 1784 a convention of delegates from most of the Suffolk County towns except Boston protested the granting to Congress of "unlimited licence" to spend Massachusetts money without consulting the people; in more prosperous times Congress might "give away ten millions in a day, without the consent or approbation of the people, and when the money is gone and expended, we grant that it is not all the county conventions on earth that can remedy it."[62]

Opinions differed about the accomplishments of the General Court of 1783-84. Western Massachusetts continued to oppose the impost; Boston supported it. A critic from Salem was astonished that the legislature dealt with federal affairs, Tory refugees, commerce, public credit, taxes, and revision of the laws "to such *universal* satisfaction in so *short* a time: there is not a single discontented person in the state! Wonderful! Wonderful!!" Dispensing with sarcasm, he asked how the state could ever produce orators and statesmen unless issues were debated at greater length.[63] Another observer praised the legislators for their diligence and good judgment, for selfish motives and passions would lengthen their deliberations: "Every day they sit it costs the Commonwealth £90. This circumstance ought to be attended to, for every one is complaining of their taxes, especially the country."[64]

Newburyport was satisfied with King. On May 14, 1784, the town meeting re-elected him to the General Court, along with Tristram Dalton, the influential speaker of the Massachusetts House of Representatives. Dalton was seventeen years older than King, but they had come to know each other well. The younger man admired the integrity and candor of his elder.[65]

62. Boston *Independent Chronicle*, May 20, 1784.

63. *Boston Gazette*, Apr. 5, 1784.

64. Boston *Independent Ledger*, May 31, 1784.

65. Newburyport Town Records, I, 425; J. G. King, Rufus King, 118; Rufus King to Aaron Porter, June 12, 1790, Porter Papers, Craigie-Longfellow House, Cambridge, Mass. Dalton later became one of the Commonwealth's first two senators under the United States Constitution, as King was to be one of New York's first two senators.

The new General Court commenced its session on May 26, and the next day the houses considered the state's public land claims west of the Hudson River. Samuel Osgood, just returned from Congress, James Sullivan, and King were appointed to a joint committee to prepare a claim to land in central and western New York based on the terms of the Massachusetts royal charter. The committee drafted a petition to Congress requesting a federal court to decide between the two states, which the legislature promptly accepted.[66]

During his second term, King served on numerous other committees, including several that dealt with financial matters: a bill for the relief of bankrupts, a new tax and tariff bill, and revision of the law governing auction sales. A number of his committee assignments related to legal matters, including a general revision of the laws, and to the administration of government, among them the method of assessing and collecting taxes, the auditing of public accounts, the financial accountability of state officials, and the creation of new counties.[67] Although there seems to be no record of the exact part King played in committee deliberations, it is obvious that they helped him to become familiar with a variety of issues and to widen his circle of political friends.

On November 3, the General Court recognized King's growing reputation by electing him as a delegate to the Congress of the Confederation.[68]

66. Jour. of Mass. House of Reps. (1784–85), 10, 13–14, Mass. State Lib.; *Journals of the Continental Congress*, XXVII, 547–49.

67. J. G. King, Rufus King, 164–72, *passim*. King also served on a joint committee which recommended that Governor Hancock ask the Governor of Nova Scotia to recall British subjects who had encroached upon the Massachusetts border, *ibid.*, 170–71.

68. Journal of Massachusetts Senate (1784–85), 196, Mass. State Lib.

CHAPTER IV

KING IN THE CONFEDERATION CONGRESS

WHEN ON NOVEMBER 3, 1784, THE GENERAL COURT MET TO FILL TWO vacancies in the Massachusetts delegation to Congress, Rufus King was the only candidate to receive a majority on the first ballot—83 of the 136 votes cast; on the second ballot, Nathaniel Gorham, a Boston merchant, was elected by a less impressive majority.[1] The appointment of a delegate as young as the twenty-nine-year-old King was unprecedented in Massachusetts, a recognition of the ability and potentialities of the young man from Newburyport, but also an indication of the unattractiveness of the post. His vigor and already proven devotion to the state's interests were qualities which could only strengthen the delegation in Congress. King promptly accepted his appointment, but Gorham declined. Subsequently Samuel Adams, Nathan Cushing, and John Lowell were elected, but all refused to serve.[2]

Seats in Congress were not prizes coveted by Massachusetts politicians. Rather than some distant outpost, they preferred Boston, the hub of high public activity in the Commonwealth, and prominent men knew that congressional seats were poorly paid from the meager funds in the state treasury. The vacancy which King filled was one of two resulting from the unwillingness of Francis Dana and Tristram

1. Jour. of Mass. Senate (1784–85), 196, Mass. State Lib.; King, ed., *King Correspondence*, I, 16*n.*

2. Jour. of Mass. House of Reps. (1784–85), 186–207, *passim*, Mass. State Lib.

Dalton to serve after they had been elected in June. When the new Congress opened at Trenton on November 1, the only Bay State delegate on hand was Dr. Samuel Holten. Other states were similarly unresponsive to federal needs; Virginia and Georgia alone were represented by more than one delegate, and there were only seven delegates present in all on that day.

King's selection as a delegate to Congress cut short his second term in the General Court. He retained the confidence of Newburyport citizens, however. Several months later they elected him to the General Court for a third time, even though it was obvious that he would be unable to serve.[3] After hurriedly winding up his law cases, he left Newburyport on November 22 for a ten-day stay in Boston before leaving New England. With his senior colleague Elbridge Gerry, and James Sullivan, one of the state's agents in the land dispute with New York, King embarked on December 3 on a sloop-packet bound for New York City. The passage was rough; a southeast gale whipped the waters so furiously that the passengers were "ready to die with sea sickness" as the ship plowed its way through Long Island Sound.[4] As the storm abated and the channel narrowed into the East River, woodland shores with clearings for houses and farms came into view. King, on his first journey south of New England, had his earliest glimpse of Long Island. After passing through the treacherous waters of Hell Gate, the packet reached Crane's Wharf at New York City on the fifth. Then King, Gerry, and Sullivan traveled across the Hudson and through New Jersey, reaching Trenton on the sixth.

In the meantime, delegates from other states had gradually assembled. By November 29, a week before King's arrival, a quorum of seven states was finally reached. By that time George Partridge had joined Holten to assure Massachusetts a vote. It had taken a month for an all but non-existent federal government to come to life, and the outlook was discouraging.

On the day of their arrival King and Gerry took their seats in Congress. Two days later, King and the other agents of Massachusetts in the dispute with New York over lands west of the Hudson

3. Newburyport Town Records, I, 444; Currier, *History of Newburyport*, I, 679. For a brief sketch of King's political development while serving in the General Court, see Welch, "Rufus King," Essex Inst., *Hist. Colls.*, 96 (1960), 246.

4. Elkanah Watson, Journal, VI, Watson Papers, New York State Library, Albany. See also Winslow C. Watson, ed., *Men and Times of the Revolution, or Memoirs of Elkanah Watson* (N. Y., 1856), 239.

met with the agents of New York to seek adjudication of the controversy. The Massachusetts commissioners included the delegates to Congress—Holten, Partridge, Gerry, and King—and in addition, Sullivan and John Lowell. The representatives of New York were Mayor James Duane of New York City, Chancellor Robert R. Livingston, Walter Livingston, and the attorney-general of the state, Egbert Benson. Benson and Chancellor Livingston were also delegates to Congress. Before Christmas, the agents of the two states had agreed upon nine judges from five states to determine the dispute.[5]

Trenton proved to be an unsuitable place for Congress. As the New Jersey legislature was currently in session, the shortage of decent living quarters seriously inconvenienced the congressional delegates. "Always more anxious about where we shall sit, than what we shall do," wrote John F. Mercer of Virginia, "our chief dispute is whether we shall spend the Winter in Philadelphia or New York." King also predicted a shift from Trenton.[6] In his first recorded vote in Congress, King joined all the delegates from north of Philadelphia in opposing a removal to that city. It was clear that the Massachusetts men preferred New York and assumed that a temporary residence in Philadelphia would only aid the efforts of Pennsylvania to keep Congress there permanently. New York, they insisted, had a more comfortable climate and equally good accommodations. They might have added that the influence of New England would be felt more strongly in the city farther to the north. In this spirit, King voted against a temporary capital at Philadelphia, at Georgetown on the Potomac, or at Trenton. On December 23 Congress voted to make New York the temporary seat of government. Removal to that city offered hope of reviving New England's flagging interest in Congress; it might even hold the union together. On the twenty-fourth Congress adopted verbatim King's resolutions of appreciation to the New Jersey legislature and the people of Trenton for their hospitality and to the state of Pennsylvania for offering the use of its public buildings in Philadelphia. It then adjourned to meet in New York on January 11.[7]

5. J. G. King, Rufus King, 183–84; *Journals of the Continental Congress*, XXVII, 709–10.

6. Edmund C. Burnett, *The Continental Congress* (N. Y., 1941), 616; Rufus King to Daniel Kilham, Dec. 12, 1784, King-Kilham Corr., Columbia Univ. Lib.

7. Burnett, ed., *Letters of Continental Congress*, VIII, 31; *Journals of the Continental Congress*, XXVII, 681, 700–03, 707–08.

The bustling commercial city at the tip of Manhattan Island heartily welcomed the Congress of the United States. The Common Council offered public accommodations, and Congress was able to hold its sessions in the new City Hall on Wall Street. Until his own house was ready, Richard Henry Lee, the president of Congress, moved into a stately home on Cherry Street owned by the widow of Walter Franklin, a merchant; it later became Washington's residence as president. Other members of Congress rented quarters that, if not as lavish as Lee's, were suitably respectable.

Rufus King found lodgings with Elbridge Gerry, who had served in Congress almost continuously since 1776. They lived in what had once been the family mansion of the Philipses, at the corner of Smith and King Streets. It was now a well-known lodging house kept by the widow Mercer and her daughters.[8] One of the boarders was the ebullient Colonel William S. Smith, the officer to whom New York had been surrendered after the peace, and who later married a daughter of John Adams. Life at Mrs. Mercer's was congenial, particularly as the gentlemen from Massachusetts got along well with the landlady's daughters. When Gerry was temporarily absent in New England, he wrote his colleague, "Give my regards to Mrs. Mercer, my love to her sweet daughters, with a cordial kiss to each of them for me, and as many as you please for yourself." King replied, referring to "our family" and to the girls' wish for Gerry's return: "Nelly is very pretty as the Spring opens," he proclaimed, "and Grace is lovely."[9] There were other girls, too, in the vicinity, with whom Gerry craved "an innocent spell of puritanical phylandering."[10] Late in 1785, Nathan Dane, newly elected to Congress by the Massachusetts General Court, stayed for a few weeks with King and Gerry, and the three delegates entertained friends at dinners, supplying dozens of bottles of porter and claret and gallons of Madeira and other spirits.[11]

8. Rufus W. Griswold, *The Republican Court; or, American Society in the Days of Washington* (N. Y., 1855), 30; W. A. Duer, *New York as it Was During the Latter Part of the Last Century* (N. Y., 1849), 9–10. Later the mansion became the Bank Coffee House. The names of Smith and King Streets were subsequently changed to William and Pine Streets, respectively.

9. Elbridge Gerry to King, Mar. 14, 1785, Gerry Papers, Lib. Cong.; King to Gerry, Mar. 24, Apr. 18, 26, 1785, King Papers, N.-Y. Hist. Soc.

10. Gerry to King, Apr. 7, 1785, Gerry Papers, Lib. Cong.

11. Grace Mercer's bills for lodging, food, etc., Nathan Dane Papers, Mass. Hist. Soc.

As a delegate, King shared the larger social life of the city and was introduced to important New Yorkers. His early acquaintance with some of the New York delegates ripened into new friendships. He had come to know Robert R. Livingston well, and now John Jay and Egbert Benson became his political intimates.

Congress met in the main hall at the east end of the second floor of the City Hall. On the walls were portraits of Washington and the King and Queen of France. On a raised platform near the south wall stood the president's chair, upholstered with red silk damask. From a silk-fringed canopy above it hung damask curtains gathered in silken cords, which served as a dignified backdrop. The members sat in richly carved mahogany chairs trimmed with red morocco leather, each with a small "bureau table" in front.[12]

Congress soon recognized King's special interest in and aptitude for commerce, finance, and diplomacy. Almost from the beginning he served on committees dealing with these subjects—the Dutch loan, the launching of the mint, the condition of the Post Office, the regulation of the Indian trade, and the reports of Adams, Franklin, and Jefferson while they were in Europe seeking commercial treaties.

The continued presence of British troops in the northwestern posts of the United States, contrary to the terms of the Treaty of Paris, was a source of deep concern. King, who from the start was actively interested in national defense and land policy, served on a committee that recommended the raising of fifteen hundred troops and the creation of new military posts to check on the British, guard the frontier at Lakes Erie and Ontario, and facilitate dealing with the Indians. Although Congress abandoned the plan for new posts and reduced to seven hundred men the force to be raised for service in the Northwest, King supported the revised bill. "A little firmness and a great deal said about candor and harmony," he later observed, "brought the measure to adoption without much difficulty."[13] The soldiers, from Pennsylvania, New York, Connecticut, and New Jersey, became the first United States army in time of peace. They were charged with protecting the northwest frontier against "intruders" and Indian raids and safeguarding the public stores.

King deplored the unwillingness of Congress to appropriate money

12. James Grant Wilson, ed., *The Memorial History of the City of New-York*, 4 vols. (N. Y., 1892–93), III, 26–27.

13. King to Elbridge Gerry, Apr. 11, 1785, King Papers, N.-Y. Hist. Soc. King suspected that British officers were under orders to hold the existing posts. King to Daniel Kilham, Dec. 12, 1784, King-Kilham Corr., Columbia Univ. Lib.

to strengthen the War Department. In March 1785 General Henry Knox was chosen Secretary of War, at the low salary of $2,450. Believing that salary should be commensurate with the importance of the office, King had on three occasions voted for a higher amount. Nevertheless he urged Knox to accept; "The present wasteing condition of the Department requires the head of a Master; if you decline, I fear we shall be driven into an election that will neither aid the Dignity nor preserve the interest of the Union."[14] The plea was unnecessary, for the General had already accepted when he received King's letter, hoping, as King did, that eventually his salary would be raised.

When these two men first met is not known, but King had long been aware of Knox's military reputation. Now he and King became warm friends, sharing similar political views. King cheerfully collaborated with the new Secretary on measures for defense against hostile Indians along the frontiers. As a result of a motion by King in Congress, Knox was authorized to prevent his officers and men from engaging in trade.[15]

In the formulation of Indian policy, King counseled caution and prudence. Congress accepted his proposal to limit the troops accompanying the commissioners to treat with the Indians of the Northwest to a single company of infantry.[16] Though much distressed by the lawlessness of Virginia frontiersmen in Kentucky and Indian reprisals along the Ohio, King was cautious about committing to this region any federal troops besides the one infantry company. He was not convinced that there was any tribal organization against the whites on the Kentucky side of the river; the murders there, he wrote, had "been perpetrated by a few vagrant Indians who are without a name or Tribe."[17] Virginia was eager for war against the Indian towns, but King was decidedly against such rashness. On his motion, Congress on June 16, 1786, asked its Indian commissioners to obtain fuller information about this violence, and their report showed that scalping and horse-stealing had occurred on both sides, but that

14. King to Henry Knox, Mar. 10, 1785, Knox Papers, Mass. Hist. Soc.

15. J. G. King, Rufus King, 356.

16. *Journals of the Continental Congress*, XXIX, 822. Congress adopted the report of a committee headed by King that this infantry company, after attending the Great Miami treaty, should be under the command of Colonel Harmar. Partly as a result of these arrangements, the Americans and the Shawnees signed a treaty at the mouth of the Great Miami early in 1786. *Ibid.*, XXIX, 822, and XXX, 185–87.

17. King to Elbridge Gerry, June 8, 1786, King Papers, N.-Y. Hist. Soc.

the Indians unfortunately took revenge upon innocent whites. In the Wabash area, the commissioners continued, the Indian nations were not hostile; the depredations had been the work of lawless "banditti" who could easily be squelched.[18] Therefore King, like Secretary Knox, opposed troop reinforcements as unnecessary and likely to provoke a full-scale war.[19] The vote of Massachusetts, however, failed to prevent the sending of more troops to the rapids of the Ohio at Louisville, and a conciliatory measure, written by King, was defeated by the five southern states.[20] Subsequently, the northern and New England states, particularly Massachusetts, resisted proposals by Virginia to authorize an invasion of the Indian country, King and his colleagues being firmly convinced that the Indians were neither organized nor the only aggressors. Politically more significant was the northerners' lack of enthusiasm for securing the frontiers of a rival section of the country.

However, when Congress later learned from its Indian commissioners that Shawnees, Chippewas, and Cherokees were seeking unity for a border war against the United States, it voted unanimously to raise 1,340 men for three years, in addition to the 700 already in federal service.[21] New Englanders, including King, were at this time more mindful of Daniel Shays's threat to the federal arsenal at Springfield, Massachusetts.[22] Nearly all the new troops were to be raised in the New England states, 660 from Massachusetts alone. It was clear that Congress intended to suppress the uprising in Massachusetts before transferring any soldiers to the West. Fortunately, Massachusetts did not need the additional forces. Moreover, the Indian pressure relaxed, and federal recruitment slowed down. Some of the new troops were disbanded in the spring of 1787. Meanwhile, the defense of the frontier was undertaken by Tennesseans and Kentuckians without any help from Congress.

In helping to shape Indian relations, King maintained a cool head,

18. *Journals of the Continental Congress*, XXX, 349–51.

19. J. G. King, Rufus King, 362.

20. Although in King's handwriting, this measure was introduced by Charles Pettit of Pennsylvania. *Journals of the Continental Congress*, XXX, 353, 374. Eventually a compromise allowed Kentucky militia to reinforce the federal troops. *Ibid.*, 380–81.

21. *Ibid.*, XXI, 892.

22. For a recent and hostile view of Knox's part in this, see Forrest McDonald, *E Pluribus Unum: The Formation of the American Republic, 1776–1790* (Boston, 1965), 149–50.

partly from a desire to secure peace on the frontiers at the lowest possible cost and partly from a determination to resist an Indian policy forced on Congress by the South. Expensive Indian wars would not only let loose trigger-happy frontiersmen but, if authorized by Congress, would further drain the federal treasury. King had no intimate knowledge of Indian life, and he never experienced border raids, but his advocacy of prudence was consistent with a just and humane Indian policy.[23]

During his first two years in Congress, he shared an all-too-common political myopia. The proceedings reflected the fears of parochial politicians, worried over expenses their states would ultimately bear and jockeying for advantage in interstate disputes. The troublesome land controversy between Massachusetts and New York was a case in point. Many Massachusetts migrants had settled on lands in a vast region west of the Hudson that later became the central part of New York State. The Massachusetts claim rested upon the original charter of 1628 whereby the Governor and Company of Massachusetts Bay had been granted lands stretching westward to the Pacific. If this claim were allowed, Massachusetts would eventually gain much-needed revenue from the area.

The Massachusetts-New York land question led to long, complicated, and technical negotiations. Congress had assumed jurisdiction over the dispute, but doubts about the extent of its power, difficulty in the selection of impartial judges, disagreement over the place where the judges should hold court, and especially the failure of some judges to accept their appointment created delays. As a delegate to Congress, and especially after his designation as one of the attorneys for his state, King became enmeshed in a political and legal snarl which absorbed the energies of leading lawyers and politicians of both states. By a close vote, Congress had chosen Williamsburg, Virginia, as the site of adjudication by a special court, but New York tried to change the location. With Gerry temporarily absent in New England, King confronted almost single-handedly what Gerry called "a phalanx of able and intriguing politicians."[24] "Never in my life," King confessed, "have I been so closely confined as since

23. In 1786 King was on committees which considered the speech to Congress by the Seneca chief, Cornplanter, and which conferred with the Wyandot leader, Scotosh: J. G. King, Rufus King, 373–77, *passim.*

24. Elbridge Gerry to King, Apr. 17, 1785, King, ed., *King Correspondence*, I, 86.

I have been in this City. You know very well my situation. Constant watching fatigues the strongest and most experienced. What must then be my condition?"[25]

After further delay, chiefly because judges were reluctant to serve on the special court, the representatives of Massachusetts and New York decided to dispense with the court and negotiate directly. Accordingly, on November 30, 1786, they met at Hartford, Connecticut. The New Yorkers were James Duane, Robert R. Livingston, Egbert Benson, John Haring, Melancton Smith, Robert Yates, and John Lansing, the first three being the principal negotiators. Representing Massachusetts were John Lowell, James Sullivan, Theophilus Parsons, and King.[26]

Both states were eager to settle their conflicting claims. The Massachusetts agents, however, doubted that their claim would be upheld by an impartial court, since the revocation of the original charter of 1628 and the acceptance of a new one in 1691 had limited the Bay Colony's jurisdiction to New England. Moreover, as recently as 1782 a federal court had ruled against Connecticut's claim to a strip of land some of her citizens had settled in the Wyoming Valley of Pennsylvania. The Massachusetts agents, therefore, were now ready to cash in on their claim for all that it would yield; the New Yorkers, for their part, wished for a clear and uncontested title. In two weeks an agreement was reached. Massachusetts yielded her claim to sovereignty over the entire territory, and New York conceded full title to almost half of the thirteen million acres involved, comprising ten townships near present-day Binghamton and six million acres to the west inhabited mainly by the Seneca and the Cayuga.[27]

The sale of this land would bring a welcome and much-needed windfall to the Bay State. Plans to speculate in the new land by means of a lottery were launched among the agents themselves before they left Hartford. Apparently, King was included in these early arrangements, but he later withdrew.[28] When in 1788 Nathaniel Gorham and Oliver Phelps organized their syndicate to buy a great tract of six million acres, King seems to have considered becoming one of the

25. King to Gerry, May 1, 1785, King Papers, N.-Y. Hist. Soc.

26. Burnett, ed., *Letters of Continental Congress*, VII, 509*n*; Amory, *Sullivan*, I, 162, 164; J. G. King, Rufus King, 209.

27. J. G. King, Rufus King, 443. For details of the settlement, *ibid.*, ch. 51.

28. *Ibid.*, 448–49; King to Theophilus Parsons, Apr. 8, 1787, King, ed., *King Correspondence*, I, 218.

proprietors. After the purchase, however, he declined to join the venture.[29] Perhaps he thought he would be charged with profiteering from a settlement in which he had participated, though to do so would not have been contrary to the business ethics of the time. More probably, he was unwilling to take the risk inherent in speculation in wilderness lands. Some of his close friends became heavily involved in land deals, but throughout his life he avoided land speculation.

During 1785, while Congress dealt with many matters of concern to particular states, including boundaries, jurisdiction, and the terms of cession of western lands to the federal government, King helped to secure the appointment of federal commissioners to survey and permanently fix the long unsettled boundary between Massachusetts and New York. He and Gerry also took timely action to stop an attempt of dissidents in Maine to secede from Massachusetts.[30] After New York had given up its shadowy claims to western lands in 1780, Congress had recommended that states with western land claims should cede them to the Union. Virginia and several other states had done so, but in November 1784 North Carolina repealed its act of cession. King, as chairman of a committee to examine North Carolina's action, reported on May 20, 1785, that the act of cession had given Congress a right to accept within one year. As no later act could alter the cession, Congress was duty-bound to accept it; he therefore recommended acceptance and a tactful application to the North Carolina legislature to rescind its repeal. Realizing, however, that such a bold stance could not be enforced, Congress voted only to appeal to the North Carolina legislature.[31] No doubt the earnest King, trained in the law and still inclined to formulate explicit legal reasons for a move, learned a lesson in political tact. Such a mild appeal to the Carolinians, even though amended to point out that other states had already ceded their claims, had no influence, and it was not until 1790 that North Carolina definitively ceded her western territory to the Union.

King's best-known work in his two and a half years in the Confederation Congress was in pushing for the exclusion of slavery in

29. Phelps to King, Apr. 5, 1788, King, ed., *King Correspondence*, I, 325; Gorham to King, Apr. 6, 1788, *ibid.*, 324–25.

30. *Journals of the Continental Congress*, XXIX, 781–86, 898; King and Nathan Dane to James Bowdoin, Dec. 5, 1785, Boston Pub. Lib.; Elbridge Gerry and King to Caleb Davis, Oct. 27, 1785, Caleb Davis Papers, Mass. Hist. Soc.

31. *Journals of the Continental Congress*, XXVIII, 381–87.

the Northwest Territory. As a boy he had known a benevolent form of slavery in his father's household in Scarborough, and after Massachusetts abolished the institution he was not much aroused by its persistence in other states since they had sole jurisdiction over slavery within their borders. But slavery in federal territory was quite a different thing, and from 1785 until his death Rufus King decried slavery on federal lands.

King seems to have been impelled into action against slavery by Timothy Pickering of Massachusetts. In March 1785, Pickering, quartermaster-general of the Revolutionary Army, who was now interested in western lands, asked Elbridge Gerry what Congress was likely to do about public land. As he was on the point of leaving New York, Gerry sent Pickering a copy of a proposed land ordinance and advised him to correspond with King. Losing no time, Pickering sent King two long letters, commenting on the land measure and lamenting Congress's rejection a year earlier of Jefferson's proposal to forbid slavery in the federal territories after 1800.[32] Indeed Pickering would have excluded slavery at once:

> The admission of it for a day or an hour ought to have been forbidden. It will be infinitely easier to prevent the evil at first, than to eradicate it or check it at any future time. . . . But why do I expostulate with you who already see all the reasons on the Subject. . . . To suffer the continuance of slaves until they can gradually be emancipated in States already overrun with them may be pardonable, because unavoidable without hazarding greater evils; but to introduce them into countries where none now exist, countries which have been talked of—which we have boasted of—as an asylum to the oppressed of the Earth—can never be forgiven. For God's sake, then, let one more effort be made to prevent so terrible a calamity.[33]

King probably did not know Pickering personally when he received this fervent appeal, but both men shared a Puritan heritage, were political conservatives from Essex County towns, and had for some time been concerned with problems of the West. Though he hardly shared Pickering's passionate moralism, his viewpoint was

32. Timothy Pickering to Elbridge Gerry, Mar. 1, 1785, King, ed., *King Correspondence*, I, 72-73; Pickering to King, two letters dated Mar. 8, 1785, King Papers, N.-Y. Hist. Soc.

33. Pickering to King, Mar. 8, 1785, King Papers, N.-Y. Hist. Soc.

similar.[34] On March 16 he presented a proposition to forbid slavery in the new states to be formed out of the western territory. It was the first public plan for the immediate exclusion of slavery in the West.[35] By a vote of eight to three (Virginia and the Carolinas opposing), Congress ordered the motion to committee. King called for the individual yeas and nays, and eighteen of the twenty-six delegates present supported the measure. As chairman of the committee to study it, King reported on April 6 a resolve which, like Jefferson's earlier plan, postponed the ban until after 1800. It also included a fugitive slave proviso. These features were designed to win support from the slave states, but Congress still took no action. Recognizing that the committee revisions were unacceptable to the northern delegations, King refrained from pressing the issue. His political sense told him the time was not yet ripe for action.

King's interest in the formulation of land policy extended beyond the slavery question. He also served on a committee that dealt with the method of settlement. The southern delegates, led by William Grayson of Virginia, favored the sale of individual lots of land, whereas the New Englanders, led by King and David Howell of Rhode Island, held out for compact township settlements. Howell, determined that grasping speculators should not profit unfairly, hoped that all citizens would be able to buy land on equal terms. "Infinite pains," he wrote, "are taken by a certain sett of men vulgarly called Land robbers or Land-sharks who have it in their power to engross the best lands."[36] Less indignant about speculators than Howell, King nevertheless wished to establish equal opportunity for western settlers.

Debate on the land ordinance was heated and prolonged. Howell called it the most complicated and embarrassing subject before Congress since the peace with England, and Grayson complained that what had been written and spoken "would fill forty Volumns."[37] Before Congress adopted the plan of selling alternate townships in

34. King to Pickering, Apr. 15, 1785, King Papers, N.-Y. Hist. Soc.

35. *Journals of the Continental Congress*, XXVIII, 164. The original motion is in Papers of the Continental Congress, No. 31, f. 327, National Archives; J. G. King, Rufus King, 229–30.

36. David Howell to William Greene, Apr. 29, 1785, Burnett, ed., *Letters of Continental Congress*, VIII, 106–07. The New England land promoters did not assault Congress until after the passage of the Land Ordinance of 1785.

37. William Grayson to Timothy Pickering, Apr. 27, 1785, *ibid.*, 106.

checkerboard pattern, King vainly sought to limit further the area of land to be sold by sections, but he accepted the final compromise and was fairly satisfied.[38] "I am persuaded great benefits will result from it," he wrote Gerry. "You will find that it bears strong features of an eastern System. When I tell you the history of this ordinance you shall acknowledge that I have some merit in the business."[39]

Two provisions of the committee report revealed the virtues and limitations of New England Puritanism: the reservation in each township of one section for a public school, and another for religious purposes. King favored these provisions and no doubt insisted upon their inclusion in the report. Although Congress found no objection to the education clause, it struck out the provision for religion. William Samuel Johnson of Connecticut and King tried to substitute the term "charitable" for "religious," but failed.[40]

In upholding the principle of state aid to religion, King adhered to the traditional concept in most of the states and found himself for the first time in direct opposition to James Madison. The Virginian, who was not then in Congress although he had been a prominent wartime member, exclaimed to Monroe: "How a regulation so unjust in itself, so foreign to the Authority of Congress, so hurtful to the sale of the public land, and smelling so strongly of an antiquated Bigotry, could have received the countenance of a Committee is truly matter of astonishment."[41] To King, of course, it was perfectly natural.

He could not be charged with antiquated bigotry if one accepted the dominant attitudes of late eighteenth-century America. An Episcopalian, he remarked that he had never wished to see the "lawn sleeves" of Episcopal bishops in America. "I never liked the Hier-

38. *Journals of the Continental Congress*, XXVIII, 339 (for King's motion, see 337–38). When Richard Henry Lee informed General Washington that all the members but one assented to the ordinance, he almost certainly meant Howell, and not King. Lee to Washington, May 7, 1785, Washington Papers, Lib. Cong. Burnett, *Continental Congress*, 625, assumed that King was the determined opponent of the ordinance at this point, but the *Journals of the Continental Congress*, XXVIII, 335–36, 339, do not seem to support this conjecture. See J. G. King, Rufus King, 244*n*.

39. King to Elbridge Gerry, May 8, 1785, King Papers, N.-Y. Hist. Soc.

40. J. G. King, Rufus King, 239, 240. For the generally similar views of these men, see George C. Groce, Jr., *William Samuel Johnson, a Maker of the Constitution* (N. Y., 1937), 129, and William Samuel Johnson to King, Mar. 2, 1798, King Papers, N.-Y. Hist. Soc.

41. James Madison to James Monroe, May 29, 1785, Burnett, ed., *Letters of Continental Congress*, VIII, viii.

archy of the Church—an equality in the teachers of Religion, and a dependence on the people, are republican sentiments—but if the Clergy combine, they will have their influence on Government."[42] These words, penned at the very time the land ordinance was under discussion, were not those of a bigot, but neither did they imply a wall of separation between church and state.

On May 20, 1785, Congress finally passed its far-reaching ordinance for the survey and sale of western lands. It was, as King observed, a compromise of opinions, but he rightly foresaw that it would result in great benefit to the country.[43] In 1787 King served on one of the committees appointed to formulate a more definite and comprehensive plan of territorial government to supplement and in part supersede Jefferson's initial proposals in the Ordinance of 1784. He helped to keep alive two features of the 1784 ordinance: the provision that guaranteed that no act of a territorial legislature should be construed to affect federal lands and the one preventing lands of nonresident owners from being taxed higher than those of residents. Although this was pleasing to speculators, King thought it but simple justice. He seems to have shared Pickering's impression that pioneer settlers were nearly as uncontrollable as the Indians.[44] These measures, and a motion, seconded by King, for the free navigation of the waters tributary to the Mississippi and the St. Lawrence, were finally embodied in the Ordinance of 1787.[45]

The Northwest Ordinance, excluding slavery from the Northwest Territory, was adopted on July 13, while King was absent at the federal Convention in Philadelphia. What he had contended for two years earlier—the *immediate* prohibition of slavery in these federal lands—had been proposed at the last moment by his Massachusetts colleague, Nathan Dane. Dane had omitted the controversial antislavery article from his original draft, but finding sentiment in Congress unexpectedly favorable, he later introduced it, and it was

42. King to Elbridge Gerry, May 8, 1785, King Papers, N.-Y. Hist. Soc.

43. King to Timothy Pickering, May 30, 1785, *ibid.*

44. *Ibid.*, and Pickering to King, June 4, 1785, *ibid.* Although not a speculator himself, King was not hostile to land promoters, many of whom were New Englanders. In *Rise of the West, 1754–1830* (N. Y., 1965), 129, Francis S. Philbrick regards King as the leader of those who wished to provide stronger governments in the West in order to control the settlers. Probably so, though the evidence is not conclusive as to King's initiative.

45. For a detailed account of King's activities mentioned here, see J. G. King, Rufus King, ch. 52.

agreed to without opposition.[46] The change in congressional opinion reflected the influence of northern land promoters and the growing likelihood that northerners would pour into the old Northwest. At this time the Ohio Company was pressuring Congress to authorize its purchase of a million and a half acres in the territory, and it is not unlikely that the persuasive arguments of Manasseh Cutler, the company's lobbyist, concerning the terms on which his clients would purchase influenced the delegates to accept the antislavery provision. Southern planters' anticipation of competition in the Northwest was another element. Grayson admitted that the southern delegates agreed to the clause "for the purpose of preventing Tobacco and Indigo from being made on the N. W. side of the Ohio as well as for several other political reasons."[47]

If King was solicitous about the development of the West, he was far more concerned about the prosperity of the East. As a coastal New Englander, he had all his life been exposed to ocean shipping, trade, and the legal complications of commerce upon which he built his career as a lawyer. His closest political associates were similarly responsive to maritime issues. As New Englanders sharing a sectional bias, these men doubted that commerce would thrive if entrusted to the leadership of southerners, who considered shipping of secondary importance and who had ideas that seemed harmful to the trade of the North.

Nowhere was King's position more obvious than in the Jay-Gardoqui negotiations. On May 15, five days before the passage of the Land Ordinance of 1785, Don Diego de Gardoqui arrived as Spanish minister to the United States. On July 20, Congress authorized John Jay as secretary of foreign affairs to negotiate with him on matters in dispute between the two countries. In the previous year, Spain had refused to allow American shipping to pass freely on the lower Mississippi River, and Gardoqui was specifically instructed not to make any concession on the navigation of the river. Moreover, Spain refused to accept the thirty-first parallel, established

46. Dane to King, July 16, 1787, King, ed., *King Correspondence*, I, 290.

47. William Grayson to James Monroe, Aug. 8, 1787, Burnett, ed., *Letters of Continental Congress*, VIII, 632. For the Ohio Company lobbying, see William Parker Cutler and Julia Perkins Cutler, *Life, Journals and Correspondence of Rev. Manasseh Cutler, LL.D.*, 2 vols. (Cincinnati, 1888), I, 350–52. A convenient, brief account of the relation of easterners and land speculators to the ordinances of 1785 and 1787 is in Jensen, *New Nation*, 354–58. Cf. Philbrick, *Rise of the West*, 127–32.

by the Anglo-American peace treaty, as the boundary between Florida and the United States. Both countries, however, sought a commercial treaty.

Secretary Jay was required to report to Congress before making any proposals to the Spanish envoy and before concluding agreements with him. Frustrated, he asked Congress for greater freedom of negotiation. King sat on two committees concerned with the proceedings. One of these, of which Monroe was chairman, freed Jay of a number of restrictions but bound him more tightly to the main subject of his negotiations: the right of the United States to its territorial boundary at the thirty-first parallel and to the free navigation of the Mississippi. And still he was not to sign anything without the express approval of Congress.

The discussions dragged on for nine months. Gardoqui refused to concede free navigation of the Mississippi south of the Spanish border, a point for which Jay steadily contended. At length the Secretary decided that a commercial treaty with Spain could be obtained only by dropping the demand for free navigation of the river, and on May 29, 1786, he suggested that Congress appoint a secret committee to instruct him on each point of the proposed treaty. Monroe, who suspected Jay of intriguing to have his instructions changed "so as to occlude the Mississippi," considered this a maneuver to shift responsibility, relieving the Secretary of the obligation to seek the opening of the river. According to Monroe, Rufus King was "associated in this business." Indeed King was eager to cooperate. In a lengthy speech on May 30 he tried to convince Congress of the need for a reciprocity treaty with Spain, and the next day he was appointed head of the committee to which Jay's proposal was referred.[48]

King's views of the Mississippi question coincided with Jay's, though no clear evidence points to collusion. King showed little direct interest in the opening of the Mississippi River trade, and he seriously doubted that westerners would remain in the Union. The activities and interests of the people on both sides of the Appalachians, he predicted, would be "so different and probably so opposite, that an entire separation must ensue." If the Mississippi were

48. James Monroe to George Washington, Aug. 20, 1786, and Monroe to James Madison, May 31, 1786, Burnett, ed., *Letters of Continental Congress*, VIII, 447, 375; *Journals of the Continental Congress*, XXX, 323. King's colleagues on the committee were Monroe and Pettit of Pennsylvania.

freely used at this time, he would consider "every emigrant to that country from the Atlantic States as forever lost to the Confederacy. . . . Commerce would not be across the Appalachian Mountains, but wholly confined to the Mississippi." He wondered whether it was wise to encourage Americans to settle beyond the mountains, even if the sale of lands there reduced the domestic debt. If the western people were "cut off for a time from any connection, except with the old States across the Mountains," he argued somewhat ambiguously, "a Government might be instituted so connecting them with the Atlantic States as would be highly beneficial to them both and promise a considerable trade."[49]

To King the important objective was a commercial treaty with exact reciprocity. He wished to stipulate that masts and timber for Spanish ships be bought in the United States and paid for in specie and that the Philippines be opened to American vessels. For its part, the United States, without relinquishing the right to free navigation of the Mississippi, would agree not to exercise it for twenty or twenty-five years, a concession Jay no doubt had urged upon the secret committee. "Would not such a treaty be of vast importance to the Atlantic States, particularly the Western division of them?" wrote King to Gerry. "Would not the Fish, Flour and other products of the U. S. acquire thereby a manifest superiority in Spain over similar commodities of any other country? Would not the conventional forbearance of the use of the Mississippi implicate most strongly the right of the U. S. independent of the Convention or Treaty?"[50] Conceding that popular opinion throughout the country favored free navigation and admitting its future importance to the West, he nevertheless saw no way to induce Spain to agree to it. A temporary concession on this score, he thought, would be wise.

Opinions about the Spanish negotiation were inflamed by sectional prejudices. King would accomplish his purpose, Monroe sourly observed, if he secured a market for fish and diverted western commerce toward the Hudson.[51] King countered that the Virginia delegates were probably deeply interested in Ohio and Kentucky lands. No wonder they insisted on the immediate, free navigation of the Missis-

49. King to Elbridge Gerry, June 4, 1786, King Papers, N.-Y. Hist. Soc.
50. *Ibid.*
51. This was a snide comment on King's marriage in March 1786 to a wealthy New York girl. James Monroe to James Madison, May 31, 1786, Burnett, ed., *Letters of Continental Congress*, VIII, 377.

sippi. But the sale of western lands, King believed, did not depend on the river trade; the actual settlers would buy them anyway, if the price were reasonable. Yielding to Spain on the Mississippi question would temporarily cut off the western population from the river trade, but it might strengthen the bonds of East and West across the mountains. He feared, too, that if a treaty were not effected, Spain would try to forestall United States expansion by a closer tie with Great Britain.[52]

Southerners saw no advantage in a treaty which would benefit primarily New England and the middle states if the price were the shutting off of the great river. Monroe charged that Jay, supported by the Massachusetts delegation, had managed a dishonest intrigue, the "most illiberal" that he had ever seen from that state. Excepting Gorham from his indictment, and believing Dane to be at least honest, the Virginian singled out King as one whose political honesty he doubted.[53]

On the secret committee, King and the like-minded Charles Pettit were able to defeat Monroe, whose impotence fed his suspicions and antagonisms. At King's request, Congress discharged the committee, whose report was then debated. The Massachusetts delegates headed the drive to repeal the instruction binding Jay to obtain the free navigation of the Mississippi. King, who thought that no sensible man north of the Potomac would disapprove of their action, proceeded to draft some new instructions to Jay. He presented them to Congress on August 16 and defended them in a long speech. Spain was the best market for American fish, he argued. A treaty with her was of the utmost consequence to New England but would benefit all the states. Temporary renunciation of Mississippi navigation was only an agreement "to forbear the use of that which we could not at present enjoy," and Spain would continue to exclude the Americans until they asserted their right by arms. Moreover, Spain was by no means a contemptible enemy, and France would favor if not join her, since the European maritime powers considered America a rival and never wished the United States to be powerful. "Refusing to treat on the terms proposed," he declared, "is sacrificing the interest and happiness of a Million to promote the views of speculating landjobbers." To break off negotiations would lead Spain to strengthen her

52. King to Elbridge Gerry, June 4, 1786, King Papers, N.-Y. Hist. Soc.

53. James Monroe to Thomas Jefferson, July 16, 1786, Burnett, ed., *Letters of Continental Congress*, VIII, 404.

forces at New Orleans. The Americans would try to force a passage, precipitating a war. No man east of the Delaware would vote for a war which so sacrificed the interests of the eastern states. After bitter debate, King's motion to repeal Jay's instruction was adopted, the seven northern states supporting it, the five southern states opposing it. Thus on August 29 Jay was authorized to "forbear" American navigation rights.[54]

In the belief that the proposed commercial treaty might be made less unpalatable to the South and that Jay would have more bargaining power now that he was freed of the Mississippi instruction, King moved that Jay be required to insist on the thirty-first parallel as the Florida boundary. The southern delegates were not mollified, however, and this feature was accepted by the same seven to five division.[55]

Southern efforts to force a reconsideration of the repeal of Jay's instruction were foiled by parliamentary maneuver. On King's motion, Congress barred further discussion of the validity of the repeal by vote of only seven states. In the meantime, the Secretary was in the dilemma of having to deal with an intransigent Spain on the one side and an extreme and unabated division of opinion in his own country. By the spring of 1787, after the mercantile cause had lost support in Congress, a wave of anger followed the seizure by the Spanish authorities at Natchez of the cargo of a North Carolina merchant who had tried to send it down the Mississippi for export. When on April 18 Madison proposed that Jefferson, then Minister to France, should go directly to Madrid and seek concessions that Jay had been unable to obtain, King successfully moved for a delay; five days later Jay reported his objections to the scheme, and the idea was dropped. However, delegates from seven of the eight states represented in Congress on May 10 united to reopen the question of repeal. The next day the Georgia delegates moved that the repeal did not authorize the Secretary to permit the impairment or abandonment of the right of free navigation, nor did it give up any right to territory. King then made a motion which would in effect emasculate the measure by striking out crucial parts of it. Three states, including his own, assured the success of this tactic; the Georgia resolve, as

54. King to Nathan Dane, Aug. 17, 1786, *ibid.*, 437; J. G. King, Rufus King, 404; C. Thomson, "Minutes of Proceedings," Aug. 16, 1786, Burnett, ed., *Letters of Continental Congress*, VIII, 429–30; *Journals of the Continental Congress*, XXXI, 595, 694–97.

55. *Journals of the Continental Congress*, XXXI, 568–69.

amended, asserted that Congress did not authorize Jay to enter into any stipulation with the Spanish envoy.[56] This watered-down and completely stultifying outcome ended the long and frustrating attempt to make a treaty with Spain. The unresolved issues awaited a fresh effort twelve years later under more favorable circumstances.

56. J. G. King, Rufus King, 413–14, 419–22, 425–26; James Madison, "Notes of Debates," *Journals of the Continental Congress*, XXXIII, 734–36; *ibid.*, XXXII, 278–79, 288–90.

CHAPTER V

THE CRISIS OF THE CONFEDERATION

NEW YORK WAS A GAY CITY. DURING HIS FIRST MONTHS THERE IN THE winter and spring of 1785, Rufus King was impressed by the number of parties, public assemblies, and concerts. In this state capital and seat of Congress, frequent public functions added to the festivities of the rich, and aspiring politicians hobnobbed with the great and near-great and drank Madeira with foreign diplomats.[1] King, who took his public responsibilities most seriously, had little time for leisure, and his natural reserve no doubt inhibited a sudden plunge into the new social whirl. Late in the year, however, he went to the refurbished John Street Theater and was charmed by the Old American Company directed by Lewis Hallam and John Henry. King enjoyed the theater more than any other amusement in the city.[2] He did not allow his stern Puritan upbringing to inhibit his pleasure at these performances, which he had not been able to see in Newburyport or Boston.

Attending the theater was a gala occasion. Hallam and Henry of-

1. For an excellent account of the city at this time see Sidney I. Pomerantz, *New York an American City, 1783–1803: A Study of Urban Life* (N. Y., 1938), ch. 9.

2. King to Daniel Kilham, Dec. 8, 1785, King, ed., *King Correspondence*, II, 609. Typically bare of descriptive details, King's letters mentioned none of the actors, nor did they refer to a single play by name.

fered everything from popular comedies, farces, and comic operas to tragedies, from Sheridan and Goldsmith to Shakespeare. If two plays were presented in the evening, a long intermission permitted gentlemen to step out to an adjoining building for "spirits, punch, grog, jellies, cakes and fruit."[3] There is no record that King experienced these delights, but his interest in the stage was genuine. Early in 1788, John Henry, inquiring about a theater in Portsmouth, New Hampshire, flattered him as "our Gracious Patron" and "one of the most liberal minds of the Western World."[4]

King was not at first seriously drawn to the opposite sex. At Mrs. Mercer's boarding house where he and Gerry lived for a time, the landlady and her two daughters, Nelly and Grace, formed part of what King called "our family," but the relationship, though friendly, was not one to encourage intimacy. So far, his only serious love had been Abigail Lee. King promptly denied a rumor that he had fallen in love again. "At present I think it improper to bow to beauty, or to bend to fortune," he wrote; "so negligent have I been on this subject, that . . . I think of neither except when I think of home."[5] He remembered his many friends in Newburyport and inquired of their doings. Anticipating the day when he would rejoin them, he announced to Daniel Kilham, "Not even the Ladies of this city, agreeable as many of them are, shall with all *their Frailties* detain me. I am, thank God, no prisoner—my system [scheme of life] will not admit of the idea. Both you and I have passed that feverish age, which leads to indiscreet attachments and subjects the Reason to the passions."[6]

After about a year at Mrs. Mercer's, King moved to the home of a respected and well-known merchant, John Alsop, on Smith Street (later William Street) at the corner of Maiden Lane. Alsop had amassed a fortune chiefly in the dry goods trade, and was president of the New York Chamber of Commerce when King first met him. He had been prominent in committees of correspondence elected in the city in 1774 and 1775 and had been a delegate to the first and

3. N. Y. *Daily Advertiser*, Jan. 13, 1786. For actors and performances see George C. D. Odell, *Annals of the New York Stage* (N. Y., 1927), I, which draws heavily upon contemporary newspapers.

4. John Henry to King, Jan. 23, 1788, King Papers, N.-Y. Hist. Soc.

5. King to Kilham, Apr. 26, 1785, King-Kilham Corr., Columbia Univ. Lib. For references to Abigail see King's letters of Mar. 8, Apr. 26, Sept. 19, Oct. 10, Dec. 4, 1785, *ibid.*

6. King to Kilham, Dec. 4, 8, 1785, *ibid.*

second Continental Congresses until the adoption of the Declaration of Independence. Active in the colonial cause, he nevertheless held to a conservative belief in the empire and hoped for a reconciliation with Great Britain. The irrevocable act of independence, and particularly its unanimous approval by the New York constitutional convention at Kingston, led him to resign his seat in Congress. When the British army occupied New York City, Alsop retired to Middletown, Connecticut, home of his brother Richard, a wealthy merchant.[7] After the peace, he reoccupied his house in New York, although he was no longer active in business. His wife, Mary Frogat, had died in 1772, when their only child, Mary, was three years old. Young Mary spent the war years with her father at Middletown and returned with him afterward to New York.

Black-haired, blue-eyed Mary, a quiet and sensitive girl with a radiant charm, was sixteen years old in 1786. Rufus King was thirty and a courteous, discreet, and discerning young man. The two soon fell in love. In March, John Jay passed on the gossip to Catherine Livingston that Miss Alsop would soon be married to one whose talents and manners did credit to her judgment.[8]

On March 30, 1786, six days after King's thirty-first birthday, he and Mary were married by the Reverend Samuel Provoost, the rector of St. Paul's Chapel who was soon to become the first Episcopal bishop of New York. The wedding may have taken place in the chapel, but judging from Alsop's invitation to General Samuel B. Webb "to see Mr. King take his [Alsop's] daughter by the hand and to pass the Evening," it was at the Alsop home. Members of Congress, among them James Monroe, attended. A daughter of one of the six bridesmaids later recalled that "the youth, beauty and fortune of the bride had made her a great belle and her marriage was a serious disappointment to many aspirants. The wedding was very splendid . . . and at the supper was produced for the first time wine which had been purchased and put aside at the birth of the bride, for this very occasion. The pipe containing it had been bricked up in one of the arches in the house . . . and had escaped the scrutiny of

7. Authorities differ on whether John Alsop was born in Connecticut or New York. See W. Barrett (pseud. of Alfred J. Scoville), *Old Merchants of New York City*, 5 vols. (N. Y., 1863), II, 294–95; J. G. King, Rufus King, 316–18; King, ed., *King Correspondence*, I, 131*n*; Wilbur C. Abbott, *New York in the American Revolution* (N. Y., 1929), 148.

8. John Jay to Catherine W. Livingston, Mar. 20, 1786, Matthew Ridley Papers, Mass. Hist. Soc.

the British officers, who had made their headquarters there. The rest of Mr. Alsop's wine was not so fortunate."[9]

The day after the wedding, the newlyweds went on what today would be considered an odd honeymoon. Accompanied by bridesmaids and groomsmen, they drove for an "excursion" to Jamaica on Long Island, amid a deep and unseasonable snowstorm. Three days later, the Kings were again in the city. "I am happy," King exulted to Gerry, and his underscored words displayed an emotion usually suppressed in his letters.[10]

For some time the Kings lived in the Alsop house on Smith Street. King had not given up the idea of returning to Massachusetts, but social obligations, as well as his public responsibilities, kept him and his bride in New York. As they entertained the customary well-wishers, King was pleased by the polite attention of so many people but glad when the prolonged amenities came to an end. It was two weeks before he notified his relatives in Maine of his marriage; physical separation and diverging interests had pushed them into the background of his active and more sophisticated life. When he finally wrote to his brother-in-law Southgate, he took care to describe John Alsop as a former delegate to Congress, a "very respectable and eminent merchant," now retired with "a very handsome fortune" and enjoying the fruits of an industrious and virtuous life. Strangely, King did not write directly to his stepmother. He nevertheless hoped to bring Mary to New England and introduce her to his family and friends, but it was many months before the Kings were able to leave New York City.[11]

The marriage of Rufus King and Mary Alsop was more than a love match. King had married wealth; Arthur Lee asserted that King had married a lady with fifty thousand pounds, and James Monroe ob-

9. N. Y. *Daily Advertiser*, Apr. 3, 1786; J. G. King, Rufus King, 318–19; John Alsop to Samuel B. Webb, Mar. 27, 1786, owned by James G. King, New York; Mary A. Patrick to Charles King, undated, King, ed., *King Correspondence*, I, 130*n*. In this volume the wedding date is given erroneously as Mar. 31, *ibid.*, 130.

10. King, ed., *King Correspondence*, I, 131*n*; King to Elbridge Gerry, Apr. 5, 1786, King Papers, N.-Y. Hist. Soc.

11. King to Elbridge Gerry, Apr. 5, 9, 1786, King Papers, N.-Y. Hist. Soc.; King to Robert Southgate, Apr. 12, 1786, King, ed., *King Correspondence*, I, 132; King to Aaron Porter, Apr. 13, 1786, Porter Papers, Craigie-Longfellow House. King intended to bring his bride to Massachusetts in June, but he changed his mind lest his presence there be interpreted by the General Court, then sitting, as a bid for re-election as a delegate. King to Gerry, May 14, 1786, King, ed., *King Correspondence*, I, 136.

served that Mary was "a woman of fortune."[12] King's was only one of many prominent interstate marriages in 1786. Gerry, Monroe, and Samuel Osgood married New York girls, and John Adams's daughter became the bride of Colonel William S. Smith, another New Yorker. John Jay, pleased with such alliances, believed they tended to break down parochialism and to bind the people as Americans to one nation, and Adams wrote King, "It will be unnatural if federal Purposes are not answered by all these Intermarriages."[13]

Mrs. King was widely admired by New York society, but her retiring nature set her apart. She was not addicted to the personal display so often encountered among the wealthy. She did not need it. A striking beauty, she had been carefully educated under her father's watchful eye to combine character and education with her generous natural endowments. Her finely sculptured features, brunette complexion, and dignified bearing were later captured in portraits by John Trumbull, who came to know her through his friendship with King.[14]

The Kings moved in the most fashionable New York society, which included the Duers, the Livingstons, the Jays, members of Congress and their wives, and other public officials, American and foreign. Sometimes Mary King entertained her own guests. Once, soon after their marriage, her husband dashed off a letter to Gerry to the accompaniment of "three or four chattering girls." Invitations to dine out were customary and frequent, and the wine flowed freely in the homes of such great entertainers as the Jays, the Temples, and the Knoxes.[15] King's acceptance by the controlling families of the city made him a more effective delegate to Congress. At ease among

12. Arthur Lee to Nancy Shippen, July 11, 1789, Ethel Armes, ed., *Nancy Shippen; Her Journal Book . . . with Letters to Her and About Her* (Phila., 1935), 267. Two months after King's wedding, Monroe sourly observed to James Madison that the Massachusetts delegate had "married a woman of fortune in New York so that if he secures a market for fish and turns the commerce of the Western country down this river [the Hudson] he obtains his object." May 31, 1786, Burnett, ed., *Letters of Continental Congress*, VIII, 377.

13. John Jay to John Adams, May 4, 1786, Henry P. Johnston, ed., *Correspondence and Public Papers of John Jay*, 4 vols. (N. Y., 1890–93), III, 194–95; John Adams to Rufus King, June 14, 1786, King Papers, N.-Y. Hist. Soc.

14. Griswold, *Republican Court*, 99–101, describes Mary King and contains an engraving of one of Trumbull's two portraits of her.

15. King to Elbridge Gerry, Apr. 16, 1786, King, ed., *King Correspondence*, I, 167. On Mrs. Jay's extensive "invitation list" for 1787 and 1788 were the names of more than a hundred persons or couples, including John Alsop and the Kings. Griswold, *Republican Court*, 98–99.

lawyers and merchants, he found support for his defense of mercantile interests.

King's friends in New York, as in New England, could count on his regular attendance in Congress. Poor attendance continually harassed that body. The state legislatures were slow in electing delegates, and the delegates, once elected, were irregular in their attendance. Since seven states were necessary for ordinary business and nine for important decisions involving commerce, finance, military affairs, or treaties, Congress was frequently forced to adjourn from day to day for lack of a quorum. In the spring of 1786 a committee studied the power of Congress to compel attendance. King, a member of this committee, summed up the situation: "Three days since October only have nine states been on the Floor. Eight are now here; when we shall have nine is a melancholy uncertainty." He proposed an adjournment if, by an appointed day, the states were not sufficiently represented. "Something of this kind must be done," he wrote Gerry. "It is a mere Farce to remain here as we have done since last October. Foreigners know our situation, and the friends of free Governments through the world must regret it."[16] In a vigorous report, the committee on attendance maintained that an absent delegate was likely "to be represented to his Country as an unworthy Servant."[17] Congress adopted a much toned-down version, resolving that the Union had a right to demand of each state performance of the duties stipulated in the Articles of Confederation, and that it became the duty of the states to send delegates promptly. In spite of all efforts, however, the seventh Congress of the Confederation had no quorum from its opening day, November 6, 1786, until January 17, 1787, two and a half months later.

Unlike many of his fellow delegates, the conscientious King attended almost constantly. He served three terms, the maximum allowed by the Articles of Confederation, and during the first was present at every session. When on June 16, 1785, the General Court of Massachusetts chose its delegates, he received 142 of a possible 150 votes, an overwhelming display of confidence. At the same time the legislature cast 116 votes for Nathaniel Gorham of Charlestown, 101 for Theodore Sedgwick of Stockbridge, and 83 for Nathan Dane of

16. King to Elbridge Gerry, Apr. 30, 1786, King Papers, N.-Y. Hist. Soc. As no mention of a specific motion to adjourn *sine die* appears in the Journals of the Congress, probably King offered it merely in the course of debate.

17. *Journals of the Continental Congress*, XXX, 338.

Beverly; all were elected on the first ballot.[18] John Hancock, who had recently resigned as governor, was elected on the second ballot but because of ill health did not attend.[19] In the following June, King, Gorham, and Dane were re-elected, and Sedgwick was replaced by Dr. Samuel Holten, who had been a delegate some time before.[20] It was only during his last term that King was ever absent from Congress: in September 1786 he visited the Pennsylvania legislature in an effort to persuade it to pay its impost quota; in November and December, he went to Hartford to help settle the Massachusetts-New York land controversy; and from May to September 1787, he was a delegate to the federal Convention in Philadelphia. In each case, he was absent on pressing public business.

Massachusetts well illustrated the indifference of state legislatures to the affairs of Congress. King feared in June 1785 that his state would be unable to fill its delegation with able men, for they would only serve if the Commonwealth did not force them to spend their own money.[21] On several occasions Massachusetts delegates were unable to collect their pay and had to rely on their personal resources. Before he had been in Congress for a year, King had to draw upon his own funds to cover expenses, and after protesting to the state treasurer, he threatened to return home. Delegates from other states lived comfortably at public expense, but Massachusetts, King complained, "neither pays any thing to the federal treasury, nor supports her Delegates." He could maintain himself and freely would do it, but, he wrote Gerry, "if a dissolution must come, and dissolve our Government will, unless the several states immediately exert themselves in its favor, it behooves every one to withdraw in season, to Effect, if possible, some sort of personal Security."[22]

18. "Monthly Chronology," *Boston Magazine*, 2 (June 1785), 239.

19. Congress chose Hancock as its president, a move in which King seems to have been instrumental. When Hancock failed to attend, Congress elected Gorham, the senior Massachusetts delegate, in his place.

20. Jour. of Mass. House of Reps. (1786–87), 137; J. G. King, Rufus King, 342–43. Strong prejudice in the interior of the state against lawyers was largely responsible for the failure to re-elect Sedgwick, whose home was in Berkshire County. Although the individual votes are not recorded, it is likely that King and Dane lost some votes because they were lawyers. Holten was a physician.

21. King to Elbridge Gerry, June 5, 1785, King Papers, N.-Y. Hist. Soc.

22. King to Thomas Ivers, Aug. 29, 1785, Burnett, ed., *Letters of Continental Congress*, VIII, 205; King to Ivers, Oct. 9, 1785, King Papers, Boston Pub. Lib.; King to Caleb Davis, Nov. 3, 1785, Caleb Davis Papers, Mass. Hist. Soc.; King to Elbridge Gerry, Apr. 30, 1786, King Papers, N.-Y. Hist. Soc. Although in June 1786 the General Court raised the pay of the delegates, payments continued to lag, and a year afterward King reminded the state treasurer that his

Much of King's work as a delegate necessarily reflected the needs of Massachusetts. Though his concern for the larger interests of the Confederation developed quite early, he remained devoted essentially to New England's welfare. On his initiative the Massachusetts delegates presented to Congress the results of an on-the-spot investigation of alleged encroachments over the Maine boundary by British subjects from New Brunswick. The inquiry had originally been suggested by Congress, and King hoped to make the controversy a federal affair, enabling John Adams, the American Minister in London, to protest to the British government.[23] Though Secretary Jay favored setting up garrisons to protect the frontier, Congress adopted the milder Massachusetts motion instructing Adams to present the American case to the British government.

A few weeks after Adams arrived in London, he wrote to his friend Gerry, "You will give me great pleasure by persuading Mr. King to write to me. I have heard a great character of him, and what is more, a good one." Anticipating congressional criticism of his diplomacy, Adams hoped that Gerry and King would become effective sources of information.[24]

King responded with a long and deferential letter in which he told Adams that all the states east of Maryland agreed with the Minister's views on commercial policy, but the "false commercial reasonings and ill-founded policy" in the southern states had led to actions which would be a cause of bitter regret in the future. If the southerners declined to vest adequate commercial powers in Congress to counter British commercial discrimination against the United States, the eastern states were "*competent* to form, and in the event must form, a subconfederation remedied of all their present embarrassment." Although King had been reading Adam Smith's *Wealth of Nations*, which had caused him momentarily to doubt the propriety of commercial preference—"If his theory is just, our plans are all

---

arrears were much larger than those of his colleagues; it was not until July 1789 that Massachusetts made the final payment to King for his services as a delegate. Before he learned of that, he had taken his seat in the new U.S. Senate. King to Ivers, Aug. 1, 1786, Jan. 7, 1787, King Papers, Boston Pub. Lib.; King to Alexander Hodgden, June 24, 1787, Dreer Collection, Historical Society of Pennsylvania, Phila.; King to Hodgden, Apr. 27, 1788, King Papers, Boston Pub. Lib.; Christopher Gore to King, July 26, 1789, King Papers, N.-Y. Hist. Soc.

23. King to Samuel Adams, Feb. 25, 1785, Burnett, ed., *Letters of Continental Congress*, VIII, 42; *ibid.*, 220 and *n.*

24. John Adams to Elbridge Gerry, June 26, Aug. 26, 1785, James T. Austin, *The Life of Elbridge Gerry . . .*, 2 vols. (Boston, 1828–29), I, 477–81.

wrong," he had written Gerry—he now took the view that a new nation required commercial treaties. He went even further; if the old Revolutionary spirit of retaliation could be reactivated by the pride of a new nation and the idea of its honor and glory, "the present embarrassments of trade and the vain sophism of Europeans relative thereto [would] not only direct but drive America into a system more advantageous than treaties and alliances with all the world—a system which shall cause her to rely on her own ships and her own mariners, and to exclude those of all other nations."[25]

"Your letter has given me great Light," Adams replied, "and opened a field to view of the highest importance for me to look into." American policy might be made effective, he thought, if the commercial states followed the plan King mentioned, and the other five merely placed heavy duties upon British ships and prohibited them from importing anything but the products of Great Britain.[26] His hope that King would write often and unreservedly was gratified, and these two men of Massachusetts who had much in common kept up an extensive and fruitful correspondence. Their legal training, patriotism, solicitude for commerce, confidence in each other, their common friends, and perhaps memory of the suit Adams had prosecuted in behalf of King's father forged a political friendship which, if not intimate, was deep and lasting.[27]

Angered by the exclusion of American ships from the British West Indies, the merchants of Boston decided to boycott British goods. They set up a committee of correspondence and petitioned the General Court to exert its influence to strengthen Congress for launching effective countermeasures. Urged on by the newly elected Governor, the conservative James Bowdoin, the General Court proposed a convention of all the states to revise the Articles of Confederation in order to give greater powers to Congress. Bowdoin forwarded to the Massachusetts delegates the legislature's resolutions and copies of relevant letters to the executives of the other states.[28]

25. King to John Adams, Nov. 2, 1785, King to Elbridge Gerry, June 5, 1785, King Papers, N.-Y. Hist. Soc.

26. John Adams to King, Dec. 23, 1785, *ibid.*

27. In 1787 King was instrumental in securing a congressional resolution of thanks for Adams's patriotism, perseverance, integrity and diligence in the able and faithful performance of his duties in Europe. J. G. King, Rufus King, 220–21. For King's comment on Congress's action, see King to John Adams, Oct. 27, 1787, King Papers, N.-Y. Hist. Soc.

28. King, ed., *King Correspondence*, I, 58.

King, Gerry, and Holten went into a hurried consultation after receiving these documents. They deliberately withheld them and after a calculated delay explained to Bowdoin their reasons for postponement. Among other objections, they alluded to the danger of surrendering commercial authority to the Union, pointing out that powers once delegated to the Confederation could not be revoked without unanimous consent. Any plan to vest Congress with greater commercial powers, they argued, should be temporary until it could be tested. Further, a convention to revise the Articles might end in the fatal subversion of republican government by centralizing aristocrats eager for federal offices, and Americans would then be ruled by an aristocracy with a standing army and numerous pensioners and placemen. Certain that the present Confederation with all its inconveniences was preferable to the dissension, animosity, and ultimate ruin which a convention would produce, the delegates asked the Governor to present their views to the legislature.[29]

Two weeks later, King reiterated these opinions in a letter to Nathan Dane, a member of the General Court who had recently been elected to Congress. It was desirable, King wrote, that Congress have additional commercial powers, but for a limited time only, perhaps fifteen years. A general revision would entail serious difficulties and result in a less republican government. Under wartime necessity, the larger states had assented to the equal representation of the smaller ones, but if the question were reopened, the original objections of the large states would be reinforced by "the increasing principles of aristocracy," and the outcome would be total disunity. In his reply, Dane summarized the motives of the Massachusetts legislators, conceding that they had, in effect, responded to the pressure of the merchants without considering fully the implications of a call for a convention.[30]

After Governor Bowdoin transmitted the official letters of the delegates, the General Court abandoned its resolution for a convention. King, Holten, and Gerry had successfully, though tactfully, challenged the judgment of their state legislature. Although Gerry probably took the initiative, King obviously approved. His expressed fear of an aristocracy, reinforced by Gerry's vigorous republicanism,

29. Elbridge Gerry, Samuel Holten, and King to James Bowdoin, Aug. 18, 1785, Burnett, ed., *Letters of Continental Congress*, VIII, 188–90, 206–10.

30. King to Nathan Dane, Sept. 17, 1785, Dane Papers, Lib. Cong.; Dane to King, Oct. 8, 1785, King Papers, N.-Y. Hist. Soc.

was genuine and not merely a popular posture.[31] Furthermore, he saw no way whereby the interests of Massachusetts could be protected by a Congress in which one-third of the delegations opposed commercial regulations. The southern states, relying on the export of tobacco, wheat, rice, and indigo, wanted as few restrictions on trade as possible.[32]

Recognizing that no commercial treaty with Britain could be expected as long as Congress lacked power to regulate commerce, King toyed with the possibility of the subconfederation he had mentioned to Adams. The Articles of Confederation authorized alliances among the states if approved by Congress, and the eastern states might thus obtain the power jointly to regulate their trade. Such a commercial convention, he confided to Caleb Davis, his political contact in Boston, would not only overcome their hardship but "raise them to a degree of power and Opulence which would surprize and astonish—Politicians in Europe see it, and fear it, more than we appear to wish it."[33]

Some southerners, notably Monroe, mistakenly assumed that King advocated disunion. Given to seeing ulterior motives and suspecting plots, the Virginian inferred from "the intrigues of designing men" that New England congressmen were scheming behind the scenes for a separation of the states east of the Hudson.[34] It was true that disunion sentiment was widespread in Massachusetts at this time, and Theodore Sedgwick, one of the state's delegates in Congress, privately favored "contracting the limits of the confederacy to such as are natural and reasonable."[35] Undoubtedly King was privy to his

31. On the following Fourth of July, King ruefully observed the Cincinnati celebrating in New York "with a splendor exceeding any thing within the practice of Government" and drawing the applause of the crowd. "The chapter of these Knights," he informed Gerry, "appointed a deputation of four members to present the anniversary congratulations to the president and members of Congress. They attended the Levee, and I was witness to the degradation of Government in seeing them received." King to Elbridge Gerry, July 4, 1786, King Papers, N.-Y. Hist. Soc. Somewhat later King changed his mind. In Jan. 1787, according to David Humphreys, King and several others who had been "mortally opposed" to the Cincinnati looked "with considerable confidence to that quarter for our political preservation." Humphreys to George Washington, Jan. 20, 1787, Washington Papers, Lib. Cong.

32. King to Daniel Kilham, July 25, 1785, King-Kilham Corr., Columbia Univ. Lib.

33. King to Caleb Davis, Nov. 3, 1785, Caleb Davis Papers, Mass. Hist. Soc.

34. James Monroe to Patrick Henry, Aug. 12, 1786, Monroe to Thomas Jefferson, Aug. 19, 1786, Monroe to James Madison, Sept. 3, 1786, Burnett, ed., *Letters of Continental Congress*, VIII, 424, 445, 461.

35. Theodore Sedgwick to Caleb Strong, Aug. 6, 1786, *ibid.*, 415–16.

colleague's opinion, and on the floor of Congress he himself invoked the danger of northern disunion to frighten the southern delegates into recognizing the importance of a Spanish treaty. As the most active New Englander in Congress, he may have discussed a subconfederation while conferring with Jay on the Mississippi question. A congressionally sanctioned subconfederation was, however, very different from disunion; far from wishing to break up the confederation, King hoped it could be strengthened. As he had suggested to Caleb Davis, perhaps the mere threat of a subconfederation would turn this trick. If the southern politicians found the commercial states intent on combining, he thought they would accede to the necessary measures in Congress.[36]

In the meantime, King believed, the European powers would seek to injure the United States. Loss of her American colonies and difficulties with Ireland made it politically inexpedient for England to conclude a commercial treaty with the American envoy in London. Moreover, Great Britain and France were jealous of American enterprise and the probable future naval power of the United States. "It would not be surprising if they united in advancing each the commerce of the other," he speculated, "if thereby they could suppress or injure the commerce of America." Europeans, he asserted, held America in contempt not only for lack of congressional power over commerce and finance, but for sending ministers abroad without competent salaries and for the continual criticism of New Englanders by southerners, who in turn were ridiculed as "fools and empty coxcombs." A strong policy of commercial retaliation, whatever the obstacles, seemed to King the wise and patriotic, as well as economically beneficial, course for the United States. He visualized fleets of American ships, multitudes of American seamen, and a flourishing American trade if only Americans would revive the old patriotic spirit and restrict their commerce to their own shipping.[37]

36. King to Caleb Davis, Nov. 3, 1785, Caleb Davis Papers, Mass. Hist. Soc. In Rufus King, 491–504, James G. King considers in detail King's relation to the idea of subconfederation and alleged northern separatism.

37. King to Daniel Kilham, Oct. 12, 1785, King-Kilham Corr., Columbia Univ. Lib.; King to Caleb Davis, Nov. 3, 1785, Caleb Davis Papers, Mass. Hist. Soc.; Elbridge Gerry to King, May 19, 1785, typescript, Gerry Papers, Lib. Cong. In his letter to Kilham, King was unenthusiastic over the commercial treaty recently concluded between the United States and Prussia: "Prussia understands the principles of war better than those of commerce. The treaty gives an important friend to the United States, so far as paper, ink, and seals can convey, but will in a very small degree advance their commerce."

A rather narrow patriotism dominated King's mind. He lacked the cosmopolitan outlook of a Jefferson or a Franklin. In his identification of New England's interests with American well-being he never understood or appreciated southern sectional apprehensions. Besides his admitted prejudice against the French, he beheld with a suspicious eye even those foreign officers who had cast their lot with America during the war. "We all have our preferences and aversions, and perhaps in general they are both alike unfounded," he confessed to Gerry. With the single exception of Lafayette, whom he respected, he had always preferred to confide in American citizens rather than in the "most plausible or experienced Foreigners" in the country. When in 1785 Congress defeated a motion to pay $25,000 to Baron von Steuben, the "drillmaster of the Revolution," in recognition of his services, all four New England delegations voted against this large sum, and King voted against later proposals to pay Von Steuben considerably less. Like many New Englanders, he was not partial to the able Prussian officer who had offered his services in the American cause. He regarded Von Steuben as an adventurer and soldier of fortune who cultivated the appearance of gentility and philanthropy. In Europe he had received less money and flattery than in America, and King thought that the generosity of Congress had buoyed him "to the preposterous Belief that his military talents are superior to those of any soldier in America."[38]

King's bias against foreigners was matched by an equally strong sympathy for deserving patriots. As chairman of a special committee, he recommended that Congress reward Samuel Fraunces, the New York tavern keeper who had sheltered American and French prisoners during the British occupation of the city and who had supplied General Washington with important intelligence. Accepting King's report, Congress voted a handsome increase in the rent it was paying for the use of Fraunces's rooms as offices. To Thomas Paine, the Revolutionary pamphleteer, King was ready to do modest justice, although there was an ocean of difference in the personalities and views of the two men. As chairman of a committee to talk with the author of *Common Sense* and *The American Crisis*, King drafted a resolution referring to his "ingenious and timely publications" and

38. King to Elbridge Gerry, Nov. 5, 1786, King Papers, N.-Y. Hist. Soc.; King, ed., *King Correspondence*, I, 15*n*; *Journals of the Continental Congress*, XXVIII, 194, 198, XXIX, 771–74.

recommended a "liberal gratification." Congress adopted the resolution and granted Paine $3,000.[39]

Although flooded with private claims arising from wartime services or hardships, Congress was confronted first with the more crucial problems of obtaining funds and preserving its credit. Aside from the payments on the public debt, the Confederation required funds for day-to-day maintenance of government, diplomats abroad, defenses on the frontiers, and protection of trade. Such funds could only come from the states, and it was, of course, impossible to force delinquent states to make their payments. In 1784, Congress had decided that new requisitions would not be made upon states that had paid their full quota until all other states had made up their deficiencies; moreover, advances by states beyond their quotas would be credited on the next requisition. Some states, therefore, presented claims as advances to be credited on the 1785 requisition. South Carolina, having obtained a credit equal to its entire quota, contended that it ought not to pay anything on the requisition of 1785. Disheartened, King wished that Congress would free the current requisitions from their ties to previous ones, and he wrote to Gerry that "confusion and intricacy" would result if each new requisition were to "operate as a ballance Bill to all preceding demands." He was against indulging the delinquent states, some of which had not complied with the requisition of 1784; he supported every possible advantage to the federal treasury and, like many others, favored a more equitable system of apportionment.[40] The requisition of 1785, which he helped to prepare, called for payment of three-fourths of the unpaid requisitions and an additional $3,000,000. Quotas were readjusted, and Gerry and King were happy to report that Massachusetts had obtained an abatement of more than $55,000 of its quota.[41]

Absorbed in virtually every problem concerning Confederation finances, King became an acknowledged expert on treasury matters. Of his committee assignments, by far the largest number were related to federal finances, and his lifelong interest in the subject was un-

39. *Journals of the Continental Congress*, XXVIII, 208, XXIX, 662–63; J. G. King, Rufus King, 260–61, 264–65. King was willing to vote for financial awards, but he was economy-minded and opposed what he regarded as overly liberal payments.

40. King to Elbridge Gerry, May 27, 1785, King Papers, N.-Y. Hist. Soc.; Burnett, *Continental Congress*, 620; J. G. King, Rufus King, ch. 29.

41. Burnett, *Continental Congress*, 621; Elbridge Gerry and King to Massachusetts Assembly, Oct. 27, 1785, Boston Pub. Lib.

doubtedly heightened at this time. His diligence in attendance, caution, lack of flamboyance, and mastery of legal intricacies brought him thankless hours of conferences to relieve the embarrassed treasury.[42]

Though Congress had in 1783 proposed that the states empower it to levy impost duties and to collect a supplementary fund to help pay off the federal debt, progress was slow. Early in 1786, on King's motion, Congress directed its secretary to report on the status of the proposal. He announced that eight states had agreed to the impost but that only three had acceded to the fund. On February 9, King was made head of a committee to consider Confederation finances, particularly a recommendation that New York and Georgia act immediately to grant the impost power. His report crisply and persuasively urged payment of quotas by delinquent states and adoption of the impost plan by those that had not already done so. Receipts from the requisitions in the past fourteen months, he reported, had been at the rate of only $371,052 a year, insufficient "for the bare maintenance of the Federal Government on the most economical establishment and in time of profound peace."[43]

King's report amounted to another appeal, this time more urgent, for congressional power to collect the impost, a general import duty of 5 per cent. Because Pennsylvania and Maryland had supported the impost only if the other states would agree to the supplementary fund, the report urged unconditional acceptance of the impost. Finally, it asserted that as long as Congress was denied the means of paying its obligations, it could not be responsible for "those fatal Evils which will inevitably flow from a breach of Public faith, pledged by solemn contract, and a violation of those principles of Justice, which are the only solid Basis of the honor and prosperity of Nations." After minor verbal changes, the report was adopted apparently without dissent.[44]

By May, New York was the only state that had not in some form

42. See J. G. King, Rufus King, 247–52, 276–90, 297–312, 378–89; Richard Welch, Jr., "Rufus King," Essex Inst., *Hist. Colls.*, 96 (1960), 248.

43. *Journals of the Continental Congress*, XXX, 66. John B. McMaster, *History of the People of the United States*, I (N. Y., 1883), 359–60, gives an enthusiastic account of King's report.

44. *Journals of the Continental Congress*, XXX, 62, 68, 75. The quoted words are taken from a Treasury Board report probably written by King's friend, Samuel Osgood, the chairman of the board. As King lodged with Osgood for a few weeks at this time, he may have had a hand in drafting the Treasury Board's report. J. G. King, Rufus King, 311*n*. For a good account of the impost controversy, 1781–87, see Main, *Antifederalists*, ch. 4.

complied with the congressional appeal. The New York legislature on May 4 granted certain imposts on its own terms, making the collectors amenable to its own but not congressional authority and allowing duties to be paid in New York bills of credit. Thereupon Congress appointed a committee, with King as chairman, which reported that New York had not, in fact, vested Congress with power to levy import duties. The committee pointed out that if one state permitted paper payments, so could others, and Congress would be left holding state-issued paper which would be wholly inapplicable to pay federal debts. Congress twice recommended that Governor George Clinton call the New York legislature into special session, and twice the Governor, mindful of local politics and the loss of a lucrative tax resource in the port of New York, declined to do so. There the matter rested. An able general and ardent patriot in the Revolution, Clinton was now a narrow partisan of local interests, and his tactics only hastened a growing movement to strengthen the federal government.

King, nettled by the manner in which some states had qualified their acceptance of the impost, might well have reflected upon his own earlier conduct. While in the Massachusetts General Court he had led the fight against granting Congress the impost power. His provincialism in the winter of 1783–84 resembled Clinton's in 1786. Nearly two years of experience in Congress had widened the New Englander's perspective, and the frustrations of the Confederation government had brought about a fundamental change of mind.[45]

Perhaps heartened by the success of its mission in March which had induced the New Jersey Assembly to rescind a resolution of noncompliance with federal requisitions, Congress commissioned King and James Monroe to ask the Pennsylvania legislature to repeal the clause which restricted its approval of the impost. A concession by Pennsylvania might influence New York, though the prospects faded as Clinton's adamant stand became known.[46]

45. For King's view of the controversy between Congress and New York, see King to Elbridge Gerry, Aug. 26, 1786, King Papers, N.-Y. Hist. Soc.: "I presume I shall not be suspected of any great partiality for this State when it is known that I have not been the last man in urging the adoption of this measure."

46. Another reason for the mission was Pennsylvania's decision to deflect much of her quota of the 1784 requisition to the payment of her own citizens' claims against the federal government. These claimants had been turned away empty-handed by the embarrassed federal treasury, but no matter how just their claims, it was obvious that if one state distributed its quota among its citizens, others would do likewise, and state contributions to the federal government would cease.

On September 13, King and Monroe addressed the Pennsylvania Assembly in a tense atmosphere. Overanxious to make a good impression, King wrote out and memorized his speech, contrary to his usual procedure. The novelty and urgency of the occasion and the hushed audience that jammed the State House unnerved him. As he rose to address the speaker, he became flustered and forgot his lines. Confused and deeply humiliated, he asked Monroe to carry on while he sat down and regained his composure. When the Virginian concluded, however, King spoke extemporaneously with brilliant effect. One listener thought his words would "insure applause even from an Attic audience," and newspapers echoed the acclaim. Indeed, the *New-York Journal* expected the Assembly to respond favorably. The Pennsylvania House, it said, "was so filled with sophistical air, that many present were obliged to swallow such large draughts as will probably operate . . . to cause a discharge of a quantity of metalic substance from the bowels of the state treasury office." But the legislators were eager to go home and deferred the matter until the next session, in effect rejecting the plea of Congress.[47]

Despite the failure of the mission, King had turned his miserable fumble into a personal triumph. He determined never again to memorize a speech but to master his subject by minute and elaborate study, to anticipate all points of view, to make copious notes for later drastic condensation, adding here and there a nice phrase or apt quotation. For the final delivery he would trust to the inspiration of the occasion.

While in Philadelphia awaiting the decision of the legislature, King talked with Alexander Hamilton and Egbert Benson, New York's deputies on their way home from the Annapolis Convention. After Virginia and Maryland conferees had agreed in 1785 upon regulating navigation on the Potomac and Chesapeake Bay, Virginia had invited all the states to a convention to discuss trade and the grant of commercial power to Congress. Delegates of only five states—New York, New Jersey, Delaware, Pennsylvania, and Virginia—attended the convention sessions on September 11–14, 1786. Unable to carry out the announced intention, the delegates adopted Hamilton's draft resolution asking all the states to send delegates to a new conclave at Phil-

47. King, ed., *King Correspondence*, I, 124–27; Welch, "Rufus King," Essex Inst., *Hist. Colls.*, 96 (1960), 249–50; Burnett, ed., *Letters of Continental Congress*, VIII, 465–66; Phila. *Independent Gazetteer*, Sept. 16, 1786; *New-York Journal*, Sept. 21, 1786.

adelphia in May, to discuss there not merely commercial problems but all measures needed to make the Articles of Confederation "adequate to the exigencies of the Union." Hamilton had played a key role in urging a wider basis of action, but his and Benson's description of the Annapolis Convention did not impress King. That very day, he dashed off a letter to Governor Bowdoin, announcing that only five delegations had attended, that their powers had varied, and that they had gone beyond the original intent and recommended a general revision of the Confederation. "Foreign nations had been notified of this convention," he added glumly, and "the Friends to a good federal government through these states [had] looked to it with anxiety and Hope; the History of it will not be more agreeable to the former, than it must be seriously painful to the latter."[48]

Though initially hopeful, King had very early grown skeptical that the Annapolis meeting could succeed. In June he had not only feared that it would do little to bring about essential changes, but had also doubted Virginia's sincerity in promoting federal powers over commerce.[49] After the fiasco at Annapolis, he wrote John Adams that it had ended "without credit or prospect of having done much good."[50] He also disapproved of the call for a convention to revise the Articles, and he did what he could to prevent it. On October 11, in an address before the Massachusetts House of Representatives, he argued that Congress was the proper body to propose changes in the Articles. A month later, his junior colleague Dane echoed him. Evidently impressed, the General Court postponed action on the recommendation of the Annapolis Convention. The Massachusetts delegates also blocked an early congressional endorsement of the proposed Philadelphia convention; since King was the most influential man in his delegation at this time, it is a fair inference that he was the decisive force in delaying action.[51]

48. King to James Bowdoin, Sept. 17, 1786, Burnett, ed., *Letters of Continental Congress*, VIII, 468–69. Forrest McDonald argues persuasively that Hamilton sought to thwart the purpose of the Annapolis Convention by securing a quick adjournment before delegates from Rhode Island and Massachusetts arrived, thereby promoting his own wider object. *E Pluribus Unum*, 290. Cf. Stanley Elkins and Eric McKitrick, "Founding Fathers: Young Men of the Revolution," *Pol. Sci. Qtly.*, 76 (1961), 209–10.

49. King to Jonathan Jackson, June 11, Sept. 3, 1786, Burnett, ed., *Letters of Continental Congress*, VIII, 389–90, 459.

50. King to John Adams, Oct. 2, 1786, King Papers, N.-Y. Hist. Soc.

51. Material in this paragraph is based on "Substance of the Hon. Mr. King's Communications to the Legislature," *Boston Magazine*, 3 (Sept.–Oct.

Within a few weeks, however, King began to change his mind, as he heard about the first rumblings of Shays's Rebellion. The year 1786 was one of bitter internal strife in Massachusetts. The General Court, too eager to reduce the state debt, had not allowed enough for depreciation of the currency; taxes were the highest in New England, and the tax laws weighed heavily on the farmers, members of the debtor class, who discovered that the courts dealt harshly with debtors. Farmers found it increasingly difficult to make payments on their mortgages and looked to the legislature for relief from the menace of foreclosures. Creditors, committed to deflation, opposed such a policy. When the General Court adjourned in July without easing the burden of the rural population, discontented farmers in the central and western parts of the state went into action. In Worcester and Hatfield they held protest meetings to demand paper money. The movement spread as family farms were lost and unfortunate debtors were imprisoned or sold out to service to work off their debts.[52] Veterans of the Revolution could not remember similar distress under George III.

People crowded to the extraordinary county conventions to voice grievances which, if listed end to end, might have stretched from Springfield to Boston: the money shortage, the failure to redeem depreciated paper, the grant of the impost to the federal government with priority over local claims, wasteful expenditures and high salaries of public officials, "British influence" and a trend toward aristocracy, the ascendency of Boston, the state Senate, and the courts. Dislike of lawyers was never more heartfelt. Vexed by litigation with its accompanying fees and costs, the farm people regarded lawyers as willing instruments of oppression.[53]

In the calmer atmosphere of New York, Rufus King read newspaper accounts of meetings in Worcester, Middlesex, and Bristol counties. "What does all this mean?" he inquired of Gerry, then in

1786), 404–07; Burnett, ed., *Letters of Continental Congress*, VIII, 479; Jour. of Mass. House of Reps. (1786–87), 352, 366, Mass. State Lib.; Stephen Higginson to Henry Knox, Feb. 8, 1787, Thomas W. Higginson, *The Life and Times of Stephen Higginson . . .* (Boston, 1907), 113–14.

52. Richard B. Morris, "Insurrection in Massachusetts," in Daniel Aaron, ed., *America in Crisis; Fourteen Crucial Episodes in American History* (N. Y., 1952), 21–49, and especially 23–24; Robert J. Taylor, *Western Massachusetts in the Revolution* (Providence, 1954), 110–11.

53. McDonald, *E Pluribus Unum*, 143, 289; Main, *Antifederalists*, 57; Nevins, *American States*, 535.

Massachusetts. "Are our Countrymen incapable of a free Government—or does all originate from the defect of the federal Constitution?"[54] Apparently he began to believe that the weakness of the Confederation was loosening respect for all authority, but he also thought Congress's lack of commercial power blocked the return of prosperity. He predicted that Rhode Island's paper money would become worthless, a lesson to the "turbulent characters" agitating the conventions in Massachusetts.[55]

During August and September, as the tumult in Massachusetts showed no signs of abating, King grew ever more distrustful of the people's capacity for self-rule. He saw in the mass meetings, county conventions, and local intimidation of the courts an attack upon what he as a lawyer and legislator considered the ordered welfare of the community. His abhorrence of violence was reinforced by the memory of the cruel mob attack on his father, the flaming barn, the threats, and the final humiliation which hastened his death. He was fully aware of the bitterness of the common people against lawyers. His natural sympathy lay with merchants and creditors, who trusted in orderly and legal procedure, and his marriage only a few months earlier to the daughter of an affluent merchant and his friendship with mercantile New Englanders and New Yorkers intensified his bias.

On September 26 several hundred angry men under Captain Daniel Shays paraded through the streets of Springfield, where the Supreme Judicial Court was about to hold its session, and confronted the militia at the courthouse. Two days later the court was forced to adjourn. Before he knew the details of these events, but fearing the worst, King prayed that the uproar would die down. "It will be humiliating indeed," he wrote, "if the Blood and Treasure expended so gloriously by our country should establish our Disgrace and furnish just grounds of exultation to the Advocates of Tyranny and Despotism."[56] Although he disapproved of the disorders, he admitted that the provocation had been great. Perhaps the legislature had taxed the people too heavily. He calculated that almost all of the million and a half dollars paid into the state treasury that year was derived from property and poll taxes, perhaps nearly equal to one-third of the income

54. King to Elbridge Gerry, Aug. 5, 1786, King Papers, N.-Y. Hist. Soc.
55. King to Gerry, Aug. 26, 1786, *ibid.*
56. King to Theodore Sedgwick, Sept. 29, 1786, Sedgwick Papers, Mass. Hist. Soc.

of all the people of the state.[57] Thus since Massachusetts had about 400,000 inhabitants, the taxes for 1786 would average about twenty dollars for every household of five. These heavy taxes, together with the relentless pressure of creditors, had led to the popular obstruction of justice and the closing of courts in Middlesex, Bristol, Worcester, Hampshire, and Berkshire counties.

Shortly after the September outbreaks, King hastened to Boston. He was ostensibly reporting to the legislature on federal affairs and how they affected the state, but his timing gave the trip special significance. He appeared in the House on October 11 before a crowded audience, attracted partly by the critical situation of the Confederacy and partly by his reputation as an orator. After reviewing the outstanding governmental problems, chiefly financial, he turned to the commotion in Massachusetts. Congress, he said, viewed it as the most important subject ever to come to its attention. Every delegate took a personal interest in it, realizing that ultimately his own life, liberty, and property were at stake. He intimated that Congress would firmly support the state's moves to put down lawlessness; if the government should be opposed by force, the Confederation would back it up. If the state yielded to the insurgents, however, all the other governments would be swept away. He suggested darkly that the disunity of the people might lead to measures that otherwise "could never be effected by the enemies of our country. When Congress should know this; when they should see government prostrated in the dust, what would be their feelings? They were not authorized to see any government subverted." Finally, he apologized for his intensity; he spoke out of a fear that "palliatives might be adopted where vigour was required."[58]

While in Boston, King attended a secret conference of political leaders called by Governor Bowdoin. The Governor laid before them a letter from Henry Knox, Secretary of War, urging Massachusetts to raise a military force if necessary to protect the arsenal

57. King to John Adams, Oct. 3, 1786, King Papers, N.-Y. Hist. Soc. For a sympathetic and readable account of Shays's Rebellion as an outgrowth of widespread popular grievances, see Marion L. Starkey, *A Little Rebellion* (N. Y., 1955). See also Morris, "Insurrection in Massachusetts," in Aaron, ed., *America in Crisis*, 21–49, and Taylor, *Western Massachusetts*, 128–67.

58. Boston *American Herald*, Oct. 16, 1786. The address is reprinted in Burnett, ed., *Letters of Continental Congress*, VIII, 478–81. Evidently the measures King alluded to were the indefinite postponement of debt payments and the issue of paper money.

at Springfield and curb the insurgents. In view of the large and heterogeneous membership of the legislature and the continued need for secrecy, the conferees agreed that the state could raise the troops only if sanctioned by a requisition from Congress.[59] In contrast to the excitement of these insiders, the people of Boston surprised King by what he took to be their apathy toward the danger facing their state.[60]

Meanwhile in New York City, Secretary Knox was preparing to ask Congress for more federal troops to protect the military stores at Springfield. Two days after he made the request, a congressional committee urged the enlargement of the federal forces to meet the threat of hostilities by the Shawnee Indians in the West. Ostensibly to protect the frontiers, but with both dangers in mind, Congress voted to raise 1,340 additional troops. The stipulation that 1,220 were to be contributed by the New England states, and half of these by Massachusetts, was a tacit recognition of Shays's Rebellion.

King had returned to New York in time to join in the deliberations of Congress. His sense of urgency, his report of the secret meeting in Boston, and his continued collaboration with Knox directly influenced Congress to authorize enlistments even beyond what the Secretary had requested. He did more. Since the tax burden in the Bay State was already heavy, he suggested that an army to suppress the rebellion be financed by private loans, urging Gerry to loosen the Massachusetts money bags: "You must impress upon the minds of *our moneyed friends the indispensable necessity* of a Loan."[61]

King feared that representatives from the turbulent townships would probably sympathize with the farmers whose votes had put them in office. Without advocating any specific program, he warned his old Newburyport friend, Daniel Kilham, now a member of the General Court, that the national safety depended in large measure upon what the Massachusetts legislators did. The insurgent leaders, he told Kilham, had publicly admitted their belief that since all men were equal, property should be equally divided, and that they looked upon enforced payment of debts as no more than plunder

59. Report of Secretary Knox, *Journals of the Continental Congress*, XXXI, 887.

60. King to Daniel Kilham, Oct. 29, 1786, King-Kilham Corr., Columbia Univ. Lib.

61. King suggested that Congress reimburse them from the current federal requisition. King to Elbridge Gerry, Oct. 19, 1786, King Papers, N.-Y. Hist. Soc. For an adverse appraisal of Secretary Knox's activity, see McDonald, *E Pluribus Unum*, 149–50.

and robbery. If the General Court failed to take vigorous action against the spread of such pernicious notions, there was "good reason to despair of the Commonwealth and to give up all to Anarchy and confusion."[62] Already inclined to sympathize with the insurgents, Kilham no doubt reacted skeptically to King's pressure; their friendship soon lapsed.

To Theodore Sedgwick, an extreme conservative whose safety in Stockbridge seemed uncertain, King avowed his own changing credo:

> I myself have been an advocate for a Government free as air; my Opinions have been established upon the belief that my countrymen were virtuous, enlightened, and governed by a sense of Right and Wrong. I have ever feared that if our Republican Governments were subverted, it would be by the influence of commerce and the progress of luxury. But if in opposition to these Sentiments the great Body of the people are without Virtue, and not governed by any internal Restraints of Conscience, there is but too much room to fear that the Framers of our constitutions and laws have proceeded on principles that do not exist, and that America, which the Friends of Freedom have looked to as an Asylum when persecuted, will not afford that Refuge.[63]

King professed compassion for those he classed as ignorant, misguided, or simply thoughtless, but he expected their leaders to be more rational and to uphold the authority of legal machinery. A good Lockean, he maintained that by the nature of the social compact every citizen was bound to submit to the laws of the majority. There could be no grievances against such laws or their execution. If the majority disapproved them, let the new legislature repeal them; a law could last only one year if the majority agreed that it was inconvenient or unwise. King could not, however, imagine a law so bad that it would be intolerable for one year. What reason was there for the complaints and rash acts of the "opposers of our Government?"[64]

62. King to Daniel Kilham, Oct. 29, 1786, King-Kilham Corr., Columbia Univ. Lib.

63. King to Theodore Sedgwick, Oct. 22, 1786, Sedgwick Papers, Mass. Hist. Soc. For Sedgwick, see Richard E. Welch, Jr., *Theodore Sedgwick, Federalist: A Political Portrait* (Middletown, Conn., 1965).

64. King to Daniel Kilham, Nov. 19, 1786, King-Kilham Corr., Columbia Univ. Lib.

When he discovered that Baron von Steuben was critical of using troops against the rebels, he was incensed at what he considered the attempt of an outsider to take personal advantage of the disturbances in Massachusetts. In frequent conversation, and as "Bellisarius" in the press, Von Steuben sided with the discontented New Englanders and raised embarrassing questions about Congress's hasty authorization of an increase in federal troops. "Although the secret proceedings of Congress," he wrote, "are impervious to our view; surely when the drum beats, we may be permitted to ask what means the noise." Where was the enemy? It could not be a foreign power, nor could it be the Indians. Was the force to be turned against the insurgents? "Bellisarius" called it absurd to think so, for, as he slyly wrote, the insurrection was ended and its leaders jailed. Not without humor he concluded that the troops must be destined for "some secret expedition." Rufus King, who was contemptuous of the Baron, likened him to Cataline who had turned demogogue in the Roman Republic: "The same Dispositions and the like desperate Fortune mark the man who openly justifies the Conduct of the Insurgents, and who will head them, if their cause prospers."[65]

On October 22, the day after Congress had authorized a special requisition and loan to cover expenses of recruitment, Governor Bowdoin, apparently in accordance with a preconcerted plan, appealed to the General Court for troops and funds, emphasizing the Indian danger in the West. The legislature, not entirely aware of the main reason behind the Governor's request, enacted a measure to raise the six hundred men required for federal service and authorized a loan of £2,500.[66]

Through the newspapers and letters from Gerry, Christopher Gore, James Sullivan, Thomas Dwight of Springfield, and others, King kept in touch with political and military events in his home state. In January he wrote directly to General Benjamin Lincoln, then in the field against the insurgents, asking for his estimate of the military prospects.[67] The most active dispenser of news of the uprising, King was careful to keep members of Congress informed of

65. "Bellisarius," in N. Y. *Daily Advertiser*, Nov. 1, 1786; King to Elbridge Gerry, Nov. 5, 1786, King Papers, N.-Y. Hist. Soc.

66. J. G. King, Rufus King, 522–23.

67. King to Benjamin Lincoln, Jan. 21, 1787, Burnett, ed., *Letters of Continental Congress*, VIII, 531–32.

the changing situation, so that if necessary they might more readily vote further aid to Massachusetts.[68]

As federal machinery came slowly to the defense of the federal arsenal at Springfield, Governor Bowdoin decided to mobilize the Massachusetts militia to repress rebellion. In January he raised an army of 4,400 men under General Lincoln's command and issued state warrants for the arrest of the insurgent leaders. On the twenty-third, the presence of Lincoln's troops assured the opening of the county court at Worcester. On the twenty-fifth, Captain Shays made his long-expected march on the Springfield arsenal, but the Massachusetts militia sent two warning shots over the heads of the rebels. When the first wave surged forward again, a third volley killed three men and quickly dispersed Shays's twelve hundred followers, who retreated northward. Near Hadley, Lincoln sent a flag of truce to Shays offering amnesty for all enlisted men who laid down their arms. Shays countered with a demand for a general pardon, asking the General to suspend military operations until the legislature could act. When Lincoln rejected this appeal as a delaying device, Shays withdrew to Petersham. Lincoln's troops after a forced overnight march surprised the Shaysites on February 5 and broke the insurrection.

That same day, the General Court, unaware of what had happened at Petersham, declared a state of rebellion, and Governor Bowdoin dispatched the news to Congress. King was delighted; the declaration of rebellion had done honor to Massachusetts, he exulted, and Lincoln had "answered the most sanguine expectations of his friends."[69]

Terms of an amnesty were soon arranged. The legislature put a price on the heads of Daniel Shays, Luke Day, Adam Wheeler, and Eli Parsons, who had eluded capture. The rank and file who took an oath of allegiance were pardoned but were placed on probation for three years, during which they might not serve on juries, hold any office, vote for any civil or military officer, teach school, or sell liquor. King doubted the wisdom of disfranchisement but was otherwise extremely pleased with the action of the General Court.[70]

68. King to Charles Thomson, Dec. 10, 1786, Papers of Continental Congress, No. 59, III, Lib. Cong.; Burnett, ed., *Letters of Continental Congress*, VIII, 529, 543; King to Thomas Dwight, Jan. 22, 1787, King Papers, N.-Y. Hist. Soc.

69. King to Elbridge Gerry, Feb. 11, 1787, Gerry Papers, Pierpont Morgan Library, N. Y. C.

70. King to Elbridge Gerry, Feb. 18, 1787, King Papers, N.-Y. Hist. Soc. Cf. King to Thomas Dwight, Feb. 18, 1787, Gratz Coll., Hist. Soc. of Pa.

On February 19, King argued in Congress against Charles Pinckney's attempt to bring about, as an economy measure, the immediate suspension of any new federal enlistments. King affirmed that the real purpose of federal intervention had been not to meet an Indian threat but to strengthen the hand of Massachusetts, and that military preparations had indeed bolstered the state's ability to suppress the insurrection. To stop federal enlistments would imply disapproval and desertion of the state troops stationed in turbulent districts and might rekindle the spark of rebellion. Pinckney insisted that, on the other hand, the United States was not bound to support the punitive measures of Massachusetts, and that if new disturbances ensued, that state alone would be responsible. By a close vote, his proposal was defeated.[71]

With tranquility fully restored in Massachusetts, King informed Congress on March 28 that his delegation no longer opposed the halting of federal enlistments. On April 9, Congress not only stopped additional enlistments but ordered the discharge of all troops enlisted in Massachusetts except for two artillery companies. Massachusetts and Rhode Island cast the only votes against this sweeping measure. King tried in vain to have an infantry company retained in his state; not only did he think it prudent to keep the soldiers in readiness for an emergency, but he also considered their sudden release as unnecessarily hard on those who had sacrificed their private interests to serve as officers.[72] Of the rank and file he made no mention.

Shays's Rebellion profoundly altered King's views on the convention for revising the Articles of Confederation. For long months he had felt the frustrating impotence of Congress and recognized the great need for reform, but it was the insurrection in Massachusetts

71. James Madison, "Diary of the Debates of the Congress of the Confederation," in Jonathan Elliot, ed., *Debates in the Several State Conventions on the Adoption of the Federal Constitution*, 2d ed., 5 vols. (Phila., 1836), V, 94–95; *Journals of the Continental Congress*, XXXII, 64. Although, according to Madison, King "reminded" the delegates that the real purpose of federal intervention had been to help Massachusetts, and although a secret committee of Congress had also mentioned the uprising, Joseph P. Warren, "The Confederation and the Shays Rebellion," *American Historical Review*, 11 (1905), 42–67, has shown that Congress actually did fear Indian trouble in the West.

72. King to Elbridge Gerry, Apr. 9, 1787, King Papers, N.-Y. Hist. Soc.; King to Jeremiah Wadsworth, Apr. 11, 1787, Wadsworth Papers, Connecticut Historical Society, Hartford. For a concise account of King's part in the debate and action on federal enlistments early in 1787, see *Journals of the Continental Congress*, XXXII, 158–59, and J. G. King, Rufus King, 526–32.

and the apparent inability of the Confederation to provide what he considered adequate help or assurance of security to his home state that jolted him onto a more nationalistic path. If his fear of anarchy was exaggerated, it was none the less real.

"I revolutionized his mind," Alexander Hamilton supposedly remarked of his efforts to overcome Rufus King's opposition to reform by convention.[73] This smug assertion, if Hamilton actually used these words, claimed too much. Although Hamilton no doubt used his logical and persuasive powers to good effect, King had become increasingly receptive to the idea of a convention in the early months of 1787, and he listened to the New Yorker more sympathetically than he had in Philadelphia when Hamilton had reported on the Annapolis meeting. By May 1787 they had become close friends, and King had come to favor the idea central to Hamilton's political faith—a strong national government based on, and designed to safeguard, the power of property. Almost the same age, both men were trained in the law, and both had married into the same influential ruling class in New York City. Hamilton, in the early months of 1787, sought with all the force of his logic, wit, and hospitality to win over wavering congressmen to the theme of a more perfect union, but to claim that he "revolutionized" King's mind is extravagant; Rufus King had already begun to assume a new role in American political life.

Early in January he was certain that the Confederation had reached a crisis. As Virginia and Pennsylvania appointed delegates to the Philadelphia Convention and as Hamilton lobbied to secure a delegation from New York, King's opposition softened. "If Massachusetts should send deputies," he wrote Gerry, "for God's sake be careful who are the men; the times are becoming critical: a movement of this nature ought to be carefully observed by every member of the Community."[74] A month later he was ready to support the Philadelphia Convention. He hoped "sagacious men" would grasp the opportunity, but he was far from confident that they would succeed. "I am rather inclined to the measure from an Idea of pru-

73. John C. Hamilton, *History of the Republic of the United States, as Traced in the Writings of Alexander Hamilton and of His Contemporaries*, 6 vols. (N. Y., 1857–60), III, 239. The sole authority for the statement is Hamilton's son, who was biased against King.

74. King to Elbridge Gerry, Jan. 7, 1787, King, ed., *King Correspondence*, I, 201.

dence, or for the purpose of watching," he explained, "than from an expectation that much Good will flow from it."[75]

Five states had already agreed to send deputies to Philadelphia when the Massachusetts delegates, Dane and King, moved on February 21 that Congress recommend a convention without specifically mentioning the Annapolis invitation. Their purpose was to endorse the Convention in such a way as to make effective their view that Congress alone had the authority to initiate a revision of the Articles. Some of the members thought that King and Dane were personally opposed to any convention, and William Irvine of Pennsylvania thought the New England delegates joined the Convention movement only when they saw its inevitability. But Madison was correct in assuming that they were responding to a growing disposition in their legislature to send deputies to Philadelphia.[76] Congress accepted the Massachusetts resolution, thereby issuing its own call for the Convention.[77]

Two weeks before the General Court voted to send deputies to the Philadelphia Convention, King was mentioned as a prospective deputy, although the most prominent candidates were Gerry and Francis Dana. On March 3 the legislature chose Dana on the first ballot, and Gerry, Gorham, King, and Caleb Strong on the second. King remained skeptical of the success of the impending meeting. "What the Convention may do at Philadelphia is very doubtful," he observed. "There are many well disposed men from the Southern States, who will attend the Convention; but the projects are so various, and all so short of the best, that my fears are by no means inferior to my Hopes."[78]

75. King to Gerry, Feb. 18, 1787, King Papers, N.-Y. Hist. Soc.

76. *Journals of the Continental Congress*, XXXII, 73; James Madison, "Notes of Debates," *ibid.*, XXXIII, 723–24; William Irvine to James Wilson, Mar. 6, 1787, Burnett, ed., *Letters of Continental Congress*, VIII, 551. Responding to the favorable report of a joint committee, the Massachusetts legislature voted on Feb. 22 to send deputies to the Philadelphia Convention.

77. *Journals of the Continental Congress*, XXXII, 73–74. The editor of the *Journals* states erroneously that Philadelphia was not specified in King and Dane's original motion. See J. G. King, Rufus King, 557.

78. King to Theophilus Parsons, Apr. 8, 1787, King, ed., *King Correspondence*, I, 218.

CHAPTER VI

THE PHILADELPHIA CONVENTION

HEAVY RAIN DID NOT DAMPEN THE SPIRITS OF THE TWENTY-NINE DELEgates who met in the Pennsylvania State House on Friday morning, May 25, 1787. On that day, a week and a half after the date appointed for the opening of the federal Convention, representatives from eight states were present when the Convention was officially organized. Seven states had a quorum of delegates—New York, New Jersey, Pennsylvania, Delaware, Virginia, North Carolina, and South Carolina. Rufus King, who had arrived on May 21, was the only New Englander in Philadelphia on opening day.

Embarrassed and concerned about the interests of the eastern states, King had written only the day before to his friend Jeremiah Wadsworth in Hartford, Connecticut, "Pray hurry on your Delegates. Some personal Sacrifices perhaps may stand in the way of their immediate attendance. But they ought not to yield to such Considerations. Believe me it may prove most unfortunate if they do not attend within a few days."[1] By Monday Gorham and Strong had arrived, giving Massachusetts a quorum of delegates and enabling her to become the eighth state to be represented. On the twenty-ninth Gerry completed the delegation.

Rufus King was only thirty-two, ten or more years younger than the other delegates from Massachusetts and one of the youngest

1. King to Jeremiah Wadsworth, May 24, 1787, Wadsworth Papers, Conn. Hist. Soc. Poor health prevented Dana from attending.

members of the Convention. He was already an accomplished orator. William Pierce of Georgia noted his handsome features, his "strong expressive Eye," and his "sweet high toned voice." When King debated, the Georgian noticed "something peculiarly strong and rich in his expression, clear, and convincing in his arguments, rapid and irresistible at times in his eloquence." Yet, despite his persuasiveness and natural, easy posture, he sometimes displayed a "rudeness of manner." All in all, however, Pierce concluded that the Massachusetts man might "with propriety be ranked among the Luminaries of the present Age."[2] The Georgian was less impressed by the others from Massachusetts: Gorham, a good debater who lacked elegant style, had "an agreeable and pleasing manner"; Strong, though an eminent lawyer, was a feeble speaker; and Gerry was conscientious and persevering, but a hesitant speaker, unconcerned with oratorical flourishes.[3]

All four Massachusetts delegates had important social and political connections in their home towns and were financially independent. Gerry came from an affluent mercantile family, and as the holder of well over $50,000 worth of continental and state paper, he was the largest owner of public securities at the Convention. Gorham, the son of a packet-boat operator, was a self-made man whose fortune in shipping had been wiped out by the ravages of the British armies in 1775 but who had more than recouped his losses through privateering and speculation during the war. Strong was a prosperous country lawyer whose income was modestly supplemented by fees earned as attorney for Hampshire County.[4]

Like Strong, King had made money from practicing law. He was not, however, very wealthy at this time.[5] What remained of his inheritance was in Maine farmland and salt marsh, not readily convertible into cash or securities. As a delegate to Congress, he had several times been forced to rely upon his own resources, accumu-

2. William Pierce, "Characters in the Convention of the States Held at Philadelphia, May 1787," Max Farrand, ed., *Records of the Federal Convention of 1787*, 3 vols. (New Haven, 1911), III, 87.

3. *Ibid.*, 87–88.

4. Forrest McDonald, *We the People: The Economic Origins of the Constitution* (Chicago, 1958), 43–45.

5. In his *Economic Interpretation of the Constitution of the United States* (N. Y., 1913), 150–51, Charles A. Beard states that King owned personalty in mercantile, manufacturing, and shipping enterprises, and that he had loaned considerable sums at interest. While largely true for a later period in King's life, Beard's statement clearly but erroneously implies that King had far-flung assets in 1787.

lated in a profitable legal business. Even while the Philadelphia Convention was in progress, he complained of heavy expenses and asked the treasurer of Massachusetts for £200, a small fraction of what the state owed him for services in Congress.[6] He appears to have had few or no public securities before 1786, though he acquired some over the next five years.[7] Some time before May 1791 he invested $3,000 in the Bank of New York, and he probably paid at least $5,000 for New York state securities from 1786 to 1788.[8] Thus at the time of the Convention, he was moderately well off, and it was only later that he became a very wealthy man. His holdings in New York securities would turn out to be profitable when the federal government took over the state debts in 1790, but as a conservative investor he counted upon steady dividends rather than a speculative rise in value.[9] Through his wife's inheritance in 1794, King would come into a considerable fortune which he could use for making private loans at interest and further investments in securities and, more modestly, in commerce.[10]

The most important business on the first day of the Convention

6. King to Alexander Hodgden, June 24, 1787, Dreer Coll., Federal Convention, Hist. Soc. of Pa.

7. On Nov. 1, 1784, an interest certificate worth somewhat more than $4 was issued to King, but I have found no other evidence that King bought public securities in Massachusetts. Register of Certificates issued, pursuant to Act of Congress passed the 28th April 1784, for interest due to 31 December 1782, on Loan Office Certificates, and Certificates of other liquidated debts, contracted in the State of Massachusetts . . . , fol. 75, Record Group 53, "Old Loans" Records of the Bureau of the Public Debt, National Archives.

8. Henry W. Domett, *A History of the Bank of New York, 1784–1884* (N. Y., 1884), 137, 139; McDonald, *We the People*, 42.

9. King exchanged more than $10,000 of New York State securities in 1791. Treasury Department, Loan of 1790 6 Per Cent Stock, Ledger A, 1797–1835, Vol. XXII, New York, fol. 14, Record Group 53, "Old Loans" Records of the Bureau of the Public Debt, National Archives. The New York securities did not appreciate much in value after 1787 because the state had funded its debt and its share of the national debt in 1786; and until 1790, when the federal government assumed the debt, the state regularly paid interest. According to McDonald, *We the People*, 42, funded New York securities after 1786 were unavailable for much less than ten shillings on the pound; King's paper profit, therefore, was only about $1,300 in four years. If one accepts this estimate, the market value of King's $10,000 of securities in 1791 was about $6,500. *Ibid.*, 42*n.* For further data on King's holdings of public securities in the early 1790's, see other records of the Loan of 1790, particularly the volumes for New York, as follows: XXV, fol. 60; XXVI, fol. 14; XXVIII, fols. 1, 14, 175; XXXI, fol. 56; DLI, fols. 104, 351, 466, 492, Record Group 53, "Old Loans" Records of the Bureau of the Public Debt, National Archives.

10. King Papers, Vol. 37, No. 84, *passim*, N.-Y. Hist. Soc.

was the election of George Washington as presiding officer. Washington appointed George Wythe, Alexander Hamilton, and Charles Pinckney to prepare standing rules and the orders of procedure. On May 28 the committee presented its proposals, one of which would have authorized the polling of individual members and the recording of their votes. King objected, arguing that such polling was unnecessary and improper, and that frequent changes of opinion would fill the minutes with contradictions. In agreeing, George Mason of Virginia pointed out that a public record would inhibit the delegates from changing their minds and would be used by opponents of the finished product. The Convention unanimously rejected the proposed rule.[11] Throughout the Convention state delegations voted on a one state–one vote basis, with the delegation being polled to determine the majority view on each issue. To encourage the fullest freedom of debate, the Convention adopted a secrecy rule, providing "that nothing spoken in the house be printed, or otherwise published or communicated without leave."

With the ground rules worked out, the Convention turned to the first order of business, the Virginia plan which Governor Edmund Randolph outlined in an elaborate speech. Although Randolph proposed only that the Articles of Confederation be corrected and enlarged, his plan, worked out in detail by James Madison, suggested far-reaching changes. They included a bicameral legislature, representation based on state contribution or free population, direct popular election of the lower house, election of the second house by the first from a list of persons nominated by the state legislatures, a national executive and judiciary, and ratification of the Convention's proposals—after approval by Congress—by state conventions expressly chosen by the people.

During the debates on the Virginia plan, King tended to judge proposals according to their practicability. He was critical, for instance, of basing apportionment in the national legislature only upon quotas of contribution to the treasury; the continually varying sums, he observed, would complicate the system, and the revenue might be so collected that the state contributions would not even appear.[12] When Richard Spaight of North Carolina moved that the upper house be chosen by the state legislatures, King called the scheme im-

11. Madison's notes, Farrand, ed., *Records of the Federal Convention*, I, 10.
12. Madison agreed with King, and the matter was postponed, *ibid.*, 36. Cf. McHenry's notes, *ibid.*, 43–44.

practicable unless the chamber were very large or proportional representation of the states abandoned. Spaight withdrew his motion.[13] On matters of procedure, King was a watchdog for orderly progression. He did not hesitate to wave a proposal aside as premature, and he agreed with Madison and Wythe that the delegates should adopt basic principles before flitting from one detail to another.[14]

King indicated fairly early his aim to give stability to the central government by providing a long term of office for the proposed national executive. Silent during the debate, he voted for a seven-year term, as did Gorham, but Massachusetts lost its vote when Gerry and Strong voted against the long term.[15] This split vote of the Massachusetts delegation foreshadowed a deepening rift that was to weaken the state's influence in the Convention.

King's faith in a strong executive was so deeply rooted that it occasionally led him to an extreme position. When on June 4 James Wilson moved to give the executive an absolute veto, only three delegates supported it: Wilson himself, Alexander Hamilton, who seconded it, and King.[16]

That same day, King opposed a council of revision whereby judges would assist the executive in reviewing the laws. He was satisfied that judges would scrutinize the laws if challenged in the courts and would "no doubt stop the operation of such as shall appear repugnant to the constitution."[17] Madison argued strongly for a council of revision, but Gerry thought that the executive would be more impartial if he were not "covered by the sanction and seduced by the sophistry of the Judges." King added that if a single executive veto afforded more responsibility, by the same token judges would be more responsible if divorced from the executive power. This time King was on the side of the large majority, which voted

13. Madison's notes, *ibid.*, 51–52.

14. Pierce's notes, *ibid.*, 58, 59, 60. After the Convention adjourned for the day on May 31, some of the delegates, including King, with his wife, attended a tea party given by the fashionable Nancy Shippen. Armes, ed., *Nancy Shippen Journal*, 249.

15. King's notes, Farrand, ed., *Records of the Federal Convention*, I, 72; King, ed., *King Correspondence*, I, 590. Cf. Madison's notes, Farrand, ed., *Records of the Federal Convention*, II, 59.

16. King's notes, *ibid.*, I, 108; King, ed., *King Correspondence*, I, 591.

17. Pierce's notes, Farrand, ed., *Records of the Federal Convention*, I, 109, also 94, 98, 105, 107.

to eliminate the proposed council.[18] He stood firmly for the separation of executive and judicial powers and for the principle of judicial review.

On June 9 the shrewd William Paterson of New Jersey moved to consider the voting rule in the proposed legislature, thereby touching off some of the most heated debates of the Convention. Paterson, whom Pierce considered as one "whose powers break in on you, and create wonder and astonishment," attacked the Virginia plan. He insisted that the Convention's job was to amend the Confederation, not to change it into a national government and thus strike at the very existence of the smaller states. New Jersey would never confederate, he asserted, on a plan which apportioned representation to the free population or to the tax quota of the states; he "had rather submit to a monarch, to a despot than to such a fate."[19] Two days later King observed that the Convention should make up its mind whether it favored a national government or the continuation of the confederation principle. He moved that the lower house of the national legislature be elected not as under the Articles of Confederation, but "according to some equitable ratio of representation." The motion passed seven to three, as the larger states rallied to its support.[20]

18. Madison's notes, *ibid.*, 138–40. In supporting a move by Wilson and Madison to authorize the creation of inferior federal courts, King remarked that it would cost "infinitely less" to establish such courts than to support the appeals that would otherwise be necessary. The measure was overwhelmingly approved, despite Butler's objection that the people would "revolt at such encroachments." *Ibid.*, 125.

19. *Ibid.*, 177–99. For Pierce's sketch of Paterson, see *ibid.*, III, 90. The generally accepted interpretation of the Virginia and New Jersey plans as large and small state plans, respectively, has recently been challenged. See John P. Roche, "The Founding Fathers: A Reform Caucus in Action," *American Political Science Review*, 55 (1961), 806; McDonald, *E Pluribus Unum*, 164–70, 296. The real issue was not what kind of national government would be created, but whether there would be a national government at all. McDonald emphasizes that the New Jersey plan granted many significant powers to the central authority and would have made congressional laws paramount to state laws and binding upon individuals as well as states. Moreover, he states that in demanding representation in the legislature in proportion to their population, Virginia, Pennsylvania, and Massachusetts really were seeking to enhance the influence of their own states, not the power of the nation. Although I agree that the delegates of these states acted in what they considered their states' best interests, it does not follow that some were not national-minded. The nationalist stance of Rufus King, for instance, was no mere pose.

20. Yates's notes, Farrand, ed., *Records of the Federal Convention*, I, 204–05; Madison's notes, *ibid.*, 200.

At this time King guardedly touched upon the Convention proceedings and prospects in two letters to his Massachusetts friends, Theodore Sedgwick and Henry Knox. Congratulating Sedgwick on his election to the Massachusetts legislature, King expressed the hope that the General Court would "check the madness of Democracy" and send to Congress "men of Consequence, not Dunces." Moderation and firmness were essential, he wrote; "I wish you may have as good a proportion of these excellent qualities as truly characterizes our Convention." He was silent about the debates, remarking only, "I think there is some foundation to hope for Good–I am precluded from communicating, *even confidentially*, any particulars."[21] He intended to ask Sedgwick in confidence for opinions upon certain anticipated points of debate, but he apparently changed his mind for there is no evidence that he sent any such questions to Sedgwick.

To Secretary Knox, King reported slow progress, and, although unwilling to predict the outcome, he noted that nothing very important had "issued unfavorably."[22] King's relations with Knox are of unusual interest. Although not a delegate to the Convention, the Secretary had been in Philadelphia for a meeting of the Cincinnati, and after returning to his office in New York, he and his wife were again in Philadelphia by the middle of June, possibly fellow-lodgers with the Kings. Whether or not the Kings and the Knoxes occupied the same quarters, the two men saw each other and talked together.[23] Despite the secrecy of the Convention's deliberations, Knox was not uninformed of what went on behind the closed doors. King himself was habitually discreet, and the few letters he wrote during the Convention were wholly proper and devoid of significant detail, but he may have leaked some information in conversations with Knox. At any rate, the Secretary wrote a letter to Washington which indicated considerable knowledge about the plan of government being discussed in the Convention. According to his most recent biographer, his main source of information was King, but Elbridge Gerry, another personal friend, also kept him posted.[24]

21. King to Theodore Sedgwick, June 10, 1787, Sedgwick Papers, Mass. Hist. Soc.

22. King to Henry Knox, June 3, 1787, Knox Papers, *ibid.*

23. *Ibid.*

24. Henry Knox to George Washington, Aug. 14, 1787, Washington Papers, Lib. Cong.; Douglas S. Freeman, *George Washington, a Biography*, 7 vols. (N. Y., 1948–57), VI, 94*n*; North Callahan, *Henry Knox, General Washington's*

On June 15 Paterson introduced the New Jersey plan, which was designed to preserve the equality of the states in the Confederation. Fundamentally, this plan was not the ideological opposite of the Virginia plan. It was no less nationalist, but in maintaining equality of the states it would have lessened the power of Virginia, Pennsylvania, and Massachusetts. Its supporters attacked what they took to be the political liabilities of the Virginia plan rather than the proposed scope of national authority.[25] To Hamilton, equality of the states was an abomination. On June 18 he argued for five hours against both the New Jersey plan and the Virginia plan and in favor of a consolidation of power in the central government.[26] The delegates listened respectfully, if perhaps wearily, but were unconvinced. The precocious New Yorker's extreme nationalist ideas were not even discussed. The next day Madison joined in the attack on the Paterson plan. King moved that the New Jersey plan be declared inadmissible and that the Virginia plan be reported by the Committee of the Whole. By a vote of seven to three, the motion passed, with New Jersey, Delaware, and New York—despite Hamilton—in the minority.[27]

The clash over rival plans led to a debate on the nature of sovereignty in which the "nationalists" did most of the talking. Wilson tried to reassure the opponents of the Virginia plan that he did not wish a national government to swallow up the state governments. Hamilton explained that though he favored abolishing the states, he regarded as necessary some kind of subordinate jurisdictions.[28] King hoped the delegates could agree on terminology. The meaning of the words states, sovereignty, national, and federal, he remarked, had often been applied inaccurately. The states, he contended, lacked the peculiar features of sovereignty: they could not make war, peace, alliances, or treaties. Considered as political beings, "they were dumb, for they could not speak to any foreign Sovereign whatever. They were deaf, for they could not hear any propositions from such Sovereign. They had not even the organs or faculties of defence or

General (N. Y., 1958), 265. William Pierce of Georgia may have violated the secrecy rule. See Nathan Dane to King, June 19, 1787, King Papers, N.-Y. Hist. Soc.

25. See the convincing argument of John P. Roche, "The Founding Fathers," *Amer. Pol. Sci. Rev.*, 55 (1961), 805–07.

26. Farrand, ed., *Records of the Federal Convention*, I, 282–311.

27. Madison's notes, *ibid.*, 314–22; Yates's notes, *ibid.*, 327. Maryland was divided.

28. Madison's notes, *ibid.*, 322–23.

offence, for they could not of themselves raise troops, or equip vessels, for war. On the other side, if the Union of the States comprises the idea of a confederation, it comprises that also of consolidation. A Union of the States is a union of the men composing them, from whence a *national* character results to the whole." Congress could act alone without the states, and if the states retained part of their sovereignty, "they had certainly divested themselves of essential portions of it. If they formed a confederacy in some respects—they formed a Nation in others." As a practical matter, he doubted the wisdom of doing away with the states, but he favored taking away much of their power.[29]

Luther Martin, attorney-general for Maryland, retorted that separation from Great Britain had placed the former colonies in a state of nature in their relationship to each other; in forming the Confederation they had acted as equals; now they met to amend it as equals. He could never accede to a scheme that would "lay 10 States at the mercy of Virginia, Massachusetts, and Pennsylvania."[30] If he spoke as an abstract political theorist, Martin was also mindful of his state's powerful neighbors and of Maryland's role in inducing Virginia to give up its western land claims.

Once King might have agreed with Martin, but no longer. Having jealously upheld the right of Congress alone to propose amendments to the federal system, he now asserted that the Convention held a similar power to make drastic revisions. Obviously his viewpoint had changed markedly during the preceding months. His manuscript notes of the Convention contain only two of his speeches, including the discourse on sovereignty, but it is uncertain whether this version of the speech is the one delivered. In any event, it is clear that he viewed the Confederation as deriving its authority from the people as well as from the states.[31] King rejected on pragmatic grounds objections to the right of the Convention to consider a new government:

> But admit[t]ing that the Articles of Confederation and Perpetual Union, or the powers of the Legislature did not extend to the proposed Reform; yet the public Expectations and the public Danger requires it—the system proposed to be adopted

29. *Ibid.*, 323–24. Cf. Yates's notes, *ibid.*, 328–29.

30. Madison's notes, *ibid.*, 324. Cf. 329, and Yates's notes, *ibid.*, 437–41.

31. King Papers, N.-Y. Hist. Soc. The transcription in King, ed., *King Correspondence*, I, 602–03, has a few inaccuracies.

> is no scheme of a day, calculated to postpone the hour of Danger, and then leave it to fall with double ruin on our successors—It is no crude and undigested plan, the Child of narrow and unextensive views, brought forward und[er] the auspices of Cowardice and Irresolution. it is a measure of Decision, it is the foundation of Freedom and of national Glory—it will draw on itself, and be able to support the severest scrutiny and Examination—It is no idle Experiment, no romantic Speculation—the measure forces itself upon wise men, and if they have not firmness to look it in the face and protect it—Farwel to the Freedom of our Government—our military Glory will be tarnished, and our boasts of Freedom will be the scorn of the Enemies of Liberty.[32]

His fervent peroration reveals him as one of the outstanding speakers of the Convention, ranking with Gouverneur Morris and Hamilton—though with more consistency than the former and less brilliance than the latter—in an era when forensic ability was highly prized.[33]

On June 20 the cautious Oliver Ellsworth of Connecticut moved to strike out the word "national" from the Virginia plan. This might reassure the small states that they would not be gobbled up by the large ones. Fundamentally the dispute was not over the proper term but over whether the new government should operate on the states or directly on the citizens. For the moment, the Convention circumvented the problem by unanimously eliminating the word "national," and thereafter the terms "federal" and "general" came to be used when men spoke of the government of the United States.[34]

32. King Papers, N.-Y. Hist. Soc.; King's notes, Farrand, ed., *Records of the Federal Convention*, I, 332. King knew, of course, that national power would be welcomed by Boston merchants, who hoped for an orderly, uniform tariff system, for an effective navigation law to counter British and French commercial discrimination, and for a navy whose existence would reduce insurance rates. See Elkins and McKitrick, "The Founding Fathers," *Pol. Sci. Qtly.*, 76 (1961), 198, which, however, does not mention King.

33. The French reformer, J. P. Brissot de Warville, *Nouveau Voyage dans les Etats-Unis de l'Amerique Septentrionale*, 3 vols. (Paris, 1791), I, 170, met King at Hamilton's dinner table in 1788 and noted his reputation as "the most eloquent man in the United States." In taking notes of the Convention debates, Madison and Yates were mainly concerned with the substance of what was said, and their records of King's speeches impart almost no sense of his oratorical method. However, they capture something of his careful organization of ideas and precise choice of words. As noted by Welch, "Rufus King," Essex Inst., *Hist. Colls.*, 96 (1960), 265, we must, for the most part, take King's eloquence on faith.

34. Yates's notes, Farrand, ed., *Records of the Federal Convention*, I, 344.

The cool springtime had by now given way to a hot summer, and the delegates sweltered, their tempers flaring, in the debates on the Virginia plan from June 20 to July 12. King agreed with Wilson that the election of the proposed House of Representatives by the people, not the state legislatures, was essential. The legislatures, King thought, would select men subservient to their own views, and he pointed to the danger of subservience to the states if the representatives' salaries were paid by the state governments.[35] In this he was in accord with Randolph, Madison, and especially Hamilton who had also urged that qualifications for federal legislators should not be so restrictive as to make them ineligible to other offices. "We refine too much by going to *utopian* lengths," Robert Yates quoted King as saying, and, according to Madison's account, he asserted that it would discourage merit and afford a pretext to the executive to make bad appointments. Political connections formed by "intimate association of offices" would strengthen government, King contended; therefore, let preferment be open to all men.[36] Hamilton went even further. He admitted the danger of men holding two offices, but an overly restrictive system would be worse: "Take mankind as they are, and what are they governed by? Their passions. There may be in every government a few choice spirits, who may act from more worthy motives. One great error is that we suppose mankind more honest than they are. Our prevailing passions are ambition and interest; and it will ever be the duty of a wise government to avail itself of those passions, in order to make them subservient to the public good."[37]

While King was moving steadily toward a strong nationalist position, though never as far as Hamilton, he could not swing the Massachusetts delegation over to his side. Gorham usually agreed with him, but Strong, who had initially impressed him most favorably, tended to side with Gerry, who, clinging to the narrow republicanism of a New England town meeting, now came out for limitations upon office holding.[38]

On the last day in June, the Convention again focused its attention upon representation, taking up Ellsworth's motion for an equal vote

35. Madison's notes, *ibid.*, 359, 372.

36. Yates's notes, *ibid.*, 379, 393; Madison's notes, *ibid.*, 376.

37. Yates's notes, *ibid.*, 381–82. Hamilton believed, however, that once a member of the federal legislature took his seat, he should vacate every other office. *Ibid.*, 382.

38. Madison's notes, *ibid.*, 388.

for each state in the upper house of the legislature. After objections from Wilson, Madison, and Davie of North Carolina, the unruffled Franklin urged compromise. "When a broad table is to be made," the eighty-one-year-old savant remarked, "and the edges [of the planks do not fit] the artist takes a little from both and makes a good joint. In like manner here both sides must part with some of their demands, in order that they may join in some accommodating proposition."[39] He offered a solution: that the states have equal numbers of senators and that, in whatever affected state sovereignty, the senators vote equally by states, but in money matters in proportion to state contributions to the federal treasury.

In contrast to Franklin's calm demeanor King burst forth in a spirited argument for voting in the upper house based on population. Uncompromising and rather ironic in tone, he opposed making "another [Confederation] Congress" of the proposed Senate, saying he was "filled with astonishment that if we were convinced that every *man* in America was secured in all his rights, we should be ready to sacrifice this substantial good to the phantom of *State* sovereignty." His feelings were "harrowed," his fears for the country greater than he could express. He considered this "the last opportunity of providing for its liberty and happiness." When a just government representing the people was within reach, he was amazed that it should be sacrificed to an illusion of the ideal freedom and importance of the states.[40] If the Convention agreed to Ellsworth's motion, he implied, the delegates might as well go home.[41]

King's display of temper led the small-state delegates to reply in kind. The impetuous Jonathan Dayton of New Jersey snapped: "When assertion is given for proof, and terror substituted for argument . . . they would have no effect however eloquently spoken."[42] He accused King of trying to undermine the equality of the states, and Luther Martin tersely echoed the charge.[43] As the tension heightened, Gunning Bedford of Delaware challenged King even more sharply. "We have been told with a dictatorial air that this is the last moment for a fair trial in favor of a good Government. It will be the last indeed if the propositions reported from the Committee

39. *Ibid.*, 488.
40. *Ibid.*, 489–90.
41. Yates's notes, *ibid.*, 499.
42. Madison's notes, *ibid.*, 490.
43. Yates's notes, *ibid.*, 499.

go forth to the people. . . . The Large States dare not dissolve the confederation. If they do the small ones will find some foreign ally of more honor and good faith, who will take them by the hand and do them justice."[44]

After saying that he was for preserving the states, in a subordinate role but with possible guarantees against federal encroachment, King denied Bedford's charge of being dictatorial: "This intemperance had marked the honorable gentleman himself. It was not he [King] who with a vehemence unprecedented in that House had declared himself ready to turn his hopes from our common Country, and court the protection of some foreign hand—This too was the language of the Honorable member, himself. He was grieved that such a thought had entered into his heart. He was more grieved that such an expression had dropped from his lips. The gentleman could only excuse it to himself on the score of passion. For himself whatever might be his distress, he would never court relief from a foreign power."[45]

Immediately thereafter, the Convention wisely decided to let time and reflection soothe the frayed nerves of excited men on that last Saturday in June, and adjourned until Monday. In the heated atmosphere of conflicting opinions and bitter personal retorts, the debate of June 30 had reached a peak of intensity never afterward attained on the Convention floor.

Ellsworth's proposal to allow each state one vote in the upper house was put to a vote on Monday, July 2. The result was a tie, five states to five, with one delegation divided, and the Convention was deadlocked. To suggest some compromise, a grand committee of one member from each state was appointed, and the delegates adjourned until Thursday to allow time for the committee to do its work and for the members of the Convention to celebrate the Fourth of July.

The committee's report recommended representation in the lower house based on population and an equal vote for each state in the upper house. This was clearly a victory for those who feared domination of the Union by Virginia, Pennsylvania, and Massachusetts.

44. Madison's notes, *ibid.*, 492. The words "with a dictatorial air" may well have been inserted in a later revision. *Ibid.*, 492*n.*

45. *Ibid.*, 492–93. The last two sentences are added from Yates's notes, *ibid.*, 502. See 493*n.* Bedford later claimed that his reference to a foreign power had been misunderstood, *ibid.*, 531.

Gouverneur Morris opened fire on the report and argued that property should be considered as well as population in determining apportionment.[46] King agreed: the number of inhabitants was not the proper index of ability and wealth. Like Morris, he believed that property was the primary object of society and that it ought to be taken into consideration.[47]

On the sixth, the Convention, on Morris's motion to work out the basis of representation for each state in the lower house, elected King to a special committee with Morris, Gorham, Randolph, and Rutledge (all delegates from large states). In debate on the report of the new committee, which suggested fifty-six delegates for the thirteen states, Paterson objected to the vagueness of its provision for future changes in population and wealth. He added that he could not consider Negro slaves as anything but property, since they were not free agents and were at the disposal of their masters. Madison was willing to let the number of free inhabitants determine representation in the lower house but wished the upper house to be based upon the entire population, including slaves. Pierce Butler of South Carolina thought it just and necessary to consider wealth in apportioning representation.[48]

King, ever the realist, pointed out that since the southern states were the wealthiest, they would not confederate with the northern ones unless their superior wealth were recognized. If the northern states expected commercial or other advantages, they must allow some advantages in return. Of the thirteen states, eleven had agreed to consider slaves in the apportionment of taxes. Taxation and representation, he said, ought to go together.[49] The Convention then selected a new grand committee to revise the previous report, and King, as chairman, reported on July 10.

Like the previous report, King's assigned a specific number of representatives to each state, but increased the total to sixty-five and modified the representation accordingly. When Rutledge and Charles Pinckney of South Carolina moved to reduce the representation of New Hampshire and increase that of the South, King defended the claims of New Hampshire and of the North. The question was not one of a difference of interests between large and small

46. Madison's notes, *ibid.*, 533.
47. *Ibid.*, 541.
48. *Ibid.*, 561–62.
49. *Ibid.*, 562.

states, but between the southern and the eastern (northern); he was ready to assure the security of southern interests, but no principle would justify a southern majority. The proposed apportionment, he asserted, provided as much equality as possible.[50]

The next day the Carolinians, insisting that Negroes be considered equally with whites in apportioning representation, precipitated a discussion of the "three-fifths rule." Gorham reminded the delegates that the Confederation Congress had adopted this rule—that three-fifths of the Negroes be included in the apportionment of taxes.[51] King, already opposed to fixing numbers as a basis of representation, was even more opposed if Negro slaves, who were denied the vote, were counted. Population, he held, was an uncertain index of wealth; even assuming it to be adequate at present, he did not expect it to remain so; hence he disapproved of what was called the "rule of numbers." Moreover, he objected to counting any slaves at all for representation. In the temporary allotment of representatives then under discussion, the southern states would have more delegates than they were entitled to on the basis of their white and three-fifths of their black inhabitants.[52] Asserting that a union without justice could not last long, King warned: "He must be short sighted indeed who does not foresee that whenever the Southern States shall be more numerous than the Northern, they can and will hold a language that will awe them into justice."[53] By a vote of six to two on July 12, the Convention decided to base representation and direct taxation upon the white (free) and three-fifths of the Negro (slave) population; it also voted to require a periodic census.[54] The vote of Massachusetts was divided, but how its delegates split is not recorded. King probably voted against the plan. However, it is conceivable that his disapproval of slavery might have been counterbalanced by recognition that a flexible formula of apportionment was the only practical way of securing sectional agreement.

Far from pleased with the course of the Convention,[55] King was

50. *Ibid.*, 566.
51. *Ibid.*, 580.
52. *Ibid.*, 586.
53. *Ibid.*, 595.
54. *Ibid.*, 596.
55. *Ibid.*, II, 5–7. King had fretfully informed Secretary Knox, "I wish [I could tell you] that we had progressed a single step since you left us . . . . If I had returned to N.-YK with you or with our very able and segacious Friend Hamilton, I should have escaped much Vexation, enjoyed much pleasure and have gratified the earnest wishes and desires of Mrs. King." King to Henry Knox, July 11, 1787, Knox Papers, Mass. Hist. Soc. In reply to King's gloomy

particularly dissatisfied with the plan which called for the equality of states in the upper house. When Charles Pinckney moved on July 14 to apportion the seats on a sliding scale from one for the smallest states (Delaware and Rhode Island) to five for the largest (Virginia), the Massachusetts delegate joined Madison and Wilson in supporting the move, while Dayton and Sherman argued for equality of votes.

King argued that it would be better to "submit to a little more confusion and convulsion" than to yield to the evil of an equal vote for each state.[56] But he denied that the general government would encroach upon the states. Madison essentially agreed and incidentally pointed out, as King had done a few days earlier, that the real difference lay between slave and free states, not between large and small ones.[57] Wilson added that he could not support a system based on a "fundamental and perpetual error"; equality of votes in the senate was not necessary to preserve the states.[58] Pinckney's motion was beaten, with six states, including Massachusetts, voting against it. Although his colleagues Gerry and Strong sought an accommodation

letter, Knox observed that the "vile state governments" were "sources of pollution" which would "contaminate the American name, perhaps for ages." Knox to King, July 15, 1787, *ibid.* King was likewise concerned over America's reputation abroad, and his anxiety was sustained by the urgent tone of letters he received from Massachusetts. See James Sullivan to King, June 14, 1787, Theodore Sedgwick to King, June 18, 1787, Christopher Gore to King, June 28, 1787, and Nathan Dane to King, July 5, 1787, all in the King Papers, N.-Y. Hist. Soc.

56. Madison's notes, Farrand, ed., *Records of the Federal Convention*, II, 5–7.

57. *Ibid.*, 10. For King's statement on this subject on July 10, *ibid.*, I, 566. King was concerned with another sectional issue, the West, and on several occasions worried lest new western states some day overshadow the original seaboard states. He seconded Gerry's motion on July 14 that in the lower house the representatives of the newer states should never outnumber those of the states which ratified the Constitution. When Sherman of Connecticut objected to the proposed discrimination against "our children and grand Children, who would be as likely to be citizens of new Western States as of the old States," King did not reply, perhaps recalling Jeremiah Wadsworth's warning that Sherman was "as cun[n]ing as the Devil, and if you attack him, you ought to know him well; he is not easily managed, but if he suspects you are trying to take him in, you may as well catch an Eel by the tail." *Ibid.*, II, 3. Jeremiah Wadsworth to King, June 3, 1787, King Papers, N.-Y. Hist. Soc. When Gerry's motion was put to a vote, the Massachusetts delegation supported it, but it was defeated five to four, with New Jersey the only northern state voting with the majority. Madison's notes, Farrand, ed., *Records of the Federal Convention*, II, 3. On this question Sherman was outvoted by his colleagues, Ellsworth and W. S. Johnson. The three united, however, in their desire to protect the Western Reserve and the interests of Connecticut holders of western lands. See McDonald, *E Pluribus Unum*, 174–79, 299.

58. Madison's notes, Farrand, ed., *Records of the Federal Convention*, II, 10.

with the small states, King advocated a clearly national government with proportional representation in both branches of the legislature. "This question was taken," he wrote, "and to my mortification by the Vote of Massachusetts lost on the 14th. July."[59]

Two days later, by a five-to-four vote, the Convention adopted an amended version of the full committee report, agreeing to the "Great Compromise" which gave the states equality in the Senate and, for the House, provided representation according to population.[60] Until the adoption of this compromise, the Convention had been like a boat floating motionless in mid-stream while its strongest oarsmen pulled strenuously toward opposite banks. Madison, Wilson, and King exerted themselves to the last against compromise. They were influenced by what they considered the practical interests of their states, but more importantly, they were guided by their theoretical preconceptions, their experiences with the inadequacies of the existing Congress, and their vision of the United States as a nation. Defeated, they acquiesced in compromise; the alternative was a break-up of the Convention.

Once it had solved the difficult problem of representation, the Convention spent the next ten days revising parts of the Virginia plan. On the election and term of office of the chief executive, opinions were extremely varied. Impeachment was a key topic of debate. When Gerry argued that impeachments were necessary ("A good magistrate will not fear them. A bad one ought to be kept in fear of them."),[61] King replied that "an extreme caution in favor of liberty might enervate the Government." If he merited it, the executive could be re-elected; if not, he could be voted out. Unless he held office during good behavior, he should not be impeachable, for impeachment by the legislature would destroy his independence and violate the "primitive axiom" of the separation of powers. King would rely upon "the vigor of the Executive as a great security for the public liberties."[62]

In the discussion on July 26 of a proposed landed property qualification for legislators, King played only a minor part, but his single observation is most revealing. Such a requirement, he said, might be very dangerous because it would exclude the "moneyed interest."[63]

59. King's notes, *ibid.*, 12; Madison's notes, *ibid.*, 11. Gorham was absent.

60. Madison's notes, *ibid.*, 15. The Massachusetts delegation was divided: Gerry and Strong voted aye, Gorham and King nay.

61. *Ibid.*, 66.

62. *Ibid.*, 66–67.

63. *Ibid.*, 123.

This view no doubt reflected his long association with merchants, security-holders, and lawyers in New England and, more recently, in New York. Although his own wealth was not in land, it seems unlikely that he gave conscious consideration to personal advantage. His opposition to confining eligibility for legislative office to freeholders was not, however, on democratic grounds; it remained for Franklin to uphold the hardy virtues and great integrity of the "lower class of Freemen."[64]

Slavery and the slave trade figured prominently in the debate on August 8, as the delegates considered the report of the Committee on Detail. More temperate than Gouverneur Morris, who proclaimed that he had rather let himself be taxed "for paying for all the Negroes in the United States, than saddle posterity with such a Constitution,"[65] King confined himself to an attack on the constitutional sanction of the slave trade. Decrying the importation of slaves as "a most grating circumstance," he said that he had not strenuously opposed it earlier because he had hoped to find "a readiness which had not been manifested, to strengthen the General Government and to mark a full confidence in it." The report of the committee had ended his hopes. The hands of the legislature were completely tied; the importation of slaves could not be prohibited, and exports could not be taxed. Was this reasonable? Should one section of the country be bound to defend another section which not only increased the danger to the former but withheld compensation for this burden? If slaves were to be imported, should not the exports produced by their labor afford a revenue "to enable the General Government to defend their Masters?" The northern states would never accept so much inequality and unreason. He had hoped that at least a time limit would have been placed upon the importation of slaves. "He never could agree to let them be imported without limitation and then be represented in the National Legislature. Indeed he could so little persuade himself of the rectitude of such a practice, that he was not sure he could assent to it under any circumstances. At all events, either slaves should not be represented, or exports should be taxable."[66]

King's speech may well have influenced the Convention's final decision to place a twenty-year limit on slave importations. On August 22, five days after King returned from a brief trip to New York,

64. *Ibid.*, 208.
65. *Ibid.*, 223.
66. *Ibid.*, 220.

the delegates again wrangled over the slave trade.[67] Pointing out that Maryland and Virginia had already forbidden the direct importation of slaves, Mason of Virginia earnestly denounced the traffic. Sherman and Ellsworth of Connecticut, fearful lest South Carolina be alienated, did not wish to meddle with this troublesome matter. Their caution seemed justified when Charles Cotesworth Pinckney asserted that South Carolina and Georgia could not do without slaves and contended further that slave importations would be of advantage to the whole country.[68] In reply to the Georgia and Carolina delegates, King ignored the moral implications and said the subject "should be considered in a political light only." If two states would not accept the Constitution, the other states would find their own reasons for opposing it. To exempt slaves from import duties while all other imports were taxed created "an inequality that could not fail to strike the commercial sagacity of the Northern and middle States."[69] A committee of eleven, including King, was finally chosen to wrestle with this and two other issues, including a proposed provision that no navigation act should be passed without the assent of two-thirds of those present in each house.[70]

The committee, besides advising against the navigation act provision, recommended a compromise which would permit slaves to be imported until 1800 but would subject them to import duties. On the twenty-fifth, the Convention postponed the terminal date to 1808, despite Madison's pungent objection that twenty years would "produce all the mischief that can be apprehended from slave importation."[71] New Jersey, Pennsylvania, Delaware, and Virginia voted against the measure, the three middle states because of strong

67. Abraham Yates, Jr., to Jeremiah Van Rensselaer and Henry Acthandt, New York, Aug. 29, 1787, Burnett, ed., *Letters of Continental Congress*, VIII, 641–42. King and his wife went to New York probably at her insistence. Mary King was not happy in Philadelphia, where she was relatively unknown and unable to see her old friends and her elderly father. There is no evidence that King planned the trip for political reasons, but he may have talked in New York with Knox or Hamilton, who had come there at about the same time.

68. Madison's notes, Farrand, ed., *Records of the Federal Convention*, II, 370–72. For a political deal between Sherman of Connecticut and Rutledge of South Carolina involving a *quid pro quo*—protection of Connecticut's landed interests in return for support of South Carolina's position on export duties and the slave trade—see McDonald, *E Pluribus Unum*, 177–79.

69. Madison's notes, Farrand, ed., *Records of the Federal Convention*, II, 373.

70. *Ibid.*, 374–75.

71. *Ibid.*, 415.

antislavery sentiment and Virginia because she needed no more slaves. New England voted solidly with Maryland, the Carolinas and Georgia in favor of the proposal. Obviously, the New Englanders reluctantly realized that extending for eight more years the legal power to bring in slaves was essential to the success of the compromise. King, while not oblivious to the moral issue, was chiefly concerned with preserving the sectional balance, and there is little doubt that John Langdon of New Hampshire and William Samuel Johnson of Connecticut, the two other New England antislavery men on the committee which recommended compromise, felt the same way. Political expediency triumphed over moral righteousness, but in no other way could the delegates have reached a practicable solution.

Although he was very much a New Englander at heart, King steered his course constantly in the direction of a national government. He seconded Rutledge's motion on August 18 for a grand committee to consider federal assumption of state debts, reasoning that the creditors of the states, who had been the strongest enemies of a federal tariff, would oppose the transfer of financial power to the Union without simultaneously transferring state debts.[72] After adopting the motion, the Convention elected King to the committee, whose report favoring congressional power to discharge state debts ran into criticism and was tabled.[73] The attempt to have the federal government assume state obligations was abandoned.

On King's motion of August 28, the Convention, by a vote of six to five, agreed to prohibit the states from taxing exports.[74] On the same day King tried to incorporate into the Constitution a clause prohibiting the states from interfering with private contracts. His closeness to the merchants and creditors in his home state, his failure to appreciate the debtor psychology which underlay Shays's Rebellion, and his preoccupation with the fiscal problems of the Confederation Congress stiffened his advocacy of brakes upon the free-wheeling inflationary economics of state legislatures. In debating the question, he pointed out that Congress had adopted such a limitation in the

72. *Ibid.*, 327–28. Massachusetts, with a large debt, stood to gain by federal assumption of it.

73. *Ibid.*, 355–56. Subsequently, Butler and Mason fired additional salvos at the proposal, the Carolinian opposing "payment to the Blood-suckers who had speculated upon the distresses of others," and the Virginian protesting the wording as likely to "beget speculations and increase the pestilent practice of stock-jobbing." *Ibid.*, 392, 413.

74. *Ibid.*, 442.

Ordinance of 1787 for new states to be created in the Northwest. Gouverneur Morris, who frequently agreed with King, thought this prohibition too far-reaching, though his colleague James Wilson favored it. Madison believed that its advantages would overcome its possible inconveniences but suggested that only a veto over state laws would be effective. To Mason's objection that the hands of the states would be tied, Wilson replied that the clause would forbid only "*retrospective* interferences." In place of King's motion, the Convention adopted Rutledge's proposal to prohibit the states from passing bills of attainder and *ex post facto* laws.[75]

Although King's move for an explicit prohibition against state action on contracts was not discussed again on the Convention floor, the idea was revived two weeks later by the Committee of Style appointed to shape into final literary form the substance of what had been agreed upon. King, Madison, Hamilton, and Johnson of Connecticut served on the committee but the most active draftsman was Gouverneur Morris, who devised much of the phraseology of the finished document. Unauthorized by the Convention, the committee made a single important addition to the text, a phrase, reminiscent of King's earlier motion, which forbade the states from enacting laws "altering or impairing the obligation of contracts."[76] Exactly how this clause came to be inserted after its previous defeat is a mystery. King was persistent and persuasive; one can imagine that, with the probable support of Hamilton and Madison, he convinced Morris of its vital importance. On the other hand, the prime mover may have been Wilson, who, though not on the committee, was the attorney for the Bank of North America, whose charter could be revoked at will by the Pennsylvania legislature.[77] Whoever took the initiative, the committee wrote into the document a part that had not been sanctioned by the Convention, and that clause was ultimately accepted without objection by the men who signed the Constitution.

King was more scrupulous about procedure when it came to the method of ratifying the Constitution. At the close of the August 30 session, the delegates were debating whether they should require ap-

75. *Ibid.*, 439–40.
76. Farrand, ed., *Records of the Federal Convention*, III, 597.
77. McDonald, *E Pluribus Unum*, 187*n*. Clinton Rossiter asserts flatly that King persuaded his committee colleagues to add the clause, *1787, The Grand Convention* (N. Y., 1966), 230.

proval by seven, eight, nine, or ten states in order to make the new document effective, when Carroll of Maryland moved that all thirteen states be required to ratify. Since the existing Confederation had been created unanimously, he said, unanimity was needed to dissolve it. King thought Carroll's motion necessary, for otherwise the Constitution would "operate on the whole though ratified in part only."[78] King pondered the question overnight and proposed the next day that the operation of the new government be limited to those states which ratified the Constitution, a practical solution to the problem he and Carroll had raised. The delegates overwhelmingly approved, and later that day they agreed upon requiring the assent of nine states.[79]

As to the method of ratification, King stoutly upheld the use of conventions chosen especially for that purpose. Leaving it up to the states to decide in their own way was "equivalent to giving up the business altogether." Only conventions would avoid the obstacles entailed in action by the legislatures, he thought. If the Constitution itself did not positively require ratification by convention, its enemies would oppose that method.[80] Madison, Gorham, and Charles Pinckney spoke in favor of conventions. The Marylanders, McHenry and Martin, objected, Martin insisting on referring the new instrument to the state legislatures and both refusing to countenance anything that would violate the Maryland constitution. According to Madison, King then remarked that the Massachusetts constitution "was made unalterable till the year 1790, yet this was no difficulty with him. The State must have contemplated a recurrence to first principles before they sent deputies to this Convention."[81]

During the first week of September, the Convention filled in the gaps in the plan before it. On the sixth, King and Gerry moved that no person should be appointed an elector who was "a member of the Legislature of the U.S.," or who held "any office of profit or trust under the U.S.,"[82] and this provision was unanimously accepted. Madison and King helped to shape the quorum rule to apply in case a close contest should throw the election of the president into the House of Representatives.[83] King defended the principle of presi-

78. Madison's notes, Farrand, ed., *Records of the Federal Convention*, II, 469.
79. *Ibid.*, 475, 477.
80. *Ibid.*, 476.
81. *Ibid.*, 476–77.
82. *Ibid.*, 521.
83. *Ibid.*, 527–28.

dential appointments with the advice and consent of the Senate against the idea of a privy council chosen for this purpose. He objected to the requirement of a two-thirds vote in the Senate for approving treaties, arguing that it would enable the minority to block the majority will.[84] When the North Carolina delegates moved to require a two-thirds vote on peace treaties affecting territorial rights, King warned of the need to "look out for securities for some other rights" and tried to broaden the motion to include "all present rights of the U. States."[85] New England fishermen and their rights were on his mind.

From time to time during the course of the Convention, delegates discussed the length of the president's term of office. On one occasion, after a seven-year term had been voted down, King went so far as to suggest a twenty-year term, calling this lengthy period "the medium life of princes." Madison thought King might possibly have been ridiculing previous motions to make the executive ineligible for re-election.[86] Since he wished to ensure the president's re-eligibility, King may indeed have spoken ironically, but it is also possible that he seriously wanted to ensure a long term in order to give stability and continuity to the executive power. On September 6, the Convention finally decided upon a presidential term of four years, a relatively short period, but made him eligible for re-election.[87]

In the remaining weeks of the Convention, only three delegates represented Massachusetts, Caleb Strong having left because of illness in his family. Though he favored the Constitution, unfounded rumors linked his sudden departure with discord and probable failure behind the closed doors of the Convention.[88] A moderate western-Massachusetts Federalist, Strong was less eager for a national government than either King or Gorham, and on several occasions he and Gerry had voted against them, dividing the state's deputation. Gerry and King had been close friends in Congress, had lived together for a time at Mrs. Mercer's in New York, and had worked efficiently as a team, but their frequent differences of principle in

84. *Ibid.*, 539, 540.
85. *Ibid.*, 543.
86. *Ibid.*, 102.
87. *Ibid.*, 525; "Journal of the Convention," *ibid.*, 517, 520.
88. Abraham Yates, Jr., to Jeremiah Van Rensselaer and Henry Acthandt, Aug. 29, 1787, Burnett, ed., *Letters of Continental Congress*, VIII, 641–42.

the Philadelphia Convention not only prevented their voting effectively as a delegation but placed a strain upon their earlier intimacy.[89] Because prior to January 1787 they had kept up a vigorous opposition in Congress to the movement for a Convention, the extent of their current disagreements related to King's progress along the nationalist path was not yet publicly known.

The final days of the Philadelphia Convention were spent in scrutinizing the report of the Committee of Style. Precisely how great a share Rufus King had in shaping the final draft of the Constitution cannot be determined. It is unlikely that the wording of the Constitution owes more to his initiative than perhaps the clause prohibiting states from impairing the obligation of contracts. Precision and clarity were qualities he admired, and his effectiveness in the committee probably lay in what he could contribute to logical arrangement and unambiguous terminology. The felicitous style of the Constitution was largely the handiwork of Gouverneur Morris.

King's preference for directness and precise terminology implied no wish to be overly specific. Madison's proposal that the new Congress have the power to grant charters of incorporation he considered unnecessary: "The States will be prejudiced and divided into parties by it—In Philadelphia and New York, It will be referred to the establishment of a Bank, which has been a subject of contention in those cities. In other places it will be referred to mercantile monopolies."[90] On the procedure for submitting the Constitution to the present Congress, King shrewdly suggested being both general and specific. He considered it more respectful to submit the Constitution "generally," rather than in a form that would "expressly and necessarily" require its approval or disapproval. Ratification by nine states, he thought, would be enough to validate the instrument, but he believed it "more proper" to incorporate the requirement into the Constitution itself than to leave it to a mere recommendation.[91]

This remark exposed once more the widening chasm between King and Gerry who immediately urged "the indecency and pernicious tendency of dissolving in so slight a manner, the solemn obligations of the articles of confederation." If nine of the thirteen states

89. Gerry had rented a house in Spruce Street, where he had brought his family, but there is no hint in the surviving records of his relations with the Kings outside the Convention hall.

90. Madison's notes, Farrand, ed., *Records of the Federal Convention*, II, 616.

91. *Ibid.*, 561.

could dissolve the compact, he protested, six of the nine could just as easily dissolve the new one.[92] Since the beginning of the year, Gerry had not journeyed far along the road to nationalism, but King had come in sight of his nationalist goal. He and Gorham would sign the Constitution; Gerry would not.

Before the signing of the Constitution, King suggested that the official records of the Convention be either destroyed or left in the custody of the president. To publicize the proceedings, he feared, would play into the hands of the opponents of ratification. After Wilson spoke in favor of King's second suggestion, the Convention agreed to turn over to Washington its journal and other papers.[93] The finished Constitution was then signed by all the members present (thirty-nine delegates from twelve states) except Gerry, Mason and Randolph. By affixing their names, King and Gorham had the satisfaction of preserving, in general, the interests of Massachusetts as well as contributing to the enlargement of federal authority over commerce and to the creation of a stronger government.

In the first rank among those who forged the Constitution were Madison and Wilson, and perhaps Gouverneur Morris. Washington exerted a steadying influence as the dignified president of the Convention, and Franklin, physically weak but mentally alert, lent his wit and experience at crucial points in the debates. Among the most influential secondary leaders were King, Mason, Randolph, Rutledge, Charles Pinckney, Sherman, and Gorham. King was in general agreement with Madison and Wilson in pushing for a stronger union, but he was less inclined than they to compromise. He was not always patient, but his arguments were usually less emotional than those of Morris, with whom he basically agreed. If his creative contributions cannot be found in the grand architectural plan of the new edifice, they are most certainly embedded in its bricks and masonry.

Morris, Sherman, Ellsworth, and Martin spoke more often than King, but their ideas were less readily accepted. Morris, as chairman of the Committee of Style, and Sherman, who suggested the compromise on representation, contributed to the constructive work of the Convention, but Ellsworth and Martin functioned mainly as critics. Mason, Randolph, and Gerry, despite their ultimate dissatisfaction, offered valuable suggestions. King, however, effectively

92. *Ibid.*
93. *Ibid.*, 648.

argued for many of the proposals which became part of the finished Constitution: he upheld the principles of the separation of powers, a strong and independent president, and, in general, provisions essential to a strengthened central government. Partly as a result of his exertions, the importation of slaves was restricted, and the clause preserving the sanctity of contracts from state action reflected his influence. His steady championship of the nationalist view assured his reputation among men of his generation and after.

When the Convention adjourned on September 17, King joined the other delegates at the City Tavern for a convivial dinner before leaving Philadelphia.[94] He and Gorham, Johnson of Connecticut, and William Few of Georgia were on hand in New York when the report of the Philadelphia Convention was read to Congress on September 20.[95] Among the members who were present to debate it six days later were twelve who had been in the Convention. On the twenty-eighth, Congress, without expressing judgment on the Constitution, unanimously resolved to pass it on to the state legislatures for submission to specially called conventions.

94. McHenry's notes, *ibid.*, 650.

95. Pierce of Georgia had left the Convention early in July and had been attending Congress for some weeks before Sept. 20.

CHAPTER VII

RATIFICATION IN MASSACHUSETTS

KING DID NOT REMAIN LONG AT HIS SEAT IN THE CONFEDERATION CONgress, for he had cast his lot with the new Constitution and was eager to promote it—and himself. In the middle of October he set out for Boston and Newburyport. There he busied himself for several weeks, explaining and advocating the Constitution, in preparation for the state convention called for January 9. On November 20, Newburyport chose its delegates: Benjamin Greenleaf, Theophilus Parsons, Jonathan Titcomb, and Rufus King. Greenleaf, a prominent merchant and the father-in-law of Parsons, easily received the most votes—141; King the fewest—only 80.[1] King's poor showing is not surprising in view of his absence for three years in Congress and the rarity of his visits to his home town, where he was now almost a total stranger. He was lucky to be chosen at all; had he not hurried back to Newburyport to mend his political fences he might not have been elected. His marriage into a wealthy New York family and his more recent association with influential persons outside Massachusetts buttressed the feeling that he no longer truly represented Newburyport. Moreover, some of his fellow citizens may have considered it unwise to elect a man who had been a framer of the docu-

1. Newburyport *Essex Journal*, Nov. 21, 1787; Newburyport Town Records, I, 500–01.

ment to be scrutinized.[2] For a person of such broad experience in federal affairs, King must have been disappointed at the weak vote of confidence in him.

Four days after his election he left for New York to join his wife, who was expecting their first child in January. When Gore and Gorham, who had also been chosen as delegates, learned that he might not return to Massachusetts in time for the opening of the convention, they pressed him to be on hand early in January before the sessions began. "No consideration" could "be an inducement to you to stay at New York after the first of January," Gorham pleaded. "You can have no idea how much depends on your presence." Although the Federalists had fared well in the Boston area, he predicted that a "black cloud" would descend from the three western counties.[3] As the days passed in December, King's friends in Massachusetts grew ever more anxious for his presence. On the twenty-ninth, Gorham again implored his old colleague to return and plainly suggested that his absence was already injuring him politically. Local Federalists were saying that King had become an alien who would not exert himself in the Bay State. The situation demanded candid and prudent leadership, and Gorham had faith in King's skill at political management. "You know some of our Friends are not good Steersmen. Most of the Eastern members are wrong; nobody can deal with them so well as you," he wrote. "Pray persuade Mrs. King to consent; you never can have a greater call."[4]

King's dilemma was solved on January 3, when his wife gave birth to their first child, a boy. They named him John Alsop in honor of his maternal grandfather. After waiting a few days to assure himself of Mary's good health, the happy father left for Boston. He took his place in the convention on January 12, three days after its opening meeting but before the delegates seriously set to work.

Of the more than 360 delegates, a clear majority were at the outset opposed to the Constitution, and had a vote been taken then, it would

2. Some time after the Massachusetts ratifying convention opened, Elbridge Gerry wrote that he would not have accepted a seat in the Convention under any circumstances, as he had been a member of the Philadelphia Convention. Perhaps he was also rationalizing the fact that he had not been elected to the Massachusetts convention. Gerry to William Cushing, Jan. 21, 1788, Gerry Papers, Pierpoint Morgan Lib.

3. Nathaniel Gorham to King, Dec. 12, 1787, King Papers, N.-Y. Hist. Soc. Cf. Christopher Gore to King, Dec. 9, 30, 1787, *ibid.*

4. Gorham to King, Dec. 29, 1787, *ibid.*

have been decisively defeated. Many opponents were worried that the centralization of power in a national government would jeopardize local interests, and they maintained that the absence of a federal bill of rights endangered individual liberties.[5] Delegates from the farming areas, particularly in the region between the coastal towns and the Connecticut Valley, held opinions shaped by widespread poverty, the burden of accumulated debt, the pressure of creditors, dislike of lawyers and moneyed men, and a sense of social injustice heightened by the stern suppression of Shays's insurrection.[6] At least twenty-nine of the delegates had actually served in the insurgent forces, and several others had attended county conventions.[7]

Facing this formidable group of skeptical and suspicious men was a solid phalanx of Federalists, chiefly from the wealthy seaboard cities, the trading towns of the Connecticut Valley, and the more prosperous farm districts. Among the experienced lawyers and politicians who supported the new Constitution were King, Gorham, and Strong, fresh from the Philadelphia Convention, former Governor Bowdoin, Gore, Parsons, Francis Dana, Theodore Sedgwick, Fisher Ames, and Tristram Dalton. Governor Hancock, one of the Boston delegates, was ill with gout and his attitude was not yet known. Samuel Adams, though possibly open to conversion, sided with the Antifederalists; King described him as "full mouthed against the Constitution."[8]

The convention opened its proceedings in the Representatives'

5. In "Men of Little Faith: the Anti-Federalists on the Nature of Representative Government," *William and Mary Quarterly*, 3d Ser., 12 (1955), 3–43, Cecelia M. Kenyon argues convincingly that, in general, the Antifederalists did not fear aristocracy *per se*; they feared power that they could not control for themselves and therefore wished to keep governments limited and tied to local interests. See pp. 13, 15, 19, and 22 for specific illustrations drawn from the Massachusetts convention. For the struggle in Massachusetts, Samuel B. Harding, *The Contest over the Ratification of the Federal Constitution in the State of Massachusetts* (N. Y., 1896) is still valuable. See also Robert A. East, "Massachusetts Conservatives in the Critical Period," in Richard B. Morris, ed., *Era of the American Revolution . . .* (N. Y., 1939), 349–91, for the background.

6. Main, *Antifederalists*, 202–03, 205–10. Most delegates from the interior of Maine were Antifederalists. Despite Gore's intimation to King that the Maine delegates would oppose the Constitution because they favored separate statehood, there is no positive correlation between these two attitudes, *ibid.*, *207n*; King, ed., *King Correspondence*, I, 312.

7. Main, *Antifederalists*, 207. In Virginia the anxious Madison learned that 18 or 20 had been active Shaysites. James Madison to George Washington, Feb. 3, 1788, Washington Papers, Lib. Cong.

8. King to Jeremiah Wadsworth, Jan. 6, 1788, Wadsworth Papers, Conn. Hist. Soc.

Chamber in the Old State House and chose Hancock to preside. As the Governor was still confined to his home, Chief Justice Cushing, the vice-president, took the chair. The chamber was so crowded that the convention moved to the larger Brattle Street Meeting House, but poor acoustics caused a return on January 12 to the Old State House. On that day 329 delegates had taken their seats, including Rufus King, who had arrived in Boston the night before. The scene was familiar to him; he had sat in this room three years earlier as a member of the General Court.

On January 14 the convention set to work. No sooner had the delegates listened to the first reading of the Constitution and voted to consider it paragraph by paragraph, than the Antifederalists moved that Elbridge Gerry be requested to attend. Gerry had refused to sign the instrument and had publicly come out against it, arguing that it gave Congress sweeping powers and failed to safeguard the rights of individuals in federal courts.[9] Unwilling to let a minor issue become a test of strength, the Federalists acquiesced in the Antifederalist maneuver. They were reluctant at the outset to excite those who, according to King, were "certainly not the most enlightened part of the Convention."[10]

King participated in the first prolonged debate, over the biennial election of representatives in Congress. Annual elections were customary in Massachusetts; the state's delegates to the Confederation Congress were chosen for only one year, though eligible for three successive terms. It took some hardihood to counter the popular faith that annual elections were the best way to keep government close to the people. King agreed that representatives should not be removed from the salutary check of frequent elections, but he argued that delegates should be in office long enough to acquire information needed for sound judgment of issues. Two years, he thought, was not too long in view of the complicated interests of the United States and the demands of foreign relations. An increase in the powers of Congress would increase the duties of congressmen, who consequently needed a reasonable time to keep themselves informed.[11] The Antifederalists were unconvinced; Abraham White of Norton

9. Arthur N. Holcombe, "Massachusetts and the Federal Constitution of 1787," in A. B. Hart, ed., *Commonwealth History of Massachusetts . . .*, 5 vols. (N. Y., 1927–30), III, 366–407.

10. King to James Madison, Jan. 16, 1788, Madison Papers, Lib. Cong.

11. *Debates, Resolutions and other Proceedings of the Convention of the Commonwealth of Massachusetts. . . 1788* (Boston, 1808), 42–45; Boston *Massachusetts Centinel*, Jan. 19, 1788.

expressed the fear that "Congress might perpetuate themselves and so reign emperours over us."[12]

After moving again from the cramped State House, this time to the Reverend Jeremy Belknap's large meetinghouse on Long Lane, Federalists and Antifederalists switched sides in an amusing exchange on the qualifications of representatives. The self-made General Samuel Thompson of Topsham, one of the more effective of the Antifederalists, argued for a property qualification. The ultra-conservative Theodore Sedgwick ironically professed surprise that gentlemen who so ardently championed popular rights should wish to exclude a *good* man because he was not a *rich* one.[13] King added that he had never known that property was an index to abilities; men without property often had superior knowledge and rectitude, he asserted, and those who had most injured the country had usually been rich men.[14] Such statements were remarkable coming from one so closely identified with property interests and so aroused by Shays's Rebellion. Aside from their tactical value in addressing a largely hostile audience, they reveal King as a moderate man, a reconciler of extremes in order to secure practical action.

When the delegates took up the Constitution's provision for apportionment of representatives and taxes according to the number of free persons, indentured servants, and "three fifths of all other persons," King felt obliged to answer some thorny remarks on slave representation. Despite his personal aversion to the Philadelphia Convention's decision, he explained that taxation and representation went hand in hand; the three-fifths or "federal" ratio had been adopted "because it was the language of all America." Under the Articles of Confederation the state quotas for the general welfare and for defense were to have been assessed according to the surveyed and improved lands in each state, but, said King, Congress had never been able to follow that rule, "the returns from the several states being so very imperfect."[15] When William Widgery of New Gloucester, an outspoken opponent, asked whether a six-year-old

12. Boston *Massachusetts Centinel*, Jan. 19, 1788.

13. *Debates of Convention, 1788* (1808), 62.

14. *Ibid.* King also defended the absence of a disqualification for age by stating that since longevity varied according to climate, such a disqualification would apply unequally to all parts of the continent, *ibid.*; Boston *Massachusetts Centinel*, Jan. 26, 1788.

15. *Debates of Convention, 1788* (1808), 62–63. Cf. T. Parsons, "Minutes," in *Debates and Proceedings in the Convention of the Commonwealth of Massachusetts, held in the Year 1788* (Boston, 1856), 299.

boy was to be considered a free person under the federal ratio, King replied that all persons born free were to be considered freemen. To make the idea of taxation by numbers more intelligible he made an arresting comparison: five Negro children in South Carolina would be subject to as much tax as the three governors of New Hampshire, Massachusetts, and Connecticut.[16] Samuel Nasson, a trader and storekeeper from Sanford, sharply replied that a good rule worked both ways, pointing out that Massachusetts would pay as much tax "for three children in the cradle as any of the southern States will for five hearty working Negro men."[17]

Federalist speakers, among them King, Gore, and Parsons, also tried to show the advantage to the northern states in the apportionment of representatives before the taking of the first federal census. Gerry, who since his admission as a guest of the convention had sat silently "biting the head of his cane," was asked why Georgia was allotted three representatives and Massachusetts eight, when the former had been assessed at only one-thirteenth the sum of the latter. Gerry was not permitted to reply directly, so he read a statement the following day, explaining that because of rapid immigration Georgia would be entitled to three representatives. Supporting his former colleague, King adverted to the difficulties of Congress in reaching an equitable apportionment under the Articles of Confederation: unable to secure surveys by the states of land and houses, Congress had consulted no rule but merely adopted the expedient of taxation according to ability to pay.[18]

Just as he upheld the two-year term for representatives, King defended the six-year term for senators. He argued that the term was not as long as it seemed; if one considered the case of the first senators chosen under the Constitution, "one class is to serve two years, another four, and another six years; the average, therefore, is four years," he contended somewhat disingenuously. When Colonel William Jones of Bristol deplored the absence of the power to recall senators, King replied that the state legislatures would keep an eye on them. If legislatures instructed erring senators, would this not be

16. *Debates of Convention, 1788* (1808), 63; Parsons, "Minutes," *Debates of Convention, 1788* (1856), 300.

17. *Debates of Convention, 1788* (1808), 66. The Boston *Independent Chronicle*, Jan. 24, 1788, reported the same remark but with a slight variation in wording.

18. J. Belknap to E. Hazard, Jan. 20, 1788, "Correspondence between Jeremy Belknap and Ebenezer Hazard," *Belknap Papers* (Mass. Hist. Soc., *Collections*, 5th Ser., 3 [1877]), II, 7; *Debates of Convention, 1788* (1808), 72–73.

a check? he asked. "When they hear the voice of the people solemnly dictating to them their duty, they will be bold men indeed to act contrary to it." Conveniently overlooking his and Gerry's pocketing of the General Court's instruction to push for a federal convention, he added: "These will not be instructions sent them in a private letter, which can be put in their pockets; they will be publick instructions which all the country will see; and they will be hardy men indeed to violate them." Furthermore, senators needed time to form mature judgments, especially in advising the president and helping to shape treaties advantageous to the United States.[19]

Dr. John Taylor of Worcester County was not convinced by King's argument. Though senators were classed, they were really to be chosen for six years.[20] Sensing that King's labored explanation had made an unfavorable impression on the Antifederalists, Caleb Strong asserted that the Philadelphia Convention had relied on the report of a committee on which Gerry had served. Gerry did more than take the hint. Without being asked, he announced that he was preparing a letter on the subject, whereupon Judge Dana, Parsons, and several other Federalists objected to his making a statement without first having been asked in writing. Tempers rose as Dana and Gerry confronted one another, and clusters of delegates swarmed around the two angry men, finally separating them amid cries for adjournment. The altercation aroused intense feelings on both sides, and it was fortunate for the Federalists that Gerry decided not to appear again on the convention floor. He deeply resented the way in which he had been thwarted in his attempts to explain his actions at the Philadelphia Convention and to communicate "important truths." King feared the dispute might prematurely reveal a division, since the Federalists supported Dana and their opponents, Gerry. As for his former friend and colleague, King wrote sadly: "Gerry's conduct cannot be excused and convinces me of one thing, that he will not hesitate in small matters."[21]

19. *Debates of Convention, 1788* (1808), 75–76; Parsons, "Minutes," *Debates of Convention, 1788* (1856), 307; Robert E. Reeser, Rufus King and the Federalist Party (unpubl. Ph.D. diss., U.C.L.A., 1948–49), 68.

20. *Debates of Convention, 1788* (1808), 76.

21. J. Belknap to E. Hazard, Jan. 20, 1788, "Correspondence between Jeremy Belknap and Ebenezer Hazard," *Belknap Papers*, II, 8; King to James Madison, Jan. 20, 1788, Madison Papers, Lib. Cong.; King to [Horatio Gates or Henry Knox?], Jan. 20, 1788, King Folder, N. Y. Pub. Lib. For a fuller account of Gerry's side of the affair, see Austin, *Life of Elbridge Gerry*, II, 71–73.

To the Federalists, the opponents of the Constitution seemed unreasonably suspicious and fearful that popular liberties would be subverted. It was an all too obvious fact that Antifederalists in Massachusetts distrusted men of property and education.[22] The Reverend Jeremy Belknap, who sat each day in the tightly packed gallery of his meetinghouse, noted that Federalist speakers repeated the same arguments day after day to combat objections which he thought arose from an enmity to any and all government. "They [the Antis] *will* not be convinced, they *will* not be silenced," wrote the observant minister, making no effort to hide his Federalist sympathies.[23]

Questions raised by the opponents of the Constitution frequently reflected their fears. On January 21, for example, John Taylor asked whether the federal power to regulate elections would not result in senators and representatives fixing elections to keep themselves in office. King replied that this power related only to "the *manner* of election, not the *qualifications* of the electors. The qualifications are of age and residence," he said approvingly, but differences in state electoral procedures made it impracticable for the states to fix the place and manner of elections.[24]

Later that day, in a debate on the powers of Congress, General Brooks of Medford suggested that the general articles of the Constitution should be restricted. In a lengthy response, King sketched the historic inadequacy of requisitions in the United Provinces of the Netherlands and pointed out that in America, though Massachusetts had paid her quota to the federal government, other states had shamefully neglected to pay theirs. Two states, he asserted, had "not paid a single farthing" since the beginning of the Confederation.

> What method then can we devise to compel the delinquent states to pay their quotas? Sir, I know of none. Laws, to be effective, therefore, must not be laid on states, but upon individuals. It has been objected to the proposed constitution, that the power is too great, and by this constitution is to be sacred. But if the want of power is the defect in the old confederation, there is fitness and propriety in adopting what is here pro-

22. King to James Madison, Jan. 20, 1788, Madison Papers, Lib. Cong. Cf. King to Madison, Jan. 27, 1788, *ibid.*; Henry Knox to George Washington, Feb. 10, 1788, Washington Papers, Lib. Cong.

23. "Correspondence between Jeremy Belknap and Ebenezer Hazard," *Belknap Papers*, II, 9.

24. *Debates of Convention, 1788* (1808), 78–79. Cf. Parsons, "Minutes," *Debates of Convention, 1788* (1856), 308–09.

posed. . . . It is an objection in some gentlemen's minds, that Congress should possess the power of the purse and the sword. But, sir, I would ask, whether any government can exist, or give security to the people, which is not possessed of this power. . . . To conclude, sir, if we mean to support an efficient federal government, which under the old confederation can never be the case, the proposed constitution is, in my opinion, the only one that can be substituted.[25]

King's cogent reasoning and earnest conviction in what was probably his best speech in the convention impressed many listeners, but it is doubtful that he won many converts. The Antifederalists remained skeptical of the Constitution and confident of their strength; no doubt they were pleased when Amos Singletary of Sutton said in reply to King that he thought "no more power could be given to a despot, than to give up the purse-strings of the people."[26]

When Samuel Nasson moved on January 23 to reconsider the decision to discuss the Constitution paragraph by paragraph, the Federalists were put clearly on the defensive. Discussion of the Constitution as a whole would have led to a premature vote for ratification or rejection—in all likelihood, rejection. Such a vote would have gratified delegates from distant points who were eager to complete their business and go home. From the beginning, the Federalists had carefully avoided any clear test of strength. They now were relieved when Samuel Adams, supported by King and others, argued against Nasson's motion and convincingly urged a thorough examination of the Constitution. Situated as he was between the two opposing camps, the popular hero of the Revolution saved the day for the Constitution, as the convention voted down the move to reconsider.

The Antifederalists asked many questions, some of them designed to embarrass their foes. Gorham, Strong, and King, all of whom had been delegates to the Philadelphia Convention, frequently rose to reply. In some instances they had to correct gross misinterpretation or insinuation stemming from ignorance or from a desire to needle the Federalists into uttering politically damaging statements. If at first King had been unwilling to respond to queries, the hostile

25. *Debates of Convention, 1788* (1808), 83–86; Boston *Independent Chronicle*, Jan. 31, 1788. Cf. Parsons, "Minutes," *Debates of Convention, 1788* (1856), 310.

26. *Debates of Convention, 1788* (1808), 90. Cf. King to James Madison, Jan. 20, 1788, Madison Papers, Lib. Cong.

American Herald asserted that he soon became expert at answering them.[27] The Reverend Belknap wrote: "Rufus King shines among the Feds with a superior lustre. His speeches are clear, cool, nervous [animated], pointed, and conclusive."[28]

King did much more than deliver speeches and answer questions. As the ablest of the four Massachusetts deputies to the Philadelphia Convention, he was at the center of Federalist councils in Boston. His correspondence with Madison and Knox occasionally illuminates the inner politics of the Massachusetts convention. Every three or four days he wrote to Madison, who sent excerpts from his letters to General Washington at Mount Vernon. The Virginia Federalists had other informants at Boston, but they seem to have placed special reliance upon King's reports. His accounts were straightforward and usually unembellished, and his predictions were cautious and temperate.[29]

After a week of debate, King described to Madison the difficulty in combating the Antis. "If the opposition was grounded on any precise points, I am persuaded that it might be weakened, if not overcome," he explained. "But every attempt to remove their fixed and violent jealousy, seems, hitherto, to operate as a confirmation of that baneful passion. The opponents affirm to each other that they have an unalterable majority on their side. The friends doubt the strength of their adversaries, but are not entirely confident of their own."[30]

An interesting expression of the Antifederalist bias which so irritated King (who a year earlier might have agreed with it) came from Amos Singletary: "All gentlemen had said about a bill of rights to the Constitution, was, that what is written is written; . . . we were

27. Boston *American Herald*, Jan. 21, 1788.

28. "Correspondence between Jeremy Belknap and Ebenezer Hazard," *Belknap Papers*, II, 11. Belknap also mentioned that Theophilus Parsons did yeoman work for the Constitution.

29. James Madison to George Washington, Jan. 28, 1788, Washington Papers, Lib. Cong. Cf. Madison to Washington, Feb. 1, 1788, *ibid.* For King's correspondence with Henry Knox, see especially King to Knox, Jan. 27, Feb. 3, 1788, Knox Papers, Mass. Hist. Soc.

30. King to Madison, Jan. 20, 1788, Madison Papers, Lib. Cong. However, on the same day King wrote more optimistically to an old Maine friend, George Thatcher of Biddeford, then in New York as a delegate in Congress: "I find that my own mind, notwithstanding its Doubts, balances in favor of the Idea that the constitution will be adopted." "The Thatcher Papers. Selected from the Papers of Hon. George Thatcher, and communicated by Captain William F. Goodwin, U. S. A.," *Historical Magazine*, 2d Ser., 6 (1869), 266.

giving up all power, . . . the states will be like towns in this state. Towns . . . have a right to lay taxes, to raise money, and the states possibly may have the same. We have now . . . a good republican Constitution, and we do not want it guarantied to us." Singletary did not understand "what gentlemen meant by Congress guarantying a republican form of government"; he wished they "would not play round the subject with their fine stories, like a fox round a trap, but come to it. Why don't they say that Congress will guaranty our state constitution?"[31]

After the convention had been sitting for two weeks, the Federalists began to despair of obtaining a majority for the Constitution without some concession to their adversaries. They decided to couple ratification with a recommendation of future amendments embodying some of the main objections. This idea was not entirely original. As early as the previous September, Richard Henry Lee of Virginia had composed some amendments and in October had suggested to Samuel Adams that "a Capital state or two" propose amendments and "express willingness to agree with the plan so amended."[32] Also in October, Gerry had sent a letter to the Massachusetts legislature, listing objections to the Constitution but suggesting that, if properly amended before it was ratified, it might yet be adapted to governmental needs and the preservation of liberty. This communication probably stiffened the criticism of the Constitution, particularly in the lower house, to which numerous Shays sympathizers had been elected in the spring. Gore felt that its publication in the newspaper injured the Federalist cause.[33] Three days after the formal opening of the ratifying convention, a writer in the pro-Federalist *Massachusetts Centinel* had predicted that the delegates would probably be strongly urged to accept the Constitution and at the same time to propose amendments. A week later, the Secretary of the Commonwealth, who was in effect Governor Hancock's secretary, saw hope for adoption of the Constitution if the most "sanguine" Federalists agreed to amendments.[34] These Federalist stalwarts, however, were not yet ready for such a move.

31. *Debates of Convention, 1788* (1808), 135–36.

32. Lee to Adams, Oct. 5, 1787, James C. Ballagh, ed., *The Letters of Richard Henry Lee*, 2 vols. (N. Y., 1911–14), II, 447.

33. Christopher Gore to King, Dec. 30, 1787, King Papers, N.-Y. Hist. Soc.

34. Harding, *Contest over Ratification*, 84; John Avery to George Thatcher, Jan. 19, 1788, "Thatcher Papers," *Historical Magazine*, 2d Ser., 6 (1869), 265–66.

It soon became apparent that a group in the convention favored adoption of the Constitution subject to amendments. This element bridged the gap between the ardent Antifederalists who would reject the new instrument at once and the most stubborn Federalists unwilling to make any concessions. Gradually the Federalist leadership sensed the need for compromise. "Our prospects are gloomy, but hope is not entirely extinguished," King wrote to Madison on January 23. "We are now thinking of amendments to be submitted, not as a condition of our assent and Ratification, but as the opinion of the convention, subjoined to their ratification. This scheme may gain a few members, but the issue is doubtful."[35] In this pessimistic tone King conveyed the earliest hint that the Federalist strategists were considering compromise. They now decided to try to win over the members who were willing to adopt the Constitution subject to amendments. Madison discounted King's pessimism as flowing from the anxiety of a naturally cautious man; other letters from Boston expressed more confidence in the outcome.[36] By January 27 even King had become more hopeful. "The opposition are less positive of their strength," he informed General Knox, "and those Few among them who are honest and capable of Reflection appear uneasy concerning the Fate of the Question." He now had reason to think that the Antifederalists would no longer insist upon total rejection of the Constitution.[37]

The Federalists found in Governor Hancock an ideal person to present the compromise proposal. He was not a Federalist, and he was not known to favor the new instrument. A popular leader in state politics, he was certain to influence the convention by whatever stand he took. Though confined at home with gout, he had been elected president of the convention, for, as Gore put it, there was advantage in his name whether he attended or not.[38] He sat out the first three weeks of the convention, but he was pliant, susceptible to flattery, and ambitious, and King was convinced that he was sitting on the fence; as soon as either side attained a majority, the Governor's health would "suffice him to be abroad."[39]

35. King to James Madison, Jan. 23, 1788, Madison Papers, Lib. Cong.

36. James Madison to George Washington, Feb. [n.d.], 1788, Gaillard Hunt, ed., *The Writings of James Madison*, 9 vols. (N. Y., 1900–10), V, 94.

37. King to Henry Knox, Jan. 27, 1788, Knox Papers, Mass. Hist. Soc.

38. Christopher Gore to George Thatcher, Jan. 9, 1788, "Thatcher Papers," *Historical Magazine*, 2d Ser., 6 (1869), 263.

39. King to George Thatcher, Jan. 20, 1788, *ibid.*, 266.

Before the Governor appeared at the convention, the Federalist chieftains, evidently including King, made a deal with him. Hancock's price was the support of James Bowdoin's friends—that is, the Federalists—in his re-election for governor. This the Federalists promised. They also held out to him the possibility of the vice-presidency of the United States under the new Constitution or, if Virginia should not ratify, the presidency.[40] In return, Hancock would publicly support the new instrument and present to the convention as his own a number of amendments agreed upon by the Federalist leaders. Theophilus Parsons was the principal author of these amendments, but King and others also helped draft them.[41] "If Mr. Hancock does not disappoint our present expectations, our wishes will be gratified," King predicted to Madison, but, he added with typical caution, "his character is not entirely free from a portion of caprice."[42]

On the morning of January 31, Federalists were tense with expectation. Tristram Dalton had written to a friend at a late hour on the thirtieth that Hancock had attended "as President in Convention, and, if he may be depended on, he will give countenance to the proposed Constitution. . . . I will tell you, as a confidential communication, that Mr. S. Adams will come out in favor of the Constitution. This and the Governor on our side will settle the matter favorably.—All this is scarcely known out of our caucus, wherein we work as hard as in Convention."[43]

The audience that filled the gallery on the thirty-first heard a final reading of the Constitution, a motion for adoption, and a prearranged speech by General William Heath urging adoption, together with recommended amendments. At the midday recess many onlookers, eager to keep their places, had their noon meal brought in.[44] In the afternoon, Governor Hancock carried out his part of the bargain. Swathed in flannels, he rose from the president's chair and read a

40. King to Henry Knox, Feb. 3, 1788, Knox Papers, Mass. Hist. Soc.; F. S. Drake, *Life and Correspondence of Henry Knox* . . . (Boston, 1873), 98; J. G. King, Rufus King, 789.

41. Parsons, ed., *Memoir of Parsons*, 71, 85–86; Nathaniel Gorham to Henry Knox, Jan. 30, 1788, Knox Papers, Mass. Hist. Soc.

42. King to James Madison, Jan. 30, 1788, Madison Papers, Lib. Cong.

43. Tristram Dalton to Michael Hodge, Jan. 30, 1788, in Eben F. Stone, "Parsons and the Constitutional Convention of 1788," Essex Inst., *Hist. Colls.*, 35 (1899), 94.

44. Henry Jackson to Henry Knox, Feb. 3, 6, 1788, Knox Papers, Mass. Hist. Soc.

plan calling for ratification, coupled with the recommendation of nine specific amendments to Congress and the other states.[45] These proposals included a declaration that all powers not expressly delegated to Congress were reserved to the states, the basis of what eventually became the Tenth Amendment, and a requirement that indictment by a grand jury precede trial for any capital or gravely punishable crime, a provision later incorporated into the Fifth Amendment. Among the other recommendations were the exclusion from federal courts of suits between citizens of different states involving property of relatively small value; jury trial of every issue of fact arising in common law actions in federal courts, if requested by either party; prohibition of acceptance by federal officeholders of titles or offices from a foreign ruler or state; prohibition of congressionally created commercial monopolies; and prohibition of direct taxation, though if federal income from tariffs and excises proved insufficient, requisitions might be levied on the states, and Congress might assess delinquent states.[46]

Samuel Adams now came out in support of Hancock's propositions.[47] On Adams's motion, the convention discussed the Governor's proposal and appointed a committee to consider the amendments. A majority of this committee were Federalists, including former Governor Bowdoin, Parsons, Dana, Strong, and Sedgwick; its favorable vote on the amendments was inevitable. Immensely relieved, King wrote to Madison that the Federalists believed the influence of Hancock and Adams would ensure a favorable result, and Madison copied the letter for Washington's perusal.[48] Abandoning his habitual

45. Austin, *Life of Elbridge Gerry*, II, 75; Harding, *Contest over Ratification*, 76, 88; "Official Journal of the Convention" in *Debates of Convention, 1788* (1856), 78–81; J. G. King, Rufus King, 791.

46. For the text of the nine amendments, see "Official Journal," in *Debates of Convention, 1788* (1856), 79–80, and 83–84 with slight committee revisions. See also Elliot, ed., *Debates*, II, 177.

47. Two days before the convention met, a Federalist-inspired meeting of Boston townspeople had expressed approval of the Constitution, and Adams subsequently felt obliged to uphold his constituents' wishes. Hancock also may have been swayed by this meeting. Harding, *Contest over Ratification*, 95–97; McDonald, *We the People*, 184; Main, *Antifederalists*, 205. According to John C. Miller, *Sam Adams, Pioneer in Propaganda* (Stanford, 1936), 382, Federalists knew that Adams's opposition had been removed ten days before he openly promoted ratification.

48. King to James Madison, Feb. 3, 1788, Madison Papers, Lib. Cong. According to his endorsement on this letter, Madison sent it to a fellow Federalist in New York, probably Hamilton, with the request that he read it immediately and return it by the bearer, who would wait for it.

reserve, King exulted to General Knox, "Hancock has committed himself in our favor, and will not desert the cause. . . . The Federalists are united in that system; and as Adams has joined us on this plan, we are encouraged to think our success is probable." He predicted that Hancock would be universally supported by Bowdoin's friends.[49] Federalist shrewdness had saved the day; the presidential prize was alluring bait.

The amendments, slightly modified, were reported favorably to the convention, and Parsons, Strong, Dana, and Fisher Ames urged acceptance. On February 5 the Antifederalists, in a final delaying action, moved for an adjournment, but the motion was easily defeated as many moderates swung behind the Federalists.[50]

On the afternoon of February 6 the convention ratified the Constitution by the close vote of 187 to 168. Many doubtful delegates had been conciliated and were willing to follow the lead of the two popular Revolutionary patriots, Hancock and Adams, and adoption of the amendments furnished the necessary excuse to their constituents. After the final vote, Widgery, Nasson, and other Antifederalist leaders announced that they accepted the will of the majority and would loyally support the new government. King was jubilant. He passed along the news to Madison, noting the minority's graceful acceptance of the decision. He now had no doubt that the people of Massachusetts would readily approve the work of their delegates, and he closed his letter with an unusual "God bless you."[51] To reinforce the New Hampshire Federalists, King sent word of the ratification to his friend John Langdon, who was largely responsible for his state's subsequent acceptance of the Constitution. King also wrote to Washington, who saw at once how much the result would affect Federalist fortunes in doubtful states.[52] Indeed, had the Constitution been defeated in Massachusetts, it could not have gone into effect.[53]

49. King to Henry Knox, Feb. 3, 1788, Knox Papers, Mass. Hist. Soc. "We tell him that if Virginia does not unite, which is problematical, that he is considered as the only fair candidate for President," *ibid.* For further insight into Federalist activity, see transcription of Henry Knox to Robert R. Livingston, Feb. 10, 1788, Livingston letterbook, 1779–1799, Bancroft Coll. of R. R. Livingston Papers, N. Y. Pub. Lib.

50. Henry Jackson to Henry Knox, Feb. 6, 1788, Knox Papers, Mass. Hist. Soc.

51. King to James Madison, Feb. 6, 1788, Madison Papers, Lib. Cong.

52. King to Langdon, Feb. 6, 1788, King, ed., *King Correspondence*, I, 319; King to George Washington, Feb. 6, 1788, Washington Papers, Lib. Cong.; Washington to King, Feb. 29, 1788, King Papers, N.-Y. Hist. Soc.

53. Harding, *Contest over Ratification*, 114–15; Main, *Antifederalists*, 200–01.

The Massachusetts convention was easily the largest and most widely representative of all the ratifying conventions. The first state to propose amendments, Massachusetts set an important precedent, as the Federalists braced themselves in the crucial states of Virginia and New York. Apart from the belated support of Hancock and Adams, the success of the friends of the Constitution in the initially suspicious and hostile Boston convention cannot be attributed to any one person. King ranked with Parsons, Bowdoin, Dana, Dalton, and Sedgwick in formulating the strategy of the Federalists. Private persuasion reinforced public oratory, and he was adept at both. With his skill in answering prickly questions on the convention floor, and with the authority of his active role at Philadelphia behind him, he was a most effective public exponent of the Constitution. Although the measure of his help to Parsons in the preparation of the amendments behind the scenes will never be known, there is no doubt about his full participation in the inner councils of Federalist leadership.

Acceptance of the Constitution checked the anarchic tendencies of some whose grievances were apparent to all and the parochialism of many more whose interests dictated resistance to change. Opposition to the new instrument stemmed far less from its defects than from a grass-roots fear of loss of local political influence. Fortunately for the Federalists, more than fifty towns had failed to send delegates to the convention, most of whom probably would have been in the enemy camp. The Federalists had advantages of superior social and economic position, greater financial resources, better political organization, more influence over the press, and the ablest speakers in the convention.[54] Even so, their victory was narrow.

On the seventh of February the delegates walked to the State House, where the High Sheriff of Suffolk County proclaimed the ratification. The convention was then formally dissolved, and the members shared refreshments, provided by prominent Bostonians, in the Senate chamber. Conciliatory toasts were drunk, and "all appeared willing to bury the hatchet of animosity, and to smoke the calumet of union and love."[55] Bells pealed, cannon were fired, and the people indulged in "demonstrations of joy." The next morning, a triumphant procession of a thousand artisans, mechanics, and farmers formed at Faneuil Hall and marched for five hours to the applause of cheering bystanders. When the marchers returned to

54. Main, *Antifederalists*, 209.

55. See Boston *Massachusetts Centinel*, Feb. 9, 13, 1788, for this quotation and subsequent details; Elliot, ed., *Debates*, II, 183.

Faneuil Hall, the merchants gave them plenty of punch and as much wine, cake, and cheese as they wanted.[56] To mark the ratification, Long Lane, the site of Jeremy Belknap's meetinghouse where the Constitution had been adopted, was renamed Federal Street.

56. William Widgery to George Thatcher, Feb. 8, 1788, "Thatcher Papers," *Historical Magazine*, 2d Ser., 6 (1869), 270–71. Widgery had opposed the Constitution "like a *new light* fighting the Devil," wrote Jeremiah Hill to George Thatcher, Jan. 1, 1788, *ibid.*, 262.

CHAPTER VIII

NEW YORK AND THE UNITED STATES SENATE

WHEN THE NEWBURYPORT DELEGATES REACHED HOME, THEY WERE MET at Newbury Green by the tradesmen and officers of the militia, and were cheered by an enthusiastic crowd. King, however, was no longer thinking of Newburyport as his permanent residence. While in Boston he had inquired about the purchase of a house in Cambridge, where he would be nearer the political center of the state. But his first wish was to return to his family, and at the earliest opportunity he departed for New York.[1] For several months he and Mary settled down to a comfortable home life. On April 5, Bishop Provoost baptized their three-month-old son, with Alexander Hamilton and General and Mrs. Knox as sponsors. George Thatcher, a Massachusetts friend and a delegate to Congress, reported to his wife that King and "his honey" were well, that they had a "fine little boy," and that King was "quite the domestic man and fond father."[2]

Not a man to allow his family felicity to interfere with politics, King kept in touch with Massachusetts affairs and did what he could

1. Newburyport *Essex Journal*, Feb. 13, 1788; Christopher Gore to King, Feb. 13, 1788, King Papers, N.-Y. Hist. Soc.

2. George Thatcher to Sarah Thatcher, Sept. 22, 1788, Thatcher Papers, Mass. Hist. Soc. A record of the baptism of John A. King appears in the family Bible of Rufus King's third son, James Gore King, now owned by the present James Gore King.

to assist Federalists in other states. To John Langdon, his New Hampshire friend, he sent a copy of a political speech by a New York Federalist and suggested its publication. "Our hopes are great that Maryland will be right, Luther Martin notwithstanding," King remarked, "but we are not so confident of Maryland as we once were of New Hampshire." In New York the outcome was "exquisitely problematical," with both parties working hard and each confident of success.[3] On May 4, King notified Langdon that Maryland had ratified, that the prospects were good in South Carolina and improving in Virginia, and that New York City was overwhelmingly Federalist and he was inclined to believe the state would adopt the Constitution.[4] He asked Madison to keep him posted on developments at the Richmond convention just as he had earlier sent the Boston news to Virginia.[5]

At the end of May, Rufus and Mary King left little John with his grandfather Alsop and took a trip to Boston, a visit doubtless motivated by politics. The New York Federalists relied upon King as an interstate contact man. If New Hampshire ratified, the necessary nine states would have acceded; in any event the New Hampshire decision would greatly influence the outcome in New York. To the success of the new Union, even after nine states ratified, the adherence of New York and Virginia would be essential. When the New Hampshire convention reassembled in June, King sent Langdon the news of South Carolina's ratification, which he had learned from General Pinckney. By stretching Madison's guarded optimism, he assured his New Hampshire friend that Virginia, too, would accept the Constitution. He arranged with Langdon to relay news of New Hampshire's ratification by express to Springfield, where Henry Knox would pass it on to Hamilton at the New York convention in Poughkeepsie. Seeking to bolster the New York Federalists, he informed Hamilton that he had talked with men from all parts of Massachusetts and was "completely satisfied that the consti-

3. King to John Langdon, Apr. 16, 1788, King Papers, N.-Y. Hist. Soc. Langdon predicted a Federalist victory in his state. Langdon to King, May 6, 1788, *ibid.*

4. King to Langdon, May 4, 1788, *ibid.*

5. King to James Madison, May 25, 1788, Madison Papers, Lib. Cong.; Madison complied, Madison to King, June 4, 9, 13, 18, 22, 25, 1788, King Papers, N.-Y. Hist. Soc.

RUFUS KING
Miniature by John Trumbull, 1792
Yale University Art Gallery

tution is highly popular, that its opponents are now very few, and that few hourly diminishing."[6]

About the middle of June, the Kings left Boston for Newburyport, where King introduced Mary to his old friends. It was there that he learned of New Hampshire's ratification; the news persuaded him that New York would not now reject the Constitution. When he returned to Boston, he wrote to Madison, thanking him for his frequent reports on the proceedings at Richmond, culminating with the news of Virginia's ratification.[7] After a leisurely trip from Boston to New York, the Kings arrived at their home to find the Federalists jubilantly celebrating another victory. On July 26, the delegates at Poughkeepsie had accepted the Constitution by the close vote of 30 to 27. The Antifederalists had failed in tactics similar to those previously used in Massachusetts, and Federalists had talked of secession by the southern counties if New York failed to ratify.[8] Hamilton's tireless efforts and the news of ratification by New Hampshire and Virginia had tipped the balance. New York was the eleventh state to adhere to the new system.

During the late summer the Kings relaxed in New York. George Thatcher regularly visited them and played with John as if the baby were his own. To his wife he had written earlier in the year, "Tell Betsy King [Rufus's half-sister] her sister is a beauty. She is vastly the best looking woman I have seen since I have been in this city. . . . She is a good hearted woman, and, I think, possesses all that Benevolence and kind, friendly disposition, that never fail to find respectable admirers."[9] King, who had called on Thatcher daily during his con-

6. King to Alexander Hamilton, June 12, 1788, Hamilton Papers, Lib. Cong.; Charles C. Pinckney to King, May 24, 1788, King to John Langdon, June 4, 10, 1788, Langdon to King, June 21, 1788, Madison to King, June 4, 1788, King Papers, N.-Y. Hist. Soc.; King to Henry Knox, June 16, 1788, Knox Papers, Mass. Hist. Soc.

7. King to Knox, June 16, 1788, Knox Papers, Mass. Hist. Soc.; King to Nathan Dane, June 27, 1788, Dane Papers, Lib. Cong.; King to Madison, July 20, 1788, Madison Papers, Lib. Cong. The Records of St. John's Lodge of the Society of Free and Accepted Masons, Newburyport, owned by the Lodge, show that King attended his last meeting at this time.

8. John Jay to George Washington, May 29, 1788, Washington Papers, Lib. Cong.; Francis Hopkinson to Thomas Jefferson, July 17, 1788, and John Brown Cutting to Jefferson, Aug. 30, 1788, Julian P. Boyd, ed., *The Papers of Thomas Jefferson*, 17 vols. (Princeton, 1950—), XIII, 370, 549–50.

9. George Thatcher to Sarah Thatcher, n.d. (probably Jan. 1788), Thatcher Papers, Mass. Hist. Soc.

finement after a smallpox inoculation, found him an equally loyal friend, and both enjoyed riding through the country together in King's carriage.[10] Despite their friendship and common "down east" origin, the sedentary and introspective Thatcher preferred reading to theater and entertainments, whereas King, though interested in books, loved the stage, parties, and full dress dinners.[11]

At a dinner given by the Jays in September, the Kings met the French journalist Brissot de Warville. To the Frenchman, New York represented the height of English luxury and fashion in America, where the ladies wore "the most brilliant silks, gauzes, hats, and borrowed hair," and the men, more simply attired, "[took] their revenge in the luxury of the table." The presence of Congress, he noticed, attracted the greatest celebrities, among whom he had met "particularly Messrs. Jay, Maddison, Hamilton, King, and Thornton."[12]

By returning to New York that summer, King played into the hands of his rivals in Massachusetts, who made political capital of his renewed absence from the state. As rumors spread that his "apparent intentions" of residing permanently in Massachusetts were merely calculated to deceive the voters, Knox urged him to act quickly to "counteract the poison." Nathaniel Gorham and Christopher Gore were also worried.[13] With his political future at stake—it was clear to all that King wished to be one of the first two United States sena-

10. George Thatcher to Sarah Thatcher, Aug. 17, Sept. 8, 22, 1788, and undated letter (*supra*, *n9*), *ibid.*

11. George Thatcher to Sarah Thatcher, Feb. 24, Oct. 9, 14, 1788, Feb. 15, 1789, and undated letter (*supra*, *n9*), *ibid.*

12. Griswold, *Republican Court*, 91; J. P. Brissot de Warville, *New Travels in the United States of America performed in 1788* . . . (London, 1792), 156–57, 163.

13. Henry Knox to King, Aug. 17, 1788, King Papers, N.-Y. Hist. Soc.; Gore to King, Aug. 30, 1788, *ibid.*; King, ed., *King Correspondence*, I, 343–44. To facilitate his return to the Boston area, Gore arranged to buy for King the John Cushing house in Cambridge, which King had inquired about early in the year; in Oct. he urged King to be on hand before the General Court convened for the elections. On previous occasions King had refrained from visiting his home state on the eve of an election in which he was involved. In this instance he yielded to the pleas of Gore, Gorham, and Knox, though he did so mainly to complete the negotiations for the Cushing house. He had already asked Gore to buy the house, but vexing questions arose over the title and the time of taking possession. King, ed., *King Correspondence*, I, 343–44; King's endorsement on Gore's letter to him, Oct. 12, 1788, King Papers, N.-Y. Hist. Soc.

tors from Massachusetts—he responded to their prompting and set out for Boston, arriving on October 20.

Two years before, King had remarked that, although the prospects for a lawyer were brighter in New York, he thought he would never move away from Newburyport; immediately after his marriage he had written that he preferred Newburyport to any other town.[14] Now, however, despite his many friends and connections in Massachusetts, he saw many reasons for choosing New York. His wife and father-in-law were there, the city offered more business and professional opportunities, and during his three years in New York he had formed strong personal and political ties. When he arrived in Boston, he discovered the extent to which his political friends had deserted him, and he sensed that local opposition was too great a liability; no such handicap would burden him in New York City. He therefore dropped plans to buy a house in Boston and returned to New York well before the Massachusetts senatorial election.

Denial of advancement in Massachusetts was, in the long run, fortunate for King. His friends in New York were eager to welcome him as a permanent resident; his work in Congress and his recent efforts on behalf of a stronger federal government had made him a valuable asset to the Federalist cause in New York. If some of his old associates like Parsons deserted him, new ones like Hamilton and Jay befriended him, and he, in turn, sought the counsel of these New Yorkers. Hamilton's great influence in the Federalist party was an excellent portent of King's prospects of holding some federal office, and other influential politicians prized King's cooperation.

An opportunity presented itself late in 1788. Colonel William Duer, an important Federalist, approached King with a scheme to form a syndicate of American citizens to buy up part of the United States debt due to France. Robert and Gouverneur Morris, Henry Knox, Jeremiah Wadsworth, and Samuel Osgood were among those involved. The original plan included the appointment of Gouverneur Morris as United States minister to the Netherlands to facilitate the operation. Duer asked King to participate but received an ambiguous

14. King to Daniel Kilham, Oct. 10, 1785, Apr. 5, 1786, King-Kilham Corr., Columbia Univ. Lib.; King to Elbridge Gerry, April 30, 1786, King Papers, N.-Y. Hist. Soc. His father-in-law was convinced that King would not be content unless he moved to Boston. John Alsop to Isaac Wharton, Oct. 20, 1788, King Papers, Vol. 69, N.-Y. Hist. Soc.

and indefinite reply. On December 20, Duer again sounded him out, proposing, at the suggestion of Knox and Wadsworth, that King allow himself to be put forward instead of Morris for appointment as minister to the Netherlands. King told the Colonel that he was "not indisposed to a foreign appointment," that the honors and duties of the office would be his "sov[e]reign rule of Cond[uct]," and that it would be a "great satisfaction" to him if, consistent with the duties and dignity of the office, he could promote the interests of his friends. However, he wished "not to be considered as giving an answer any way at present." Obviously he was unwilling to antagonize Morris, with whom he had cooperated in the Constitutional Convention. He hesitated until he could consult Jay and Hamilton, whose views weighed heavily with him.[15] Nothing came of the project, so far as King was concerned, but it may have influenced him later in backing Morris as American minister to France.

By the end of March 1789, King had definitely made up his mind to become a permanent resident of New York. Gore was disappointed by his friend's decision, but he finally recognized that New York City, the seat of the United States government, was King's logical choice.[16] To his brother-in-law Southgate, King expressed regret that he was destined to remain so distant from relatives and old friends in Maine.[17]

His decision was a triumph for his wife and father-in-law. The aged Alsop was dependent on his daughter's care, and at the time of her marriage had urged King to stay in New York. Although Alsop would have gone to Boston had the Kings moved there, he would have been unhappy away from his old neighbors and his business interests, some of which he soon turned over to the care of his son-in-law.[18] Mary King, besides looking after her father, was pregnant during the winter months of 1788–89 and reluctant to move. Her son John was fourteen months old when, on March 16, she gave birth to a healthy infant she named Charles. (Alsop celebrated the

15. King's memorandum, Dec. 21, 1788, King Papers, N.-Y. Hist. Soc.

16. Christopher Gore to King, Apr. 5, 1789, *ibid.*

17. King to Robert Southgate, June 7, 1789, King, ed., *King Correspondence*, I, 351.

18. *Ibid.*, 132, 340; John Alsop to Isaac Wharton, Oct. 20, 1788, King Papers, Vol. 69, N.-Y. Hist. Soc. Alsop to Elias Boudinot, June 2, 1788, *ibid.*, concerns an early instance of a business matter attended to by King.

family's good fortune by purchasing tickets in the English lottery for his two grandsons.)[19]

King rapidly adjusted himself to a New York residence, and New York adjusted itself to him. Dispensing with a customary requirement, the state Supreme Court admitted him to the New York bar. As George Thatcher wrote his wife, this unusual act did King great honor. New York had "made a considerable acquisition in him," while Massachusetts had "suffered a great loss."[20]

In New York state, political factions were sharply divided. The Federalists achieved a small but decisive majority in the state Senate in the elections of 1788, and in New York County, where they were strong, their candidates easily won seats in the Assembly. The lower house, however, was controlled by the Antifederalists who had become so strong upstate that they elected assemblymen in Albany and Montgomery counties, normally under the influence of the Federalist, General Philip Schuyler. Governor George Clinton, persistently Antifederalist, not only swayed the Assembly but controlled the state patronage with a firm hand. He was president of the Council of Appointment, to which the Assembly elected four Antifederalists in January 1789, giving their party complete control. As a member of the Council of Revision, Clinton also reviewed the work of the legislature.[21]

Now that New York had adopted the federal Constitution, the choice of United States senators was of crucial importance to both the Clinton and the Schuyler-Livingston forces. New York's vital interests in the Union were at stake, and neither faction wanted the inevitable patronage to fall into the hands of its rival. Before the meeting of the legislature of 1789, the Clintonians had confidently expected to elect two Antifederalists to the United States Senate. If the state Senate and the Assembly voted together, as anticipated, Clinton would have his way. But this was the first election of United States senators, and there was no rule on the manner of election.

19. King, ed., *King Correspondence*, I, 351; John Alsop to Sargent Chambers & Company, July 8, 1789, King Papers, Vol. 69, N.-Y. Hist. Soc.

20. George Thatcher to Sarah Thatcher, May 14, 1789, Thatcher Papers, Mass. Hist. Soc. The requirement of the law of Feb. 20, 1787, that judges examine candidates for the New York bar was waived for King.

21. Jabez D. Hammond, *History of Political Parties in the State of New York . . .*, 2 vols. (Albany, 1842), I, 31–32; Nevins, *American States*, 295–96.

The Federalists insisted upon separate balloting by the two houses as in Massachusetts. Melancton Smith, the skilled Antifederalist debater from Duchess County, was a leading opponent of this method. "The scheme now on foot to give the Senate a negative," he wrote, "will add amazing force" to the tendency toward aristocracy. "A few men combining in the Senate may forever put their veto upon any choice, until it falls upon such men as would serve their purposes. . . . I trust the Assembly will never yield the point, be the consequences what they may. Better have no Senators for a Century to come than establish a principle, which when once granted never can be reclaimed."[22] The Federalists were equally adamant. Neither party would yield, and the session ended without a choice of senators.

The dispute over the method of electing United States senators was in large part incidental to the Clinton-Schuyler rivalry. Political factionalism was an old story in New York. Before the Revolutionary War, the province had been the scene of contention between the powerful Livingston and De Lancey families, but the latter, becoming Tories, were wiped out by the Revolution. In opposition to the Livingstons, the Schuylers, and their family affiliations, a leader of the yeomanry, George Clinton, was swept into power in 1777 as New York's first governor under the new state constitution, and he had been Governor ever since. Able, genial, and popular in most of the state, he controlled a far-flung network of henchmen, and he confidently approached the 1789 campaign for his fifth term. "You well know the art and cunning of Clinton and his party, and that they are using every possible exertion for his reelection," warned the old Federalist, General Samuel Webb. "We must work double tides to defeat them. In this quarter we have nothing to fear, he is most heartily despised, except by a few Sycophants, whom he has put in office and their dependants 'whose price of Office has been Obedience to their Chief.' "[23] The difficulty of unseating the Governor was fully appreciated by Schuyler, Hamilton, Chancellor Livingston, and John Jay. They mounted a propaganda campaign to defeat Clinton, and in Federalist New York City he was universally condemned.[24]

22. Melancton Smith to Gilbert Livingston, Jan. 1, 1789, Melancton Smith Papers, N. Y. State Lib.

23. Samuel B. Webb to K. K. Van Rensselaer, Mar. 22, 1789, Emmet Collection, N. Y. Pub. Lib.

24. James M. Hughes to John Smith, Jan. 22, 1789, Miscellaneous Manu-

The chances of toppling Clinton were so slim that the Federalist leaders resorted to an ingenious maneuver. On February 11 several hundred party stalwarts, including Hamilton, Duer, Robert Troup, William Constable, and Aaron Burr (who at this time was collaborating with Hamilton and his friends), gathered at Bardin's Tavern in New York City and nominated Judge Robert Yates for governor. Yates had resigned from the Constitutional Convention in Philadelphia and had zealously fought against ratification in the Poughkeepsie convention, but he had shortly afterward urged all to support the new Constitution.[25] By selecting Yates, the Federalist strategists hoped to split Clinton's followers and detach enough of them to give the Federalists a victory.

A number of assemblymen were also to be elected. On April 2 a group of Federalist planners held a joint meeting of three committees: one of merchants, one of mechanics, and one for "correspondence and election" which included Hamilton, Duer, and Constable. They agreed upon a list of candidates for the Assembly most of whom had been proposed earlier by an informal meeting of leading merchants. The name of Rufus King headed the list of eight.[26] The next day a large meeting of merchants at Rawson's Tavern nominated substantially the same group of men, King's name again heading the list, and a few days later, a meeting of the mechanics adopted, with one exception, the same slate.[27]

Elections were held at the end of April, but the race for the governorship was so close that the outcome was not certain until June, when it was finally announced that Clinton had squeaked through with 6,391 votes to Yates's 5,962. Perhaps 60 per cent of the state's freeholders had cast their ballots. Payments of lost election bets were said to have exceeded £1,000; the size of Yates's vote was the talk

---

scripts—John Smith (of Mastic), N.-Y. Hist. Soc. Smith was an assemblyman. "They are trying to kill Clinton politically but won't succeed," predicted Samuel A. Otis of Massachusetts to Nathan Dane, Mar. 28, 1789, Dane Papers, Lib. Cong.

25. N. Y. *Daily Advertiser*, Feb. 12, 1789; Hammond, *History of Political Parties*, I, 39–40; Alexander C. Flick, ed., *A History of the State of New York*, 10 vols. (N. Y., 1933–37), VI, 38–39; Nevins, *American States*, 297.

26. Miscellaneous Manuscripts—Alexander Hamilton, folder marked 1757–1784, N.-Y. Hist. Soc.

27. N.-Y. *Daily Advertiser*, Apr. 10, 1789. On Apr. 15 a meeting of "respectable freeholders" included King on a somewhat different list of nominees. *Ibid.*, Apr. 18, 1789.

of the taverns. Merchants, gentlemen, and artisans celebrated the uncanny political generalship of the thirty-two-year-old Hamilton, who had exploited the Federalist trend since the Poughkeepsie convention and whose planning and organization had nearly upset what has been called "the most effective political machine in America."[28]

Hamilton's guidance was apparent, too, in the votes for the legislature, where the Federalists maintained their dominance in the Senate and gained control of the Assembly. In New York City, all nine Federalist candidates for the Assembly were elected. King got 1,173 votes, only three fewer than the frontrunners Gulian Verplanck (soon to be elected speaker) and John Watts.[29] Hamilton's father-in-law, Philip Schuyler, was re-elected to the state Senate. Three of the five congressmen were Federalists, including Hamilton's and King's friends, Egbert Benson and John Laurance.

Governor Clinton called a special meeting of the new legislature early in July to break the continuing deadlock over the method of choosing United States senators. Schuyler suggested that each house nominate two senators and if the nominations were different, the Senate would elect one of the Assembly's nominees and the Assembly one of the Senate's; Clintonians rejected it, however.[30] They might better have accepted it, for after the spring election the Federalists had enough votes to sway both houses and were less inclined to compromise. At this session of the Assembly, Rufus King helped to draft a respectful reply to the Governor's address to the legislature, was appointed to a committee to digest the rules and orders of the Assembly, and was chosen one of the commissioners with power to declare the consent of the legislature to the creation of a separate state of Vermont.[31]

Almost a month before the meeting of the legislature, Governor Clinton had quietly called on King, who happened to be absent from his house but returned the call the next day, June 12. After the usual pleasantries, Clinton spoke of the choice of senators, remarking that the Republicans were not united upon their candidates, that John Lansing would not serve, and that Melancton Smith had antagonized

28. *Ibid.*, June 4, 1789; *N.-Y. Journal*, June 4, 1789; Nevins, *American States*, 301.

29. *N.-Y. Journal*, June 4, 1789.

30. N. Y. *Daily Advertiser*, Apr. 7, 1789.

31. *Ibid.*, July 13, 1789; *Journal of the Assembly of the State of New-York*, 13 sess., 1st meeting, 13 (July 10, 1789).

many Antifederalists by acceding to the ratification of the federal Constitution. He then asked King if he knew who had been mentioned as candidates. King replied that he had not talked with any members of the Assembly, had heard only the "loose conversation of unimportant politicians," and "knew nothing of the private opinion of influential men." General Schuyler, Judge Yates, Lansing, Duane, Judge Morris, and Chancellor Livingston had been suggested, said King. After dismissing Lansing as unavailable, Clinton questioned whether any state judge ought to participate in federal legislation, eliminating Yates and Morris. He then stated his opinion that powerful offices should not be concentrated in the hands of a single party or family association; with Schuyler, Duane, and Livingston in mind, he remarked that abilities and wealth already gave them great influence, and if in addition they monopolized the highest offices, the "public Liberty" might be jeopardized. Evidently a movement to make Duane a senator had already been launched, and, according to the Governor, Duane claimed the office as his right, although it was not the right of any man to be senator.[32]

The Governor remarked that some politicians thought New York should elect a merchant to the Senate, but it had been difficult to find a suitable candidate; he had heard King's name mentioned but knew that King was not a mercantile man. Responding to this gentle probe, King merely observed that this possibility had been mentioned to him, though not by a member of the Assembly; because he was a recent citizen of the state, however, he did not wish to interfere with the claims of old and respected New Yorkers. As recorded by King, Clinton responded "that the novelty of my Inhabitancy could be no Objection—that I was a member of the Assembly, and that he had ever considered that appointment as sufficient authority for him to appoint any person to an Office for which he might in his Judgment appear capable."[33]

Reverting to his initial theme, the Governor recounted the rivalry of the De Lanceys and Livingstons in colonial times, and asserted that since the fall of the De Lanceys "all the great and opulent families" had united in one confederacy. He aimed to "keep a constant eye to the measures of this Combination," and he thought the

32. Substance of a Conversation with Gov. Clinton, June 12, 1789, King Papers, N.-Y. Hist. Soc.

33. *Ibid.*

people should guard against its machinations.[34] Apparently, Clinton hoped that King's candidacy would offset the influence of the Schuyler-Livingston faction. He said he had heard King's name mentioned not by assemblymen from New York City, but by "some Gentlemen from the Country," an obvious suggestion that his nomination would have wide support. He went even further, remarking that he thought the assemblymen should reach an understanding on candidates before the meeting of the legislature in July.[35]

That Clinton, who had doggedly thwarted an increase in federal power for so long, should appeal to King may seem surprising, but it was a characteristically shrewd move. As a newcomer to New York politics, King might yet be drawn into an alignment with the Clinton forces and perhaps bring with him adherents from the mercantile community. If King could be built up, the ambitions of the "great and opulent families" might be checked. Now that New York had accepted the United States Constitution, it would be prudent for the Clintonians to modify their extreme parochialism by backing a man with strong ties to the merchants and lawyers of New York City, one who would win a following in the city and uphold the state's commercial interests in federal matters involving revenue and treaties.

Clinton may have been the first to mention King for the Senate. However, the informal discussion of his name which preceded this notice suggests that the idea of making him a United States senator had already been privately discussed. For quite different reasons, Hamilton favored the choice of King, who had become his fast friend and who shared in considerable degree his views of men and measures.

When the special session of the legislature met in July, the Federalists first approached Judge Yates, the defeated candidate for governor, and offered to make him one of the United States senators. Yates declined, preferring to remain on the state Supreme Court. Thereupon the Federalist leaders unanimously determined to support Schuyler and, by a vote of twenty-four to twenty, chose James Duane over King. At this caucus, King accepted the result, saying he was ashamed to oppose Duane and considered the matter settled.[36]

34. *Ibid.*

35. *Ibid.*

36. Robert Troup to Alexander Hamilton, July 12, 1789, Harold C. Syrett, Jacob E. Cooke, *et al.*, eds., *The Papers of Alexander Hamilton*, 11 vols. (N. Y., 1961—), V, 359–61.

Newspaper accounts soon led the public to assume that Schuyler and Duane would be elected.[37] Hamilton, however, attempted to thwart the nomination of Duane, an older man with great prestige but one who would be less responsive than King to his persuasions. As the mayor of New York City, then an appointive position, Duane was popular among the dominant merchants and lawyers, and Hamilton spread the idea that Duane would be a poor choice for the Senate because "some very unfit character" probably would succeed him as mayor. He abandoned his efforts, however, when he learned from Burr that the Federalists in both houses planned to support Schuyler and Duane.[38]

The balloting in the legislature reveals that King's friends were active from the outset, though at first they lacked the strength to get him nominated. On July 14, a move in the Assembly to substitute him for Schuyler failed, and the House as anticipated accepted the General. An attempt to replace Duane with King also miscarried, and the Mayor was nominated.[39] The next day, however, the Senate elected Schuyler but rejected Duane by a single vote. Senator Ezra L'Hommedieu of Southold, Long Island, an experienced state legislator, was proposed in place of Duane; although Federalist by inclination, L'Hommedieu had a mind of his own and did not feel bound to support Duane.[40] Philip Livingston moved to substitute King, but the Senate voted down the motion and chose the Long Islander.[41] That day, Hamilton heard from Schuyler of the ambitions of L'Hommedieu and also another state senator, Lewis Morris. Passing on the news to King, Hamilton confided that their friend Robert Troup "tells me that L'Hommedieu is opposed to you. He made our friend Benson believe that he would even relinquish himself for

37. *N.-Y. Journal*, July 16, 1789. See Christopher Gore to King, July 26, 1789, and W. Wetmore to King, July 29, 1789, King Papers, N.-Y. Hist. Soc.

38. Alexander Hamilton to King, July 15, 1789, King Papers, Vol. 28, N.-Y. Hist. Soc.

39. *N. Y. Assembly Journal*, 13 sess., 1 meet., 22–23 (July 14, 1789).

40. Grandson of a Huguenot refugee, L'Hommedieu had helped frame the state constitution, had served in the Assembly and, since 1783, in the state Senate. He also had been a delegate to Congress, where he sometimes refused to follow the lead of the persuasive Duane and the dominating Robert R. Livingston. C. B. Moore, "Biography of Ezra L'Hommedieu," *New York Genealogical and Biographical Record*, 2 (1871), 7. See Edmund C. Burnett in *DAB* s.v. "L'Hommedieu, Ezra."

41. *Journal of the Senate of the State of New-York*, 13 sess., 1 meet., *passim; N.-Y. Journal*, July 23, 1789 (erroneously cited in King, ed., *King Correspondence*, I, 354*n*, as the *Democrat*). This newspaper recorded some of the votes inaccurately.

you."[42] King's adherents must have worked feverishly overnight to counteract the moves toward L'Hommedieu and Morris, for on the sixteenth, the Assembly rejected L'Hommedieu, easily defeated the nomination of Morris, and finally voted unanimously for Rufus King.[43] The Senate concurred by a vote of eleven to eight, and King joined Schuyler as one of New York's first two United States senators.[44]

In this intricate maneuvering, a few facts stand out. In the state Senate, nearly all of the Clintonians opposed King and supported L'Hommedieu. Although he voted to reject Duane, L'Hommedieu himself cast no ballots either for or against King, and his own candidacy confirms the suspicions of Schuyler, Hamilton, and Troup that he was an obstacle to King's election.[45] In the Assembly, L'Hommedieu mustered less support than Duane, the favorite from New York City. When this was apparent, the members from the city region shifted their strength to King, and Governor Clinton had the satisfaction of seeing Duane defeated. What Clinton thought of L'Hommedieu is not known, but he could not have been overly displeased by King's victory in the Federalist-dominated legislature.

The sudden rise in New York politics of this transplanted New Englander was impressive. Jefferson's informant in London, John Brown Cutting, called King's election to the United States Senate "the most signal instance of disregard to local attachments and prejudices" that he had ever observed in any state of the Union.[46] Only a month after establishing his permanent residence in New

42. Alexander Hamilton to King, July 15, 1789, King Papers, Vol. 28, N.-Y. Hist. Soc. For Troup's letter to Hamilton, see Syrett, *et al.*, eds., *Hamilton Papers*, V, 359–61.

43. *N. Y. Assembly Journal*, 13 sess., 1 meet., 25 (July 16, 1789).

44. *N. Y. Senate Journal*, 13 sess., 1 meet., 16 (July 16, 1789).

45. In his *Alexander Hamilton* (Boston, 1882), 80–82, Henry Cabot Lodge asserted that Hamilton forced King's appointment as senator, thus giving the Schuyler faction both senators, alienating the Livingstons, and strengthening Burr, probably enough to cause his defeat of Schuyler two years later. It is doubtful that Hamilton alone could have engineered King's election. Not all the Livingstons were alienated: in the state Senate, Philip Livingston not only supported Schuyler but moved to substitute King's name for L'Hommedieu's, and on the final vote, he supported King. Chancellor Livingston, it is true, became disgruntled because he was not offered high federal office, but he was not a candidate for the United States Senate, and his conversion from Federalism to Republicanism occurred somewhat later. Burr no doubt gained popularity for reasons other than disgruntled Livingstons.

46. John Brown Cutting to Thomas Jefferson, Sept. 15, 1789, Boyd, ed., *Jefferson Papers*, XV, 427.

York, King had been elected to the legislature. His notably short career as assemblyman—ten days—may have broken a record. He did not even act on the committees to which he had been appointed.

On July 23, King left Albany. Two days later, he took his seat in the United States Senate at Federal Hall in New York City. Schuyler appeared on July 27, and the next day the two men drew lots to determine their tenure of office; the fifty-six-year-old General and veteran of New York politics drew the two-year term, and his thirty-four-year-old colleague the comfortable six-year term.[47]

As he began his new duties, Rufus King had ample reason to reflect upon the course of his life during the past year, to be satisfied that he had cast his lot with New York, and to take some delight in his good fortune. Only eight months earlier, Massachusetts had elected its senators, and he had not been chosen. Now he received the plaudits of old New England friends. William Wetmore, the Boston lawyer, wrote of his chagrin and disappointment that King's success had been attained outside Massachusetts. "Your friends rejoice," he concluded, "that N. Y. has done you Justice which the people here were ready to offer but were prevented by the vile and secret, tho successful artifices of three or four vipers."[48]

The junior Senator from New York had hardly taken his seat in Federal Hall before he was asked to use his influence. His intimate friend Christopher Gore, perhaps the first to ask him for a job, sought to become United States district attorney for Massachusetts, and was soon appointed.[49] Nathaniel Gorham, doubtful that the House of Representatives would adopt his proposal for a special commission to determine precisely the boundary between western New York and United States territory, was worried lest the vast Phelps and Gorham land interests suffer from a line drawn too far east, where the Pennsylvania congressmen wanted it. Preferring a governmental settlement to a lawsuit, Gorham wrote to Phelps that he thought their best chance was in the Senate, where Schuyler and King were "able advocates and understand the subject well."[50] When the Senate considered the question, Maclay of Pennsylvania reported, King and Schuyler managed the debate. The Pennsylvanians put up a spirited opposition, Maclay protesting so ardently that he got a sore throat;

47. *Annals of Congress*, I, 52; King, ed., *King Correspondence*, I, 354.

48. William Wetmore to King, July 29, 1789, King Papers, N.-Y. Hist. Soc.

49. Gore to King, Aug. 11, 22, Dec. 3, 1789, *ibid.*

50. Nathaniel Gorham to Oliver Phelps, July 31, 1789, Phelps and Gorham Papers, Box 17, N. Y. State Lib.

they won the land they claimed, a triangle of territory fronting on Lake Erie, and were able to thwart the plans of Phelps and Gorham.[51]

During the summer of 1789, the Senate, meeting behind closed doors, debated commercial, military, and administrative measures and proposed amendments to the Constitution. King, having missed the deliberations of the spring and early summer, played no part in the Senate's enactment of the judiciary bill and other early measures, but he was soon active in debate and committee work. He found himself among familiar faces. In the Senate were Langdon of New Hampshire, Ellsworth and Johnson of Connecticut, Paterson of New Jersey, Robert Morris of Pennsylvania, George Read and Richard Bassett of Delaware, Butler of South Carolina, and Few of Georgia, all of whom had been in the Philadelphia Convention. Of course he knew the men from Massachusetts, Caleb Strong and Tristram Dalton. With such men King served on one committee or another: to consider the tariff, regulations for foreign shipping and the coastal trade, expenses of Indian negotiations, safekeeping of government records, appropriations, payments to invalid pensioners, and the size of the army. On two occasions he was one of the Senate managers of conferences with the House.[52]

King's part in the deliberation over proposed amendments to the Constitution is not revealed by the meager records, except in two instances. He favored a unanimous jury for the conviction of criminals, a requirement barely defeated by the Senate, and he voted with the majority against a measure to require the consent of two-thirds of the members present in both houses of Congress to permit a standing army in peacetime.[53] In these instances he showed a lawyer's concern for liberty and a Federalist's aversion to an overly rigid limitation on the exercise of national power.

Establishing the salaries of senators and representatives was a troublesome detail that evoked strong opinions from King and others. When Maclay proposed five dollars a day, Robert Morris accused him of trying to curry popular favor and proposed eight dollars. Supporting Morris, Izard of South Carolina complained of senators who "lodged in holes and corners, associated with improper company,

51. William Maclay, *Journal*, ed. Charles A. Beard (N. Y., 1927), 121–22.

52. *Journal of the Senate of the United States*, 1 Cong., 1 sess., 87, 94, 96, 114, 128, 129, 152, 153.

53. *Ibid.*, 130–31, 148. The army proposal also limited wartime enlistments to the duration of a war.

and conversed improperly, so as to lower their dignity and character." Seeing time wasted with proposals of various amounts, King moved for commitment, and the Senate promptly appointed him as committee chairman. "By the complexion of the committee," recorded the testy Maclay, "it would seem the Senate want their wages enlarged."[54] King's committee recommended six dollars, but the Senate postponed a decision until it determined an appropriate differential between the pay of senators and congressmen. Maclay opposed any discrimination between them; the Senate was no more dignified than the House. Convinced that worth was being equated with wealth, and dignity of character with expensive living, he lectured the senators on the basis of true dignity, which was unattainable through "extravagant expense, haughty and distant carriage, with contemptuous behavior to the mass of mankind." An angry debate erupted, followed by a vote, of which King disapproved, to pay congressmen five dollars. As Maclay noted, "King and sundry others called for the yeas and nays with an avidity that I never observed before."[55]

King favored generous salaries as necessary to attract able men into federal service. His experience in Massachusetts and in the Confederation Congress had convinced him that niggardliness with public servants was false economy. Salary ought to be commensurate with the dignity of an office. When the Senate allotted four thousand dollars to the chief justice and only three thousand to the associate justices of the Supreme Court, he voted to give them another five hundred dollars, and he seconded Morris's proposal to raise the pay of the attorney-general to two thousand dollars, a measure passed by the vote of the Vice-President.[56]

In stressing the dignity of office, King not only expected public figures to behave with propriety but also thought they deserved respectful treatment. With Izard and Johnson, he upheld a clause in a penal bill making it a crime to defame a foreign minister. Vice-President Adams, mindful of his own diplomatic experience, pointed

54. Maclay, *Journal*, 131–32; *U.S. Senate Jour.*, 1 Cong., 1 sess., 106. The other members of the committee were Morris, Izard, Carroll of Maryland, and R. H. Lee of Virginia.

55. *U. S. Senate Jour.*, 107, 109, 110–11; Maclay, *Journal*, 136–38. In the debate on $6 for senators, according to Maclay's *Journal*, 138, Izard, King, and Morris "said every rude thing they could" to him and abused him for his "nonsense" and "stupidity."

56. *U. S. Senate Jour.*, 140–41; Maclay, *Journal*, 153–54. The motion to raise the judges' salaries failed.

out that etiquette and ceremony demanded such a provision, but the Senate evidently did not take it so seriously and voted it down.[57]

One subject the senators did take seriously was the future seat of the federal government. The first session of Congress was marked by an intense struggle in both houses over the location of the national capital, in which local pride, sectional interests, personal fortunes, and financial policy became inextricably mixed. New Yorkers wanted their flourishing seaport city to remain the federal residence, Pennsylvanians pushed for a site on the Delaware or the Susquehanna, and southerners hoped for Baltimore or a site on the Potomac. Learning that the House had selected a location on the Susquehanna, Robert Morris and others who favored Philadelphia went to work in the Senate; Maclay, who held out for the Susquehanna, noticed Morris busily calling out members from the Senate floor, among them Grayson, Read, Butler, James Gunn, and King.[58] After much wrangling but no final decision on the residence bill, the Senate adjourned to watch the well-advertised launching of Deeker's balloon which caught fire and collapsed.[59]

That day the New England delegates met with King and John Laurance, who represented the New York delegates, to counteract a scheme of the southern members and those from Pennsylvania to fix the permanent capital on the Potomac and make Philadelphia the temporary seat of government. The conferees authorized King and Representative Benjamin Goodhue of Massachusetts to offer the Pennsylvanians support for the east bank of the Susquehanna if the latter would agree to a temporary residence in New York.[60] However, when King and Goodhue met the Pennsylvania delegates, Madison burst in upon them before the subject was broached and so

57. Maclay, *Journal*, 134.

58. *Ibid.*, 154. At issue was a provision in the Senate's residence bill requiring the consent of Maryland and Pennsylvania to the removal of legal barriers to the navigation of the Susquehanna. This provision was carried, only five senators voting against it: Morris, King, Schuyler, Johnson (Conn.), and Dalton (Mass.).

59. "Yesterday, at 4 o'clock P.M. departed in a blaze, to the great astonishment of thousands, the much CELEBRATED BALLOON, constructed under the admired abilities of Mr. DEEKER, whose eccentric ingenuity was displayed in acquiring a brilliant sum, which perfectly accorded with his N.B. that he should leave the city after his descent—into the *purses* of the generous and disappointed spectators." *N.-Y. Journal*, Sept. 24, 1789.

60. King's memorandum, Sept. 23, 1789, King Papers, N.-Y. Hist. Soc. This and another memorandum dated Sept. 22, 1789, may be found in King, ed., *King Correspondence*, I, 370–75.

embarrassed the Pennsylvanians that they broke off the conference.[61]

The next day Robert Morris told King that the Pennsylvanians agreed to the bargain proposed by him and Goodhue, although "how they got clear of their allies" puzzled Fisher Ames, who had joined the New York-New England coalition. With Pennsylvania, New York, and New England votes, the House of Representatives passed a bill naming the Susquehanna as the permanent capital, but made it contingent upon the removal by both Maryland and Pennsylvania of all legal impediments to navigation on the river.[62]

Quietly, King and Schuyler asked the Pennsylvania delegates about the implications of this proviso. As King already knew, Morris opposed it, fearing injury to commerce on the Delaware and hoping to pressure Maryland into authorizing a canal between the Chesapeake and Delaware bays. If the proviso could not be eliminated, he was ready to abandon the Susquehanna for the Germantown district on the Delaware near Philadelphia. All the other Pennsylvania delegates except Maclay agreed, so Morris offered his vote and those of the Pennsylvania congressmen and the two Delaware senators, against the removal of Congress from New York before January 1793, if the New York senators would vote for Germantown as the permanent residence. King and Schuyler then consulted the New York congressmen, all but one of whom advised a vote for Germantown if the Senate struck out the Susquehanna.[63]

The Senate did eliminate the Susquehanna, and the New York senators voted, as planned, for Germantown. The city was approved by the Senate on September 24 with the vote of the Vice-President. "This day marked the perfidy of Mr. Morris in the most glaring colors!" lamented Maclay, the lone Pennsylvania holdout. "Notwithstanding his promises . . . he openly voted against the Susquehanna. King, Schuyler, and all the New England men except Dr. Johnson, voted against it . . . . Our ruin is plotted, contrived and carried on in

61. *Ibid.* It is not known whether the Virginian was invited or introduced himself. King told the embarrassed Pennsylvanians that New York would make no offer until assured that Pennsylvania had made no commitments. He warned that the eastern states might not remain united in the future. After talking with his colleagues, Morris asked King and Goodhue not to act until he could again confer with them. See Irving Brant, *James Madison*, 6 vols. (Indianapolis, 1941–61), III, 279.

62. King's memorandum, Sept. 23, 1789, King Papers, N.-Y. Hist. Soc.; Seth Ames, ed., *Works of Fisher Ames*, 2 vols. (Boston, 1854), I, 71.

63. King's memorandum, Sept. 23, 1789, King Papers, N.-Y. Hist. Soc.; Maclay, *Journal*, 155–57, 161–62.

conjunction with the Yorkers."[64] The measure, revised by the Senate, came back to the House, where Madison, acting for the southern bloc, secured an amendment, and when Congress adjourned, the issue remained unsettled.

Before the end of the first session of Congress, the theatrical season had resumed, affording a happy diversion from official business, and Washington's presence in New York lent prestige to the stage. His interest in the drama was well known, and advance notice of his attendance attracted crowds to the performances of the Old American Company in the little John Street Theater. On the evening of November 24, after the presidential levee, Rufus and Mary King went to the theater with President and Mrs. Washington. The audience was unusually large that night, partly to watch a performance of Thomas Wignell, the finest comedian in America, but more to observe the celebrities. When the presidential party entered, the orchestra struck up the "President's March," composed for the occasion, and the audience gave the Chief Executive a standing ovation. George and Martha Washington, Abigail Adams, General and Mrs. Schuyler, Alexander and Elizabeth Hamilton, the Kings, and two other guests sat in the President's box. What they saw was far from profound drama, but was typical of the time. The bill opened with *The Toy; or a Trip to Hampton Court*, "as now performing at the Theatre Royal, Covent Garden." This was followed by *The Critic; or a Tragedy Rehearsed*, a two-act comedy by Oliver Goldsmith, "with a Grand Sea Engagement, and an Attack upon Tilbury Fort by the Spanish Armada, with the total Defeat of the Fleet, by Fire-Ships, Cannon and Bombs, from the Fort." The concluding piece, *Darby's Return*, was a "comic sketch, interspersed with Music."[65]

Diversions of another sort were the formal dinners given by the President and his wife. Washington was anxious to make the presidency "respectable," and his dinners were elaborate. Guests were announced by footmen in powdered wigs, tables were lavishly spread, and the President's order for twenty-six dozen bottles of claret and an equal amount of champagne suggests something of the scale of his official hospitality. During the year 1789 the President lived in the Osgood house on Cherry Street, but as it was neither

64. Maclay, *Journal*, 158–59.

65. Odell, *Annals of the New York Stage*, I, 243, 279; Benson J. Lossing, ed., *Diary of George Washington, from 1789 to 1791; Embracing the Opening of the First Congress . . .* (N. Y., 1860), 56–57; N. Y. *Gazette of the United States*, Nov. 28, 1789; N. Y. *Daily Advertiser*, Nov. 24, 1789.

as spacious nor as handsome as he wished, he moved in the following February to the Macomb house on Broadway, not far south of Trinity Church. Formerly occupied by the French Minister, this residence had spacious high-ceilinged "public rooms" for levees and for dinners where as many as twenty-seven sat at table.[66]

King attended a number of these dinners, sometimes with his wife and sometimes alone. From December to July he was present on at least six Thursday evenings, with the Vice-President, cabinet officers, senators and congressmen, justices of the Supreme Court, Governor Clinton, federal Judge Duane (formerly Mayor of the city), Bishop Provoost, and others.[67] The President was not always at ease; one evening, according to Senator Maclay, he fidgeted and drummed on the table with his fork or knife. If Maclay himself could not bear the forced pleasantries of such occasions, King enjoyed them. His formality, interest in fashion, and meticulous attention to social niceties typified "respectable" behavior, and his graceful manner and aristocratic bearing accorded with his sense of dignified personal and public deportment. He would have agreed with Abigail Adams's description of the President as "polite with dignity, affable without familiarity, distant without Haughtyness, Grave without Austerity, Modest, wise and good."[68]

Mrs. Adams and Mrs. Washington developed their own round of ceremonies, with weekly dinners, teas, and receptions. At smaller and more intimate parties and afternoon teas, the ladies—Mrs. King among them—exchanged pleasantries. Outside the official circle, larger assemblies were held every two weeks and balls every month. So festive was New York that even the dour Maclay called the city's allurements "more than ten to two compared with Philadelphia," whose Quaker severity, he thought, had "proscribed all fashionable dress and amusements."[69]

66. Freeman, *George Washington*, VI, 226, 252, 253.

67. Lossing, ed., *Diary of Washington*, 60, 62, 98, 115, 120, 141.

68. Abigail Adams to Mary Cranch, Jan. 5, 1790, Stewart Mitchell, ed., *New Letters of Abigail Adams, 1788–1801* (Boston, 1947), 35; Maclay, *Journal*, 201. For King's graceful manner, see Samuel A. Otis to Elbridge Gerry, Jan. 5, 1784, Gerry Papers, Pierpont Morgan Lib. For King's formal politeness, see Andrew Craigie to Timothy Pickering, July 19, 1785, Pickering Papers, Mass. Hist. Soc.

69. Abigail Adams to Mary Cranch, Apr. 21, 1790, Mitchell, ed., *New Letters of Abigail Adams*, 46; Alexander White to Horatio Gates, Mar. 13, 1790, Emmet Coll., N. Y. Pub. Lib.; Maclay, *Journal*, 331.

CHAPTER IX

DOMESTIC ISSUES

1790-1792

OF THE MANY POLICY QUESTIONS BEFORE CONGRESS IN THE EARLY 1790'S none was more fundamental than finance and public credit, and it was fortunate for Hamilton that Rufus King was in the Senate championing his ideas. In his report to Congress on the funding of the debt, the Secretary of the Treasury held that the honor and the credit of the country depended upon funding the principal and paying the defaulted interest on the Continental debt. Fairness to all creditors required that there be no discrimination between the original purchasers and the present holders of federal obligations. In addition, he argued, the United States must assume the states' wartime debts and unpaid interest.[1]

If Hamilton's proposals for handling the federal debt did not cause serious division of opinion,[2] his recommendation of assumption of state debts encountered conflicting state interests and also hastened the buying up of state securities by shrewd speculators. Noting the rise in value of public debt certificates and having heard that William Constable, Robert Morris's New York partner, had a contract for

1. Whether the federal government should take over the state debts was not a new question. During 1789 it had been discussed privately by politicians and public creditors, and in Massachusetts the General Court hesitated to arrange for payment of the state debt until it learned what Congress would do.

2. Ferguson, *Power of the Purse*, 304, 305, asserts that most members of Congress shared a conception of public policy that favored immediately the interests of commerce and property, and he regards as mistaken the supposition that Hamilton's federal debt proposals seriously divided either Congress or the people.

$40,000 worth, Senator Maclay thought the funding report would "damn the character of Hamilton as minister forever." Senator Benjamin Hawkins of North Carolina told of meeting on his way to New York two expresses carrying large sums of money to buy southern securities. Representative Jeremiah Wadsworth of Connecticut had dispatched two vessels to the South with cash to purchase certificates. Condemning these private financial manipulations, southern congressmen decried the injustice of rewarding rich men while penalizing war veterans who had parted with their depreciated paper for next to nothing. Northern representatives, including Boudinot, Sedgwick, Ames, and Laurance, admitted the hardship of the original holders but argued the impossibility of finding out who the original holders were, since innumerable certificates had been issued in the names of government clerks. A refund, they said, would lead to fraud and perjury on a wide scale.[3]

In March, Maclay discerned a "rendezvousing of the crew of the Hamilton galley," and in April he testily remarked on the forlorn appearance of the Hamiltonian "gladiators," by whom he meant King, Schuyler, Ellsworth, Strong, Paterson, and Izard. "The Secretary's people," he recorded, "scarce disguise their design, which is to create a mass of debts which will justify them in seizing all the sources of Government, thus annihilating the State Legislatures and creating an empire on the basis of consolidation." King's and Ellsworth's "toolism" in supporting administration measures was evident to anybody, he thought.[4]

If Maclay was correct in ascribing strongly nationalist views to King, his picture of the New York Senator as Hamilton's tool was etched too deeply with the acid of hatred and contempt. King agreed with Hamilton's financial objectives, and he exerted himself heartily to bring about the assumption of state debts. His association with leading creditors and his past efforts to strengthen the credit of the federal government were no secret, but neither was his political alliance with Hamilton in New York.

The Hamilton clique was not immune from attack outside the walls of Federal Hall. One day in April, King "looked like a boy that had been whipped, and General Schuyler's hair stood on end as if the Indians had fired at Him," according to Maclay, who ascribed

3. Maclay, *Journal*, 173, 174–75; Brant, *James Madison*, III, 292–93, 295.
4. Maclay, *Journal*, 202–03, 228–29, 230, 244.

their agitation to newspaper charges against them.[5] A sarcastic writer in the *New-York Journal* had proposed the nomination of Schuyler, King, and Laurance for the state legislature, since "all our great men" were in Congress, and state affairs would suffer if the people did not also elect these worthies to high state office. Sniping at King's recent residency in New York, he suggested importing

> some hopeful youth, from the mines of Cornwall, or the fens of Lincolnshire, or possibly . . . we may find some person belonging to one of the states, who may be disappointed in a seat in the house of Representatives for his own state, and we may get him elected by our legislature to the Senate. That such a person may be a stranger, or soiled, or not thought worthy of the honor, or that it would be impolitic, or ungrateful, or absurd, or laughable, to give him a preference to all the *old servants* of the state, is nothing at all; we have a case exactly in point—*no one* can complain.[6]

The bill for the assumption of state debts was defeated in the House on April 12 by only two votes.[7] But the battle was not over, and, much to the puzzlement of the public, assumption soon became entangled with the bill to fix the seat of the federal government. After a House vote to hold the next session of Congress in Philadelphia, Fisher Ames, who suspected Pennsylvania of bargaining to oppose assumption if it could have the temporary capital, exclaimed, "*we* are sold by the Pennsylvanians, and the assumption with it." This "despicable grog-shop contest, whether the taverns of New York or Philadelphia shall get the custom of Congress," he wrote, "keeps us in discord, and covers us all with disgrace."[8]

If it would prevent assumption and result eventually in the removal of Congress to the Potomac, the Virginians were eager to concede the temporary residence to the Philadelphians. Thus, pushing for an immediate settlement of the temporary capital, Lee moved in the Senate to postpone the choice of a permanent residence. Izard

5. *Ibid.*, 228–29.

6. *N.-Y. Journal*, Apr. 8, 1790.

7. In the House debate, congressmen reflected the economic interests of the various states: those from states hoping to gain favored the bill, those from states likely to lose opposed it, and those from states not greatly affected were indifferent. See Ferguson, *Power of the Purse*, 307–18.

8. Fisher Ames to Thomas Dwight, June 11, 1790, Ames, ed., *Works of Ames*, I, 79–80.

and Butler of heavily indebted South Carolina led the assumptionist fight to combine the questions of permanent and temporary capitals. They rounded up allies, including Johnson of Connecticut, who was carried into the Senate ill with influenza, heavily bundled and wearing his night cap, and attended by two doctors. As a result, postponement was defeated, strengthening the belief that a small Senate majority was more interested in assumption than in the residence question.[9]

The next day, the House voted that Congress move to Baltimore, a move favored by the assumptionists. By a margin of two votes, however, the Senate again postponed action on the temporary residence. King proposed to Senator John Henry of Maryland that New York vote for Baltimore as a permanent seat if Maryland supported New York City as the temporary residence. After Henry declined, King and his friends made a similar proposal to the senators of Georgia, the Carolinas, Connecticut, and Massachusetts. The six southerners assured King that if the measure could be carried they would agree to it. Ellsworth and Johnson of Connecticut went along, as did the Rhode Islanders, who had now taken their seats for the first time. Massachusetts balked, however.[10]

King recognized that to the Bay State senators, assumption was the important issue. He appealed to one of them, Caleb Strong, alleging that the opposition to it was weakening every day. Perhaps assumption should be separated from the residence question, but if they must be connected, he suggested, assumption might win more votes by a decision for New York as the temporary and Baltimore as the permanent capital than by an immediate removal of Congress to Philadelphia. "The Dilemma is New York and Baltimore, or Philadelphia—if one does not succeed, the other will. The Delegates of Massachusetts may conceive it is best to take no part in this question; but in this Dilemma not to agree to New York and Baltimore, is embracing Philadelphia." Moving to Philadelphia left open the matter of permanent residence. Would it not be best to decide the question now? "New York will ask nothing which will promote her interest, unless that of the United States is also promoted," he concluded, "but she must possess unusual apathy not to feel, and with pretty strong

9. King's memorandum, June 8, 1790, King Papers, N.-Y. Hist. Soc.; Maclay, *Journal*, 227–28; Brant, *James Madison*, III, 312.

10. King's memorandum dated June 30, 1790, and his undated "Memorandum addressed to Strong. . . ," (perhaps June 8 or 9), King Papers, N.-Y. Hist. Soc.

emotions, that a measure which seems calculated to accomplish both, should be lost by the votes of those whose interest she anxiously desired to advance."[11]

Evidently Hamilton persuaded the Massachusetts senators not to cooperate in King's plan. The Secretary had come to the conclusion that the funding of the debt, including assumption, could succeed in Congress only with votes from Virginia, and that meant acceptance of a southern site for the permanent capital. About June 20, Hamilton and Madison dined at Jefferson's house and worked out a deal: two Virginia congressmen would change their votes on assumption, and Hamilton would see to it that the permanent seat of government would be on the Potomac; to secure the support of Robert Morris and the Pennsylvanians, Philadelphia would be the temporary capital for ten years.[12]

Hamilton called on King at his home and told him that lesser goals must be sacrificed to the primary national object of the funding system, including assumption. He did not like the Philadelphia-Potomac arrangement, but it would ensure passage of the financial measures, which otherwise would be defeated. King protested, but to no avail, and later lectured to Hamilton that "great and good schemes ought to succeed on their own merits and not by intrigue or the establishment of bad measures." That his friend had stooped to bargain struck King as beneath the dignity of a statesman. His own viewpoint, he told the Secretary, was national, but if local considerations were to prevail, he would have to submit and adopt state or local views, as others found it in their interest to do.[13] His chagrin at Hamilton's legerdemain was the reaction of an independent spirit, not the response of a cog in a Hamiltonian machine.

On June 30 the Senate accepted Philadelphia as the temporary seat of government with Vice-President Adams tipping the scale, and the next day, by a vote of fourteen to twelve, it adopted the Potomac site as the permanent capital. King was dismayed at the sudden fading of New York's hopes for at least a temporary residence. According

11. *Ibid.* The quotations are from the memorandum addressed to Strong. This is printed in King, ed., *King Correspondence*, I, 381–83. On the matter of assumption, Massachusetts, like South Carolina, had huge debts remaining from the Revolution, and her politicians hoped to unload them on the federal government. See Ferguson, *Power of the Purse*, 307–09, 313, 315–17.

12. Brant, *James Madison*, III, 315–17; John C. Miller, *Alexander Hamilton: Portrait in Paradox* (N. Y., 1959), 251.

13. King's memorandum, June 30, 1790, King Papers, N.-Y. Hist. Soc.

to Maclay's malicious account, he "took up his lamentations. He sobbed, wiped his eyes, and scolded and railed and accused first everybody and then nobody, of bargaining, contracting arrangements and engagements that would dissolve the Union. He was called on sharply. He begged pardon, and blackguard-like, railed again." As the senators left their chamber after the stormy session, King glared at Maclay, Maclay insulted King, and King at the foot of the stairs sarcastically blurted, "let us now go and receive the congratulations of the city for what we have done."[14] Maclay rudely walked away.

Some days later feelings had calmed down, and the two men chatted informally and in apparent good humor. According to Maclay, King asserted that a bargain on the residence had been made to win over at least one vote in place of his own, since he would most likely vote against assumption if Congress went to Philadelphia. Maclay was astonished at King's admitting what "in fact, amounted to this: that he had engaged his vote for the assumption if the residence stayed in New York."[15] This interpretation shows how little Maclay understood the New Yorker's character. King may have threatened to oppose assumption if coupled with the residence question, but he could hardly have determined to sabotage a measure he so ardently approved. It is more plausible that Hamilton, knowing he could not rely on King's vote, traded an extra vote or two for Philadelphia in return for support of assumption.[16]

If he was dissatisfied with Congress's departure to Philadelphia, King battled loyally for Hamilton's financial program. Like the Secretary, he accepted human self-interest as an axiom of political life. The financial plight of the Confederation had led both men, Hamilton first, King eventually, to conclude that a consolidation of governmental obligations was needed to strengthen the central government, insure its credit, and give it permanence. Approving Burke's dictum that "experience, not abstraction" should be man's guide, King saw no substitute for effective power. Wise leaders would act according to the ambitions and interests of men. Government, there-

14. Maclay, *Journal*, 305.

15. *Ibid.*, 312.

16. On June 28 the Senate had voted, by 13 to 12, to make New York the temporary capital, but the next day eliminated that city, as Gunn of Georgia, who had been absent, tied the votes, and the vice-president cast his vote against New York. Then, when Philadelphia was chosen, Butler of South Carolina, who had favored New York, switched to Philadelphia. *Ibid.*, 301–04; *Annals*, 1 Cong., 2 sess., 997–1000; *N.-Y. Journal*, July 2, 1790.

fore, must attract talented individuals into its service, and people of "good sense and property" must rally to its support.[17] Although he did not elaborate this theme, King made it an article of faith to which his entire public career was testimony.

When the funding bill came before the Senate, it provoked a lengthy discussion of the rate of interest to be paid. King threw his weight behind Hamilton's proposal of 6 per cent, but he appears to have been ready to settle for 4 per cent immediately with an additional 2 per cent in ten years. Failure to compensate the public creditors fully, he held, was not only disgraceful and unjust but would weaken their attachment to the government. On every roll call bearing upon the funding, King voted for liberal terms to creditors.[18]

The fact that the senators debated behind closed doors led one public creditor to complain about "a few knowing ones" able to give tips to buyers or sellers of securities. "Not having the honor of an acquaintance with Mr. K——, Mr. M——, General ——, Colonel ——, etc.," the outsiders could not possibly explore the reasons for alleged agreements or votes in the Senate.[19] Thus, King, Morris, Schuyler, and Hamilton led the "knowing ones," and it was widely believed that insiders had profited from prior information about the funding program. As Assistant Secretary of the Treasury, John Duer (who resigned before he could be called to account for violating a law forbidding treasury officers from buying and selling securities) had attracted a following of moneyed men who, like himself, invested heavily in the public debt, hoping to cash in when the new government refinanced existing obligations. If facts concerning Hamilton's program leaked out, the likely source was Duer. Hamilton was careful to keep his own hands clean, though his enemies charged that he gave inside information to Schuyler, who by 1791 owned more than $60,000 in government paper. Schuyler, however,

17. King to James Madison, Jan. 27, 1788, King Papers, N.-Y. Hist. Soc. The quotation from Burke appears on an undated loose leaf inserted in King's notebook, owned by James G. King. "Wisdom, in the antient Mythology, was represented as armed because experience had proved that good Examples and noble Precepts fail of their Efficacy, unaccompanied by a Power to enforce them." King's notation, Mar. 1816, King Papers, N.-Y. Hist. Soc.

18. See, for example, votes on June 21, July 19, 28, 1790, *Annals*, 1 Cong., 2 sess., 991, 1013–15, 1020–22. For a concise account of the funding controversy, see Ferguson, *Power of the Purse*, ch. 13.

19. *New-York Daily Gazette*, June 19, 1790.

had long held public securities and as early as 1782 had tried to promote his son-in-law's early plan to fund the debt.[20] As for King, there is no indication that he pocketed any money through his friendship with Hamilton or his acquaintance with Duer, though his own familiarity with some of the intricacies of finance may have suggested profitable opportunities. He owned government paper but in accord with his cautious nature held it for income. There is no record of speculative activity.

On July 21, the Senate passed the funding bill by a vote of fourteen to twelve, after Maclay had made a long and impassioned speech against it. Its advocates, knowing that they had the votes, paid no attention to him, nodded, whispered to one another, and even left the chamber. "The majority are solid, and Hamilton has bought them," the testy Pennsylvanian concluded, apparently without evidence.[21] The New England senators, except the two from Rhode Island and one from New Hampshire, voted for the bill, as did the senators of New York, New Jersey, and South Carolina. While the Virginians, North Carolinians, and Georgians were united in opposing it as a scheme to enrich mostly northern and "eastern" speculators, King and the other Hamiltonian "gladiators" were satisfied that the United States would meet what they considered the just claims of its creditors.

As signed by the President, the funding act, which included the assumption of state debts, provided for a loan of $21,500,000. Subscriptions to this loan were to be paid for at par in certificates of indebtedness and outstanding Continental money. Each subscriber would receive new certificates, two-thirds of which would bear interest at once, and the remaining third, known as deferred stock, would bear interest after ten years. In each case the rate was a generous 6 per cent.[22] Hamilton probably looked upon the funding program primarily as an instrument of power. If it raised the debt higher than necessary to establish the national credit, it afforded a major advantage in attracting moneyed men to the administration by creating

20. Miller, *Alexander Hamilton*, 246*n*.

21. Maclay, *Journal*, 330. The roll call on this bill may be found in *Annals*, 1 Cong., 2 sess., 1016 (July 21, 1790).

22. The text may be found in *Annals*, 1 Cong., 2 sess. (appendix, 2243–51). James Schouler, *History of the United States of America under the Constitution*, 7 vols. (N. Y., 1880–1913), I, 149, concisely describes the act.

profitable opportunities for investment or speculation in the funds, in land, or in manufactures.

The Bank of the United States was another device to bind wealth to government. Although a bank was perhaps not needed for the funding of the debt, it was a convenient agency to attract the capital of merchants and speculators. Early in 1791 a Senate committee consisting of Strong, Morris, Schuyler, Butler, and Ellsworth, all of whom shared Hamilton's ideas on strong central government, reported a bill substantially as the Secretary had proposed it.[23] The bank was to have a capital of $10,000,000, of which $8,000,000 would be open to individual subscribers by the payment of one-fourth in gold or silver and three-fourths in United States securities. The government was to subscribe the remaining $2,000,000 in cash. On the Senate floor, Maclay moved to permit the public to subscribe on the same terms, without having to pay specie. This brought about an oratorical free-for-all, with every speaker claiming to be an expert in public finance. The public subscription was intended only as a deposit, said Ellsworth, who saw no disadvantage to the people in being excluded from subscribing to three-fourths of it in public securities. "King El[l]sworth, and Strong all harped on this string with the most barefaced absurdity that I ever was witness to in my life," recorded the dour Maclay, who thought King in particular wanted the public to support the bank with specie, while speculators reaped the profits of its operation.[24]

Agreeing with the principles on which the bank was based, King and half of the senators also hoped to charter the bank for a long term. By a bare majority, the Senate voted to extend the life of the institution to twenty-four years, but the next day it reconsidered and decided upon a twenty-year term. An attempt by southern senators to limit the bank to ten years was easily beaten, and on January 20 the bank bill passed without a roll call in substantially the form in which it had been proposed.[25]

The day the Bank of the United States subscription books were

23. Bray Hammond, *Banks and Politics in America From the Revolution to the Civil War* (Princeton, 1957), 115. Hammond devotes three chapters to the founding, development, and operation of the Bank of the United States, including the relationship of politics to banking from 1791 to 1816.

24. Maclay, *Journal*, 359–60, 361.

25. *U. S. Senate Jour.*, 1 Cong., 3 sess., 33, 35–36, 37; *Annals*, 1 Cong., 3 sess., 1745–46, 1748; Maclay, *Journal*, 362.

opened, July 4, 1791, was a holiday for hopeful investors, who eagerly snapped up the offering. All the shares available to the public were subscribed within an hour.[26] King and the New York financiers had reason to apprehend the growth of Philadelphia as a rival banking center, with its Bank of North America, chartered ten years earlier by the old Congress as the first private commercial bank in the United States, and now the new Bank of the United States, with its much wider scope of operations.

Already interested in banking, King had been elected on May 10, 1791, as a director of the Bank of New York. This bank had obtained a corporate charter only two months earlier, but it had been in operation since 1784 and was the oldest in the state. Of its nearly two hundred shareholders at the time of incorporation, five, including Rufus King, held twelve shares apiece; only seven other stockholders held larger amounts.[27]

On October 21, King was chosen as one of the twenty-five directors of the Bank of the United States. Among the ten who received the highest number of votes were King; Philip Livingston, who as a state senator had pushed King for election to the United States Senate; Nicholas Low, a New York City merchant and later King's financial agent; Herman Le Roy, another wealthy and influential New York merchant; Thomas Willing, president of the Bank of North America and the first president of the Bank of the United States; and Senator Samuel Johnson of North Carolina. The remaining fifteen directors included King's friends, Congressmen John Laurance of New York and Jeremiah Wadsworth of Connecticut, and George Cabot, newly appointed Senator from Massachusetts.[28]

The sale of Bank of United States scrip on the Fourth of July, 1791, touched off an orgy of speculation such as had never been seen in America. The president of the Philadelphia Stock Exchange was said to have cleared $40,000 in a single month by dealing in scrip,

26. Hammond, *Banks and Politics*, 123.

27. Domett, *History of Bank of New York*, 122, 137–40; Wilson, ed., *History of the City of N. Y.*, III, 78; Bank of New York, Minute Book of Directors' Meetings, owned by the bank and used with its kind permission. The shareholders held a total of 723 shares, each share having a par value of $500. By 1796 King held only 4 shares. Nicholas Low to King, Nov. 3, 1796, King Papers, Vol. 37, N.-Y. Hist. Soc.

28. *N.-Y. Journal*, Oct. 26, 1791; Burton Alva Konkle, *Thomas Willing and the First American Financial System* (Phila., 1937), 142.

and stories of fantastic fortunes made overnight induced members of Congress, businessmen, clerks, shopkeepers, even apprentices and farmers to borrow money in order to become rich.[29] Astonished and appalled, King voiced to Hamilton his concern over the extent of the mania.[30] The Secretary, however, showed no alarm. A little speculation, he thought, would be good for the Bank and the country by helping to raise the price of public securities and thereby freeing more capital for investment. Soon, however, he felt impelled to speak out. As he explained, "a bubble connected with my operations is of all the enemies I have to fear, in my judgment, the most formidable—and not only to promote, but as far as depend on me, to counteract delusions, appears to me to be the only secure foundation on which to stand."[31] Like the sorcerer's apprentice, Hamilton felt responsible for, and frustrated by, the flood tide of speculation rising around him.

King had correctly gauged the temper of the delirious speculators. He advised Hamilton to be careful what he said in answering accusations that he was manipulating the money market. The Secretary complained that his statements had been misquoted and denied that he had given a standard of prices lower than the current market value of securities. He listed for King his own standard of prices for various types of paper, so that King could contradict charges that the Secretary of the Treasury was deliberately depressing the funds.[32]

As the boom showed signs of breaking, King was almost pleased. The damage might not be too extensive, he reassured Hamilton, and small investors would learn not to plunge into unknown depths: "The fall of Bank certificates may have some good affects, it will operate to Deter our industrious citizens from meddling in future with the funds, and teach them contentment in their proper vocations." The sufferers would "neither excite nor deserve commiseration." The most timid, he observed, would have the chance to retire "with something less money and much more wisdom than they have brought into the market." Things would turn out well in the end, and there was no reason to fear a precipitous fall in stock prices. "The

29. Miller, *Alexander Hamilton*, 269.

30. King's letter to Hamilton apparently is lost. Hamilton's reply, July 8, 1791, King Papers, Vol. 28, N.-Y. Hist. Soc., alludes to a "certain subject," which I have inferred was the speculation.

31. Hamilton to King, Aug. 17, 1791, *ibid.*

32. *Ibid.*

Business was going on in a most alarming manner, mechanicks deserting their shops, Shop keepers sending their goods to auction, and not a few of our merchants neglecting the regular and profitable commerce of the City—a check was necessary—the explosion will restore order, and we shall return to our regular pursuits."[33]

The panic was short lived, thanks to Hamilton's timely action. Through the Bank of New York, the treasury entered the bond market and spent more than $200,000 from the sinking fund to support government bond prices. Some of the speculators had been ruined, but most investors happily found the prices of government and bank stock leveling off well above what they had been before the boom.[34]

No sooner had the speculative mania subsided than another event disconcerted King and Hamilton. The directors of the Bank of the United States decided to set up a branch in New York City with almost twice the capitalization of the Bank of New York. As a director of both banks, King was perched uncomfortably. He appears to have suggested that the New York institution offer some of its stock to the Bank of the United States. "Anxious to cultivate a good understanding and to obviate if possible a competition between the Two Banks," King's fellow directors in New York made the offer, but the federal bank turned it down.[35] Several weeks later, King transmitted from Philadelphia to his colleagues at the Bank of New York the outlines of a plan to unite the federal and state institutions, but, although the New York directors approved it, nothing came of the plan.[36] King escaped from his personal dilemma when his term as a director of the Bank of New York ended in May 1792.

Hamilton, to the surprise of many, championed the state banks. In particular, the Secretary favored the Bank of New York, which he had helped to establish; in depositing government funds and drawing foreign bills of exchange, he threw business to the local institution.

33. King to Hamilton, Aug. 15, 1791, Hamilton Papers, Lib. Cong. For determination of the date of this letter, see Syrett *et al.*, eds., *Papers of Hamilton*, IX, 61.

34. Miller, *Alexander Hamilton*, 271.

35. Bank of New York, Minute Book of Directors' Meetings, Oct. 31 and Nov. 17, 1791, Bank of New York.

36. *Ibid.*, Dec. 15, 20, 1791. The minutes do not reveal the details of the outline King transmitted. It is unlikely that King was the author of the plan, but he probably approved of it. A few months later, his Massachusetts friend Gore favored the idea of the federal bank taking over the state banks. Christopher Gore to King, Apr. 1, 1792, King Papers, N.-Y. Hist. Soc.

Had the treasury not supported it, the Bank of New York might well have been destroyed by the federal colossus.

Although conservative in financial affairs, King, like Hamilton, remained on friendly terms with speculators, a course which probably won him as many enemies as friends. Gore suggested that he participate in another scheme to take over the United States debt to France, but, as when Duer had approached him in 1788, he wisely avoided involvement. In 1793, however, he pushed the reappointment of Andrew Craigie, a successful speculator, to the directorship of the Boston branch of the Bank of the United States.[37]

At the end of 1793 the Senate took up a proposed amendment to the Constitution forbidding any officeholder in the Bank of the United States from being at the same time a member of Congress. At about this time, King resigned as director of this bank, partly because he wished to act freely upon the proposed amendment without incurring insinuations of self-interest.[38] The Senate defeated the amendment by a single vote; King, of course, voted against it. Perhaps as vital to his decision to resign from the bank was his belief that it needed the concentrated attention of more directors who were residents of Philadelphia.[39] As a New Yorker, he spent only part of the year at the seat of the bank's operations, and soon, he professed, he would spend all his time in New York.[40]

In spite of his growing political influence, King was tempted to return to private life as his family claimed more of his attention.[41] In 1790 Mary King gave birth to Caroline, their only daughter,

37. Christopher Gore to King, May 15, 1792, *ibid.*; King to Craigie, Jan. 15, 1793, King folder, Long Island Collection, Queens Borough Public Library, New York. The King Papers in the New-York Historical Society contain no letters of King between June 7, 1789 and Jan. 20, 1792, and it is therefore difficult to elucidate his position on many public and financial questions in this period.

38. John Laurance to King, Jan. 12, 1794, King Papers, N.-Y. Hist. Soc.; King, ed., *King Correspondence*, I, 397, 513–14.

39. King to John Laurance, Dec. 22, 1793, Herman Le Roy to King, Dec. 20, 1793; Isaac Wharton wrote to King, Oct. 21, 1793: "The Approbation we have received from *you* and our Brother Directors *in New York* is highly gratifying to Us." King exerted himself to secure the appointment of John Laurance as a director. Robert Troup to King, Jan. 1, 13, 1794, all King Papers, N.-Y. Hist. Soc.

40. King to John Laurance, Dec. 14, 1793, *ibid.*

41. "It is not without the most painful sacrifice that I continue in Congress," King had affirmed in 1792. "I had much anxiety to see a Government established which would afford a prospect of Stability and Peace; and I have not been without zeal in the progress of this important event." King to Robert Southgate, Jan. 20, 1792, King, ed., *King Correspondence*, I, 404.

and the next year a third son, James, was born.[42] Another son, Henry, was born in July 1792 but died two months later. The elderly John Alsop, under whose roof the family still lived, was an additional care for Mrs. King, as was her husband's young half-brother Cyrus, who in the summer of 1790 came from Maine to live with the Kings while he attended Columbia College. Indebted to his stepmother for having fostered his own education at Harvard, King had undertaken to pay Cyrus's expenses and had encouraged him to come to New York to study under fraternal supervision. The boy's mother was uneasy at his being in that city, which she imagined to be a den of vice, but she was confident that if he lived with the Kings he would be properly protected. "Your kind and best of brothers, what do I say a more than father, I need not tell you to mind and improve by his counsel. I know he will take all the pains in the world in order that you may make a respectable figure in life." Dutiful and serious, Cyrus ingratiated himself, and King, pleased with the boy's behavior and educational progress, supplied him with money to meet all his needs.[43]

King was a member of the New York Society Library, which owned three thousand volumes shelved in the City Hall. Its roster of members included most of New York's leading citizens—merchants, politicians, officeholders, lawyers, and physicians. King joined its purchasing committee in August 1791 and served for a year as a trustee. Among the books he borrowed, some no doubt for Cyrus, were Montesquieu's *Spirit of the Laws*, a life of Plato, Lord Sheffield on commerce, Robertson's *Navigation*—which he renewed four times, Anburey's *Travels*, a few novels and plays, Chesterfield's letters, Blair's *Lectures on Rhetoric and Belles Lettres*, Noah Webster's grammar, and textbooks in algebra and geometry.[44]

42. Caroline died in 1793. James was later given a middle name, Gore, in honor of his godfather, Christopher Gore.

43. King to Cyrus King, June 6, 1790, quoted in James G. King's notebook, Letters, etc., of Rufus King and his Family, I, 47–48, Mary Black King to Cyrus King, Sept. 27, 1790, owned by James G. King; Mary Black King to Cyrus King, Mar. 2, 1791, Feb. 22, May 23, 1792, Sept. 2, 1793 (copied from extracts from the originals owned by Mrs. John H. Thomas), in James G. King's notebook (*supra*), 31–35, 39. Cyrus King to William King, n.d., 1793, *ibid.*, 67 (copied from Elizabeth Porter King's sketch of her father, Cyrus King, in 1849, now owned by Mrs. John H. Thomas).

44. Ledger of books borrowed from the New York Society Library, New York, 1789–1792. This, the first ledger, is owned by the Library. A. B. Keep, *History of the New York Society Library* ([N. Y.], 1908), 212, 215, 216, 222–27, 555. King seems to have dropped his membership sometime in 1793.

In spite of occasional complaints that heavy public responsibilities wearied him, his life was centered in politics. He had become an influential legislator, a practiced debater, a member and often chairman of important committees shaping bills before the Senate, occasionally one of the managers to iron out differences with the House, and an expert on protocol. As a tactician, he was deft in parliamentary maneuver and a stickler for exact detail. In one instance, he moved to strike out part of the previous day's minutes and insert another clause. "I saw the thing was preconcerted," the rancorous Maclay recorded, "done contrary to all rule."[45] Another time, when King sought to correct the minutes, the Pennsylvanian grumbled, "King is a singular man. Under the idea of correcting the minutes he introduces matter totally new. It is not correcting matter of form, but total alteration and adjection of new matter. I opposed him . . . and yet it was carried, but amended afterward and placed nearer the truth."[46] Jefferson later recounted at second hand a story that Gunn of Georgia had once remarked to Hamilton, "I wish, Sir, you would advise your friend King to observe some kind of consistency in his votes. There has been scarcely a question before the Senate on which he has not voted both ways. On the representation bill, for instance, he first voted for the proposition of the Representatives and ultimately voted against it." Hamilton was said to have replied candidly that it was never intended that the bill should pass.[47]

Every year King supported motions to remove the secrecy surrounding the Senate debates. In 1791 he welcomed resolutions from the New York legislature favoring open discussions in the United States Senate. "Having for some time thought that it would be expedient that the legislative debates of the Senate should be public," he and Schuyler wrote upon receipt of the resolutions, "it affords us much satisfaction that our sentiments on the subject concur with [yours]."[48] He did not, however, approve of newspaper publicity as a substitute for the printing and circulation of a complete Senate

45. Maclay, *Journal*, 169.

46. *Ibid.*, 374–75.

47. Franklin B. Sawvel, ed., *The Complete Anas of Thomas Jefferson* (N. Y., 1903), 45, entry for Dec. 25, 1791. For the contention of King and Ellsworth that the Senate was not a continuing body and that each session should be started *de novo*, see Maclay, *Journal*, 175–76.

48. King and Philip Schuyler to Isaac Roosevelt and John Watts, Feb. 23, 1791, printed in *N.-Y. Journal*, Mar. 3, 1791, and Phila. *Gazette of the United States*, Mar. 5, 1791.

journal.[49] Aware of the distortions of the partisan press, he preferred to keep the record straight and preserve the independence of senators' judgments from day-to-day popular pressures. By voting to open the doors, King lined up on the side of his most ardent critics, yet a majority of the senators succeeded in keeping the debates secret.

Among the important measures discussed in the second session of the First Congress was a naturalization bill requiring two years' residence before immigrants could become citizens of the United States. King did not join those who advocated a longer residency requirement.[50] Nor did he favor a property qualification for citizenship, as urged by Ellsworth of Connecticut and supported by southern senators to forestall possible assaults on slavery by hostile newcomers. To King, who was not especially sympathetic toward easing immigration standards, the holding of property was a common law right and a matter for the states to deal with.[51]

He also considered slavery a local rather than national problem. Opposed to slavery himself, as his past activities in the old Congress and in the Philadelphia Convention of 1787 had demonstrated, he was no abolitionist and did not wish to risk disruption of the Union he had so eagerly championed. On February 15, 1790, Vice-President Adams read in the Senate petitions and memorials of the Quaker-dominated antislavery society of Philadelphia. Izard and Butler of South Carolina denounced the society, Butler accusing Franklin (who was influential in the group) of trying to overturn the Constitution he had once consented to. King rose to defend the correctness of the view that Congress had no power to interfere with slavery but said nothing of Franklin, whom he disliked. "King is courting them," Maclay whispered to Robert Morris, but when asked to defend Franklin, Morris replied, "I will be silent from the same motive that makes him [King] speak."[52] The Senate adjourned without taking action.

49. *Annals*, 2 Cong., 2 sess., 637–638, Feb. 4, 1793. For King's efforts to open the Senate debates, see *ibid.*, Feb. 25, 1791, Mar. 26, 1792, Feb. 4, 1793; *U. S. Senate Jour.*, Feb. 25, 1791.

50. "We Pennsylvanians," wrote Maclay in his *Journal*, 205, "act as if we believed that God made of one blood all families of the earth; but the Eastern people seem to think that he made none but New England folks."

51. *Ibid.*, 208, 212. Henry, King, Strong, Ellsworth, and Johnson had been appointed as the committee to consider the bill. King's views were shared by Johnson and Henry; Strong was inclined to agree with Ellsworth.

52. *Ibid.*, 192.

To King, a far more appropriate subject for Senate discussion was the defense of the frontiers. As a staunch supporter of the administration, he favored strong defenses for the United States. The essence of Washington's policy was to make peace with the Indians all along the frontier by acknowledging their territorial rights and assuring them of American recognition, but to destroy those Indians who went on the warpath and thereby to set a deterrent example to less aggressive tribes. King helped to translate these principles into legislation. He voted for the purchase of land at West Point for a military academy; he opposed reducing the size of frontier regiments; and, to minimize the likelihood of conflict, he voted for stricter regulation of the Indian trade.[53]

If he hoped to build up national strength in the interior, he was even more concerned with improving America's commercial position abroad. In general, he approved of the tariffs on foreign goods entering the United States. When Jefferson's recommendations favoring special consideration for French shipping reached the Senate, they were referred to a committee of which King and Ellsworth were members. Both senators were unsympathetic toward France, and their unwillingness to make the desired concessions helped to kill the proposal in the upper house.[54]

King's protectionist sentiments sprang from his optimism over the prospects of the nation whose institutions he was helping to fashion. He rejoiced at the growth of American trade and the investment of native instead of British capital in American enterprises. By late summer 1792, he exulted over the soundness of public credit and the founding of new banks, notably branches of the Bank of the United States in Boston, New York, Baltimore, and Charleston. Claiming that they had already helped commerce, he predicted that they would soon encourage the expansion of manufactures and agriculture. "The settlement of new lands is only equalled by the increase of our

53. *U. S. Senate Jour.*, June 25, 1790, Feb. 21, 1791; *Annals*, Feb. 17, 23, 1792, Feb. 26, 1793. Cf extract from King to Alexander Hamilton, March 24, 1791, Syrett *et al.*, eds., *Papers of Hamilton*, VIII, 212–13, which reveals anxiety over possible Indian attacks in New York state.

54. After a calculated delay, the Senate recommended that the French be informed "in the most friendly manner" that they would be denied favored treatment. *Journal of the Executive Proceedings of the Senate*, I, 77, Feb. 26, 1791; *Annals*, Mar. 3, 1791; Maclay, *Journal*, 393–94; Alexander DeConde, *Entangling Alliance, Politics and Diplomacy under George Washington* (Durham, N. C., 1958), 150.

population," he wrote proudly to Gouverneur Morris. "You hear of companies formed and forming in all the states for the improvement of our inland navigation, and thus the most distant lands will become almost as valuable as those nearest to our principal markets." Contrary to Freneau's assertions in the *National Gazette* that the country was dissatisfied, King went on, "we are and have reason to be, the happiest people in the World. Our government is established, it performs as much as its friends promised, and its administration has evidently advanced the prosperity of its citizens."[55] Like all partisan spokesmen, he gave his party full credit for the healthy state of the economy, but he also accepted as quite normal the political opposition to Federalist policy; in a free country such rivalry had always prevailed, and always would.

Two days after King had sung the praises of the burgeoning United States, Hamilton wrote to Jay, now the Chief Justice, of a crisis in the affairs of the country demanding "the most mature consideration of its best and wisest friends." He was worried over the sullen resistance in western Pennsylvania to the federal excise tax on whisky. Aroused farmers, brimming with resentment over a tax on one of their major products, had a different view of the country's economic health. On August 21, angry men had met at Pittsburgh and drawn up resolutions denouncing the tax and declaring that they would use legal means to obstruct its collection. Hamilton favored vigorous countermeasures and wished to have Jay's support. Would a presidential proclamation alluding to the "criminality" of such proceedings be effective? If force should be necessary, should the President go in person to the scene of the commotion? "Perhaps it will not be amiss for you to consult with Mr. King," the Secretary of the Treasury suggested. "His judgment is sound—he has caution and energy."[56]

The New York Senator at this time was aware of complaints in the back counties of Pennsylvania, Virginia, and the Carolinas, but he was not worried. As the law became better understood, and if it were mildly but steadily enforced, he thought opposition would soon evaporate. He predicted that the tax would benefit the people by curtailing the baneful practice of home distilling and making the

55. King to Gouverneur Morris, Sept. 1, 1792, Gouverneur Morris Papers, Columbia Univ. Lib.

56. Alexander Hamilton to John Jay, Sept. 3, 1792, Hamilton Papers, Lib. Cong.

production of liquor "a branch of Labor, instead of . . . a ruinous employment pursued by every family."[57]

Jay, after conferring with King in New York, advised Hamilton against immediate action and recommended that the President refer the matter to Congress at the opening of the next session. This sharing of responsibility was preferable to an immediate strong declaration against the malcontents, which would merely furnish opponents with "materials for deceiving the uninformed part of the community, and in some measure render the operations of administration odious."[58]

President Washington, however, agreed with Hamilton and issued a proclamation stating that the law would be enforced and warning against "unlawful combinations and proceedings." Privately he expressed the hope that it would be unnecessary to use federal troops, but if force was required, he thought it should be authorized by Congress.[59] As it happened, it was not until two years later that the government resorted to military force.

During the year 1792 few events were of more immediate concern to Rufus King than the canvass of votes in the race for the governorship of New York. No election in the entire history of the state has aroused more partisan fury than the gubernatorial contest of April 1792 between George Clinton and John Jay, but it was what happened after the votes were counted that caused the greatest furor.

The state board of canvassers, a joint committee of the legislature, found that Jay had won a majority of the votes, but seven of the canvassers, who were Clinton supporters, wished to throw out the votes of Otsego, Tioga, and Clinton counties on technicalities; the other four canvassers contended that these votes should be included in the count. In Otsego County, a majority of about four hundred votes had been cast for Jay, and in Tioga and Clinton the results did not materially diminish Jay's majority.[60] Hence, if the votes from these three counties were allowed, Jay would be the new governor; if rejected, Clinton would be re-elected.

57. King to Gouverneur Morris, Sept. 1, 1792, Gouverneur Morris Papers, Columbia Univ. Lib. King did not appreciate the fact that in the West liquor served as a standard of value and medium of exchange.

58. Jay to Hamilton, Sept. 8, 1792, Hamilton Papers, Lib. Cong.

59. George Washington to Hamilton, Sept. 16, 1792, cited in Freeman, *George Washington*, VI, 372.

60. Hammond, *Political Parties in New York*, I, 62–63.

The crucial Otsego County was a Federalist bastion, largely because of the activities of Judge William Cooper (the father of James Fenimore Cooper), who was such a Jay partisan that he had threatened to ruin tenants and debtors if they did not vote as told.[61] Under the law, the sheriff of each county had the duty of putting the ballots into a box and sending them to the state secretary to be handed over to the canvassers. Richard R. Smith had been appointed to hold office as sheriff of Otsego County for one year until February 18, 1792. He had declined a reappointment five days before the end of his term, and a new sheriff had not been appointed when the election took place. Continuing to act as sheriff, Smith received the ballots, boxed them, and forwarded them by a deputy to be counted. For some reason, he left out the votes of one town and sent them in a separate sealed package, though the law required all votes to be put into the same box. In Tioga County, the sheriff's deputy fell ill while delivering the ballots and handed them over to his clerk for transmission. In Clinton, the sheriff turned over the ballots to a man not deputized for their transmission.[62]

Unable to agree on whether the votes from the three counties should be allowed, the canvassers sought the opinions of their United States senators, King and Aaron Burr (who had succeeded Schuyler). Both men were lawyers of wide reputation, but if the canvassers thought their advice would solve the dilemma, they were indeed naïve. King and Burr conferred, but they differed in opinion as widely as the canvassers. Burr was uneasy: if he found for Clinton he would antagonize his Federalist friends; if he found for Jay he would alienate his Antifederalist friends. He therefore tried to avoid taking a stand and suggested that he and King decline to give their advice. King saw no reason to back out and was determined to give his own interpretation of the law, so Burr had to do likewise.[63]

King was a champion of Jay and a political adversary of Clinton, despite the Governor's hope in 1789 that the transplanted New Englander might become his adherent. Former Senator Schuyler had

61. Chilton Williamson, *American Suffrage, From Property to Democracy 1760–1860* (Princeton, 1960), 160, citing *N. Y. Assembly Journals*, 1792, 70–93, 188–203.

62. Data in this and the previous paragraph are based on Hammond, *Political Parties in New York*, I, 66.

63. Matthew L. Davis, ed., *Memoirs of Aaron Burr*, 2 vols. (N. Y., 1836–37), I, 332–33, 355–57; William B. Hatcher, *Edward Livingston: Jeffersonian Republican and Jacksonian Democrat* (Baton Rouge, 1940), 22.

repeatedly urged King to come to New York before the election and join more actively in the campaign for Jay. "He would do much good,—and prevent evils which a set of unprincipled villains contemplate," the General had written to Hamilton.[64] From Burr, on the other hand, the Federalists expected no help. According to Robert Troup, an influential Federalist lawyer, the submission of the dispute to King and Burr was a Clintonian trick, "a cloak for the Canvassers to cover their villainy in rejecting the votes of Otsego. They knew Burr to be decidedly with them, and that he would give them an opinion to justify their views."[65]

Soon after the election, Edward Livingston asked Troup for his opinion of the Otsego returns and was surprised to hear their legality upheld. This sent the Chancellor, Edward, and Brockholst Livingston into a huddle with Governor Clinton, and they challenged the legality of the votes from Otsego. To reassure himself, Troup spent an evening with King and Judge Egbert Benson, examining the legal aspects of the case, and the three agreed in their interpretation of the law.[66]

King's formal opinion to the canvassers was essentially that which Troup had given to Livingston. With respect to Otsego, King inferred from the Constitution and laws of the state that a sheriff could hold office for four years unless his successor had taken office. Because four years had not expired since the appointment of Sheriff Smith, and as his successor had not taken office, Smith was the lawful sheriff when the votes were forwarded. King added that the office of sheriff had been frequently held for more than a year under one appointment, and he could not consider Smith's statement of disinclination to be reappointed as a resignation or surrender of the office. Even if Smith were not *legally* sheriff, King continued, he was in fact the sheriff, and such acts of a *de facto* sheriff as tend to public utility and are essential to preserve the rights of others are valid. However, the votes Smith failed to place in the ballot box ought not to be canvassed. The votes from Clinton and Tioga counties should be allowed, King asserted, the former because a sheriff could deputize by word of mouth, and the latter because, though it was doubtful that a sheriff's deputy could deputize someone else, the election law

64. Philip Schuyler to Alexander Hamilton, Mar. 25, 1792, Hamilton Papers, 2d Ser., Lib. Cong.

65. Robert Troup to John Jay, June 10, 1792, Johnston, ed., *Papers of Jay*, III, 428.

66. Troup to Jay, May 20, 1792, *ibid.*, 424–27.

should be construed liberally to make effectual the right of suffrage.[67]

Burr asserted that the Otsego votes should be rejected, since no New York statute specifically authorized a sheriff to exercise his functions after his term expired. The common law, therefore, was applicable, and by it the sheriff ceased to exist officially when his term ended. Burr denied that Smith was sheriff *de facto*. With respect to the Clinton and Tioga ballots, Burr virtually agreed with King but was more positive in denying the right of a deputy sheriff to authorize a special deputy to perform an important trust. Taken as a whole, Burr's opinion was centered upon technicalities and it served the Clinton cause well. By contrast, King's broad construction was an attempt to protect the rights of voters from the misconduct or negligence of those charged with the duty of delivering the ballots. His opinion served as a rallying cry for Jay's followers.

When in June the pro-Clinton majority of the canvassers finally decided to reject the votes from the three counties, the four minority members made a futile protest. King knew it would be impossible to change the minds of the Clintonian canvassers; according to Mrs. Jay, he remarked that Clinton was as lawfully governor of Connecticut as of New York, but he knew of no redress.[68] And indeed there was no appeal, for by law the decision of the canvassing committee was final. Furious Federalists, however, were unwilling to accept the result; they protested in articles signed "Brutus" or "Gracchus," distributed among themselves a circular letter, held conclaves to plan their next moves, and proposed that the legislature order a new election. One of them suggested confidentially that, if a new election were not feasible, the legislature might order a *quo warranto*, which would leave the legality of Clinton's election in the hands of the judiciary.[69] In New York City, a Federalist stronghold, public meetings in the City Hall were so packed that the crowds overflowed into the streets, and testimonial dinners were given to Jay, whose chances for the presidency of the United States were

67. King, ed., *King Correspondence*, I, 411; Hammond, *Political Parties in New York*, 66–67. King's opinion to the canvassers may conveniently be found in Davis, ed., *Memoirs of Burr*, I, 336–38.

68. Mrs. John Jay to Jay, [June 11], 1792, Johnston, ed., *Papers of Jay*, III, 433.

69. Josiah Ogden Hoffman to Peter Van Schaack, June 26, 1792, Miscellaneous Manuscripts—Nicholas Low, N.-Y. Hist. Soc.; Josiah Ogden Hoffman to Stephen Van Rensselaer, June 24, 1792, Miscellaneous Manuscripts—Stephen Van Rensselaer, *ibid.*; cf. Hoffman to Van Rensselaer, June 20, 1792, Miscellaneous Manuscripts—H, *ibid.*

thought to hinge upon this election. In Albany and elsewhere, Clinton's aroused enemies planned efforts to unseat him. So active were the Jayites that Edward Livingston proposed Clintonian counter-demonstrations, and a public dinner was held for Clinton to the accompaniment of booming cannon.[70]

Meanwhile, calmer leaders wondered where all the agitation would end. Hamilton wrote King from Philadelphia that public indignation should be kept alive but warned that it might get out of hand. "Tis not to be forgotten that the opposers of Clinton are the real friends to order and good Government; and it will ill become them to give an example to the contrary." Uncertain of the specific objects of the anti-Clinton movements, he asked his friend, "What *can* you do? What do you *expect* to effect?"[71] King endorsed this letter: "I had no agency in promoting the measures adopted respecting the decision of the Canvassers. I have however felt the utmost indignation." On July 10 he replied, "Hitherto I have been quite aside, and have not engaged in the controversy," and he left no doubt that he feared the possibility of violence:

> If [the Federalists decide upon action] under any authority of law I shall rejoice, because I consider the Determination to be a precedent dangerous to free elections—still however I do not clearly see the prudence of an appeal to the People—yet others have no doubts on that subject, and there is reason to conclude that Mr. Jay deems the occasion such as will justify the step, should it be found that the powers of government are insufficient to afford a Remedy—he has an idea of a convention for the sole purpose of canvassing the canvassers and their decision. But Mr. Clinton is in fact Governor, and though he may not be free from anxieties and doubts, he will not willingly relinquish the office—the majority, and a very great one are now against him—should he persist and the sword be drawn, he must go to the wall—but this my dear sir, is a dreadful alternative. . . . If this case will justify a recurrence to first Principles, what are we not to expect from the disputes which must and will arise in the Succession to the Presidency? and how are we able to place confidence in the security of our Government?[72]

70. Edward Livingston to Robert R. Livingston, July 14, 1792, and Henry Livingston to Walter Livingston, July 19, 1792, Livingston Papers, N.-Y. Hist. Soc.; Wilson, ed., *History of the City of New-York*, III, 83–84.

71. Alexander Hamilton to King, June 28, 1792, King Papers, Vol. 28, N.-Y. Hist. Soc.

72. King to Hamilton, July 10, 1792, Hamilton Papers, Lib. Cong.

A postscript described how the "Friends of Liberty" had met Jay as he returned to town: "I took Benson with me in my carriage—the concourse was immense, and Mr. Jay has been received with the ringing of Bells, firing of cannon, huzzaing and clapping of hands. The shout was for 'Jay and Liberty.' " Hamilton agreed with King, continuing to hope that the anger over the Clintonians would be kept alive but within bounds—"and this for National purposes, as well as from a detestation of their principles and conduct." Force, he thought, ought to be employed only in cases of "great magnitude and urgent necessity." He opposed the calling of a convention to revise the state constitution, because in the heat of the moment it might make hasty, unwise, or too far-reaching changes. In Philadelphia, Hamilton had talked with resolute Federalists and found that they shared his opinions. As for Jay, who had ardently encouraged his partisans, Hamilton observed that the Chief Justice's character might "suffer by the idea that he fans the flames a little more than is quite prudent. I wish this idea to be conveyed to him with proper *management*."[73]

King evidently tried to calm Jay's feelings and voice Hamilton's concern lest the commotion in New York injure their party in the coming federal election. Within a week, Jay was on his way to Philadelphia to confer with the Secretary. His adherents went ahead with plans to persuade the legislature to call a convention to annul the canvassers' decision. King doubted that they would succeed, and events proved him right.[74]

As Washington's first term as president drew to a close, it was obvious that he would be re-elected, but the deep rift between Federalists and Republicans focused attention on the vice-presidency. John Adams's chief rival was George Clinton, Governor of New York by courtesy of seven canvassers. If Adams should be unseated as vice-president, King feared, it would be only a first step toward a thorough change of administration.[75] Jefferson and Madison, Burr

73. Hamilton to King, July 25, 1792, *ibid.*

74. King to Hamilton, July 29, 1792, *ibid.*; King to Gouverneur Morris, Sept. 1, 1792, Gouverneur Morris Papers, Columbia Univ. Lib. Though King believed that a majority of the people in the state disapproved of the canvassers' decision, he anticipated a Clintonian majority in the Assembly.

75. King suspected Burr as well as Clinton of angling for the vice-presidency, and he dreaded the prospect of a coalition of Republicans effected by Clinton, Burr, Dallas, and Jefferson. "If the enemies of the Government are secret and united we shall lose Mr. Adams," he wrote Hamilton, Sept. 17, 1792, Hamilton Papers, Lib. Cong.

in New York, and Alexander J. Dallas in Pennsylvania were already organizing the opposition. "Though we may be wearied with politicks, and disgusted with politicians," King wrote, Adams supporters must act to preserve government and order by checking the maneuvers to get rid of their man.[76] He was relieved when, on February 13, 1793, seventy-seven electors were found to have cast their ballots for Adams and only fifty for Clinton. Virginia's twenty-one electors, however, had voted solidly for Clinton, a dark prophesy for the future of Federalism. As expected, Washington was unanimously returned to the presidency, but the ship of state was heading into turbulent seas.

76. King to Jeremiah Wadsworth, Sept. 23, 1792, Wadsworth Papers, Box 141, Conn. Hist. Soc. Government and order were, of course, synonyms for Federalist administration. Cf. King to [probably] John Langdon, Sept. 30, 1792, King Papers, N.-Y. Hist. Soc., which alludes to Burr's ambitions.

CHAPTER X

NEUTRALITY AND GENÊT

WASHINGTON HAD HARDLY TAKEN THE OATH OF OFFICE AS PRESIDENT when France felt the first tremors of revolution. In defiance of King Louis XVI, the delegates of the Third Estate declared themselves the true representatives of the people, created a national assembly, and swore not to separate until they had given France a constitution. In July a mob stormed the Bastille, and peasants rioted on the estates of their landlords. During the summer, France was converted into a limited monarchy, as her untried leaders glimpsed the dawn of a new day for their country and for humanity.

Americans at first greeted the French Revolution enthusiastically. With French help, they had emerged from their own revolution as champions of liberty and foes of arbitrary government, and they saw in the events unfolding across the sea a salutary effect of their example. Lafayette, who had fought under Washington, was now a leader of the liberal monarchists in his native country and symbolized to Americans the spirit of a kindred people. Jefferson, having recently returned from his post in France to become Secretary of State, was eagerly sympathetic with the Revolution, and by the end of 1791 Madison was exulting that it had succeeded beyond the most sanguine hopes. President Washington followed the events in France with keen interest, if less enthusiasm. Hamilton, who in the first flush of excitement had told Jefferson that his heart was wholly with the French in their war against tyranny, soon became apprehensive that enthusiasts for popular rights would lead the people down the road to a worse despotism.[1]

If Rufus King shared in the delight that France had struck a blow for freedom, he gave no sign of it. His experience in public life placed him on the side of efficient and orderly government and support of legal processes, no matter how popular the agitation for change. His horror at mob violence, his prejudice against the French, and his awareness of the pro-French feelings of the Secretary of State contributed to his taking part in frustrating the hope of Jefferson's candidate, William Short, to succeed Jefferson as the American minister to France.

Early in 1792, King was instrumental in securing senatorial consent to the appointment of the able but controversial Gouverneur Morris to that post. Morris's distrust of democracy had been obvious to all at the Constitutional Convention, where King had come to know him. He was a sparkling conversationalist, with a lively imagination and great personal charm. Morris made no effort to hide his mistrust of popular causes. At the time Washington sent his name to the Senate, he was shuttling between Paris and London, having been abroad since 1789 on private business (including efforts to sell American lands and—on behalf of a syndicate of which he was a member—to buy up the American debt to France). Since John Adams had left England in 1788, all diplomatic relations between the United States and Great Britain had ceased, and early in 1790 the President had requested Morris to ascertain whether the British government intended to carry out unfulfilled terms of the Peace of Paris, whether it would agree to a commercial treaty, and if it would send a minister to the United States. Morris failed to accomplish his purpose in the face of the evasive maneuvers of the ministry, a fact held against him by his detractors in the Senate, who also charged him with levity, indiscretion, and haughtiness toward those who disagreed with him. In France, they pointed out, he was known as an aristocrat hostile to the Revolution, and therefore unsuitable to represent the United States. His defenders emphasized his ability and wide knowledge of public affairs and were able to effect confirmation by a vote of sixteen to eleven. Interpreting the opposition as simply a reaction to Morris's personal idiosyncracies, the President, who was friendly to the new Minister, gently warned him that it was "indispensably necessary that

1. Brant, *James Madison*, III, 372; Miller, *Alexander Hamilton*, 363–64.

more circumspection should be observed by our Representatives abroad than they conceive you are disposed to adopt."[2]

On the day he received his credentials, Morris thanked King for influencing the appointment and urged him to send timely news of conditions in the United States. King's letters, he wrote, would help him combat the opinions of "numerous Idlers, whose Pursuit of Knowledge rarely extends beyond a Newspaper Paragraph, who have more influence on national Councils than is generally imagined, and especially in France, where everything is talked of and hardly anything is understood." With partisan warmth, Morris poured out his feelings: "I think if you and I should chance to grow old and converse together, it will be no small Consolation to reflect that those Measures which have rendered our Country great and happy were carried in Spite of the Opposition of our Enemies whom we have pitied without Contempt tho they have hated without Cause."[3] He likewise wished to correspond with Hamilton, who probably had initially induced Washington to appoint him. Hamilton agreed to do so, and suggesting the use of a cipher, furnished a list of pseudonyms for administration officials, senators, and congressmen. King appeared as "Leonidas."[4]

The appointment of Morris proved unwise. It raised suspicions of factionalism at home, and in France the new Minister soon made himself *persona non grata.* To Jefferson he was a "high-flying monarchy man," who poisoned the President's mind.[5] The French government asked for his recall six months after his arrival, but Washington retained him until Edmond Genêt was dismissed in 1794.

When news of the storming of the Tuileries Palace and the September Massacres at Paris reached the United States at the end of 1792, many sympathizers began to waver; and when in April Americans learned that Louis XVI had lost his head on the guillotine and that France had declared war on Great Britain and Spain, a deep split occurred. Federalists, neither admirers of France nor proponents of popular revolution, openly expressed their hostility, while Jeffersonians continued to champion what they saw as humanity's cause.

2. George Washington to Gouverneur Morris, Jan. 28, 1792, in Beatrix Davenport, ed., *A Diary of the French Revolution by Gouverneur Morris*, 2 vols. (Boston, 1939), II, 401–02.

3. Gouverneur Morris to King, Apr. 6, 1792, King Papers, N.-Y. Hist. Soc.

4. Alexander Hamilton to Gouverneur Morris, June 22, 1792, in Davenport, ed., *Diary of the French Revolution by Gouverneur Morris*, II, 388–89.

5. Sawvel, ed., *Anas of Jefferson*, 69, entry for Mar. 12, 1792.

The new French declaration of war raised awkward questions of policy for the United States, which remained a formal ally. In the treaty of alliance of 1778, whereby France had openly supported the American Revolutionary cause, the United States had guaranteed France's possession of her West Indian islands and permitted her privateers to be equipped in American ports. If France should now demand it, how could Washington's administration honorably refuse to defend the French islands from almost certain assault by the British Navy? After consulting his divided Cabinet, the President proclaimed the neutrality of the United States, though in deference to Jefferson, who had hoped to bargain for concessions from England, the proclamation carefully omitted the word neutrality.

King, while favoring neutrality, was disturbed at the wording of the proclamation. "I could have wished to have seen in some part of it the word 'Neutrality' which every one would have understood," he complained to Hamilton whose defense of the administration's choice of wording did not wholly satisfy him.[6] The situation "will not, perhaps, justify us in saying 'the Treaties are void,' " the Senator replied, "and whether we may contend in favor of their suspension is a point of delicacy, and not quite free from doubt." With his usual prudence, however, King ended by urging caution and delay in applying the neutrality proclamation.[7] He also suggested that a report of Le Brun, the French Minister of Foreign Affairs, to the National Convention showing the bad faith of the monarchy towards the United States might be used as evidence that France herself had sabotaged the treaty. He pointed to an inconsistency between France's treaty commitments to England and to the United States, and asserted that a French violation of a single obligation "would give us the power to renounce the whole Treaty." After perusing American shipping laws, he concluded somewhat hesitantly that prizes brought into American ports by a belligerent could not be protected by the American flag, even though they might be owned by United States citizens.[8]

King's criticisms of France were balanced by a mild sympathy for England, which was strengthened by reports from masters of American ships arriving from the British Isles, of the complete exemption of American vessels from interference by the Royal Navy. From this situation, he wrote Hamilton, "we may make pretty certain infer-

6. King to Alexander Hamilton, Apr. 24, 1793, Hamilton Papers, Lib. Cong.
7. *Ibid.*
8. *Ibid.*

ences," and added, "I wish I could give assistance to the measures and maxims you will pursue. We must not become entangled with this mad war."[9]

The unpopularity of a neutral posture led King to take up his pen in support of the President. "If we are bound by Treaty to perform services to some, and to refuse them to other nations," he declared, "we hold the public faith and the national honor too precious to hesitate to perform our engagements. If on the other hand, we are altogether free from engagements of preference, the country at large cannot too early be informed that such is the case."[10] In defending the neutrality policy, King emphasized and undoubtedly exaggerated the influence of American commerce upon Europe:

> It cannot be for the interest of any of the maritime powers to disturb our repose, since our friendship is of importance to all of them. If we sought for proofs to satisfy us on this point, we have them in the conduct of Great Britain. No one who remembers the embarrassments to which our ships were subjected a few years since, when that power was arming against Spain, can fail being struck with the difference in their present conduct. The press is now as hot as at any former time. The American Navigation is exempt from search and our Flag receives its due and proper respect in the different parts of that dominion. We owe to England and to every other power with whom we have no Treaties friendship and impartiality—to those with whom we have Treaties, we owe the same friendship and impartiality, together with whatever else we are obliged to afford them.[11]

Examining the extent of American obligations to France, he admitted the value of French aid during the Revolutionary War but also noted that the dismemberment of the British Empire was "an event to which France could not have felt an entire indifference," and that subsequently France had been "uniformly and systematically" unfriendly to the growth of American power and prosperity. He saw no reason to abandon strict impartiality and warned against making "a love affair of the French Revolution, or [engaging] in war from an excess of sensibility and sentiment."[12]

The American guarantee of the French West Indies, King asserted,

9. *Ibid.*

10. Undated article written for publication, in King, ed., *King Correspondence*, I, 440–41. I have not found this article in print.

11. *Ibid.*, 441.

12. *Ibid.*, 444.

was a defensive one. As it had been made in order to effect the independence of the United States, the obligation might now be considered expired. But should the treaty still be operative, King insisted upon proof that France was not the aggressor in the present war. Even if the treaty were upheld, France's enemies commanded the seas, preventing defense of her island colonies and rendering "performance . . . impossible on our part." France would be wise to grant independence to her West Indies.[13]

King argued that if the American treaty with France were considered still in force, the United States would not, according to international law, violate its neutrality by denying British and Dutch ships the right to refit and bring prizes into its ports while at the same time opening them to the French.[14] He questioned France's intention to observe the terms of the treaty which favored the United States. By the spirit of the treaty, France ought to have helped the United States to obtain a share in the Newfoundland fisheries; but, he alleged, the French court had spared no measure to exclude the United States from them. France had also violated the spirit of the alliance, he asserted, by obstructing American claims to the east bank of the Mississippi. More specious was his insinuation that France should have helped drive the British out of the northwestern posts, which they still held after the Revolutionary War, because by the treaty France was bound to guarantee to the United States the possession of her entire territory. France, moreover, had signed with England a commercial treaty inconsistent with her treaty of commerce with the United States. Instructions of the French Crown affecting policy toward America, unearthed by the new republican government, made it appear that the National Convention wished to nullify the American treaty in the hope of obtaining more beneficial arrangements. Cautiously, King suggested that if France's lack of good faith had vitiated the treaty, the United States would be justified in renouncing it and declaring its impartiality toward the belligerents, and he hinted that the President might consider negotiating treaties with other nations. Above all, the United States must avoid being drawn into a bloody war of uncertain duration.[15]

Meanwhile, the new French Minister to the United States, Edmond

13. *Ibid.*
14. *Ibid.*, 445.
15. *Ibid.*, 446–48.

Genêt, had landed in Charleston, where he had received a tumultuous welcome, become a popular idol, and set about outfitting privateers to prey on British shipping. That the United States government had not yet officially received him in no way deterred Genêt from equipping privateers and sending them out to sea. At the time of the neutrality proclamation, he was on his way northward, attracting curious crowds eager to hear the loquacious representative of the new French republic.

In contrast to the civic fêtes accorded Genêt, the President determined on a policy of noninvolvement as he planned with his Cabinet Genêt's official reception. Hamilton asked King's advice, and the Senator told him that the government should "qualify" Genêt's reception, thus avoiding pressure to make premature commitments. As it turned out, King shared the opinion of Washington and Hamilton that America's official greeting should be cool, calm, correct, and no more.[16] In the middle of May, more than five weeks after his debarkation at Charleston, Genêt reached Philadelphia. When he presented his credentials as the French minister, the President received him with an icy formality which was unmistakable and in sharp contrast to the tumultuous ovations which had marked his trip from Charleston.

Undeterred by Washington's reception, Genêt recklessly flaunted his own interpretation of French rights in America. He enjoyed for a few weeks the confidence of the Secretary of State, and he basked in the warmth of popular pro-revolutionary enthusiasm, whipped up by Freneau's *National Gazette*, a paper which was supported by Jefferson and Madison but which was a thorn in the President's side. Washington refused to allow French prizes to be brought in for sale in American ports or to permit the outfitting of French privateers in these ports. Nevertheless Genêt arranged for the *Little Sarah*, a small English merchant vessel captured by the French frigate *L'Embuscade* and brought to Philadelphia as a prize, to be converted into a privateer renamed the *Petite Democrate*. To detain it without the use of force, Governor Mifflin of Pennsylvania sent Alexander J. Dallas, his secretary of state, to ask Genêt to hold the vessel in port. Genêt refused and denounced Washington as a dupe of anti-French advisers. Informed by Mifflin, Jefferson hurried to Genêt, who told

16. King to Alexander Hamilton, Apr. 24, 1793, Hamilton Papers, Lib. Cong.

the Secretary that the crew would resist the use of force but indicated that the ship was not yet ready to sail. Jefferson interpreted this as a promise that it would stay in port.[17]

The episode of the *Petite Democrate* led to Genêt's downfall. Hamilton and Secretary of War Knox had little faith in Genêt's word and urged the fortification of Mud Island in the Delaware River, which commanded the passage to the sea. Jefferson disagreed, and Washington decided against force. Although notified that he was not to allow that ship or others of similar status to depart, Genêt defied American policy, and the *Petite Democrate* slipped out to sea. This mockery of American neutrality determined the President to be rid of Genêt, and the Hamiltonians seized upon the details of the Frenchman's words and acts to turn popular feeling against him and the French alliance. King was actively engaged in the attack. He saw no reason for public protests against the Executive's actions and from New York warned Hamilton of the plans of Melancton Smith, Brockholst Livingston, and others for a huge meeting to welcome Genêt to the city. French warships had already sailed into the harbor, and two to three hundred opponents of the administration could be expected to greet their hero. "These gentlemen will not be stopped by Trifles," King asserted; "they already affirm that the Cause of France is that of America." If the Executive did not use his powers quickly and vigorously to check the influence of the French Minister it might be too late. Although the Chamber of Commerce planned a counter-demonstration in support of the neutrality proclamation, King believed it was wrong for a public gathering to assume such responsibility. "It was never intended that the executive should sit with folded arms, that the Government should be carried on by Town Meetings and those irregular measures which disorganize the Society, destroy the salutary influence of regular Government, and render the Magistracy a mere pageant."[18]

Even before this, rumors spread that Genêt would appeal to the people over the head of the President. Hamilton and Knox had heard second hand from Governor Mifflin that the French Minister had made such a statement to Dallas during a midnight interview over the detention of the *Petite Democrate*. Hamilton had imparted this explosive story to King and John Jay before they left Philadelphia

17. DeConde, *Entangling Alliance*, 218–19.
18. King to Alexander Hamilton, Aug. 3, 1793, Hamilton Papers, Lib. Cong.

for New York where the Senator and the Chief Justice circulated it among their friends. Rumors spread like a contagion, raising eyebrows of incredulous or outraged listeners.[19] Asked by certain skeptics whether the rumors were true, Jay and King at the proper moment vouched for their authenticity. On August 12 a "card" appeared in the *Diary*, a New York newspaper:

FOR THE DIARY.

Messrs. PRINTERS,

CERTAIN late publications render it proper for us to authorize you to inform the Public, that a report having reached this City from Philadelphia, that Mr. Genet, the French Minister, had said he would Appeal to the People from certain decisions of the President; we were asked, on our return from that place, whether he had made such a declaration—we answered, THAT HE HAD, and we also mentioned it to others, authorising them to say that we had so informed them.

JOHN JAY,
RUFUS KING.[20]

New York, August 12

Widely reprinted in Federalist newspapers, this certificate had a devastating effect upon Genêt's adherents, who melted away in awed silence.[21] A few, like Monroe, considered it a trick which would recoil upon its authors, but any such hopes were ultimately disappointed.[22] The issue of the French alliance had been effectively personalized: it was Genêt versus Washington. To counter the strategy of Hamilton, Knox, Jay, and King, a few Republican papers and some members of the democratic societies denounced the "certificate men"

19. Maude H. Woodfin, Citizen Gênet and his Mission (unpubl. Ph.D. diss., University of Chicago, 1928), 364; DeConde, *Entangling Alliance*, 285–86.

20. New York *Diary or Loudon's Register*, Aug. 12, 1793, as quoted in full in *Historical Magazine*, 10 (1866), 329, and in King, ed., *King Correspondence*, I, 459. Cf. Rufus King's manuscript endorsed: "Certificate tendered to Mr. Denning to sign," Nov. 8, 1793, King Papers, N.-Y. Hist. Soc.

21. On July 31 Hamilton himself, writing as "No Jacobin" in Dunlap's N. Y. *Daily Advertiser*, mentioned Genêt's threat. The "No Jacobin" articles, appearing from July 31 to Aug. 23, were later reprinted in the Phila. *Gazette of the U. S.* As the President's Cabinet agreed on Aug. 1–2 to ask for Gênet's recall, it is obvious that Hamilton was playing politics; it is probable that Hamilton had not informed Jay and King of the Cabinet decision when they published their certificate.

22. James Monroe to Thomas Jefferson, Sept. 3, 1793, cited by DeConde, *Entangling Alliance*, 290.

as actors in a Federalist plot to undermine the French alliance and ruin Genêt. The French Minister himself came to believe that the certificate was part of the administration's plan to replace the French alliance with a British one.[23] Furious, Republicans demanded proof of the charge against Genêt. In the issue of the *Diary* containing their certificate, a writer, calling himself "Impartial," had pointed out that Jay and King had mentioned neither time, place, manner, nor the occasion of Genêt's alleged utterance, and he called for the evidence.[24]

King asked Hamilton for details, and the Secretary responded with a long letter, underscoring certain passages for the Senator to use as he saw fit, the remainder to be revealed confidentially to "persons whose discretion may be relied on, and whose knowledge of it may be useful." Hamilton concluded, "I am of opinion with you, that the charge ought to be insisted upon."[25] In another letter, the Secretary assured King that he and General Knox would come forward as witnesses if it should prove necessary, as indeed it did.[26] Jay and King decided to publish the underscored parts of Hamilton's account of the Genêt affair as the framework of a new statement stressing that since Dallas's authority to interview Genêt had been derived from Washington, the Frenchman was therefore flouting the President. On December 2, the *Daily Advertiser* printed a small "extra," containing a long explanation by Jay and King of the circumstances of Genêt's threat. This account, based on Hamilton's letter, gave the full story and was followed by a certificate of Hamilton and Knox that they had supplied the information and that it was from the Secretary of State that they had learned of Genêt's incendiary statement to Dallas.[27]

In introducing the sequence of events, the New Yorkers played loudly on the patriotic motif:

> When at Philadelphia, in July last, we frequently heard that Mr. Genet the French Minister, had on a certain occasion said "that he would appeal from the President to the People"—an appeal by a foreign minister from the President to the People

23. G. C. Genêt, *Washington, Jefferson, and "Citizen" Genêt, 1793* (N. Y., 1899), 28, cited by DeConde, *Entangling Alliance*, 287*n*.
24. Cf. "Philo-Impartial," in the N. Y. *Daily Advertiser*, Aug. 14, 17, 1793.
25. Hamilton to King, Aug. 13, 1793, Hamilton Papers, Lib. Cong.
26. Hamilton to King, Aug. (n.d.) 1793, *ibid*.
27. Supplement to the N. Y. *Daily Advertiser*, Dec. 2, 1793. A copy is in the file of the N.-Y. Hist. Soc. King, ed., *King Correspondence*, I, 458–62, reprints it.

> appeared to us as a serious and alarming measure: that a foreign minister, finding it impossible to bend the government to his purposes, should turn from it with disdain to the Citizens at large, and before them impeach the wisdom or virtue of the administration, would be a proceeding evidently and necessarily productive of parties, practices, and intrigues highly detrimental to the peace and independence of the country, and in a variety of respects offensive to the dignity and sovereignty of the nation, as well as humiliating and injurious to its constituted authorities.
>
> We left that city well convinced that Mr. Genet had made such a declaration. On our return to New York, we found a report of that declaration had preceded us, and that it made the same impression upon others that it had made upon us. We were asked whether it was true. We answered that it was. To many, a declaration so extraordinary did not appear probable, and our having asserted it to be true was questioned. We were called upon in the public papers to admit or deny that we had made such an assertion. That call merited attention.[28]

Jay and King explained somewhat disingenuously that their original certificate had been intended as an assertion of fact and not a public charge against Genêt. Now the situation was different. Hamilton and Knox had implicated Dallas, Governor Mifflin, and Jefferson, all Republicans. Much to the discomfiture of King and Jay, however, the Secretary of State kept discreetly silent. Ever since June, Jefferson had been growing more impatient with the French Minister. As the administration had asked for Genêt's recall early in August, the Secretary of State saw only harm in prolonging the controversy—harm both to the country and to the Republicans.[29] By refusing to confirm the Hamilton-Knox statement, Jefferson and Mifflin avoided playing into the hands of the Federalists; regarding Genêt as a liability, and wishing to be rid of him, they feared any move which might injure the French alliance or their political following.[30] Dallas denied that Genêt had made the alleged declaration and complained that Hamil-

28. *Ibid.* Punctuation has been changed slightly for the sake of clarity.

29. Dumas Malone, *Jefferson and His Time*, 3 vols. (Boston, 1948–62), III, 123, though sympathetic toward the Secretary of State, admits that patriotic and partisan motives were intertwined.

30. DeConde, *Entangling Alliance*, 292–93. Jefferson acknowledged privately that Dallas had informed him that the French Minister had made the threat. For Jay's complaint about Jefferson, see Jay to King, Dec. 19, 1793, King Papers, N.-Y. Hist. Soc.

ton, Knox, Jay, and King had, without consultation or permission, publicized his official and confidential communications to Mifflin and Jefferson.[31]

"Whatever Mr. Dallas' statement of the interview in question be supposed to prove," King rejoined, "it will by no means disprove his former declaration that Mr. Genêt had said that he would appeal from the President to the People." Writing in the *American Minerva*, King compared Jefferson's report to the President (recording Dallas's remarks on Genêt's threat) with Dallas's later denial in order to show the latter's "apostacy." Jefferson's account, the Senator explained, "is contemporary with the transaction which it relates; it is from an authority of the greatest truth and precision; and moreover instead of a mere distant recollection, is part of a report made in the course of official duty and under the obligation of an oath." Dallas had visited Genêt in New York months later, King pointed out, and it was only after this interview that he had backed the Minister's denial of a threat to appeal over the President's head.[32]

Although satisfied that Dallas's "Jesuitical publication" had been ably contradicted, King's friends were uneasy over the continued silence of Jefferson and Mifflin. Jay and Judge Egbert Benson thought the Secretary of State and the Pennsylvania Governor should be forced to state the facts.[33]

They had good reason to worry, for Genêt meanwhile sought to have King and Jay prosecuted for libel. At his request, a copy of his letter to Attorney-General Randolph asking for the prosecution was laid before the President by Jefferson, who afterward equivocally informed Randolph that Washington recommended legal action, especially as it concerned "a public character peculiarly entitled to the protection of the laws," but on the other hand, "as our citizens ought not to be vexed with groundless prosecutions," this recom-

31. Dallas's statement to the public, dated Dec. 7, 1793, is reprinted in King, ed., *King Correspondence*, I, 464–69. In the words of his biographer, Dallas's statement was "foggily legalistic." Raymond Walters, Jr., *Alexander James Dallas: Lawyer, Politician, Financier, 1759–1817* (Phila., 1943), 49.

32. N. Y. *American Minerva*, Dec. 11, 1793, reprinted in King, ed., *King Correspondence*, I, 462–64. King relied on Hamilton's summary of Jefferson's report.

33. Herman Le Roy to King, Dec. 15, 1793, Jay to King, Dec. 12, 1793, Benson to King, Dec. 18, 1793, King Papers, N.-Y. Hist. Soc. Mrs. King, fretting in New York City over her husband's exposure to public gaze in Philadelphia, wished him to move from the City Tavern to a more secluded private house. John Alsop to King, Dec. 12, 1793, *ibid.*

mendation should not apply if the Attorney-General considered it inapplicable.[34]

When they learned of this, Jay and King were incensed. The President, it seemed, had yielded to the Secretary of State, whom they considered partisan, and would be a party to a vendetta against patriotic citizens. Jefferson's letter, with the apparent approval of the Chief Executive, "authorised inferences unfavorable to our characters," the New York Senator concluded.[35] He and Jay wrote to the President, complaining of the action taken in his name, and asked him to direct Jefferson to give them a certified copy of his report to the President concerning his interview with Dallas. They asked Washington's permission to publish the document. Thus the issue was joined.

Randolph, who like Jefferson had been castigated in the Jay-King letter, tried to induce the President to justify his and the Secretary's conduct. Hamilton advised Washington to send Jay and King the document they wished but without acknowledging their imputation of injustice. Knox, seeking to avoid a showdown, wanted to bury the matter quietly: let Jay and King take back their letter and propose a personal interview with the President "to heal the wound inflicted by the letter." This the New Yorkers refused to do, but they offered to discuss the issue with the President if *he* invited them.

Accordingly, Washington invited them, and the two irritated dignitaries unburdened themselves. In defending his conduct, the President spoke of the difficulty of his situation and of his need for "great caution"; Jefferson and Randolph, he contended, had meant nothing "incorrect or unfriendly," and he complained of the severity of the letter Jay and King had sent him. Jay, stressing his and King's disinterested patriotism, asserted their claim to "the full Force and disclosure of those Truths which would justify us in the presence of our fellow citizens." Now that Genêt had tried to use the administration to humiliate them, said Jay, they did not expect to see the facts suppressed or misrepresented. Washington tried to smooth Jay's feelings, expressing his friendship for him and his respect and regard for King. Jay then suggested that the President furnish him and King

34. Jefferson to Edmund Randolph, Dec. 18, 1793, reprinted in King, ed., *King Correspondence*, I, 476.

35. Statement in King's hand, Dec. 18, 1793, King Papers, N.-Y. Hist. Soc. Reprinted in King, ed., *King Correspondence*, I, 476. This statement is the basis of this and subsequent paragraphs.

with a copy of Jefferson's report—or at least the portion relating to Genêt's threat; in return, he and King would turn over the original draft of their letter to the President. Washington agreed.

A few days later King called on the President and handed him the original Jay-King letter. Washington then produced a written defense of his conduct, and gave it to King to read. The Senator returned it, and the President gravely threw both documents into the fire; several days later he sealed the bargain by giving King the promised extract of Jefferson's report.[36]

As for Genêt, it soon became apparent that if he were sent home, as his newly arrived replacement, Fauchet, demanded, he would be guillotined. The President, with the support of his Cabinet, dismissed Genêt, who was given asylum in America. Genêt settled down and married a daughter of Governor Clinton but still denied that he had threatened an appeal to the people in his nocturnal rendezvous with Dallas.[37] He dropped his proposed lawsuit against Jay and King, and Fauchet made clear that he would not resume it. So ended the painful quarrel. King and Jay felt personally vindicated, Washington had made his peace with them, and the Federalists had successfully exploited the advantage that Genêt and the pro-French enthusiasts had presented them.

The political animosities stirred up by Genêt flared again late in February 1794, in the debate over Albert Gallatin's eligibility to sit in the United States Senate. Although the Pennsylvania legislature had elected Gallatin to the Senate, Federalist senators questioned his right to a seat on the ground that, as an immigrant, he had not been a citizen of the United States for the nine years required by the Constitution. A native of Switzerland, Gallatin had arrived in America in 1780 at the age of nineteen, and had lived in Massachusetts, Virginia, and Pennsylvania. He did not, however, take an oath of allegiance until 1785. His supporters claimed that, as a minor who had arrived during the Revolution, he had acquired state citizenship, and that under the Articles of Confederation an inhabitant of a state was entitled to all the privileges of a citizen in another state.

36. King, ed., *King Correspondence*, I, 478; DeConde, *Entangling Alliance*, 296.

37. The Cabinet had been divided on how Genêt should be dismissed; Knox and Hamilton—the latter after conferring with King and others—advised the President to dismiss Genêt without any reference to Congress. This the President did. As late as 1823, Genêt maintained his innocence. *Albany Argus*, Sept. 29, 1823, cited by DeConde, *Entangling Alliance*, 296*n*.

Rufus King, mindful of Federalist interests and suspicious of the influence of continental Europeans upon American life, led the attack against Gallatin's right to be a senator. His arguments interpreted strictly the legal requirements for citizenship in a state, and he asserted that if Gallatin's claim were allowed, all persons who happened to have been in the United States before the adoption of the Constitution would automatically have become American citizens: "The weary Traveller in his first slumber, and while he still fondly dreamed of his beloved home, was changed, and although he slept a Briton he awoke an American citizen. The magic is so pleasing that one could almost wish the Dream was real."[38]

Though the discussion centered upon technicalities, nobody doubted that the real contest was political. Having helped the Pennsylvania Republicans in the election of 1792, and having recently married a daughter of James Nicholson, a New York Republican leader, Gallatin had gained the reputation of an uncompromising opponent of the administration. He had criticized Hamilton's financial measures on the floor of the Pennsylvania Assembly, had cooperated with Alexander J. Dallas and other Republican politicians, and had helped to draw up resolutions denouncing the whiskey tax. With his keen understanding of fiscal affairs, Republicans counted upon him to carry through a Senate investigation of Hamilton's management of the treasury. Federalists recognized in him a dangerous antagonist and Gallatin knew that the outcome of his case would be determined strictly by party considerations. Although the Federalists held a slender majority, he hoped for a tie which might be broken in his favor by the conscientious Vice-President.[39] Aaron Burr, whose political shifts had already alienated some of his former friends, championed the Swiss immigrant, as did Taylor and Monroe of Virginia, while Ellsworth and Strong, among other Federalists, agreed with King in opposing Gallatin's claim.

The debate attracted more attention than usual, for it was the first open to the public. After a full week of rhetoric, Vice-President Adams wrote that "a great impression had been made upon the public by the learning, eloquence, and reasoning of some of the senators." The Senate, by a partisan vote of fourteen to twelve, denied Gallatin

38. King, ed., *King Correspondence*, I, 535. This volume reproduces King's notes of his speech. The manuscript is in the King Papers, N.-Y. Hist. Soc.

39. Raymond Walters, Jr., *Albert Gallatin, Jeffersonian Financier and Diplomat* (N. Y., 1957), ch. 5 *passim.*

his seat. Accepting the result, Adams wondered whether American conditions had not degenerated to a point where "popularity was more courted than truth."[40]

40. John Adams to Abigail Adams, Mar. 2, 1794, in C. F. Adams, ed., *Letters of John Adams, Addressed to His Wife*, 2 vols. (Boston, 1841), II, 145. On this as on previous occasions, King had voted to open the doors of the Senate. King, ed., *King Correspondence*, I, 539. Many years later, on June 30, 1826, Gallatin wrote to the editors of the Washington, D. C. *National Intelligencer* that he had always regarded the question of his eligibility as doubtful and had never found fault with those who opposed him. "In fact," he asserted, "the doubt arose within myself, and I stated publicly the objection which might be raised when I was first put in nomination. . . . Had I been silent no opposition would have taken place." Gallatin Papers, Lib. Cong.

CHAPTER XI

KING AND JAY'S TREATY

EVEN AS THE CONFLICT OVER ALBERT GALLATIN REACHED ITS CLIMAX, ominous news of British attacks upon American shipping on a massive scale reached Philadelphia. Britain had loosed her naval power to prey upon American trade with the French West Indies. News of ship seizures, of American crews thrown into prison, and of confiscation of American property aroused a tide of anger that swept from New England to Georgia, and Madison introduced in the House resolutions calling for retaliation: higher tonnage taxes on ships of countries having no commercial treaty with the United States and port restrictions on the shipping of nations whose ports discriminated against American vessels.[1] Reports that the Governor-General of Canada, in a provocative speech to western Indians, had predicted war between Britain and the United States brought American resentment to the boiling point.

Federalists were in a quandary. They did not want war, yet they thought Madison's resolutions would invite war without adequate preparations for defense. While hoping that Britain would relax her maritime policy, they joined the growing clamor for defense measures. Prepared for the worst, King advocated stronger harbor defenses, the equipping of stout frigates, the raising of an army, and the levying of extra taxes. Only through strength could the United States compel respect for its maritime rights.[2] He tried to secure the ap-

1. Brant, *James Madison*, III, 389.
2. King to Christopher Gore, Mar. 10, 1794, King Papers, N.-Y. Hist. Soc.

pointment of a reliable Federalist to superintend the construction of at least one frigate at New York—a job, he felt, that should not be directed by anyone who did not have "that faithful regard to order and good government so indispensable at this Period of revolution and Change."[3]

At local rallies and in legislative halls, alarmed citizens demanded quick action. Aroused Federalists joined with Republicans in a surge of patriotic feeling, though the cooperation was painful to some. "I am to sup with a set of Jacobins at the large house opposite me this Evening," grumbled one rich broker, "and I would almost as leave be whipped as go."[4] As King anticipated, a House bill to construct a navy was approved by the Senate without much opposition. King served on a Senate committee that examined a bill to strengthen harbor defenses, which was quickly passed.[5] The House authorized a large appropriation for the army, and Madison's relatively mild "restrictive" resolutions were scrapped, as both houses approved a thirty-day embargo, regarded by the Federalists as at least preferable to continued British confiscation of American cargoes. England might regain her senses if her lucrative American commerce were checked, and hundreds of idle ships might have a less risky future.[6]

King wished to avert a break with England and resented having to flow with the Republican tide toward war. At his Philadelphia lodgings on March 10, he, Ellsworth, Cabot, and Strong delegated Ellsworth to urge upon President Washington the need to calm the public, while at the same time proposing vigorous defense measures and the appointment of an agent to the West Indies to assess American shipping losses and assist aggrieved merchants and seamen. Ellsworth was to suggest that the President send a special envoy to England to adjust the differences between the two countries while pointing to either Hamilton or Jay as ideal for such a mission. As agreed, Ellsworth recommended Hamilton to the President, who admitted doubts that Hamilton had the confidence of the country and refused to commit himself.[7] Meanwhile, King got Robert Morris to

3. King to [probably James Watson of Albany], Mar. 14, 1794, Long Island Coll., Queens Borough Pub. Lib. For Watson's refusal, see his letter to King, Mar. 22, 1794, King Papers, N.-Y. Hist. Soc.

4. Herman Le Roy to King, Feb. 28, 1794, King Papers, N.-Y. Hist. Soc.

5. King to [James Watson], Mar. 14, 1794, Long Island Coll., Queens Borough Pub. Lib.; *Annals*, 3 Cong., 1 sess., 70, 71, 485–98, 499, Mar. 10, 12, 17, 19, 1794.

6. *Ibid.*, 504, Mar. 13, 1794.

7. King, ed., *King Correspondence*, I. 517–18; James Monroe to Thomas Jefferson, Mar. 4, 1794, Jefferson Papers, Lib. Cong.

support the mission to England, and when asked by Washington, Morris spoke decidedly in favor of Hamilton.[8] For a long time, Hamilton had seen the need for the mission, but in view of his own political unpopularity, he wrote to the President proposing Jay.[9]

King, as well as Hamilton, saw that there would be less opposition to Jay's appointment. When the Chief Justice arrived in Philadelphia for circuit court duty, he visited King, who informed him that the Federalists insisted on him or Hamilton. The Secretary of the Treasury had an intimate knowledge of Cabinet affairs and of commerce, said King, but Jay had the advantage of "weight of character abroad as well as at home"; besides, Hamilton was essential at his present post.[10]

When Washington offered him the mission, Jay demurred, fearing that resolutions before the House to cut off British imports and sequester British debts would render the mission futile, but on April 15, a determined team consisting of Hamilton, King, Cabot, Strong, and Ellsworth visited the reluctant Chief Justice and pressured him to take the appointment. The next day, Jay told the President he would accept. On April 20, by vote of eighteen to eight, the Senate concurred in his nomination as envoy extraordinary to London.[11] A few days later Jay urged King to accompany him, but tempting as it seemed, both family affairs and the slim margin of Federalist preponderance in the Senate caused him to refuse.[12]

8. Without committing himself to Morris, Washington invited Jay to dinner that evening. John A. Carroll and Mary W. Ashworth, *George Washington*, VII, 166.

9. For the elements entering into Hamilton's decision, see Broadus Mitchell, *Alexander Hamilton*, 2 vols. (N. Y., 1957–62), II, 335.

10. King's manuscript relating to events from Mar. 10 to Apr. 21, 1794, King Papers, N.-Y. Hist. Soc. Printed in King, ed., *King Correspondence*, I, 517–23.

11. King, ed., *King Correspondence*, I, 520–22. The day after his confirmation, Jay discussed his mission with Hamilton, King, Ellsworth, and Cabot. They agreed that the President need not consult the Senate in drafting the envoy's instructions, and that any treaty secured by Jay should be signed, subject to later Senate approval. Reviewing all the outstanding points of dispute between Great Britain and the United States, they agreed that if the British fulfilled the terms of the treaty of 1783 and paid compensation for the capture of American vessels, the United States might allow the British up to half a million pounds sterling for losses due to non-payment of pre-Revolutionary debts. *Ibid.*, 523.

12. John Jay to King, Apr. 29, 1794, King Papers, N.-Y. Hist. Soc.; King to Jay, May 2, 1794, Jay Papers, Columbia Univ. Lib. King informed Jay in this letter that Chancellor Livingston was a likely contender to replace Gouverneur Morris, whose recall France had requested. Livingston had joined the Republicans. Should he be opposed? Jay's somewhat equivocal reply raised the question of Livingston's successor as chancellor; King would be a good choice. Jay to King, May 3, 1794, King Papers, N.-Y. Hist. Soc.

King earnestly tried in his own way to promote mutual understanding between the United States and Great Britain. On April 7 he conferred with George Hammond, the British Minister, on the differences between the two nations. Hammond maintained that Americans had no true complaint until British appeals courts had decided upon their claims, and King countered that the large number and peculiar nature of the cases, considered in the light of official British orders, demanded compensation. The Minister replied that his government would not agree to this, but King persisted, calling it a small matter in view of the larger issue of restoring good relations.[13]

As volunteers worked on fortifications and wondered whether war would break out, party spirit gripped America. On the floor of the Senate, the humorless John Taylor of Caroline burst out in denunciation of the "mild and supplicating course" taken by the United States and demanded that Britain be made to adhere to its treaty obligations. Before seeking redress for ship seizures, he fumed, the United States should settle old scores with the British: compensation for slaves carried off in the Revolutionary War and the continued retention of the Northwest posts. Moreover, Jay's mission promised to sacrifice the welfare of the South to the interests of northern merchants.[14]

A few days after Taylor's tirade, King invited him into the privacy of a Senate committee room and gravely raised the question of dissolving the Union. It was utterly impossible, he said, for the Union to continue: the South and the North had never agreed, and the South had hindered every operation of government. Whenever the South Carolina legislature replaced Federalists Izard and Smith in the Senate, the southern factionalists would dominate the federal government, and northerners would never submit. A separa-

13. King, ed., *King Correspondence*, I, 523–25. Saying that he was pleased that the President planned to send an envoy to England, Hammond remarked that he had already informed Lord Grenville, the British Foreign Secretary, that the probable emissary would be Jay, Hamilton, or King. *Ibid.*, 525. All three were well-known Anglophiles, and Hammond was on friendly terms with Hamilton and probably King. King's pro-British perspective is incidentally mentioned in Joseph Charles, "The Jay Treaty: the Origins of the American Party System," *Wm. and Mary Qtly.*, 3d Ser., 12 (1955), 623–24.

14. King's notes: In Senate, May 6, 1794, King Papers, N.-Y. Hist. Soc. Taylor and Monroe were the only senators who voted to present a bill suspending the fourth article of the Peace of Paris (which aimed to prevent impediments to the recovery of debts). Many Republicans were conveniently absent when the roll was called. *Ibid.*

tion by mutual consent would be preferable to the use of force. In the midst of their discussion, Oliver Ellsworth entered the room—Taylor thought by prearrangement. King repeated what he had said, Ellsworth concurring, and then suggested that Congress work out a plan to divide the Union. Shocked, Taylor rejoined that opposing interests could be reconciled if the parties would shed their mutual suspicions. The public debt, he asserted, was the main cause of division, because the Federalists were suspected of wishing to use it as a political machine instead of reducing it or paying it off. Would not suspicion be allayed if the army and its supporting taxes were decreased while proceeds from the sale of public land were applied to paying off the debt? King objected that such differences of opinion were not the only questions which divided the country. North and South never had and never would think alike. As for himself, King would consent to a decrease in the army after a year, but he would not approve of a land office. Moreover, he suspected Madison of harboring mischievous plans, but when Taylor pressed him for details, he refused to elaborate. The only solution to irreconcilable political differences, he repeated, would be severance of the Union. On this sharp note the interview ended.[15]

King's suggestion that the Union be dissolved deeply impressed Taylor. An early opponent of the Constitution, he had accepted the logic of events and had emerged as a spokesman for the agrarian South against centralized government and Hamiltonian finance, but he was not prepared to hear northern Federalists talk of a separation at the Hudson, the Delaware, or the Potomac. Aghast, he suspected even more than King and Ellsworth told him—that a "British interest" lurked behind their behavior, that Britain and the North might join forces to defeat southern interests. He wrote a confidential memorandum of the conversation and sent it to his friend Madison, now the leader of the Republicans in the House, who was less impressed and later appended these words: "The language of K. and E. probably in terrorem."[16]

Madison was right. Although Taylor suspected King and Ellsworth

15. Memorandum by John Taylor, dated May 11, 1794, John Taylor of Caroline, *Disunion Sentiment in Congress in 1794 . . .*, ed. Gaillard Hunt (Washington, 1905), *passim.* Taylor had published in 1793 a pamphlet attacking Hamilton's fiscal measures and claiming that the moneyed interests dominated Congress.

16. *Ibid.*, introduction, 13.

of plotting disunion, the two northern men had deliberately tried to frighten the Virginia Senator into a more pliable stance. Taylor's influence and important connections in Virginia, as well as his closeness to Madison and Monroe, might foster a conciliatory spirit among southern Republicans. If the two northern senators seriously contemplated a breakup of the Union, there is no corroborating evidence, and King's later consistent support of the Union suggests that in 1794 he was simply using the threat of separation as a drastic political tactic.[17]

During the summer and autumn of 1794, the aroused farmers of western Pennsylvania, still smarting under the excise tax, gathered again to prevent its enforcement. Alarmed, the President called out fifteen thousand militia from four states and, when negotiations with the "whiskey rebels" broke down, ordered the insurrection suppressed. "This business must not be skinned over," Hamilton wrote to King. "The political putrefaction of Pennsylvania is greater than I had any idea of. Without vigour everywhere our tranquillity is likely to be of very short duration, and the next storm will be infinitely worse than the present one."[18] Like the Secretary of the Treasury, King feared the worst and urged that troops be kept indefinitely in the disaffected area to "discourage future opposition to the Laws, and countenance good men in Supporting them."[19]

When Congress convened in November 1794, King, Ellsworth, and Izard drafted a formal reply to President Washington's opening address, in which they alleged that overt resistance to the law had been fostered by "certain self-created societies relative to the laws and administration of the Government," whose proceedings were "founded in political error, calculated, if not intended, to disorganize our Government, and which, by inspiring delusive hopes of support,

17. Gaillard Hunt thought Madison's interpretation of the Taylor interview was correct but also considered it "impossible to escape the conclusion that King and Ellsworth were at this time seriously thinking of the desirability of breaking up the Union." He noted their close political cooperation with George Cabot and Caleb Strong, two New Englanders who, during the War of 1812, "stood in the front line of the disunion forces." *Ibid.*, introduction, 14. It might be pointed out that King cooperated politically with Federalists of varying viewpoints, and although he remained friendly with Cabot and Strong, he never abetted New England separatism after his conversion by early 1787 to Hamiltonian Federalism.

18. Alexander Hamilton to King, Oct. 30, 1794, King Papers, N.-Y. Hist. Soc.

19. King to Cyrus King, Nov. 8, 1794, copied in 1933 by James G. King from the original in the possession of the late Moses Hale Douglass of Brandon, Vt.

have been influential in the scene of insurrection."[20] The Senate went on record as approving the President's action.

A few days later, King's ailing father-in-law, John Alsop, died at the age of seventy. Earlier in the year, Alsop had hoped King would resign from the Senate, return to a more normal family life in New York, and devote himself wholly to managing their finances.[21] When Alsop died on November 22 King hastened to New York. Mrs. King "required all my Consolation," he wrote to his half-brother Cyrus after the funeral. "You knew the singular worth of this good man, and can feel our loss."[22]

John Alsop left no will, and it fell to King to administer a substantial estate, much of it in real property and in bonds secured by mortgages. As administrator, King took on the irksome duty of collecting debts due his father-in-law and was as vexed as Alsop had been at the slowness of debtors to pay.[23] His father-in-law's mortgages and government securities substantially enhanced King's fortune.[24] In the previous three or four years he had amassed wealth by shrewd and cautious investment in real estate and personal loans, and by the appreciation of his holdings in the New York state debt, assumed at face value by the federal government under Hamilton's funding program.[25]

King could have resigned from the Senate without financial worry, but he was both conscientious and interested in public affairs, and as he returned to his lodging house in Philadelphia, he was already looking beyond the three months that remained of his term in the Senate.[26] Philip Schuyler, who had been sorely disappointed when

20. Aaron Burr failed in an attempt to have this portion of the response expunged. The Senate address, which probably was drafted by King, may be found in King, ed., *King Correspondence*, I, 578–80.

21. John Alsop to King, Mar. 12, 1794, King Papers, N.-Y. Hist. Soc.

22. King to Cyrus King, Nov. 27, 1794, owned by James G. King of New York. It is uncertain whether King was in Philadelphia or had reached the family home in New York before Alsop died.

23. Letterbook of John Alsop, King Papers, Vol. 69, *passim*, N.-Y. Hist. Soc. Alsop claimed to have lost half of his property during the Revolutionary War, yet he retained a considerable fortune as long as he lived.

24. King Papers, Vol. 37, *passim*, *ibid.*

25. During 1792, King had more than $10,000 worth of 6 per cent stock under the Treasury Department loan of 1790. Ledger A, 1797–1835, Vol. 22, New York, Folio 14, Record Group 53, "Old Loans" Records of the Bureau of the Public Debt, National Archives. A few weeks before Alsop died, King loaned Robert Troup $5,000. Troup to King, Oct. 4, Nov. 7, 1794, King Papers, N.-Y. Hist. Soc.

26. King was staying at Mrs. Williams's. See John Alsop to King, Nov. 11, 1794, King Papers, N.-Y. Hist. Soc.

Burr had been elected to succeed him in that body, thought it essential to keep King at the focus of power, and the New York Federalists were determined to secure his reappointment. "We have reason to conclude that success will attend our endeavours for the reappointment of Mr. King," the General wrote to Hamilton. "We shall however keep a close attention to the object as we have to do with wiley adversaries."[27] The Clintonians spared no pains to frustrate their efforts, but on January 27 the legislature re-elected the Federalist Senator, by a majority of five in the Assembly and two in the state Senate over Thomas Tillotson, brother-in-law of Chancellor Livingston.[28] "This is a great point gained," wrote Vice-President Adams.[29] Although gratified, King bared his deeper feeling to his old friend Gore: "Without affectation I can say to you that I am wearied with this kind of life, which has nothing new to afford me, and which demands of me sacrifices that I become daily more unwilling to make."[30]

Hamilton needed his sturdy supporter in the Senate. Shortly before resigning from the treasury, he had proposed paying off the federal debt without resorting to new sources of revenue. When Congress rejected his recommendation of payments to those creditors who had not converted their securities under the funding plan, Hamilton, now out of office, fumed at this "unnecessary, capricious and abominable assassination of the National honor." "I conjure you, my friend," he wrote King, "make a vigorous stand for the honor of your country. Rouse all the energies of your mind, and measure swords in the Senate with the great Slayer of public faith, the hacknied *Veteran* in the *violation* of public engagements," an allusion to Burr who had helped to throw out the Otsego returns that would have made Jay the governor of New York in 1792.[31]

A call to battle against Burr had special meaning at this time, for plans were already advanced to name the Republican Senator governor at the spring election. If Van Gaasbeek, King's Federalist lieutenant at Kingston, was correct, Burr's supporters would switch

27. Philip Schuyler to Alexander Hamilton, Jan. 5, 1795, Hamilton Papers, 2d Ser., Lib. Cong. This letter is misdated 1794.

28. King, ed., *King Correspondence*, II, 1–3, which states the majorities incorrectly; N. Y. *American Minerva*, Jan. 27, Feb. 10, 1795.

29. Adams, ed., *Letters of John Adams to his Wife*, II, 175.

30. King to Christopher Gore, Feb. 14, 1795, King Papers, N.-Y. Hist. Soc. Cf. King to Alexander Hamilton, May 2, 1796, Hamilton Papers, Lib. Cong.

31. Alexander Hamilton to King, Feb. 21, 1795, King Papers, Vol. 28, N.-Y. Hist. Soc.

to Jay, if the Chief Justice returned in time from England and if Burr himself decided not to run.[32] Burr spread the opinion that Jay would not return before the election, that it would be folly to run him *in absentia*, and that it was doubtful that he could win.[33] Hamilton, who had emphatically declined to enter the race, came out decidedly for Jay, as did King.[34]

Early in March, King reached New York City and at once plunged into the campaign for Jay's election. Clinton, in the face of sharp divisions, had at last eliminated himself. While Burr had support in both camps, the majority of Republicans nominated Judge Robert Yates. Although Yates was popular, Jay enjoyed the sympathy of many New Yorkers who thought of him as the rightful governor who had been cheated out of his office three years before. If Jay remained in England too long, however, his chances might evaporate, and King moved to scotch rumors that the Chief Justice would long be absent and contradicted false stories of the terms of his newly negotiated treaty. To the trusted Van Gaasbeek, King let it be known that the articles of Jay's Treaty would be kept secret until the Senate met in June, well beyond the April elections.[35] Federalists assiduously spread the word that the Chief Justice would soon return, though they were painfully aware that every day without him meant votes for Yates.[36] Jay was still out of the state when the voters went to the polls. On May 26, he was declared the winner, and two days later, after a year's absence, the new Governor landed at New York, where his partisans received him amid ringing bells and booming cannon.[37]

The proposed treaty had reached the United States in March, two months ahead of Jay, but President Washington wisely kept it under wraps until a special session of Congress met in June. When the

32. Peter Van Gaasbeek to King, Mar. 18, 1795, King Papers, N.-Y. Hist. Soc.
33. Aaron Burr to Stephen Van Rensselaer, Dec. 30, 1794, Van Gaasbeek Papers, File 2781, MS 777, Senate House Museum, Kingston, N. Y.
34. *Ibid.*; draft of Peter Van Gaasbeek to Stephen Van Rensselaer, Dec. 30, 1794, R. R. Hoes Collection, *ibid.*
35. King to Peter Van Gaasbeek, Mar. 25, 1795, Record Group 7, Item 65, Papers of Peter Van Gaasbeek, Doc. 116, Franklin D. Roosevelt Library, Hyde Park, N. Y.; King to Oliver Wolcott, Mar. 19, 1795, Wolcott Papers, VI, Conn. Hist. Soc.
36. Ezekiel Gilbert to Peter Van Gaasbeek, Apr. 26, 1795, R. R. Hoes Coll., Senate House Museum, Kingston, N. Y.; King to Van Gaasbeek, Mar. 24, 26, 1795, King Papers, Henry E. Huntington Library, San Marino, Cal.
37. Hammond, *Political Parties in New York*, I, 91.

Senate convened to consider the treaty, Republican senators charged that Jay had betrayed the country and launched a special attack upon Article XII, which limited American ships trading with the British West Indies to seventy tons—trade in canoes, as Madison remarked. Hamilton himself considered this article inadmissible. To save the treaty, which dismayed even the Federalists, some senator, probably King, cleverly offered a motion in two parts: first, that the Senate approve all of the treaty except Article XII, and second, that it recommend further negotiation on the West Indies trade. Although this motion had no effect on the Republicans, it helped to diminish criticism within Federalist ranks. Only the combined strength of all the Federalists, marshaled by King, Ellsworth, and Cabot, killed Burr's motion for postponing further consideration and requesting the President to reopen negotiations. On June 24, after eight days of debate, the Senate struck out the offensive twelfth article and consented to the treaty by a vote of twenty to ten, the barest two-thirds majority.[38]

King was convinced that eventually all points in dispute between Great Britain and the United States would be adjusted, but the immediate task was to explain the treaty satisfactorily to the American public. Despite the Senate's foolish attempt to restrict distribution of the text, the general contents of the treaty were already known: senators had allowed friends to read their personal copies, and passionate opponents were already snatching the opportunity to smear the treaty.[39] King advised Washington and Secretary of State Randolph to release an official copy for publication, but it was too late.[40]

38. *Annals*, 3 Cong., 2 sess., 862–63, June 24, 1795; King, ed., *King Correspondence*, II, 9–10; Alexander Hamilton to King, June 11, 1795, King Papers, N.-Y. Hist. Soc.; Carroll and Ashworth, *George Washington*, VII, 251–53; DeConde, *Entangling Alliance*, 112; Bradford Perkins, *The First Rapprochement; England and the United States, 1795–1805* (Phila., 1955), 31, citing Ralston Hayden, *The Senate and Treaties, 1789–1817 . . .* (N. Y., 1920), 76.

39. King showed Hamilton a copy but did not give it to him, which was no more than what other senators were doing. Hamilton, *History of the Republic*, VI, 223. For King's optimism regarding adjustment of the points in dispute, see King to Cyrus King, June 25, 1795, copied by James G. King in his notebook, Material on the Life of Rufus King, I, 14. The original was owned in 1933 by the late Moses Hale Douglass.

40. Peter V. Daniel, Jr., ed., *A Vindication of Edmund Randolph, Written by Himself and Published in 1795* (Richmond, Va., 1855), 19; Edmund Randolph to King, July 6, 1795, King Papers, N.-Y. Hist. Soc., in reply to King's letter of July 1.

A Virginia Republican Senator furnished a copy to the editor of the Philadelphia *Aurora*, who published the full text as a pamphlet.

Throughout the land, popular reaction was unmistakably hostile to the treaty. In New York state the angry denunciations outweighed the enthusiastic statements of those ready to accept the pact. Although James Kent thought it "founded on fair and honest principles," conceding "no more than what justice and true Policy might reasonably have required," Chancellor Livingston believed it sacrificed every essential interest and prostrated the honor of the nation.[41] A kinsman, Maturin Livingston, observed that Jay was burnt in effigy in Philadelphia on the Fourth of July and would have met the same fate in New York had he not been Governor.[42]

The Federalists, though unprepared for such a popular outcry, rallied their forces. Under the guidance of Hamilton and King, a group of New York City merchants met at the Tontine Coffee House on July 17 to counter an anti-treaty meeting scheduled for the next day. On the morning of the eighteenth, a pro-treaty address was published, and the city was flooded with handbills pleading that the treaty was not as bad as supposed and urging discussion of it. A large crowd gathered in front of the City Hall, and at the stroke of twelve Hamilton mounted a stoop and, aided by King and two others, began to defend the treaty. He was heckled, hissed, hooted, and coughed at. Brockholst Livingston objected to time-wasting discussion of a treaty which had been published for two weeks. Thereupon Peter Livingston, carrying a flag on a long pole, led about half the crowd in a parade to the Battery, where they formed a circle and ceremoniously burned a copy of the treaty. Meanwhile, Hamilton introduced a resolution said to have been written by King, which the chairman tried to read aloud, to the effect that it was unnecessary to give an opinion of the treaty. At that, part of the assemblage went wild, yelling, "Tear it up! We will hear no more of it!" and they carried a motion to appoint a committee to draft resolutions condemning the treaty. The treaty-burners had by now returned from the Battery, accompanied by seamen from French ships in the harbor. As the excitement mounted, arguments gave way to violence,

41. James Kent to Moss Kent, July 2, 1795, Kent Papers, Vol. 2, Lib. Cong.; transcript of Robert R. Livingston to James Madison, July 6, 1795, Robert R. Livingston letterbook, 1779–99, Livingston Papers, N. Y. Pub. Lib.

42. Maturin Livingston to Robert R. Livingston, July 15, 1795, Livingston Papers, N.-Y. Hist. Soc.

and Hamilton was struck in the head by a stone. He called out to the "friends of order" to follow him, and they marched away, leaving the field to the enemy. "The English party," wrote Edward Livingston, had "counted on Hamilton's eloquence and personal influence. If that should fail their next resource was to raise a disturbance in the meeting and throw all the odium of it on the republicans—they partly succeeded in the last Object. They created confusion."[43]

King put it differently. "From the Resentment, and past defeats of our Jacobins," he informed Christopher Gore, "it was natural to expect a very considerable effort on this Occasion. They had concerted their plans, and by manifesting a noisy opposition in the large Towns at the same Time, they expected to surprize and gain the public Opinion. Industry and arts will continue to be employed for this purpose, and you are right in saying that the moment demands all the Patience and Firmness of virtuous men to bear up against the torrent."[44]

The noise and confusion at the meeting on July 18 had precluded all serious discussion of the treaty, and the gathering broke up. Later in the afternoon, several of the principals met at the entrance to Edward Livingston's house, where Peter Livingston got into a heated personal dispute with Josiah Hoffman, a Hamilton admirer. King and several others tried to quiet them, but Hamilton himself lost his temper and offered to fight the whole party one by one.[45]

In the press, the Republicans had seized the initiative, but the Federalists soon caught up. The chief anti-treaty essays came from Chancellor Livingston, writing as "Cato." Using the pen name of

43. Edward Livingston to Margaret Beekman Livingston, his mother, July 20, 1795, Livingston Papers, *ibid.* For contemporary accounts of the fracas, see the N. Y. *Argus, or Greenleaf's New Daily Advertiser*, July 20, 1795; N. Y. *American Minerva*, July 18, 1795; Benjamin Walker to Joseph Webb, July 24, 1795, Worthington C. Ford, ed., *Correspondence and Journals of Samuel Blachley Webb*, 3 vols. (N. Y., 1893–94), III, 197–98; King, ed., *King Correspondence*, II, 20.

44. King to Gore, July 24, 1795, King Papers, N.-Y. Hist. Soc.

45. Edward Livingston to Margaret Beekman Livingston, July 20, 1795, Livingston Papers, *ibid.* Tempers stayed high over Sunday, and on Monday the Republicans held a second meeting at the City Hall, boycotted this time by the chastened Federalists. Resolutions against the treaty were promptly adopted for forwarding to the President of the United States. Not to be outdone, the Chamber of Commerce met Tuesday evening, listened to a deliberate reading of the treaty, and passed favorable resolutions to be sent to the president. N. Y. *Argus*, July 23, Aug. 7, 1795; N. Y. *American Minerva*, July 22, 24, 1795; King to Christopher Gore, July 24, 1795, King Papers, N.-Y. Hist. Soc.

"Curtius," Noah Webster, aided by James Kent and others, defended the pact, but the most important pro-treaty essays were the "Camillus" letters.[46]

Although Hamilton wrote most of the "Camillus" papers, King, and to a lesser extent Jay, collaborated. King penned the substance of numbers 23–30, 34, and 35, or ten in all, examining the maritime and commercial articles. Jay consulted with Hamilton and King on most if not all the letters. According to John Adams, King later told him that Jay was to have written the concluding essay, "but being always a little lazy, and perhaps concluding . . . that it might be most politic to keep his name out of it, and perhaps finding that the work was already well done, he neglected it."[47]

"Camillus" concentrated upon the advantages of the treaty, ignored its shortcomings, and, on the whole, brilliantly defended a document which was widely considered inconsistent with American interests and treaty commitments to France. Hamilton pleaded its constitutionality, and King's analysis of its commercial and maritime features cast the treaty in a favorable light. The assignment proved invaluable in terms of King's subsequent career, leaving him with a sound grasp of international law as it applied to trade and navigation.[48]

President Washington procrastinated in signing the treaty, allowing King time to urge friends into concerted action. He pointed out to Massachusetts connections the need to organize the merchants to counteract the impression created by the town meeting that Bos-

46. The first 25 numbers of "Camillus" were printed in the N. Y. *Argus*, the remaining 13 in the N. Y. *American Minerva*, and the series was widely reprinted in other cities and published as a pamphlet, *A Defence of the Treaty of Amity, Commerce, and Navigation, entered into between the United States of America and Great Britain, as it has Appeared in the Papers under the Signature of Camillus* (N. Y., 1795). The first Camillus article appeared in the *Argus* on July 22, simultaneously with the third article by Cato.

47. John Adams to Abigail Adams, Jan. 31, 1796, Charles F. Adams, ed., *The Works of John Adams, Second President of the United States*, 10 vols. (Boston, 1850–56), I, 485–86; King, ed., *King Correspondence*, II, 12–13, VI, 55. In Hamilton's papers, Lib. Cong., are drafts of numbers 23–30, 34, and 35 in King's hand. They differ, however, from the printed versions of these numbers which emerged as the result of collaboration.

48. More than 20 years later, King would recall the experience: "Principles were established and Usages and Regulations discovered relative to maritime and commercial Law which have given me greater confidence in acting and deciding on these intricate matters than I feel on almost any other subject." King to William Coleman, undated but probably Feb. 9, 1817, King Papers, N.-Y. Hist. Soc. Printed in King, ed., *King Correspondence*, II, 13, and VI, 55.

tonians unanimously condemned Jay's diplomacy. Christopher Gore and George Cabot did their work well in Boston and nearby towns, where some who had bitterly criticized the treaty were induced to say that if the President signed it, they would cordially support it.[49]

In mid-August the President reluctantly signed. "That which from its uncertainty has been the source of Fear and Hope is now made certain," King wrote. "The arts and Intrigues which have been practiced on this occasion exceed belief. It would be some consolation that all had proceeded from honest Error; but I fear that Charity which covers a multitude of Sins will be insufficient to save the Integrity of all."[50]

At the same time, Edmund Randolph suddenly resigned as secretary of state.[51] Washington offered the post to William Paterson of New Jersey, Thomas Johnson of Maryland, Charles Cotesworth Pinckney, and Patrick Henry, but all of them declined. "What am I to do for a Secretary of State?" the President asked Hamilton. "Would Mr. King accept it? You know the objection I have had to the nomination to office [of] any person from either branch of the Legislature; and you will be at no loss to perceive that at the present crisis another reason might be adduced against this appointment. But maugre all objections, if Mr. King would accept, I would look no further." Washington wished Hamilton to sound out King.[52]

49. King to Gore, July 24, 1795, Cabot to King, July 25, 27, 1795, King Papers, N.-Y. Hist. Soc.

50. King to Caleb Strong, Aug. 17, 1795, Caleb Strong Papers, Forbes Library, Northampton, Mass. Secretary of State Randolph's countersignature was obtained by the President on Aug. 14, but apparently Washington did not affix his own name until Aug. 18. Carroll and Ashworth, *George Washington*, VII, 291.

51. Secretary of War Pickering and Secretary of the Treasury Wolcott, both recent appointees, convinced Washington, on flimsy and ambiguous evidence, that Randolph had tried to sell official information to Fauchet, the French Minister. The President confronted Randolph, in the presence of Pickering and Wolcott, with one of Fauchet's dispatches to his superiors in Paris, which had been intercepted by the British and turned over to Wolcott by George Hammond, the King's envoy. The humiliated Secretary of State resigned that day, Aug. 19. Federalists erroneously presumed that Randolph had opposed Jay's Treaty and sympathized with France, hence their acceptance of his disgrace as necessary to save the Hamiltonian system and to counteract French influence in the United States. In fact, Randolph had approved the treaty, and soon after he left office, he told King that he saw no reason to change his opinion. Randolph to King, Aug. 16, 1795, King to Christopher Gore, Aug. 25, 1795, King Papers, N.-Y. Hist. Soc.

52. George Washington to Alexander Hamilton, Oct. 29, 1795, Hamilton Papers, Lib. Cong.

More than two years earlier, while vainly beseeching Jefferson to stay on in the post, the President had alluded to the difficulty of securing a successor and mentioned Jay's high opinion of King.[53] When Jefferson vacated the office, Madison believed that King or Rutledge would be appointed.[54] Now, after the storm over Jay's Treaty, King's New England friends expected his appointment, and Senator James Gunn of Georgia begged him to accept the post if the President offered it. "Colonel Hamilton will take your place in the Senate and all will be well," wrote the glib Georgian. "If ever the Executive wanted aid, this is the moment."[55]

After speaking with King, Hamilton reported to Washington that the Senator would not accept. He was unwilling, as Hamilton explained, to be the target of "the foul and venomous shafts of calumny, which are continuously shot by an odious confederacy against virtue."[56] The two New Yorkers had discussed other likely candidates for the office, but Hamilton concluded that the President would have to be satisfied with a second-rater. Under the circumstances, Secretary of War Pickering, who had agreed to temporarily assume the state department business, was prevailed upon to become the new Secretary of State.

After Jay's retirement as chief justice, Washington had offered the post to the brilliant John Rutledge of South Carolina, who had sat on the court before his resignation in 1791 to become a judge in his home state. Rutledge, however, had attacked Jay's Treaty in an hour-long speech at St. Michael's Church in Charleston, "sufficient to raise the tombs in the nearby graveyard."[57] Federalists were maddened, and their newspapers, seizing upon reports disparaging the judge's personal conduct and alleging that he was prone to fits of insanity, mercilessly flayed him. As a senator who would be passing upon Rutledge's qualifications, King asked Hamilton's opinion of

53. Thomas Jefferson's memorandum of conversation of Aug. 6, 1793, Jefferson Papers, Lib. Cong. Jefferson did not record his response to the hint.

54. James Madison to Thomas Jefferson, Sept. 2, 1793, Hunt, ed., *Writings of Madison*, VI, 195.

55. Christopher Gore to King, Sept. 13, 1795, Gunn to King, Aug. 22, 1795, King Papers, N.-Y. Hist. Soc.

56. Alexander Hamilton to George Washington, Nov. 5, 1795, Washington Papers, Lib. Cong.

57. Richard H. Barry, *Mr. Rutledge of South Carolina* (N. Y., 1942), 356. Charlestonian hostility to the treaty was shared by Federalists and Republicans alike. Charles C. Pinckney, a spirited Federalist, refused either to support or oppose it. Charles C. Pinckney to J. Read, Sept. 26, 1795, Emmet Coll., N. Y. Pub. Lib.

the judge. Rutledge's "imprudent sally upon a certain occasion," Hamilton replied, would not by itself be sufficient to disqualify him, but if it were really true that he was "sottish," that his mind was impaired, or that he had "exposed himself by improper conduct in pecuniary transactions," Hamilton would reject him.[58] On December 15, the Senate voted fourteen to ten against confirming Rutledge, the supporters of the treaty, including King, Cabot, Strong, and Ellsworth, throwing their weight against him. Ostensibly the Carolinian was rejected on account of alleged insanity, but there is little doubt that the real reason was his denunciation of Jay and of the treaty. The Senate's action was a foregone conclusion, and King had no regrets. Laconically, he informed Hamilton, "Rutledge was negatived yesterday."[59]

In the face of the Hamiltonian view that it could not presume to veto the means for execution of treaties, the Republican-dominated House of Representatives did just that, beginning in March 1796 with a resolution requesting that the President release Jay's diplomatic papers for inspection. When Washington refused, the House, under Madison's leadership, reprimanded the President and by a vote of fifty-seven to thirty-five asserted its right to reject the treaty.[60] For weeks it debated a motion to put the treaty into execution, the expected defeat of which would force the abandonment of what had already been proclaimed to be in effect.[61]

As he followed the House debates, Hamilton saw the need for political action and urged King to arouse public support for the Chief Executive: "We must seize and carry along with us the public opinion—and loss of time may be loss of everything."[62] The Senator responded by arranging a meeting of merchants in Philadelphia, who obliged with resolutions demanding the execution of the treaty. In

58. Alexander Hamilton to King, Dec. 14, 1795, King Papers, Vol. 28, N.-Y. Hist. Soc.

59. King to Alexander Hamilton, Dec. 16, 1795, Hamilton Papers, Lib. Cong.

60. Unasked, Hamilton sent drafts of a refusal message to the President and another copy to King. Stephen G. Kurtz, *The Presidency of John Adams, The Collapse of Federalism, 1795–1800* (Phila., 1957), 43. At this time, King thought the House request was probably "not only innocent but meritorious," and he predicted that the House would disapprove the treaty but provide the funds needed to carry it into effect. King to Cyrus King, Mar. 12, 1796, copied by James G. King in 1933 from the original owned by the late Moses Hale Douglass.

61. DeConde, *Entangling Alliance*, 135. Ratifications had been exchanged in Aug. 1795, and the treaty was proclaimed in effect on Mar. 1, 1796.

62. Alexander Hamilton to King, Apr. 15, 1796, King Papers, Vol. 28, N.-Y. Hist. Soc.

New York, Hamilton's lieutenants had no difficulty as they roamed the city soliciting signatures to petitions favoring appropriations for the treaty. Philip Schuyler, who circulated copies upstate, believed that many signers had been influenced by the fear of war with Britain if the House did not uphold the treaty, a fear that was carefully fostered by Federalist orators and newspapers.[63] With the public clamor continuing, Hamilton hoped that Fisher Ames and other Federalist congressmen would play for time, and that King would do his part by keeping the Senate from adjourning until the House session had ended.[64]

Senator Henry Tazewell of Virginia observed that because bills had been bottled up in committees, the Senate had nothing to do; he therefore called on the committees to report and particularly on King, who sat on most of them. According to Tazewell, King admitted that the committees were holding back their reports pending the House vote on the treaty appropriation. If the appropriation did not carry, he said, the committees might as well disband and consider the Union as dissolved. Tazewell, astonished, asked if he understood correctly. King rose again and repeated his words. The next day, Cabot used even stronger language and, Tazewell reported, threatened a dissolution of the government.[65] Such threats were part of a calculated effort to impress southern Republicans.

King and Hamilton concocted other maneuvers, in case the petition campaign and the protest meetings failed to impress the House. The Senator held in reserve a scheme for a Senate amendment that would add Jay's Treaty to the House appropriation bill covering Pinckney's Treaty with Spain, negotiated at San Lorenzo the previous October. If that failed, King was prepared to add both these treaties to the appropriation for the treaty with Algiers or even lump all pending treaties into a single bill.[66]

63. Hamilton to King, Apr. 20, 1796, Hamilton Papers, Lib. Cong.; Schuyler to Hamilton, Apr. 25, 1796, cited by Kurtz, *Presidency of John Adams*, 54–55.

64. Alexander Hamilton to King, Apr. 15, 20, 23, 1796, King Papers, N.-Y. Hist. Soc.; King to Hamilton, Apr. 20, 1796, and Hamilton to King, Apr. 24, 1796, Hamilton Papers, Lib. Cong.

65. Sawvel, ed., *Anas of Jefferson*, 191. Tazewell's account is recorded by Jefferson in the entry dated Mar. 1, 1798, and if it is incorrect in detail it is probably correct in substance. Hamilton had advised King to prevent adjournment of the Senate until the House term had ended. Hamilton to King, Apr. 15, 1796, King Papers, N.-Y. Hist. Soc.

66. King to Alexander Hamilton, Apr. 20, 1796, Hamilton Papers, Lib. Cong. See also Kurtz, *Presidency of John Adams*, 59–60.

These tactics proved unnecessary. The petitions and public meetings, despite Republican counteractivity, effectively mobilized pro-treaty opinion. Cleverly and vigorously, King and Hamilton heightened the effect of merchant, broker, and banker protest by marshaling skilled mechanics and artisans, giving voice to those normally inarticulate. Reason seems to have won converts, but so did blatant exploitation of prejudices, picturing the treaty's opponents as "negro representatives, . . . british Debtors, fraudulent bankrupts . . . , anti-federal Tribes, factious demigouges, french *partizans*, imported Scots, Irish, English malcontents etcccc."[67] Sectional jealousies, fear of war, and mistrust of foreign influences were inflamed, but clear-thinking Americans saw the need for a unified government policy. Even in Albert Gallatin's Republican district of western Pennsylvania, a petition to Congress maintained that Jay's Treaty did not justify the spectacle of a government at war with itself, with one branch thwarting another.[68]

Under this pressure of petitions, with signatures totaling several thousand, Madison, Gallatin, Edward Livingston, Speaker Dayton, and other House Republicans began to waver.[69] Grass-roots politics, national pride, and the fear of war determined the outcome more fundamentally than the brilliantly persuasive speech of Fisher Ames, who on April 28 brought tears to many eyes and has been credited with bringing about a last-moment shift in alignment in the House of Representatives. The next day, in the Committee of the Whole, Chairman Frederick Muhlenberg courageously cast the deciding vote for the appropriation, and on the thirtieth, by a division of fifty-one to forty-eight, the House formally approved funds for Jay's Treaty.[70]

During the height of the treaty struggle in the House of Representatives, Hamilton, King, and John Marshall were looking ahead toward the coming presidential election. Hamilton and King sug-

67. Ezekiel Gilbert to Peter Van Gaasbeek, Apr. 17, 1796, Hoes Coll., Senate House Museum, Kingston, N. Y.

68. Kurtz, *Presidency of John Adams*, 64, suggests that Hamilton or King might have drawn up this petition. There is no concrete evidence that King drafted it, but it calls to mind his willingness to lump together the Jay and Pinckney treaties. The petition asserted that by its action the House threatened to close the Mississippi to westerners and to prevent the growth of the West Indies trade, etc.

69. Some petitions, of course, urged defeat of the appropriation for the treaty, but it appears that most of them favored the treaty, or at least were pro-Washington. *Ibid.*, 66, 72; DeConde, *Entangling Alliance*, 137.

70. *Annals*, 4 Cong., 1 sess., 1280, 1291.

gested to Marshall that he approach the old patriot, Patrick Henry, as a possible Federalist candidate, despite Washington's preference for Adams. Apart from Hamilton's dislike of the Vice-President, both New Yorkers believed that a New Englander would be less likely to win than a southerner who had the confidence of northern Federalists. Henry had shifted his position since 1788 and now supported the national administration while retaining his great popularity in the South. Marshall consulted Henry Lee, and both tactfully sounded out Henry without mentioning the source of the offer, but the sixty-year-old Revolutionary statesman firmly refused to run.[71]

If a southerner was to be their candidate, the New Yorkers had to move fast. Doubtful of Henry's acceptance, King had described for Hamilton the merits of Thomas Pinckney of South Carolina, who was highly regarded by southern congressmen, and whose treaty with Spain was as popular as Jay's was not. By the Spanish treaty the United States had won recognition of the free navigation of the Mississippi, the right of deposit near its mouth, and a favorable Florida boundary settlement. Pinckney was still abroad as Minister to England, but he would soon return. "To his former Stock of Popularity he will now add the Good-will of those who have been peculiarly gratified with the Spanish Treaty," King reasoned. "Should we concur in him, will he not receive as great, perhaps greater, southern and western Support than any other man?"[72] Hamilton agreed at once: "I am entirely of opinion that P.H. declining, Mr. P— ought to be our man."[73] In the months that followed, Hamilton used all his wiles in a scheme to catapult Pinckney into the presidency, a move that not only failed, but contributed to the disastrous split within the Federalist party. Anticipating that Vice-President Adams would have little southern support because of Jefferson's sectional popularity, the Hamiltonians worked on northern and southern electors to

71. Marshall to King, May 24, 1796, King Papers, N.-Y. Hist. Soc., endorsed by King: "Answered 1 June. regretting etc and observing that it would be requisite to fix on another Person without Delay." For correspondence concerning Henry, see Marshall to Hamilton, Apr. 10, 1796, and King to Hamilton, May 2, 1796, Hamilton Papers, Lib. Cong.; Marshall to King, May 24, 1796, King Papers, N.-Y. Hist. Soc. See also King, ed., *King Correspondence,* II, 45–48, and Kurtz, *Presidency of John Adams*, 102–03. Jefferson heard reports of the offer and, though he regarded it as insincere, concluded that the New Yorkers would do anything to split Virginia's ranks. Kurtz, *ibid.*, citing Jefferson to James Monroe, July 10, 1796, Jefferson Papers, Lib. Cong.

72. King to Alexander Hamilton, May 2, 1796, Hamilton Papers, Lib. Cong.

73. Hamilton to King, May 4, 1796, *ibid.*

cast their second ballots solidly for Pinckney, so that they would, in effect, elect the Carolinian as president.[74] King, however, seems to have had no part in the intrigues which developed out of his suggestion.

In fact, King had grown weary of politics. He had accepted reappointment to the Senate without great enthusiasm, and neither he nor his wife was content with his long absences from home while Congress was in session. "Having observed that nearly one Half the session passes before we go seriously to business," he had written in January, he would remain with his family as long as possible.[75] In May he wrote to Hamilton, "You must know that I am a little tired with this separation from my Family and drudging in the Senate—the work now before us being finished, I think I am entitled to a Dismission—It would be agreeable to me to spend a few years abroad, and if I do not misconceive the interests of the Country, I think I could render some service to the Public at the present period in England." Hamilton should confer with Jay, and only if both approved should the President be approached.[76]

King assumed correctly that Hamilton and Jay would favor his appointment to the Court of St. James. Taking Jay's concurrence for granted, Hamilton wrote to Secretary of State Pickering, suggesting King as the ideal successor to Pinckney: "If we had power to make a man for the purpose, we could not imagine a fitter than Mr. King. He is tired of the Senate, and I fear will resign at all events. I presume

74. For the so-called "Pinckney plot," see Kurtz, *Presidency of John Adams*, 104–05, 112–13. Kurtz says, "The problem was that of instilling party regularity as a necessity in the minds of New Englanders who could not be expected to look the other way while so obvious a steal was being carried off." *Ibid.*, 105. No doubt, many Federalists saw Pinckney as their only hope of staving off a victory for Jefferson. Kurtz ranks this dark-horse project with "Hamilton's great failure of 1800" as a major cause of the collapse of the Federalist party. *Ibid.*, 113.

75. King to Theodore Sedgwick, Jan. 9, 1796, Sedgwick Papers, Mass. Hist. Soc. (In this letter King suggested that Sedgwick discuss Jay's Treaty with men like Ellsworth, Cabot, and Strong, and he enclosed some of the Camillus letters.) The Kings had spent the summer of 1795 out of town, probably at Morrisania, where Rufus King had been on a committee that petitioned for a bridge over the Harlem River, but later in the year he resigned, knowing he would be absent when the Senate met. King to James Morris, Nov. 27, 1795, King Papers, Library of the University of Texas, Austin. This collection includes the petition, signed by King and Aaron Burr, among others.

76. King to Alexander Hamilton, May 2, 1796, Hamilton Papers, Lib. Cong. King's Philadelphia address at this time was 104 Spruce Street.

he would accept the mission to England. Can there be any doubt that it will be wise to offer it to him?"[77] Agreeing that King was the best possible choice, Pickering wrote to the President, "A minister of his abilities, experience, and law knowledge, would seem peculiarly desirable at this time."[78]

When Washington pondered Pinckney's replacement, he at first doubted the political wisdom of appointing King. Jefferson and other Republican chieftains suspected King as well as Hamilton of harboring monarchist sympathies, and they knew him to favor England over France. "You know as well as I," the President confided to Hamilton, "what has been said of his political sentiments, with respect to another form of government; and from thence, can be at no loss to guess at the Interpretation which would be given to the nomination of him." The President was fully convinced of King's abilities, however, and there was no doubt in his mind of the New Yorker's fitness for the diplomatic post. Until he made his choice, however, Washington urged that King not resign from the Senate, lest the resignation be interpreted as part of a concerted plan.[79]

Five days later Hamilton sent the President a long letter arguing for King's appointment: the Senator was the best choice of those willing to go; Washington's doubts might apply to everyone "fit for the mission by his conspicuousness, talents, and dispositions"; and if the President listened to partisan Republican insinuations, the government would lose its most competent and faithful agents. "Mr. King is a remarkably well informed man, a very judicious one, a man of address, a man of fortune and oeconomy, whose situation affords just ground of confidence; a man of unimpeached probity where he is best known, a firm friend to the Government, a supporter of the measures of the President, a man who cannot but feel that he has strong pretensions to confidence and trust."[80]

77. Alexander Hamilton to Timothy Pickering, May 10, 1796, Henry C. Lodge, ed., *The Works of Alexander Hamilton*, 12 vols. (N. Y., 1904), X, 164–65. Jay had earlier recommended King to the President as one of the best qualified to serve on the commission concerned with debts and ship seizures under the terms of Jay's Treaty. John Jay to George Washington, Jan. 26, 1796, Higginson, *Life of Stephen Higginson*, 188.

78. Timothy Pickering to George Washington, May 12, 1796, Octavius Pickering and Charles W. Upham, *Life of Timothy Pickering*, 4 vols. (Boston, 1867–73), III, 291.

79. George Washington to Alexander Hamilton, May 15, 1796, Hamilton Papers, Lib. Cong.

80. Hamilton to Washington, May 20, 1796, Washington Papers, Lib. Cong.

The plea was unnecessary; on May 19, the day before it was written, Washington had sent King's name to the Senate, which confirmed his appointment the next day. On the twenty-third, King resigned from the upper house, much to the dismay of politicians like New York's Congressman Ezekiel Gilbert, who asked, "Who can or will supply with equal fitness from New York the place of King in the Senate, where since the Vacancy of Elsworth, he is justly deemed the main pillar of that important branch of the Government."[81] King's old friend Christopher Gore, recently appointed one of the commissioners under the seventh article of the Jay Treaty, was delighted that they would be together in England, and Mrs. Gore was more reconciled to the trip when she learned that the Kings would be neighbors in London.[82]

The truth was that King intensely wanted the mission to England. Had Washington offered the post to him instead of Pinckney in 1792, he would have taken it.[83] Now, four years later, he snapped at the opportunity to apply for it. Ever since his college days he had been interested in international relations, and his early political experiences in the Massachusetts General Court and the Congress of the Confederation had intensified his concern for America's reputation abroad. Correspondence with John Adams in London and Gouverneur Morris in Paris sharpened his interest in diplomatic problems, and both the Genêt episode and the battle over Jay's Treaty had dominated his thinking during his last three years in the Senate. He had become an expert in commercial and maritime law, and his firmness and courtesy were essential diplomatic qualities. Finally, his zealous defense of Jay's Treaty would commend him to the British government, while at home, as merchants and shippers looked anxiously to the federal government for recovery of their losses from ship seizures, Washington could be confident that King would serve the nation well.

81. Ezekiel Gilbert to Peter Van Gaasbeek, May 20, 1796, Hoes Coll., Senate House Museum, Kingston, N. Y. Ellsworth had become Chief Justice of the United States in Mar.

82. Gore to King, May 27, 1796, King Papers, N.-Y. Hist. Soc.

83. King to William Coleman, undated but probably Feb. 9, 1817, *ibid.*

CHAPTER XII

ENGLAND: A NEW SCENE

THE AMERICAN SHIP *James* SLIPPED OUT OF NEW YORK HARBOR ON A cloudy June 20, 1796. On board were Rufus and Mary King, their four small sons, John, who was eight, Charles, seven, James, five, and Edward, one, and King's twenty-four-year-old half-brother Cyrus, who was taken along as the Minister's secretary. After a calm, even tedious, voyage, Captain Conckling guided the vessel toward the town of Hastings on the English Channel, where the King family disembarked four weeks later. They arrived in the narrow, noisy streets of London on July 23, after riding sixty-four miles through hills and valleys bursting with luxuriant crops.[1]

King brought with him the official letter recalling Thomas Pinckney, whom he very much wished to meet, no doubt in part to prepare the Carolinian for his anticipated role in the coming presidential election, but mainly to discuss pending diplomatic issues and to learn more about the British officials with whom he was likely to be concerned. As directed by Secretary of State Pickering, Pinckney turned over to King his correspondence concerning British-American relations.[2]

1. Cyrus King to Hannah Storer, Aug. [n.d.] 1796, transcript misdated 1776, in vol. I of a MS. biography of Cyrus King, Hale-King Papers, Bowdoin College Library, Brunswick, Me. Cyrus King, who had graduated from Columbia College two years before, interrupted his subsequent law studies in Maine to avail himself of the experience and sophistication to be gained with his brother in London. After only a year in London, however, he returned to Maine, where he married Hannah Storer and eventually became a Federalist Congressman.

2. Timothy Pickering to Thomas Pinckney, May 23, 1796, Pinckney Family Papers, Lib. Cong.

Probably through the assistance of the Gores, who were already in London, the Kings took a house at 18 Baker Street. It proved unsuitable, however, and six months later they moved to 1 Great Cumberland Place which remained their London address. Baggage proved an irksome problem. King had brought to England a rather large quantity of wine, but for some reason it was not delivered to him until late in the year, and then only after he had twice asked government officials to intercede for him. A feather bed, several mattresses, and a small trunk filled with linen were missing, and as late as October King was forced to ask Captain Conckling whether they had been left on board the *James*.[3]

In furnishing his residence, King gave exact instructions to agents in Paris for the purchase of china, urns, vases, ornamental figurines, and mirrors. For dinner settings he wanted white with a gold edge, though his wife preferred a more ornate pattern. The Minister's conservative taste dictated that the ornaments be "chaste and pretty," and he set a limit of £250 for the table and dessert set. "I think it an expensive affectation that frequently carries people to the first manufacturer," he asserted, "when a second or third in Reputation will give the same article in every respect, except the criticism of a Virtuoso, as good. It is perhaps well that Persons of great Fortune should encourage the fine arts, but I am not one of the order, and it would ill suit my Finances to be tributary to the laudable rivalry of the manufacturers." By the standards of the British aristocracy, the American envoy was not rich, though he lived comfortably, and he would entertain guests with simple and unostentatious dignity. His salary of £2,025 per year, paid quarterly, proved insufficient to cover necessary expenses, and it was only by the liberal use of his personal wealth that he maintained his household and performed official functions during the ensuing eight years.[4]

The new Minister had reached London during the slack summer season. Most key government officials were out of town, although an audience with King George III was hastily arranged by Lord Grenville, the Foreign Secretary, before the monarch left for Weymouth.

3. King, ed., *King Correspondence*, II, 73; King to George Hammond, Sept. 27, 1796, and King to George Rose, Oct. 18, Nov. 8, 1796, King Papers, Vol. 63, N.-Y. Hist. Soc.; King to Joseph Conckling, Oct. 20, 1796, letterbook owned by James G. King.

4. King to Richard Codman, Nov. 6, 1796, letterbook owned by James G. King; King to Nicholas Low, Jan. 19, 1797, *ibid.*; Charles J. Ingersoll, *Recollections . . .* (Phila., 1861), 357–58.

King sought a conference with Grenville himself, and on August 9 obtained the first of many interviews.

William Wyndham Grenville was four years younger than King, highly intelligent, widely respected, but cold in appearance and so forbidding in personality that a Cabinet member's wife could complain that during an entire day at his home she had never exchanged a word with him. Insufferably dogmatic and argumentative, he scorned the advice of colleagues and was contemptuous of public opinion, yet he had certain admirable qualities. Unlike the many ambitious self-seekers and hangers-on who burdened British administration, Grenville devoted himself wholeheartedly and efficiently to the Pitt ministry, giving fully of his time and energy and even carrying his work home to Cleveland Row or Dropmore, his country home, in the evening. The ministry relied heavily upon his discerning judgment, buttressed as it was by a mastery of detail. King and Grenville were both exceedingly conscientious, methodical, and well-informed, and if little personal attachment grew from their relationship, they respected one another. In their conception of the nature of society and in their abhorrence of the French Revolution they had much in common.[5]

Admitted to upper-class circles, King enjoyed the hospitality of distinguished Englishmen both in and out of the government. From the beginning of his mission, he was befriended by Sir Charles Blagden, a well-known physician and Secretary of the Royal Society, to whom he later introduced Robert R. Livingston, the American Minister at Paris after Jefferson's election to the presidency. Years later he recalled that he had lived on friendlier terms with British officials than had any other foreigner of his time, and he had also associated with many of the outstanding literary figures of the day.[6]

5. My description of Grenville is based largely upon the masterly short sketch of him in Perkins, *The First Rapprochement*, 18–19. When in 1798 Grenville sent King a copy of a speech on France, the latter agreed completely with its opinions and commented: "Only by this animated firm and explicit manner of treating the detestable principles which threaten the existence of every society, as well as human happiness" could one expect to see them resisted. *Ibid.*, 46–47, 198, citing Grenville to King, Private, Mar. 29, 1798, and King to Grenville, Private, Mar. 30, 1798, Boconnoc MSS., America 1793–1803, Lostwithiel, Cornwall. In sending King his speech, Grenville had written, "I have thought your friendship to me would give it in your eyes more interest than it would otherwise be entitled to."

6. King to Robert R. Livingston, Mar. 10, 1802, Livingston Papers, N.-Y. Hist. Soc.; King, ed., *King Correspondence*, II, 51.

One of his warmest friends was William Wilberforce, the crusader against the slave trade, supporter of William Pitt, and adept parliamentarian who had much private influence with men in office. The same age as Grenville, Wilberforce had known the cold and formal Foreign Secretary since they were boys, and he told King that young Billy Grenville "had seedlings in his Character . . . as the acorn contains the Oak." From time to time, King and Wilberforce dined together, but despite their kindred political sympathies, interest in Anglo-American friendship, and mutual horror of the French Revolution, they were temperamentally different. Unlike the Englishman, King was no evangelical reformer and felt little urgency to end the slave traffic. When, however, at Jefferson's request in 1802, he tried to negotiate with the British Sierra Leone Company for the right to ship slaves and freedmen from the United States to Africa, the American Minister turned to Wilberforce for aid—in vain, as it turned out. After the fall of the Pitt government, Wilberforce helped King to establish informal contact with the Addington ministry.[7]

King, whose conversion to Anglicanism while at Harvard College had been a link in the chain of his English sympathies, appreciated Wilberforce's moral earnestness and approved his evangelical fervor as serving the purposes of the Episcopal Church. He ruefully recalled that the mansion built by Wilberforce's father for Dr. Conyers, a preacher at Helmsley, had been vacant for many years: "Religion then was all the fashion, and the inhabitants fed richly on daily ordinances and expositions. Too richly, perhaps, as most of them appear to have been palled. The fallen state of that town ought to warn congregations in the established church who are deprived of evangelical pastors, against the evil of dissenting; for the Helmsley people, impatient with Dr. Conyers's successor, . . . built a dissenting chapel, and crowded to it in shoals. After many vicissitudes of preachers and preaching, it is shut up, and the people go nowhere, but content themselves with railing at formal ministers and blind guides."[8] In

7. King's notebook, memorandum of Apr. [n.d] 1797, King Papers, Vol. 73, N.-Y. Hist. Soc.; Wilberforce to King, Jan. 24, 1801, Dec. 3, 1802, King Papers, Vol. 25, *ibid.*; King to Wilberforce, Jan. 8, 1803, and Wilberforce to King, Private, Jan. 11, 1803, King, ed., *King Correspondence*, IV, 205–07; King to Wilberforce, Jan. 8, 1802 [probably 1803], R. I. Wilberforce and S. Wilberforce, eds., *The Correspondence of William Wilberforce*, 2 vols. (Phila., 1846), I, 186–87.

8. King to Wilberforce, Apr. 5, 1802, Wilberforce, eds., *Correspondence of William Wilberforce*, I, 187–88.

religion as in government, order and discipline seemed necessary foundations of the good society, and he found much to admire in Wilberforce's moral and religious zeal.

Quite different, more profound intellectually, and even closer to King was the learned Sir William Scott. A legal expert, Sir William was appointed in 1798 as a judge of the High Court of Admiralty and served for thirty years. He won great distinction as a formulator and interpreter of maritime and international law, subjects of intense interest to Rufus King. Scott ardently hoped for friendly relations between his country and the United States. After failing to convince the Admiralty that it should compel cruisers to carry prizes only to islands where Admiralty jurisdiction had been established, he apologized to King: "It is solely on *your account* that I was anxious to obtain a different Rule to be adopted; I dread the Hazard of Constitutional Questions between us and the disinherited Colonies."[9]

King's cultivation of prominent Englishmen far outside the diplomatic circle, such as the scientist Sir Joseph Banks, helped to advance his country's reputation and the regard in which he himself was held. Not many Americans penetrated the reserve of the British upper classes. As he later wrote to Madison, "The English, though a cold and proud people, place little value amongst themselves upon the Knowledge or the observance of mere ceremony: Etiquette, as they often say, is good for nothing except as a guard to keep off impertinence, conceit and rudeness. They live very little with the Corps Diplom. and few foreigners travel, none reside in their Country."[10]

Despite high wartime taxes, London's fashionable society lived

9. Sir William Scott to King, May 21, 1801, King, ed., *King Correspondence*, III, 453–54. The warm friendship of these two men is suggested in Scott to King, Aug. 12, 1809, *ibid.*, V, 168–69.

10. King to James Madison, Dec. 22, 1803, Jefferson Papers, Lib. Cong. At the round of dinner parties to which the American Minister was invited, the conversation, though usually political, ranged over many topics—from King George's health to the behavior of Lady Cornwallis, the income of English lawyers, or the freedom of the press. On one occasion, all agreed that the newspapers had become a tyrannical engine of oppression. At a dinner attended by Lord Melbourne, Wilberforce, and Louis Otto, the French representative in London, King questioned the truth of an account that King Charles II had been subsidized by French money. Otto said he had no doubt of it, and later murmured to the American, "Even some of your Patriots did the same thing. They applied to us (the French Embassy in America) in their way." King did not reply to Otto's remark that a minister had only one course of action, namely, to give money. King's notebook, entry for Dec. 28, 1801 and *passim*, King Papers, Vol. 73, N.-Y. Hist. Soc.

well, even extravagantly. To King, who was no stranger to fine living, it was incomprehensible. "This is the third winter I have passed in London," he reflected in 1799, "and it exceeds in every respect in point of Expense either of the former—more Entertainments, more expensive Dresses, greater shew of fine Carriages and Luxuries; in short, a much greater display of luxury than has appeared for several years."[11]

Of necessity, the American Minister lived more modestly, but this was no hardship for King who preferred restraint and moderation in his mode of life. In outward appearance he was indistinguishable from many of the less extravagant English gentlemen. His choice of wine showed preference for the popular claret, Burgundy, and champagne, and his cellar was well stocked. Before coming to England he had been a heavy smoker and had filled his study rooms with tobacco fumes, but discovering that the British gentry frowned upon smoking, he gave up the habit. "Hard times, no segars in England! Smoking quite savage!!!" he exclaimed in a letter written four months after his arrival.[12] He could have been admitted to exclusive clubs, but he was not a "joiner." He chose not to accept election to a new club on Bond Street, which counted the Duke of Somerset and Lord Morpeth among its members and fixed its fee at two guineas above that charged by other clubs in order to ensure its "intended Superiority . . . over any other" in London.[13]

As the representative of a foreign state, King attended many a government function. He paid formal visits at the homes of each of the Cabinet ministers, and appeared at the King's levee, along with other foreign diplomats, the English Cabinet members, the bishops and archbishops, the Lord Chancellor and the judges of Westminster Hall. Envoys of other nations rarely mingled with the English ministers, however, except when their host was the Foreign Secretary, who gave entertainments to celebrate the birthdays of the King and Queen. Describing the reception given for diplomats' wives, King

11. King to Theodore Sedgwick, May 2, 1799, Sedgwick Papers, Mass. Hist. Soc.

12. King to Theodore Sedgwick, Nov. 6, 1796, postscript, Box C, *ibid.*; King, ed., *King Correspondence*, III, 5. For wines, see King to Richard Codman, Nov. 6, 1796, letterbook owned by James G. King; Joseph Pitcairn to King, Mar. 5, May 16, 1797, King Papers, N.-Y. Hist. Soc.; King's memorandum book, entry for Nov. 9, 1796, owned by James G. King; King, ed., *King Correspondence*, II, 73.

13. John Martindale to King, Jan. 31, Feb. 14, June 25, 1800, King Papers, N.-Y. Hist. Soc.

observed that there was no system of precedence, "the assembly being literally a scene of Confusion" in the Queen's drawing room. In celebrating the marriage of a member of the royal family, the wives of diplomats were placed in the same rank with their husbands, but on ordinary social occasions, a man's title was what counted most, not his office. "Mrs. King reminds me," he wrote, "that this was always the Case at the Dinners of the Lord Chamberlain, as well as those of [Lord Grenville and Lord Hawkesbury, his successor]."[14]

Although a man of polished manners and dignified bearing, the American envoy possessed no gift for small talk. He attended the Lord Mayor's ball but did not dance and proved to be less a master of banter and wit than his successor, James Monroe.[15] He was more at ease in the company of politicians, though he did not share an equal intimacy with all of them. Small wonder that Republican newspapers labeled him an Englishman at heart, while Federalists, whom they called "Anglomen," toasted "Our King in Old England."[16]

An accomplished orator, the American Minister frequented the debates in Parliament. The first time he heard William Pitt in the House of Commons, he thrilled with excitement. With Christopher Gore he often sat under the gallery, listening to the Prime Minister contend with Charles James Fox on the conduct of the war against France. Pitt's eloquence sprang from the impressive way in which he marshaled facts at a time when cheap and flimsy demagoguery often passed for argumentation. Gore was astonished at Pitt's acumen and eloquence, but King, though impressed, remarked that Hamilton would have done better than either Pitt or Fox.[17]

Most of the American envoy's activities centered about his combined residence and office in Great Cumberland Place. Here he

14. In 1803, after Anthony Merry, the British Minister to the United States, took offense at Jefferson's casual way of receiving him, Secretary of State Madison inquired of King, recently returned to America, about precedence and etiquette at public ceremonies in England. Madison to King, Private, Dec. 18, 1803, *ibid.* The quotations are from King's reply. King to Madison, Dec. 22, 1803, Jefferson Papers, Lib. Cong.

15. Christopher Gore to King, Nov. 16, 1803, King Papers, N.-Y. Hist. Soc.

16. Ingersoll, *Recollections*, 70–71, 147; Sawvel, ed., *Anas of Jefferson*, 194; Perkins, *First Rapprochement*, 47.

17. Bradford Perkins, The First Anglo-American Rapprochement, 1795–1805 (unpubl. Ph.D. diss., Harvard University, 1952), I, 177, citing James Greig, ed., *The Farington Diary*, 8 vols. (N. Y., 1923–28), I, 181–82; Timothy Pickering to Christopher Gore, Jan. 31, 1827, and Gore's endorsement of his reply, Pickering Papers, Mass. Hist. Soc.

entertained British and American guests, officials with whom he associated, diplomats passing through London, and businessmen. Here he performed many favors, capably assisted by Mrs. King as hostess.[18] The Kings and the Gores were, as friends and neighbors, frequently together and were sometimes joined by the proud and impulsive artist, Colonel John Trumbull, whom they had known years earlier in Boston.

Trumbull had been secretary to John Jay during the latter's mission to England, and he and Gore had since become members of the Anglo-American commission on claims arising out of captures at sea. He continued to paint, however, and in 1800 and 1801 completed bust-length portraits of Rufus and Mary King and their four children.[19] Emotional and unpredictable, Trumbull baffled his friends, including King, who once left him a note on finding him away from home: "D[ea]r Colonel: If your ways are not, your hours are past finding out."[20] While in England, the forty-four-year-old artist-commissioner married a strikingly attractive but socially unacceptable lady of twenty-six, supposed by some to have been an illegitimate daughter of Lord Thurlow. King and Gore attended the wedding on October 1, 1800. As they waited with the clergyman at St. Mary's Church in Hendon, the girl was whisked to the portico in a coach, which sped away. King gave away the bride, though he did not know her. Immediately after the ceremony he asked Trumbull who she was. "Mrs. Trumbull, Sir," the groom replied.[21]

18. Count Rumford wrote King that his daughter had been "deeply impressed with a sense of kindness she experienced from you and your Lady." Count Rumford to King, Aug. 26, 1799, King Papers, Vol. 25, N.-Y. Hist. Soc. The Count sent models of field pieces for presentation to the Secretary of War. Count Rumford to King, Aug. 31, 1799, *ibid.*

19. Theodore Sizer, ed., *Autobiography of Colonel John Trumbull, Patriot, Artist, 1756–1843* (New Haven, 1953), 192*n*; New-York Historical Society, *Annual Report for the Year 1958* (N. Y., 1959), 17. The portraits of John and Edward King are owned by the New-York Historical Society. One of Trumbull's two portraits of King is owned by Yale University, the other by Charles King Lennig, Jr., of Chestnut Hill, Philadelphia. For Trumbull's role as the fifth commissioner, or umpire, under the seventh article of Jay's Treaty, see his account in the Trumbull Papers, Lib. Cong.

20. King to John Trumbull, Mar. 30, 1800, King Papers, Library of the University of Texas.

21. King, who probably learned the girl's identity but kept his mouth shut, told the story of the wedding to Gulian Verplanck, who repeated it to William Dunlap. *The Diary of William Dunlap*, ed. Dorothy C. Barck, 3 vols. (N. Y., 1930), III, 738–39. Trumbull claimed he had known the girl a long time and did not suddenly marry without reflection. John Trumbull to Jonathan Trum-

From time to time the King family escaped official burdens by fleeing to the country. In the fall of 1797, they spent a few weeks in Wales, but miserable weather spoiled this jaunt.[22] Summers were first spent at Randalls, a rented estate near Leatherhead, Surrey, about eighteen miles southwest of London, and easily reached by the stagecoach leaving the Golden Post, Charing Cross, three times a day. During later vacations, the Kings lived at Mill Hill, near Hendon, Middlesex, not far from London. They went to the seashore, frequently accompanied by the Gores, either to Brighton on the south coast or, more often, to Margate, about fifty miles from London, below the mouth of the Thames. In 1799 a swollen, rheumatic knee from an old sprain obliged King to hobble about on crutches, and on the advice of his surgeon, he bathed for several weeks at Brighton beach, where he grumbled about the dampness and sudden changes of climate.[23] From Brighton he wrote to the owner of his rented Mill Hill estate, asking what to pay the gardener. "If he works with the same alacrity that he talks, he must be an excellent servant," the American told the landlord.[24]

Not all of King's own servants proved satisfactory. He retained Pinckney's coachman for three years, but the butler had barely been hired when he "took French leave." The Minister offered to raise the wages of another butler if he proved his worth, but before the year was out, King had written across his memorandum in large letters "Bad Servant." Although the first footman did not last long, two others stayed for more than two years.[25]

An incident involving Harris, his loyal footman, suggests the envoy's magnanimity. Having caught a woman stealing from the house, Harris was summoned to appear in court to testify against her, but King asked George Hammond to inform the magistrate that his

---

bull, Jan. [n.d.], 1808, Trumbull Coll., Historical Manuscripts, Yale Univ. Lib. For the fullest account of Mrs. Sarah Hope Harvey Trumbull, see Sizer's edition of the *Autobiography of John Trumbull*, 350–65. The Kings became her loyal friends.

22. "The rains were incessant, and we had only Six or Eight bright days," was King's sole recorded reaction to the journey. Notebook, King Papers, Vol. 73, N.-Y. Hist. Soc.

23. J. Munro to King, June 26, 1802, King Papers, N.-Y. Hist. Soc.; notebook, entries for Oct. 15, 1798, Oct. 2, 1799, *ibid.*, Vol. 73; letters addressed to King, 1798–1802, *passim*, King Papers, N.-Y. Hist. Soc.; King to Egbert Benson, Aug. 21, 1799, postscript, letterbook owned by James G. King.

24. King to Samuel Davis, Aug. 8, 1799, letterbook owned by James G. King.

25. King's memorandum book, *passim*, owned by James G. King.

servants were not obliged to obey the order. "You know, my Dear Sir," he wrote the Undersecretary for Foreign Affairs, "that I am not inclined to make questions of this sort, and motives of compassion alone influenced me to forbid my Servant to prosecute this poor woman whose distresses most likely forced her to transgress."[26]

Of deep concern to the American Minister was the proper education of his children. His own education had been sedulously fostered by his stepmother, and he had responded with parental concern by putting his half-brother Cyrus through Phillips Academy at Andover and Columbia College. For two years his two older sons studied with a Mr. Winter in Kensington, until they were ready for one of the "public" schools. In the summer of 1797, accompanied by the Gores, the Kings visited Eton, but it seemed to Rufus King that ten or twelve years of a boy's life was too long a period for "the mere acquisition of dead Languages," even though he recognized the school's social advantages. Two years later, after inquiring about other schools, King decided upon Harrow for John and Charles who were eleven and ten respectively. Although aware of possible social benefits, King wanted primarily the careful discipline and demanding scholarship which he felt Harrow would insist upon in preparation for undergraduate education at Harvard. He had an understanding with Dr. Drury, the head of the institution, that the boys would be advanced as rapidly as their abilities permitted.[27] Under Drury's supervision, a tutor would, he hoped, lay the "foundation of an Education upon which their future Condition and Character must chiefly, and, I might add, solely depend."[28]

At Harrow the King boys made a promising start. Their first tutor sent favorable reports to their father, noting in particular that John was good-natured and conscientious and that Charles was unusually steady. King wished his boys to express themselves cogently, and was pleased to learn in 1801 that they would be reading English twice a week with Dr. Drury and, according to their father's desire, would submit occasional compositions. Among their schoolmates were boys

26. King to George Hammond, Oct. 14, 1798, Foreign Office, General Correspondence, America, Ser. II, F.O. 5/24, f. 397, Public Record Office, London.

27. King's endorsement on Nelson Kerr to King, Nov. 20, 1799, letterbook owned by James G. King; notebook, entry for July 29, 1797, King Papers, Vol. 73, N.-Y. Hist. Soc.; King, ed., *King Correspondence*, III, 4; King to Cyrus King, May 2, 1800, owned by James G. King.

28. King to Dr. Drury, June 15, 1799, letterbook owned by James G. King.

who later became famous, Lord Byron, Sir Robert Peel, Lord Aberdeen, and Lord Palmerston. Active games like hare-and-hounds were popular at Harrow, and there were the usual scrapes. John once thrashed a classmate who had unmercifully fagged a freshman, and both boys carved their initials upon paneled walls.[29]

King was pleased that John and Charles were happy at Harrow and that they had responded warmly to their tutor, the headmaster's son, Henry Drury. "I shall be particularly thankful to you for every instance of kindness with which you may indulge them," he wrote to Drury. "I place them in your hands, both as their friend and Instructor."[30] King wanted his two older sons to stay at Harrow until they had acquired the firm foundation in classical languages that in 1803 was regarded as the only sound education.[31]

It was typical of Rufus King to limit his boys' expenses to what he considered fitting and described as "decent," barring unnecessary or "foppish" expenses. When he learned that John was buying books, he remarked that the acquisition of a private library, except textbooks, should be deferred until the boy's judgment was mature enough to distinguish substantial from frivolous literature.[32]

In order to broaden their education, King arranged to have the boys tutored during their holiday periods. He wished them to learn French and Spanish and also instructed the Abbé Ruffini, in whose charge he placed them, to further their knowledge of geography and mathematics. They were not, however, to be "so entirely occupied during their Holidays as to be unable to amuse themselves in a way suitable to their age." The boys were free to go out with their friends in the daytime but were to be generally chaperoned in the evenings. Trips to the theater and out-of-town excursions were left to the dis-

29. Nelson Kerr to King, Nov. 20, 1799, Feb. 16, Mar. 14, 1800, *ibid.* Henry Drury to King, Apr. 26, 1801, *ibid.*; King, ed., *King Correspondence*, III, 4*n*; J. H. Van Amringe, "Charles King, LL.D.," *Columbia University Quarterly*, 6 (1904), 121; Gertrude King Schuyler, "A Gentleman of the Old School," *Scribner's Magazine*, 55 (1914), 619.

30. King to Henry Drury, draft, May 16, 1803, King Papers, N.-Y. Hist. Soc.

31. If King had doubted the value of too exclusive a concentration on Latin and Greek, he did not deny the importance of classical training. According to Timothy Pickering's son John, who succeeded Cyrus as King's secretary in London, it was Vicesimus Knox's *Liberal Education* which converted the American Minister from his earlier prejudice. John Pickering to Timothy Pickering, Aug. 24, 1800, owned by the present John Pickering, Salem, Mass. Mrs. King owned two volumes of Knox's *Essays Moral and Literary* (London, 1785), and they are now in the King Collection, N.-Y. Hist. Soc.

32. King to Christopher Gore, Dec. 7, 1803, King Papers, N.-Y. Hist. Soc.

cretion of the Abbé. Meals were to be plentiful but plain, "in the English manner," with only occasional wine, clothing to be neat and clean, and at regular intervals the boys were to have their teeth examined by the surgeon-dentist in White Horse Street.[33]

King had long lamented the state of American education and could agree with his friend Gore that only the inculcation of sober attitudes and good moral habits would enable their country to survive its internal political conflicts, its government to gain stability, and its people a fixed character.[34] The American envoy hoped that Harrow would provide for John and Charles what could not be found in America, and he remained concerned lest his sons not work to their capacity.[35] Planning beyond their schooling in England, he inquired in 1800 of young John Quincy Adams, the United States Minister at Berlin, about German universities. Adams's reply typifies the outlook common to most New England Federalists: "With regard to the purposes of instruction, the University of Göttingen is universally admitted to be the best in Germany; but the wild and mischievous doctrines, religious and political, which have produced such pestilential effects in Europe, are said to flourish there with the rankest luxuriance. There is probably no university in Germany, but is deeply infected with the same evil." At Göttingen, wrote the President's son, most of the professors were "Jacobins in political doctrines, and at the utmost deists in religion." Generally, they were disciples of "a certain professor Kant of Königsberg, who passes for a prodigy of metaphysical depth because he writes a jargon that no human being can understand."[36] King thought no more of a German education for his sons. He was a Lockean empiricist who believed that experience in the sensory world was the great teacher. Years later, he quoted Edmund Burke approvingly: "We may not apply unqualified metaphysical principles to Affairs. Experience not abstraction ought to be our Guide in practice and in Conduct."[37]

Rufus and Mary King were equally watchful over the younger members of their growing family, and they were proud to learn that James's schoolmaster considered him unusually precocious, "a

33. King to [Abbé Ruffini], draft, May 9, 1803, *ibid.*
34. Christopher Gore to King, Sept. 6, 1803, King to Gore, Dec. 7, 1803, *ibid.*
35. King to Henry Drury, June 3, 1802, owned by James G. King.
36. John Quincy Adams to King, May 1, 1800, King Papers, Huntington Lib.
37. King's notebook, loose leaf insert, undated, possibly 1820, owned by James G. King.

prodigy in learning for his years." Early in 1802, after studying Latin, Greek, and French for a year at a smaller school and learning to dance, James was sent to Paris for further schooling. The Kings' fourth son, Edward, a baby when the family had arrived in London, started school in England, but their last child, Frederick, was born in 1802, too late for an English education. When the American envoy and his wife toured the Continent they entrusted the two youngest boys to the childless Mrs. Gore.[38]

King had for some time been hoping to visit the Continent, but the war made it unwise for him to leave his post in London. In the spring of 1802, however, the Peace of Amiens had been concluded, and much of King's most pressing work had been accomplished, so President Jefferson gave him permission to make the trip. He left Gore as chargé d'affaires in London and, with his wife, two young American friends, two servants, and traveling carriages, embarked at Harwich on August 15.

At Rotterdam the party visited naval docks and arsenals, the marketplace, the stock exchange, and the birthplace of Erasmus which had become a gin shop whose proprietor proudly displayed the room and bed where the great humanist scholar was born. In Delft for a brief pause, the tourists read inscriptions on historical monuments, including one to Hugo Grotius, whom King had admired since he began to study international law. Long fascinated by history and politics, the envoy walked through the palace where William the Silent had been assassinated, the guide pointing out the bullet holes in the wall. Ever interested in business affairs, King noted that the manufacture of Delft earthenware had fallen into decay as imported chinaware won popularity.[39]

For part of their journey, the company traveled by canal boat, but mostly they went by land, the Kings in an English chariot, the two young men in a Flemish cabriolet, and a courier and mulatto servant riding ahead on horseback.[40] At The Hague, where they stopped at the Maréchal de Turenne, the travelers saw the "House in the Wood,"

38. J. Winter to King, Aug. 8, 1800, letterbook owned by James G. King; Thomas Browne to King, June 12, 1801, *ibid.*; Mary A. King to [?], Aug. 23, 1802, King Papers, N.-Y. Hist. Soc. In this, one of the few known letters of Mrs. King, she expresses great reluctance to leave the children.

39. My account of this trip is based chiefly upon King's disappointingly brief and incomplete unpaged diary, King Papers, Vol. 78, N.-Y. Hist. Soc.

40. William M. Meigs, *The Life of Charles Jared Ingersoll* (Phila., 1897), 33–34. The two men in the cabriolet were Ingersoll and a Mr. Smith of Baltimore.

with its paintings by Dutch masters and Oriental panels and curtains. Here, as elsewhere, King was less moved by the aesthetic nature of what he saw than by its historical interest; he noticed a globe made of Dutch oak into which Flemish and Dutch patriots had driven nails to symbolize their unity in asserting their independence from Spain. In Leyden, the party visited the university, the botanical garden, and book shops and attended church, where King noted the congregation sitting with their hats on while the "bellman with his pole and sack was the whole time passing up and down the church soliciting contributions." They toured a naval school at Amsterdam and saw its large gallery of portraits. They were impressed with the well-built, clean, and orderly appearance of Dutch cities, with their canals bordered with fine trees, and with the well-stocked meat and fish markets and the excellent Dutch breweries.[41] At the theater, King thought the acting undistinguished, the speech poor, and the audience boorish. Visiting Dutch bankers was more congenial, and the envoy's brief diary of the trip includes a full page on Dutch commercial laws and two pages on the Amsterdam Bank. In contrast to Amsterdam and Rotterdam, Antwerp appeared to him a dead city, with few warehouses and stores, its buildings fallen into decay, its great church stripped of its famous Rubens paintings, and the inhabitants without ambition to revive their town as a great commercial center.

Traveling south toward Brussels between rows of elms and poplars, the Kings were impressed with the rich, cultivated fields and the varied and lush crops. While in England, King had become much interested in gentleman farming and had been a guest of Coke of Norfolk, whose Holkham estate was a renowned showplace. Having accepted "foreign honorary membership" in the British Board of Agriculture, King had been invited by Sir John Sinclair, the president of the board, to a "grand meeting of farmers" including Arthur Young, the leading advocate of advanced methods. William Strickland had asked the American envoy to write an introduction to a new edition of his papers on American agriculture.[42]

King and his wife fell in love with Brussels in particular. Its

41. Mary A. King to [?], Aug. 23, 1802, King Papers, N.-Y. Hist. Soc.

42. King to Thomas Coke, July 29, 1810, library of the Earl of Leicester, Holkham; W. O. Hassall, "Coke of Norfolk," *The Countryman*, 31 (1945), 29; John Sinclair to King, Mar. 29, Nov. 16, 1797, letterbook owned by James G. King; William Strickland to King, May 22, Nov. 11, 1800, King Papers, Vol. 25, N.-Y. Hist. Soc.

approaches were lined with beautiful trees, and, like most Flemish towns, it was surrounded by wall and moat. The ramparts afforded a pleasant promenade, but war and revolution had taken their toll. Some of the trees had been cut down and statues and monuments mutilated or destroyed. Though retaining much of its architectural splendor, the Habsburg palace just north of the city had been stripped of its furnishings. Most of the titled owners of former estates had fled to Vienna, and their houses were for sale; monks and nuns had been ejected from their monastic buildings, and King could not help noting that "every object which marked a superiority of Enjoyment or Taste of one portion of the Citizens over the others had been injured or destroyed."

Brussels to Liége, to Aix-la-Chapelle, thence to Cologne ("cultivated like a garden"), to Bonn, Coblenz, and across the Rhine to Wiesbaden where King laid his diary aside, telling us nothing of the trip up the Rhine or the magnificence of the Alps. From one of the travelers, young Charles J. Ingersoll, we learn that the Kings were in Frankfurt on Main, Basel, Lausanne, and Geneva, before ending their tour at Paris.[43] They stayed for a month with Robert R. Livingston, who had taken up residence in the French capital while negotiating for the purchase of New Orleans. Conscious that he was accredited to the Court of St. James, King declined an opportunity to be received by the First Consul, Bonaparte. After visiting with their son James, the Kings returned to London on November 17.[44]

43. Meigs, *Life of Ingersoll*, 34.

44. Robert R. Livingston to Morgan Lewis, Dec. 7, 1802, Livingston Papers, N.-Y. Hist. Soc.; King, ed., *King Correspondence*, IV, 165, 180.

CHAPTER XIII

ANGLO-AMERICAN ISSUES

AS A DIPLOMAT, RUFUS KING RAISED THE CREDIT AND DIGNITY OF THE United States in the eyes of Englishmen. He reached London at a crucial time, when Britain and France were gripped in war, when the effects of Jay's Treaty poisoned the diplomacy of the French Republic toward his country, when unresolved issues between the British and the Americans were to be settled by arbitration boards, and when the rights of a vigorous young neutral power required forceful assertion. He remained at his post through a stormy period, witnessing the rise of Napoleon Bonaparte, the resignation of the Pitt government in England, and the transfer of power in his own country from the Federalist administrations of Washington and Adams to Jefferson's Republican administration, which wisely kept him in England until, at his request, he returned in 1803.

With tact and skill, he attended to thousands of petty matters, from securing passports to interceding for individuals caught in situations of embarrassment, hardship, or injustice. He controlled a fund for the support of Lafayette after his release from an Austrian prison, directed the procurement of muskets through agents on the Continent, and watched closely over financial operations affecting the value of American securities on the English market. Businessmen consulted him, and he was on excellent terms with the London merchants trading with the United States. He cooperated with the American consuls and served as a funnel of important information for the American envoys in Lisbon, Madrid, Paris, The Hague, and Berlin.

Cautious and methodical, he kept careful records and reported his acts fully to the Secretary of State.

A unique problem for the American Minister was the disposition of Maryland's bank stock. He persistently sought to recover for that state the value of its colonial investment in shares of Bank of England stock held by British agents acting as trustees in England. At the close of the Revolution, the trustees refused to surrender the stock to Maryland until claims against the new state were settled. Legal and diplomatic appeals on behalf of Maryland had failed to effect the transfer, and Secretary of State Timothy Pickering asked King to renew the demand and obtain from the British government an explicit acknowledgment of the obligation to pay the debt with interest. In 1797, King almost obtained the release of the securities, but new claims raised against Maryland blocked action. Renewing his efforts in 1801, he eventually prodded the Addington ministry into initiating judicial proceedings to transfer the shares to the Crown, which would then convey them to Maryland. The long legal process had not been completed when King left England in 1803, but the Foreign Secretary gave assurance that the British government would act as he wished, and Maryland eventually recovered her full investment, which, with interest, was worth about £200,000.[1]

During his first few months in England, King concentrated on the issue of impressment of American seamen into the Royal Navy, upholding the principle that the American flag protected citizens who sailed under it. At his first interview with Lord Grenville, the Foreign Secretary in the Pitt ministry, he presented a list of Americans detained aboard British warships, with a view to securing their early release.[2] Subsequently he turned over to the Foreign Secretary more lists of seamen claiming to be United States citizens and asked him to expedite their interrogation.[3] Although some Americans had been taken by press gangs in the early 1790's, impressment had not at first been a serious problem. However, early in 1796, the Royal Navy, having drained the seaport towns of seamen, began to seize men from

1. The bank stock issue may be followed in King, ed., *King Correspondence*, II, 144–45, 202, 265–66, 273–74, 281–82, 473; III, 137, 271–74; IV, 156–57, 190–91, 247–48, 321.

2. King to Grenville, Aug. 8, 1796, King Papers, Vol. 63, N.-Y. Hist. Soc. King's memorandum of the interview is printed in King, ed., *King Correspondence*, II, 616–20.

3. For example, King to Grenville, Sept. 28, 1796, King Papers, Vol. 63, N.-Y. Hist. Soc.

ships on the high seas and stepped up impressments from American ships in British ports. The American people were outraged, and Congress authorized a system of certification to enable Americans to prove their citizenship and funds to employ agents to secure the release of those impressed. As a senator, King had doubted the practicability of this law; as a diplomat, he found it completely inadequate. Proving citizenship to the satisfaction of the British was a frustrating experience. Almost anyone, the American Minister observed, from the secretary of state to a lowly parish clerk, could grant naturalization certificates, which varied in form and were often based on dubious proof, mostly on the simple oath of a seaman. The certificates were consequently disregarded.[4]

Grenville told King that Englishmen had been obtaining certificates of American citizenship and asserted that such documents issued by American consuls were not binding upon the British government. Even if the consuls had the right to issue them, which he denied, he considered them worthless because they did not afford satisfactory evidence of nationality. At the Foreign Secretary's request, King informed the American consuls in Britain that they were exceeding their authority; he thus put an end to consular issuance of "protections," as they were called.[5] He also wrote to Jonathan Dayton, the Speaker of the House of Representatives, urging revision of the unworkable law,[6] but Congress did not act until 1799, and even then it failed to tighten the regulations enough to convince the British government that it should recognize the protections.

Early in 1797, King complained to Grenville that it was impossible for him to attend personally to the many cases of seamen seeking naturalization certificates. He tried again, without much hope, to persuade the British ministry to change its mind about consuls issuing protections upon sufficient proof. As expected, the Foreign Secretary declared that his government considered the American consuls' indiscreet and incautious. King had already concluded that every American seaman should be required to obtain a certificate of citizenship only from a collector of a port, who would endorse upon

4. King to Jonathan Dayton, Dec. 6, 1796, Private, King Papers, N.-Y. Hist. Soc.; Timothy Pickering to King, Jan. 17, 1797, King Papers, Huntington Lib. The unwillingness of John Trumbull, appointed under the law as agent in Great Britain, to serve, forced King for a time to supervise personally and coordinate the work of American consuls on behalf of American seamen.

5. Grenville to King, Nov. 3, 1796, King Papers, Vol. 51, N.-Y. Hist. Soc.

6. King to Jonathan Dayton, Dec. 6, 1796, Private, King Papers, N.-Y. Hist. Soc.

the crew list of any ship the names of such crew members as had proven American citizenship. He said nothing about this to Grenville, hoping in vain for Congress to change the law.[7]

Although Britain did not claim the right to impress American citizens, Grenville denied that a British subject could divest himself of allegiance to his sovereign by becoming a naturalized American.[8] In practice, when men were desperately needed, British commanders took the seamen they wanted without listening seriously to their protests. It was difficult enough to distinguish between American citizens and British subjects, and necessity took precedence over legal niceties in time of war. Frauds, involving the wholesale issuance of protections and their sale to Englishmen, gave the Admiralty ample pretext for the taking of any able-bodied American sailor who could not prove his citizenship beyond a doubt.

The impressment of American seamen was most common in the West Indies, where Admiral Hyde Parker rigidly resisted American efforts to have them freed. Except briefly at first, Colonel Silas Talbot, the American agent for seamen in the West Indies, met with great difficulty, and the unfortunate seamen had no recourse but to appeal to the Admiralty through Rufus King. Thus, from the time of his arrival in London, King compiled lists of impressed sailors, obtained proofs of citizenship, forwarded weekly requests to the Admiralty, and pleaded with Grenville to speed the men's release.[9] He was relieved of the day-to-day burden of these cases when Major David Lenox arrived in England in April 1797 as special agent for

7. King's notebook, entry for Jan. 24, 1797, King Papers, Vol. 73, N.-Y. Hist. Soc.; King to Jonathan Dayton, Dec. 6, 1796, Private, *ibid.*; King, ed., *King Correspondence*, II, 122.

8. Grenville to King, Nov. 30, 1796, Mar. 27, 1797, *American State Papers, Foreign Relations*, 6 vols. (Washington, D. C., 1833–59), II, 149, 150. I cannot accept Burt's contention that the principle of nationality played no part in the quarrel over impressment. A. L. Burt, *The United States, Great Britain, and British North America from the Revolution to the Establishment of Peace after the War of 1812* (New Haven, 1940), 212. As Burt states, the British never claimed the right to impress American seamen but impressed them as British subjects; yet an important question was: could a British subject, if liable to be impressed, become a citizen of the United States after the achievement of American independence? See Perkins, *First Rapprochement*, 61.

9. During these eight months, the American Minister obtained the discharge of 86 of the 271 men claiming to be Americans. The British claimed 37 as deserters. No decision was made on the remaining 148, the vessels on which the men were detained having in many instances sailed before the seamen could be interrogated at King's request. King to Timothy Pickering, Apr. 13, 1797, King Papers, Vol. 51, N.-Y. Hist. Soc.

impressed American seamen and was allowed by Grenville to correspond directly with Evan Nepean, secretary to the Lords Commissioners of the Admiralty. Impressed with Lenox's intelligence, discretion, and attention to details, King found him a valuable aide.[10]

The best efforts of United States officials could only bring about the release of individual seamen, and no amount of persuasion could induce the British to renounce the policy of impressment. Many tragic cases of hardship and inhumanity, including detention of impressed seamen for years on British frigates, even death in battle aboard ships of the Royal Navy, justified continued protests by the American Minister. If the British government sometimes recalled a commander, it did so only upon American protest against a ship or her commander by name, and no decisive measures to curb the most unscrupulous officers were taken. Those officers were aided when Grenville informed the Admiralty that protection papers issued in the United States were no longer acceptable as proof of American citizenship. Some Americans "volunteered" for service in the Royal Navy, and King told Grenville that if Great Britain were correct in refusing to release Americans because they had voluntarily taken service on British ships (as some did), she was mistaken in impressing British seamen from American vessels, since all her seamen on American ships were there voluntarily![11] Depending for national survival upon a well-manned and powerful naval force, the Pitt government would not accept any limit to the practice of impressment, and American attempts to negotiate such limits were confounded with a demand for the restoration of British deserters.

King understood Britain's position, but confident at first that the Pitt administration wished to cultivate American good will, he made it a point to be both firm and conciliatory.[12] He pushed for an agreement which would set standards for distinguishing between Ameri-

10. Timothy Pickering to King, Apr. 22, 1797, King Papers, Huntington Lib.; King to Pickering, July 16, 1799, Private King Papers, Vol. 65, N.-Y. Hist. Soc.; King, ed., *King Correspondence*, III, 117–18; Perkins, *First Rapprochement*, 65, 66, 201. According to a chart dated Sept. 15, 1801, Lenox secured the release of 1,042 seamen, about 47 per cent of all the applicants. The Admiralty refused to release 552 and detained another 624 as requiring further evidence. King Papers, Vol. 35, N.-Y. Hist. Soc.

11. King to Grenville, Nov. 30, 1796, King Papers, Vol. 63, N.-Y. Hist. Soc. Cf. King to Grenville, Oct. 7, 1799, *ibid.*, Vol. 65; Perkins, *First Rapprochement*, 67.

12. King to Timothy Pickering, Oct. 16, 1796, King Papers, Vol. 63, N.-Y. Hist. Soc.

can and British seamen, but he soon grew pessimistic. By the summer of 1799, thoroughly disillusioned, he reported to Secretary of State Pickering:

> As you know, I have attempted again and again but without success to convince this Government that both Justice and a friendly Policy required of them to agree with us in a Convention . . . that should at the same time give to them as well as to us adequate and reasonable security in regard to our respective Interests. Latterly I have ceased to urge it from a full persuasion that my Exertions would be fruitless; nor do I believe that any such agreement will ever be made during a war.[13]

Late in 1800, the American envoy proposed to Grenville three articles to be added to Jay's Treaty, one of which stipulated that neither country should permit the impressment of the other's nationals out of merchant ships on the high seas, though seamen might be impressed within the territorial waters of either nation.[14] The Pitt government fell, however, before any action was taken. King urged the same proposal upon Lord Hawkesbury, Grenville's successor in the new Addington ministry. As Hawkesbury did not commit himself, King discreetly asked Thomas Erskine, formerly an opponent of Pitt in the House of Commons, to intercede with Admiral St. Vincent, the new First Lord of the Admiralty, whose views the American considered crucial.[15] St. Vincent passed the buck to Hawkesbury, and nothing materialized.[16]

13. King to Timothy Pickering, July 15, 1799, *ibid.*, Vol. 63. Cf. King to Pickering, Mar. 15, 1799, *ibid.*, Vol. 64. Pickering fully supported King's firm but friendly tactics. Pickering to King, Aug. 6, 1799, King Papers, Huntington Lib.; King, ed., *King Correspondence*, III, 146. To the American Minister at Lisbon, King reiterated his disgust, adding: "Our system of Protections is in my Eyes a pernicious one, but as it has the sanction of Government, we are bound to support it." King to William Loughton Smith, Sept. 30, 1800, King Papers, Vol. 65, N.-Y. Hist. Soc.

14. King's memorandum, Dec. 19, 1800, King Papers, Vol. 65, N.-Y. Hist. Soc.; King to Timothy Pickering, Jan. 23, 1801, *ibid.*, Vol. 66.

15. King to Hawkesbury, Mar. 10, 1801, King to Thomas Erskine, Mar. 11, 1801, Confidential, *ibid.*, Vol. 66.

16. In a letter which Erskine turned over to King, St. Vincent sharply alluded to American abuses: "Mr. King is probably not aware of the abuses which are committed by the American Consuls in France, Spain and Portugal, from the generality of whom, any Englishman, the consul knowing him to be such, may be made an American for a dollar. I have known more than one American Master carry off Soldiers in the Regimental arms and accoutrements from the Garrison of Gibraltar, and there cannot be a doubt, but the American

In May 1803, at the very end of his mission, as war clouds ominously gathered to shatter the Peace of Amiens, King made a last attempt to commit England to stop impressment on the high seas. He again sought Hawkesbury's ear and conferred directly with Addington, the timid and unimaginative Prime Minister.[17] The next day he discussed the subject with the First Lord of the Admiralty, who raised qualifications and promised to think it over after consulting Lord Hawkesbury.[18] Two days later the envoy appealed again in a private note to St. Vincent,[19] and once more in an interview the day before departing from London. The First Lord consented to the terms of a convention but soon had second thoughts and that night wrote to King that the ban on impressment must not extend to instances occurring on the narrow seas, as these were considered within the dominions of Great Britain. The crestfallen envoy, who had thought a major settlement was within his grasp, could not accept St. Vincent's limitation and dropped the negotiation.[20]

The lives and destinies of seamen were of first importance, but King acted as firmly on behalf of American merchants and shippers whose vessels and cargoes had been seized by the British. As suits for

---

Trade is navigated by a Majority of British Subjects, and a considerable one too. . . . I entertain a very high respect for the public and private Character of Mr. King . . . and you may rest assured that whenever Lord Hawkesbury makes a communication to me on this Subject, I will do everything consistently with my duty to the Public to cement the union between the two Countrys." St. Vincent to Thomas Erskine, Mar. 13, 1801, King Papers, Vol. 25, N.-Y. Hist. Soc.

17. "Addington seemed to agree with me," King recorded, "and he said he would confer again with Lord St. Vincent, who hesitated in agreeing to my Proposal that no such impressment should be made by either side." King's notebook, entry for May 12, 1803, owned by James G. King.

18. Entry for May 13, 1803, *ibid.*

19. King to St. Vincent, May 15, 1803, King Papers, N.-Y. Hist. Soc.

20. King to James Madison, July [n.d.], 1803, copy in King's hand, *ibid.*, Vol. 55, in which he wrote: "As I had not supposed from the tenor of my conferences with Lord St. V— that the doctrine of *mare clausum* would be revived against us on this occasion, but believed that England would be content with the limited jurisdiction or dominion over the seas adjacent to her territories, which is assigned by the law of nations to other States, I was not a little disappointed on receiving this communication; and, after weighing well the nature of the Principle and the disadvantage of its admission, I concluded to abandon the negotiation, rather than to acquiesce in the doctrine it proposed to establish." Had he remained longer in England, King later believed, he might have been successful. James Madison to James Monroe, Oct. 10, 1803, Madison Papers, Lib. Cong.; King to Timothy Pickering, Jan. 31, 1809, King, ed., *King Correspondence*, V, 130.

the recovery of property met with irksome delays, the American Minister vigorously urged Grenville to use his influence to speed up the trials:

> These causes are very important both in number and value. Many of them for a very long time have been ready for Trial; in all of them the Claimants are exposed to heavy expenses in the prosecution of their Claims, and in some instances they are threatened with heavy losses by the detention of their property, in consequence of which other of their commercial concerns are deranged and placed in a ruinous situation. . . . It would ill become me, my Lord, to inquire into the causes of the delays complained of, if on investigation these complaints shall appear to be well founded; but it is my duty to state to your Lordship that a long catalogue of American Causes, in which the Captures took place so long ago . . . and in which the Claimants for a long time have been prepared for Trial, remain undecided.[21]

While officially complaining of British seizures and delayed trials, he admitted privately that some of the captures had been "but too well justified." Certain Americans, hoping to make a killing from high freight charges, lent their names to cover French goods; thus, early in King's mission, a few profiteers jeopardized the legitimate trade of American vessels.[22] Yet, despite the sharp practices of some, American merchants had ample reason to protest the high-handed captures of their ships by swarms of British privateers and the seizure of alleged contraband bound for enemy ports.

Grave and persistent diplomatic problems for King were Britain's claim that enemy property carried in neutral ships was subject to seizure, and British enforcement of the rule of 1756 that prevented neutrals from carrying on in wartime a trade denied to them in peacetime. The policy was designed to prevent France and her allies from saving their colonial trade by letting neutral, notably American, merchantmen do the carrying. The re-export from the United States of West Indian products lent itself to fraud, and since it was virtually impossible to obtain evidence on the high seas, British frigates understandably brought American vessels into port for adjudication.

Within narrow limits, the Pitt government gave belated evidence of its willingness to act favorably on King's protests, but the Ameri-

21. King to Grenville, Jan. 24, 1797, King Papers, Vol. 63, N.-Y. Hist. Soc.
22. King to John Quincy Adams, Nov. 10, 1796, *ibid.*

can was never able to secure from the British an acceptable definition of contraband. As directed by Pickering in 1799, he pointed out that the New Orleans deposit area should be considered an extension of the United States, since goods passing through it did not come under Spanish authority; but the British would not then accept that interpretation. When in 1800 King again raised the question, Grenville agreed to the American view, but he resigned before formal action could be taken.[23] Too late for King's satisfaction, Britain finally accepted the American contention in the same month that the United States purchased Louisiana.

The British government slowly responded to American protests against unjustifiable ship seizures. Without making it a fixed policy, the ministry intervened at times to rebuke overzealous or grasping commanders on the seas, and occasionally it recalled a particularly offensive officer. At King's request, Captain Pellew of the frigate *Cleopatra* was recalled in 1801, and when Admiral Parker, his superior at Halifax, allowed him to proceed to the West Indies, the Admiral, too, was ordered home. As King reported to Secretary of State Madison, Parker's conduct had "in other instances been exceptionable in not restraining the plundering Spirit of the Officers under his Command," and the Admiralty, in recalling him, had been convinced that he had "participated too much in the avaricious passions of his subordinate officers."[24]

King repeatedly urged reform of the vice-admiralty courts. The harsh character of the condemnation proceedings and the mediocrity of the judges in these courts in the West Indies frustrated and infuriated American shippers. As the judges depended upon fees, they were tempted to convict, and judicial procedure amounted in many cases to systematic plunder.[25] In 1801, the American Minister went beyond the Foreign Office and indirectly approached Lord St. Vin-

23. Timothy Pickering to King, May 11, 1799, Pickering Papers, Mass. Hist. Soc.; John Marshall to King, Sept. 20, 1800, Department of State, Instructions to Ministers, V, National Archives, Cf. King to James Madison, May 10, 1803, King Papers, Vol. 55, N.-Y. Hist. Soc. On instructions from Pickering and later Marshall, King worked for a formal article on contraband, but nothing came of his efforts. Perkins, *First Rapprochement*, 83.

24. King to James Madison, May 19, 1801, King Papers, Vol. 66, N.-Y. Hist. Soc. Cf. Timothy Pickering to King, Aug. 6, 1799, King Papers, Huntington Lib.

25. Between 1795 and 1801, 80 per cent of some 225 decrees involving Americans carried to the High Court of Appeals were reversed to afford relief to the American owners. Perkins, *First Rapprochement*, 82.

cent, still First Lord of the Admiralty, who appeared somewhat sympathetic. Shortly afterward, Sir William Scott incorporated several of King's suggestions in a bill he introduced in Parliament. As adopted, the measure authorized only three vice-admiralty courts in the Western Hemisphere, and it abolished the nefarious fee system.[26] If this belated reform reflected sensitivity to the persistent complaints of Rufus King, it probably also reflected the election of the anti-British Jefferson as president of the United States and the fear that America might join the Armed Neutrality against England.[27]

The American envoy was intensely chagrined by the incompetence of Sir James Marriott, a justice of the High Court of Admiralty, who was so old and feeble that he could not keep up with the court calendar and contributed conspicuously to the long, exasperating delays in the appeal of seizure cases. Even Grenville admitted embarrassment when King mentioned to him in 1796 that more than thirty cases had been ready for trial for nearly a year without being acted upon. A week later, King repeated his grievance while at dinner with Grenville and the Lord Chancellor, who also confessed embarrassment but said that if the American would prefer a complaint, the Privy Council could require the judge to sit more frequently; in fact, the Council had already hinted to Marriott that requests for instructions regarding the cases before him would be favorably entertained. That judges might be instructed how to decide struck King as "quite repugnant to Justice," but he hoped that official pressure would speed up the appeals.[28]

To King's disgust, Marriott was allowed to continue his bumbling for nearly two years. In September 1798, King wrote again to Grenville, insisting that Marriott's increasing infirmities incapacitated him, and that his presence on the bench was inconsistent with a belligerent's obligation to create courts where neutrals could expect relatively quick decisions. Already chagrined, the Foreign Secretary hoped the judge could be induced to resign, but when Marriott held out for a huge pension, Grenville virtually forced him out of office by order-

26. St. Vincent to Thomas Erskine, Mar. 13, 1801, copied in King Papers, Vol. 54, N.-Y. Hist. Soc.; William Scott to King, May 21, 1801, *ibid.*, Vol. 34; H. M. Bird to King, June 2, 1801, *ibid.*, Vol. 34; Perkins, *First Rapprochement*, 85.

27. See Perkins, *First Rapprochement*, 85.

28. King's notebook, entries for Dec. 16, 22, 1796, King Papers, Vol. 73, N.-Y. Hist. Soc.

ing public criticism of him.[29] Representatives of other nations, individual claimants, and even the captors had complained, but it was primarily Rufus King's interposition which led to Marriott's retirement.

Ameliorative action to relieve the hardships of American shippers was taken in response to King's protests, but the Pitt government acted only when it felt the complaints were justified and the remedies not harmful to Britain's conduct of the war. By applying the doctrine of continuous voyage, the Admiralty hoped to limit the lucrative re-export of colonial produce from the United States. However, in the case of the *Polly* in 1800, Sir William Scott decreed that the captor must prove that a shipper intended to evade regulations, and since it was difficult to obtain proof, the effect of that decision was greatly to encourage American commerce. King took pains to secure the publication of Scott's judgments, and for the next five years British seizures declined.[30]

The American Minister kept a watchful eye on the seizure commission authorized by Article VII of Jay's Treaty to make awards for captured American vessels whose owners claimed to have been unfairly treated in British courts, and to satisfy the much smaller British claims for American seizures in violation of neutral obligations. The five-man commission sat in London, its two American members being William Pinkney of Maryland and King's friend, Christopher Gore, both lawyers; and its two British members John Nicholl and John Anstey, both experts in maritime law and, in King's opinion, "esteemed, enlightened, candid, and honorable men."[31] The fifth commissioner or umpire, chosen by lot, turned out to be the American, John Trumbull, who was acceptable to the British despite his unfamiliarity with law, diplomacy, and commerce. In conferences with the Foreign Secretary and other high British officials, King successfully supported the American members' contentions. The Pitt government, he reported to Pickering in 1798, had sincerely tried to remove obstacles to the faithful execution of the terms of the treaty. For reasons beyond its control, the commission

29. King to Grenville, Sept. 6, 1798, *ibid.*, Vol. 64; Perkins, First Anglo-American Rapprochement, II, 340–41.

30. Perkins, First Anglo-American Rapprochement, II, 341–42; King to Timothy Pickering, Feb. 28, 1800, King Papers, Vol. 65, N.-Y. Hist. Soc.; Perkins, *First Rapprochement*, 86–89.

31. King to John Jay, Aug. 25, 1796, Jay Papers, Columbia Univ. Lib.

suspended its meetings the next year, but after patient negotiation King secured the resumption of its sittings in 1802. It eventually awarded about $6,000,000 to American and about $110,000 to British claimants. Throughout the period of his ministry, King was a persistent and respected intermediary, whose training had equipped him to understand the issues involved and whose friendship for Gore and Trumbull, high regard for Nicholl and Anstey, and good working relations with British officials helped him to foster the work of the seizure commission.[32]

Another arbitral board, acting under Article V of Jay's Treaty, successfully determined which river was the St. Croix named by the 1783 peace treaty as the northeastern boundary of the United States. To obviate the laborious task of locating the exact latitude and longitude of the head of every stream which might be the St. Croix, the commissioners proposed that the two countries simply agree to set up a permanent marker at the source agreed upon. In this Rufus King played a modest part as the American negotiator. He intimated to Grenville the advantage of acting before the Senate adjourned, and resisted the Foreign Secretary's suggestion that the negotiation be transferred to America. In two months they reached a preliminary accord, in time for Senate ratification in June 1798. Thus the work of the St. Croix commission was hastened, and several months later an amicable compromise was worked out, which established a portion of the Maine-New Brunswick boundary, though the remainder of this line was not to be determined for nearly half a century.[33]

In 1801, Secretary of State Madison asked King to initiate exploratory talks with Lord Hawkesbury looking toward a settlement of the Canadian-American boundary far to the West—between the Lake of the Woods in Ontario and the source of the Mississippi. The envoy was also directed to discuss the ownership of certain islands in Passamaquoddy Bay, including Deer, Moose, and Campobello, off the coast of Maine and New Brunswick. Finding Hawkesbury "entirely unacquainted" with these matters and unlikely to pursue them, King

32. King's notebook, entries for Dec. 16, 18, 1796, Vol. 73, King to Timothy Pickering, Aug. 3, 1798, Vol. 52, King to James Madison, Apr. 23, 28, 30, 1803, King Papers, N.-Y. Hist. Soc.; Perkins, *First Rapprochement*, 142–43 and *passim.*

33. King to Grenville, Feb. 2, 5, 1798, Vol. 63, Grenville to King, Feb. 5, 1798, King to Timothy Pickering, Mar. 14, 1798, Vol. 52; Grenville to King, Mar. 8, 1798, King Papers, N.-Y. Hist. Soc.

requested from Madison more explicit instructions.[34] The Secretary of State responded in June 1802, suggesting that the northwest boundary line run from the source of the Mississippi to the western shore of the Lake of the Woods and then along that bank to the northwestern corner of the lake. With respect to the Northeast, he forwarded the opinion of James Sullivan, an expert on the Maine boundaries, that American claims to all but Moose Island were weak; he worked to obtain the free navigation of Passamaquoddy Bay in order to protect American shipping there, and pressed for title to Campobello Island. By the time Madison's orders reached London, King had left for his vacation on the Continent, and on his return he was asked to discuss Passamaquoddy with Thomas Barclay, an Englishman from Nova Scotia, who was in England in February 1803. They soon agreed on everything but Campobello.

Although King did not plan to hold out for that island, he foresaw the usual delays in Lord Hawkesbury's office. Nothing, he thought, would impede a settlement "except the difficulty of engaging the Minister to bestow upon the Subject sufficient time to understand it."[35] After repeated conferences Hawkesbury finally agreed to the terms of a convention not very different from Madison's original instructions to King. Campobello was to be British, but the boundary was to run north and east of it, assuring to the United States a shipping channel open at low tide. Commissions were authorized to fix the Maine boundary. In the Northwest, the boundary line was drawn from the source of the Mississippi directly to the northwest corner of the Lake of the Woods. After another month's delay, King and Hawkesbury signed the engrossed copies of the convention, so that at the close of his mission the American had the satisfaction of winning an agreement that promised to decide small but vexing boundary issues largely on American terms, a convention which he felt would be ratified with no trouble.[36]

34. King to James Madison, Dec. 31, 1801, *ibid.*, Vol. 66.

35. King to James Madison, Feb. 28, 1803, *ibid.*, Vol. 67. Madison later directed King to concentrate on the northeastern boundary. Madison to King, Dec. 16, 1802, Western Americana Collection, Yale Univ. Lib.

36. King to Hawkesbury, Apr. 11, 1803, and draft convention, King Papers, Vol. 67, N.-Y. Hist. Soc.; King to James Madison, May 13, 1803, Department of State, Despatches from Great Britain, Vol. 10, National Archives; King's notes of conference with Hawkesbury, May 12, 1803; King, ed., *King Correspondence*, IV, 256.

Unfortunately, the Louisiana Purchase occurred before Congress could act and thereby poisoned the fruit of King's negotiation. In 1802 the American Minister to France had sought to acquire the mouth of the Mississippi; while in Paris that autumn, King had discussed the subject with him and had recognized that if the United States and Great Britain agreed on the source of the river so as to give Britain access to its navigation, Livingston's hand would be strengthened. However, the American purchase of the entire Louisiana country with its vague northern boundary changed the situation. After ratifying the Louisiana treaty in October 1803, the Senate balked at the King-Hawkesbury convention, which it considered a few days later. Many senators feared that Article V of the Anglo-American agreement might prevent the United States from gaining a more favorable boundary later by weakening possible claims to land north and west of the Lake of the Woods. At the request of John Quincy Adams, chairman of a Senate committee to consider the problem, Madison inquired of King whether he and Lord Hawkesbury had known of the Louisiana Purchase when they signed their convention. King, now at home in New York, replied that the text of the convention had been drafted weeks before the conclusion of the Louisiana treaty and had been signed before news of the latter reached London. This information failed to quiet the objections; the Senate ratified the convention conditionally, rejecting Article V. The Republican senators voted solidly against the controversial article, thus emphasizing an issue that could be raised to embarrass King in the event of his presidential candidacy in 1804. Britain refused to accept conditional ratification.[37]

The American Minister was much concerned with another joint commission, which met in Philadelphia to look into the claims of British creditors seeking payment of American pre-Revolutionary debts. Before it could examine the wildly inflated claims of the British creditors, this commission had to determine whether state laws or other legal impediments blocked efforts to collect, and whether, when collection was attempted, the debtor was solvent. It became hopelessly lost in a maze of specific details, and the American and

37. Perkins, *First Rapprochement*, 146–48; Burt, *United States, Great Britain, and British North America*, 195–97; Arthur B. Darling, *Our Rising Empire, 1763–1803* (New Haven, 1940), 191.

British members exchanged acrimonious charges. In the summer of 1799, the Americans walked out during a particularly bitter dispute, and the Philadelphia meetings broke down.[38] Grenville replied by halting the sessions of the seizure commission in London.

Grenville and King were each inclined to support the views of their own countrymen, but they were far more conciliatory than the members of the debt commission. In February 1800 the American envoy presented to the Foreign Secretary certain procedural rules for the commission, framed by Pickering—but in such terms that King had little hope of acceptance. When they were refused, the American Minister kept channels open and conferred again with Grenville, who at an earlier meeting had casually mentioned a lump sum settlement. King now asked if Grenville had meant that his government would consider ending the dispute this way. Although not personally in favor of this method, Grenville admitted that others in the Cabinet thought it possibly the best solution. King at once sent this news to the State Department, intimating that it might lead to a satisfactory settlement.[39]

The idea of paying a lump sum seemed to President Adams worthy of serious attention, and in spite of anticipated difficulties, he assented. If the negotiation failed, Adams was content, as he put it, to "leave it to Mr. King to do the best he can" in determining how a new board of debt commissioners should be set up.[40] On August

38. The American commissioners were Thomas FitzSimons, a businessman and former Pennsylvania Federalist Congressman, and James Innes, who died and was replaced by Samuel Sitgreaves, a Federalist lawyer. The English members, whom King at first thought willing to cultivate friendlier relations between the two countries, were Thomas Macdonald, a prominent barrister, and Henry Pye Rich, a merchant and former British consul in Holland. King to Timothy Pickering, Nov. 12, 1796, King Papers, Vol. 51, N.-Y. Hist. Soc. A fifth commissioner, nominated by Macdonald and Rich and formally chosen by lot, was John Guillemard, a British merchant then in America. The minute book of the commissioners, now in the Huntington Library, affords detailed evidence of the recriminations within the commission.

39. King to Timothy Pickering, May 25, 1799, Vol. 53, statement presented by King to Grenville, Feb. 18, 1800, Grenville to King, Apr. 9, 1800, Private, Pickering to King, Apr. 22, 1800, all King Papers, N.-Y. Hist. Soc.; Perkins, *First Rapprochement*, 117–20.

40. John Adams to John Marshall, Aug. 1, 1800, Adams, ed., *Works of John Adams*, IX, 68–69. The President feared that when this point of dispute was settled, the British would invent another; but such fear, he remarked to the Secretary of State, "cannot be gravely urged as a reason against settling this quarrel. I am willing you should write to Mr. King instructions on this head." Adams to Marshall, Aug. 11, 1800, *ibid.*, 73–74.

23 Secretary of State Marshall sent word that the United States would pay a sum up to one million pounds, and King accordingly held conversations with Grenville, Hammond, and John Anstey, who had been named to work out the details.[41]

Just as success was in sight, the Pitt government fell, and the new Addington ministry, preoccupied with weightier matters, paid little attention to America. Lord Hawkesbury, Grenville's successor, was in no hurry to inform himself of the debt negotiation and ignored Anstey, who was still meeting with King. The disheartened American envoy thereupon dealt directly with Hawkesbury and with Addington himself. Hawkesbury's procrastination and failure even to discuss the question in the Cabinet exasperated King, who visited Addington at Downing Street, handed him a *précis* of the debt situation, and warned that further delay might injure Anglo-American harmony.[42] King also asked Undersecretary George Hammond, who favored a settlement on the terms offered, to express himself to Hawkesbury. Assuming that the Foreign Secretary would consult his predecessor, King sought out Lord Grenville:

> I told him [the envoy recorded] that I came to complain that since he left the office of foreign affairs, our Business . . . had stood still; . . . we had a right to demand an answer, especially as the Affairs had been many months under consideration; that I could go no farther. I believed fully that I had been authorised to go far enough; that the claim was in fact the remnant of old scores, and moreover that I had no reason to expect that a larger sum would be given; that the unsettled state of the Business was disadvantageous to both Countries, and that an erroneous Settlement was better than none. . . . Lord Grenville said he was ready to admit all I had said.[43]

41. Marshall to King, Aug. 23, 1800, *American State Papers, Foreign Relations*, II, 386–87.

42. King to James Madison, Apr. 20, 1801, State Department Archives, England, Vol. 9, which is accompanied by copies of the King-Anstey correspondence; King to Hawkesbury, Apr. 1, 1801, King Papers, Vol. 66, N.-Y. Hist. Soc.; King's memorandum of interview with Addington, Apr. 8, 1801, *ibid.*, Vol. 73. The document delivered to Addington is in *ibid.*, Vol. 66 and is printed in King, ed., *King Correspondence*, III, 423–24.

43. King's memorandum of Apr. 20, 1801, King Papers, Vol. 73, N.-Y. Hist. Soc. King also appealed to the Chancellor: "It is quite probable that the Creditors, if consulted, may demand a larger compensation than I am authorized to offer; but experience has taught me that the expectations of interested Persons can seldom be received as rules of Justice, and never as grounds of accommodation depending on mutual concession; the sum we offer is, in our

While the envoy was trying to overcome British inaction, the new Jefferson administration in America offered the fixed sum of £600,000, provided the seizure commission was reactivated. Addington somewhat grudgingly agreed to this figure if the terms of payment could be satisfactorily adjusted and if the United States would guarantee that American courts would be open in the future to British creditors. King objected to Hawkesbury that his country could not accept any new stipulations, and that the sum offered was strictly for the full satisfaction of all claims recoverable at the end of the Revolutionary War which still could not be recovered through ordinary legal procedure. Hawkesbury asked the American to draw up a convention embodying the substance of their talk for submission to the Cabinet. Securing the Foreign Secretary's assent to the immediate reassembling of the seizure commission, King went to work. In drafting the proposed convention, he prudently avoided the appearance of solicitude about the seizure commission because he knew it would encourage attempts to commute American claims against the British. Commutation of British claims without implying commutation of American claims, he informed Madison, had been "one of the most delicate parts of the negotiation."[44]

Still there were stumbling blocks. Last-minute objections were raised in the Cabinet, notably to the reactivation of the seizure commission. When Hawkesbury told him that the subject would again have to go before the Cabinet, King was piqued: "I asked when this would be done and expressed pretty strongly my impatience at the delays which had taken place; he replied that he could not name a day, but that it should be soon. It is now evident that little attention has been bestowed upon our affairs, the [peace] negotiation with France having excluded the Consideration of all other Subjects."[45] In the middle of December, Hawkesbury suggested a complicated method of payment, but through discussions with the Chancellor, Lord Eldon, King got the ministry to abandon that plan.[46]

---

view, a liberal one, considering that the debt still outstanding is the remnant of old Scores, and, to use a homely expression, the fag end of the ancient dealings of the two Countries." King to Lord Eldon, May 3, 1801, *ibid.*, Vol. 66.

44. King to James Madison, Aug. 24, 1801, *ibid.*

45. King's memorandum, Oct. 2, 1801, *ibid.*, Vol. 54. Another memorandum of this interview is in Vol. 73.

46. King's memorandum, Dec. 15, 1801, *ibid.*, Vol. 73; King to James Madison, Jan. 9, 11, 1802, *ibid.*, Vol. 55. For a convenient review of King's efforts in Oct. 1801, see King, ed., *King Correspondence*, III, 527–36.

At long last, in January 1802, the debt convention was signed: the United States would pay the £600,000, its courts would be open in the future to British creditors, and the London seizure commission would reconvene at once. "No one knows more thoroughly than you do," King wrote to former President Adams, "the source of those difficulties, often discouraging and sometimes disgusting, which continue to encumber our negotiations with this Government; the affair of the Debts, of all others, was the most likely to revive feelings and prejudices not yet extinguished, and which have been suffered to do so much real disservice to both countries."[47] Nevertheless perseverance had led to success. Having completed the important negotiation, King reflected that it was "the Duty of every one entrusted with what concerns the welfare of his Country, in the midst of despair to perform all the offices of hope."[48]

Not the least of King's vexations while in England were the demands of the rulers of the Barbary states, who for years had levied tribute upon legitimate governments as the price of trading in the Mediterranean. By a recent treaty with the Dey of Algiers, the United States had obligated itself not only to make a cash payment of approximately $800,000, but also to bow to the novel disgrace of an annual tribute in cash and goods. Only a month after King arrived in London, David Humphreys, the United States Minister to Portugal, urged him to induce the Baring banking house to honor drafts enabling payment. The Barings did not have sufficient American funds to cover the amount, but King nevertheless persuaded them to make an advance. He was worried, however, that the low stock prices in London and the high prices at Leghorn, Italy, where dollars could be obtained, would be unfavorable to his country.[49] Although King's relationship with the Barings was excellent, dealing with Algiers was frustrating in the extreme. The Dey raised his sights, and the final terms included, as well, the obligation to build a frigate for the Algerian navy and to supply naval stores, all of which cost more than the navy the United States was building for itself.

When the Barings sold the remainder of the 6 per cents remitted to them on account of the Barbary treaties, the low price of the se-

47. King to John Adams, Jan. 12, 1802, King Papers, Vol. 67, N.-Y. Hist. Soc. Cf. King to John Marshall, Jan. 12, 1802, *ibid.*

48. King to James Madison, Jan. 11, 1802, Private, *ibid.*

49. David Humphreys to King, Aug. 25, 1796, Mar. 21, 1798, Rare Book Room, Yale Univ. Lib.; King to Oliver Wolcott, Jr., Sept. 9, 1796, Private, Wolcott Papers, Vol. 6, Conn. Hist. Soc.

curities and the unfavorable exchange rate distressed King, who was obliged to secure additional credit from the Messrs. Baring.[50] In time, he felt even more uncomfortable. The Dey, impatient with the delay in sending ships from the United States for his fleet, was beginning to take reprisals against American vessels; and William Loughton Smith, who succeeded Humphreys at Lisbon, warned King to alert Americans to the new threat.[51] When, at the Dey's behest in the summer of 1799, the United States Consul-General at Algiers asked Smith to buy brass cannon in England, to be paid for when delivered, King advised against it:

> When we have once concluded a Peace with the Barbary Powers, which in my judgment should be purchased with money or the Productions of our own Country, we ought to avail ourselves of the circumstances of our great distance and of our being ourselves obliged to purchase in foreign Countries the articles that the Barbary Powers might otherwise ask of us, to avoid their capricious and irregular demands. . . . If we yield to the execution of an order of this kind, we establish a Precedent that it will be difficult to get rid of, and our Consul will be engaged in perpetual and expensive Brokerage for the Dey and his Ministers. How far we have already gone in this course I know not; if we have begun, the sooner we stop the better; and if we have not begun, I am confident that we ought not to.[52]

This counsel was effective. Smith accepted King's judgment, and the matter was dropped.

Unexpectedly, in the spring of 1800 and for more than a year afterward, the Minister to England found himself involved in the purchase of costly presents for another troublesome potentate, the Bey of Tunis. William Eaton, the American consul at Tunis, had concluded a peace with the Bey, but the slowness of the United States in delivering the stipulated military and naval stores and the customary

50. "I do not know that the Business could have been managed better than it had been by Col. Humphreys," King wrote to the Secretary of the Treasury, "but one feels a little concern in being in any way connected with an unfortunate transaction in which you have neither power nor responsibility." King to Oliver Wolcott, Jr., Aug. 6, 1797, Wolcott Papers, Vol. 6, Conn. Hist. Soc.

51. Smith to King, Nov. 2, 1798, King Papers, Huntington Lib.

52. King to Timothy Pickering, July 15, 1799, King Papers, Vol. 65, N.-Y. Hist. Soc. See also King to Smith, July 15, 1799, *ibid.*, and Smith to King, postscript dated Aug. 3, 1799, to letter of July 29, 1799, King Papers, Huntington Lib.

"present" of jewels jeopardized the settlement; Eaton wished King to buy jewels and other articles estimated by the Bey to be worth $40,000. King, however, refused to act without an explicit request from Smith in Lisbon and notified the Secretary of State that if he was expected to use his discretion in the future he must be kept fully informed of America's Barbary affairs.[53]

Even when he learned that the President thought it prudent to buy the articles, he hesitated to execute the commission for the jewels. He obtained an estimate of the cost: no less than £7,000. Surprised that Eaton had tried, through the agent of a British commercial firm, to arrange the purchase himself, King refused to supply the money and asked one of the partners of the firm to suspend shipments. He suggested to Eaton that there might be some way of avoiding the gift of the jewels; perhaps the presents already being shipped from England and America would enable the consul "to obtain a release from this pretended engagement." Though Eaton could not be blamed for "the imprudence or looseness of engagements made by other Persons," King tactfully wrote him, it would be "a high proof of your Talents if you should be able to extricate us from Inconveniences proceeding from their misconceptions and errors."[54] Later, when the Secretary of State sanctioned Eaton's efforts to procure the jewels, King took steps to obtain them, but he still encouraged Eaton to get rid of at least part of the obligation.[55]

Upon receiving direct instructions from the state department, King made elaborate arrangements for the costly gifts. He went directly to the manufacturers to avoid agents' commissions, and his trouble and anxiety were said to have enormously entertained his family and friends. He shopped from jeweler to jeweler but learned that the jewels would have to be specially made.[56] Then he placed

53. King to Timothy Pickering, May 25, 1800, King Papers, Vol. 53, N.-Y. Hist. Soc.

54. King to William Eaton, Nov. 24, 1800, *ibid.* In a letter to William Loughton Smith, Oct. 8, 1800, *ibid.*, King had suggested that Eaton be apprised that it would take a year to mount the jewels and obtain other items at great difficulty and expense, and that Eaton should discourage the expectation of future gifts.

55. King to William Eaton, Dec. 28, 1800, *ibid.* King warned that United States tribute should not exceed the payments by Denmark and Sweden, which had complained that American lavishness toward the Barbary powers had disturbed their economical dealings with those pirates. *Ibid.*

56. Beckles Willson, *America's Ambassadors to England, 1785–1928, A Narrative of Anglo-American Diplomatic Relations* (N. Y., 1929), 72–73.

orders for silk and woolen cloths worth a thousand pounds, a diamond ring, gold watches set with diamonds, a gold snuff box set with diamonds, and guns and pistols mounted with gold and set with diamonds. Having before experienced shortages of funds, he reminded his government of each transaction, so that he would have adequate means.[57] He requested of Addington that England use her influence with the Barbary powers on behalf of the United States, and the British authorities issued orders to supply American frigates at Malta, Minorca, and Gibraltar.[58] Worried over the safe delivery of the precious cargo, King enlisted the commander of a squadron of American frigates bound for the Mediterranean to help in forwarding a mounted sabre from Malta, where it had been taken by a British warship, and apprised him of a future shipment to Malta for transfer to Tunis.[59] When the Bey complained to Eaton that the woolen cloth was inferior to what he had expected, King ordered a replacement, but he warned Eaton that there would be no other changes.[60] Finally, by March 1802, all the presents had been sent. Their richness and elegant craftsmanship, the American Minister had been assured, were superior to anything of the sort ever made before. "And so indeed they ought to be," he remarked with curt finality, "considering the sum of money they cost us."[61]

King's national pride and strong sense of frugality caused him to wince at the weakness of his country in dealing with the Barbary states. The Pasha of Tripoli had been at war with the United States for more than a year, and when the Sultan of Morocco also declared war in 1802, King marked it as "another proof, if another be wanting, that our security against the Barbary powers must depend upon force and not upon Treaties, upon ships of war instead of Presents and subsidies."[62]

57. King to James Madison, Apr. 26, 1801, King Papers, Vol. 54, N.-Y. Hist. Soc.

58. King's notebook, entries for May 24, 30, 1801, *ibid.*, Vol. 73.

59. King to Commodore Richard Dale, July 10, 1801, *ibid.*, Vol. 54.

60. King to William Eaton, Aug. 20, 1801, *ibid.*

61. King to Eaton, Mar. 16, 1802, *ibid.*, Vol. 55.

62. King to James Madison, July 19, 1802, *ibid.* Jefferson and Madison came to the same conclusion and energetically carried on the Tripolitanian War, winning a favorable peace in 1805, but the United States continued to pay tribute to other Barbary states until 1815, when a final treaty was concluded with Algiers.

CHAPTER XIV

FRANCE, REVOLUTION, AND THE NEW WORLD

AS HE FOLLOWED THE COURSE OF EVENTS ON THE CONTINENT, THE American envoy watched with deep concern the diplomacy of the French Directory, the progress of the war, and the military and political exploits of Napoleon Bonaparte. Hostility to the American interpretation of the Franco-American alliance of 1778 and to Jay's Treaty had painfully strained French relations with the Washington and Adams administrations, and the continuing Anglo-French conflict subjected many American ships to seizure and confiscation by French officials and sea captains.

King had scarcely assumed his duties in London when he had reports of a French order to stop all neutral vessels with cargoes bound for British ports. The order, he observed, simply presented "to private cupidity a pretence for the interruption and spoliation of our Trade."[1] Within a few weeks French privateers in the West Indies were busily capturing and condemning American ships.

These attacks occurred at a time when France chose to intervene in the domestic politics of the United States. Professing that his country wished to live in harmony and friendship with France, Rufus King nevertheless shared the Federalist animosity toward Adet, the French Minister at Philadelphia, who (like his predecessor, Fauchet) had worked for the defeat of Jay's Treaty and in 1796 attempted to in-

1. King to James Monroe, Oct. 7, 1796, King Papers, Vol. 51, N.-Y. Hist. Soc.

fluence the presidential election in Jefferson's favor. Although Adet's functions as minister had been suspended, his informal activities were reported by Federalists in America to King, who spurned friendship with France if the price was the subjection of American affairs to the Directory's guidance.[2] "I detest the idea that either France or England should really have any influence in the Government of America. I will not believe that such is our degraded Condition." However sincere the friendship of Americans for the French people, "our own character, our honor, our national independence not only of France but of all the rest of the world, are infinitely more dear to us than the interest we have taken in whatever concerned France. This will be proved beyond a doubt if France persists."[3]

Despite news early in 1797 of the wholesale operations of French agents and privateers in the West Indies, and the expulsion of the American envoy, General Pinckney, from Paris, King advised against retaliatory or provocative acts.[4] When he learned that a committee of London merchants had petitioned the British government to authorize convoys of American ships and cargoes, he disapproved the project. The British, he knew, would order a convoy if he asked for it, but he told Grenville that the time was not ripe and that such a decisive measure should be initiated by the United States government.[5] When a year later he learned of a new French decree that made liable to confiscation a ship and all its cargo if even a minute quantity of British goods was found on board, he abandoned his hesitation and urged American sea captains to join convoys.[6]

Long before the American Minister acted, French shipping policy had grown noticeably harsher. By a decree of March 2, 1797, the Directory unilaterally modified the Franco-American treaty of 1778 so as to require for every American vessel a *rôle d'équipage*, a ship's register or crew list, of a type unknown in the United States and which stipulated signature by a public official who had no counterpart in the United States. Since American ship captains possessed no

2. King to David Humphreys, Dec. 29, 1796, *ibid.* The Federalists, wrote Hamilton, were "labouring hard to establish in this country principles more national and free from foreign ingredients." Alexander Hamilton to King, Dec. 16, 1796, *ibid.*, Vol. 41.

3. King to Charles C. Pinckney, Jan. 14, 1797, *ibid.*, Vol. 51.

4. King, ed., *King Correspondence*, II, 148–49.

5. King to Timothy Pickering, Mar. 12, 1797, King Papers, Vol. 51, N.-Y. Hist. Soc. King asked Pickering for guidance lest the future justify a reconsideration.

6. King to consuls in England, Feb. 13, 1798, *ibid.*, Vol. 52; King's notebook, entries for Feb. 15, Mar. 20, 1798, *ibid.*, Vol. 73.

such document, their vessels were liable to capture. French policy also came to embrace the broad assumptions that any American citizen holding a commission from enemies of France (as well as seamen aboard their ships) was punishable as a pirate and that enemy goods sailing under a neutral flag were subject to confiscation. In June 1797, Pickering reported to Congress that in one year, more than three hundred American vessels had been captured by French cruisers, while others had been seized by Spanish privateers.[7] Occasionally a predatory commander would torture an American skipper. After thumb screws had been used on the master of the *Cincinnatus*, King observed:

> It is impossible that these barbarous outrages should be authorized; indeed the concealment observed by the Perpetrators of them, who refused to tell their names, or the port of their Equipment, evince that they are not so. A general peace, if concluded on the basis of reciprocal justice may secure to us an exemption from the System of Plunder and Barbarity into which Europe seems in danger of relapsing.[8]

President Adams, determined to resist the demands for war aroused by French plundering, appointed three commissioners to negotiate a new treaty with France: General Pinckney, who was still in Europe, John Marshall, and Elbridge Gerry. Marshall, a Federalist like King, was learned in the law of nations. Gerry, who had been King's intimate colleague in the Confederation Congress, showed too much independence for many of his old Federalist friends.[9] While temporarily residing at The Hague, Pinckney wrote to King for his impressions of Gerry. The reply was that Gerry was a man of integrity, patriotism, and honor, and that these qualities would serve to extenuate "those subordinate defects to bear with and to get over which requires only patience and a little management." As for Marshall, King paid him a high tribute: "his head is one of the best organized of any one that I have known."[10]

7. Samuel F. Bemis, ed., *The American Secretaries of State and Their Diplomacy*, 10 vols. (N. Y., 1927–29), II, 214–15.

8. King to Timothy Pickering, Apr. 19, 1797, King Papers, Vol. 51, N.-Y. Hist. Soc.

9. Adams nevertheless had confidence in him, cautioning him only that it was important to preserve harmony among all America's ministers abroad. John Adams to Elbridge Gerry, July 17, 1797, Huntington Misc. Collection, Huntington Lib.

10. Charles C. Pinckney to King, Aug. 14, 1797, King Papers, Huntington Lib.; King to Pinckney, Oct. 17, 1797, King Papers, Vol. 51, N.-Y. Hist. Soc.

From the very beginning of the French mission King had serious doubts of its success, but he cooperated in every possible way. He found an occasion to write a curious letter of congratulation to Talleyrand upon his appointment as minister of foreign affairs. Having met the Frenchman in America, King thought he could express himself with a frankness which, as he wrote, "you approve and practice, and which always belongs to important occasions," and he professed to be confident that Talleyrand would restore friendship between their countries.[11] If King believed that his deliberate flattery would have any effect upon Talleyrand, it showed a poor reading of the character of one who, as Napoleon later remarked, was like a cat, always able to land on his feet.

At his London listening post, King carried on a lively correspondence with Pinckney, Marshall, and Gerry, with William Vans Murray, who maintained another observation point in the Low Countries, and with Timothy Pickering, the Secretary of State. King politely offered to do favors in London for his former colleague, Gerry, and invited him for a visit on his return.[12] At first King's letters to the emissaries at Paris were almost entirely limited to factual information, but on November 24 he expressed his personal hope for peace. War would retard America's economic progress and dangerously divide the people at home. "I make these observations," he explained, "in order that you may justly estimate such information as with a view to the negociation in your hands, I may send you; for with all our impartiality, our prejudices will sometimes colour not only what passes through our minds, but even the objects that fall beneath our senses."[13] This equivocal statement may have encouraged Gerry to take a more flexible stand than Pinckney and Marshall wished, and to the latter it may have sounded like a counsel of appeasement. Pinckney, regarding King's words as "enigmatical," suggested that a fuller expression of his views would be helpful. This unexpected request, together with the British rejection of the Directory's proposal of peace

11. King to Charles Maurice de Talleyrand-Périgord, Aug. 3, 1797, King Papers, Vol. 51, N.-Y. Hist. Soc. This was written before King received a letter from General Pinckney suggesting that he write to the French Foreign Minister. Charles C. Pinckney to King, Aug. 14, 1797, King Papers, Huntington Lib.

12. King to Elbridge Gerry, Sept. 2, 1797, King Folder, Long Island Coll., Queens Borough Pub. Lib.

13. King to Pinckney, Marshall, and Gerry, Nov. 24, 1797, King Papers, Vol. 51, N.-Y. Hist. Soc.

based on a bribe and lingering reservations about Gerry, led King to backtrack. As he reported unofficially to Pickering, his own opinions had been "misconceived and treated with more respect by Mr. Gerry than they merited. I have corrected this error in a Letter to our Envoys."[14] He informed the three commissioners: "Earnestly as we desire the preservation of peace, the time is near at hand, when we must look and act with firmness upon the *alternative*. France may be inclined to practice a dilatory and insidious policy; it is in your power to disappoint the former, and I have the consolation to believe that the latter will be attempted in vain."[15]

He cautioned Pinckney, Marshall, and Gerry to act together, not to treat with any unauthorized persons, and not to accept bribes such as France had offered to England. In a confidential note to Pinckney on December 24, King disclosed his misgivings about Gerry and his fear that the Directory would exploit that envoy's "few little defects of character." King changed the cipher he and Pinckney had been using and cautioned the General to keep up the appearance of harmony. In a letter to Gerry the same day, he emphasized American difficulties with France and expressed pessimism about the negotiation, for, in truth, he had concluded that the mission would fail.[16]

He was shocked and dismayed by Gerry's independent action in April. After the emissaries had refused to consider a *douceur* as a preliminary to serious discussions, Pinckney and Marshall prepared to leave Paris, but Gerry made it clear that he would remain and deal alone with the Directory, a stand which shocked King who pleaded with his old associate not to play Talleyrand's game. "The proposal to send away two and retain one of you is treacherous, and if acceded to may be injurious," he warned; it would also be "disgusting and universally condemned by our Country."[17] Three days

14. King to Timothy Pickering, Dec. 23, 1797, *ibid.* Pinckney's letter to King was dated Dec. 14, 1797, *ibid.*

15. King to Pinckney, Marshall, and Gerry, Dec. 23, 1797, Confidential, *ibid.*

16. *Ibid.*; King to Charles C. Pinckney, Dec. 24, 1797, *ibid.*, in which he upheld Gerry's integrity but described his mind as "neither ingenuous nor well organized, but habitually suspicious, and, when assailed by personal vanity, inflexible." King remembered well Gerry's conduct in the Massachusetts ratifying convention.

17. King to Elbridge Gerry, Apr. 13, 1798, *ibid.*, Vol. 52. Gerry's decision reached King by way of a letter from Pinckney, dated Apr. 4. King had written tactfully to Gerry on Apr. 2. King, ed., *King Correspondence*, II, 302–04.

later he urged the Secretary of State to order Gerry out of France.[18] Pickering scarcely needed prodding and on June 25 recalled the envoy. King, convinced that it was time to "give up half-way measures with half-way men," believed Gerry's reply to Talleyrand's "XYZ" demands had placed him "in a more degraded light than I ever believed it possible that he or any other American could be exhibited."[19] In fact, however, Gerry had been careful to protect his country's interests and, while staying on in Paris, had refused to act as more than a channel of communication. In mid-August he was on his way home. He stopped momentarily in Portsmouth harbor, England, and exchanged outwardly friendly messages with his old Massachusetts colleague, but the two did not meet.[20]

Despite the gravity of the situation, King took pride in his belief that most Europeans, whatever their feelings about the United States, approved the open and dignified rebuke given to France. The resistance of the United States contrasted strikingly with the supine submissiveness he observed on the Continent. "It would be hardly decent to express what I think of the weakness, corruption, and indecision of most of the Continental Governments," he wrote to President Adams. "The aristocracies are as unwise and as base as their Princes; and if Europe shall be rescued from the Barbarism with which Philosophy is about to overrun it, it will be effected by the moderation and virtues of the People, who in Spain, Italy and throughout Germany are less guilty and more meritorious than their Magistrates and Rulers." In this sad situation only England could be relied upon. Its resources, the firm stand of its government, the adaptability of its laws, and the support of its people could alone offer reasonable hope for eventual security, he asserted. The President, who considered King to have

18. King to Timothy Pickering, Apr. 16, May 11, 1798, King Papers, Vol. 52, N.-Y. Hist. Soc.

19. King to Alexander Hamilton, May 12, July 14, 1798, Hamilton Papers, Lib. Cong. Cf. King to Noah Webster, June 15, 1798, Noah Webster Papers, N. Y. Pub. Lib.

20. Elbridge Gerry to King, July 16, Aug. 15, 1798, King Papers, Huntington Lib.; King to Gerry, Aug. 15, 1798, King Papers, Vol. 52, N.-Y. Hist. Soc. In view of the anti-French bias of Pinckney and Marshall, Gerry believed that as a known friend of France, he might succeed in treating alone with the Directory. To justify himself, he sent King copies of his correspondence with Talleyrand. For the XYZ Affair and Gerry's viewpoint, see Alexander DeConde, *The Quasi-War, The Politics and Diplomacy of the Undeclared War with France, 1797–1801* (N. Y., 1966), 36–73, and especially 58.

been at times "a little subject to croaking," accepted this solemn appraisal as very sound.[21]

King's dismay at the disruptive effects of the French Revolution influenced his attitude toward the turbulence in Ireland in 1797 and 1798. French exploitation of Irish hopes for independence gave to the insurrection of 1798 an importance which the American Minister was quick to perceive. As early as May 1797 he regarded Irish activities as more intensive and systematic than had been supposed, and he feared that certain Americans had been employed as French agents in fomenting revolution in Ireland.[22] A year later he wrote Pickering of Ireland's miserable condition, with every day bringing "new proofs of the intimate connection that subsists between the Chiefs of the Malcontents and the Directory."[23]

When the British were on the verge of suppressing the rebellion, King feared that thousands of Irish fugitives might flee to the United States. "Their Principles and Habits would be pernicious to the Order and Industry of our People," he advised the Secretary of State, "and I cannot persuade myself that the Malcontents of any character or country will ever become useful Citizens of ours."[24] After the British broke the force of the insurrection, the American envoy, labeling its leaders as "without character and without any intellect," smugly wrote Hamilton that there was only one remedy for Ireland: like Scotland, it must become an integral part of the British Empire, or it would continue "ignorant, ill governed, oppressed and wretched."[25] As Scottish emigrants had carried certificates from their religious societies testifying to their sobriety and good character, King suggested to Pickering that the United States require a similar document of all immigrants, including a statement that the individual had neither been convicted of a crime nor expelled from his country. "I am, I confess, very anxious on this subject," observed King; "the contrast between New England and some other Parts of the U. S. is, in my view, a

21. King to John Adams, Jan. 26, 1799, King Papers, Vol. 53, N.-Y. Hist. Soc.; Adams to Timothy Pickering, Apr. 13, 1799, Adams, ed., *Works of John Adams*, VIII, 631.

22. King's notebook, entry for May 1, 1797, King Papers, Vol. 73, N.-Y. Hist. Soc.

23. King to Timothy Pickering, May 11, 1798, *ibid.*, Vol. 52.

24. King to Pickering, June 14, 1798, *ibid.*, Box 7.

25. King to Alexander Hamilton, July 2, 1798, *ibid.*, Vol. 28.

powerful admonition to us to observe greater caution in the admission of Foreigners among us."[26]

As the American Minister was expressing these xenophobic opinions, Congress passed the notorious Alien and Sedition Laws and raised the residence requirement for naturalization from five to fourteen years. Had King remained in the Senate, he would no doubt have voted for them. "You cannot be too careful in the introduction of proper Provisions in the revision of the naturalization law," he remarked in the summer of 1798, "and the situation of our Country requires that you should vest the Executive with power over Aliens who are among us."[27]

When the Virginia and Kentucky legislatures passed their resolutions protesting the Alien and Sedition Laws, King was only slightly less outspoken than Murray at The Hague, who alluded to their "absurd and ruinous principles," or than John Quincy Adams in Berlin, who called them the outgrowth of "either an incurable distemper or at least one from which recovery is very distant."[28] What surprised King most was the boldness of the Virginia and Kentucky opposition to the administration, and he could only account for what he called "inflammatory proceedings which discredit and injure us so much abroad" as aimed at winning the congressional election, after which political passions might subside.[29]

By the end of July 1798, the Irish rebellion had been extinguished, and King sent word to Pickering that many of the leaders would be exiled. If, as he feared, they sought asylum in the United States, he hoped the President would have the power to exclude them.[30] He attentively read the testimony before the Secret Committee of the Irish Parliament and promptly forwarded it to the Secretary of State, convinced that the insurrectionists held ideas like those current in France—"so false and so utterly inconsistent with any practicable or settled form of Government."[31]

26. King to Pickering, July 19, 1798, Private, *ibid.*, Box 7.

27. King to Theodore Sedgwick, June 6, 1798, Sedgwick Papers, Box C, Mass. Hist. Soc.

28. William Vans Murray to King, Apr. 22, 1799, King Papers, Huntington Lib.; John Quincy Adams to King, Feb. 4, 1799, *ibid.*

29. King to John Jay, Mar. 18, 1799, in William Jay, *The Life of John Jay*, 2 vols. (N. Y., 1833), II, 290.

30. King to Timothy Pickering, July 28, 1798, King Papers, Vol. 52, N.-Y. Hist. Soc.; King to Pickering, Aug. 3, 1798, Private, *ibid.*, Box 7. Cf. King to Alexander Hamilton, July 31, 1798, Hamilton Papers, Lib. Cong.

31. King to Pickering, Sept. 13, 1798, King Papers, Vol. 52, N.-Y. Hist. Soc.

King's apprehension had become so great that he asked the Duke of Portland at the Home Office to persuade His Majesty not to permit the Irish state prisoners to go to the United States. "I certainly do not think they will be a desirable acquisition to any Nation," he ventured, "but in none would they be likely to prove more mischievous than in mine, where from the sameness of language and similarity of Laws and Institutions they have greater opportunities of propagating their principles than in any other Country."[32] Portland, who respected King so highly that he had recommended him to Oxford for an honorary degree, cordially assured him that his wish would be respected.[33] When newspapers continued to mention preparations for sending the prisoners to the United States, the envoy again addressed the Duke. Portland at once wrote to Cornwallis, now Lord Lieutenant of Ireland, mentioning the American Minister's concern, stating that His Majesty had no power to banish any of his subjects to any other country without its consent, and warning that "not one of the Traitors . . . shall be suffered upon any account whatever" to depart for the United States without the King's express permission.[34]

The American Minister's intervention against the emigration of radical Irish leaders was one of his most controversial acts. He had taken the initiative and was pleased at the outcome. As he later boasted, his interposition had won him the "honor" of the Irish leaders' "cordial and distinguished Hatred."[35] William L. Smith, in Lisbon, thanked him for having "stopped the devouring locusts in their pestilential flight and given them another direction."[36] In America, the Federalists were jubilant. "If the Seditious were hardy enough to Denounce you for the great service you have rendered the Coun-

32. King to Portland, Sept. 13, 1798, *ibid.* After he had acted, King received a letter from John Quincy Adams in Berlin suggesting the same idea and adding, "We have too many of these people already." Adams to King, Aug. 27, 1798, King Papers, Huntington Lib. William L. Smith, before learning of King's action, wrote him from Lisbon, "For God's sake, use your influence with Lord Grenville to prevent the U. Irishmen from going to America." Smith to King, Nov. 2, 1798, *ibid.*

33. Portland to King, Sept. 23, 1798, Private, King, ed., *King Correspondence*, II, 640–41; Perkins, *First Rapprochement*, 46.

34. King to Portland, Oct. 17, 1798, King Papers, Vol. 52, N.-Y. Hist. Soc.; Portland to Cornwallis, Oct. 17, 1798, *ibid.*, Box 7.

35. King to Theodore Sedgwick, Mar. 21, 1799, Sedgwick Papers, Box D, Mass. Hist. Soc. With a touch of sarcasm, King wrote Hamilton, "Probably our Patriots will think my conduct presumptuous." King to Hamilton, Nov. 9, 1798, Hamilton Papers, Lib. Cong.

36. Smith to King, Dec. 22, 1798, King Papers, Huntington Lib.

try in shutting its doors against Irish Desperadoes," George Cabot crowed, "you would still have reason to be content, for the praises of the good would be increased in proportion to the clamours of the vicious."[37] President Adams was relieved to be rid of the problem. Secretary of State Pickering instructed King to secure names and descriptions of the prisoners, lest they emigrate elsewhere and indirectly enter the United States.[38] The Republicans, who did not share King's social and political attitudes, played another tune. As they saw it, the envoy's partisan maneuver blocked additional Irish support for them in the United States.

The Irish in both Ireland and America never forgave Rufus King. Like Banquo's ghost, the charge that he was anti-Irish and opposed to the right of political asylum arose after he returned home to plague him in domestic politics. King did not believe in an unqualified right of asylum. He would exclude the Irish revolutionaries because he considered them pawns of French policy and unwitting collaborators in the scheme to upset solid and time-tested values. That they would flock to the Jeffersonian standard like children to a parade seemed only too probable to Rufus King, who remained a party man as well as a patriot.

All revolutions do not appear in the same light, and the envoy in London was intensely concerned over the future of restive Spanish America. "It should be known to you that South America is on the Eve of Revolution," he wrote to Pinckney, Marshall, and Gerry in April 1798:

> England has prepared, and waits only for the Events that the march of the French army into Spain will effect, to send an expedition to commence the revolution which shall make South America independent. If it is not assisted to become independent by England, the work will be done by France, who will introduce there her detestable principles, divide it into small Republics, put bad men at their head, and by these means facilitate her meditated Enterprizes against us. We have an immense Interest in the Event, as well as the manner in which it shall be accomplished. England will at Philadelphia ask the Co-operation of the United States. . . . France expects to find "un point d'appui" in Louisiana, and to begin from thence her operations against the United States. . . . The French System once established

37. Cabot to King, Feb. 16, 1799, King Papers, Vol. 41, N.-Y. Hist. Soc.
38. Timothy Pickering to King, Feb. 5, 1799, King Papers, Huntington Lib.

in South America and the West Indies, we shall be in perpetual risque. On the other hand, the independence of South America on wise principles will put an end to the old Colony and Commercial System, and with obvious Combinations presents wealth and security to the United States, and a new Balance among nations.[39]

This remarkable message clarifies the American Minister's anxiety over French policy, his warnings to Pickering and Hamilton to be on guard against the machinations of French agents in the United States, and, at least in part, his interest in the revolutionary intrigues of Francisco de Miranda, a native of Caracas and the first of the great revolutionaries in Latin America.[40] Miranda was in England early in 1798, striving to win support for a plan to invade the South American mainland. On January 30, the Venezuelan called on King, who suspected that his visitor had been encouraged by the Pitt government, which was hopeful of detaching South America from Spain. The American Minister was courteous and attentive, soliciting information, without committing himself or his country.[41] When King returned the visit, the Venezuelan said he had asked the British to supply eight thousand foot soldiers and two thousand seasoned cavalry, and a small naval squadron to appear off the coast of Peru; he wanted from the United States "50,000 woodsmen—or soldiers who understand new countries" and, hopefully, many of the old captains and majors who had served in the Revolutionary War. As the Spanish forces were weak, he assured King, the emancipation of South America would be bloodless.[42] In a third interview, Miranda tried to sound out the American envoy, who frankly stated that he did not know his government's attitude toward revolution in South America and therefore could express no opinion.[43] Having carefully informed Lord Grenville that his sole purpose was to obtain exact information for his government, he established friendly relations with the Ven-

39. King to Pinckney, Marshall, and Gerry, Apr. 2, 1798, King Papers, Vol. 52, N.-Y. Hist. Soc.

40. For King's warnings against French agents masquerading as consuls, see King to Pickering, July 2, 1798, and King to Hamilton, July 2, 1798, King, ed., *King Correspondence*, II, 356–57.

41. King's notebook, entry for Jan. 30, 1798, King Papers, Vol. 73, N.-Y. Hist. Soc. To King, Lord Grenville seemed distrustful of the Venezuelan and, at least for the moment, unenthusiastic about his scheme. Entries for Feb. 1, 15, 1798, *ibid.*

42. Entry for Feb. 8 or 9, 1798, *ibid.*

43. Entry for Feb. 12, 1798, *ibid.*

ezuelan adventurer, with whom he had at least ten conferences between January 1798 and October 1801.

Although King was cautious in dealing with Miranda, he saw advantages in Anglo-American cooperation, and he was disturbed, therefore, when the British Foreign Secretary told him that if Spain preserved her independence from France, Britain would not actively aid revolution in Spanish America. King considered the possibility of a secret understanding between Britain and Spain,[44] but he thought it probable that Spain would succumb to French power, and that England would eventually appeal to the United States for cooperation in securing South American independence. If so, he wrote Pickering, the United States should join the enterprise "under the influence of that wise and comprehensive policy, which, looking forward to the destinies of the New World, shall in the beginning by great and generous deeds lay deep and firm the foundations of lasting concord between its rising Empires."[45]

The American Minister was full of enthusiasm for Latin American independence. That Spanish America might fall into French hands was a vivid nightmare for him. Quite naturally, his interest in Miranda deepened throughout 1798, as the United States drifted into an undeclared naval war with France.[46] He was not alone. His friend John Trumbull thrilled to the Venezuelan's plan, and Hamilton in New York exchanged letters with King which alluded mysteriously to the nation's stance toward Spanish America.[47] Like King, Hamilton feared French designs on Louisiana, and he agreed that his own country should take the initiative.[48] A war to capture the mouth of the Mississippi would, moreover, strengthen the Federalist party; as Theodore Sedgwick later asserted, it would have aroused a patriotic

44. Entry for Feb. 15, 1798, *ibid.*

45. King to Timothy Pickering, Feb. 26, 1798, Vol. 52, *ibid.*

46. For the "immense interest" of the United States in Spanish American revolutions, see King to Pickering, Apr. 6, 1798, *ibid.* For King's reaction to Grenville's views, see King to Pickering, Aug. 17, 1798, *ibid.*

47. John Trumbull to King, Aug. 22, 1798, *ibid.*, Box 7; John Trumbull to Jonathan Trumbull, Apr. 5, 1799, Trumbull letterbook, 1796–1802, Lib. Cong.; Hamilton to King, May 12, Aug. 22, 1798, Hamilton Papers, Lib. Cong.; King to Hamilton, July 7, Sept. 17, Oct. 20, 1798, *ibid.*

48. As he prepared for war against France, Hamilton hoped to seize Louisiana and the Floridas, thus securing for the United States the key to the West, and at the same time covering himself with martial glory. To his credit, however, he refused to participate in Miranda's scheme without his government's approval of the project. Hamilton to Miranda, Aug. 22, 1798, Hamilton Papers, Lib. Cong.

fervor such as would make unnecessary the Alien and Sedition Laws—"without them we might have hanged traitors and exported Frenchmen."[49]

President Adams, taking a more deliberate view, decided to ignore Miranda's project, and consequently King received no official instructions on the subject. Scarcely concealing his disappointment, the envoy privately protested to Pickering, "You are silent concerning South America. I have again and again touched upon it. I have wished to say much more but I have not thought it prudent to. England is ready. She will furnish a fleet and military stores and we should furnish the army. A map of the country that some time since I procured is in the hands of the engraver."[50]

For several months King tried to keep the project alive. He urged Hamilton to use his influence with the Secretary of State, asserting that the time for action had arrived. "Without superstition, Providence seems to have prepared the way, and to have pointed out the instruments of its will," he wrote. "Our children will reproach us if we neglect our Duty, and Humanity will escape many scourges if we act with wisdom and decision."[51] If the United States did not guide the revolution in South America, he maintained, France would do so, to the disadvantage of American liberties.[52]

Although troubled over his inability to arouse the Adams administration to move toward the glorious goal of an independent New World, King conducted himself correctly, refusing to make any commitment to the Venezuelan. After Miranda lost hope of British assistance, King upheld his honesty, continued to befriend him, aided him to secure passports, and saw him in later years in both England and America.[53]

That the normally level-headed American envoy pursued an en-

49. Sedgwick to King, Jan. 20, 1799, King Papers, Vol. 41, N.-Y. Hist. Soc.

50. King to Timothy Pickering. Oct. 20, 1798, Private, *ibid.*, Box 7. President Adams was bent on having a pacific settlement with France and was unwilling to advance the fortunes of his rival Hamilton. Miranda's supporters in England and America would not participate in his scheme unless the British and United States governments cooperated, and neither government was willing to act alone. For further light on Adams's position, see DeConde, *Quasi-War*, 117–19.

51. King to Alexander Hamilton, Jan. 21, 1799, Hamilton Papers, Lib. Cong.

52. King to Theodore Sedgwick, Mar. 21, 1799, Sedgwick Papers, Box D, Mass. Hist. Soc.

53. King's notebook, entry for May 11, 1799, and undated entry, May 1799, Vol. 73, King to Francisco de Miranda, Sept. 1, 1799, Vol. 53, King Papers, N.-Y. Hist. Soc.

trancing vision can be explained only by his deep anxiety over French influence in the New World, his assumption that Britain probably would support South American revolution, his awareness of the wartime preoccupation of Europe, and his pride in the rising power of the United States. Little did he anticipate that, after the "XYZ" fiasco, President Adams would single-mindedly push for a peaceful accommodation with France. Little did he perceive in this connection the wide rift between Hamilton and the President, between the militarists eager for war and the forces of moderation in his own party, between Federalist sedition-hunters and Republican defenders of civil liberty.

King's attentiveness to New World revolutions extended to Santo Domingo, where the former slave, Toussaint L'Ouverture, had defied French authority and made himself master of that Caribbean island. Learning of an agreement between a British commander and Toussaint that the latter promised to open his ports to English ships, the American Minister made it clear to the British government that if Toussaint were recognized as the ruler of an independent state, the United States would demand similar trading privileges and the protection of its commerce from privateers based on the island. Grenville proposed a British-American company to monopolize the trade with Santo Domingo, but King pointed out that monopolies were unpopular in America and that constitutional objections would be raised in Congress. Instead, the American suggested that an independent Santo Domingo be induced to open its trade to all British and American nationals. More flexible than Grenville, Pitt was willing to consider this alternative, and King had the satisfaction of nipping in the bud a monopoly scheme that would have limited American trade with Toussaint to produce and livestock, an arrangement from which few Americans would have profited.[54] The United States and Great Britain subsequently agreed on terms which would leave the carrying trade with the island in the hands of only American and British shippers.

King had little respect for Toussaint, and he did not relish the thought of social and racial insurrection. In alerting Grenville to the possibility that a free Santo Domingo might open the way to a revolution in Jamaica, the American envoy emphasized that, unlike

54. King's notebook, entries for Dec. 6, 1798, Jan. 6, 10, 1799, Vol. 73, King to Timothy Pickering, Jan. 10, 1799, *ibid.*, Vol. 53; Perkins, *First Rapprochement*, 106–10.

France, the United States had not fomented rebellions in the colonies of other powers, and "there was no likelihood of our becoming zealous in the Propagation of the new Doctrines of Liberty and the Rights of Man."[55] He told Henry Dundas, the War Secretary, that the restoration of French power could best be prevented by taking advantage of the Negroes' jealousy of their former masters, and by developing commerce with the black insurgents which would encourage them but at the same time confine them to cultivating the soil.[56]

The American envoy's almost pathological fear of French ascendancy in America was fed by the possibility that Santo Domingo might some time be used as a base of operations against the mainland of North America, and that the Spanish would prove an ineffective check to France in the New World. The view that France was seeking to repossess the Louisiana country was firmly held in the United States, and early in 1797 Pickering informed King of rumors that Spain had already agreed to cede Louisiana and the Floridas; if so, he hinted, the envoy might help to block completion of the deal.[57] It was not until 1800, by the secret treaty of San Ildefonso, that Spain assented to the return of Louisiana.

The treaty's general outlines were known by May 1801 when King and Lord Hawkesbury discussed their implications. When the Foreign Secretary hinted at a possible British expedition to occupy part of the territory in order to protect Canada and the West Indies, King quickly responded that his country was content with the Floridas in Spanish hands but would be unwilling to see them transferred except to the United States.[58] On at least two later occasions, he repeated his concern to Hawkesbury over either French or British occupation of New Orleans and the Floridas. The Englishman, poring over a map, asked where New Orleans was, and King, pointing it out, enlarged upon the value to France of Louisiana if New Orleans and the Floridas were added. As he recorded the conversation:

> His Lordship seemed to have never considered the subject and remarked that it must be a very long time before a country

55. King's notebook, entries for Jan. 10, 1799, Dec. 26, 1801, King Papers, Vol. 73, N.-Y. Hist. Soc.
56. Entry for June 15, 1799, *ibid.*
57. Timothy Pickering to King, Feb. 15, 1797, King Papers, Huntington Lib.
58. King's notebook, entry for May 30, 1801, Vol. 73, King to James Madison, June 1, 1801, Vol. 54, King Papers, N.-Y. Hist. Soc.

> quite a wilderness could become of any considerable value. I observed that we saw the subject in a very different Light and were desirous that this Region should remain in the quiet hands of Spain, and then asked if Spain should continue to desire it, as well as we, and we should employ such influence as we might have, to engage France to extinguish the Cesion, whether England would cooperate at Amiens by using her influence in favour of the Restoration of this Country to Spain. Lord H. said he would give no answer on that point.[59]

News of Napoleon's preparations for a large land and sea expedition bound for Santo Domingo and perhaps the Mississippi area disturbed King, who was not much relieved by French assurances that the force was intended only for the reconquest of the island. The Addington government, engaged in peace-making, was playing for stakes closer to home and obviously was less aroused over Louisiana than the American Minister. He reported to Madison that during the Anglo-French negotiations, neither side had mentioned a word respecting Louisiana.[60] He expressed independently his basic agreement with Jefferson's warning in 1802 that if France took possession of New Orleans "we must marry ourselves to the British fleet and nation."[61] "The more the subject is considered," King asserted, "the more its importance will unfold itself . . . ; in its consequences it must unavoidably lead to a total change of our political system; I hope not internally, but I am thoroughly mistaken or such will be its effects in regard to our foreign connexions."[62]

Throughout 1802 and as long as he remained in England, King kept up a steady correspondence with Robert R. Livingston, the former Chancellor of New York, whom Jefferson had appointed as minister to France. He urged Livingston to make a strong, dignified protest, with pointed allusions to the "pernicious influence" of French control of Louisiana to which the latter replied that no argument would be effective with Bonaparte, who had cast his eyes upon that

59. King's notebook, entry for Nov. 25, 1801, King Papers, Vol. 73, N.-Y. Hist. Soc. Cf. entry for Sept. 22, 1801.

60. King to James Madison, Oct. 31, Nov. 20, 1801, Vol. 54, *ibid.*

61. Thomas Jefferson to Robert R. Livingston, Apr. 18, 1802, Paul L. Ford, ed., *The Writings of Thomas Jefferson*, 10 vols. (N. Y., 1892–99), VIII, 145.

62. King to Robert R. Livingston, Apr. 25, 1802, Livingston Papers, N.-Y. Hist. Soc.

land ever since he had lost his grip upon Egypt.[63] Neither King nor Livingston knew for certain whether the Floridas as well as Louisiana had passed into French hands, but since the value to Spain of the Floridas was dependent upon Louisiana, King believed that France would take title to them whenever she chose. This must be prevented. The Floridas "must and will ultimately belong to us," he avowed, as he firmly opposed giving any guarantee of them. Should another war break out between France and England, King predicted that Spain, as in the past, would join France, that England probably would take possession of New Orleans and the Floridas, and that if the United States had previously guaranteed the Floridas, she would be called upon to fulfill her engagement.[64]

King's correspondence was most helpful to the American Minister at Paris. London was alive with news from many quarters, and King was in a position to pass along more information from British Cabinet members and newspapers than Livingston could learn through the Consulate and the government-controlled press. In the autumn of 1802, while vacationing on the Continent, King anxiously inquired at post offices in Germany, Switzerland, and France for letters from Livingston, climaxing his trip with a month's stay in Paris, where the two diplomats reviewed the entire Louisiana and Florida question. After the envoy to London returned to his post, the correspondence was resumed.[65]

It was not until 1803 that the Addington ministry began to take

63. King to Livingston, Jan. 16, Mar. 23, 1802, Livingston to King, Jan. 25, 1802, *ibid.* When commenting on Hawkesbury's stated belief that Toussaint would destroy the French forces launched against him, King remarked that "nothing short of complete proof will convince an Englishman that others will succeed better than his countrymen did." King to Livingston, Apr. 25, 1802, *ibid.* Later, King wrote: "Toussaint's submission will not relieve France from the maintenance of a large military force in Hispaniola, which must be def[ended] from the U. S. but it will enable her to detach a considerable body of troops to the Mississippi, and it seems quite probable that no farther delay will now be suffered to intervene in taking Possession of Louisiana." King to Livingston, June 18, 1802, *ibid.* In this connection, he sent certain secret papers to Livingston with instructions to burn them, which Livingston did. *Ibid.*; Livingston to King, June 30, 1802, *ibid.*

64. King to Livingston, July 12, 1802, *ibid.* Livingston agreed with King. Livingston to King, Aug. 2, 1802, *ibid.*

65. For this correspondence, see Livingston Papers, N.-Y. Hist. Soc., esp. Livingston to John Armstrong, Sept. 1, 1803, for Livingston's appreciation of King's aid.

an active interest in Louisiana. King apprised Livingston on March 11 that Britain was considering an expedition to New Orleans,[66] and asked: "If you are authorized to negotiate a purchase, would not the occupation by the English benefit your bargain, it being well and previously understood that if we obtain the Title they would give us the Possession?"[67] Two weeks later, at a dinner given by the American merchants in London, Addington adverted to an English seizure of New Orleans in case of war. King immediately objected:

> The occupation of New Orleans would be a step of much inquietude to us, without a previous, confidential, and explicit disclosure of their views at Washington; we were content with the possession of Spain who was quiet, and we had patience, knowing that time increased our strength, as well as of itself would unavoidably place that country in our hands, but that we should feel differently were it occupied either by France or England.[68]

Addington, in reply, was conciliatory according to King's report: "Be assured that we would not have Louisiana if it were offered to us; we do not want it ourselves, nor are we willing the French should have, but we are perfectly content and shall be ready in any way to assert that you should have it, because we believe that you would and could defend it." He assured King that nothing would be done about Louisiana without the knowledge and, he hoped, the consent of the United States.[69]

While King kept Secretary of State Madison informed of British intentions regarding Louisiana, James Monroe crossed the Atlantic as a special emissary to assist Livingston in the purchase of New Orleans and the Floridas. In anticipation of a possible cession, King informed Livingston and Monroe that if war broke out in Europe, the British

66. Renewal of the war with France seemed inevitable, and since the United States might seize New Orleans, Addington and Hawkesbury considered taking Louisiana and handing it over to the Americans. This would have two advantages for England: French mainland operations would be forestalled, whereas if Britain waited for the Americans to act, Napoleon might gain a foothold on the Gulf coast; secondly, in return for their assistance, the United States might be more favorably inclined toward the British, and perhaps even offer commercial concessions in her new territory.

67. King to Robert R. Livingston, Mar. 11, 1803, King Papers, Vol. 55, N.-Y. Hist. Soc.

68. King's notebook, entry for Mar. 26, 1803, *ibid.*, Vol. 73.

69. *Ibid.*

would occupy New Orleans but that if France ceded the area to the United States, British knowledge of the fact would forestall an attack on New Orleans.[70] Indeed, five days later, Addington and Hawkesbury assured King that if the United States acquired Louisiana an English expedition there would be out of the question.[71]

Upon completion of the Louisiana Purchase, Livingston and Monroe wrote to King suggesting that he should tell the British government that care had been taken not to infringe upon any British right to the navigation of the Mississippi. This news the American Minister promptly revealed to Hawkesbury.[72] When King George learned of it, he was pleased that Britain's interests had been respected, and he commanded Hawkesbury (the Foreign Secretary wrote to King) "to assure you, Sir, that the Sentiments which you have expressed in making this communication are considered by his Majesty's Government as an additional proof of the Cordiality and Confidence which you have uniformly manifested in the whole course of your public Mission, and which have so justly entitled you to the Esteem and Regard of his Majesty's Government."[73]

King was pleased and yet dubious about the Louisiana treaty. He complimented Livingston and Monroe, asserting that "a little more or less money cannot be an object with a country circumstanced like ours, especially when it is applied to secure advantages so important as those which depend upon the complete navigation and control of the River Mississippi." However, he continued, "if I might be permitted to doubt respecting your treaty, it would relate to the great extension of territory that it gives us."[74] This doubt, somewhat obscured by the elation of the moment, would grow after Rufus King reached America bearing the first news of the Louisiana Purchase.

70. King to Livingston and Monroe, May 7, 1803, Livingston Papers, N.-Y. Hist. Soc.

71. King's notebook containing memorandum of letters, entry for May 12, 1803, owned by James G. King.

72. Livingston and Monroe to King, May [n.d.] 1803, and King to Hawkesbury, May 14, 1803, King Papers, N.-Y. Hist. Soc.; King to Livingston and Monroe, May 16, 1803, Livingston Papers, *ibid.*

73. Hawkesbury to King, May 19, 1803, King Papers, N.-Y. Hist. Soc.

74. King to Livingston, May 16, 1803, Secret, Livingston Papers, *ibid.*

CHAPTER XV

HOME TO FRUSTRATED FEDERALISTS

THE NEED TO REVISE THE COMMERCIAL PROVISIONS OF THE JAY TREATY which were soon to expire and to review American relations with Great Britain in the light of the recent adjustment of relations with France was clear to Rufus King, who in 1801 had been abroad for five years. In October he asked Secretary of State Madison to take the matter up with the President, noting his willingness to work closely with Robert Livingston at Paris or even to return for consultation at Washington.[1]

When Jefferson and Madison ignored his proposal, the envoy began seriously to think of home. He had originally anticipated only four years in England, and although the Republican President had allowed him to stay at his post and had approved his efforts to settle outstanding Anglo-American problems, it now appeared that King could no longer take the initiative. Unwilling to be "a mere figurant" of an administration in which he carried no weight, he felt the time ripe to re-establish himself in America.[2] His inclination to bow out was strengthened by the appointment of George W. Erving as consul at London, for between Erving and King there lay a chasm of hostility.

In April 1802, after London papers carried premature accounts that he had decided to resign, King asked Hamilton's opinion. The

1. King to James Madison, Oct. 8, 1801, Private, Madison Papers, Lib. Cong.
2. King to Alexander Hamilton, Apr. 8, 1802, Hamilton Papers, *ibid.*

former Secretary of the Treasury, now practicing law in New York, advised him to come home, where his presence might be "useful in many ways which it is not necessary to particularize." Not that a man should quit his office merely because of a change in administration, Hamilton asserted, but he ought not to lend his talents in support of "undisguised persecutors of the party to which he has been attached and [who] study with ostentation to heap upon it every indignity and injury."[3]

These words reinforced King's determination, and on August 5 he tendered his resignation. Although there was no hint of dissatisfaction in his letter to the Secretary of State, the restive envoy obviously saw no future for himself in England. As he later remarked, when Anglo-American relations had seriously deteriorated, "I did not choose to be the witness of what I foresaw would take place."[4]

In the wake of King's letter of resignation, word began to spread in Republican quarters that Federalists were planning a rejuvenation under his leadership. "You doubtless have before this understood that the plan of the Federalists is to make Mr. King *President*," the new London consul, Erving, commented to Aaron Burr. A few days later he sounded a similar alarm to Madison and Monroe.[5] Livingston, who had not given up his own ambitions, informed his New York political friends that King was planning to establish a new, moderate party: "There is no doubt that he will meet with all the support the federalists can give him and the bait may be taken by some of their opponents." He predicted to DeWitt Clinton that King would be "the forlorn hope of our feds and perhaps they could not chuse better, as he certainly has much address and may serve to catch some of the unwary among our friends."[6]

The rumors had substance insofar as the Federalists hoped to rebuild their shattered forces by capitalizing on King's reputation for

3. Hamilton to King, June 3, 1802, King, ed., *King Correspondence*, IV, 132–34.

4. King offered to stay on at least until Apr. 1803. King to Madison, Aug. 5, 1802, *ibid.*, 154–55. The quotation is from King to Timothy Pickering, Jan. 31, 1809, *ibid.*, V, 131.

5. George W. Erving to Burr, Sept. 24, 1802, Dreer Coll., Hist. Soc. of Pa. "Mr. King is at once a man of talents and politically unprincipled; artful, plausible, and insinuating, in private life perhaps he is respectable (the more politically dangerous) . . . and I do sincerely think that he should be recalled, and if possible disgraced in the public Eye." Erving to James Monroe, Sept. 29, 1802, Private, Monroe Papers, N. Y. Pub. Lib.

6. Robert R. Livingston to Thomas Tillotson, Nov. 12, 1802, Livingston to Clinton, Feb. 5, 1803, Livingston Papers, N.-Y. Hist. Soc.; cf. Livingston to Morgan Lewis, Dec. 7, 1802, *ibid.*

integrity and moderation. By January 1803, Federalist leaders were talking of General Charles C. Pinckney and Rufus King as their candidates in the next presidential election, though Theodore Sedgwick of Massachusetts believed that King should seek the governorship of New York, since it was necessary to concentrate on keeping or winning control of the state governments.[7]

For the moment, King was caught up in the details of his personal affairs. His home on Broadway in New York City had been rented to various tenants, and after it had been on the market for a year, he sold it in April 1802 to John Jacob Astor for $27,500, approximately what it had cost to build.[8] Having made up his mind to become a country gentleman in America, he asked Nicholas Low, his agent in New York, to rent a furnished house in the country and a small town house in the city, with good coach houses and stables for four horses, "for I am not, as I would not wish to be thought, quite ruined by the Expences of my mission."[9]

For some time King had dreamed of buying Hudson Valley farmland, with a sturdy house and barns, fenced fields, woodlands, and fruit trees. At first he thought favorably of Dutchess County, though it might mean political differences with the neighbors. Advising him not to purchase until he returned, Nicholas Low could hardly believe that King would settle down "among the clan of Livingstons," and moreover, like Judge Benson, Hamilton, and Robert Troup, he was apprehensive about King's living too far from New York City.[10] Later, when Low wrote him of the availability of 130 acres in Westchester County, only twenty-six miles from the city, he visualized a country seat "upon the beautiful Waters" of Long Island Sound, but he decided against buying without seeing the property. To satisfy the family's immediate needs, the agent finally rented a house two and a half miles from New York's City Hall.[11]

7. Sedgwick to Alexander Hamilton, Jan. 27, 1803, Hamilton Papers, Lib. Cong.; Sedgwick to King, July 12, 1803, King Papers, N.-Y. Hist. Soc.

8. King's agent, Nicholas Low, and his lawyer, Robert Troup, tried to hold out for $30,000, but the shrewd fur merchant, knowing that the house was not easily salable, refused to budge from his offer of $27,500. Low to King, Apr. 11, 1802, Vol. 37, Troup to King, Apr. 9, 1802, Vol. 47, King Papers, N.-Y. Hist. Soc.; King to Low, Mar. 15, 1802, letterbook owned by James G. King.

9. King to Low, Aug. 5, 1802, letterbook owned by James G. King.

10. Low to King, Aug. 15, 1798, Vol. 37, Troup to King, Oct. 2, Nov. 16, 1798, Aug. 9, 1800, Vol. 47, King Papers, N.-Y. Hist. Soc.

11. Low to King, Aug. 5, Dec. 9, 1800, *ibid.*, Vol. 37; King to Low, Sept. 24, 1800, letterbook owned by James G. King; King, ed., *King Correspondence*, IV, 220–21.

On May 4 Rufus King took formal leave of King George III. He acknowledged the kind consideration of the King and his ministers, to which the monarch replied, "I must say, Mr. King, that I am sorry for your departure. . . . For your conduct here has been so entirely proper, both as it has regarded the interest of your own Country and of this, as to have given me perfect satisfaction." The King, who a quarter of a century before had stubbornly insisted on crushing his rebellious subjects in America, expressed his wish for friendship and mutual understanding with the United States.[12]

During the next two weeks King made a last futile attempt to reach an agreement on the impressment question. He took leave of the Queen on May 12, and settled his affairs in England. On the morning of the eighteenth, he and Mrs. King, with their youngest boys, Edward and Frederick, left London for Cowes on the Isle of Wight, where the *John Morgan* was lying at anchor.[13] On the twenty-first, the ship weighed anchor for the homeward voyage.

After forty days at sea, the *John Morgan* glided into New York Harbor. Rufus King came ashore on the afternoon of June 30 to the cheers of several thousand welcomers and curiosity seekers. Apparently Mary and the children disembarked separately, for the returning Minister was escorted alone up Broadway to Nicholas Low's house, where he bowed to the crowd before entering with a dozen old friends.[14] Greetings poured in upon the Kings as they moved into their rented house overlooking the Hudson a short ride beyond the city, and the envoy was wined and dined in a continuous round of parties. "I have been forced to drink more wine than was suitable," he admitted, adding ruefully that the medicine he was taking for an inflammation of the bladder had not been given a fair chance.[15]

Two weeks after King's arrival at New York, the merchants spon-

12. King's Political Notes, London, 1803, and Record of Letters Written, 1803–06, etc., owned by James G. King; King, ed., *King Correspondence*, IV, 249–50.

13. The two older boys, John and Charles, were left to finish their studies at Harrow, which George III thought a mistake: "All wrong, Mr. King," the monarch remarked; "the boys should be educated in the country in which they are to live." *Ibid.*, 250. Cf. Schuyler, "A Gentleman of the Old School," *Scribner's Magazine*, 55 (1914), 611–19. King's third son, James, was still at school in Paris, where he was under the care of Livingston and Daniel Parker, the Paris representative of the Barings.

14. Eliza Southgate Bowne, *A Girl's Life Eighty Years Ago; Selections from the Letters of Eliza Southgate Bowne* (N.Y., 1888), 160. The Kings called on Eliza, their 20-year-old niece, and her husband Walter Bowne, a New York merchant. *Ibid.*, 162, 163.

15. King to Christopher Gore, Aug. 30, 1803, King Papers, N.-Y. Hist. Soc.

sored a grand public dinner in his honor. Two hundred guests gathered at Leavitt's Hotel for the festivities. King offered a toast to the city of New York, and the assemblage drank to "Rufus King—May foreign Nations ever recognize in the American Envoy the firm Patriot, the able and dignified Statesman," and saluted him with six cheers.[16] This reception was nonpolitical. Republicans and Federalists alike were attentive to the former Minister, whose urbanity and moderate manners won friends, if not active partisans, though Edward Livingston was quick to see in King the Federalist candidate for president.[17]

Living in temporary quarters, King felt unsettled for some months. Books remained unopened in the trunks, and furniture brought from England lay in storage. He looked at houses, inquiring about prices and rents, and regretted that he had sold his Broadway home. After years of the cool English climate, Manhattan's summer heat seemed insufferable. Servants posed a problem: a Negro woman the Kings had brought with them became disgruntled and was fired, but a French cook, hired for $20 a month, proved satisfactory, particularly for his palatable soups.[18]

Late in 1803 the King family rented Peter Livingston's house on Broadway and moved into town, leaving young Edward behind to be tutored by a clergyman a few miles outside the city.[19] It was not until December that King unpacked his baggage. Opening a case supposed to contain an expensive clock and matching girandoles bought

16. *New-York Evening Post*, July 13, 1803; King, ed., *King Correspondence*, IV, 289; Bowne, *A Girl's Life*, 168–69; Barrett [pseud.], *Old Merchants of New York*, V, 153. Tobias Lear, one of the guests, noted the "unbounded applause" when an American air was substituted for the second of two songs extolling the prowess of Great Britain. Lear to James Madison, July 19, 1803, Private, Madison Papers, Lib. Cong.

17. Edward Livingston to Robert R. Livingston, July 18, 1803, Livingston Papers, N.-Y. Hist. Soc. King was pleased with the Jefferson administration's civility towards him, relieving him of the need to report in person in Washington, and allowing his bulky baggage to enter the country duty free. King, ed., *King Correspondence*, IV, 280–81; James Madison to King, July 5, 1803, Albert Gallatin to King, July 6, 1803, King to Christopher Gore, July 10, 1803, King Papers, N.-Y. Hist. Soc.

18. King to [Christopher Gore], July 10, 12, 1803, *ibid.*

19. Mary King wrote her son in England that his father usually spent 12 hours a day in his chair. "As his Knee has given him no trouble, I have advised his using it a little more, and occasionally he has walked for an hour or two, but not often." Mary A. King to Charles King, Dec. 6, 1803, copy by James G. King, from the original owned by Mrs. Margaret Brewster Dunn, Hillside, N. J.

in Paris, he was dismayed to discover the old clothing of a Mr. and Mrs. Apthorp of Boston. When he removed his books from the trunks, he was angered to find several damaged volumes, some unbound—contrary to his orders—and others missing. He wrote angrily to his Paris bookseller to complain of the "blunders and misfortunes" attending his large and costly order but was calm enough a few weeks later to write a friend, "I am snug by my fire side, with my books about me."[20]

Deciding to build his own house, King indirectly approached Charles Bulfinch, who had recently designed the State House in Boston. The Boston architect considered New York builders an unreliable lot, but promised a sketch. Although it is not clear whether King accepted it, or a plan submitted by Daniel Wadsworth of Hartford, or some other design, he had a substantial three-story town house built for him in 1805 at the corner of Church and Robinson[21] Streets. In its chimneys he installed grates brought with him from England, and over the fireplaces handsome marble mantels from Italy. "You are building a house, I hear," wrote young Charles Ingersoll, "Pray Heaven the Jacobins mayn't burn or demolish it. Not that I mean to say you have the honor of being preeminently obnoxious to them, for I even understand the contrary."[22]

During the winter of 1803–04, King stayed aloof from politics, but other Federalists kept his name alive. On February 22, 1804, Timothy Pickering presided over a Federalist dinner in Washington, at which General Charles C. Pinckney and King were named as candidates for the presidency and vice-presidency to oppose Jefferson and George Clinton whom Republicans chose as their second candidate. They ignored Vice-President Burr, whom Jefferson had not forgiven for trying to deprive him of the presidency in 1801. Seeking another avenue to office, Burr decided to run for the governorship of New York. With Clinton out of the running and what then seemed the

20. King to Mr. Franklin, Dec. 15, 1803, King to Mr. Hottinguer, Dec. 21, 1803, King to Charles Pouget [or Pougins], Dec. 16, 1803, King to Charles J. Ingersoll, Dec. 21, 1803, King Papers, N.-Y. Hist. Soc.

21. Later the western half of Barclay Street.

22. Joseph Hale to King, Mar. 2, 1804, King to Daniel Wadsworth, Feb. 22, 1804, Wadsworth to King, Mar. 4, 1804, King to Christopher Gore, Jan. 26, 1806, and quotation from Ingersoll to King, June 11, 1805, King Papers, N.-Y. Hist. Soc. The house was erected on two lots acquired from Trinity Church for $4,300. Conveyances (June 27, 1804), Microfilm Roll No. 347, Liber 229, pp. 47, 51, Hall of Records, New York City.

weak candidacy of Morgan Lewis, a Republican and son-in-law of Robert R. Livingston, Burr won strong Federalist support.

To prevent the New York party from becoming the personal following of Aaron Burr, Hamilton begged King to make the race. "There is no other man among us, under whose standard either fragment of the democratic party could as easily rally," he wrote him.[23] The same day, David B. Ogden, another New York Federalist, visited King to urge the same. King was caught in an embarrassing position between one faction which wished him to be governor of New York and another which was eager to see him vice-president and wished him to support Burr. That he was on good terms with both groups was evidence of the respect he commanded. He determined to remain above this internal factionalism, alienate as few as possible, and strengthen his party for the impending federal election. He probably doubted that he could be elected governor, and he therefore told Ogden that he saw "unsurmountable objections" to giving his consent.[24]

Had King entered the race, it is unlikely that he could have won. There was little chance of Burr's withdrawal; the Federalists were weak in New York, and although the Republicans were divided, they would have closed their ranks against an opponent clearly identified as a Federalist, even a moderate one. As the election turned out, Lewis easily defeated Burr, his majority increased by the votes of Federalists who saw no hope for their own party in the state or, like King and Hamilton, viewed Burr as an unprincipled adventurer.

King's unwillingness to run for the governorship may also have been influenced by his growing awareness that certain New England Federalists preferred secession from the Union to continued subjection to Virginia's Jeffersonian leadership. The self-righteous and choleric Timothy Pickering, now a Senator from Massachusetts, was a ringleader in a conspiracy to organize the five New England states, New York, and New Jersey into a separate union under the guidance of Burr, if the latter was elected governor of New York. King may have learned of the scheme before March 4 when Pickering revealed it to him. Characterizing the President as a "coward wretch"

23. Alexander Hamilton to King, Feb. 24, 1804, King Papers, Vol. 28, N.-Y. Hist. Soc.

24. King to Hamilton, Feb. 24, 1804, King Papers, N.-Y. Hist. Soc. Cf. King to Hamilton [?], Mar. 1, 1804, *ibid.* Reeser, Rufus King and the Federalist Party, 215.

who, "like a Parisian revolutionary monster prating about humanity," took "infernal pleasure in the utter destruction of his opponents," Pickering asked: "Without a separation can those [seven northern] states ever rid themselves of negro presidents and negro congresses, and regain their just weight in the political balance?" The Senator claimed he did not know a thoughtful New Englander who was not "anxious for the *great event*."[25]

The New Yorker replied with great circumspection, merely remarking that Pickering's opinions "ought to fix the attention of the real friends of Liberty in this quarter of the Union, and the more so as things seem to be fast advancing to a crisis."[26] Of his abhorrence of disunion and mistrust of Burr, King mentioned nothing to the bitter New Englander. The less extreme George Cabot, while hoping Burr would win in New York, did not believe New Englanders were ready for secession; as he wrote King from Boston, the project seemed impracticable, too bold to succeed, and ruinous to the public careers of its advocates.[27] King's opposition to separatism, however, was more firmly rooted in devotion to the Union than in the likelihood of the plan's failure. He made no public statement.

On his way home after Congress adjourned, Senator John Quincy Adams stopped for a few days in New York City, where he paid several visits to Rufus King. On the evening of April 8, he found the New Yorker in his library, talking with Timothy Pickering about the scheme to separate the northern states. Pickering, who had seen Hamilton the same day, soon left, and Adams spent the rest of the evening with his host. Discussing the plan for disunion, King emphatically declared, "I disapprove entirely of the project; and so, I am happy to tell you, does General Hamilton." Adams said he was delighted; he, too, opposed it and was worried that in Connecticut and Boston it was considered seriously.[28]

Adams and King talked a long time about the purchase of Louisiana, which had been the immediate stimulus to New England disunionism, and both agreed that the annexation of Louisiana would inevitably lessen the weight and influence of the North in the affairs

25. Pickering to King, Mar. 4, 1804, King Papers, N.-Y. Hist. Soc.
26. King to Pickering, Mar. 9, 1804, *ibid.*
27. Cabot to King, Mar. 17, 1804, *ibid.*
28. John Quincy Adams, "Reply to the Appeal of the Massachusetts Federalists" (1829), in Henry Adams, ed., *Documents Relating to New England Federalism, 1800–1815* (Boston, 1905), 147–48.

of the nation, augment slave representation, and endanger the Union by stretching boundaries so far as to weaken the country's defenses against invasion. Yet America had no choice; the only alternative, they admitted, was possession of the territory and the mouth of the Mississippi by Napoleon. They believed, however, that the extension of national power and security would eventually outweigh the northeastern states' loss of influence, and at least France had been converted from a formidable danger in America to a "natural ally." In any event, King and Adams regarded a break-up of the Union as "a remedy more desperate than any possible disease."[29]

Meanwhile, Hamilton mustered all his energy to defeat Burr's bid to become governor. Although the decisive victory of Morgan Lewis was in reality the outcome of effective vote-getting by the Clinton-Livingston combination, Hamilton took evident satisfaction in crushing Burr's political fortunes. During the campaign, an Albany newspaper published an allegation that Hamilton had declared Burr "a dangerous man, and one who ought not to be trusted with the reins of government," and Burr demanded an unqualified acknowledgement or denial. Before replying, Hamilton asked King whether he was bound to give a definite answer, and his friend advised him firmly not to.[30] Encouraged, Hamilton declined to reply to Burr's questions, which were based upon inferences from remarks allegedly heard in an unspecified conversation. When Burr insisted upon an explicit retraction, denial, or avowal, Hamilton refused. The Vice-President then challenged him to what became the most famous duel in American history.

In accepting the challenge, Hamilton ignored King's unsolicited advice against it. More than that, he determined to withhold his fire, and he revealed this decision to a single "judicious friend," Rufus King. Horrified, King protested that Hamilton "owed it to his family and the rights of self-defence" to fire at his opponent, but reasonable expostulation had no effect upon Hamilton whose proud sense of personal honor would not permit a suspicion of cowardice, and who in his last letter announced that Christian scruples had convinced him to risk his own life rather than incur the guilt of taking another's.[31] "With a mind the most capacious and discriminating that

29. *Ibid.* The quoted words are Adams's.

30. King to Charles King, Apr. 2, 1819, and lengthy endorsement by Charles King, Apr. 7, 1819, King Papers, N.-Y. Hist. Soc.

31. *Ibid.*; Mitchell, *Alexander Hamilton*, II, 530–33; Miller, *Alexander Hamilton*, 572.

I ever knew," King wrote, Hamilton had governed himself by "certain rules upon the subject of Duels, the fallacy of which could not fail to be seen by any man of ordinary understanding; with these guides it is my deliberate opinion that he could not have avoided a meeting with Col. Burr, had he even declined the first challenge."[32]

Seeing that Hamilton could not be dissuaded, King left for Boston shortly before July 11, the day of the fatal duel at Weehawken.[33] After Hamilton's death, some people, unaware of what had gone on between the two devoted friends, blamed King for not trying to prevent the duel, and for seeming to wash his hands of the affair by departing on the eve of the tragedy. Yet, in fact, King was engulfed in sadness. Inscribed in one of his notebooks, under the name "Hamilton," are these lines:

> In every virtuous act, and glorious strife,
> He shone the first and best—
> Homer—il.2 208
>
> Each rising sun beholds my ceaseless grief
> And night returning brings me no relief.[34]

Like many northerners, including Hamilton himself, King detested dueling. He considered it not a proof of courage but a violation of man's civil, moral, and religious duty. "No person can hold in deeper Abhorence than I do the practise of Duelling," he asserted, "and our lamented friend was not unacquainted with my Opinion upon this Subject."[35]

32. Allan McLane Hamilton, *The Intimate Life of Alexander Hamilton* (London, 1910), 380. The author states, I think erroneously, that King wrote these words to Charles King on Apr. 2, 1819. Substantially the same words appear in King's hand on the back of his draft of a letter to Matthew Clarkson, Aug. 24, 1804, King Papers, N.-Y. Hist. Soc. It is not known to whom they were written.

33. The exact date of King's departure is uncertain. It was asserted in 1819 that he had left the day before the duel. Dorothy C. Barck, ed., *Letters from John Pintard to his Daughter, Eliza Noel Pintard Davidson, 1816–1833 . . .* (N.-Y. Hist. Soc., *Collections*, 70–73 [1937–40]), I, 173. In 1825 Pickering wrote that Judge Egbert Benson told him King had left New York "on the Friday preceding the Monday of the fatal duel." Timothy Pickering to William Coleman, July 1, 1825, Pickering Papers, Vol. 18, Mass. Hist. Soc. The duel, however, occurred on a Wednesday.

34. King's notebook on Gibbon's Rome, etc., owned by James G. King.

35. King to Matthew Clarkson, Aug. 29, 1804, N. Y. Society Lib.

Although King evidently had planned his New England trip in April, the purpose being to visit the Gores, who had returned from England, and his relatives in Maine,[36] he undoubtedly had a political purpose as well. He hoped to thwart, or at least restrain, a planned conclave of Federalist leaders at Boston where it was intended to further Pickering's plot for a northern confederacy. The day before the duel, in his last political letter, Hamilton pleaded with Theodore Sedgwick against dismemberment of the Union as sacrificing great advantages without any counterbalancing gain and as serving to concentrate the poison of democracy. "*King* is on his way for Boston," he added, "where you may chance to see him, and hear from himself his sentiments."[37]

The journey to New England gave King a long-sought chance to chat with old friends and associates. With his wife and Judge Benson, he headed first for Hartford, where he had several political cronies and Mary King had relatives. At the Connecticut capital he received letters from New York confirming rumors of Hamilton's death. King was deeply shocked by the loss of a friend to whom he had so often turned for advice. As the circumstances of the duel were not widely known, he was eager to prevent misrepresentation and sought to have the true story publicized by Oliver Wolcott, Jr., and by Nathaniel Pendleton, who had been Hamilton's second in the duel and was one of his executors.[38] Though Hamilton owned land, he had gone deeply into debt and had not adequately provided for his wife and children. King thought the state of New York ought at least to help pay the debts, but he volunteered to subscribe $1,000 to a private fund to support the family.[39]

Delayed by attacks of intermittent fever on the way from Hartford, the Kings arrived on July 22 at the new mansion of the Gores in Waltham, where for the better part of five weeks they resumed the intimate companionship of their London days. In mid-August

36. Christopher Gore to King, Apr. 27, 1804, King Papers, N.-Y. Hist. Soc.

37. Alexander Hamilton to Sedgwick, July 10, 1804, Sedgwick Papers, Mass. Hist. Soc.

38. Of his fallen hero's scruples King wrote, "I have some recollection that in his dispute with Monroe, he made this distinction, that he would neither give nor refuse a challenge." King to Oliver Wolcott, July 16, 1804, Wolcott Papers, Vol. 7, Conn. Hist. Soc.

39. King to Oliver Wolcott, July 23, Aug. 8, 1804, Wolcott to King, Aug. 14, 1804, *ibid.* King was one of eight individuals subscribing $1,000 apiece, their $8,000 being half the amount pledged by all the subscribers by Aug. 14. *Ibid.*

King and Gore were among those who, by invitation, visited the Boston public schools. At this time, young Daniel Webster, studying law in Gore's Boston office, noticed that a man in plain gray clothes entered and, on learning that Gore was out, sat down to wait. Webster, who had been reading alone in the office, recalled later, "I went on with my book, till he asked what I was reading, and, coming along up to the table, took the book and looked at it. 'Roccus,' said he, '*de navibus et nando*. Well, I read that book too when I was a boy'; and proceeded to talk not only about 'ships and freights,' but insurance, prize, and other matters of maritime law, in a manner 'to put me up to all I knew,' and a good deal more. The grey-coated stranger turned out to be Mr. Rufus King."[40]

Early in September the Kings set out for Maine. King was entertained at Salem, and on the fifth, his home town of Newburyport gave him a public dinner in Washington Hall, which resounded to songs and patriotic toasts.

After his brief visit to Dummer School, King and his party crossed the Piscataqua into his native district where he no doubt recalled other incidents of his childhood. There at last he greeted his stepmother, his brothers and sisters, and their families and introduced his wife and Judge Benson, who accompanied the traveling party. On the twenty-ninth, King and Benson were publicly received in Portland.[41]

Back in Boston by the middle of October, King was guest of honor at an elaborate public dinner on the seventeenth. About two hundred people, including Governor Caleb Strong, other high officials, and clergymen, graced the newly enlarged and decorated Concert Hall. The toasts were appropriate to a Federalist political rally: the Washington and Adams administrations were called the morning and evening stars of America's national glory; "The *State of New York*. Too respectable to be the *Dupe of Virginia*"; "May those Yankees who cannot endure Federal *Sunshine*, go to Louisiana for MOONSHINE"; "May we cultivate and defend the soil we *already possess*, without paying or fighting for what we can *neither cultivate nor defend*"; "BONAPARTE. May he learn *justice* from the British Government, and *meekness* from ours."[42]

40. King to Wolcott, July 23, 1804, *ibid.*; King, ed., *King Correspondence*, IV, 418–19; Charles W. March, *Reminiscences of Congress* (N. Y., 1850), 20–21.

41. *Newburyport Herald*, Sept. 7, 1804; Boston *Columbian Centinel*, Oct. 6, 1804.

42. Boston *Repertory*, Oct. 19, 1804.

Seeing in the affair "an extraordinary contempt for every thing that regarded American glory" and "a charming tone of sycophancy for the British government," the *Independent Chronicle*, speaking for Republicans, thought it more appropriate for London than Boston. Noting that the good citizens of Massachusetts would credit the "tories" with eagerly seizing all opportunities to be "sentimentally seditious," the Republican journal charged the Essex Junto with using the visit of King and Gore as a vehicle for abusing the Jefferson administration, and observed that former President Adams and his son had been absent from the festivities. The younger Adams had left for Congress the evening before the dinner, a departure which, if delayed, might have proved embarrassing, for he would have been identified with an assemblage of "inveterate tories and British factors with more zeal than character." The former President, on his part, felt obliged to publicize his reply to the committee on arrangements, declining the invitation because of illness.[43] Two weeks after the occasion, John Adams had recovered his health sufficiently to be hailed at a public dinner to celebrate his seventieth birthday, with King an honored guest.[44]

After an absence of almost four months, the Kings returned to New York early in November. King plunged into conferences on Hamilton's financial affairs and worked with Gouverneur Morris on a plan to raise money for Elizabeth Hamilton and her children.[45] Politics he left to others. Almost certainly without his knowledge, he was nominated in the state legislature to oppose the Republican congressman and scientist, Samuel L. Mitchill, for the seat in the United States Senate vacated by John Armstrong, who had been appointed to succeed Livingston as minister to France. Mitchill won decisively. That only three state senators and fourteen assemblymen voted for King was conclusive proof of the prostration of Federalism in New York.[46]

If King carefully skirted New York's political strife, he nevertheless accepted nomination for high national office. Ratification of the Twelfth Amendment in September meant that he would be the

43. Boston *Independent Chronicle*, Oct. 20, 25, 1804; King, ed., *King Correspondence*, IV, 425.

44. *Ibid.*, 426.

45. Gouverneur Morris, Diary, entries for Nov. 12, 15, 1804, Lib. Cong.

46. Samuel L. Mitchill to Catherine A. Mitchill, Nov. 17, 20, 1804, Mitchill Papers, Museum of the City of New York; *Albany Centinel*, Nov. 13, 1804; King, ed., *King Correspondence*, IV, 426. The election was held on Nov. 9.

Federalist candidate for the vice-presidency. Many in his party disliked the new constitutional amendment separating the candidates for president and vice-president, thinking that it gave distinct advantage to the party in power, and no doubt he shared that opinion. Gouverneur Morris thought King agreed with him that the Constitution was about to be overturned. If some naïve partisans thought of General Pinckney and Rufus King as political saviors of the country, King recognized that the nominations were a barren honor. He expected Jefferson's re-election and saw everywhere only the dimmest prospects for Federalism. All of New England except Massachusetts and Connecticut had gone Republican, and he had little doubt that these strongholds would be lost before long. Still he was incapable of the wild denunciations of democracy uttered by Pickering, Uriah Tracy, Roger Griswold, and other New England extremists who dallied with disunionism.[47] In December, Jefferson was returned to office by carrying 162 of the 176 electoral votes, Clinton winning the vice-presidency by the same margin. King and Pinckney were accorded only the 14 electoral votes of Connecticut and Delaware. In their sweeping triumph, the Republicans controlled both houses of Congress with huge majorities.

Since his return from England, King had not lost interest in Francisco de Miranda's aim of revolution in South America. "An immense number" of Americans, he had predicted, would be electrified by news of a filibustering expedition and would "take up their Bed and walk."[48] Miranda, despairing of decisive intervention by the British government, sailed under an assumed name to the United States and, on November 10, 1805, the day after he disembarked at New York, called upon King to brief him on the latest revolutionary plans and to ask for help. He handed the former diplomat a long letter from Nicholas Vansittart, who, as a commercial expert for Addington's ministry, had been friendly with both Miranda and King. Now a member of Parliament, Vansittart described English opinion on rebellion in Spanish America, noting that while merchants were eager

47. King's notebook containing memorandum of letters, entry for Aug. 22, 1804, owned by James G. King; King to Robert R. Livingston, Aug. 22, 1804, Livingston Papers, N.-Y. Hist. Soc. Tracy, fretting at the "daily scourge of Democratic nonsense and wickedness," asserted that Rhode Island and Vermont were so devoted to Virginia that "if she asked them to Castrate themselves they would struggle for a preference for loosing first their testicles." Tracy to King, Jan. 3, 1804, King Papers, N.-Y. Hist. Soc.

48. King to Christopher Gore, Jan. 4, 1804, King Papers, N.-Y. Hist. Soc.

to exploit rich new markets, others shrank from countenancing revolution. "You will be the best judge" of the support Miranda might muster in America, the Englishman suggested to King, "and your influence will be of the utmost importance to him."[49]

Though sympathetic with Miranda's cause, King was unwilling to encourage a filibuster without the administration's approval. He responded warily to the Venezuelan's entreaties and refused to ask friends for aid on his own initiative; he advised Miranda to confer with the President and the Secretary of State. Before Miranda departed for Washington, King sent Vansittart's letter along to Madison, thus leaving no doubt of the New Yorker's desire to avoid suspicion by informing the administration of the circumstances of Miranda's mission.[50]

After talking with Jefferson and Madison, the Venezuelan returned to New York, convinced that the government, though refusing official aid, would wink at actions by private individuals. Again he asked King to approach friends for money, and again the New Yorker declined, replying that the administration had not hinted to any of his friends that they might discreetly supply the expedition.[51] King was unwilling even to talk with Miranda's New York associates, among whom were two Federalists, Samuel A. Ogden, a merchant, and William S. Smith, surveyor of the port, who supplied men, ships, and funds.[52] Bitterly disappointed, Miranda notified Vansittart that King and Gore "who had promised much" had done nothing.[53]

A few weeks after Miranda sailed on the *Leander* for Santo Do-

49. Nicholas Vansittart to King, Aug. 14, 1805, Box A, *ibid.*; William S. Robertson, *The Life of Miranda*, 2 vols. (Chapel Hill, 1929), I, 292.

50. King to Christopher Gore, Mar. 9, 1806, Box A, King to James Madison, Nov. 25, 1805, Private, King Papers, N.-Y. Hist. Soc. Madison returned the letter, with a polite but noncommittal acknowledgment. Madison to King, Dec. 4, 1805, Private, *ibid.* For further details, see King, ed., *King Correspondence*, IV, 577–86. King declined to give Miranda a letter of introduction, and he did not expect the government to encourage the Venezuelan. Anne Cary Morris, ed., *The Diary and Letters of Gouverneur Morris. . .* , 2 vols. (N. Y., 1888), II, 470. Gore introduced Miranda's agent to some potential supporters in Boston, but they declined to participate in the filibuster. Gore to King, Dec. 10, 1805, King Papers, N.-Y. Hist. Soc.

51. King's memorandum on the back of Miranda to King, Dec. 30, 1805, King Papers, Box A, N.-Y. Hist. Soc.; Robertson, *Miranda*, I, 295–97.

52. King to Christopher Gore, Mar. 9, 1806, King Papers, Box A, N.-Y. Hist. Soc.; Robertson, *Miranda*, I, 297–99.

53. Miranda to Nicholas Vansittart, Jan. 4, 1806, in Robertson, *Miranda*, I, 298.

mingo, Ogden and Smith were arrested and haled into court and King was implicated. When called to a hearing, he informed the district attorney that he had recommended to Miranda full disclosure of his plans to the government, and that the Venezuelan had later reported to him that the government, while not sanctioning the filibuster, would "assist at Miranda's procuring the supplies from individuals, provided the same was done discreetly."[54] Seeing in the proceedings a calculated attempt to smear the Federalists in New York City, King confided to Gore: "I felicitate myself that the sentiments I entertain of our Chief have kept me within the limits of extreme Caution. I cannot with honour be a volunteer on this occasion against Government, but if I am called as a Witness on the Prosecution they institute, all Reserve will be at an end; the whole must be told, and being told cannot leave any doubt of the unworthy Conduct of Government in this Affair."[55]

Smith and Ogden were eventually acquitted, and the excitement generated by what Gore called the government's "persecution" gradually died down. Miranda's expeditionary force, too small to be effective, ended in pitiful failure, but King still looked to the future. "Were I an English Minister," he wrote to Vansittart, "I would not rest till the Resources of South America were wrested from the hands of France, for they can no longer be regarded as those of Spain."[56]

King's suspicion of the Republican administration, so apparent in the Miranda episode, was only a mild reflection of his aversion and contempt for a regime which seemed to him bent on proscribing the opposition and undermining the foundations of government. In 1805 he congratulated the impeached Supreme Court Justice Samuel Chase upon his acquittal, praising the judge's defense of the "just and necessary power of the judiciary" and calling it "an everlasting Record of the unworthy Motives" of his persecutors.[57] For the next eight years, King was deeply critical of Jeffersonian and Madisonian policies, his determined aloofness from politics only fostering the frustration of his fellow Federalists.

54. King, ed., *King Correspondence*, IV, 577–86. After King was informed that his testimony was relevant only to the *Leander*'s destination (Santo Domingo and thence to Caracas), the record of the examination was destroyed. *Ibid.*, 586. Miranda sailed from New York on Feb. 2, 1806.

55. King to Christopher Gore, Mar. 9, 1806, King Papers, Box A, N.-Y. Hist. Soc.

56. King to Nicholas Vansittart, Sept. 30, 1806, King Papers, N.-Y. Hist. Soc.

57. King to Samuel Chase, Mar. 6, 1805, *ibid.*

CHAPTER XVI

COUNTRY GENTLEMAN

WITH NO IMMEDIATE PROSPECT OF PUBLIC OFFICE, RUFUS KING BECAME absorbed in personal affairs and in civic, church, and educational projects. He was a charter member of the Academy of Fine Arts, which was organized in 1801–02 under the inspiration of Robert R. Livingston. Except for John Trumbull, few of the charter members were connoisseurs. King was chosen a director and vice-president in 1804, was re-elected as both the next year, and seems to have attended about half the society's meetings before dropping out in 1807.[1] The few recorded comments about the painting, sculpture, and architecture he saw in the Low Countries indicate that King's appreciation of art was limited and related mainly to its historical interest. Among the several thousand books in his library, only a score dealt with the arts, though well-printed works in expensive bindings delighted him.[2] The one artist with whom he was on intimate terms was Trumbull, who shared his Federalist political sympathies and whose broad historical canvasses appealed to King's patriotism. Trumbull's portraits of members of the family had for King more sentimental than artistic value.

1. King was still vice-president early in 1807. American Academy of Fine Arts, Minute Book, I, *passim*, N.-Y. Hist. Soc.; Robert R. Livingston to King, Apr. 27, 1804, contained in American Academy of Fine Arts, Plans, I, *ibid.* Livingston recommended to King that the group's name include the word "American," and in 1808 the society obtained a charter as the American Academy of the Arts, which, after many vicissitudes, was absorbed in 1840 by the younger National Academy of Design.
2. Author's analysis of King's library, now in the N.-Y. Hist. Soc.

A deep and abiding interest in history and an admiring friendship for Judge Egbert Benson induced King to be one of the founders of the New-York Historical Society.[3] His enthusiasm for history was reflected in the nearly six hundred historical works on his shelves. Like most educated men of his generation, King read widely among classical authors and acquired more than four hundred volumes of classics and descriptions of the ancient world. Gibbon's *Decline and Fall of the Roman Empire* he considered immortal. For several years he kept notebooks, jotting into them excerpts from the writers he admired, particularly Gibbon, which were useful in preparing speeches. One such extract, "a permanent interest very frequently ripens into a sincere and useful friendship," mirrored his pragmatism; another appealed to his deep sense of responsibility: "It is dangerous to entrust the conduct of nations to men who have learned from their profession to consider reason as the instrument of dispute, and to interpret the laws according to the dictates of private interest."[4]

King, who was neither particularly spiritual in outlook nor well versed in theology, regarded the church as an institution necessary to ensure morality, the very foundation of social stability, and as a source of personal comfort. He had been a warden of St. Paul's Church, Newburyport, and later as a New Yorker had joined the socially prominent congregation of Trinity Church, whose rector had officiated at his marriage. His father-in-law had been a parishioner, as were many of King's friends. In 1805 he became a warden of Trinity, and during the next seven years he was five times appointed as Trinity's lay delegate to state conventions of the Protestant Episcopal Church. He served on at least three important diocesan committees: to finance a new chapel, to consider applications from churches for funds, and to aid destitute clergymen in the New York diocese. In 1806 and 1807 he was a member of the trustees' Society for Promoting Religion and Learning in the State of New York.[5] To all of these he brought valuable knowledge of finance and a sound business sense. Although King declined appointment to the board of the American Bible Society, he approved its work, and the

3. Benson presided at the organization meeting on Dec. 10, 1804, of this second oldest historical society in the United States. Minutes, 1, 2, owned by the Society.

4. King's notebook on Gibbon's Rome, 1799–1802, owned by James G. King; King's notebook, King Papers, Vol. 75, N.-Y. Hist. Soc.

5. Extracts from the minutes of the vestry of Trinity Church, communicated to the author by Helen Rose Cline, parish recorder.

fact that he had been approached suggests something of his reputation as an active Christian layman.[6]

Before his town house was completed, King renewed the search for a country home where he could spend most of the year in privacy. He abandoned earlier dreams of a princely estate overlooking the Hudson or of a site on Long Island Sound and took title in November 1805 to a substantial but unpretentious house and barn on ninety acres of land in Jamaica, Long Island, twelve miles from the city. Combining the sturdiness of the Dutch tradition and the refinement of the Georgian style, the building was more than fifty years old when King acquired it, and at one time had been an inn or tavern. King described it as "not fashionable but convenient."[7]

Even if the Kings' new home was several miles from the waterfront and lacked a commanding view, it was a bargain at $12,000 and had other advantages. A daily stagecoach rumbled along the road to Brooklyn, making connection with the ferry to New York. Within easy reach were church, schools, and physicians, important to Mrs. King, whose health was beginning to fail. For her husband's sporting interests, Long Island afforded excellent riding and hunting. He loved horses and hunting for grouse, woodcock, and other small game and was considered a fine marksman. In later years farmers remembered him with his sons riding over the North Shore hills, where beautiful woodlands relieving the monotony of the open Jamaica countryside sloped to the waters of the Sound. The village of Jamaica was attractive, impressing an English visitor in 1810 with its "elegant" buildings and "seminary for education." This was Union Hall Academy, of which King and later his son John became trustees.[8]

6. King, ed., *King Correspondence*, IV, 535–36.

7. Late in the 18th century, the property had been bought by Christopher Smith, but John Alsop, King's father-in-law, controlled it through a heavy mortgage. Smith, though the owner of 10 slaves, died in debt, and it was from his estate that King, as the highest bidder at public sale, bought the property in two parcels for $12,000. Microfilm QC-5 (Deeds) of Liber M, 96–100, Register's Office, Queens County, Jamaica, N. Y.; Harold D. Eberlein, *Manor Houses and Historic Homes of Long Island and Staten Island* (Phila., 1928), 158; "Federal Census, 1800, Queens County, Long Island, New York," *N. Y. Gen. and Biog. Record*, 54 (1923), 120, 210–13.

8. John Melish, *Travels in the United States of America. . .* , 2 vols. (Phila., 1812), I, 385; printed announcement of Union Hall Academy, Apr. 17, 1819, on the reverse of which, in manuscript, is John A. King to Morris S. Miller, Oct. 4, 1819, Miscellaneous Manuscripts, N. Y. Pub. Lib. Over the years, King's younger sons and several grandchildren studied at Union Hall Academy. King to Theodore Sedgwick, July 28, 1824, Sedgwick Papers, Box 2, Mass. Hist. Soc.

The fifty-nine-acre farm around King's country home was mostly open and flat, its few trees offering almost no shelter from the parching summer sun. However, on the hills to the north, King owned thirty-one acres of woodland, with a fine view of the country and seashore.[9] The house itself lay in a bare field, about a hundred yards from a white picket fence along the road, flanked by two horse chestnuts and some old apple trees. In the spring of 1806, when his family moved in, King had started alterations, adding a new kitchen with pine timber cut from his own woods, oak planks for beams, and dressed shingles purchased from a neighbor.[10]

The house was dignified and comfortable, and its new owners later remodeled the dining and bedrooms to suit the needs of a large family that often entertained guests. The very unpretentiousness of his home, in contrast to Gore's brick mansion in Waltham, suited King, who approvingly quoted Cicero's dictum that a citizen's dignity should be adorned by his house, not derived from it.[11] From the Doric-columned portico one entered a central hall, where, on the left, King placed a desk, with impressive busts of his heroes, Washington and Hamilton, on either side, near pictures of his favorite race horses. To the left of the hallway, in the drawing room, were English Chippendale chairs and a sofa, brightly upholstered in golden damask, which the Kings brought with them on returning to America. Other furniture was made locally, a few pieces by the New York cabinetmaker, Duncan Phyfe. The dining room, to the right of the hall, was small and was enlarged in 1810 when King altered the bedrooms above it.[12]

Diagonally across the hall, behind the drawing room, was the library. Here for many years the master of the house read and studied, conversed privately, and relaxed on his couch. About him were ceiling-high bookcases, sufficient for his books and pamphlets. Even-

9. In 1810 and 1811, King added 16 more acres of woods in Jamaica and another 16 in Flushing. Microfilm QC-5 (Deeds) of Liber M, 96–100, 101–04, 105–08, 109, Register's Office, Queens County, Jamaica, N. Y.

10. George Codwise to King, Jan. 7, 1806, and King's endorsement on Codwise to King, Jan. 13, 1806, King Papers, N.-Y. Hist. Soc.; *Homes of American Statesmen: with Anecdotal, Personal, and Descriptive Sketches, by Various Writers* (N. Y., 1860), 358. The chapter on King's Jamaica estate was written by his son, Charles King.

11. King's notebook, King Papers, Vol. 75, N.-Y. Hist. Soc.

12. Eliza Gracie Suydam, *A Descendant of Kings, a Memoir* [1941], owned by James G. King; King to John Trumbull, July 25, 1810, King Papers, N.-Y. Hist. Soc.

tually his collection numbered more than five thousand volumes, nearly a quarter of them on politics or public affairs; almost a thousand were travel accounts and geographical descriptions; histories came next, then books on commerce and finance, followed in decreasing numbers by writings of the *philosophes*, works on science, the ancient classics, international relations, law, war, novels and criticism, religion and morals, poetry, dictionaries and other literary aids, essays, volumes on botany and horticulture, biography, memoirs, and theater. A few were presentation copies: Count Rumford's essays, Sir John Sinclair's pamphlet on longevity, and Lord Sheffield's defense of Britain's navigation and colonial system. Others were in sets attractively bound in leather. Four lavish and expensive folios of engravings of art masterpieces were among the most handsome volumes. So were John Blair's strikingly illustrated account of the world from its presumed creation in 4004 B.C. to 1800 A.D. and William Curtis's *Flora Londoniensis*, two thick folios of exquisite color plates. After King's death, the collection was evaluated at $5,530, in retrospect certainly an underestimate.[13]

Rufus and Mary King loved the country and were well versed in the lore of nature. They spent many hours and large sums in renovating lawns, planting trees, and transplanting many of their shrubs from the nearby woods and meadows. He cherished his garden and farm, but it is likely that he rarely turned a shovel himself. As planner and superviser, he directed the planting of oaks, sycamores, and other deciduous shade trees; fir and pine of varieties unobtainable on Long Island he secured from a friend in New Hampshire; laurel, larch, silver fir, hemlock, spruce, and white pine he imported from the woods of his native Maine. In the orchard were apple, peach, apricot, and other fruit trees. The strawberry plants yielded a fine crop. In the fields King planted clover, timothy, English hay, cereal crops, potatoes, and various vegetables, and he kept horses, cows, sheep, hogs, and bees.[14]

The longer he lived in the country the more absorbed he became in farming and horticulture. Once, years after moving to Jamaica, he

13. Estimate by G. H. Carvill and F. G. King, Oct. 13, 1827, King Papers, Vol. 74, N.-Y. Hist. Soc. The books mentioned in this paragraph are in the King Collection, *ibid.*

14. *Homes of American Statesmen*, 360–61; King's Memoranda concerning the Propagation of Trees and Shrubs, 1806, King Papers, Box 81, N.-Y. Hist. Soc.; Robert Ernst, "Jamaica Gentleman," *Adelphi Quarterly*, 4 (1961), 7–13.

toured the grounds with the scholarly Portuguese diplomat, the Abbé Corréa, conversing not on international problems but on Linnaeus's system of classification, on agriculture, climate, soils, and manures. The amateur Portuguese botanist remarked that King's estate provided specimens of most of the flowers and trees of the central and eastern United States. King's achievements in scientific farming were no greater than those of other gentlemen farmers of his time, but if he admitted to only a modest knowledge, he nevertheless gained a considerable local reputation and in 1819 was chosen the first president of the Queens County Society for the Promotion of Agriculture and Domestic Manufactures.[15]

King also developed an interest in animal husbandry. In 1810 he asked Thomas Coke of Norfolk, who had been his host in England, to buy him four cows "of the most approved sort for milk and form." There is no record of the cattle being received, but six years later Coke sent him two North Devon cows, whose mahogany color, fine proportions, and docile nature so pleased their new owner that he imported more in answer to a local demand for pure stock. King considered it important for the United States to domesticate Spanish merino sheep in order to increase the native supply of wool. He hoped to see both woolen and cotton manufactures develop to a point of national self-sufficiency.[16]

Rural life did not completely isolate King from his old friends in town. For a number of years he spent winters in New York City, enjoying the warm comradeship of Nicholas Low, Egbert Benson, and Gouverneur Morris. Frequently he drove from his town house to Morrisania for a day or two, to share with his expansive host the conviviality of dinner, wine, and conversation. By this time Morris was probably more interested in horticulture than he had been in 1789, when he had claimed "no knowledge of botany except to distinguish onions and cabbages from oak trees."[17]

15. *Homes of American Statesmen*, 361, 363; King to Richard Peters, Feb. 24, 1816, in collection labeled "Scrapbook, T.W.C.M.," N. Y. Society Lib.; David S. Bogart to King, June 24, 1819, King Papers, N.-Y. Hist. Soc.

16. King to Thomas Coke, July 29, 1810, library of the Earl of Leicester, Holkham, printed in *The Countryman*, 31 (1945), 29–30; *Homes of American Statesmen*, 361–62; King to John A. King, Apr. 17, 1823, Jesse Buel to King, Mar. 21, 1825, King Papers, N.-Y. Hist. Soc. King to John Trumbull, Oct. 29, 1810, Vol. 80, *ibid.* It is not clear from existing records whether King himself owned merino sheep.

17. Gouverneur Morris, Diary, *passim*, Lib. Cong. The quotation may also be found in Morris, ed., *Diary of Gouverneur Morris*, I, 94.

In 1806, shortly after moving to Jamaica, King was elected a trustee of Columbia College, a family institution for old New Yorkers. As King's College, it had always maintained a close connection with Trinity Church, which continued to exert a strong influence upon it after it was reorganized as Columbia in 1784. The college's trustees were socially prominent men, mostly Episcopalians and decided Federalists. Among them were King's friends, Morris, Judge Benson, Oliver Wolcott, Jr., Robert Troup, and Cornelius Bogert. It is quite probable that King influenced Benson and Bogert to become residents of Jamaica, Bogert in 1809, and the judge some years later. Bogert, who enjoyed hunting with King, was a conservative lawyer and a former Tory, who in 1821 stoutly defended property qualifications for voting and deplored "the influx of foreign vagabonds."[18] While King had graduated from Harvard, his connections with Columbia were strong; he had given a Columbia education to his half-brother Cyrus, and much later, his second son, Charles, was to serve for thirteen years as a trustee and for fourteen years as president of the college.

Dissatisfied with the quality of the student body, the trustees appointed a committee under King's chairmanship to investigate and consider appropriate remedies. On its recommendation, the trustees strengthened the curriculum and stiffened the admission requirements, directing the faculty not to admit any boy who could not meet established standards in mathematics as well as demonstrate familiarity with the Greek and Latin authors specified in the regulations for admission. The faculty took exception to this reflection upon its conduct of the admission examinations, but the trustees were unmoved and adopted resolutions, subsequently reported by King's committee, which set even higher standards of student discipline and training.[19]

Perhaps the most troublesome of the trustees' problems concerned

18. When the Bogerts bought their property in Jamaica, Mrs. King considered Mrs. Bogert "a great acquisition to our circle of acquaintance." Mary King to Mrs. John Trumbull, July 3, 1809, Dreer Coll., Hist. Soc. of Pa. For Bogert's conservatism, see Bogert to King, Jan. 8, 1821, King Papers, N.-Y. Hist. Soc.

19. Minutes of the Trustees of Columbia College, II, 347–48, 352, 354, 356–57, 359–60, 367–85, 387–88, Columbiana Coll., Low Memorial Library, Columbia Univ.; N. F. Moore, *A Historical Sketch of Columbia College* (N. Y., 1846), 76–77; [Columbia Univ.], *A History of Columbia University, 1754–1904 . . .* (N. Y., 1904), 87.

the religious affiliation of Columbia's president. An Episcopalian had always held this office, even after the college's reorganization, but a Presbyterian faction of the trustees now wished to be rid of all vestiges of Episcopal–specifically Trinity Church–control. For three years, beginning in 1808, a controversy raged over the possible candidacy of John Mason, a Presbyterian divine who served on King's committee to reform the curriculum. A vigorous and ambitious man of forty, Mason confided to King that if he did not obtain the presidency, he would abandon his career and prepare himself for the law. As a moderate Episcopalian, skilled in negotiating, King was thrust into the fray as mediator between the reformers and those whom Mason labeled the "College-Vatican."[20]

Through King, the Episcopalian majority offered to make the president of Columbia, in effect, a figurehead if the office were restricted to members of their denomination and to create a new post of vice-president, to be held by a non-Episcopalian, who would wield the effective executive power. What seemed to the Episcopalians reasonable and generous was at first unacceptable to Mason, though eventually the substance of their proposal prevailed; when in 1811 the Episcopal Reverend William Harris was chosen president, Mason accepted an appointment as provost. Something of the sensitivity which King brought to his role as mediator is suggested in his memorandum of an interview with Mason:

> [He] could not be unapprized of difficulties which I had to overcome: that the Division and Rivalry between the Episcopalians and the Presbyterians were such as that a common Opinion seemed hopeless–that the Episcopalians feared that the College would be turned into a theological Institution directed by Dissenters–and that connected as I was with the Episcopalians, it would be difficult to take any part that would appear like dissection. If the Division were not so considerable, if the Feelings of Gentlemen on both sides were less lively and strong, in a word, if the College had not in fact become a bone of contention between the Episcopalians and the Dissenters, I should have no hesitation as to the course I ought to take–that in my Opinion the College should have nothing to do with the Reasons and Arguments in support of Episcopacy or the Tenets of the Dissenters; that a collegiate Education was to fit the Candidates

20. King's memorandum, Feb. 6, 1810, John M. Mason to King, June 23, 1809, King Papers, N.-Y. Hist. Soc.

> for the different learned professions—and not to teach any of the Professions; so far as regards the Evidence of the Christian Religion was concerned, let it be inculcated, but as respects the different professions among Christians, leave the students to their own Choice.[21]

Although a loyal supporter of Trinity Church, King knew that a peaceful solution would in fact give the non-Episcopalians the real power of governing Columbia. As he wrote to his fellow trustee, Gouverneur Morris, the Revolution had wiped out the preeminence of the Episcopal Church in New York, yet the Episcopal clergy still wanted to "continue at the head of the College as a privileged order, a pretension which you must at once see would meet with opposition."[22]

Mason's remark that "certain intriguing men" had looked for years with rapacious eyes upon Columbia's property and were hoping to destroy the college altogether was not without substance. In 1817 King served on a committee which reported adversely to the trustees on a resolution of the regents proposing to consolidate Columbia with a college on Staten Island and recommending that the trustees negotiate with Trinity Church both for removal of Columbia from the city and for relinquishment of the requirement that its president be an Episcopalian. In rejecting the proposal, the committee not only alluded to the inconvenience of Staten Island, but also defended the college for the quality and morality of its students and faculty. Columbia had impartially educated persons of all religious and political persuasions without seeking to change their convictions, the committee maintained; moreover, to obtain Trinity's consent to a removal from New York City would mean sacrificing at least one-fourth of the college's property, to say nothing of the expense of erecting buildings on Staten Island. When the trustees backed their committee, the scheme died. Nevertheless as late as 1819 Columbia was still being attacked as a relic of royalty that no good Republican ought to support.[23]

21. King's memorandum, Feb. 6, 1810, *ibid.*

22. King to Morris, Mar. 21, 1810, Gouverneur Morris Papers, Columbia Univ. Lib.

23. John M. Mason to King, Feb. 19, 1810, Confidential, King Papers, N.-Y. Hist. Soc.; Henry Rutgers to DeWitt Clinton, Mar. 23, 1810, Clinton Papers, Columbia Univ. Lib.; Minutes of the Trustees of Columbia College, Columbiana Coll., Low Mem. Lib., Columbia Univ.; Charles King to Rufus King, Feb. 15, 1819, King Papers, N.-Y. Hist. Soc.

King was intensely irritated by the attacks upon Columbia as a citadel of privilege. Believing that democratic pressures already had done great injury to American education, he declared that the country's forefathers had founded colleges amid great difficulties, while posterity had neglected them. Instead of regarding colleges as schools of wisdom and virtue, he explained to Noah Webster, "we behold them as Nurseries of Inequalities and Enemies of Liberty, and here as elsewhere, the unnatural Genius of Equality, the arch *Enemy* of the moral world, is permitted to seek her visionary Level, not by elevating what Ignorance and vice have degraded, but by degrading what knowledge and virtue have elevated."[24]

His labors as a trustee of Columbia for eighteen years, and for Trinity Church were King's most significant philanthropic interests, but he did not overlook his Long Island village of Jamaica. Not only was he a trustee of the private Union Hall Academy, but he was elected each year from 1815 to 1819 as one of the three commissioners of common schools. Later he contributed to the purchase of a new fire engine, invested in the Jamaica turnpike, and exerted his influence to inaugurate a daily mail service between the village and New York City. Most important to King and his family was Grace Church, which adjoined his property. After transferring his membership from Trinity, he liberally supported this local Episcopal church and became one of its wardens. He liked and respected Gilbert Sayres, the rector, a young Columbia graduate, who was outspokenly against intemperance, war, and slavery. When the congregation outgrew its small building, King was instrumental in designing a new one, contributed $500, and obtained a substantial gift from Trinity Church Corporation toward the erection of the more modern structure, which was completed in 1822.[25]

King's sustained interest in education was nourished in part by his concern for the three boys who had remained in Europe to complete

24. King to Noah Webster, [May 25, 1807], King Papers, N.-Y. Hist. Soc.

25. Jamaica Village Records, Book 600: 29, 31, Bureau of Municipal Investigation and Statistics of New York City, Room 510, Municipal Building, New York City. (King's son, John, who moved to Jamaica in 1816, was a trustee of the village and of the township's common lands in the 1820's. Jamaica Town Records, Book 452: 238, *ibid.*) King's account book, 1806–25, entries for May [n.d.] 1823 and June 16, 1823, owned by James G. King; Eliphalet Wickes to King, Apr. 20, 1820, King Papers, N.-Y. Hist. Soc.; "A Short History of Grace Church Parish, Jamaica, Long Island," compiled from Horatio Oliver Ladd, *The Origin and History of Grace Church, Jamaica, New York* (n.p., 1940), 10; Jamaica *Long Island Farmer*, cited by Henry Onderdonck, *Queens County In Olden Times . . .* (Jamaica, N. Y., 1865), 107.

their schooling. After finishing their studies at Harrow, John and Charles were sent to a school in Paris, where their resentment at being treated like children worried their temporary guardian, Daniel Parker, Paris agent of the house of Baring. Parker was relieved when King decided late in 1805 to place Charles with a banking firm in Amsterdam and pressed John to return to America for college and training in the law. John came home from Paris early the next year, and a few months later the restless and impatient Charles was ordered home from Amsterdam by his father.[26]

Meanwhile in the spring of 1805, Robert R. Livingston recrossed the Atlantic, bringing with him the Kings' third son, James, who was enrolled at Harvard that fall. The Gores in Waltham kept a watchful eye on him. King was somewhat apprehensive over James, particularly when he became involved in a student attempt to resist the college authorities during an examination, but Gore wrote reassuringly that, though "fond of Frolic and amusement," the young man was "remarkably clever in avoiding the Results incident to such a Temper, and full of management in extricating Himself from Difficulty."[27]

The youngest boys, Edward and Frederick, remained at home under the care of their mother and of a faithful domestic, Eve Bush, who, according to a family story, was a deserted orphan girl whom they had discovered one evening under a bush by the roadside, and whom they had named and adopted as a servant.[28]

The tranquility of King's private life was threatened when war broke out again in Europe and American shipping was subjected to

26. King to Sir Francis Baring, Feb. 8, 1805, King to Mr. Le Roy, Oct. 31, 1805, King to Mr. Hope, July 20, 1806, King to Charles King, July 20, 1806, in King's notebook containing memo of letters, 1803, owned by James G. King; Daniel Parker to King, Jan. 25, 1806, King Papers, N.-Y. Hist. Soc. John did not attend a college but soon began his law studies.

27. King to Christopher Gore, Oct. 28, Nov. 9, 1805, Gore to King, Jan. 13, 1806, Apr. 17, Dec. 28, 1807, King Papers, N.-Y. Hist. Soc.

28. Mary A. King to Charles King, Dec. 6, 1803, transcript, *ibid.*, Box 81; Edward H. Brush, *Rufus King and His Times* (N. Y., 1926), 125–26. This story, which asserts that Eve Bush was a little girl barely able to talk when the Kings found her, was told by a great-granddaughter of Rufus King. Eve Bush died in 1846 at 74, according to her headstone in Grace Churchyard in Jamaica. Having been born about 1770, she could not have been a little child barely able to talk when the Kings adopted her, but the rest of the story may be accurate. For Mrs. King's domestic inclinations, see Mary A. King to Charles King, Dec. 6, 1803, *supra*, Mary A. King to Mrs. John Trumbull, July 3, 1809, Dreer Coll., Hist. Soc. of Pa., and James Kent to Elizabeth Kent, Apr. 20, 1804, Kent Papers, Vol. 3, Lib. Cong.

renewed attack. As businessmen and shippers clamored for negotiations with England, New York merchants privately approached King about his willingness to go abroad once more. Determined to send a special envoy to England, and knowing that King would be well received by the British government, President Jefferson asked if he would accept the mission. King was reluctant to do so; there was small hope of reaching a satisfactory agreement now that Britain was at war, and he doubted that the President would give him a free hand so long as Monroe was in London as the American minister. He agreed to accept only if he were permitted to take full responsibility for the negotiation, leaving it to the President and the Senate to judge his handiwork. When told that he would have to conform to specific instructions, he declined, and in April 1806 Jefferson nominated William Pinkney as special envoy to cooperate with Monroe.[29]

Within two weeks of Pinkney's appointment, New York had a sharp taste of the war. Three British frigates stationed off Sandy Hook fired on a small coaster, killing one of three men aboard. The dead man's body was exposed to a horrified, gaping crowd on one of the city's wharves. At a Federalist-led meeting at the Tontine Coffee House the next day, King was named to a committee which drafted a report castigating the administration for leaving the New York harbor defenseless.[30]

King doubted that the Republican leadership had a clear plan for the country. He thought the President's acts "feeble, hypocritical and mean" and considered him remiss in allowing a quarrelsome Republican Congress to take the initiative. The nation was at the mercy of "casual, intemperate, and inefficient measures of unexperienced individuals."[31] While not hopeful about negotiations with England, King thought it unwise and inconsistent for Congress at the same time to pass a nonimportation law whose purpose was to bludgeon the

29. King, ed., *King Correspondence*, IV, 457, 472; William Plumer, Diary, II, pt. 1, 430–31, entry for Apr. 22, 1806, William Plumer, Autobiography, 176, Lib. Cong.; King to Christopher Gore, Dec. 25, 1805, Secret, King Papers, N.-Y. Hist. Soc. Hearing a rumor that King would be sent to England, Monroe mordantly protested against appointing "a man hostile to his government, ready to engage in any intrigue, with people here or in France to overset both [governments]." Monroe to Thomas Jefferson, June 15, 1805, Stanislaus M. Hamilton, ed., *The Writings of James Monroe*, 7 vols. (N.Y., 1898–1903), IV, 456–57.

30. *Niles' Register*, 4 (1813), 74–75, contains this report and attendant resolutions; Bowne, *A Girl's Life*, 212.

31. King to Timothy Pickering, Mar. 13, 1806, and Feb. 7, 1806, Pickering Papers, Mass. Hist. Soc.

British government into concessions. That ill-advised act, he wrote Sir Francis Baring, the London banker, "must not . . . occasion temper on the side of England. The two countries should be friends, and a captious temper should not be permitted to prevent them being so."[32] Jefferson, however, insisted that Great Britain abandon impressment and pay for renewed ship seizures, and when Monroe and Pinkney negotiated a treaty without these terms he refused to submit it to the Senate and instructed the envoys to reopen discussions. This proved fruitless, as King might have predicted.

Anti-British furor in America reached a new peak when in June 1807 the frigate *Leopard* fired upon the U.S.S. *Chesapeake* off Hampton Roads, killing three and wounding eight men, and removed four alleged deserters from the Royal Navy. The President promptly ordered British warships out of United States territorial waters. Like most Americans, King was outraged by the wanton assault upon a United States warship, but he considered the *Chesapeake's* master, Commodore James Barron, "guilty of gross military indecorum in engaging Seamen, knowing them to be deserters from the English Ships of War." Barron's "misconduct," however, he considered "no justification of the attack on the Chesapeak." King expected the British to make reparation, but he knew from his own experience in England that they would not give up the practice of impressment. He deplored the war fever, refused to believe that England wished war with the United States, and hoped that Congress would restrain its more belligerent members. A war would be disastrous, he thought, and he determined to resist it.[33]

The need to revive the Federalist party was clear. Ever since the death of Hamilton, the party in New York had remained demoralized, King's own aloofness having contributed in large measure to its impotence in Albany.[34] At a rally of New York City Federalists in

32. King to Sir Francis Baring, Sept. 30, 1806, in King's notebook containing memo of letters, 1803, owned by James G. King.

33. King to Christopher Gore, Sept. 11, 1807, King Papers, N.-Y. Hist. Soc., for the quotation; King to William King, Dec. 8, 1807, William King Papers, Maine Hist. Soc.; King to Timothy Pickering, Dec. 31, 1807, Pickering Papers, Box 28, Mass. Hist. Soc.; King to Pickering, Jan. 7, 1808, King Papers, N.-Y. Hist. Soc.

34. "The feds appear sanguine here, but I think have not the stamina of exertion in them. Their strongest men have held back. Rufus King for instance. This I think evinces that the leaders do not believe in success." "G. S." to William P. Van Ness, Apr. 18, 1806, William P. Van Ness Papers, N. Y. Pub. Lib.

the spring of 1807, King was induced to head the list of local candidates for the state assembly. The slate was designated the "American ticket," a name, as Robert Troup observed, "free from the hobgoblins attached by many to Federalism."[35] DeWitt Clinton, Mayor of New York City, nephew of the Vice-President, and in the minds of contemporaries the leading Republican in the state, was not fooled. He and the bulk of his followers hoped to elect Daniel D. Tompkins governor, and, knowing that Morgan Lewis could be re-elected only with Federalist votes, they arrayed themselves solidly against the "American ticket." The Federalist slate was labeled a "Tory ticket," one Republican broadside proclaiming, "One hitch more and . . . with great propriety they might put a King on it."[36]

While New York Federalists appealed to nationalist sentiment and spurned the foreign-born, the Clintonians followed the Mayor's lead in deliberately cultivating them. Clinton, a discerning politician of Irish ancestry, was a lifelong friend of the Irish and reaped political dividends by investing his sympathy in the newcomers, particularly those United Irishmen who managed to reach America after the abortive revolution of 1798. Their leaders were William J. Macneven, a physician, and Thomas Addis Emmet, an articulate lawyer.

Emmet and James Cheetham, editor of the *American Citizen*, led the attack upon King. In the columns of this shrill Clintonian sheet, Emmet called King a "royalist" and an acknowledged enemy of liberty who had protested to the British government against the shipping of Irish state prisoners to the United States. To Cheetham and Emmet, King had clearly been the "political dupe" of the British court, who had cooperated "to torture oppressed Ireland and keep her bleeding patriots in dungeons"; yet this "servile courtier of Mr. Pitt" and "adorer of British men and British measures" was charged, quite illogically, with advocating war to satisfy his personal ambition.[37]

35. Troup to King, Apr. 11, 1807, King Papers, N.-Y. Hist. Soc. For King's nomination, see King, ed., *King Correspondence*, V, 14, 15. The designation "American ticket" was used for several years.

36. Dixon Ryan Fox, *The Decline of Aristocracy in the Politics of New York* (N. Y., 1919), 80, which presents interesting details of the campaign. A Republican handbill calling Rufus King "the friend of Tory principles," etc., is reproduced in Noble E. Cunningham, Jr., *The Jeffersonian Republicans in Power; Party Operations, 1801–1809* (Chapel Hill, 1963), 295.

37. N. Y. *American Citizen*, Apr. 1, 10, 1807. For other anti-King articles, see the issues of Apr. 4, 6, 8, 11, 13, 14, 20, 23, and 29.

Anything that might be dredged up and distorted was embodied in the persistent indictment of King as a British tool and an enemy of the common people. He was pictured as "a mere drone, himself rioting in wealth acquired by wedlock, while his poor family in Massachusetts, his brothers and sisters, linger out, unnoticed by him, a miserable existence." With somewhat more truth, he was accused of having been, as a senator, the confidential friend and adviser of George Hammond, the British Minister to the United States, with whom he had held midnight conferences "to palm upon us the British treaty."[38]

When King failed to reply to this fusillade, he was charged with affecting a pompous silence. Although he composed a reasoned and temperate defense of his interference to prevent the exile of the Irish prisoners to the United States, he finally determined not to publish it. The coarse and ribald attacks—in particular those of Emmet, who had written him provocative letters—he deeply resented, but he resolved "to enter into no explanations, leaving the Public to decide between me and these foreigners."[39]

The public decided in favor of the foreigners. The "American ticket" was beaten, and despite the city's majority for Lewis, Tompkins won the governorship. With the help of French-born Genêt, who had reason to hate King, and Cheetham, the English-born editor, the Irish-born Emmet had won his assault upon those who decried them as "imported patriots." Still an alien but already a member of the local bar, Emmet attained great influence in New York, where the future lay with the Irish immigrants. If King's name sounded magical to the Federalists, its presence on their slate was a mistake which probably lost more votes than it gained. Three of the city's Federalist candidates for the Assembly polled more votes than he did.[40]

After the President signed the Embargo in December 1807, impotent New York Federalists raged anew. A response to the British proclamation of October 17 requiring the fullest exercise of the right of impressment over neutral merchantmen, the Embargo forbade American ships to sail for foreign ports and required American

38. *Ibid.*, Apr. 20, 25, 1807. King had indeed been friendly with Hammond; that he had held private conferences related to Jay's Treaty is entirely probable.

39. *Ibid.*, Apr. 28, 1807; King to Christopher Gore, Apr. 10, 1807, King Papers, N.-Y. Hist. Soc. For Emmet's second letter to King, published in the N. Y. *American Citizen* on Apr. 9, see King, ed., *King Correspondence*, V, 15–23, and for King's unpublicized defense of his conduct, *ibid.*, 24–28.

40. Official returns were printed in the N. Y. *American Citizen*, May 2, 1807.

coastal shipping to post high bond as a guarantee that cargoes would be landed at United States ports. Imports in foreign vessels, not specifically prohibited, were made almost impossible by the banning of exports in foreign bottoms. Within a month the merchants of New York were complaining of their distress.[41]

Gradually they began to stir. On February 10, King attended a Federalist caucus at the home of Richard Harison that considered supporting Vice-President George Clinton, a New Yorker, for the presidency and, according to one of Madison's informants, sent a delegation to form a coalition with their erstwhile foes, the Clintonians. King doubtless opposed such collaboration, even if it promised to transfer national leadership from Virginians to New Yorkers. At his town house on March 6, several of the city's leading Federalists discussed whether or not to nominate Federalists or, in King's words, whether to "put good men in power or remain quiet Spectators." Deciding to put up a fight, these insiders later nominated another "American ticket," this time without naming King, and condemned the "visionary maxims and pernicious measures" of the Jefferson administration. In the spring election, their party made remarkable gains, winning contests in the city and in Queens County on Long Island, and although the Republicans retained their majority in the Assembly at Albany, the Federalists substantially increased their representation. As DeWitt Clinton had predicted, they profited from the distress caused by the Embargo.[42] In another year they would win control of the legislature for the first time in a decade.

In the national capital and throughout the country, the Republicans were torn by faction. Madison, who was Jefferson's choice as his successor, was opposed by the anti-administration followers of John Randolph of Roanoke and John Taylor of Caroline, and by northerners sympathetic to Vice-President George Clinton. One rumor had it that the Madisonians would hold out attractive bait to lure New Englanders and Federalists. "They talk clandestinely of a compromise—meaning Rufus King as Vice President as an Equivalent," re-

41. Oliver Wolcott to Timothy Pitkin, Jan. 22, 1808, Private, Pitkin Papers, Huntington Lib. Wolcott was at this time a merchant in New York City.

42. "H" [John H. Douglass?] to James Madison, Feb. 11, 1808, Madison Papers, N. Y. Pub. Lib.; Gouverneur Morris, Diary, entry for Mar. 6, 1808, Gouverneur Morris Papers, Lib. Cong.; *N.-Y. Evening Post*, Apr. 19, 30, 1808; DeWitt Clinton to George Clinton, Apr. 3, 1808, Clinton Papers, Vol. 4, Columbia Univ. Lib.; Hammond, *Political Parties in New York*, I, 265; David H. Fischer, *The Revolution of American Conservatism: The Federalist Party in the Era of Jeffersonian Democracy* (N. Y., 1965), 80, 115.

ported a Washington correspondent of the Connecticut Federalist, Timothy Pitkin. Smarting under the effects of the Embargo, northern Republicans nominated Clinton, to whom some New England Federalists, George Cabot and Harrison Gray Otis among them, were ready to throw their support rather than name a candidate of their own party.[43]

The proposed coalition with the Clintonians was unacceptable to most Federalist leaders. In the third week of August, some thirty-five Federalist notables from eight states held a secret convention in New York City. It is not known whether King attended, but he obviously agreed with the New York delegates, who refused to support Clinton. The conclave renominated Charles C. Pinckney and King as its candidates for president and vice-president.[44]

The selection of these veterans, who had no chance of victory, reflected a determination to keep the Federalist party a separate organization rather than let it sink in the northern seas of Clintonian Republicanism. Madison and Clinton were easily elected, their opponents receiving only forty-seven electoral votes apiece. The result did not surprise King. Being out of political favor, as he wrote, "I pass my time in the bosom of my Family, thinking and saying as little as I can upon the subject of politicks."[45]

Though remaining in retirement, he fumed helplessly, like other Federalists, at the anti-commercial policies of those whom they dubbed "our rulers." He fully accepted George Cabot's dour view that the evils of Jeffersonian policies were "the natural offspring of our vices, vanity, and folly as a people."[46] He joined in condemning the Embargo as impractical and ruinous, and demanded its repeal. "It is high time to discard visionary Experiments—for God's sake let the Federalists abstain from any share in them," he wrote Pickering.[47]

43. Archibald Lee to Timothy Pitkin, May 31, 1808, Pitkin Papers, Huntington Lib.; Samuel Eliot Morison, *The Life and Letters of Harrison Gray Otis, Federalist, 1765–1848*, 2 vols. (Boston, 1913), I, 307–08.

44. King to Christopher Gore, Sept. 27, 1808, King Papers, N.-Y. Hist. Soc.; Morison, *Otis*, I, 304–07; Fischer, *Revolution of American Conservatism*, 86–87. Theophilus Parsons and others of the "Essex Junto" did not feel bound by the decision of the New York conference. See Gore to King, June 16, 1808, and King to Gore, Sept. 27, 1808, King Papers, N.-Y. Hist. Soc.

45. King to George Hammond, Dec. 12, 1808, King Papers, N.-Y. Hist. Soc.

46. George Cabot to Oliver Wolcott, Dec. 28, 1808, H. C. Lodge, *The Life and Letters of George Cabot* (Boston, 1877), 403.

47. King to Timothy Pickering, Dec. 1, 1808, Pickering Papers, Mass. Hist. Soc.

From fragmentary information about French attempts to pressure the United States into war with Great Britain, he adjudged the administration's response to be weak and cowardly. Napoleon's Berlin Decree, which subjected to confiscation American shipping between English and French-held ports, not only violated neutral rights, King asserted, but contravened the Franco-American Convention of 1800. The British Orders in Council, which also struck at American shipping, were in his opinion merely retaliatory, but in so rationalizing the British action, he conveniently overlooked the fact that the Berlin Decree was in part a retaliation for Fox's blockade five months earlier. As for the United States, King thought it should have armed itself and cut off all trade with France: "Had we so done, there would have been no orders in Council, no Embargo, and probably before this we should have been again in Peace with France."[48] Like other northerners with mercantile ties, and like Federalists everywhere, including Chief Justice Marshall, he saw in the tenacious enforcement of the Embargo provocation for war with England, which, he feared, would strike first when convinced that American policy complied with French demands for the closing of United States ports to British ships.[49] America's official impartiality toward the belligerents seemed to King like submission to France and offended his patriotic pride:

> I was born an American, I have passed the meridian of the life of man, and during my whole life have been the attentive and careful witness of every important transaction of independent America: although some events have occurred during the last 40 years which I could have earnestly wished might not have happened, never until I read these debates and heard the language of the administration, did I feel myself completely humbled, for I had not before seen reason to doubt the Integrity of my Country.[50]

By staying out of politics and expressing only occasionally in public his animosity toward the Republican leadership, King did Federalism a disservice. Since 1805 the better-known Federalist chieftains

48. *Ibid.* See King's argument, "Retaliation a Law of Peace as Well as War," King, ed., *King Correspondence*, V, 142. For his learned and extended analyses, see *ibid.*, 114–21, 138–42.

49. King to Timothy Pickering, Jan. 7, 1808, John Marshall to Pickering, Dec. 19, 1808, Pickering Papers, Mass. Hist. Soc.

50. King, ed., *King Correspondence*, V, 140.

had become more narrow, despairing, and unreasonable, and the carping criticism uttered by rigid men like Pickering in the Senate and by Barent Gardenier and Josiah Quincy in the House reflected their inability or unwillingness to use the organizational techniques so well exploited by the Republicans. King was on friendly terms with extremist critics, shared most of their views, and regularly exchanged letters with Pickering, but his moderation and common sense were sorely needed in party councils where both were markedly absent.[51]

During his ten years out of office, King kept up a correspondence with such English friends as Sir Francis Baring, Sir William Scott, Vansittart, and Wilberforce, expressing hope for a restoration of good relations with Great Britain. "Virtuous men" in America, he wrote George Hammond, were solicitous of England's welfare. "If England be dishonoured or fall, the best security of this and other Countries against the ambition of France is lost." Shortly after the breakdown of negotiations between Madison and George Rose, the special British emissary, in March 1808, King wrote at Pickering's request a letter stressing the need for peace and friendly relations between the two nations. Pickering handed it over to Rose, who thanked him for permission "to keep that gentleman's letter, which, I am sure, will carry high authority where I can use it confidently."[52]

The repeal of the Embargo a year later, the substitution of a less stringent nonintercourse law, and the negotiations of the British Minister to the United States, David M. Erskine, with Secretary of State Robert Smith seemed to promise a change for the better. Resting on the Englishman's unauthorized assurance that the British would revoke their Orders in Council so far as they applied to the United States, the Erskine agreement with the Madison administration gave rise to premature jubilation for it was soon repudiated by Foreign Secretary Canning. Both Republicans and Federalists could claim credit. "One side rejoice because they think the Embargo et

51. Cf. Bradford Perkins, *Prologue to War; England and the United States, 1805–1812* (Berkeley, Calif., 1961), 34–35, and Louis M. Sears, *Jefferson and the Embargo* (Durham, N. C., 1927), 201–04. A distinction must be drawn between old-school Federalists, like King, and a younger generation of Federalists who actively engaged in organizational work in numerous localities. See Fischer, *Revolution of American Conservatism*, an important new study.

52. King to Hammond, Feb. 20, 1808, typescript, owned by James G. King; Rose to Timothy Pickering, Mar. 18, 1808, Pickering to Rose, Mar. 13, 1808, Pickering Papers, Mass. Hist. Soc.; Pickering to George Cabot, Mar. 16, 1808, in Lodge, *George Cabot*, 388.

cetera has brought England to terms," King observed, and "the other side rejoice because they believe that the opposition to the late Measures of Congress has obliged the administration to abandon their system, and to accept a Reconciliation with England."[53] Canning, however, disavowed the Erskine agreement, because it did not accord with certain stipulations that he had demanded of the United States, including the free admission of British trade to American ports at the same time that French trade was excluded, and authorization of the Royal Navy to capture American vessels trading illegally with France. When he learned of these conditions, King showed as he had earlier that he was no uncritical Anglophile. He could never approve the use of British ships to enforce American law, for it was clear to him that the United States would have been humiliated and dishonored, had it accepted such a surrender of its sovereignty.[54]

Whatever he may have felt about British policy, King had nothing but contempt for Madison's diplomacy. Even if the nonintercourse law allowed the export of American goods to all countries except Great Britain and France, this would provide insufficient tariff revenue and would keep alive popular prejudices. Ineffective commercial restrictions remained in force, he asserted, through "mere pride and Interest of party"; Madison had no distinct policy, he thought, other than to stay in power and drift along without breaking relations with England or France. After Congress reopened trade with the belligerents in May 1810, King saw little change in what he considered the administration's pro-French orientation. "Bonaparte has seized our Ships and Cargoes, and we bear it like Philosophers," he complained, but if England had done the same, the Republicans in America would have had "town meetings, and Harangues, and Processions, and Laws, and Proclamations, and noise, and names and all other Expressions of Displeasure."[55]

53. King to John Trumbull, Apr. 24, 1809, King Papers, Vol. 80, N.-Y. Hist. Soc.; Perkins, *Prologue to War*, 218–19.

54. King to Trumbull, July 31, 1809, King Papers, Vol. 80, N.-Y. Hist. Soc. After rejecting the Erskine agreement, Canning sent to America as a special envoy the arrogant Francis James Jackson, whose appointment as minister to the United States King had successfully opposed in 1801.

55. King to Trumbull, Nov. 22, 1809, Jan. 24, May 25, 1810, *ibid.* King regarded Madison as "a well meaning little man when left to himself," who could "write a pretty Essay, or make, if he has time to prepare it, a handsome speech"; but he was "of feeble temper and apt to submit himself to a Leader." Jefferson, on his return from France, "had the Goodness to become the

Federalists played a guessing game, as the administration kept them in the dark about its transactions. King's chief Washington informant, the splenetic Senator Pickering, discovered in each diplomatic act new grounds for suspicion. From private sources, newspapers, and public documents, Pickering and King pieced together their impressions of what was happening, reinforcing each other's prejudices. They concluded that the administration was deliberately conspiring with the continental powers of Europe, and saw as part of this plot the arming of merchant ships. King's belief that France dictated American policy was fortified by a steady flow of letters from Gore, who in 1809 was Governor of Massachusetts, and from John Trumbull in England, an Anglophile who poured his contempt upon the "supernatural wisdom" of Madison.[56]

Over strong but futile Federalist protests, Congress barred both French and British warships from American waters when it reopened commerce with the two countries in 1810. Macon's Bill No. 2, which empowered the President to reimpose nonintercourse upon whichever nation failed to revoke or modify its orders injuring American shipping, was to King not only mischievous but an unconstitutional encroachment of Congress upon the Executive's power to conduct foreign relations. Subsequently King was critical of Madison's reinstatement of nonintercourse with Great Britain on the basis of the Duc de Cadore's flimsy assurance that France would repeal her Berlin and Milan decrees.[57] For the government to accept the Frenchman's statement, in the face of evidence to the contrary, was to King proof of willful and harmful Francophilia. Prejudice against England and sympathy for France had warped, if not destroyed, public opinion in America:

> Men whose minds remain free are discouraged from making those Efforts in favour of Truth and Justice, which the dangers upon whose brink we stand would otherwise impel them to make—quiet men, whose personal prudence [is the ruling mo-

Keeper of poor Madisons Conscience." King's manuscript, undated but probably 1804 or 1805, King Papers, Box A, N.-Y. Hist. Soc. For a sympathetic treatment of Madison's policy towards France, see Irving Brant, *James Madison*, V, esp. 41, 58, 63–64, 147–48, 338–39.

56. King to Timothy Pickering, Jan. 26, 1810, Pickering to King, Feb. 2, 1810, also see many letters from Gore and from Trumbull to King, all King Papers, N.-Y. Hist. Soc.

57. King's manuscript, President's Proclamation, *ibid.*

tive] of their Conduct, are from the hope of Ease deterred from expressing their sentiments–Office seekers and those who desire popular favour, and are unwilling to incur popular Displeasure, hold their peace. Men of sound understanding and who perceive the Delusion of the times and the Gulf which opens to receive us, doubting the impartiality or the capacity of the People, resign themselves to an unmanly despair and like the ignorant Clown, call upon Jupiter for help and Deliverance.[58]

58. King's manuscript, French Decrees and English Orders, *ibid.*, Box A.

CHAPTER XVII

KING AND THE WAR OF 1812

RUFUS KING DID NOT BELIEVE THAT NAPOLEON HAD ABANDONED HIS policy out of respect for the United States. He saw instead that the French Emperor refused to release American vessels seized before November 1810, while those putting into French ports after that month were not allowed to leave or to discharge their cargoes until news reached France that the United States had taken retaliatory measures against English commerce. American ships touching at British ports were seized, as before, and American trade with France, restricted by a system of licensing, was reduced to a trickle.

In an eagerly awaited report of November 29, 1811, the House Foreign Affairs Committee refused to censure France as it denounced the British Orders in Council and impressments, and recommended strengthening the army and navy and the arming of merchant ships. The committee's chairman, Peter B. Porter, indirectly sought King's opinion of the report and received in reply a frank and carefully composed letter. "I am unable to agree with the Committee . . . that the French decrees are revoked, or so modified as that they cease to modify our Rights," King declared; "without receding an iota from her system of war upon the English Resources," France had done just enough "to mislead a nation torn asunder by faction and blinded to her most important interests." So long as actual French seizures and confiscations continued, the British would not repeal their Orders. As to impressment, if naturalized citizens were not enlisted in the crews of American vessels, Britain would abandon the practice.[1]

If Porter's report failed to satisfy the War Hawks, it went farther than the administration wished and alarmed some Federalists and commercial firms. On its assertion of the "sacred duty of Congress to call forth the patriotism and resources of the country," King commented that if national honor demanded war, let it be declared, "for in my poor judgment, the Honor of a Nation is the only legitimate cause of war," but before going to war against England, the United States should first consider the attitude and actions of France. "Are we to submit to . . . taunts and injuries aimed directly at our Honour, and at the same time to whine and strut, and vapour about our Honour's being insulted by the orders in Council and the impressment of Seamen?" he asked. If he were in Congress, he told Porter, he would oppose war with England.[2]

By 1812 most Americans had come to accept the contention that France had not in reality repealed the Berlin and Milan decrees. Honest men in both political parties could hardly support measures against Britain while ignoring Napoleon's injuries and insults. A war against the former, they felt, was unjustifiable and would leave the country deeply divided.[3]

Despite the administration's hope that preparedness legislation might induce Britain to drop her hostile policy, the prodding of Clay, Calhoun, Grundy, Cheves, and other War Hawk leaders moved the nation along the tortuous road to war. The House quickly adopted Madison's recommendation of a sixty-day embargo, which the War Hawks regarded as a prelude to armed conflict. Moderate Republicans in the Senate, eager to prolong negotiations, succeeded in extending the embargo to ninety days, and the President signed the bill on April 4. Late in May, the *Hornet* arrived with news from England, including Foreign Secretary Castlereagh's instructions to Augustus Foster, the British Minister, reaffirming the position that, as Napoleon had not repealed his decrees, the Orders in Council could not be annulled. Madison, convinced at last that Britain would not yield to economic coercion or to threats of hostilities, presented his war

1. King to [Peter B. Porter], Dec. 10, 1811, Private, King Papers, N.-Y. Hist. Soc. King asserted that impressments were perhaps less numerous than at any previous time.

2. *Ibid.*

3. Cf. Bradford Perkins, *Prologue to War*, 366.

message to Congress on June 1. On the fourth, the House voted for war, and on the eighteenth, after spirited opposition by anti-war Republicans and Federalists, the Senate voted for war by the scant margin of three votes.

The decision for war reflected an outraged national pride at repeated maritime injuries, recognition of the failure of economic retaliation, blame of British commercial restrictions for the low prices of tobacco, cotton, and hemp, and determination to crush British influence among the Indians in the Northwest.[4] In the commercial states, however, there was no popular clamor. Northern merchants and shippers, Clintonians, and Federalists denounced the war as the sad outcome of partisan politics and inept management.

To King it was "a war of party, and not of the Country." The action of Congress, he believed, was contrary to public opinion in a country unprepared for war. Neither Congress nor the state legislatures, he asserted, could legally compel the essentially defensive militia to march upon Canada, the logical objective of a land attack. He predicted that a regular army would be enlisted only with the utmost difficulty, that people would not lend money and would resist new taxes, that America's association with Napoleon would increase popular discontent, and that the war would become ever more oppressive. Thus, he reasoned, if Britain merely let events take their natural course, the United States soon would be forced to seek peace.[5]

During the summer of 1812, New York Federalists tried to capitalize upon the anti-war feeling in the city. William Coleman, the editor of the *Evening Post*, called on King on July 27 and induced him to serve on a committee to draft resolutions and an address for a mass meeting. Turning to presidential politics, Coleman told him that Federalist congressmen, despairing of the election of a Federalist president, had deliberated with party leaders in New York

4. For several recent interpretations, in addition to Perkins, *Prologue to War*, see Roger H. Brown, *The Republic in Peril: 1812* (N. Y., 1964), Reginald Horsman, *The Causes of the War of 1812* (Phila., 1962), and Norman K. Risjord, "1812: Conservatives, War Hawks, and the Nation's Honor," *Wm. and Mary Qtly.*, 3d Ser., 18 (1961), 196–210. Harry L. Coles, *The War of 1812* (Chicago, 1965), 27–37, discusses the problem of causation.

5. King to Christopher Gore, July 17, 1812, King Papers, N.-Y. Hist. Soc.; undated manuscript inserted in King's notebook (1820), in which King asserted that war was "justifiable only on the Principle of self Preservation." Owned by James G. King.

to obtain their support for DeWitt Clinton, the state's powerful Lieutenant-Governor. Clinton was ready to promise, if elected, to make an immediate peace with England.[6]

Late in the evening of July 31, while spending the night at Archibald Gracie's country mansion overlooking the East River, King was visited by Dr. Mason, the Provost of Columbia, who had been discussing the college's affairs with Clinton. Mason told him that the anti-war Republican welcomed Federalist support in his bid for the presidency of the United States and asked whether King would confer with Clinton. King replied that he wished first to consult Jay, Gouverneur Morris, Matthew Clarkson, Richard Varick, and Richard Harison, with whom he would collaborate in preparing resolutions for the forthcoming peace demonstration. Three days later at Morrisania, King, Morris, Jay, and Clarkson debated the wisdom of a conference with Clinton. King opposed it, arguing that Clinton was no different from other factional leaders and would abandon his followers, who in turn would desert him—"more certainly as soon as he united with the rival Faction for any purpose." As long as the Republican leaders, Armstrong, Spencer, Tompkins, and Taylor, were against him, he was "not worth accepting." King held that it was more important for Federalists to maintain their integrity than to win power with the help of dissident Republicans. Moreover, the Clintonians might well embarrass the Federalists by misrepresenting their motives. Jay and Morris were inclined to meet with Clinton, reasoning that to refuse his offer not only would give offense, but might encourage him to make a bid for the vice-presidency in place of Elbridge Gerry, and thereby eliminate all prospects for a peace party. Reluctantly King acquiesced, but only if the conference were limited exclusively to unifying the peace advocates and possibly communicating with similar groups in other states.[7]

On August 5, Clinton went to Morrisania, where he joined King, Jay, and Morris at the dinner table. The four then retired to the library, where Morris read the proposed peace resolutions. Clinton

6. King's memorandum dated July 27, 1812, King Papers, folder for June 1812, N.-Y. Hist. Soc.

7. This paragraph is based on King's memoranda of July 31 and Aug. 3, 4, and 5, 1812, *ibid.* Varick and Harison agreed to the plan on Aug. 4. Clinton had previously intimated to Morris that Gerry had accepted the Republican nomination for the vice-presidency conditionally and was ready to withdraw in Clinton's favor. *Ibid.*, Aug. 5, 1812.

said he approved of them but suggested postponing the peace meeting while he rallied the Republicans behind him. He told his skeptical listeners that he was not merely temporizing and, according to King, "he would have received what should have satisfied him, especially as he was yet a young man" if he had agreed to support Madison's administration, but in view of the President's "incapacity" he could not do so; "that he was separated from the administration forever; that he pledged his honor that the Breach was irreparable: that for political Reasons he found it expedient to avoid publicity on this subject."[8]

As a result of this conference, King worked to prevent postponement of the public meeting, for he had become convinced that the advocates of peace should act while excitement was still high and that delay would only promote Clinton's personal advancement and would be misunderstood by the Federalists. Others agreed, and on August 18, two weeks after the Clinton interview, the "Friends of Liberty, Peace, and Commerce" held their rally.

That morning the pro-administration *Public Advertiser* warned that the "enemies of the government, cooperating in secret with the deep and crafty, though the professed, yet hypocritical partizan republicans of this city, will be furnished with a rich repast on the luxurious imagery which will be displayed . . . against their government by the venomous slander of some lurking villains who still remain engrafted upon the rotten and corrupt stem of toryism in New York."[9] In the afternoon a large crowd at Washington Hall adopted eight resolutions (five of them drafted by Jay, King, Morris, Clarkson, Harison, and Varick) condemning Madison's "fatal" anti-commercial policy, stressing the country's financial and military unpreparedness for an offensive war, and calling for a network of committees of correspondence to cooperate with the "friends of peace" in other communities to work for "such *constitutional* measures as may secure our liberties and independence, and preserve our Union."[10]

King became an active propagandist for the Friends of Liberty,

8. *Ibid.*, Aug. 5, 1812.
9. N. Y. *Public Advertiser*, Aug. 18, 1812.
10. *N.-Y. Evening Post*, Aug. 18, 1812; Alden Bradford, *History of the Federal Government, . . . 1789–1839* (Boston, 1840), 188–89. Washington Hall, a Federalist rallying place at the corner of Broadway and Reade Street, was built in 1809, a year before Tammany Hall was begun.

Peace, and Commerce, though he thought the *Evening Post* had exaggerated his zeal at the rally. In an "Address to the People of the State of New York on the present state of affairs," printed over the signature of "An American," he proclaimed it impossible to trust and respect a government that so lacked power or will. "Confide, then fellow citizens, in yourselves," he concluded. "Unite! unite! and save yourselves."[11] In an undated manuscript written in a similar vein, he described the war as rash, unnecessary, and dangerous–rash, because the treasury was exhausted, arms and ammunition were unavailable, an army was not yet recruited, large sums of money were under the enemy's control, and merchant ships were dispersed over the oceans instead of being at home and arming for war; unnecessary, because an honorable and advantageous arrangement with Great Britain on impressment was still possible, and because the Orders in Council had been revoked; and dangerous to the liberty and independence of the United States because the war would destroy what was left of America's commercial capital, load the country with debts and taxes, and draw it into a "hateful connexion with France, the natural enemy of every free state."[12]

Throughout the late summer and autumn, the Friends of Peace instigated meetings in Westchester, Queens, Columbia, and Oneida counties, along the lines sketched by the New York City resolutions. Morris harangued a crowd in Westchester, and, at a rally at the Queens County Court House, King was appointed to a committee of correspondence.[13]

Some Federalists looked to King as their national standard-bearer. At Staunton, Virginia, a convention of delegates from eighteen counties of the Old Dominion recommended him for the presidency.[14] Former Secretary of the Navy Benjamin Stoddert and former Secretary of the Treasury Oliver Wolcott, Jr., hoped that the New Yorker would stand again for the vice-presidency. Theorizing that John Marshall or Judge Bushrod Washington would have the best chance of weaning Virginia from Madison, they saw King as the obvious choice for a northerner to balance the ticket. However,

11. *N.-Y. Evening Post*, Aug. 26, 1812.

12. King's manuscript, probably written in 1812 but filed in box labeled 1814–1815, King Papers, N.-Y. Hist. Soc.

13. *N.-Y. Evening Post*, Sept. 8, 9, Oct. 6, Nov. 4, 1812.

14. *Winchester* [Virginia] *Gazette*, as quoted in *N.-Y. Evening Post*, Oct. 3, 1812.

King refused to be considered. As he would not agree to the Federalist nomination of Clinton for the presidency, he thought it proper to eliminate himself altogether.[15]

These scattered efforts were doomed from the start. Most leading Federalists recognized that their party could not elect a president without combining with dissident Republicans. Since 1811 Federalists in New York had been expected to cooperate with Clinton, who opposed Madison's "anti-commercial" policies and who, once his ambition for the highest office in the land was satisfied, would, they thought, be a good chief executive. As in 1808, New Englanders, under the leadership of Otis, were ready to make a deal with a New Yorker.[16]

On September 15–17, more than sixty Federalist delegates from all the states north of the Potomac and from South Carolina convened at Kent's Tavern on Broad Street in New York City, to deliberate on party strategy. C. C. Pinckney had already refused to be a candidate again and had recommended Jay or King, neither of whom could be regarded as likely to win. Beyond dragging out of the closet the old arguments of 1808, some delegates made much of Clinton's promise to administer the government satisfactorily to the Federalists and to sue for peace.[17]

King attended this convention, where unimpressed by the assurances, he descanted upon Clinton's unscrupulousness and vacillation in recent years. To elect him would be to substitute Cesare Borgia for James Madison. In almost the words Hamilton had used against Burr, it was said, King denounced Clinton as a dangerous demagogue; any respectable Federalist was preferable, he believed, because such a choice would maintain party unity and principle until a more opportune occasion arose. Things could not get better until they had grown worse.[18]

15. King, ed., *King Correspondence*, V, 266, 272, 281*n*; Benjamin Stoddert to James McHenry, July 15, 1812, Bernard C. Steiner, *The Life and Correspondence of James McHenry* (Cleveland, 1907), 581–83.

16. "Letters of Samuel Taggart, Representative in Congress, 1803–1814," American Antiquarian Society, *Proceedings*, 33 (1923), 371; Morison, *Otis*, I, 309, II, 62; Fischer, *Revolution of American Conservatism*, 87–90.

17. Morison, *Otis*, I, 309, 316–17; King, ed., *King Correspondence*, V, 268–70, 280–81.

18. King, ed., *King Correspondence*, V, 276*n*, 281*n*; Henry Adams, *History of the United States During the Administrations of Jefferson and Madison*, 9 vols. (N. Y., 1889–91), VI, 410; King to Christopher Gore, Sept. 19, 1812, King Papers, N.-Y. Hist. Soc.

A majority of the delegates disagreed with King, but the convention, nevertheless, adopted ambiguous resolutions: that it was inexpedient to nominate Federalist candidates but that the party should support those who would "pursue a different course" from Madison's and that a committee should be appointed to ascertain the choice of electors in the key state of Pennsylvania, name the candidates worthy of support, and inform the electors in the other states. No two delegates seemed to agree upon the precise meaning of these resolutions, and at least one member did not think they precluded the possibility of a Federalist candidate. King, however, was certain that the Federalists, to all intents and purposes, were now committed to Clinton. Wolcott was so disgusted that he suggested forming a society with Gouverneur Morris as its chaplain to pray for them that they might be delivered from their own worst enemies—themselves.[19]

The Federalists tried to keep their conclave a secret but, as in 1808, the news leaked out. The *National Intelligencer*, an organ of the administration, published a reasonably accurate account, but Otis denied its assertion that a bargain had been struck with Clinton at this meeting.[20] The *Public Advertiser* published another version, stating that, with the exception of King and Mayor Wharton of Philadelphia, the Federalists had unanimously nominated Clinton. It reported King as having offered, if the delegates would abandon Clinton, to try to "reconcile their conduct to every thing honorable, without shadow of shame, or loss of principle," but that if they insisted on Clinton, they should "no longer consider him as one of *their* party." Robert G. Harper, a delegate from Maryland, claimed that the only dissenters were King, Radcliff of New York, and Sitgreaves of Pennsylvania. Whoever they were, the objectors were clearly a tiny minority. Though opposed to the Federalists, the *Public Advertiser* paid high tribute to King for his stand against the "state juggler and would-be-president."[21]

King regarded the presidency issue as unimportant in comparison with the need to reform the Constitution: to change the apportionment of representation and perhaps to define more precisely the

19. King, ed., *King Correspondence*, V, 280*n*; Morison, *Otis*, I, 309–11; Fischer *Revolution of American Conservatism*, 89–90; Oliver Wolcott to George Gibbs, Nov. 7, 1812, Wolcott-Gibbs Family Correspondence, Lib. Cong.

20. *N.-Y. Evening Post*, Oct. 20, 23, 1812.

21. N. Y. *Public Advertiser*, Sept. 19, 30, 1812; R. G. Harper to John Lynn, Sept. 25, 1812, in Steiner, *McHenry*, 584.

mechanism of presidential elections so as to prevent manipulation by party machines. While the Republicans were in power, such changes would not take place, but he declared that Madison's re-election would lead to national degradation and public disgust, enabling the Federalists eventually to gain possession of the government with popular support as great as that given Jefferson in 1800. Such was the only chance of reform without violence and civil war, for "next to the power of the Sword is that of a depressed party, when risen to a triumphant one."[22]

King's aristocratic bias blinded him to any virtues of democratic political organization. Like so many of the older Federalists, he would not stoop to rough-and-tumble politicking among the rank and file. To do so would be to associate himself with factionalism, political bribery, and emotionalism. Because the Republican party worked well at the grass roots, King saw it as a willing host to the spreading contagion of ambitious, unprincipled, and greedy men. In congratulating his brother Cyrus upon his election to Congress, he pointedly remarked that the public welfare was promoted both by the choice of good men and the "exclusion of men of mischievous politicks."[23]

While King played the part of Cassandra, Clinton was appealing for Federalist votes on the promise of an early peace and for Republican votes on the basis of Madison's incompetence. Military reverses along the Canadian frontier brightened Clinton's star, and in the December election he carried every state north of the Potomac except Pennsylvania and Vermont, but he was nineteen votes short of a majority in the electoral college. While Madison was re-elected, the Federalists doubled their strength in the new Congress, a resurgence that swept King back into office.

On February 2, 1813, the New York state legislature returned King to the United States Senate, seventeen years after his resignation to accept the mission to England. Because the Federalist majority in the Assembly at Albany was not large enough to carry a joint session, King's nomination in the state Senate had been regarded as a mere courtesy, but when the houses balloted jointly, sixty-eight votes were

22. King to Christopher Gore, Sept. 19, 1812, King Papers, N.-Y. Hist. Soc. King declared it possible that Madison might arrange a French alliance, resulting in French troops on American soil, civil strife, and British military intervention. *Ibid.*

23. King to Cyrus King, Dec. 25, 1812, owned by James G. King. For the problem of Federalist organization, see Fischer, *Revolution of American Conservatism.*

cast for King, sixty-one for General James Wilkin of Orange County, and three ballots were blank. The result surprised all but a few insiders.[24]

What had led to the election of an outstanding Federalist critic of the war by a preponderantly Republican legislature? The Tammany faction claimed that it was the price Clinton paid for Federalist support in November; Martin Van Buren, a rising young rival of Clinton, later recalled charges that King's appointment had resulted from "one of those profligate interchanges of public favour for private ends between men possessing different political sentiments which are so justly odious to the people" and was carried out by men in Clinton's confidence with the cooperation of certain leading Federalists.[25] "We are astonished or at least disappointed," a fellow Tammany man wrote to Van Buren. "I am very glad you mentioned the blank voting, as the Martling [Madisonian, or Tammany] men had begun to lay the fault to the Clintonians, and regret that King is elected. . . . We are all in a dilemma, and they (the Martlingites) solve it only by saying it was agreed in the Presidential election that Mr. King should be Senator."[26]

Clintonians, on the other hand, laid the result to a bargain between the Republican agents of the Bank of America and the Federalists, whereby the latter would vote for the incorporation of that institution, and the bank's political sponsors would secure the choice of a Federalist as senator. Wilkin, the defeated candidate, was convinced that King had won through the influence and votes of the bank's friends. Although the details will never be known, this explanation is the most likely one.[27]

24. King, ed., *King Correspondence*, V, 293; *N.-Y. Evening Post*, Feb. 4, 1813; Fox, *Decline of Aristocracy*, 173.

25. Martin Van Buren, *Considerations in Favour of the Appointment of Rufus King. . .* (n. p., 1819), 23–24; Hammond, *Political Parties in New York*, I, 343–44; Fox, *Decline of Aristocracy*, 173.

26. Charles Holt to Martin Van Buren, Feb. 3, 1813, Van Buren Papers, Lib. Cong.

27. Jabez D. Hammond, a knowledgeable contemporary, was inclined to accept this explanation, noting that Clinton would not have sacrificed his steady friend Wilkin, who had presided over the legislative caucus that had nominated him for the presidency. Hammond was ready to believe, however, that "the knowing ones" in the Republican party had reason to doubt whether a Republican could be elected as senator. Wilkin lacked the standing and influence which several other state Republicans had, and Hammond concluded that had they been sure of electing a Republican senator, someone else probably would have been nominated. *Political Parties in New York*, I, 344–45.

King himself apparently had no knowledge of any negotiations with bank men. His character was widely respected and his opposition to private bargaining by public men well known; nobody in any party or faction suspected him of complicity. Clinton, despite the blame cast upon him by Van Buren, also seems to have been personally innocent of the deal. He opposed an improper extension of banking privileges, even to his own supporters.[28]

Election for the third time as a senator from New York surprised King. He had heard his name mentioned but had not taken it seriously because he knew that the legislature's Federalists alone could not elect anyone. Victory with "democratical assistance" was embarrassing; in view of his disapproval of Federalist support of Clinton, he had tried to avoid any appearance of inconsistency. Beyond his reluctance to come out of retirement, he had premonitions of a lonely time in the Senate, with so many new and younger men he did not know, for he would be the only senator who had sat in that body while Washington was President. To his former Massachusetts colleague, Governor Caleb Strong, he suggested that his old friend Gore be appointed to the Senate if, as seemed likely, the incumbent Senator Lloyd should resign. When Lloyd did resign, Strong appointed Gore, who accepted reluctantly and only after King's persistent pleading.[29]

As they rode into the Federal District late in May 1813, King and Gore caught their first glimpse of the city of Washington. The capital, with its vast empty spaces, was chilling in contrast to Philadelphia, Boston, or New York, not to mention London. Hotels and boarding houses were scarce, and the two men with their wives, accustomed to gracious living in comfortable homes, were fortunate to find suitable quarters at Crawford's Hotel, a well-furnished mansion in nearby Georgetown.[30]

Crawford's became a mecca of newly elected Federalist legislators.

Dorothie Bobbé, *DeWitt Clinton* (N. Y., 1933), 189, accepts the bank deal as the true explanation. Cf. De Alva S. Alexander, *A Political History of the State of New York*, 4 vols. (N. Y., 1906–23), I, 211–12; Fox, *Decline of Aristocracy*, 173.

28. Hammond, *Political Parties in New York*, 344*n*; Van Buren, *Considerations in Favour of Rufus King*, 24; Bobbé, *DeWitt Clinton*, 189.

29. King, ed., *King Correspondence*, V, 294, 297–99; King to Caleb Strong, Mar. 5, 1813, Confidential, Strong Papers, Forbes Lib.

30. Mrs. King and Mrs. Gore maintained a private parlor which occasionally served as a drawing room.

Congressman Daniel Webster and New Hampshire Senator Jeremiah Mason were fellow lodgers who often dined with King and Gore. Among its many other guests in 1814 were Senator Robert Goldsborough of Maryland, Congressmen Gaston of North Carolina, Lewis of Virginia, and Miller of New York. The atmosphere may have suited King, but it was hard on his wife, who vastly preferred the quieter life at Jamaica. Now frail and in chronically poor health, she was no longer eager to entertain and soon grew tired of Washington. Only the companionship of the Gores made the exile from her Long Island home tolerable.[31]

As King presented his credentials to the Senate on May 28, he faced only two men he had long known: Gore and the Vice-President, Elbridge Gerry, who had long since trodden the Republican path and was now in the chair formerly occupied by George Clinton, who had died in office in 1812. The Republicans controlled the Thirteenth Congress, but King's influence in the Senate soon carried weight. He was respected by men of both parties, some still thinking of him as a future president.[32] Congressman John Lovett of New York considered him "the very *Oracle* even with the Democracy," which "would be heartily glad to hustle poor Madison and this scant-patterned old skeleton of a French Barber, Gerry, off hand and make Mr. King factotum in all things."[33]

The New York Senator played an influential part in a running controversy between the upper house and the President. Although the Republicans held a margin of two to one in the Senate, anti-administration figures like Samuel Smith, William Branch Giles, Michael Leib, Nicholas Gilman, and King's New York colleague, Obadiah German, were ready to cooperate with the Federalists. Their main object was to embarrass and discredit Madison, whose nomination of Jonathan Russell to fill a proposed new post as minister to Sweden gave them an early opportunity.[34]

31. Gilbert J. Clark, ed., *Memoirs of Jeremiah Mason* (Boston, 1917), 98; Cyrus King to Hannah S. King, [n. d.] 1813, copy, evidently by his daughter, Elizabeth Porter King, Bowdoin College Library.

32. Cyrus King to Elizabeth King Porter, July 23, 1813, contemporary copy by Dorcas King Leland, owned in 1958 by Arthur Lord, Newton, Mass.

33. John Lovett to Solomon Van Rensselaer, June 22, 1813, Catharina V. R. Bonney, *A Legacy of Historical Gleanings*, 2 vols. (Albany, 1875), I, 301.

34. Irving Brant, who warmly defends Madison's wartime policies in *James Madison*, VI, devotes an entire chapter to the President's struggle with the Senate.

King and Goldsborough concocted a resolution asking the President to inform the Senate whether Russell, former chargé d'affaires at Paris, had ever admitted or denied the Duke of Bassano's statement that he had told Russell of the repeal of the Berlin and Milan decrees before it was made public. This resolution, adopted on June 2, was intended to give the impression that Madison had concealed the repeal decree, although it was an open secret in Congress that the decree was pre-dated and hence nonexistent until its publication. Another resolution, debated in secret session, asked the President to furnish to any senator, on request, an extract of his message concerning Russell's nomination. King considered Sweden a second-rate power, a center of foreign intrigue and corruption, whose trade with the United States was paltry; in view of the need for strict wartime economy, he asked why the United States should incur the increased cost of a minister plenipotentiary.[35] With Wells and Giles, King was appointed to confer with Madison, but the President was seriously ill, and committee chairman Wells declined Secretary of State Monroe's offer to discuss the matter. On July 9, by vote of twenty-two to fourteen, the Senate turned down Russell's nomination.[36]

Another hassle occurred after the President accepted a Russian offer to mediate between the United States and Great Britain, and nominated Albert Gallatin, Senator James A. Bayard, and John Quincy Adams as commissioners to negotiate treaties of peace and commerce with Britain and a commercial pact with Russia. Nobody objected to Adams, who was already in St. Petersburg as minister to the Tsar's court. As Bayard was a Federalist, some in his party were at first uneasy that he might have formed a private understanding with the administration.[37] Gallatin, however, was the Secretary of the Treasury, responsible for financing the war, and Madison's valued adviser; his nomination raised a constitutional question, though he had already departed on his mission.

Like other Federalists, King disapproved of Russian mediation, believing that a more satisfactory peace could be obtained through

35. *Annals*, 13 Cong., 1 sess., 91–92, June 2, 1813; King, ed., *King Correspondence*, V, 324–37.

36. *Annals*, 13 Cong., 1 sess., 94–98.

37. K. K. Van Rensselaer to James A. Bayard, Apr. 17, 1813, James A. Bayard to K. K. Van Rensselaer, Apr. 24, 1813, draft, James A. Bayard to Samuel Bayard, Apr. 23, 1813, James A. Bayard Papers, Lib. Cong.

bilateral negotiations with England. He offered three resolutions in the Senate: one called for the diplomatic correspondence between the United States and Russia, another called for copies of the envoys' commissions, and the third asked the President whether Gallatin retained his post in the treasury, and if so, "under what authority and by whom" the powers and duties of that office would be carried on in his absence.[38] Although the first two resolutions failed, the third was adopted. In reply, President Madison stated that the office of the Secretary of the Treasury had not been vacated and that Gallatin's duties were being performed in his absence by William Jones, Secretary of the Navy, under authority of a 1792 law.

This gave King the opportunity to make a long speech in the Senate against Gallatin's appointment as envoy while holding the treasury position. Opening with sly innuendo about the extension of executive power, he argued that the 1792 law was intended to cover absences through personal necessity such as illness, not one "created by the President himself," and that Madison had overlooked an amendment in 1795 which limited the appointment of a deputy to six months, after which the office became vacant.[39] The Senate referred Gallatin's nomination to a select committee, which reported that the offices of secretary of the treasury and envoy extraordinary were incompatible. Adopting the report, the Senate authorized the committee to confer with the President, but when Madison told the committee that, under the circumstances, the Senate had already deprived him of its "aid or advice," it reported against the nomination. By a vote of eighteen to seventeen the upper house rejected Gallatin, then easily confirmed Adams and Bayard.[40]

In taking his stand, King conveniently overlooked the fact that Federalist administrations had twice appointed a chief justice as envoy extraordinary, Jay in 1795 and Ellsworth in 1799. Republicans had then offered objections similar to those King now presented, and older Republicans with long memories might well have suspected that the New Yorker acted from petty and spiteful motives. Gallatin

38. For King's view of the Russian mediation, see King to Oliver Wolcott, June 6, 1813, Wolcott Papers, Vol. 23, Conn. Hist. Soc., and King to Christopher Gore, Aug. 29, 1813, King Papers, N.-Y. Hist. Soc. For King's three resolutions, see *Annals*, 13 Cong., 1 sess., 84, June 2, 1813.

39. "Notes of a Speech against Gallatin's Appointment as One of the Envoys to Russia while holding Secretary of Treasury's Position," King, ed., *King Correspondence*, V, 313–18; Brant, *James Madison*, VI, 182–83.

40. *Annals*, 13 Cong., 1 sess., 86–89; Brant, *James Madison*, VI, 191.

was more magnanimous; although attributing his rejection chiefly to King, he was not piqued and even spoke highly to James Bayard of the New Yorker's talents.[41] In contrast, the Secretary's friend, fur merchant John Jacob Astor, called King a liar who was unashamed "to ask any member for a voat for the Presidency," and condemned the Senate for its "strange if not wickd" proceedings.[42]

There can be no question that King was playing politics, probing the strength of the anti-Madison Republicans and laying the groundwork for a possible Federalist revival. Never appreciating Gallatin's fine qualities, he had succeeded, nearly twenty years before, in excluding the Swiss-born Republican from the Senate, and now suspected him of "an intricate intrigue" to land the appointment as a peace commissioner. This suspicion, shared by other Federalists, was based in part upon a statement of Gallatin's enemy, Secretary of War Armstrong, that Daschkoff, the Russian chargé at Washington, had intervened with David Parish of Philadelphia and Gallatin to secure the latter's appointment, and that the Russian had obtained a slice of a recent $16,000,000 loan. It was also based upon the sudden change in the administration's financial fortunes after the Russian offer of mediation. Desperate attempts to float the government loan had been rescued from failure only after Gallatin had raised the interest and discount to 7½ per cent, and Parish and Stephen Girard, assisted by Astor, took the entire unsubscribed loan. That the Philadelphia bankers had made the Secretary's appointment as commissioner a condition of their loan seemed a reasonable conclusion to hostile Federalists.[43]

While the controversy over Gallatin raged in Washington, opposition to the war flamed in New York. Anti-war Republicans joined Federalists in blaming Madison for the inadequate defenses of the state, particularly for failure to fortify New York harbor. The Common Council of New York City drafted a memorial to Congress asking for federal protection and sent a delegation to Washington to

41. Elizabeth Donnan, ed., *Papers of James A. Bayard, 1796–1815* (American Historical Association, *Annual Report*, 1913, II), 476.

42. Astor to Albert Gallatin, Aug. 9, 1813, Gallatin Papers, N.-Y. Hist. Soc.

43. King, ed., *King Correspondence*, V, 320; King to Oliver Wolcott, June 27, 1813, Wolcott Papers, Vol. 23, Conn. Hist. Soc.; King's memorandum on Gallatin's mission, King Papers, N.-Y. Hist. Soc.; Brant, *James Madison*, VI, 158. Gallatin had indeed sought the peace mission, believing that continuation of the war would exhaust America's resources, and he was confident of his ability as a negotiator.

confer with King. After prudently ascertaining that the Secretary of War had recommended raising two thousand troops to defend the city and harbor, King presented the memorial to the Senate on June 16.[44] He shared the Common Council's alarm, as the British strengthened their naval forces in the Chesapeake Bay area while the President was ill and his Cabinet torn by the rivalry between secretaries Monroe and Armstrong.[45] Eight months later, King defended Senator Goldsborough's attempt to have the government print a memorial of the Maryland House of Delegates complaining of inadequate defenses and asking for federal assistance. In an extemporaneous speech, the New Yorker stoutly upheld the right of remonstrance and declared it "a mere question of prudence how far any State would bear the present state of things." Daniel Webster, who was listening, reported, "You never heard such a speaker. In strength, and dignity and fire; in ease, in natural effect, and gesture as well as in matter, he is unequalled."[46]

If the country's defenses were grossly inadequate, so were its finances. King was willing to cooperate with the administration if it worked to establish an equitable and permanent tax system. When Republican senators admitted to him that the repeal of the old internal taxes had been a mistake, he told them he would participate "in all such measures as may correct past Errors." This was more than most Federalists were ready to do.[47] King joined them, of course, in their chant of woe against the "weakness" and "timidity" of the nation's "rulers," but his particular objection to tax bills was their limited duration of one year beyond the end of the war. As he explained in July 1813, he voted against four tax measures because they did not provide a permanent system of revenue, and he predicted that by the end of the year the treasury would have no income either

44. *Annals*, 13 Cong., 1 sess., 27; King to DeWitt Clinton, June 14, 1813, Clinton Papers, Vol. 5, Columbia Univ. Lib.

45. King to Oliver Wolcott, June 26, 1813, Wolcott Papers, Vol. 23, Conn. Hist. Soc. King had no confidence in either Monroe or Armstrong.

46. Daniel Webster to Ezekiel Webster, Feb. 5, 1814, Fletcher Webster, ed., *The Private Correspondence of Daniel Webster*, 2 vols. (Boston, 1857), I, 241. King's remarks were not printed in the *Annals*, 13 Cong., 2 sess., 622, which reported the debate and defeat of the motion.

47. King to Oliver Wolcott, June 10, 1813, Wolcott Papers, Vol. 23, Conn. Hist. Soc.; Stephen Van Rensselaer to David Parish, June 13, 1813, Misc. MSS, Stephen Van Rensselaer, N.-Y. Hist. Soc. For the financing of the war, see Paul Studenski and Herman E. Krooss, *Financial History of the United States . . .*, 2d ed. (N. Y., 1963), 75–81.

from import duties or loans. As a sound-money man and a stickler for strict adherence to contractual obligations, he wished his party would play a positive role in federal finance. Excluding consistency, "which in a good cause is worth something," he wrote Gore, Federalists should always help in enabling the government "to perform its Contracts."[48]

The Federalists nevertheless opposed the administration's financial measures, though King, Gore, and Wells of Delaware approved a general assessment bill in July 1813. When it came to specific taxes, however, the New Yorker voted with his Federalist colleagues against a direct tax and against taxes on bank notes, carriages, stills, domestically refined sugar, auction sales, retail wine and liquor sales, and foreign imports, all carried by the Republican majority in the summer of 1813.[49] The next year he continued to oppose tax levies as inequitable or as temporary expedients and not part of a carefully planned tax structure, but in January 1815 he voted for a $6,000,000 direct tax as the basis of a system to revive and support public credit. Most Federalist senators were against it.[50]

In March 1814 King reported that a proposed $25,000,000 loan was insufficiently supported by tax moneys, and he opposed the pledging of the treasury's sinking fund to pay the interest and principal. By resorting to loans to pay interest on previous loans, he declared, the administration had borrowed millions without adding to the sinking fund, and by pledging that fund to sustain this new loan, the government would so injure its credit that eventually nobody would lend to it. Let Congress pledge funds from taxes to amortize the loan. For this purpose he offered an amendment to provide a new sinking fund by setting aside some of the internal revenues imposed during the previous session.[51]

48. King to Oliver Wolcott, July 17, 1813, Wolcott Papers, Vol. 23, Conn. Hist. Soc.; King to Christopher Gore, Aug. 29, 1813, King, ed., *King Correspondence*, V, 342.

49. *Annals*, 13 Cong., 1 sess., 47, 58, 59, 68, 71.

50. King's speech on taxation and public credit, delivered in the Senate early in Jan. 1815, aroused favorable newspaper comment, and the pro-administration Washington *National Intelligencer*, Jan. 7, 1815, praised King for telling the senators it was their duty to enable the President to act. In King's scrapbook, King Collection, N.-Y. Hist. Soc., is a clipping of the substance of this speech; see also *Niles' Weekly Register*, Jan. 14, 1815, 313, 318.

51. King's manuscript, 1814, including the substance of his speech on a loan bill and notes on the debate, Mar. 18, 1814, King Papers, N.-Y. Hist. Soc. A portion of the notes is not in King's hand. King to Oliver Wolcott, Mar. 10, 14, 1814, Wolcott Papers, Vol. 23, Conn. Hist. Soc.

The Senate rejected King's sinking fund plan, as well as several other amendments he offered, and passed the loan bill. None were fully satisfied, and King was one of six who voted against it.[52] His negative vote, together with his stand on the sinking fund, stamped him in Republican minds as an incorrigible obstructionist. He would not support any financial program that did not rest upon permanent internal taxes, and he correctly predicted that after the war the Republicans would throw the burden of taxation upon the merchants.[53]

Throughout 1814 moneyed men and politicians weighed the merits of a new national bank. King regretted the death of the first Bank of the United States in 1811. He had assisted in establishing it, and he looked favorably upon the idea of a new national bank with expanded capital resources as valuable to the government and "a ligament of Union among the States."[54] Nevertheless he was suspicious of bank proposals coming from Republicans, most of whom had in the past been hostile to the Bank of the United States, and he politely declined to meet with a group associated with John J. Astor.[55] His correspondence with Oliver Wolcott, Jr., and with Charles Wilkes of the Bank of New York revealed mutual concern over the soundness and timeliness of Secretary Dallas's plan for a new national bank, and King encouraged Wilkes's effort to draft a petition of New York bankers against it.[56] It was obvious that King had been outvoted, when in December a special committee, of which he was chairman, reported a bill for a Bank of the United States essentially as recommended by Dallas. He argued on the Senate floor to reduce the bank's capital from $50,000,000 to $20,000,000, but the administration phalanx defeated the motion, and two days later, on the ninth, the bank bill passed. Together with four Republicans, King and a solid bloc of Federalists voted against it.[57]

In the House, a bill acceptable to most Federalists was adopted:

52. *Annals*, 13 Cong., 2 sess., 674–75; *Niles' Register*, Mar. 26, 1814; Adams, *History of the U. S.*, VII, 390.

53. King to Oliver Wolcott, Feb. 24, Apr. 10, 1814, Wolcott Papers, Vol. 23, Conn. Hist. Soc.

54. King to Oliver Wolcott, Feb. 8, 1814, *ibid.*

55. King to Astor, Sept. 1, 1814, King Papers, N.-Y. Hist. Soc. King conscientiously criticized the Astor group's bank plan without committing himself.

56. Oliver Wolcott to King, Dec. 6, 1814, Charles Wilkes to King, Nov. 3, 11, 19, 1814, *ibid.*

57. *Annals*, 13 Cong., 3 sess., 119, 123, 125, 126–27; King, ed., *King Correspondence*, V, 442. For Federalists' attitude toward a bank in this period, see Hammond, *Banks and Politics*, 238–39.

the bank would have $30,000,000 of capital, one-fourth in specie and three-fourths in government securities; it could not suspend specie payments, nor was it obliged to lend three-fifths of its capital to the government. On January 20, the Senate accepted the House bill by a vote of twenty to fourteen, King having played an influential part in reversing its previous stand. Madison, despite a bankrupt treasury, saw no advantage in this emasculated bank and vetoed the bill, asserting that the bank would not revive public credit, provide a national medium of circulation, or help the treasury obtain loans, and that after the war the bank would grow rich without comparably benefiting the government. Despite King's reply to the President's objections, the Senate failed to override the veto.[58] The New Yorker was far from dismayed; if a bank plan of very limited value to the government had been rejected by the Chief Executive, Congress had thwarted a clearly inflationary scheme that would have helped the treasury only momentarily and would have enriched a few insiders at the expense of the public credit.

Madison's commercial and naval policies seemed to King as ruinous as his financial measures. Long an advocate of naval power, the Senator from New York wished to strengthen the navy directly instead of depending upon privateers. He voted against granting bounties to owners, officers, and crews of American privateers, partly, no doubt, because he thought the practice wasteful, but also because it would interfere with naval recruitment.[59] Like other commerce-conscious Federalist senators, he teamed up with dissident Republicans in July 1813 to defeat an administration embargo on shipping, but five months later these anti-Madison forces were unable to prevent a new embargo, which Senator Jeremiah Mason called "a kind of self-immolation, like that practiced by the inhabitants of Japan, who destroy themselves to resent an affront on their honor."[60] King would have agreed.

Scarcely two weeks after Madison signed the embargo act, news reached America that British Foreign Secretary Castlereagh, though

58. *Annals*, 13 Cong., 3 sess., 173–74, 175, 177–78, 207–14. The Senate received Madison's veto on Jan. 30, 1815. King's answer to it, on Feb. 2, is reprinted in King, ed., *King Correspondence*, V, 553–61. King replied in detail to the President's specific objections, and he defended limitations on the bank's operations.

59. *Annals*, 13 Cong., 1 sess., 82.

60. *Ibid.*, 100–01, and 13 Cong., 2 sess., 561. For Mason's comment, see *ibid.*, 558.

declining Russian peace mediation, had offered direct negotiations with the United States. Reports that Napoleon had been decisively beaten at Leipzig and was in headlong retreat, coupled with the American loss of Fort Niagara and the devastation of Buffalo and other towns along the northern frontier, dimmed hopes for success in the war with Britain. On January 6 the President told Congress he had accepted Castlereagh's offer. The Senate quickly confirmed the nomination as peace commissioners of Adams and Bayard, who were still abroad; Jonathan Russell, who was at the same time finally confirmed as minister to Sweden; and Henry Clay, who was strongly opposed by Federalists. When it was learned that Gallatin expected to remain for some time in Europe, the President nominated him also. The legal limit of six months on absences from a federal post, emphasized earlier by King, had expired, and with the appointment of Senator George W. Campbell as the new secretary of the treasury, the Senate approved Gallatin.[61] In April overwhelming majorities in both houses of Congress repealed the embargo, as well as a nonimportation law passed late in January. The President signed the repeal on the fourteenth, making the path clear for peace negotiations.

Prospects of a peace satisfactory to both Britain and the United States were far from bright. Neither power was willing to yield on impressment, a major issue. King, who professed to be baffled by the inconsistency of the administration, interpreted Madison's new policy of abandoning commercial restrictions as a face-saving device to obtain from Britain some stipulation which could be used as "an apology" for the war. Judging by what he learned from Sir William Scott, Britain's specialist in maritime law, King expected the negotiations to break down if each side clung to its own doctrine of maritime rights. The British would not be willing to give up impressment even if the United States agreed to ban British-born seamen from American ships.[62]

Before the negotiations began at Ghent, King had a long conference with John Jacob Astor, friend of Gallatin and supporter of the administration, who, in a private letter to Secretary Monroe, proposed acknowledging the right of impressment. Astor buttressed his argument with statements by English and Swedish merchants and

61. For particulars, see Brant, *James Madison*, VI, 240–41.

62. King to Gouverneur Morris, Jan. 26, 1814, G. Morris Papers, Columbia Univ. Lib.

by politicians in both parties in the United States, including King, who he asserted "would let Great Britain have her men from our ships." If the American commissioners could yield gracefully, King would approve a treaty which acknowledged the right of impressment.[63] The Senator's willingness to accede to that right, based as it was on Britain's superior naval and military strength, was a simple recognition that the United States could not force a powerful adversary to weaken herself. More than a decade earlier, while in England, he had vainly tried to induce Lord Hawkesbury to abandon impressment; in 1814 the United States had even less bargaining power, as northern shipowners well understood.

Astor's plea was unnecessary, for Monroe had already instructed the American commissioners to drop the impressment issue if necessary, and on the basis of Gallatin's letters from London, sent new instructions on October 4 which dropped other mandatory requirements as well. The abandonment of what had been adhered to for so long was justified by the President as a pragmatic response to the restoration of peace in Europe, which portended no further occasion to dispute the issues of impressment or of blockading without an adequate force.[64] When Madison's authorization of peace on the basis of the *status quo ante bellum* was revealed to Congress, King commented sourly, "every point for which we went to war is given up. . . . the war must be continued to save us from losing what we before possessed and for the sake of obtaining something additional."[65] He was referring to the military disasters on American soil, and though he wanted peace, he could not accept "Terms of Dishonour or Degradation."[66]

King's gloom deepened in 1814. Ever since Gallatin had "deserted" the treasury, its work had devolved on "clerks and jobmen and undertakers"; it was notorious, the Senator wrote, that commissaries, district attorneys, loan officers, marshals, contractors, navy agents, postal officials, customs house officers, and tax gatherers were "taken from one class of citizens only." He was convinced that if these men

63. John Jacob Astor to James Monroe, July 22, 1814, Private, Monroe Papers, N. Y. Pub. Lib.

64. Brant, *James Madison*, VI, 333; Adams, *History of the U. S.*, IX, 32–33.

65. King to Stephen Van Rensselaer, Oct. 19, 1814, Gratz Coll., Case 1, Box 38, Hist. Soc. of Pa. Cf. King to Gouverneur Morris, Oct. 19, 1814, G. Morris Papers, Columbia Univ. Lib.

66. King to John Trumbull, Dec. 11, 1814, Gratz Coll., Hist. Soc. of Pa.

were investigated, the number of dishonest agents among them would astonish the country.[67]

> In Congress we do not rise above mediocrity; and not a few of us are positively below that standard. The scramble for place and authority is the great Object and employment of men of the greatest Influence. No country was ever more absolutely abandoned than our country. The states east of Pennsylvania have no influence; such is their division, that they might as well keep their Representatives at home as to send them to Congress. In short . . . such is . . . our deplorable condition, that the disastrous Effects of it upon our Prosperity, and upon the security of our Rights, are not only in the highest degree alarming, but no man is authorized to expect any beneficial change.[68]

King was in better humor when he and his wife settled down again at their Jamaica homestead late in April. He read with great satisfaction the latest dispatches from Europe telling of Napoleon's continued defeats and the triumphant entry of the allies into Paris. A treaty with the tyrant, he wrote, "would be insecure. I care nothing about the Bourbons, but by their reestablishment, there may be, and probably will be, a Peace of considerable duration. I therefore earnestly hope that the Allies will persevere until Bonaparte be expelled from France."[69]

When news of Napoleon's exile to Elba arrived, King and other Federalists planned a solemn celebration, to be climaxed with an appropriate oration by Gouverneur Morris. The Senator was apprehensive, however, that Morris's tone might be too anti-administration, even disunionist, and thereby injure the cause of moderate Federalism.[70] On June 29, in the crowded Presbyterian Church on Cedar

67. Undated notes made by King at the time of the Hartford Convention, King Papers, N.-Y. Hist. Soc.; King's speech on taxation and public credit, Jan. 1815, scrapbook of clippings, King Coll., *ibid.* In Dec. 1813, King had called for an examination of expenses for navy contracts and purchases of supplies. *Annals*, 13 Cong., 3 sess., 138.

68. King to Oliver Wolcott, Apr. 10, 1814, Wolcott Papers, Vol. 23, Conn. Hist. Soc. King and Wolcott corresponded in mutual commiseration. Recent study indicates that there was little change in the social and educational level of public officials after 1801; see Sidney H. Aronson, *Status and Kinship in the Higher Civil Service: Standards of Selection in the Administrations of John Adams, Thomas Jefferson, and Andrew Jackson* (Cambridge, Mass., 1964).

69. King to Christopher Gore, May 24, 1814, King Papers, N.-Y. Hist. Soc.

70. King to John Jay, June 20, 1814, Jay Papers, Columbia Univ. Lib. Cf. Jay's reply, June 23, 1814, King Papers, N.-Y. Hist. Soc.

Street, Morris pronounced his "oration of triumph" after which the celebrants marched up Broadway to Washington Hall for a large banquet over which Rufus King presided. While the diners raised their glasses, a mob gathered outside, shouted insults, and threw stones which shattered windows and crashed inside, injuring a few guests before the rioters were dispersed.[71] King may have remembered the stoning of Hamilton nineteen years earlier.

While Americans generally hailed the fall of Napoleon, Great Britain, freed from the threat in Europe, concentrated on the New World theater of war. She planned new offensives against Lake Champlain, Chesapeake Bay, and New Orleans, sent to America fourteen thousand veterans of Wellington's Peninsular Campaign, and tightened her blockade. In August, while an American army was besieged at Fort Erie on the Canadian side of the Niagara, British soldiers, direct from France, landed in Maryland, routed a hastily assembled force under the incompetent General Winder at Bladensburg, and marched into Washington, putting to the torch the Capitol, the Executive Mansion, and nearly all the other public buildings. Government officials fled the scene, but President Madison soon returned with some of his Cabinet officers to view the destruction, face an angry public, and begin the task of reconstruction. As a first step, John Armstrong was replaced as secretary of war by his rival, Monroe.

Armstrong, who earlier in the year had intimated his willingness to cooperate with the Federalists against the "Virginia dynasty" at the next presidential election, tarried in New York City en route to his home and saw King several times. Astor, his suspicions raised, informed Monroe that the Armstrong-King interviews were frequent enough to occasion surprise among the Senator's friends and hinted at a liaison. However, King thoroughly mistrusted Armstrong, whom he regarded as a warmonger and self-seeker. Consequently their conversation was undoubtedly confined to the peace negotiations at Ghent, the destruction of Washington, the military prospects, and the sort of accommodations that might be provided for Congress.[72]

After the sack of Washington, New Yorkers were alarmed lest

71. Morris, ed., *Diary of Gouverneur Morris*, II, 565; N. Y. *Spectator*, July 2, 1814.

72. John Jacob Astor to James Monroe, Sept. 22, 1814, Monroe Papers, N. Y. Pub. Lib. Armstrong had arrived in New York City on Sept. 7. For King's opinion of Armstrong, and the latter's overture to the Federalists early in 1814, see King, ed., *King Correspondence*, V, 357, 363, 370–71, 390–91.

other armies be landed and the burning of towns along Chesapeake Bay be repeated at the mouth of the Hudson. Led by Mayor DeWitt Clinton, politicians dropped their differences to prepare the city for possible bombardment, and militiamen were hurriedly assembled to guard the defenses.

For King the turning point had come. At a public meeting of prominent merchants he defended the decision of the New York banks to suspend specie payments and to issue paper, and he appealed to the people's sense of duty to support the action of the banks. He considered the banks sound and assured his hearers that the emission of new notes would be limited. "The enemy is at our doors, and it is now useless to enquire how he came here—he must be driven away—and every man join heart and hand, and place shoulder to shoulder to meet him."[73] The bankers, however, refused to lend their bills without better collateral than the federal government could afford but informed Governor Tompkins that if treasury notes, endorsed by him, were deposited, they would advance enough money to the city to strengthen harbor fortifications.

Learning of this, King called on the Governor to persuade him to endorse the notes. Tompkins was reluctant, fearing that in case of failure he would be ruined. "Then ruin yourself if it becomes necessary to save the country," urged King, according to a later account, "and I pledge you my honor that I will support you in whatever you do." Although he did not offer to be a co-endorser, his appeal must have impressed the Governor, who endorsed the notes. The bankers advanced the money, work was stepped up on the defenses, and by the end of September nearly twenty thousand state militia were guarding New York City.[74] King's three oldest sons volunteered for the militia, and he himself made a liberal cash contribution; he was said to have told General Morgan Lewis, "Let a loan be immediately

73. *N.-Y. Evening Post*, Sept. 2, 1814. As the *Post* admitted, these may not have been King's precise words but represented their substance and spirit. Cf. King to Christopher Gore, Sept. 2, 1814, and King to Jeremiah Mason, Sept. 2, 1814, King, ed., *King Correspondence*, V, 413–15.

74. Hammond, *Political Parties in New York*, I, 378. A committee of the House of Representatives later reported that, when Tompkins hesitated to risk financial ruin, King "solemnly urged him to go on, and do his duty, and if ruin was the consequence, to consent to endure it, and look to the honor and gratitude of the country." *Annals*, 17 Cong., 2 sess., 909, Feb. 8, 1823. For the defense of New York City, see R. S. Guernsey, *New York City and Vicinity during the War of 1812–15 . . .*, 2 vols. (N. Y., 1889–95), and Julius W. Pratt, "The War of 1812," in Alexander C. Flick, ed., *History of the State of New York*, 10 vols. (N. Y., 1933–37), V, 242–47.

opened. I will subscribe to the amount of my whole fortune," and when the city announced a loan of $1,000,000 at 7 per cent, he actually subscribed $20,000.[75]

King's political stock rose rapidly after the assault of the British on the national capital. "The people from all parts of the country are loudly calling for a change of Administration; your name is always coupled with Mr. King's," wrote an American attaché in London to James A. Bayard, the only Federalist on the United States peace commission, and, like the New Yorker, a moderate.[76] It was rumored in the British capital that King had been called into the American government, but the wish was father to the thought.[77]

Though obscure in origin, the King boom was genuine. On August 31, the *Centinel* in Boston proposed a reorganization of Madison's Cabinet: King to be Secretary of State, Langdon Cheves to take over the treasury, John Brooks the War Department, and James Lloyd the Department of the Navy. On September 3, a leading administration paper, the Boston *Patriot*, took up the suggestion without mentioning names, and before long, Federalist journals in other states were even printing demands that the President resign in favor of the veteran Senator.[78] Late in August, several men had called on Astor in New York and declared that if Monroe took charge of the War Department (as, in fact, he did) and turned over the State Department to King, the Federalists would aid the administration in every respect. Astor reported this to Monroe, adding: "I mearly observed that if Mr. King wishd to cam [come] in with a view to the Presidency I Suposed . . . [Monroe's] pretentions and qualifications as good as Mr. Kings—but that Mr. Campbell [Secretary of the Treasury] . . . would probably Resign and in Such case if Mr. King wish to Serve the Country he might if the President tought proper to apoint him cam in that Deportment."[79] Monroe, of course, never

75. N. Y. *Spectator*, Aug. 31, 1814; *N.-Y. Evening Post*, Sept. 17, 1814. As for King's sons, John became a lieutenant in the New York Hussars, a cavalry company; Charles served briefly as a captain in a volunteer regiment; and James was appointed as an aide by Gen. Ebenezer Stephens, who commanded the militia of the city. King, ed., *King Correspondence*, V, 426–27; Fox, *Decline of Aristocracy*, 183.

76. Donnan, ed., *Papers of James A. Bayard*, II, 342.

77. *Ibid.*, 354.

78. Morison, *Otis*, II, 98*n*.

79. John Jacob Astor to James Monroe, Sept. 2, 1814, Private, Monroe Papers, Lib. Cong. The unnamed gentlemen replied that King's talents were not suitable for the treasury office, but this was an obvious dodge because King was familiar with finance.

would have consented to yield to his long-time antagonist and would have objected to King in any Cabinet post. The President retained his Virginia friend as both secretary of war and acting secretary of state. Had he appointed a prominent Federalist to the Cabinet, Madison would undoubtedly have strengthened his hand, for it would have united many Federalists behind a reorganized administration, and it might have forestalled the Hartford Convention. To sanction a bipartisan war effort, however, would be to admit past failures, and in that tense autumn, the President was in no mood to let Monroe, his choice for the succession, be outmaneuvered by Rufus King.

Early in October, Federalist senators and congressmen convened at Crawford's Hotel and adopted a policy report drawn up by King, Gore, and Daggett of the Senate, and Pickering, Pearson, and Oakley of the House. Although no single person took credit for drafting it, the report was consistent with King's often expressed views and bore the unmistakable imprint of his hand. It recommended vigorous prosecution of the war, the granting of money and men, and the strengthening of the navy, but it opposed conscription. It justified a direct tax apportioned according to population and the increase or extension of indirect taxes. In view of the "incapacity of the Executive Government, invariably manifested at home and abroad, whereby the public credit is deeply impaired, and the objects of the war, as well as of negotiation, have been alike abandoned," the report concluded that "nothing short of an entire change of the Heads of Departments" would restore public confidence and lead to peace with safety and honor.[80]

For many of the party faithful this seemed a statesmanlike position. It would give its adherents a constructive program with a positive goal, and at the same time shift more of the burden of war from commerce to agriculture. Moreover, it was designed in part to retain the loyalty of those New England Federalists dallying with disunionism.[81]

When pressed by Gouverneur Morris to participate in the Hartford Convention, which assembled on December 15, King firmly

80. Manuscript endorsed by King, dated Oct. 1814, King Papers, N.-Y. Hist. Soc. For a parallel statement by King, see King, ed., *King Correspondence*, V, 419.

81. See, however, Pickering's later statement that only a British conquest of New Orleans and the West might force the South to accede to New England's demands; he saw no alternative but separation from the Union. Hervey P. Prentiss, "Timothy Pickering and the War of 1812," Essex Inst., *Hist. Colls.*, 70 (1934), 143.

declined.[82] He frowned upon hasty decisions and reckless acts born of frustration and anger. Wincing at the outspoken disunionism voiced in the legislature of his native state, he hoped that the moderates could head off New England separatism, but, characteristically, he did not openly oppose the Hartford Convention, and privately he advised delay. Patience, prudence, and time were the resources of wise men, and "partial measures," he warned, would jeopardize comprehensive and permanent legislation. Hasty sectional proceedings should not impair needed national deliberation: "The real Patriots, the men of sound principles, are dispersed over the whole Nation. They have the same Pride of Country, the same devotion to the Principles of Freedom, the same desire that the Government of the Nation should afford equal Protection and distribute its honors with an impartial hand among the respective members."[83]

In the Thirteenth Congress, King had become the acknowledged Federalist leader in the Senate, and his prestige was never higher among the men of his party. When Vice-President Gerry died in November 1814, the New Yorker was the choice of the Federalists as the new presiding officer of the Senate, but even with the aid of their few Republican allies, they could not prevent the election of John Gaillard of South Carolina.[84]

King, like his Federalist colleagues, considered as unconstitutional any conscription of state militiamen into the United States Army. A bill from the House of Representatives called for a year's service of eighty thousand militia, the Senate held out for two years, and a conference committee compromised on eighteen months. On December 28, the House rejected the conference report, and the next day, King moved an indefinite postponement. There was no debate, and the motion quickly carried by fourteen to thirteen, in effect killing the bill. Although disclaiming any special credit, the New Yorker won

82. King showed his correspondence with Morris to Martin Van Buren, who informed John Quincy Adams. Charles F. Adams, ed., *Memoirs of John Quincy Adams, Comprising Portions of His Diary from 1795 to 1848*, 12 vols. (Phila., 1874–77), VI, 487.

83. King's manuscript on the Hartford Convention, 1814, King Papers, N.-Y. Hist. Soc. The reason King was not more outspoken may perhaps be that his friend George Cabot, who presided over the convention, was a moderate. As it turned out, the proceedings and resolutions of the convention did not reflect the views of the extremists.

84. Gaillard was elected on the second ballot with 16 votes, to 10 for King, 5 for Chase of Vermont, and 1 for Anderson of Tennessee. *Annals*, 13 Cong., 3 sess., 110–11.

the plaudits of Madison's enemies, and the Maryland House of Delegates voted him a resolution of thanks.[85]

A month and a half after the failure of the "conscription" bill, the Senate received the Treaty of Ghent. Silent on impressment, blockades, and other maritime issues over which the war had been declared, the pact simply called for a return to the situation *ante bellum*. King spoke for forty minutes, pointing out "the great blessings of the present war." His biting satire, said the *New-York Evening Post*, had scarcely ever been equaled. "Every sentence was Cantharides to the already blistered feelings of the administration."[86] That day, February 15, the Senate ratified the treaty, and two days later the President proclaimed it in effect.

Relieved at the peace, proud of Jackson's magnificent late victory at New Orleans, and pleased at the war record of the navy, the mercantile-minded Rufus King looked forward to fulfillment of America's maritime destiny. He asserted that all legislation, particularly maritime and commercial, should anticipate repeated struggles on the seas before the United States possessed "the undisputed trident." "Our system should have constant Reference to the future," he wrote, "and all should combine heads and hearts and purses to lay down and support a wise plan of national Policy never to be departed from and always to be promoted."[87]

85. *Ibid.*, 141; King, ed., *King Correspondence*, V, 454–57. Daniel Webster believed that King's motion was unpremeditated. Webster, ed., *Private Correspondence of Daniel Webster*, I, 249. In a letter to the speaker of the Maryland House, King stated his belief that the bill drafting state troops was unconstitutional, but he also asserted his sense of obligation to vote for men, money, and supplies in order to revive public credit, protect the states against invasion, and save the nation from dismemberment. King to Henry Chapman, Jan. 8, 1815, King Papers, N.-Y. Hist. Soc.

86. *N.-Y. Evening Post*, Feb. 14, 1815.

87. King to Oliver Wolcott, Feb. 26, 1815, Wolcott Papers, Vol. 23, Conn. Hist. Soc. King wrote a long letter to his son in England, giving a full account of the Battle of New Orleans. King to Charles King, Feb. 15, 1815, King Papers, N.-Y. Hist. Soc.

CHAPTER XVIII

SENATOR AND FEDERALIST STANDARD BEARER

RUFUS KING, RECENTLY HONORED WITH A FOURTH DOCTOR OF LAWS degree,[1] was sixty years old in March 1815. For most of his life he had been in robust health, but the discomfort he vaguely associated with "gravel" or "inflammation of the kidney" caused him to appreciate more than usual his return to the quiet pastoral scene on Long Island. He liked the change of pace, though he zestfully planted crops, sold produce, cut hay in the salt meadow, and performed countless tasks of farm management.

His fourth son, Edward, having completed two years at Tapping Reeve's law school, decided to practice in Ohio and proceeded in October to Chillicothe, where Governor Thomas Worthington, whom King had known in the Senate, agreed to act *in loco parentis*. In the ensuing months Edward received much parental counsel, not all of it accepted. His father pressed upon him the need to be patient, diligent, methodical, frugal, and sober, and to avoid political controversy. "To be a Lawyer of reputation," King advised, "your punctuality, industry, acquirements and talents, bottomed upon the

1. On Jan. 7, 1815, the University of Pennsylvania awarded LL.D degrees to King, Chief Justice Marshall, and Justice Bushrod Washington. While he had been abroad in 1802, Dartmouth had similarly honored King. Williams had done so in 1803, and Harvard in 1806. Minutes of the Trustees of the University of Pennsylvania, Jan. 7, 1815, as reported to the author by Leonidas Dodson, university archivist; King, ed., *King Correspondence*, IV, 538–39.

purest integrity, must be seen and understood by others. . . . Your present object is not immediate acquisition of fortune, but to acquire character, standing, and public consideration" through orderly habits, hard work, and perseverance. He urged Edward to read, write, study, and relax at regular times, and to keep a journal, for method was "the parent of order and the first law in education and business."[2]

The sober and regular habits enjoined upon Edward had been strictly practiced in the King household. Precision, purposefulness, and prudence were among the Senator's own noticeable traits, as was temperance. With few exceptions, he never allowed the consumption of hard liquor in his family, and he advised his son to drink beer or cider instead. Reserved and highly disciplined himself, he urged Edward to control his passions and his language and cautioned especially against gambling.[3]

Mary King had no need to add to the catalogue of instructions, but when she wrote her son in March 1816 she expressed concern that he made no mention of the fair sex. "With the exception of Governor Worthington's family, you say nothing about the female society of Chillicothe," she observed; "I like female society for young Men. It softens and polishes the manners even if the Ladies themselves are not very refined." Edward's mother was soon to discover why her son had mentioned only the Governor's family, for in the middle of May he married that gentleman's daughter, Sarah, "rather sooner than we had expected," wrote King, who was opposed to early marriages and had so told Edward. However, John, Charles, and James had married young, despite their father's advice, and Edward did so, too, contending that early marriage was a necessity to a lonely stranger in the West.[4]

At this time, King was in the national capital, where in December 1815 the Senate took up a new commercial treaty negotiated with England. Although it ended discriminatory duties and opened India to American commerce, the pact made no specific concessions to

2. King to Edward King, Dec. 16, 1815, King, ed., *King Correspondence*, V, 494–95. The original is in the Lilly Library, Indiana University. King to Edward King, Dec. 23, 1815, King Papers, Cincinnati Historical Society, Cincinnati.

3. King to Edward King, Jan. 1, 1816, King Papers, Cincinnati Hist. Soc.

4. Mary King to Edward King, Mar. 6, 1816, King, ed., *King Correspondence*, V, 524; King to Christopher Gore, May 27, 1816, King Papers, N.-Y. Hist. Soc.

American shipping in the British West Indies, excluded American ships from the St. Lawrence, and was silent on impressment, contraband, and blockades. The Senate ratified it without great enthusiasm. "It is scarcely worth the wax of its Seals," King remarked, "and leaves every point of Dispute and disagreement unsettled."[5]

In the Fourteenth Congress, King was nearly always in the minority on significant issues. Like most of his Federalist colleagues, he vainly opposed cutting the direct tax from six to three million dollars and extending it for another year.[6] He objected less to the amount of the tax than to capricious annual tax laws "designed to organize faction . . . for the little purposes of popularity." Internal revenue measures, a moderate tariff, and a moderate land tax he considered essential, but when he saw no chance for a permanent land tax, unpopular in the South and West, he would not support a temporary one.[7] Most Federalists disliked a protective tariff, but King was ready to accept Secretary Dallas's tariff recommendation and reluctantly voted for the tariff of 1816 as a necessary evil.[8]

Government economy and the prevention of a burgeoning bureaucracy were twin Federalist objectives. Now that peace had returned, King and other Federalist senators saw little to be gained from an enlarged military establishment. Though they contributed to the defeat of a $200,000 appropriation to build naval vessels on the Great Lakes, they failed to block the reorganization of the army and an appropriation of $1,250,000 for expenses incurred in calling up the militia during the war. King voted against adding two brigadier generals to the army engineer corps as needless and unwise, his

5. King to Edward King, Dec. 23, 1815, King Papers, Cincinnati Hist. Soc. Cf. Samuel F. Bemis, *John Quincy Adams and the Foundations of American Foreign Policy* (N. Y., 1949), 293–94. For King's helpful role in the technical maneuvering necessary to give effect to this convention, see *Annals*, 14 Cong., 1 sess., 160–61; King, ed., *King Correspondence*, VI, 2–3.

6. *Annals*, 14 Cong., 1 sess., 166. On a motion to extend the tax beyond 1815 until repealed, the Federalists divided: King, Gore, and Mason voted aye; Daggett, Dana, and Goldsborough voted nay, and the motion was defeated, 18 to 15. *Ibid.*

7. Baltimore *Federal Republican*, Feb. 28, 1816, as quoted by the N. Y. *Commercial Advertiser*, Mar. 1, 1816; King to Gouverneur Morris, Mar. 9, 1816, King, ed., *King Correspondence*, VI, 11. Unlike King, Morris had speculative interests and opposed a land tax. See Morris to King, Jan. 26, 1816, King Papers, N.-Y. Hist. Soc.

8. *Annals*, 14 Cong., 1 sess., 330–31; King to Oliver Wolcott, Feb. 18, 1816, Wolcott Papers, Vol. 23, Conn. Hist. Soc.; Wolcott to King, Apr. 2, 1816, King Papers, N.-Y. Hist. Soc.; King, ed., *King Correspondence*, VI, 17, 21.

RUFUS KING
by Gilbert Stuart, *ca. 1819*
Owned by Frederick Lennig, Andalusia, Pa.
Reproduced by Frick Art Reference Library, N.Y.C.

present attitude, which was shared by other Federalists, being strangely reminiscent of Republican protests against Federalist militarism in the 1790's.[9] Federalists also voted against increasing the salaries of the members of Congress. Like Webster in the House, King saw a need to boost the legislators' income and was ready to increase their *per diem* allowance, but he thought the salary grab imprudent and likely to arouse public disgust. "Having voted ourselves a salary of 1500 Dollars a year," he commented ironically, the session would end within a month.[10]

With most Republicans no longer opposing a national bank as unconstitutional, the House passed a new bank bill in March, substantially as recommended by Secretary Dallas. In the Senate, Federalists subjected the bill to close scrutiny, suggesting many changes but without much effect. King supported an amendment to raise the proportion of specie to be paid at the time of subscription from 5 to 10 per cent. Advising against hasty passage, he called attention to the smallness of the majority (eighty to seventy-one) which had enacted the House bill, and lectured the Senate on the Philadelphia Convention's wisdom in creating two separate branches of the legislature so that each could act independently. Referring to the Senate bill, he predicted that, since the bank's first discounts would be made to those most pressed by the state banks, the proceeds of these discounts would wind up in the vaults of the state banks. Half a million dollars, he asserted, would be entirely too small to enable the national bank to compete with these state banks. If the issue of the bank exceeded the specie paid in, the latter would find its way into the local banks; moreover, if the bank confined its discounts to the amount of paid-in specie, the institution would be of very limited use to the government. The new bank, he feared, might well become a "paper bank," and he hoped the Senate would prevent this potential disaster by increasing the amount of authorized specie payment. The Senate rejected the amendment and on April 3 passed

9. *Annals*, 14 Cong., 1 sess., 333–34, 336, 341. On a scrap of paper, which he dated Mar. 1816, King scrawled: "Standing army Introduced at the Revolution [of 1688] and by the Whigs—the only army that destroyed *Liberty* was the army of Liberty, that of Cromwell—while the army of Despotism of James 2d refused to side with him against the Country and Constitution—odisse quem Caeseris." King Papers, N.-Y. Hist. Soc.

10. King, ed., *King Correspondence*, VI, 18. The vote on the salary bill was 21 to 11. *Annals*, 14 Cong., 1 sess., 203–04.

the bank bill by a vote of twenty-two to twelve. Three Federalists voted for it, and seven, including King, voted against it.[11]

To those who might have considered King's opposition strange for one who had been so ardent an advocate of the first Bank of the United States, the New York Senator had an answer. He regarded the new institution as a tool to be manipulated by the wrong people. "Excepting the magnitude of its Capital, and the appointment by the President and Senate of a fifth of the Directors, I should assist in passing the Law," he wrote his son a week before the final vote, "but especially on the latter objection I am opposed to it. The Patronage of the Executive is already enough; the civil list, the army, the navy and the Revenue officers holding their places at pleasure, and scattered over the face of the country, are a powerful Executive influence and sufficiently so, without creating 5 Directors of the Bank of the U.S., who may overlook and in some way control the private business of every man in the nation."[12]

With wry satisfaction, King reflected upon the similarity of postwar Republican measures to Federalist legislation of the 1790's. If the labels were different, the contents were the same. The Republicans were adopting former Federalist measures despite years of protesting the evils of taxes, the army, and the navy; and the creation of the new Bank of the United States was a perfect example of Federalist policy under Republican sponsorship. "I remain the same," King smugly observed, "and if others change and do what I did, and still contend that I was wrong in doing as they do now, it is for them to make out their own Consistency."[13]

Constitutional questions always interested King, and, as the only senator in the Fourteenth Congress who had been a framer of the Constitution, he spoke with an air of authority. He was aroused when, in an obvious attempt to weaken the last national stronghold of Federalism, Senator Nathan Sanford proposed a constitutional amendment to make judges removable by the president supported by a two-

11. Annals, 14 Cong., 1 sess., 281. For King's arguments, see 237–38.

12. King to Edward King, Mar. 28, 1816, King, ed., *King Correspondence*, VI, 17. Cf. Hammond, *Banks and Politics*, 239. King had offered motions to eliminate the government directors, and when these failed he moved to prevent such directors from acting as stockholders' agents or proxies. He also supported a motion to eliminate government directors whenever the United States ceased to hold stock in the bank. *Annals*, 14 Cong., 1 sess., 255, 256, 258.

13. King to Christopher Gore, June 26, 1816, King Papers, N.-Y. Hist. Soc. Cf. King to William B. Giles, Apr. 21, 1816, Misc. MSS—King, N.-Y. Hist. Soc.

thirds vote in Congress. True to the position he had taken in the Philadelphia Convention nearly thirty years before, King denounced the resolution as violating the independence of the judiciary and warned against debating such a "sacred" part of the Constitution.[14]

Another issue which stirred King, the method of electing the president and vice-president, was timely because 1816 was an election year. Varnum of Massachusetts proposed to amend the Constitution so as to divide each state into electoral districts for the choice of both representatives to Congress and electors of the president and vice-president. Since the electoral machinery of the Republican party was dominated by the caucus system, politicians appreciated that any device that threatened to break the grip of the caucus might also weaken the party. Varnum's resolution sparked a lively debate in which lofty sentiments masked partisan purpose. The election of the president was no longer what the Constitution intended, King told the Senate.

> In conformity with the original view of the authors of that instrument, I would restore, as thoroughly as possible, the freedom of election to the people. I would make the mode of election uniform through the country by throwing the whole nation into as many districts as there are Electors, and let the people of each district choose one Elector. . . . then all the people of the country would stand precisely on the same footing; and no particular addresses could be made to the special interests and particular views of particular men or particular sections of the country.[15]

Long resentful of Virginia's influence in the Union, the New Yorker admitted that the choice of each elector within a district would destroy the power of the large states but asserted that the sacrifice of power by some states would benefit the people of the Union as a whole. Although he did not avow it on the Senate floor, he probably looked to electoral reform as one step toward ultimately eliminating slave representation.[16]

If his viewpoint coincided with partisan aims, it was honestly held

14. *Annals*, 14 Cong., 1 sess., 208. Sanford was German's successor as New York's other senator. The Senate did not act on his proposal.

15. *Ibid.*, 216. Varnum's proposal was made upon the instruction of the Federalist legislature of Massachusetts.

16. *Ibid.*, 224, 225. See there the remarks of Georgia's Senator Bibb.

and quite consistent with ideas he had expressed before. He had given his opinion in the Constitutional Convention that presidential electors should be chosen by the people, and he regarded the electoral system adopted at Philadelphia as a compromise with delegates who had favored election by the federal or state legislatures. Hence it was not at all strange that the New Yorker dwelt upon a theme he had affirmed some thirty years earlier, his fervent speeches betokening a war-begotten sense of urgency:

> Men now live who will probably see the end of our system of Government as we now go on: terminate when it will, that termination will not be favorable to public liberty. . . . Not a people on earth were more capable of high excitement than this people. . . . The march from military rule to despotism is certain, invariable. Those who think they see the probable tendency of our present system should interpose something remedial. The people in this particular are the best keepers of their own rights; and any device to remove that power from them weakens the security of it.[17]

On later occasions King voted for similar resolutions to amend the Constitution so that senators, representatives, and electors for president and vice-president would be chosen uniformly in districts. The proposal had strong support in the Senate but, like Varnum's earlier motion, it failed to win the necessary two-thirds vote.[18]

An abiding concern with constitutional problems usually transcends interest in any one constitution, and when the movement in Maine for separation from Massachusetts gathered steam, King gave some advice to his half-brother William, who was destined to become the new state's first Governor. For Maine's constitution, the New Yorker recommended an independent, responsible executive who would have time to do his job before having to seek re-election, a small legislature, and an independent judiciary. He also favored a $500 real or personal property qualification for voting and office-holding.[19]

17. *Ibid.*, 223.

18. *U. S. Senate Jour.*, 15 Cong., 1 sess., 220, and 15 Cong., 2 sess., 149–50, 221.

19. Since the annual election of a governor did not promote executive independence, King proposed a three-year term; he thought a lieutenant-governor as useless as a vice-president, which office he doubted would have been created "had not Mr. Adams' friends desired a place for him." A governor's council was "worse than useless," a source of intrigue which would destroy executive responsibility. The governor should have wide appointive

These suggestions show moderation, a desire for stability and continuity in government, acceptance of limited democracy, and a faith in disinterested leadership uncorrupted by factional influences. King was proudly conservative, and, in petty things as in large, he took a reasoned stand. Questioning, for instance, the wisdom of changing the design of the American flag, he thought the multiplication of stars and stripes might destroy the distinctness of the symbol which identified the United States on the ocean.[20]

In February 1816, New York's political situation demanded King's concentrated attention, for he was suddenly thrust into the gubernatorial contest. When the state Assembly had convened the month before, the Federalists had failed to gain control of the powerful Council of Appointment; the clerk of Ontario County had falsely certified the election of one Peter Allen to the Assembly, enabling the Republicans to elect a speaker by the margin of a single vote. The Federalists were unable to have Allen's vote thrown out, and the Republicans steam-rollered the choice of a Council. Hoping to capitalize on popular disgust, the Federalists counted on the youthful and attractive State Supreme Court Judge William W. Van Ness to be their candidate for governor, but, despite his previous agreement to run, the judge backed out.[21] For three days in mid-February, anxious Federalist leaders met in Albany where they selected a committee that vainly urged Van Ness to change his mind. The frantic politicians, unable to name anyone who commanded a majority of their votes, faced the dismal prospect of adjourning without a candidate, until John Duer offered the name of Rufus King. Assured by Duer that the Senator would not decline, the caucus unanimously approved his nomination.[22]

---

powers and a partial veto. Favoring a small legislature, King suggested that state senators be chosen by the people in large districts, and the representatives in assembly districts larger than the many small townships of Maine. Staggered terms of office would tend to make the legislature more impartial, experienced, and stable. King to William King, Aug. 24, 1816, William King Papers, Maine Hist. Soc.

20. King to John W. Taylor, Dec. 16, 1816, John W. Taylor Papers, N.-Y. Hist. Soc.

21. Van Ness held that if he resigned from the bench, he would be replaced by a Republican. Thus Republicans would gain strength in the Council of Revision (consisting of governor, chancellor, and State Supreme Court judges), which held the veto power in the state.

22. W. A. Duer to William Henderson, Feb. 16, 1816, King Papers, N.-Y. Hist. Soc.; N. Y. *American*, Jan. 1, 1820.

At once, influential New York Federalists flooded King with letters of support and entreaty. Such political friends as Chancellor Kent, Theodore Dwight, and David B. Ogden told him that the party's fortunes depended on him; Stephen Van Rensselaer offered to electioneer for him, and Judge Van Ness himself flatly asserted, "If you decline I am persuaded there is an end of the federal party in this State. We are waiting for your answer with trembling anxiety."[23]

Indignant at being nominated without his previous consent, King replied to Kent with the hope that the Chancellor would persuade Van Ness to run, but he was soon informed of disadvantages in the judge's candidacy.[24] In the background, as usual, was DeWitt Clinton. If King refused, the Clintonians would probably nominate their chief and count on Federalist votes to defeat Governor Tompkins, who hoped to be re-elected. The Tompkins Republicans even charged that the Federalists, knowing that King would not accept, had named him as a stalking-horse for Clinton.[25] In this situation, Van Rensselaer's letter to the Senator on February 29 was decisive:

> [If Clinton were nominated] many of our friends, it is to be apprehended, will support him, and in that event many will believe that your nomination has been made to make room for him. Whether any man can prevail against Tompkins, I doubt; yet the accounts from the Country induce me almost to believe in your success. Great enthusiasm is evinced every where upon your nomination being known, and I am convinced no other person would run as far. If you were the Candidate our best Characters every where would be candidates for the Legislature and with such men I think you could be of great service to the Country.[26]

23. James Kent to King, Feb. 16, 1816, Theodore Dwight to King, Feb. 16, 1816, David B. Ogden to King, Feb. 17, 1816, Stephen Van Rensselaer to King, Feb. 19, 1816, W. W. Van Ness to King, Feb. 19, 1816; the official communication, dated Feb. 16, 1816, notifying King of his nomination, was signed by H. Bleecker, J. G. Lansing, J. R. Van Rensselaer, Peter A. Jay, and John Duer; all King Papers, N.-Y. Hist. Soc.

24. King's endorsement on Kent to King, Feb. 16, 1816, and King to Stephen Van Rensselaer, Feb. 24, 1816, Confidential, *ibid.*

25. W. A. Duer to William Henderson, Feb. 16, 1816, *ibid.*; Thomas Eddy to DeWitt Clinton, Feb. 22, 1816, Clinton Papers, Vol. 6, Columbia Univ. Lib.; Fox, *Decline of Aristocracy*, 188–89.

26. Stephen Van Rensselaer to King, Feb. 29, 1816, King Papers, N.-Y. Hist. Soc.

After two weeks of hesitation, King consented to his nomination. Only an extraordinary sense of duty and a determination, as in the past, to maintain the integrity of his party led him to forego his personal preference. He did not expect to be elected.[27] In fact, his strength as a candidate put the Republicans on the defensive, and they closed ranks behind Governor Tompkins.

During the campaign, issues were lost behind a screen of character assassination. One paper printed the calumny that King had appropriated to his own use the inheritance of a widow whose claim to a legacy he had been defending. The scurrilous *Albany Register* implied that during the Revolutionary War, King had enjoyed in New York "the protection of the British armies, while his REPUBLICAN FELLOW COUNTRYMEN were wading through blood and slaughter to rescue their country from British thralldom."[28] In a move to woo the growing Irish vote, Republicans revived the shopworn issue of the Irish state prisoners of 1798. The Senator drafted a letter and a public address defending his interference against the Irish radical leaders, but he wisely accepted advice to lay them aside.[29]

The fact that King's son Charles, who had been a commissioner to investigate the shooting of mutinous American prisoners in an English military prison at Dartmoor, had reported his findings with impartiality, gave the Republicans additional ammunition: it was charged that the son had been brainwashed in the father's Anglophilia.[30]

Congress remained in session during the election campaign, and it was not until the middle of May that King reached home. Perhaps this was just as well, for early in April he learned of a threat against his life. His son John warned that a shoemaker in New York City had overheard a startling conversation in an Irish brogue: "About 9 o'clock as he was obeying the call of nature behind a pile of Boards near his house," the shoemaker heard a man say of King, "he is our

27. King to Edward King, Mar. 28, 1816, King, ed., *King Correspondence*, VI, 17. King's unpolitical wife wrote, "I must confess my patriotism is not sufficient to cause me to congratulate or wish him success." Mary A. King to Edward King, Mar. 6, 1816, *ibid.*, V, 524.

28. King's reply to the legacy charge may be found in the N. Y. *Commercial Advertiser*, Apr. 24, 1816. For the false accusation about King during the Revolution, see *ibid.*, Apr. 25, 1816, quoting the *Albany Register* [n.d.].

29. King's draft of this address is in folder dated Apr. 19, 1816, King Papers, N.-Y. Hist. Soc.; King to David B. Ogden, Apr. 19, 1816, and endorsement, *ibid.* See King, ed., *King Correspondence*, V, 529–33.

30. John A. King to King, Apr. 5, 1816, and enclosure, King Papers, N.-Y. Hist. Soc.

Enemy and has always been so and we will take his life. . . . The rifles that will do [t]his business are in Philadelphia in good hands and damn him, he will never reach home again." Following his father's suggestion, John consulted some trusted friends in New York who advised taking the shoemaker's affidavit and warned the Senator not to expose himself unnecessarily while on the trip home. John relayed this advice to Washington and offered to ride on horseback as far as Baltimore to accompany his father the rest of the way, though he did not think the threat would be carried out.[31]

Whether for safety's sake or for recreation, King and his wife took a circuitous route home. The Gores were driving to Warm Springs, Virginia, and on May 2, the Kings accompanied them as far as Harper's Ferry, proceeding north to Hagerstown and into Pennsylvania on a two weeks' leisurely back-country tour.[32] En route he received word that the Republicans had won in New York City, and while at Palmyra near Harrisburg, he wrote despondently to Gore:

> Ça ira—the first imposition, says Aristotle, is to flatter the people, and is naturally followed by violence. Liberty is too dear to be voluntarily parted with: it must therefore be gradually weakened by making the People jealous of its wisest and most sincere Defenders; so that open force may in the end be used to destroy it. . . . We have been the visionary men, who have believed, as many have, that mere Paper Constitutions, without those moral and political Habits and opinions, which alone give solidity and support to any Government, would be sufficient to protect and preserve the equal Rights of the weak against the strong, of the Honest against the Dishonest, of the wise and faithful Friends of free Government against the wicked and ambitious Men, who disregard every thing that stands in the way of their criminal Desires.[33]

On the fifteenth, after a two-hour crossing from Elizabeth Town and a brief stop at Archibald Gracie's in New York, the Kings drove home. They were greeted by John, who had recently bought a house in Jamaica near his father's estate. That day King learned the details of the Federalist defeat. As anticipated, the Republicans had swept the New York election. Even New York City chose Republican as-

31. John A. King to King, Apr. 9, 16, 1816, King to John A. King, Apr. 12, 1816, *ibid.*

32. King to Edward King, May 1, 1816, King Papers, Cincinnati Hist. Soc.

33. King to Christopher Gore, May 8, 1816, King Papers, N.-Y. Hist. Soc.

semblymen. Though he carried the city, the Senator was decisively defeated for the governorship, Tompkins rolling up a margin of nearly seven thousand votes—twice that which had made him Governor in 1813.[34] For himself, King asserted, "no Event would have been less agreeable" than to have been elected governor; it was time for the party to give up the fruitless struggle. "Federalists of our age," he concluded, "must be content with the past."[35]

In comparison with the New York gubernatorial race, the presidential election of 1816 was a drab affair, a Republican caucus on March 16 having named Monroe for the presidency and Governor Tompkins for the vice-presidency. By a sort of tacit understanding, Rufus King became the Federalist standard-bearer. His candidacy was unofficial, without the sanction of a party caucus or secret meeting as in 1812, and in only three states, Massachusetts, Connecticut, and Delaware, did the Federalists enter electoral tickets.[36]

Convinced that the party of John Adams, Hamilton, Marshall, and C. C. Pinckney had reached its end, Federalists made no serious attempt to organize a campaign. Harrison Gray Otis tried to persuade his Massachusetts colleagues to vote for Monroe rather than throw away their ballots on a hopeless candidate.[37] King himself was under no illusions. He shared the general belief that a fourth Virginian would become president: "The Presidential Election having been settled last winter at W[ashington] . . . ," he conceded, "so certain is the Result, in the Opinion of the Friends of the Measure, that no pains are taken to excite the Community on the subject. It is quite

34. In New York City, King received 1,926 votes, Tompkins 1,861. Throughout the state, Tompkins polled 45,412, King 38,647 (or 46 per cent of the vote). N. Y. *Commercial Advertiser*, May 4, 1816; N. Y. *Spectator*, May 8, 1816; N. Y. *American*, May 24, June 15, 1820; Shaw Livermore, *The Twilight of Federalism; the Disintegration of the Federalist Party, 1815–1830* (Princeton, 1962), 32–33.

35. King to Christopher Gore, May 15, 1816, King Papers, N.-Y. Hist. Soc.

36. Toward the end of the year, rumors circulated that Clinton had an understanding with the Federalists and would again seek the presidency, but that shrewd New Yorker had his eye on the governor's chair, attainable once Tompkins was propelled to Washington. DeWitt Clinton to Roger Skinner, Nov. 14, 1816, draft, Vol. 18, Skinner to Clinton, Nov. 21, 1816, Clinton Papers, Vol. 6, Columbia Univ. Lib. With Clinton off the field, the path was clear for King. For the vice-presidency, John E. Howard of Delaware was named in Massachusetts, Robert G. Harper in Delaware; the Connecticut leaders could not agree on anyone. *Niles' Register*, Dec. 14, 1816, Feb. 15, 1817.

37. Christopher Gore to King, Dec. 20, 1816, June 2, 1822, King Papers, N.-Y. Hist. Soc.; Morison, *Otis*, II, 202.

worthy of Remark that in no preceding Election has there been such a Calm respecting it."[38] Not that Monroe was a magnetic figure; on the contrary, he appeared amiable but colorless. As King later remarked, "he had the zealous support of nobody, and he was exempt from the hostility of Everybody."[39]

An apathetic country learned in December that 183 electoral votes had been cast for Monroe and only 34 for King (Massachusetts, 22; Connecticut, 9; and Delaware, 3). As Rufus King was the last Federalist candidate for president, his name symbolizes the end of an era. Some of the younger men in his party anticipated regeneration through an easing of tension and an end to proscription of Federalists under the new administration, but, in fact, Monroe's election placed the tombstone on the grave of Federalism as a national force; henceforth it survived only locally and in the personal careers of a few leading men.[40]

One such individual was King, who arrived at the capital shortly after Christmas for the new session of Congress. After an exhausting stagecoach journey he settled down as usual at Crawford's Hotel in Georgetown, but things were different. Mrs. King had not been well enough to accompany her husband, and Christopher Gore had left the Senate. Jeremiah Mason and Daniel Webster had moved to a house on Capitol Hill, and other former Crawford patrons had taken up residence at a large tavern recently erected on the Hill by Bailey, "the Virginia gambler." At Crawford's, the New Yorker occupied his old chambers and, as in the past, took breakfast and tea in his drawing room. In the dining room he joined the other lodgers, among them Alexander Hanson, former Congressman and now a Senator from Maryland, who, as editor of the Baltimore *Federal Republican*, had braved mob attacks to oppose the War of 1812.[41]

In the second session of the Fourteenth Congress, King quietly

38. King to Christopher Gore, Nov. 5, 1816, King Papers, N.-Y. Hist. Soc.

39. King to William King, Apr. 22, 1818, William King Papers, Maine Hist. Soc. Cf. King to Jeremiah Mason, Mar. [n.d.] 1818, Clark, ed., *Memoirs of Jeremiah Mason*, 187–88.

40. In his *Twilight of Federalism*, 44–46, Shaw Livermore emphasizes Federalist hopes of possible glories to be achieved under Monroe's administration. These hopes proved delusive, as Livermore subsequently points out. David H. Fischer's *Revolution of American Conservatism* has no systematic treatment of Federalism after 1816.

41. King to Christopher Gore, Dec. 26, 1816, Jan. 2, 1817, and Jan. [n.d.] 1817, King Papers, N.-Y. Hist. Soc. Although Hanson was rash and vituperative, King considered him honest and able, and later loaned him money. Hanson to King, Dec. 20, 1817, *ibid.*

played an active part. The Senate reorganized its committees in December 1816, and he was placed on two of the most important ones, finance and foreign relations, where in the years to come he would apply his knowledge and experience. In debates and roll calls on the Senate floor, he was a watchdog, sniffing out signs of wastefulness and partisan aims. He criticized as unnecessary a proposal to create a "Home Department," declaring that the State Department was competent to handle domestic as well as foreign affairs, and that more departments would not assure more effective government. If he publicly emphasized efficient operations, he privately suspected that a new department would simply increase opportunities for party patronage. He had heard that Attorney-General Rush, whom he later called a "soft and empty pedant," would be given the new office in order to make way for another as attorney-general.[42] By a large majority, the Senate defeated the bill for a Home Department, and it was not until more than twenty years later that Congress actually established a Department of the Interior.

A far more important problem in the postwar years was the protection and encouragement of commerce. King had always been intensely interested in ocean shipping, had mercantile friends, and had gained from his legal, political, and diplomatic career an insight into the complexities of international trade.[43] As a member of the Senate Foreign Relations Committee, he was troubled over the continuance of British colonial regulations which discriminated against American vessels. The committee's recommendation for higher duties on imports from territories which excluded United States ships did not go far enough, however, to satisfy merchants and ship owners, who demanded fuller retaliation.[44]

42. King to Christopher Gore, Jan. [n.d.] 1817, *ibid.* For King's speeches on the subject, see *Annals*, 14 Cong., 2 sess., 59, 74–75, and for his opinion of Rush, see King to Gore, Apr. 12, 1818, King Papers, N.-Y. Hist. Soc.

43. King had invested $20,000 in the China trade ventures of Oliver Wolcott, realizing a handsome profit of $25,000. His initial investment probably was made in 1808, and he withdrew from the enterprise before the end of 1813. His largest single cash dividend was 40 per cent in 1810. King to Oliver Wolcott, Jan. 9, 1814, Wolcott Papers, Vol. 23, Conn. Hist. Soc.; Wolcott to King, May 13, 1814, King Papers, N.-Y. Hist. Soc. King's son Charles was a partner in Archibald Gracie & Sons, having married the affluent Scotsman's daughter Eliza and become one of the "sons"; King's third son James had begun a promising mercantile life; and William King, Rufus's half-brother, was a prosperous merchant in Bath, Maine, who now was worried lest the British monopolize the lumber trade with the West Indies.

44. *Annals*, 14 Cong., 2 sess., 78, 81; *Niles' Register*, Feb. 1, 1817.

Congress responded in April 1818, when by huge majorities it enacted a stringent navigation act, the work of Rufus King. As perhaps the leading authority in the country on maritime and commercial law, he drafted and worked successfully for the passage of a bill which went beyond the interests of the merchants to build up a merchant marine and a pool of skilled seamen for the navy. The Navigation Act of 1818 closed American ports to British vessels coming from ports closed to the vessels of the United States, and required the consignees of British ships carrying American articles to give bond that the American cargo would be landed at a port that was not barred to American ships. After its passage, King proudly remarked, "I gave all my heart and all my strength, with all my hopes of success to this measure, which in principle is incomparably the most important law ever passed on this, and perhaps any other subject."[45]

Behind King's extravagance lay his knowledge of what had made the British Empire great and a vision of similar glory for his own nation. The British, by setting up far-flung outposts of trade and applying exclusive navigation laws to them, had monopolized much of the world's shipping, and as the British had broken the Dutch monopoly in an earlier age, King argued, the United States must do likewise if it would break the British hegemony. The real issue was not access to the British West Indies, he told the Senate; it was nothing less than the safety of the United States and the development of its resources, which entailed nurture of its sea power.[46] As the future source of danger would be on the ocean, the country's cheapest and most efficient defense lay in a strong navy, and as naval power was always proportionate to commercial shipping, a strong American navy depended upon a flourishing merchant marine to train its sailors.

45. King to Jeremiah Mason, Apr. 21, 1818, Clark, ed., *Memoirs of Jeremiah Mason*, 197–98.

46. *Annals*, 15 Cong., 1 sess., 329. In 1820 King played a leading role in securing a more stringent law that closed American ports to ships from all British colonies. Unfortunately, the unrealistic insistence of John Quincy Adams, supported by King, upon the complete abolition of imperial preference before lifting American tonnage and tariff charges on British shipping from the colonies led to the closing of British colonial ports in 1826. A final settlement in 1830 failed to eliminate imperial preference. Bradford Perkins, *Castlereagh and Adams: England and the United States, 1812–1823* (Berkeley, 1964), 231–37. See also F. Lee Benns, *The American Struggle for the British West India Carrying Trade, 1815–1830* (Indiana University, *Studies*, No. 56 [1923]), and Bemis, *John Quincy Adams*, 457–63.

"Money may build ships," King declared, "but the navigation of the great ocean only can make seamen, and it is in connexion with this view of the subject, that the exclusion of our shipping and seamen from the navigation between the United States and the colonies of England, derives its chief importance."[47]

That the Navigation Act was so widely supported in most of the country pleased everyone who shared its author's heightened sense of nationalism in the postwar years. The disappearance of formal party distinctions and the recognition of the vast potentialities of the United States contributed to a buoyancy long absent from the national capital. Realistically, King doubted that the new law would wring fundamental concessions from the British, yet he believed it a vital factor in the unifying and energizing of his country, or, as he expressed it, in the "formation and diffusion of national opinions, national attachments and national character . . . no nation being more homogeneous, or more firmly united."[48] He sent John Adams a copy of his Senate speech advocating the new law, and the former President, warmly acknowledging the gesture, called the speech "a Master Piece of a Master Spirit," the most accurate, judicious, comprehensive, and concise view of the subject that he had seen. Praising King for avoiding allusions to past political antagonisms, Adams added, "With you, I am astonished at the late rapid growth of a National Character; a Plant so feeble in its origin, for a long course of Years so slow in its growth and so little cultivated. . . . Your assurances of Union revive me."[49]

Others with long memories pointed out that King's restrictive measure confirmed the wisdom of Madison, who had proposed similar regulations in 1794. The Senator insisted, however, that laws should be judged by their aim; whereas his own project was aimed primarily at developing the navy, Madison's goal had been coercive, to secure indemnity for ship losses. In 1794 he had disapproved the Virginian's resolutions as tending to embroil the United States in the wars of the French Revolution.[50] Whatever the distinction, the fact remained

47. *Annals*, 15 Cong., 1 sess., 329.

48. King to Adams, July 12, 1818, King Papers, N.-Y. Hist. Soc.; King to James Barbour, Aug. 18, 1818, Barbour Papers, N. Y. Pub. Lib.

49. Adams to King, July 29, 1818, King Papers, Boston Pub. Lib. For other commendations of King, see Caesar A. Rodney to James Monroe, Nov. 4, 1818, Monroe Papers, Lib. Cong., and King, ed., *King Correspondence*, VI, 150.

50. King to Edward King, June 28, 1818, King Papers, Cincinnati Hist. Soc.; King to [William] Coleman, n.d. [1818], King Papers, N.-Y. Hist. Soc.

that the Navigation Law of 1818 applied economic pressure, and the nation was stronger than in 1794.

King foresaw some difficulty in enforcing the law, particularly in preventing smuggling across the frontier of the Maritime Provinces of Canada and a possible weakening of the law's effectiveness if the Bermuda trade, open to American vessels, expanded too rapidly. He urged Secretary of State John Quincy Adams to apply the law vigorously and conferred with him at length on its operation. To tighten the squeeze upon Britain, the Senator advised against renewing the commercial convention of 1815 and suggested that Adams seek wider trading privileges in Asia that would enable American ships to sail directly from India to China.[51] New Englanders who had formerly shipped fish and other articles in British vessels to the British West Indies gradually became reconciled to the loss of this trade, and by the end of 1818 King was encouraged by statistics revealing that British tonnage in the colonial trade had decreased, while American tonnage had increased.[52]

While under the impulse of national feeling, Congress heeded the plight of Revolutionary War veterans, many of whom were eking out a bare existence in their declining days. In 1818 King supported and voted for pensions to these men, though he would have preferred to limit the aid to needy officers. As he explained to Jeremiah Mason, the soldiers had been paid high bounties and had been clothed and fed, but not so the officers; furthermore, the law would be more costly than its advocates expected.[53] Events proved him right. The law was expensive, and it was abused; persons said to be worth $10,000 to $20,000 had claimed to be paupers in order to secure the benefits, and one pensioner was said to have deposited his

51. King to John Quincy Adams, Aug. 6, 1818, State Department Archives, Misc. Letters, Aug.–Oct. 1818, National Archives; C. F. Adams, ed., *Memoirs of John Quincy Adams*, IV, 128, 181; King to Jeremiah Mason, May 19, 1818, Clark, ed., *Memoirs of Jeremiah Mason*, 200.

52. Christopher Gore to King, Dec. 11, 1818, King Papers, N.-Y. Hist. Soc.; King to DeWitt Clinton, Dec. 21, 1818, Clinton Papers, Vol. 8, Columbia Univ. Lib.

53. For King's motion, later withdrawn, to limit the grant to half pay for life to surviving officers of the Continental Army, see *Annals*, 15 Cong., 1 sess., 138–39, 205. The final bill, as amended, passed the Senate by a vote of 22 to 10. *Ibid.*, 241. For King's opinions, see King to Christopher Gore, Feb. 26, Nov. 18, 1818, and King to Jeremiah Mason, Apr. 21, 1818, King Papers, N.-Y. Hist. Soc.

entire pension in a savings bank.[54] Two years later, the law was changed to cut down the number of recipients, and to pay no pensions until claims were substantiated. Whatever the deficiencies of the earlier law, King disliked the new one. Ascribing its passage to the empty treasury and to the fact that three of every four pensioners lived east of the Delaware River, he condemned it as a violation of the public faith.[55]

Among the most serious of the nation's financial troubles was a shortage of specie occasioned by the war. Some enthusiasts looked to the new Bank of the United States for a remedy, but to King this appeared an impossibility. "Every nostrum is not a Salutary Medicine; and I have never discovered how the Bank is to bring about specie payments," he had remarked in 1816.[56] Specie circulation could be restored more easily, he believed, through the cooperation of the state banks, but the government could help. In April 1817, on his suggestion, President Monroe obtained treasury approval for the minting of more coins.[57]

The proliferation of banks and the excess of paper soon focused public attention upon the Bank of the United States. King's prediction that it would be an instrument of speculation was all too well borne out. From the moment its doors opened, fortune-hunters swarmed upon it. As authorized by law, its private subscribers made large purchases of shares in three easy installments amounting to a total of $75 in government stock and only $25 in specie. Then the directors permitted the stockholders to pay their second installment on the security of the stock itself, and on August 27, 1817, the shareholders were authorized to discount on their stock at an advance of 25 per cent. William Jones, the Bank's president, a good-natured incompetent, allowed the institution to make loans far in excess of what was necessary and to establish numerous branches, whose direc-

54. *Niles' Register*, Oct. 16, 1819.

55. King to John A. King, Apr. 27, 1820, King Papers, N.-Y. Hist. Soc. King listed 12,174 pensioners, including 3,162 New Yorkers, living east of the Delaware, out of a total of 16,163. Undated paper, 1812, *ibid.* As New York had the largest number of pensioners, Senators King and Sanford voted against this bill, but it passed by a vote of 24 to 17. *Annals*, 16 Cong., 1 sess., 640; *Niles' Register*, Apr. 29, 1820.

56. King to William B. Giles, Apr. 21, 1816, Misc. MSS—King, N. Y. Pub. Lib.

57. King to James Monroe, Apr. 14, 1817, Monroe Papers, Lib. Cong.; Monroe to King, Apr. 28, 1817, King Papers, N.-Y. Hist. Soc. Madison and Dallas regarded the state banks as uncooperative.

tors were, even more than he, ignorant of sound banking principles. In the South and West particularly, these branches responded to the speculative mania, lending on mortgages and repeatedly reissuing their notes without much thought to their ultimate redemption.

Thoroughly alarmed, Rufus King introduced into the Senate a resolution for an investigation of the Bank's books. With a few unimportant changes, the Senate adopted it, calling upon the Secretary of the Treasury to report on the funded debt, to determine the types and amount of federal stock paid into the Bank by its subscribers, and to report the types and amount of the funded debt sold by the Bank to domestic and foreign purchasers. King's initiative inspired *Niles' Register* to proclaim, "The *spirit of enquiry* has gone abroad; truth may be manifested; and the people preserved! The sun is setting to the *day of speculation*. . . . The anxiety and alarm occasioned by Mr. King's motion, is the best evidence that can be afforded of its utility."[58]

The demand for easy credit in the South and West, the mad rush to buy land, and the heady impulse to get rich quickly were checked by the effects of a congressional order for the resumption of specie payments that caused banks to contract their credit. Large amounts of money from public land sales deposited in the branches of the Bank of the United States had given it a power over the specie in state banks, and, as these local institutions strained their resources in 1818, they increasingly resented the Bank's competitive advantage. As the state banks' criticism mounted, King advised his son Edward to resign as a director of the Chillicothe (Ohio) branch of the Bank, rather than jeopardize his reputation by having to defend an unpopular institution.[59]

The Senator condemned the speculator-directors of the Bank of the United States, who, to swell their dividends and raise the price of the Bank's stock, had made excessive loans; the excess paper, he observed, returned to the Bank and caused a similar return of state bank notes to the local banks, as the demand for specie and consequent curtailment of Bank discounts caused embarrassment and hardship to the borrowers.[60] As the House of Representatives in-

58. *Niles' Register*, Apr. 11, 1818. For the resolution, see *Annals*, 15 Cong., 1 sess., 312, 340.

59. King to Edward King, June 28, 1818, King Papers, Cincinnati Hist. Soc. Cf. King to Edward King, Jan. 18, Apr. 5, 1818, *ibid.*

60. King to Christopher Gore, Nov. 6, 1818, King Papers, N.-Y. Hist. Soc.

quired into the institution's affairs, King worried lest public anger and state bank pressure lead to another suspension of specie payments or the abrogation of the Bank's charter. If the Bank closed its doors, he predicted, so would all the banks outside of New England.

The remedy, as he saw it, was not dissolution, but reform and the restoration of public confidence; if the Bank's stockholders ousted the stock-jobbers from their directorate and could reduce its capital, and if President Monroe named sound and respectable men as government directors, all would be well.[61] When the President renominated the discredited Jones as a government director, King worked successfully to prevent confirmation.[62] Jones resigned as president and was succeeded by the able South Carolinian, Langdon Cheves, the choice of the reformers. King was pleased. From his point of view the former Congressman and jurist was an ideal choice; his conservative and restrictive policies in the next few years, together with a reorganized directorate, restored the credit of the Bank and placed it in a sound position.[63]

After each session of Congress following his election to the Senate in 1813, King had returned to his Jamaica home. In the spring and summer he carefully managed his farm, his livestock, and his gardens, rode his horses, relaxed with his books, undertook civic duties, entertained guests, and enjoyed his family. Time had wrought changes. In 1816 he learned of the death in Maine of his stepmother at the age of nearly eighty, and the next year his half-brother Cyrus died of erysipelas. By the summer of 1817, King's four older sons had married, and his four latest grandchildren—he now had twelve—had

61. Rufus King to William King, Feb. 7, 1819, King to Charles King, Feb. 6, 1819, *ibid.*; King to Jeremiah Mason, Feb. 7, 1819, Clark, ed., *Memoirs of Jeremiah Mason*, 209. King was pleased when in Mar. 1819 Chief Justice Marshall, in the case of McCulloch *v.* Maryland, upheld the constitutionality of the Bank and denied the power of a state to tax it. King to Edward King, Mar. 12, 1819, King Papers, Cincinnati Hist. Soc.

62. Thomas M. Willing to King, Jan. 11, 1819, King to Charles King, Dec. 30, 1818, Jan. 23, 1819, King Papers, N.-Y. Hist. Soc.

63. King to Edward King, Mar. 12, 1819, King Papers, Cincinnati Hist. Soc.; King to Langdon Cheves, Apr. 9, 1820, American Diplomats, Case 2, Box 9, Hist. Soc. of Pa.; Cheves to King, Apr. 13, 1820, King Papers, N.-Y. Hist. Soc. For King's relation to the reform faction, see Thomas M. Willing to King, Jan. 11, 1819, and James C. Fisher to King, Jan. 25, 30, 1819, *ibid.* For an account of the Bank in this period, see Hammond, *Banks and Politics*, ch. 10. See also George Dangerfield, *The Awakening of American Nationalism, 1815–1828* (N. Y., 1965), 75–88.

been born within the space of twelve months.[64] Later that year, when their youngest son Frederick entered Harvard, Rufus and Mary King were left alone in their home, though their eldest son John and his family lived nearby in Jamaica.

Good-natured and generous, Frederick, in common with others in the family, had what his father called "a pretty large share of vanity." In his sophomore year he was involved in a riot of freshmen and sophomores which began with bread-throwing and ended in physical combat. Although he claimed to be innocent of wrongdoing, he was suspended for three months and banished to a parsonage in Billerica, twenty miles from Cambridge. King approved the punishment, but he considered the offense merely "one of the irregularities into which young men are liable to fall."[65] Meanwhile, from his place of exile, the exuberant Frederick wrote of his "triumphal" departure from the college "amid the acclamation of hundreds."[66] At the end of his three months' rustication, the boy was reinstated but soon after resuming his studies he learned of his mother's serious illness and hastened to New York.

After the adjournment of the Fifteenth Congress, Senator King and his wife headed for Baltimore, where they embarked with their servants, horses, and carriage on a steamboat for the head of Chesapeake Bay and rode on to Philadelphia. The arduous journey was especially hard on the fragile and ailing Mrs. King, weakened by dyspepsia and showing symptoms of scurvy. A snowstorm delayed them in Philadelphia, and cold weather and bad roads slowed their journey northward. When they reached New York City on March 19, Mary King was too weak to proceed to Long Island, and, needing expert medical care, stayed in town at the home of her son Charles while her husband went on to Jamaica. Toward the end of May

64. William King to King, July 1, 1816, King to Edward King, June 5, 1817, King to Christopher Gore, July 15, 1817, King Papers, N.-Y. Hist. Soc. At the time of his death, King had 25 grandchildren. Another 13 were born later.

65. King to Edward King, Apr. 21, 1818, King Papers, Lilly Library, Indiana Univ.; King to Edward King, Jan. 10, 1819, King Papers, Cincinnati Hist. Soc. (for the quotation); King to Christopher Gore, Nov. 18, 29, 1818, King Papers, N.-Y. Hist. Soc.

66. Frederick G. King to Edward King, Dec. 2, 1818, King Papers, Cincinnati Hist. Soc. "The *Bell 'scrape'* [the removal of the Cambridge schoolhouse bell, in which Frederick had been a ringleader] which made such a *rumpus* at home, I got clear of by the aid of a little impudence (a material not wanting in the King family) and some wit in my defence before the Corporation of the College." *Ibid.*

she returned to the country, but her illness soon became grave. Her sons with their wives were constantly at her bedside, and Dr. David Hosack, the foremost New York physician, attended her every day. Though her mind was lucid, her strength ebbed, and, at the end, painful spasms tortured her wasted body.

On June 5 Mary King died. She was buried in the churchyard of Grace Church in Jamaica, within sight of the King homestead. For thirty-three years she had been the loyal companion of one whose interest in public life she could not share and for whom she had sacrificed her own preferences. Devoted to her family and home, she had reared five sons with tenderness and abiding concern.[67]

His wife's death left King in solitude and sorrow. Despite her obvious weakening over the years, he had not been prepared for her death until her last confinement to bed. "The example of her life is worthy of the immitation of us all," he wrote Edward in Chillicothe.[68] He advised Frederick, now back at Cambridge, to master his feelings and acquire "those sober and reflecting habits of thinking which will contribute to your own reputation and happiness, as well as to my support and comfort." Far from wishing to convert Frederick into a "cheerless and moping and perpetually moralizing young man," he hoped the boy would act purposefully. Only by reflection and a "fixed establishment of our sense of Duties" can we control our actions and avoid "the endless, the capricious and inconsistent impulses of our mere senses," King observed; otherwise "we in nothing differ but become inferior to the races of mere animals."[69]

67. This and the preceding paragraph are based on King to Edward King, Mar. 12, Apr. 23, 1819, *ibid.*; King to [Christopher Gore], Mar. 13, 1819, John A. King to King, Mar. 24, 1819, King Papers, N.-Y. Hist. Soc.; King, ed., *King Correspondence*, VI, 225–27; Barck, ed., *Letters from John Pintard*, I, 196. Little is known of Mrs. King, only eight of her letters having survived. The precise nature of her fatal illness is unknown.

68. King to Edward King, June 21, 1819, King Papers, Lilly Lib., Indiana Univ.

69. King to Frederick G. King, July 17, 1819, typed copy owned by James G. King.

CHAPTER XIX

FEDERALIST PATRIARCH

THE RAPID GROWTH OF THE WEST AFTER THE WAR OF 1812 AND THE admission of new western states to the Union made King apprehensive. He was one of four senators to vote against Illinois statehood despite his repeated observation that the region was destined for rapid development. Essentially his viewpoint was that of an easterner concerned about the welfare and influence of the Atlantic seaboard, oceanic commerce, and the revival of the ailing merchant marine.

While the United States was negotiating with Spain over a common boundary in the trans-Mississippi country, King was ready to accept the line proposed by Luis de Onís to Secretary Adams. "We have enough, more than enough of western territory, and it is the highest imprudence to grasp at more," he wrote privately.[1] Americans, he knew, could not be hindered from emigrating further into the interior; as the strength and political demands of the West mounted, the old states of the East would be sapped of their vigor. When United States troops reached the great fork of the Missouri and the Yellowstone, he predicted that a major Indian war was bound to break out. The result would be that the soldiers, aided by eastern money, would settle in the newly opened country.[2]

Ever hostile to land speculation, King was appalled at the speculation in western lands and had no sympathy for the thousands who

1. King to William King, Feb. 7, 1819, King Papers, N.-Y. Hist. Soc. Cf. King to [Christopher Gore], Feb. 19, 1819, *ibid.*; King to Jeremiah Mason, Feb. 20, 1819, Clark, ed., *Memoirs of Jeremiah Mason*, 215.

2. King to William King, Feb. 7, 1819, King Papers, N.-Y. Hist. Soc.

were ruined by the panic of 1819. For years he had opposed the annual postponement of overdue installment payments on public lands, and although his own motion to abolish the credit system died, its principle was enacted by the land law of 1820, which required cash payment for public lands. To encourage cash payments, King favored reducing the minimum price of these lands to $1.25 and the minimum purchase to eighty acres. These features were embodied in the new law, whose objectives coincided with his desire to enlarge the number of debt-free, responsible property owners.[3] He believed the cash requirement would thwart speculators and monopolists, but, as it turned out, widespread indebtedness made full cash payments difficult with the result that speculators combined to defeat competition at public sales and later sold land in competition with the government.[4]

Although interested in the building of roads and canals, the New Yorker was doubtful about extensive financing of them. He had voted against an appropriation in 1815 for the Cumberland Road but two years later supported the Bonus Bill, which Madison vetoed.[5] As chairman of a new standing committee on roads and canals in 1820, he reported bills for extending the Cumberland Road from Wheeling to the Mississippi and for canal routes connecting the Delaware with the Raritan and Chesapeake Bay. The Cumberland Road bill passed, and when the canal bill ran into trouble, King argued for its constitutionality and expediency; later he supported a study of the feasibility of a canal to connect Lake Erie with the

3. King to Christopher Gore, Apr. 22, 1820, *ibid.* Commenting on the debtors of the Holland Land Company in New York, King declared, "all Experience . . . condemns the constituting or suffering a large body of citizens, especially if connected in the same neighborhood, to become public debtors." King to Martin Van Buren, Mar. 27, 1820, Private, Van Buren Papers, Lib. Cong. For King's doubts about the wisdom of further surveys of public lands and his opposition to federal improvement of the Ohio, Mississippi, and Missouri Rivers, see *Annals*, 17 Cong., 2 sess., 287, 298, and 18 Cong., 1 sess., 765; King to Charles King, Apr. 5, 1824, King Papers, N.-Y. Hist. Soc.

4. King to Jeremiah Mason, Feb. 20, 1819, Clark, ed., *Memoirs of Jeremiah Mason*, 215; King to [Christopher Gore], Feb. 19, 1819, King to John A. King, Jan. 21, 1821, King Papers, N.-Y. Hist. Soc.; *Annals*, 16 Cong., 1 sess., 485–86. Like the vast majority of senators, King did not favor the right of preemption. *Ibid.*, 458.

5. *Annals*, 13 Cong., 3 sess., 188–89. King had doubts about the bonus bill but, considering the Erie Canal project and New York's interest in improved transportation in the West, he decided to support the bill. King to Thomas Worthington, Feb. 21, Mar. 1, 1817, King, ed., *King Correspondence*, VI, 60, 65*n*.

Ohio River.[6] As late as 1822, in debate on a measure to erect toll gates on the Cumberland Road and to appropriate $9,000 for repairs, he claimed that Congress had the right to grant funds for roads and canals. Detesting wasteful spending, however, and disliking roundabout methods, he opposed an allocation of another $9,000 from a military appropriation bill.[7] When Monroe vetoed the Cumberland tolls bill, King was not moved to raise any protest.

The great demand for internal improvements forced King to a thorough review of his thinking on implied powers in the Constitution. Within two years he observed that extensive congressional subsidies for roads and canals would empty the treasury "more easily and certainly" than it could be filled. Schemes would be set afoot everywhere to raid the treasury in order to build local improvements, and the inevitable effect of unlimited congressional power over such projects would be to corrupt public officials. "To survey or explore the route of Roads and Canals throughout the whole of the U. S. is a useless and unnecessary business," he maintained, "while the ascertainment of the Route of particular Roads or Canals, which it may be desirable and of common benefit to make, would be expedient, if any Power for such Purpose be given by the Constitution."[8] Reversing his earlier stand, King voted against further surveys.[9]

Commerce and navigation were always closer to King's heart than internal improvements. He remained an easterner, and one could detect the salt of the sea in his Senate voting record. On his initiative,

6. *Annals*, 16 Cong., 1 sess., 624–25, 652, 655, 677, 682, 683. King believed the extension of the Cumberland Road was in the national interest, and he hoped that topography, not local pressures, would dictate its precise location. King to editors of an unnamed newspaper, June 28, 1820, Misc. MSS—King, N. Y. Pub. Lib.

7. *Annals*, 17 Cong., 1 sess., 444, 445.

8. King to Charles King, Feb. 3, 1824, King to Christopher Gore, Feb. 1, 1824, King Papers, N.-Y. Hist. Soc.

9. *Annals*, 18 Cong., 1 sess., 568; *Register of Debates in Congress*, 18 Cong., 2 sess., 361, 666, 671. Alluding in 1825 to the defeat of a proposal in the federal Convention of 1787 to give Congress specific power to incorporate canals, Senator T. W. Cobb turned to King, saying, "At the present moment we have in this body a distinguished member of that Convention. Doubtless he will be able to inform us whether the rejection of the amendment proceeded from a belief in the Convention that the power was conferred in some other clause of the Constitution." King shook his head and was understood to have replied, "Such a thing was not thought of." Farrand, *Records of the Federal Convention*, III, 465.

Congress extended the restrictions of the Navigation Act of 1818 to additional British West Indian ports and prohibited imports from British maritime possessions in America unless produced locally and shipped directly to the United States.[10] On the eve of Maine's statehood, he helped to push through Congress a law enabling coastal vessels to sail from the state of Maine to Newburyport, Salem, or Boston without having to obtain custom-house papers on every trip.[11] Ever watchful over the interests of hard-pressed merchants after the panic of 1819, he urged the creation of a uniform national bankruptcy system. Worried lest shippers be injured by proposed duties on iron, copper plates, hemp, and paint, he insisted that "manufactures must not overturn navigation and commerce."[12]

In the case of Jackson's controversial invasion of Spanish Florida, however, King showed little respect for strict construction and in a letter to the President defended the constitutionality of the punitive expedition.[13] While he regretted the execution of Arbuthnot and Ambrister, the British traders accused of aiding the Seminoles, he believed that these men had fully identified themselves with the Seminoles' war policy and that Jackson had as much power to punish them as the Indians themselves.[14] As King sardonically observed, he could not "join the hue and cry with those who, with altogether different motives, are zealously, and for the first time in their lives the Champions of humanity, the teachers of the milder virtues, the accusers of vindictive white warriors, and Protectors of the red men. . . . The end of Mr. Monroe's term may shew that ambition is impatient and cannot feed on hope deferred."[15]

10. *Annals*, 16 Cong., 1 sess, 491–92, 497, 586, 596.

11. In this, as in other matters, the district of Maine was indebted to King, its native son, for aiding the transition to statehood. Daniel Corry to King, Nov. 30, 1819, William King to King, May 10, 1819, King Papers, N.-Y. Hist. Soc.; King to DeWitt Clinton, Dec. 21, 1818, Clinton Papers, Vol. 8, Columbia Univ. Lib.

12. *Annals*, 16 Cong., 1 sess., 564; King to Charles King, May 1, 1820, King Papers, N.-Y. Hist. Soc.; King's endorsement on John Sergeant to King, May 20, 1820, *ibid*. Cf. King to Martin Van Buren, Mar. 27, 1820, Van Buren Papers, Lib. Cong. In 1824 King succeeded in having stricken out of a Senate bill a number of specified import duties, and he voted against what became the Tariff of 1824. *Annals*, 18 Cong., 1 sess., 707, 714, 715, 744.

13. King to James Monroe, July 27, 1818, Monroe Papers, N. Y. Pub. Lib.

14. King's memorandum, Dec. 17, 1818, King Papers, N.-Y. Hist. Soc.

15. King to Christopher Gore, Feb. 7, 1819, *ibid.* Censure of Jackson would of course impute censure to Monroe and Adams. See King to William King, Feb. 17, 1819, *ibid.*

As members of an investigatory committee, the New Yorker and Senator Eaton of Tennessee failed in their effort to block a report that charged Jackson with high-handed and lawless conduct of a predetermined invasion, but their influence probably prevented any specific recommendation. Knowing that the committee was dominated by men determined to profit politically from the Jackson issue and seeing the report as designed solely to defame the General, he threatened to expose on the Senate floor "the caballing and electioneering passions and practices which are mingled in this affair."[16] While Jackson made a triumphal tour of the East and reputedly threatened to cut off the ears of the offending senators, King took satisfaction in having supported Adams's strong policy toward Spain and in having prevented a direct Senate censure of the hero of New Orleans.

In these same years, the cause of Latin American independence aroused great interest in the United States. King had sympathized with the insurgents ever since his association with Miranda at the turn of the century, believing that Spanish American independence would benefit the United States, but, doubting that in 1818 the revolutionaries were yet capable of self-government, he advised a policy of watchful waiting. As provocative statements about Spanish tyranny might lead to premature United States involvement, he opposed congressional agitation for Latin American independence. His view was based upon a realistic assessment of Spain's inability to suppress the revolts, and he was convinced that only in relying upon themselves would Latin Americans learn the patience and restraint necessary for self-government.[17]

As his term in the Senate neared its end in 1819, King made no effort to win re-election. He told his sons that he was completely indifferent to the outcome.[18] Meanwhile, as both Republican factions at Albany maneuvered for advantage, the Federalists in the legislature, led by Abraham Van Vechten, William A. Duer, Thomas

16. Adams, ed., *Memoirs of John Quincy Adams*, IV, 245, 278. Jackson wished to be introduced to King, and they probably met in Jan. 1819. J. Overton to King, Jan. 6, 1819, King Papers, N.-Y. Hist. Soc.

17. King to [Christopher Gore], Jan. 18, 1818, King to [Charles King], Feb. 10, 1819, King Papers, N.-Y. Hist. Soc.; King to Oliver Wolcott, Feb. 18, 1818, Wolcott Papers, Vol. 45, Conn. Hist. Soc.

18. "I never have held a pub[lic] situation merely for the sake of my personal gratification," King wrote to his son, "nor would I now continue to hold even the

Oakley, and King's son John, worked to prolong the Senator's tenure. The younger King resented the captivity of many Federalists in DeWitt Clinton's camp and deliberately cultivated the influence of the "Bucktails," Tammany or anti-Clinton Republicans. Alexander Hamilton's son James privately suggested to Martin Van Buren, the rising Bucktail boss, that he promote King's re-election, and the small Federalist band renominated King, hoping to secure Clintonian votes, as in 1813, and possibly those of Bucktails eager to check Governor Clinton's influence. With misguided optimism, Charles King predicted that an almost unanimous legislature would return his father to the Senate.[19]

Aware of Clinton's hostility to King, Federalists were no doubt secretly pleased when the Governor's Republican opponents spread the false word among his followers that he favored King's re-election in order to conciliate the Federalists. They sought to convince the Bucktails that by voting for the veteran Federalist, they would gain control of the influential Council of Appointment, but the Bucktail chiefs had reason to avoid the appearance of collaboration with Federalists. As Secretary of the Navy Smith Thompson informed his friend Van Buren, King's appointment would not displease the administration's supporters in Washington, but in New York state "it would disarm you of the most powerful argument you now have against your adversaries—Federal aid—Federal coalition."[20]

Fear of jeopardizing their political future by throwing votes to a Federalist, no matter how respected, was strong enough in both Republican factions—particularly the Bucktails—to prevent a choice. When the legislature balloted on February 2, neither the Clintonian

---

little Remnant of my Term in the Senate unless I believed that in doing so I shall promote the public welfare." King to Charles King, undated draft, King Papers, N.-Y. Hist. Soc. Cf. King to John A. King, Jan. 14, 1819, *ibid.* There is no reason to credit a rumor that King had come to New York to influence his renomination. See Nathaniel Pendleton to J. Ogden Hoffman, Mar. 14, 1819, Pendleton Papers, N.-Y. Hist. Soc.

19. James A. Hamilton to Martin Van Buren, Dec. 31, 1818, Private, Van Buren Papers, Lib. Cong.; Charles King to King, Jan. 20, 1819, John A. King to King, Jan. 14, 1819, King Papers, N.-Y. Hist. Soc.; Alexander, *Political History of N. Y.*, I, 267; Fox, *Decline of Aristocracy*, 207; Alvin Kass, *Politics in New York State, 1800–1830* (Syracuse, 1965), 74. The term Bucktail derives from Tammany announcements of meetings: each member would "wear a Buck's tail in his hat, the distinguishing badge of Tammany."

20. Hammond, *Political Parties in New York*, I, 482–84; Smith Thompson to Martin Van Buren, Jan. 23, 1819, Van Buren Papers, Lib. Cong.

John C. Spencer, the Bucktail Samuel Young, nor King could muster a majority.[21]

During 1819 King gradually gained support. Young Alexander Hamilton castigated Clinton for avoiding the responsibility of "preserving to our national councils a patriotic and distinguished statesman"; in June, Hezekiah Niles predicted that King would be almost unanimously elected; and by mid-November, Duer was certain that the anti-Clinton Republicans were ready to vote for King.[22] The move to King owed much to Martin Van Buren, who, in stressing the Senator's patriotic support of the War of 1812 after the assault on Washington, recognized that King could be useful not only to the country but to him as well: individual "high-minded" Federalists in the legislature were to be weaned from Clinton. Van Buren wrote a thirty-two page pamphlet entitled *Considerations in Favour of the Appointment of Rufus King, To the Senate of the United States.* Although it bore no author's name, it was widely understood to have been the work of Van Buren, who was a member of the state Senate. Copies were distributed among the legislators. The pamphlet recounted King's bold appeal to Governor Tompkins during the financial crisis of 1814, his large personal subscription to the war loan, and his inspiration of public confidence. Van Buren praised the old Federalist's integrity, talents, and fitness, his "recent and splendid exertions" in the Senate against British "encroachments," his continued patriotism, and his enjoyment of the confidence of the federal administration. King should be elected on his own merits, and not merely as a means to an end. Van Buren heavily emphasized that "Mr. King and his friends, all who have a respect for, and are influenced by his opinion, are decidedly and unequivocally opposed to the reelection of Mr. Clinton; their views are, and their conduct will be, in unison with that of the republicans of the state and union."[23]

21. For detailed information about the voting, see the *N.-Y. Evening Post*, Feb. 5, 1819. Some legislators explained privately that they had not voted for King out of fear that support of a Federalist would ruin their political fortunes in the state. *Ibid.*, Feb. 16, 1819. Cf. John A. King to King, Feb. 26, 1819, King Papers, N.-Y. Hist. Soc.

22. Barck, ed., *Letters from John Pintard*, I, 172–73; *Niles' Register*, June 12, 1819; *Albany Argus*, Aug. 3, 1819; W. A. Duer to Nathaniel Pendleton, Nov. 14, 1819, Pendleton Papers, N.-Y. Hist. Soc.

23. *Considerations in Favour of the Appointment of Rufus King, To the Senate of the United States, Submitted to the Republican Members of the Legislature of the State of New York by One of Their Colleagues*, Dec. 1819, 20; J. C. Fitzpatrick, ed., *Autobiography of Martin Van Buren* (Amer. Hist. Assoc., *Annual Report*, 1918, II), 100–01.

Another pamphlet, *Considerations Against the Appointment of Rufus King*, by "Plain Truth," reached the legislature two days before the election. Who wrote it is not known. Its case against King revived nearly all the old charges and added new ones, but it was ineffective.[24] Clinton, thinking it advantageous to keep up his Federalist connection, announced to the legislature shortly before it voted that he would support the veteran Senator's re-election, and on January 7 the *Albany Register* predicted King's election by a large majority.[25]

At noon the next day, this prediction was confirmed. As John Quincy Adams recorded it, "King, who after 10 trials last winter, could not get so many as twenty votes out of one hundred and fifty, now came in by a unanimous vote of the Senate and all but three of the Assembly."[26]

While his candidacy for re-election hung in the balance, King embarked upon the most significant crusade of his entire career. Late in February 1819, as the Senate began its angry debates over Missouri's petition for statehood, he made two powerful speeches urging the exclusion of slavery from Missouri. They were his first lengthy public statements on slavery or its extension, but they expressed ideas he had long held. In the Congress of the old Confederation he and Jefferson, on separate occasions, had proposed barring slavery from the Northwest Territory, and their efforts had led to the inclusion of the antislavery clause in the Ordinance of 1787. After the acquisition of the Louisiana country, King shared the view widely held by New England Federalists that representation there should be limited to free inhabitants, and that new states carved from it should have no slaves.

King's interest in slavery was primarily political, but his attitude was shaped by humane considerations. In the Constitutional Convention of 1787 he had voiced his distaste for the three-fifths compromise for southern representation, though he had defended it upon practical grounds in the Massachusetts ratifying convention. As a boy he had

24. *Considerations Against the Appointment of Rufus King to the Senate of the United States: Submitted to the Republican Members of the Legislature of the State of New York*, 1820. A copy is in the N. Y. Pub. Lib. Bucktails said it was written by a Clintonian; the Clintonian *Albany Register*, Jan. 11, 18, 1820, declared that a Bucktail penned it to influence Tammany members hostile to Clinton.

25. Fox, *Decline of Aristocracy*, 220; N. Y. *American*, Jan. 15, 1820.

26. Adams, ed., *Memoirs of John Quincy Adams*, IV, 517; John A. King to King, Jan. 8, 1820, King Papers, N.-Y. Hist. Soc.

known slaves in his father's household. His conservative disposition, respect for property, and legal training led him to acquiesce in the definition of slaves as property where slavery was legal. He could not defend slavery, but he did not burn with zeal for emancipation. He had freed his one known slave—conceivably an indentured servant—at Jamaica in 1812, only a few weeks before the state chose him for the third time as senator.[27] Notwithstanding his personal aloofness from the bargaining that procured his election, he had recognized that slaveholding had become a political liability in New York.

As a senator, he opposed a bill for the recovery of fugitive slaves and voted to exclude slavery from the Territory of Arkansas, but it was the Missouri question that evoked his strongest protest. Northerners had long opposed the three-fifths rule, and ever since Jefferson's election as president, slave representation had been an important element in the North-South rivalry over the balance of power in the Union. As long as Republicans controlled the government and the free states could not hope to abolish the ratio, southern leaders had no need to defend what was constitutional, but the Missouri question arose while local party alignments were shifting, ambitious men were developing sectional followings, and northern Republicans were hoping to unseat the Virginia dynasty.

In his speeches, King argued for the constitutional right of Congress to set the conditions for the admission of new states to the Union. If Congress had forborne to exercise the right in the cases of Kentucky, Tennessee, Mississippi, and Alabama, he observed, it was only because they had been created out of states where slavery was legal. The Missouri Territory was not, however, within the confines of the original states, and therefore Congress ought to act upon its right to bar slavery from Missouri as a state. The New Yorker barely touched on the morality of slavery. To do so, he asserted, would be to inflame passions "which would disturb, if not defeat the impartial considera-

27. Jamaica Town Records, Book No. 452, 135, Bureau of Municipal Investigation and Statistics of New York City, Room 510, Municipal Building, New York, N. Y. These records are more readily available in a typescript copy made in 1939 by Leland Fielder, and located in the Long Island Collection, Queens Borough Pub. Lib., N. Y., IV, 122, which records King's manumission of Margaret, who had been bought probably between 1805 and 1812. For fuller treatment of King and slavery, see Robert Ernst, "Rufus King, Slavery, and the Missouri Crisis," *N.-Y. Hist. Soc. Quarterly*, 46 (1962), 357–82, and Joseph L. Arbena, "Politics or Principle? Rufus King and the Opposition to Slavery, 1785–1825," Essex Inst., *Hist. Colls.*, 101 (1965), 56–77.

tion of the subject."[28] Accepting the unhappy fact of slavery, and noting that enlightened men sought to mitigate it, he confined his attention to its impact upon national defense and the public welfare.

The extension of the already disproportionate power of the slave states, King declared, would be not only "unjust and odious," but injurious to the public welfare. Slavery impaired the productivity and power of a nation, and experience seemed to show that slave labor did not make manufacturers prosper. If dependent upon slave labor, Missouri would be unable to recruit soldiers and seamen in wartime; her slaves would be a liability in an exposed frontier area. If slavery were forbidden in all states admitted in the future, King prophesied, the slave markets would be destroyed, and free Americans could more readily resist foreign aggression and defend themselves against domestic insurrection. "Freedom and slavery are the parties which stand this day before the Senate," he affirmed, "and upon its decision the empire of the one or the other" would be established in Missouri. "If, instead of freedom, slavery is to prevail and spread, as we extend our dominion, can any reflecting man fail to see the necessity of giving to the general government, greater powers to enable it to afford the protection that will be demanded of it; powers that will be difficult to control, and which may prove fatal to the public liberties."[29]

King frankly hoped to stir up a storm in the North. After the session ended, he worked over his speeches and in November published them as a pamphlet, which became a focus of agitation despite measured tones, sober legalism, and lack of demagoguery. Webster, Gore, and Justice Joseph Story used it to whip up opinion in Boston. Reprinted at Philadelphia, it inspired many newspaper essays, and mass meetings in Philadelphia, New York, Trenton, Baltimore, and elsewhere adopted resolutions echoing King's arguments. The Richmond *Enquirer*, on the other hand, accused King of "striking a new blow at our Constitution."[30] Observing the New Yorker's encouragement of the controversy, John Quincy Adams wondered whether King foresaw the consequences and had determined to promote them even if it meant the dissolution of the Union.[31]

28. *Substance of Two Speeches . . . on the Missouri Bill*, in King, ed., *King Correspondence*, VI, 690–703, quotation, 697.

29. *Ibid.*, 703.

30. Quoted in N. Y. *American*, Dec. 15, 1819.

31. Adams, ed., *Memoirs of John Quincy Adams*, IV, 517.

Re-election to the Senate in February 1820 enabled King to renew his demand for the exclusion of slavery from Missouri. His two-hour speech on the eleventh elicited three hours of rebuttal by William Smith of South Carolina and another hour by Edward Lloyd of Maryland on the fourteenth. On the fifteenth, Lloyd's colleague, William Pinkney, so passionately defended slavery that he soon became known as the South's leading proslavery orator. As King returned to the fray the next day, a sympathetic listener likened him to an old Roman senator wrapped in quiet dignity.[32]

In his latest speeches, in contrast to those delivered a year earlier, the New Yorker enlarged the basis of his argument by adverting to the law of nature. Since all men were born free and entitled to life, liberty, and the pursuit of happiness, he asserted, neither man nor the state could enslave a man, and hence Congress was bound to prohibit slavery in the territories:

> Mr. President, I have yet to learn that one man can make a slave of another. If one man cannot do so, no number of individuals can have any better right to do it. And I hold that all laws or compacts imposing any such condition upon any human being are absolutely void, because contrary to the law of nature, which is the law of God, by which he makes his ways known to man, and is paramount to all human control.[33]

By February 1820, human rights and liberties had become the dominant motif in King's speeches, and he drew satisfaction from the force of his oratory as he sensed the powerful effects of it. For six weeks he threw his heart and soul into the Missouri issue, discussing it with Adams, Webster, Otis, Story, and others, over the dinner table and at every other opportunity. "King has made a desperate

32. Morgan Dix, ed., *Memoirs of John Adams Dix*, 2 vols. (N. Y., 1883), I, 60.

33. Senator Smith of South Carolina reported that King said this on Feb. 11. *Annals*, 16 Cong., 1 sess., 380–81. King's speeches were not reported, but from incomplete drafts and notes, Smith's and Pinkney's rebuttals, and contemporary correspondence, one can infer that King had arrived at new high ground. See Richard Peters to Roberts Vaux, Feb. 12, 1820, Vaux Papers, Hist. Soc. of Pa.; King to Christopher Gore, Feb. 17, 1820, King to John A. King and Charles King, Feb. 20, 1820, and Box 81, *passim*, King Papers, N.-Y. Hist. Soc., which contains an undated draft, in which King wrote: "All men being by natural law free and equal, and the formation of society being for the purpose of procuring by the union of individuals safety and other advantages for each and all the Members, as in their individual and antisocial Condition one man could not rightfully make another his slave, so in their social state, they could not confer on others a Right to do what they themselves could not do—hence it follows that no Prince or Government can make and hold slaves."

plunge into it, and has thrown his last stake upon the card," wrote Adams, who noted, however, the New Yorker's "great self-control, cool judgment, and spirit-breaking experience."[34]

Southerners were increasingly resentful and called his speeches inflammatory and seditious. Madison was "truly astonished" at some of his ideas, and President Monroe thought such renewed ardor and activity lessened King's "reputation for talents and patriotism and indeed for morality." According to the President, his old New York antagonist approved immediate emancipation and considered the federal compact broken if slavery were permitted in Missouri.[35] John Pintard, the New York merchant, wrote of the torrent of abuse poured upon King, "who is called a Traitor and Moral Hypocrite by the immaculate Saints of the South."[36]

Republicans, especially southern ones, assumed that a Federalist plot was afoot. Even Senator Jonathan Roberts of Pennsylvania, who agreed with King on Missouri, grew suspicious of him and of alleged Federalist scheming.[37] That King hoped for a new sectional alignment of parties is clear, but beyond his publishing speeches and trying to impress friends with the importance of forbidding slavery in Missouri, there is no evidence of ulterior motives on his part. As the last of the active Hamiltonians, the New York Senator was a natural target, and his continued political association with certain New England Federalists may well have suggested a sectionally inspired plot to those who remembered the Hartford Convention.

At a time when the legislature at Albany instructed New York's congressmen and senators to oppose the admission of Missouri as a slave state, King's all but unanimous reappointment to the upper

34. King to Stephen Van Rensselaer, Mar. 5, 1820, postscript, Hist. Soc. of Pa.; Adams, ed., *Memoirs of John Quincy Adams*, IV, 526.

35. James Madison to James Monroe, Feb. 10, 1820, Monroe Papers, Lib. Cong.; Monroe to Madison, Feb. 19, 1820, James Madison Papers, Rives Collection, Lib. Cong.

36. Barck, ed., *Letters from John Pintard*, I, 275. King complained of southerners' tactics to win over wavering antislavery men and disparage the motives of "those who cannot be seduced." In their active correspondence with northern leaders, he claimed, they misrepresented the views of the "Friends of Liberty," needlessly revived old jealousies, ascribed to personal ambition the statesmanlike efforts of men like himself, and maliciously denounced DeWitt Clinton as having inspired the opposition to slavery and collaborated with other politicians to elevate himself into the presidency. King to Joseph B. Varnum, Feb. 27, 1820, Private and Confidential, typescript owned by James G. King.

37. Jonathan Roberts to Elizabeth Roberts, Feb. 13, 16, 27, 1820, Roberts Papers, Hist. Soc. of Pa.

house triggered charges that he harbored personal ambitions. As a Federalist, he could not hope to become president of the United States, and it was therefore alleged that he wished to head a sectional party founded on the slave issue. Jefferson ventured that King was "ready to risk the Union for any chance of restoring his party to power and wriggling himself to the head of it," and even John Quincy Adams, who had long known King, found it difficult to account for his behavior without, as he put it, "allowing something for the instigations of personal expectancy."[38]

The insinuations of personal ambition were unfounded, however. King's first Missouri speeches had been delivered shortly after his unsuccessful bid for re-election to the Senate in 1819, and in the months that followed he determined to make an even stronger appeal. As astute a politician as Martin Van Buren concluded that King was innocent of any plotting about Missouri.[39] Although deeply critical of slavery itself, the Senator from New York was primarily and most deeply aroused over the political balance of power. If Monroe and Madison erroneously attributed his zeal to self-seeking ambition, they correctly discerned his hopes for an antislavery party aimed at strengthening northern influence at Washington. King, however, overestimated popular feeling against slavery in the North. Adams, accurately gauging the temper of the times, predicted that northerners would acquiesce in the admission of Missouri as a slave state, and so they did. When the Missouri Compromise ended his futile efforts, King, fearful for his country's future, asserted that the forces of slavery—the "black strap"—would win recruits, conquer, and enslave the free states.[40]

King disappointed those reformers who hoped he would lend his name and prestige to the cause of abolition, by refusing to endorse a proposal for the gradual abolition of slavery in the national capital and by affirming that the slave states were the sole authorities over

38. Thomas Jefferson to James Monroe, Mar. 3, 1820, Monroe Papers, Lib. Cong.; Adams, ed., *Memoirs of John Quincy Adams*, IV, 517.

39. Martin Van Buren to Mordecai M. Noah, Dec. 17, 1819, Van Buren Papers, Lib. Cong. For King's aversion to office-holding for personal gratification and his genuine concern for the future of the Union, see King, ed., *King Correspondence*, VI, 191, 267, 269–70, 278–80.

40. Adams, ed., *Memoirs of John Quincy Adams*, IV, 517; King to ?, Mar. 3, 1820, King Papers, N.-Y. Hist. Soc.; Fitzpatrick, ed., *Autobiography of Van Buren*, 139.

the question of emancipation of their slaves. "I am particularly anxious not to be misunderstood," he wrote to the spokesmen of a committee in his village of Jamaica, "never having thought myself at liberty to encourage, or assent to, any measure that would affect the security of property in slaves, or to disturb the political adjustment which the Constitution has established respecting them."[41] Like New York Congressmen James Tallmadge and John W. Taylor, his counterparts in the lower house, King was a free-soiler long before free soil became a popular rallying cry. Only time would justify his conviction that the continued expansion of slavery would merely postpone the inevitable day of reckoning.

New Yorkers were less aroused over slavery in Missouri than over revising their own state constitution. After Clinton's hairbreadth victory over Tompkins for governor in 1820, agitation for constitutional change erupted with new vigor, as Tammany called for a convention to revise the constitution of 1777, which reflected the controlling influence of conservative landholders and under which the Council of Appointment had become an instrument of political control. Secure from removal, the members of this council were accused of having resisted the creation of more judgeships and thereby slowing the administration of justice. Not only was New York City strong for reform, but settlers from New England in the northern and western parts of the state demanded a constitutional system more responsive to a rapidly growing population. The Bucktail-controlled legislature passed a bill to call a convention, but Clinton, fearful that such a convention might weaken his power, cast his deciding vote against it in the Council of Revision. Early in 1821, however, the legislature submitted the question to the people, who voted overwhelmingly in favor of a convention and elected delegates in the spring.

Rufus King, who ran as a "Republican," was one of the three delegates chosen by Queens County in the spring election. Arriving at Albany on August 26, he took rooms at Cruttenden's, facing the public square, and arranged with the proprietor for a congenial group of downstate delegates to dine together at a special table. King fore-

41. King's decidedly negative endorsement on "Humanitas" to King, Mar. 10, 1820, King Papers, N.-Y. Hist. Soc.; King to John B. Coles and John T. Irving, Nov. 22, 1819, King, ed., *King Correspondence*, VI, 233–34. Cf. King to Richard Peters, Jr., Nov. 30, 1819, King Papers, N.-Y. Hist. Soc.

saw tension and bitterness in a power struggle between Clintonians and the Bucktail majority and hoped that prudent delegates would "check the excesses of such men as may be inclined to go too far in their schemes of Reform."[42]

The convention gathered on the twenty-eighth in the assembly chamber of the capitol. Former Governor Daniel D. Tompkins, now the nation's Vice-President, was chosen to preside. Martin Van Buren, who operated more behind the scenes than on the convention floor, left no doubt about Bucktail strength when all but two of the standing committees were chaired by his close associates.[43] King had an aisle seat in the front row, a few feet from the raised speaker's chair. Next to him was Henry Wheaton, lawyer, United State Supreme Court reporter, and expert in international law. Across the aisle sat Nathan Sanford, whom the Bucktails had retired from the Senate in February to make way for Van Buren. Behind King, two rows back, sat Chancellor James Kent, close to Stephen Van Rensselaer, the most important landlord in the state, whom Van Buren—acting through King—had induced to support the convention. Among others in the hall were Chief Justice Spencer, Judge William Van Ness, and Judge Jonas Platt, all forceful conservatives. The leading reformers were Colonel Samuel Young, General Erastus Root, an ardent and colorful orator, and Peter R. Livingston, a wealthy philosophical democrat. Of the Tammany men, Ogden Edwards stood out as a moderate reformer.[44]

At the outset, the convention accepted King's recommendation to establish a committee to classify parts of the existing constitution for reference to select committees. Tompkins appointed a committee of thirteen under King's chairmanship. Its work led to the creation of ten standing committees. King became chairman of the committee

42. King, ed., *King Correspondence*, VI, 396; King to Christopher Gore, June 23, 1821, King to Charles King, Dec. 24, 1820, King Papers, N.-Y. Hist. Soc. For indications of King's "homework" during the summer, see Egbert Benson to King, Aug. 17, 1821, Misc. MSS—Benson, N. Y. Pub. Lib.; Isaac Parker to King, Aug. 21, 1821, King Papers, N.-Y. Hist. Soc.

43. Tompkins was elected by a vote of 94 to 16. For an account of the convention, see Fox, *Decline of Aristocracy*, 229–70. Fox's interpretation, however, has recently been challenged. See below, n. 62.

44. Nathaniel H. Carter, William L. Stone, and Marcus T. C. Gould, *Reports of the Proceedings and Debates of the Convention of 1821. . .* (Albany, 1821) [hereafter *Debates of 1821*], frontispiece and *passim;* Fox, *Decline of Aristocracy*, 239–67. Some of the 12 other Federalists in the convention, like King, were elected as "Republicans" or independents.

on the legislative department, most of whose proposals were accepted in substance.[45]

King's role in the convention was not crucial, but he was so highly respected that his arguments on specific points carried weight. In the lengthy debate on the governor's veto, which followed the abolition of the Council of Revision, he opposed permitting a bare majority of the legislature to override, and eventually the convention voted to require a two-thirds majority, as in the federal Constitution.[46] He preferred to leave the governor's term of office at three years, but when this was turned down, he vigorously opposed General Root's attempts to establish an annual term as insufficient to enable the governor to learn the routines of his office. The tendency to revise should be "indulged with great caution," the Senator warned, "lest it lead us on to dangerous innovations. Governments are the fruit of experience: they can safely rest on those political truths to which time has added his infallible sanction; and it is only the wise combination and distribution of these truths which distinguish our free constitutions from all others." If Americans lacked "moderation and wisdom to establish, preserve, and perpetuate free governments, where, among whom, may we hope for their existence?" he asked. Whether swayed by King's eloquence or by a practical desire to compromise, eleven delegates who had previously voted for the annual term changed their votes, with the result that the convention finally settled upon a two-year term, as King had predicted.[47]

Without much effect, the old Federalist took an active part in a debate on Negro voting. When the committee on the elective franchise recommended restricting the suffrage to whites, Peter Jay moved to strike out the word "white." Colonel Young retorted that the Negroes were incompetent, that their vote "would be at the call of the richest purchaser," but Chancellor Kent objected that the exclusion of Negroes would violate the rights guaranteed to the citizens of each state under the United States Constitution. King saw voting

45. King told the delegates it was their duty to demonstrate to all men that free people were capable of self-government, and that they could "renovate" their liberties "without destroying those securities which education and manners, our laws and constitutions have provided." *Debates of 1821*, 32. The convention reduced to 8 the 17 Senate districts recommended by King's committee. *Ibid.*, 401, 474–75; Hammond, *Political Parties in New York*, II, 13–14.

46. *Debates of 1821*, 77, 89–90, 115–16, 660.

47. *Ibid.*, 547–52; King to John A. King, [Sept. 20], 1821, King Papers, N.-Y. Hist. Soc.

rights as bound up with citizenship, and he was not sure how a Negro, unless born free, could become a citizen: "A man born a slave cannot be a citizen; a red man cannot be a citizen; they cannot even be naturalized, for naturalization can only be effected under the laws of the United States, which limit it to the whites." Nevertheless, he argued, "the period is not distant when they must be. As certainly as the children of any white man are citizens, so certainly the children of the black men are citizens; and they may in time raise up a progeny, which will be disastrous to the other races of this country. I will not trouble the Convention further; but I thought it due to the occasion to express my opinion of the constitutional barriers which interpose to prevent our retaining the 'white' in the clause."[48]

He was determined that New York avoid a discriminatory clause like that in Missouri's constitution, but his private letters revealed no emotion over the Negro vote.[49] Although the convention eliminated the word "white," it limited Negro voters to male citizens of the state owning a freehold worth $250. King voted against this freehold requirement (adopted by more than a two-to-one margin) because he objected to discrimination against colored citizens.[50]

Believing that some property qualifications were desirable for all voters, King also voted against universal suffrage. Like almost all the conservatives in the convention, he disapproved the motion that the franchise be opened to anyone who served in the state militia or who, on assessment, worked on the highways. Those who were unable to vote independently and impartially, or were "habitually and necessarily influenced by other men," such as militiamen and those doing road service, should be denied the vote, he asserted. Property was a better index of capacity.[51] Universal suffrage was, in his view, dangerous. It undermined the basis of civil society and the primary objects of government, protection of property and encouragement of honest industry. If universal suffrage were sanctioned, King re-

48. *Debates of 1821*, 192.

49. King anticipated that the convention would eliminate the word "white" and substitute a clause forbidding the immigration of Negroes who were not citizens of another state. King to John A. King, [Sept. 20], 1821, King Papers, N.-Y. Hist. Soc.

50. *Debates of 1821*, 557. Only briefly did the delegates discuss slavery in New York, which, under the gradual abolition law of 1799, would formally end in 1827. *Ibid.*, 485, 486, 497–98.

51. King to Charles King, Sept. 27, 1821, King Papers, N.-Y. Hist. Soc.; *Debates of 1821*, 273–75, 283. King favored a property qualification for the franchise, which would include freeholds, leaseholds, securities, and personal effects. Convention notes, 1821, King Papers, N.-Y. Hist. Soc.

marked, he would regret having been a member of the convention. When the delegates adopted age and residence as the only qualifications for the white man, he voted in opposition.[52]

The controversy over suffrage was a scuffle compared with the battle to regulate political patronage. After the convention abolished the Council of Appointment, an attempt to create a new council drew King's fire; it would be no improvement over the old one, which had drawn to Albany many office-seekers and "experienced corps of men" to obtain and hand out offices to such an extent that the council's duties were "corruptly neglected," and the business of the legislature often subserved the "bad views which guided the suitors who assembled" there.[53] Few delegates were willing to set up a new council, and the proposal was dropped.

Most controversial was the question of selecting local magistrates, before whom, as Van Buren observed, five times as much business was transacted as in all the other courts in the state. The Bucktails favored any device which would lodge ultimate control of these appointments in Albany. Having nothing to gain from partisanship, King ably advocated, as desirable in itself, the local election of justices of the peace. The possibility that a central power at the capital might appoint 2,500 local justices evoked his sharp criticism:

> Each of these judges employs his constables or marshals, and is attended by the small lawyers who excite and sustain the suits. . . . There being on an average four justices in each town, the justices, the constables, the suitors, the pettifoggers, and the idle attendants, make together a great collection of people. Indeed, so important is this magistracy and its associates in this state, that it has been said . . . that he who can control or dispose of their appointments would possess greater influence than were he able to dispose of all the other offices throughout our state.[54]

After considering a number of possibilities, King became convinced that each town should elect its own justices. To the charge that elections by the people in their town meetings would be "aristocratic," he exclaimed: "Call a country town meeting an aristocracy!

52. *Debates of 1821*, 286–87. In his convention notes, which referred freely to feudal practices, England, and Blackstone, King underscored a quotation from Blackstone: "The true reason of requiring any Qualification, with regard to property in voters is to *exclude such as are in so mean a situation* as are presumed to have no will of their own."

53. *Debates of 1821*, 314–15; King to Charles King, Oct. 4, 1821, King Papers, N.-Y. Hist. Soc.

54. *Debates of 1821*, 315.

What, then, may it not be called! But give to this simple, primitive, and innocent association what bad name we like, still a town meeting of freemen presents a picture of order, of freedom, and intelligence, which is the envy of other lands, and which is the basis and security of our republican system."[55] As a native son of New England, he saw the town meeting as something more than a device to check the use of local judges as tools of Albany patronage; it was the ideal form of local government. Townspeople who knew each other were most capable of judging their own men. "There is," he pleaded, "a beauty and simplicity in this mode of choosing the magistrates who, we may presume, will promote peace and order, and arbitrate justly between their neighbors."[56]

The political activities of several of the state's highest judges had aroused much criticism, and a majority in the convention was determined to curb the Clintonian judiciary. The lack of the power to impeach and remove judges was a serious weakness in the existing constitution, as King well knew, yet he was fearful that instead of merely blocking political judges, the convention would go to extremes in overhauling the judicial system. When Erastus Root proposed to transfer the duties of the chancellor to the Supreme Court, while the Court of Chancery continued at the pleasure of the legislature, King questioned the wisdom of combining statutory and common law cases with equity cases and objected to giving the legislature such broad power over the judiciary.[57] Some delegates apparently were ready to abolish the existing Supreme Court in order to get rid of its judges. Partly on principle, and partly because the scheme might evoke popular sympathy for undeserving judges, King determined not to cooperate, and he was in the minority when the convention voted sixty-two to fifty-three to set up an entirely new, smaller Supreme Court.[58]

55. *Ibid.*, 316, 333, 344, 381. Van Buren opposed elected justices of the peace. He moved that in each county the board of supervisors and the court of common pleas draw up separate lists; candidates whose names were on both lists automatically would be selected, and the governor would make appointments from among the remaining candidates. With nearly all the downstate delegates voting against it, this plan was beaten by a small majority. *Ibid.*, 299, 321, 341, 382–84; King to Charles King, Oct. 21, 1821, King Papers, N.-Y. Hist. Soc.

56. *Debates of 1821*, 381.

57. *Ibid.*, 521–22.

58. *Ibid.*, 624; King to [Charles King], Oct. 24, 1821, Private, King Papers, N.-Y. Hist. Soc.

In the brief debate on church and state, both King and Chief Justice Spencer asserted that Christianity was entitled to the special protection of the law, though they did not question the principle of religious toleration. "The religious professions of the Pagan, the Mahomedan, and the Christian," King declared, were not of equal validity in the eye of the law. For Christians the deeds of this world were rewarded or punished, and the moral law rested upon that doctrine. So too, the civil law:

> Our laws constantly refer to this revelation, and by the oath which they prescribe, we appeal to the Supreme Being, so to deal with us hereafter, as we observe the obligation of our oaths.
>
> The Pagan world were, and are, without the mighty influence of this principle, which is proclaimed in the Christian system—their morals were destitute of its powerful sanction, while their oaths neither awakened the hopes nor fears which a belief in Christianity inspires.[59]

King therefore opposed tampering with the clause on religion in the existing constitution, which he believed implicitly acknowledged the truths of the religion of the gospel. Whether or not they agreed with his reasoning, the delegates were not eager for changes, and the sections on religion and ministers in the new constitution were essentially the same as in the old. On King's initiative, a proposed phrase, "ministers of religion," was changed to "ministers of the gospel," as in the original constitution.[60]

As the convention dragged on, King grew increasingly irritated over the slow progress of the debates and the informal caucuses at private lodgings which were "more attended to than concerted measures within the Capitol." "I find less communication of the views of men with whom I am supposed to cooperate than I had expected," he complained to his son. "Suspicion and jealousies are more extensive than we could have anticipated." In the depth of his despondency King confessed, "I often wish I had not come hither."[61]

Work on the new constitution came to fruition, however, when a committee which included Yates, Van Buren, Root, Kent, Jay, and King prepared a first draft. This was refined by another committee whose report became the basis of the new instrument—really a drastic

59. *Debates of 1821*, 574–75.

60. *Ibid.*, 648.

61. *Ibid.*, 313; King to Charles King, appended Oct. 2 to letter dated Sept. 30, 1821, also King to Charles King, Oct. 15, 1821, King Papers, N.-Y. Hist. Soc.

revision of the old one—which ninety-eight delegates, including King, adopted on November 10 after two and a half months' labor.

Adoption of the New York state constitution of 1821 administered a crippling blow to the old order which King represented. He recognized the inevitable, however, and the new constitution seemed to him, on the whole, an improvement over the original and in some respects even better than those of other states. Despite his lifelong preference for property qualifications, he finally settled for universal white male suffrage because it was bound up with necessary changes.[62] Although he himself returned to Washington before the constitution was submitted to the people, he urged his sons to work for its ratification. As the outcome was almost certain, many citizens did not bother to vote. Even so, the new instrument was accepted by a magnificent majority of nearly 34,000.

At the national capital, King wryly watched the scramble to succeed President Monroe. The rivalry between Crawford, the Secretary of the Treasury, and Calhoun, the Secretary of War, extended to the Senate, where the dominant Crawfordites—the "true patriots," as King sarcastically called them—tried to cut military appropriations. Martin Van Buren, neutral in the struggle, spent every waking hour as New York's freshman senator cultivating political friends. The Bucktails, according to Daniel Webster, were serving their own interest by hinting to King that he might be their presidential candidate. Webster feared that Senator King was not as "impressed with this truth as he ought to be"; it is doubtful that the seasoned political veteran was that gullible.[63]

62. "It is impossible to prevent the extension of the Right of suffrage," King observed, "and though individuals may be affected by the alterations of the judiciary, the judicial system is preserved and amended." King to [Charles King], Dec. 19, 1821, King Papers, N.-Y. Hist. Soc. By correcting the worst abuses of the appointive system, broadening the suffrage, and making government more responsible to the people, the new constitution laid the groundwork for adoption of a fully democratic electoral system in 1825. Kass, *Politics in New York*, 89–91, convincingly challenges Fox's view that anti-Clinton Bucktails and Clintonian aristocrats were locked in ideological conflict over reform. He points out that party lines were frequently crossed in the convention, that the Bucktails opposed certain democratic measures they thought would hinder them politically, and that the vast majority of Bucktails shared with the majority of Clintonian and Federalist delegates the credit for the moderate reforms that were achieved.

63. King to David Daggett, Feb. 17, 1822, Daggett Papers, Yale Univ. Lib.; King to Christopher Gore, Jan. 3, 1822, King to Charles King, Feb. 23, 1822,

King's friendship with Van Buren was one of the most remarkable of the time. The old Federalist had been grateful to the younger man for having brought about his re-election to the Senate in 1820, and as Senate colleagues they became personal friends. King was rounding out a long career that had begun when Van Buren was born; though he considered his elder as "from first to last a federalist of the Hamilton school," Van Buren, twenty-seven years younger than King, shared the older man's cultivated manners and polite conversation. King was charmed by Van Buren's urbanity, geniality, and tact, and he recognized the younger man's integrity, legal acumen, and political ability.[64]

A sense of obligation to Van Buren, as well as bias against Clintonian factionalism in New York, led King to join in an ill-advised move to prevent the appointment of Solomon Van Rensselaer, formerly a Federalist but now a convert to Clinton, as postmaster at Albany. On Van Buren's initiative, both senators urged Postmaster-General Meigs to delay making any appointment to this post. Van Buren's candidate for the postmastership was John Lansing, the former Chancellor of New York, and King frankly told Van Rensselaer that he himself preferred Lansing. Annoyed that Van Rensselaer had not initially consulted him, Van Buren, aided by Vice-President Tompkins, conducted a spiteful campaign to block the appointment. Anticipating failure, and no doubt regretting what had become an unsavory political feud, King withdrew from the fray before his colleague went over Meigs's head to the President. Monroe declined to intervene, Van Rensselaer was appointed, and a storm of well-deserved criticism descended upon the two New York senators.[65]

Van Buren seems to have genuinely enjoyed King's company, despite their differing political principles. In February 1822 he moved

---

King Papers, N.-Y. Hist. Soc.; Daniel Webster to Jeremiah Mason, Mar. 23, 1822, Clark, ed., *Memoirs of Jeremiah Mason*, 259.

64. Fitzpatrick, ed., *Autobiography of Van Buren*, 155; King to James Monroe, Apr. 2, 1823, King Papers, N.-Y. Hist. Soc. Van Buren was quite impressed with King's intelligence, dignity, plausibility, and at times eloquence as a speaker, but he thought King lacked Hamilton's intellectual vigor and comprehensiveness. *Autobiography*, 155–56.

65. Pertinent documents are in the Van Buren Papers, Lib. Cong., and the King Papers, N.-Y. Hist. Soc. See also King, ed., *King Correspondence*, VI, 437–50; Hammond, *Political Parties in New York*, II, 95–97; Robert V. Remini, *Martin Van Buren and the Making of the Democratic Party* (N. Y., 1959), 18–26.

from Capitol Hill to Bradley's Hotel in Georgetown, where King was staying, and for the remainder of the congressional session and the next one, took meals with King, Stephen Van Rensselaer (a cousin of the victorious new Albany postmaster), and Harrison G. Otis, among others; strange company indeed for a Republican party boss and organizer. After returning to Albany in May, Van Buren thanked King for his kindliness "throughout our acquaintance and particularly the last winter," and asserted that he would always regard their intimacy as one of the most fortunate incidents of his life. He would value it the more "from an entire conviction that it must last with our lives." In spite of deepening political differences and an instance of irrational vexation on the aging King's part, the cordial relationship continued.[66]

While these two men represented New York in the Senate, commercial relations with Great Britain and France once more became major diplomatic questions. In 1822 King was chairman of the Senate Foreign Relations Committee, which considered demands for repeal of the laws restricting British shipping between the United States and the British West Indies. He reported against repeal as premature until a bill opening the West Indies to American ships passed Parliament.[67] Subsequently, he reported a measure authorizing the President, if satisfied that these ports were actually opened, to lift for one year the restrictions on British vessels. The Senate adopted the bill, together with King's amendment authorizing suspension of certain duties upon French shipping in American ports whenever Secretary of State Adams and the French Minister, Hyde de Neuville, signed a commercial convention.[68] Although the British Parliament passed a navigation law, the French prolonged the negotiations over long-standing American financial claims, much to the Senator's irritation.

66. Fitzpatrick, ed., *Autobiography of Van Buren*, 153–54, 574; Bonney, *Legacy of Historical Gleanings*, I, 397–402; Martin Van Buren to King, May 31, 1822, King Papers, N.-Y. Hist. Soc.

67. *Annals*, 17 Cong., 1 sess., 293–98; King to Charles King, Mar. 23, 1822, King to [John A. King], Mar. 20, 1822, King Papers, N.-Y. Hist. Soc.

68. *Annals*, 17 Cong., 1 sess., 432, 434–35; King to Charles King, May 3, 1822, King Papers, N.-Y. Hist. Soc. King was uneasy at the French delay in satisfying American financial claims, not only for love of country but also because he had loaned large sums of money to his friend Archibald Gracie, one of the claimants. King to Charles King, Mar. 17, Apr. 15, 1822, *ibid.*; King to Hyde de Neuville, Dec. 26, 1818, King Papers, Humanities Research Center, University of Texas.

He distrusted Hyde de Neuville and expostulated with the French chargé, bluntly accusing France of calculated delay in meeting American claims and willful discrimination against American creditors.[69] In general, King loyally supported the administration's foreign policies.

In December 1823, the Senate changed the rules for the selection of its standing committees, which had formerly been elected; henceforth their members were to be appointed by the presiding officer of the Senate. Senator John Gaillard of South Carolina, acting in the absence of the Vice-President, named King to the Foreign Relations Committee but appointed James Barbour of Virginia as its chairman. Although the former Virginia Governor was an experienced Senator who had previously served as chairman of the committee, he was twenty years younger than the New Yorker. King was insulted and asked to be relieved of his committee membership.[70] The request was granted, and so ended his formal senatorial influence on the making of foreign policy.

King's final political crusade was launched against the centralization of political power in the hands of a few strategically placed men. He joined in a mounting attack upon the New York legislature's practice of appointing presidential electors and in so doing ended his political honeymoon with Van Buren. Upon learning in April 1823 that the Little Magician, who favored a congressional caucus, would use his state political machine, the Albany Regency, to win legislative support for Crawford, King determined to fight for the choice of electors by the people.[71] He was not alone. His young friend, Henry Wheaton, who had been with him at the state convention two years before, wrote trenchant propaganda for the popular choice of electors in *The Patriot*, founded by Calhoun supporters to help in thwarting Van Buren. As agitation for repeal of the state's electoral law

69. King to Charles King, Dec. 26, 28, 1822, King to John A. King, Dec. 28, 1822, King Papers, N.-Y. Hist. Soc. A clause in the new British law permitting future issuance of Orders in Council induced King to favor suspension, rather than repeal, of the American navigation laws.

70. King to Charles King, Dec. 17, 1823, Private, *ibid.* The Senate had elected King only once (Dec. 1821) as chairman of the committee. In Dec. 1822 it chose Barbour for the fourth time as chairman, and although King probably resented being replaced, he could hardly complain about the vote of his colleagues. The presiding officer's appointment of the chairman in 1823 was another matter.

71. King to John A. King, Apr. 10, 1823, *ibid.*

heightened during the summer and gave rise to a "People's Party," other newspapers took up the cry. One of these was the New York *American*, edited by King's son Charles, to whom his father fed suggestions and arguments.[72] Asserting that constitutional checks would become "a mere farce" if the caucus men had their way, the old Senator sent a stream of letters advising Wheaton, now an assemblyman, to avoid arousing rural prejudices against city or downstate legislators, and not only to oppose a state caucus but to push actively for popular choice of electors by promoting town and county meetings.[73]

When the state legislature met in January 1824, the Assembly passed a bill authorizing the choice of electors by the people, but the Senate, dominated by Crawford supporters, killed it. Popular fury was further roused by the Regency's removal of Clinton as a canal commissioner, a purely political tactic that backfired. Clinton, who favored the choice of electors by the people, was nominated for governor at a state convention in Utica and subsequently returned to the governor's chair after a two-year absence. The next year, a new legislature enacted a law creating electoral districts, and the battle for popular choice of electors was won.

Though King kept a wary eye on New York politics, he fixed his attention as senator upon the congressional caucus. The nomination of a presidential candidate by caucus no longer satisfied most Republican leaders in Congress, and it was obvious that the adherents of Adams, Calhoun, Clay, and Jackson would not abide by a device that no one of them could control. When in February a caucus nominated Crawford, only sixty-six men attended. King, who supported Adams, particularly objected to Crawford not only as another southern candidate but as an ambitious politician of mediocre ability who had connections with Van Buren. The Georgian, wrote the Long Islander, was "the most cunning and dangerous Intriguer" in the nation, whose following comprised "the ablest and most adroit Intriguers throughout the country which such a master could recruit."[74]

72. King proposed that Charles develop the inference that the United States Constitution did not give the state legislatures the power to appoint electors. King to Charles King, Sept. 29, 1823, *ibid.*

73. King to Henry Wheaton, Dec. 28, 30, 1823, Wheaton Papers, Pierpont Morgan Lib. For a recent evaluation of Bucktail policy on the choice of electors, see Kass, *Politics in New York*, 51–52.

74. King to Charles King, Mar. 16, 1824, King Papers, N.-Y. Hist. Soc.

Even more aroused over the system than the man, the old Federalist thought it not as much a question of who the president should be as whether the people or a legislative oligarchy would decide. "The Election of a Pope is purity, simplicity, and certainty, when compared with the System of Electing a President by a Caucus," he declared. "The conclave of Cardinals are enclosed, and soon walled up, while the Caucus of Congress to elect a President is composed of Members, who separate, confer with whom they please, and for one or two years carry on the Intrigue to choose a President."[75] In a long Senate speech on March 18, he denounced the caucus as an extraordinary, self-created "central power," which had taken over the direction and control of the constitutional provisions for the election of the president and endangered the careful distribution of powers under the federal system worked out in Philadelphia in 1787.[76]

Strict adherence to the Constitution was the best guarantee, the New Yorker asserted, against an unbroken succession of presidents chosen by a perpetual body whose policies and pretensions to power would be settled by "uninterrupted and secret delibrations." If this body continued unchallenged, he warned, it would solidify the power of the executive and eventually lead to demands for a single, consolidated national government. While calling for the suppression of the "central power," King advised against changing the Constitution in the midst of political excitement:

> All that is the work of man, is like him, imperfect. We probably enjoy a greater proportion of freedom and happiness than falls to the lot of other nations; and, because we desire yet more, we must be careful not to lose what we have, by hasty and partial alterations in our plan of government. [I] would, therefore, prefer to adhere, for the present, to the Constitution as it is, in hopes that adequate means may be devised to suppress this great and alarming central power, which is now oppressing the Constitution itself, by controlling and superseding its wise and well ordered provisions.[77]

75. King to [Charles King], Dec. 23, 1823, also King to Charles King, Jan. 1, 1824, *ibid.*

76. The entire speech is reprinted in King, ed., *King Correspondence*, VI, 703–10.

77. *Ibid.*, 709–10. King's speech was occasioned by a motion to postpone indefinitely several proposed amendments to the Constitution. He sent copies of the speech to New York politicians, including Erastus Root, then president of the New York Senate, and to the newly elected speaker of the Assembly. King

This was Rufus King at his best. The only remaining Senator who had been a member of the Philadelphia Constitutional Convention, he persevered as a moderate, conservative constitutionalist. Within five years he had championed the constitutional validity of free-soilism in the Missouri debates, had participated in the regeneration of the political life of New York state, and had contributed to the death of "King Caucus."

---

to Henry Wheaton, Apr. 12, 1824, King Papers, N.-Y. Hist. Soc. Thoroughly aroused, the caucus men poured upon the veteran New York Senator a torrent of verbal abuse. This made him feel all the more self-righteous. As it turned out, the caucus that nominated Crawford was the last to nominate a presidential candidate.

CHAPTER XX

A FINAL MISSION

BY THE 1820'S RUFUS KING HAD BECOME MORE PORTLY, HIS HAIR HAD thinned, his broad face had grown fleshier and somewhat more rubicund, yet his health was good for a man in his sixties. If his appearance had changed over the years, his manner was still serious and to some, perhaps, austere. Trousers, once worn only by farmers and laborers, had become the fashion, but the old Federalist clung to his generation's badge of gentility; longer than any other senator, he appeared publicly in knee breeches, silk stockings, and buckled shoes. William Pinkney, himself something of a fop, once called him "an old woman out of fashion."[1] Courtly and given to standing on his dignity, the veteran Senator seemed to younger men pompous and aloof in the dawn of a democratic era.

Early in 1824, King made up his mind to quit the Senate at the end of his term, anticipating a quiet, permanent retirement to Jamaica the next year, when he would be seventy. Although he genuinely wished to retire, he also knew he stood no chance of re-election. The peculiar circumstances of New York state politics which had returned him to the Senate in 1820 no longer existed, and neither the Bucktails nor the Clintonians were willing to renominate him.[2] Wishing to be free of other civic responsibilities, King resigned as a trustee of Columbia College. He had served for eighteen years but

1. Alexander C. Hanson to King, Sept. 9, 1818, King Papers, N.-Y. Hist. Soc.
2. Remini, *Martin Van Buren*, 226; N. Y. *National Advocate*, Jan. 25, 1825; Adams, ed., *Memoirs of John Quincy Adams*, VI, 487.

had attended few meetings after 1819 and none at all after 1822. In his letter of resignation, he apologized for his inability to take a more active part.[3]

For one who planned to remove himself from public life, he was surprisingly immersed in the coming presidential election. He favored John Quincy Adams as the only well-informed candidate and as an expert on foreign affairs but was not enthusiastic about him, perhaps because of Adams's connection with the Monroe administration, his conciliatory stand in the Missouri debates, and his broad interpretation of constitutional powers.[4] His relations with Adams had been friendly but not intimate; the Secretary thought King "one of the wisest and best among us," but suspected "a spice of disappointment in all his opinions," which he attributed to the old Federalist's failure to become president.[5] It is probable that the Senator exerted strong influence behind the scenes in the struggle for presidential electors in New York, and Adams's overnight stay in Jamaica in 1824 was certainly more than a social visit.[6] William Coleman of the *New-York Evening Post* asserted that King, through his son John, had committed three Queens County assemblymen to vote for Adams.[7]

After an unproductive first session of the Eighteenth Congress[8]

3. Minutes of the Trustees of Columbia College, III, Pt. 1, *passim*, King to Clement C. Moore, Jan. 17, 1824, Columbiana Collection, Low Memorial Lib., Columbia Univ.

4. King to Charles King, Mar. 16, 1824, King to Christopher Gore, Mar. 7, 1824, King to Elijah H. Mills, June 14, 1824, King Papers, N.-Y. Hist. Soc.

5. Adams, ed., *Memoirs of John Quincy Adams*, VI, 342.

6. William A. Duer to King, Feb. 17, 1825, King Papers, N.-Y. Hist. Soc. Adams's visit at Jamaica is mentioned in Timothy Pickering to William Coleman, July 1, 1825, Pickering Papers, Vol. 38, Mass. Hist. Soc.

7. William Coleman to Timothy Pickering, Feb. 13, 1825, Pickering Papers, Vol. 32, Mass. Hist. Soc. Subsequently, when the election was thrown into the House of Representatives, Stephen Van Rensselaer held the decisive vote in a deeply divided New York delegation. Although by his own preference for Adams, King may have indirectly influenced his friend, it is hard to believe Coleman's statement that the night before the balloting King had induced Van Rensselaer to vote for Adams, *ibid.*; cf. King to John A. King, Feb. 8, 1825, King Papers, N.-Y. Hist. Soc. Clay and Webster were more directly responsible for the result, having been closeted with Van Rensselaer on the day of the balloting; and Van Rensselaer's ballot gave New York's vote and the presidency to Adams. See Fitzpatrick, ed., *Autobiography of Van Buren*, 152; King's memorandum, Feb. 10, 1825, King Papers, N.-Y. Hist. Soc.; Livermore, *Twilight of Federalism*, 180–81; Remini, *Martin Van Buren*, 89–90.

8. The Senate ratified a convention with Great Britain to suppress the African slave trade but in effect defeated it by rejecting two articles and adding a crippling amendment. King, who favored the convention, blamed

and a summer of farming on Long Island,[9] King returned to Washington, where in December 1824 he was placed on a Senate committee to arrange for the reception of the Marquis de Lafayette. A guest of the nation, King's only French friend was tumultuously welcomed in America. The President received him and recommended a tangible congressional reward in appreciation of his services in the Revolutionary War, but a House committee delayed approval of the recommendation. Embarrassed, the Senate committee recommended a gift of $200,000 in stock and a township of land, which Congress approved, though the House required payment of money instead of stock.[10] On New Year's Day, King sat at the main table at a congressional dinner in honor of the Marquis, attended by President Monroe and most of the Cabinet.

In his last months as a senator, King served again on the Committee on Finance but otherwise was not very active. He voted against a bill to abolish imprisonment for debt, as he had previously done, but he took no part in the debate.[11] When on occasion he rose to speak, he showed an unaccustomed irritability, as when his colleague Van Buren presented a Shaker petition asking exemption from military service. Upon Van Buren's moving that the petition be referred to committee, King sprang from his seat and denounced the Shakers as a band of fanatics. He moved to lay the petition on the table, adding—according to Van Buren—that it would be but justly treated

---

the Crawfordites for sabotaging it and immediately reported to Adams that their main purpose had been to exploit the issue to the Secretary's disadvantage in the presidential election. *Journal of Executive Proceedings of U. S. Senate*, III, 385–87; King to Charles King, May 23, 1824, King Papers, N.-Y. Hist. Soc. According to Adams, Adams, ed., *Memoirs of John Quincy Adams*, VI, 350, King said that after making the slave trade piracy, "to cant at the right of searching for pirates was an absurdity," and that the convention had carefully guarded against abuses of the right of search.

9. King visited Gore in Waltham late in the summer; his presence in the Boston area may have stimulated the Massachusetts Historical Society to elect him as a corresponding member. John A. King to King, Aug. 24, 1824, King Papers, N.-Y. Hist. Soc.; "Quarterly Meeting" [Oct. 28, 1824], Mass. Hist. Soc., *Proceedings*, 1 (1791–1835), 377.

10. King to Charles King, Dec. 17, 1824, King Papers, N.-Y. Hist. Soc.; King, ed., *King Correspondence*, VI, 576; *Register of Debates in Congress*, 18 Cong., 2 sess., 55–56.

11. *Register of Debates in Congress*, 18 Cong., 2 sess., 230. King probably agreed with Hayne that the abolition of imprisonment for debt would be ineffective without a national bankruptcy law. For Hayne's speech, see *Annals*, 18 Cong., 1 sess., 483–98.

were it thrown *under* the table. "There was something so extraordinary, so unexpected and to all present so amazing in his concluding remarks, as related to myself," wrote Van Buren, "that they failed to disturb my own temper."[12] Van Buren calmly defended the Shakers' sobriety and industry and upheld their right of petition. Without dissent, the Senate referred the petition. For a time, the two New York senators did not speak to each other, but a day or two later, after adjournment, King asked to join Van Buren in his carriage where he apologized for having lost his temper.[13]

In contrast to King's pettiness over the Shaker petition was the prophetic quality of his views on slavery. During the previous summer, he had belittled the efforts of the American Colonization Society as serving only to call attention to the "desperate condition" of the slave states. Unless adequate means were adopted to mitigate or abolish slavery, he had predicted, these states would "endure Calamities that the order and Justice of Providence prepare for the oppressor."[14] Private philanthropy seemed to him doomed to fail, and he came to believe that eventually the federal government might support a plan to encourage manumissions and the emigration of slaves from the South. Convinced that at least the upper South would assent to it, he introduced on February 18, 1825, a resolution to utilize the public lands and the proceeds from their sale as a fund to aid in the freeing of slaves in the United States and in the removal of slaves and free Negroes beyond the borders of the country:

> *Resolved by the Senate of the United States of America*, That, as soon as the portion of the existing funded debt of the United States, for the payment of which the public land of the United States is pledged, shall have been paid off, then, and thenceforth, the whole of the public land of the United States, with the nett proceeds of all future sales thereof, shall constitute and form a fund, which is hereby appropriated, and the faith of the

12. Fitzpatrick, ed., *Autobiography of Van Buren*, 153–54.

13. *Ibid.*, 154. On this occasion, King acknowledged Van Buren's respect and kindness; despite their differences in the presidential canvass, he said, it was remarkable that so few incidents had threatened their friendship. In Van Buren's words, King remarked that "he owed it to me to say, before we parted, how sensible he was that we were in a very great degree indebted for that exemption to my amiable disposition and self command; and he concluded by pressing me earnestly to pay him a visit on my return home after the adjournment." *Ibid.* Van Buren, relieved and pleased, did visit King on his return to New York. It was the last time they saw each other. *Ibid.*, 154–55.

14. King to Elijah H. Mills, June 14, 1824, King Papers, N.-Y. Hist. Soc.

> United States is pledged, that the said fund shall be inviolably applied to aid the emancipation of such slaves, and the removal of such free persons of color, in any of the said States, as by the laws of the States, respectively, may be allowed to be emancipated, or removed to any territory or country without the limits of the United States of America.[15]

King knew that his bold proposal had no chance of early adoption. Saying he did not wish to debate it or ask for immediate consideration, he offered it as a guide for future action. On motion of Senator Benton, who admired the New Yorker, the plan was ordered to be printed, but it was never taken up.[16] It aroused southern ire, however, and evoked a counter-resolution by Hayne of South Carolina denying the power of Congress to create such a fund dangerous to the slave states and "calculated to disturb the peace and harmony of the Union." Hayne's proposition likewise was not acted upon.[17]

King's resolution was a fitting valedictory for the old veteran of the Missouri controversy. Climaxing the long senatorial career of one who now belonged essentially to the past, the scheme looked to the future. Expatriation of Negroes, slave or free, was no more than what many whites desired, but King's suggestion of employing the nation's greatest natural resource to foster emancipation showed that he now believed it a national responsibility to check slavery.

On the evening of March 5, two days after the expiration of the New Yorker's fourth term as senator, President Adams called on him at his rooms in Williamson's Hotel and asked him to become for a second time minister to England, a post which had previously been offered to Governor Clinton, who, as expected, had turned it down. Astonished, the old Federalist at first declined, protesting that he had made up his mind to retire from public life. Adams persisted. He stressed King's patriotic duty not to refuse important services for

15. *Register of Debates in Congress*, 18 Cong., 2 sess., 623.

16. Despite King's opposition to the admission of Missouri, he liked Benton and gave him advice and aid. Once, after Benton had spoken passionately in the Senate, King came over to him and, in a fatherly way, advised him to moderate his manner, pointing out that in the heat of debate, Benton assumed an air of overbearance and defiance that antagonized the older members. "This was real friendship, enhanced by the kindness of manner, and had its effect," Benton recalled; "I suppressed that speech, through compliment to him, and have studied moderation and forbearance ever since." Thomas Hart Benton, *Thirty Years' View, or, A History of the Working of the American Government for Thirty Years, from 1820 to 1850 . . .*, 2 vols. (N. Y., 1854–56), I, 58.

17. *Register of Debates in Congress*, 18 Cong., 2 sess., 696–97.

which perhaps no one else was as well qualified. The issues to be negotiated were all familiar to the former envoy, who still had many friends in England and was known to the British government. He would thus enjoy an unusual confidence in dealing with boundaries, navigation of the St. Lawrence, trade between British colonies and the United States, and neutral search of ships suspected of being slavers. Further, King's appointment would please the Federalists and would prove the sincerity of Adams's desire to heal party divisions, as expressed in his inaugural message. The President persuaded him to consider accepting the offer. The next day, King left Washington for the last time and returned to his Long Island home.[18]

Torn between his deepest wishes and a sense of duty, and saddened by the death of his daughter-in-law, Charles King's wife, King hesitated to send Adams a definite reply. He was seventy years old, had recently suffered a first attack of gout, and admitted that time had spared neither his body nor his mind. He was unwilling to go to England unless his son John, with wife and children, accompanied him, for he could not bear the thought of a lonely life in an empty London mansion. After consulting his family and a few friends, he finally accepted, on condition that John become secretary of the mission.[19]

King's appointment, announced in April, caused an uproar. The President's deliberately conciliatory gesture to Federalists outraged many Republicans, who seized upon it to show that the door was open to outsiders at the expense of deserving party stalwarts. South-

18. Adams, ed., *Memoirs of John Quincy Adams*, VI, 522–23; King to Christopher Gore, Mar. 22, 1825, King Papers, N.-Y. Hist. Soc.; Timothy Pickering to William Coleman, July 1, 1825, Pickering Papers, Vol. 38, Mass. Hist. Soc. King told Judge Egbert Benson, who told Pickering, that Adams had confessed that he had not thought of King for the mission until 24 hours before their conference. *Ibid.*

19. King to John Quincy Adams, Mar. 22, 1825, Adams to King, Mar. 26, 1825, King to Christopher Gore, Mar. 24, Apr. 4, 1825, King Papers, N.-Y. Hist. Soc.; Timothy Pickering to William Coleman, July 1, 1825, Pickering Papers, Vol. 38, Mass. Hist. Soc.; King, ed., *King Correspondence*, VI, 605–07. "This mission is not of my seeking," King wrote, "nothing could have been more unexpected or less desired, though the Motive of the Offer merited my Respect—a satisfactory settlement with England, and the Union of Parties, are very much to be desired. Whether either be practicable remains to be disclosed. For the first I wish for stronger Confidence . . . . As to the Reunion of Parties, it is not plain to me that it can be literally fulfilled, our system being too free for its continuation but the old Parties cannot endure." King to Harrison G. Otis, Apr. 28, 1825, H. G. Otis Papers, Mass. Hist. Soc.

erners particularly recalled King's Missouri speeches and his recent proposal to use the proceeds from public lands for the manumission of slaves. Newspapers like the Richmond *Enquirer* and Mordecai Noah's *National Advocate* in New York denounced the appointment. Although Noah's patron, Van Buren, wished King health, happiness, and honor, he apparently regarded the President's choice as unfortunate.[20] Thurlow Weed, an Adams supporter, could not imagine any reason strong enough to justify the choice of King, and James Tallmadge later wondered why the President had favored an infirm old Federalist instead of advancing his supporters in New York state.[21] If most Federalists were pleased, the suspicious Timothy Pickering saw King's appointment simply as a reward for supporting Adams during the campaign. The fact that Adams had visited King at Jamaica before the election seemed proof of connivance: "Was not the mission to England arranged at that time—provided Adams should obtain the Presidency?" he wrote.[22]

When eventually King's nomination reached the Senate, several senators tried to block it. Thomas of Illinois objected that the nominee had regretted the extension of the United States across the Mississippi and was hostile to the West. Hayne of South Carolina and Johnson of Kentucky also opposed the appointment. Even Van Buren, who voted for confirmation, was, according to King's son, "cold, very cold, indeed in his acquiescence."[23] In spite of its unpopularity, the appointment was confirmed on December 20, some six months after he had landed in England.

As King made ready for another ocean voyage, he had grave misgivings. "Our old friend Judge Benson says that no one is wise enough to foresee Events that may even be near at hand," he confided to Harrison G. Otis. "Thus a regular sort of man, who for years had been making arrangements to reside soberly and quietly in this village, is of a sudden seized with the madness of abandoning it, and of going abroad: and notwithstanding his advanced age, is busily em-

20. Martin Van Buren to King, Apr. 29, 1825, Charles King to John A. King, July 22, 1825, also Charles King to King, Mar. 9, 1826, King Papers, N.-Y. Hist. Soc.

21. Remini, *Martin Van Buren*, 95; James Tallmadge to John W. Taylor, May 13, 1826, John W. Taylor Papers, N.-Y. Hist. Soc.

22. Pickering to William Coleman, July 1, 1825, Pickering Papers, Vol. 38, Mass. Hist. Soc.

23. Charles King to King, Mar. 9, 1826, King Papers, N.-Y. Hist. Soc.

ployed in preparing to leave the Scene of his promised Repose."[24] King engaged a cabin on the *Pacific*, nonetheless.

Before sailing he became involved in an unpleasant quarrel with the heirs of Alexander Hamilton. In 1810 Judge Nathaniel Pendleton, one of Hamilton's executors, had entrusted to King a sealed package containing a draft in Hamilton's hand of Washington's Farewell Address as well as correspondence between the Treasury Secretary and the first President. Knowing Hamilton's widow to be convinced that her husband had composed the Farewell Address and believing himself that Washington had written it, the judge explained at the time that he wished to prevent the documents from falling into the hands of the Hamilton family. He feared a public controversy which might injure the reputation of Washington.[25] Hamilton's son James claimed that Pendleton had told him in 1824 that the evidence for Hamiltonian authorship of the Farewell Address was "most conclusive" and suggested that he obtain the papers from King. Remembering the remark after Pendleton's death, and at his mother's urging, James Hamilton visited King on May 20, 1825. The old Federalist refused to give up the papers or even allow them to be read. Disappointed, James sent him a letter, renewing his request for the papers, again without success. Then James's brother John rode out to Jamaica and threatened King with legal action. King was deeply affronted. Viewing seriously his obligation to Pendleton, he could not be budged, and his long friendship for the Hamiltons was vaporized in anger. Equally incensed, Mrs. Hamilton sued him.[26]

This painful episode, which so poisoned the relations of the Kings and the Hamiltons, could have been avoided. To have refused Hamil-

24. King to Harrison G. Otis, Apr. 20, 1825, H. G. Otis Papers, Mass. Hist. Soc.

25. "Why Judge Pendleton omitted to keep the papers in his own possession, or preferred their delivery to me, I can explain in no other way, than in his being liable to enquiries respecting them," wrote King to his son Charles, Nov. 26, 1825, King Papers, N.-Y. Hist. Soc.

26. Mrs. Hamilton eventually dropped the suit when, after King's return from England, he voluntarily restored the papers to her family. Embarrassed and probably convinced that he would lose the case, he saved face by stating that a recently published letter by John Jay (arguing that Washington had been the true author of the Farewell Address) had relieved him of his trust. *Reminiscenses of James A. Hamilton; or, Men and Events, at Home and Abroad, during Three Quarters of a Century* (N. Y., 1869), 24–27; James A. Hamilton to King, May 23, 25, 28, 1825, King to James A. Hamilton, May 26, 28 (draft), 1825, King Papers, N.-Y. Hist. Soc.; King, ed., *King Correspondence*, VI, 612–21.

ton's sons even a glance at the papers seems an unduly rigid interpretation of King's responsibility. Like Judge Pendleton, Jay, John Marshall, and Judge Richard Peters, King was overly anxious for the security of Washington's fame. Understandably, he feared that Hamilton's sons would publicly claim that their father had written the Farewell Address.[27] King may also have thought it impolitic to encourage the Hamiltons in anything that might revive their family feud with the Adamses.

On June 1, the day after Mrs. Hamilton's bill of injunction was served upon him, King departed from New York. With him were his son John, the latter's wife, and their four daughters. A Colombian frigate and a cutter moored off the Battery fired salutes as the harbor steamboat transferred its distinguished passenger to the *Pacific* for the ocean voyage. The seas were rough; the envoy, already suffering from intestinal troubles and gout, was seasick every day. When the packet reached Liverpool early in the evening of June 26, the feeble Minister and his party were whisked to the Waterloo Hotel, where King was too ill to accept the invitations that poured in upon him. After several days, on the advice of physicians, he traveled southward to the popular watering resort of Cheltenham, where he spent some weeks imbibing its mineral waters. His health having somewhat improved, he left on August 17 for London, where John had rented a furnished house at 20 Baker Street.[28]

The ailing diplomat was cheered by the flood of friendly letters and invitations from Englishmen he had known at the turn of the century, among them the Earl of Essex, Lord Bexley, Lord Bathurst, Alexander Baring, and George Canning, now Foreign Secretary. Lord Grenville, living in secluded retirement at Dropmore, wrote to King that it was "very gratifying" to think that Anglo-American diplomacy would "pass through the hands of a person as sincerely desirous of promoting good will and friendship between them as I well know you to be."[29]

27. Further, as a lawyer, King would have been reluctant to open any sealed package of documents.

28. King, ed., *King Correspondence*, VI, 622; *Niles' Register*, June 4, 1825; King's note on an undated scrap of paper, now owned by James G. King; King to Christopher Gore, Aug. 11, 1825, King Papers, N.-Y. Hist. Soc.; King to Archibald Gracie, Jr., July 22, 1825, King Papers, Humanities Research Center, Univ. of Texas.

29. Various letters, and specifically Grenville to King, Aug. 25, 1825, King Papers, N.-Y. Hist. Soc.

Before his presentation to the King on November 11, the American Minister prejudiced Canning against him by intervening on behalf of one Charles Bonnycastle, recently appointed as professor of moral philosophy at the new University of Virginia. The professor was the son of a mathematics teacher at Woolwich, the Royal Military Academy and naval dockyard, and had received a free education there upon signing bond not to enter any foreign service without the government's consent; nevertheless, he had sailed to America without obtaining this consent. At Jefferson's request, King sought a remission of the penalty to be imposed on Bonnycastle.[30] He twice asked Canning to intercede with a view to stopping the prosecution on the bond, but the Foreign Secretary declined to intervene, suggesting stiffly that the American envoy obtain a proper application from the professor.[31] King persisted. Sharing President Adams's desire to obliterate the scars of party division in the United States, he wrote frankly to Canning:

> I have no desire to justify the course adopted by this gentleman, indeed I see the case to a given extent, as it has appeared to you; but there are facts connected with the case with which you must be unacquainted, as they have arisen out of our domestic party divisions, in which for more than thirty years I have not belonged to the same camp with Mr. Jefferson. He has belonged to the winning party, I, to the losing one: during his prosperity I commonly lived in retirement. Nothing is however constant; things are now in a course of change, and this is evinced by the overture which Mr. Jefferson becomes the organ of making to me respecting the University of Virginia. I should have been gratified in complying with the request.[32]

Canning, who had not availed himself of the Admiralty's permission to drop the prosecution, now wrote privately to Lord Melville, First Lord of the Admiralty: "Rufus takes the refusal so much to heart that I am inclined now to relent." Instead of giving the envoy exactly what he asked, however, the Foreign Secretary proposed sub-

30. Drafts of King's letters to Canning, King Papers, Vol. 83, *ibid.*; King, ed., *King Correspondence*, VI, 631–32; Willson, *America's Ambassadors to England*, 161–63. Jefferson also asked King to handle the university's funds for the purchase in England of books and scientific apparatus.

31. King to Canning, Aug. 28, Oct. 10, 11, 1825, Canning to King, Private, Oct. 12, 1825, King, ed., *King Correspondence*, VI, 633, 635–36.

32. King to Canning, Oct. 15, 1825, Private and Confidential, *ibid.*, 636–37. A pencilled draft, nearly identical, is in Vol. 83, King Papers, N.-Y. Hist. Soc.

stituting any other man in place of Bonnycastle, whose prosecution would have to be continued, though without exacting the penalty which otherwise King would have to pay.[33] This letter lay on Melville's table for more than a month while his lordship was "shooting (or endeavoring to shoot) pheasants," but ultimately he replied that there was some doubt about the validity of the Bonnycastle bond and that he did not relish Canning's plan, which would allow "Mr. Yankee . . . to be tampering in our Establishment at Portsmouth or elsewhere in our Dock Yards." In any event, it was clear that the professor would remain in America; hence it would be better to abandon the prosecution as a personal favor to the American Minister.[34] The Foreign Secretary consequently informed King that His Majesty's government would suspend the legal proceedings against the delinquent professor. "What *could not* be conceded officially," he wrote, "is yielded to *Mr. King's personal* desire."[35]

Canning's rigid attitude was based largely on principle, but he had also been annoyed by King and was not at first in a mood to accommodate him. The American had transmitted to his government confidential letters from the Foreign Secretary to him, relating to their common aim of inducing Spain to acknowledge the independence of her lost American colonies. When Canning quite properly complained, the envoy excused himself on the ground that the Secretary's own words would produce a stronger effect upon the United States than any précis he himself could have prepared.[36] King had made a tactical blunder that stiffened Canning's attitude.

If King's persistence had borne fruit in the Bonnycastle affair, which was entirely unofficial, it failed to do so in the one official matter to which the envoy gave his full attention: indemnification for slaves and other property carried away from the United States by the British in violation of the Treaty of Ghent. Under an arbitral convention signed in 1822, a mixed commission had met at Washington to determine the amount of the award; the British commissioner

33. Canning to Melville, Oct. 18, 1825, Private, Melville Papers, William L. Clements Library, University of Michigan. Woolwich was the chief dockyard of the Royal Navy, and evidently it was the navy, not the army, which had a claim upon Bonnycastle's services.

34. Melville to Canning, Private, Nov. 21, 1825, *ibid.*

35. Canning to King, Dec. 23, 1825, Private, King, ed., *King Correspondence*, VI, 637–39.

36. Canning to King, Sept. 15, 1825, Confidential, King to Canning, Sept. 21, 1825, King Papers, Vol. 83, N.-Y. Hist. Soc.

had refused to abide by an article of the convention requiring that, if the commissioners failed to agree, the decision should be made by an arbitrator chosen by lot. The American commissioner had held that interest charges should be included in his country's claim, while his British counterpart denied that the convention authorized such payment. The result was a deadlock.

The President had privately advised King before his departure that the slave indemnity commission was "the object of most immediate urgency," and informal instructions from Secretary of State Clay had aimed chiefly at reaching a settlement.[37] As early as October 12, the American Minister intimated to Canning his hope for an adjustment of differences, and although the Foreign Secretary referred the dispute between the American and British commissioners to the Law Officer of the Crown, the matter was not acted upon for three weeks. King sharply reminded Canning of the need for a decision and on December 26 proposed that the commission be terminated and that he and the Foreign Secretary agree upon a fixed sum by way of a compromise.[38] In January, therefore, at Canning's request, the Under-Secretary for Foreign Affairs called on the American envoy, who mentioned $2,000,000. The Foreign Secretary abruptly dismissed the figure as absurdly high, pretending to imagine "some error in Mr. King's proposal."[39] But rather than making a lower counteroffer, as King anticipated, he wrote the American a week later that, since the sum of $2,000,000 was neither reasonable nor a compromise, the opening of a new discussion in London would be a waste of time.[40] Spiritedly, King replied, as Clay had intended, that interest payments were part of a "just indemnification" and maintained that Canning had overlooked compensation for at least ten years' detention of slaves, bringing the total to nearly $2,700,000: "To say that Interest, not being mentioned [in the slave convention]

37. John Quincy Adams to King, May 6, 1825, Private, *ibid*. King had sailed for England without full, formal instructions. Clay, admitting King's greater knowledge of Anglo-American commercial questions relating to the colonial trade, invited the envoy's opinions before he left for England. Henry Clay to King, May 2, 1825, Private, *ibid*., Clay to King, May 10, 1825, *ibid*., Vol. 85.

38. King, ed., *King Correspondence*, VI, 649–52; King to Canning, Nov. 25, Dec. 26, 1825, King Papers, Vol. 83, N.-Y. Hist. Soc.

39. Memorandum in the hand of John A. King, Jan. 18, 1826, King Papers, N.-Y. Hist. Soc. "If there be no error," Canning stated, "it is hardly necessary to add that such a Proposal is at once declined." Canning to King, Jan. 19, 1826, *ibid*., Vol. 83.

40. Canning to King, Jan. 25, 1826, *ibid*.

was not intended to be allowed, may it not be asked, how otherwise is the Indemnification to be measured?"[41] The Foreign Secretary, exchanging heated letters with the American Minister, refused to consider interest payments.

King reported to Clay his belief that Canning had intended the negotiations to fail, and that had a smaller amount been named, it would have met the same fate.[42] He was mistaken. An agreement between the proud and irritable Foreign Secretary and the sick, equally proud, and irascible envoy was not likely, but Albert Gallatin, his successor, would later accept a British offer of $1,200,000 or about $200,000 less than the minimum that King had been authorized to agree upon.[43]

The American Minister never took up with Canning the Maine boundary problem, the navigation of the St. Lawrence, or the duties on cargoes engaged in the West Indian trade. He had doubted from the beginning of his mission that he could effect early solutions.[44] Finding the British government preoccupied with its own pressing issues, he did not even initiate discussion of these questions.

Upset over the Foreign Secretary's brusque rejection of his offer to compromise the slave indemnity, and still in precarious health, King resigned the mission on March 20, nine months after his arrival in England. He could not, in his weakened state, face the prospect of long and futile negotiations, whatever the subject. As he wrote the President, "The Transfer to Washington of matters entrusted to me at this Post is an indignity to my feelings, and evinces a defect of confidence in me as the Representative of the United States, which I feel cannot but impair my influence in the future Execution of this Trust. A treatment so wholly undeserved I am not willing to endure."[45] Clay, in sending letters of recall, expressed Adams's satisfaction with King's ministry.[46]

41. King to Canning, Jan. 26, 1826, *ibid.*

42. King to Henry Clay, Feb. 13, 1826, *ibid.*, Vol. 82.

43. King, ed., *King Correspondence*, VI, 654*n*, 663; Adams, ed., *Memoirs of John Quincy Adams*, VII, 213; Willson, *America's Ambassadors to England*, 165.

44. King to Clay, May 6, 1825, King Papers, N.-Y. Hist. Soc.

45. King to John Quincy Adams, Mar. 29, 1826, *ibid.*, Box 84. Canning had suggested that the Anglo-American commission resume its proceedings in Washington. Canning to King, Jan. 25, 1826, *ibid.*, Vol. 83.

46. Clay to King, May 2, 1826, King Papers, N.-Y. Hist. Soc. To King's son Adams wrote: "I deeply lament the loss of your father's services to the public, but believe the nation has too strong a sense of justice to consider the misfor-

At his father's request, Frederick King, now a practicing physician in New York and recently married, came with his wife to England in order to minister en route to the returning envoy. With them and the wife and daughters of John King, who remained in England as secretary of the legation, King left London for the last time. The party embarked on the *Acasta*, which hoisted anchor at Cowes on July 8, and after a calm voyage, they stepped ashore at New York on August 15.[47]

Still very weak from his now chronic indigestion, King rested for a few weeks in the city at his son James's house on Bond Street, James's elder children having been sent away to Mrs. Gore's care. "Poor Grandpapa King," he wrote them, "could not bear any noise; he occupies Mama's Bedroom and sits in the Backroom on the same floor, all of which is set apart for his use and that of Eve Bush (my old nurse) who attends most faithfully on her old master."[48] Soon the aged gentleman returned to his home on Long Island, where he was waited upon by Eve Bush and several other servants.

At Jamaica he grew weaker. He saw little company, though from time to time his sons rode out from the city to be with him. His next-door neighbor, Cornelius Bogert, thought the old statesman's mind was impaired.[49] "There is no perennial spring of life," King himself observed despondently. "Since leaving America the tide has seemed to constantly ebb, and it cannot be long before it neaps. . . . Darkness and night seem to be near at hand. I may endure a little while longer, but it must be short; my Reason and increasing weakness tell me this Fact."[50]

Small matters loomed large to the emaciated master of the house.

---

tune of his illness as matter of censure either upon him or upon the administration." John Quincy Adams to Charles King, May 3, 1826, Private and Confidential, King, ed., *King Correspondence*, VI, 671. Before receiving King's letter of resignation, the Cabinet had considered associating another minister with him. Charles King to John A. King, Apr. 24, 1826, King Papers, N.-Y. Hist. Soc.; Daniel Webster to Jeremiah Mason, May 2, 1826, Private, Clark, ed., *Memoirs of Jeremiah Mason*, 297.

47. King to Henry Clay, June 27, 1826, John A. King to Clay, July 21, 1826, King Papers, N.-Y. Hist. Soc., N. Y. *American*, Aug. 16, 1826.

48. James G. King to Caroline King *et al.*, Aug. 19, 1826, owned by the present James G. King.

49. William Coleman to Timothy Pickering, Sept. 24, 1826, Pickering Papers, Vol. 32, Mass. Hist. Soc.

50. Entry for Oct. 11, 1826, King's journal, owned by James G. King. See also subsequent entries.

He was ever more preoccupied with his physical symptoms. On one occasion he had another attack of gout: "I am told I eat *too much pepper*. Must cut down," he recorded, adding that the cook did not cut his meat into small enough pieces for his stew. He was irascible. The kitchen help were using too much butter, he thought, so he ordered its purchase in the village as a check on their consumption. His servant William came home drunk one night, ordered the cook about, and shut her out of the parlor. After calling the servants together to stop their petty feuds, King wrote in his journal: "These are trifles; but in my state they become important. Little things which gain my attention; this forms a portion of my malady." He was irked at his son James for not immediately sending his writing desk from New York, and, learning of James's annoyance at his father's peevishness, contritely recorded, "I submit to the will of a merciful Providence, hoping that I may avoid impatience and all manifestation of the want of submission."[51]

Loss of memory and clear thinking greatly distressed King, who had always relied upon an unusually retentive mind. "Providence denies me the Preservation of Understanding and Memory," he observed. "I suffer no pain, but have little of the Comforts of memory; how the Scene will close is Known to the author who continues it, and I am resigned to his power and grateful for his Mercies. . . . God's will be done, and may I be thankful; if I could utter a wish, it should be for understanding; and that *it might have been* continued." On November 8, he recorded his almost total failure of memory and suspected, erroneously, that he was having hallucinations.[52]

Late in the year he moved to New York, where he was cared for by members of the family and examined more frequently by his son Frederick. His meager strength ebbed, however, and he no longer wished to live. He took to his bed in March and thereafter slept most of the time. Although not in pain, he lost his appetite and wasted away.[53]

On April 29, at the age of seventy-two, Rufus King died. Peace-

51. Entries for Oct. 27, 30, Nov. 1, 2, 3, 8, 10, 1826, *ibid.*; the entry for Nov. 11 mentions preparations to move into New York City.

52. Entries for Oct. 20, Nov. 8, 1826, *ibid.*

53. Entry for Nov. 20, 1826, *ibid.*; William Coleman to Timothy Pickering, Feb. 11, 1827, Pickering Papers, Vol. 32, Mass. Hist. Soc.; John A. King to Edward King, Mar. 25, 1827, Frederick G. King to Edward King, Apr. 26, 1827, King Papers, Cincinnati Hist. Soc. King evidently spent his last days in a rented house on lower Broadway.

fully resigned to the inevitable, he had been conscious, until a few hours before the end, of the presence of his sons. The funeral was held at Jamaica on May 2. According to his wish, King was buried between his wife and the first wife of his son Charles in Grace Churchyard near his Jamaica home in a grave marked by a plain white stone. In New York City the members of the Common Council voted to wear crepe mourning bands on their left arms for thirty days.[54]

As executors of the estate, John, Charles, and James followed their father's instructions and equitably apportioned his property, valued at $140,000, among his heirs. The faithful old servant, Eve Bush, received an annuity of $100 for the rest of her life.[55] Though not specifically mentioned in King's will, the farm in Jamaica fell to John, who shared his father's taste for the life of a country gentleman and who occupied the mansion for forty years afterward.

Other enthusiasms of King were reflected in his children. John, the farmer and politician, became Governor of New York; Charles, the editor, became president of Columbia College. James carried on in international business and commercial banking, which had intensely interested his father. Edward was a lawyer, as his father had been before entering public life, and a legislator in Ohio. Frederick, reflecting in some measure his father's liking for applied science, was a physician and lecturer on anatomy, who died only two years after his father. As a parent who had carefully supervised the education of his sons, Rufus King was rewarded by their varied and useful lives.

54. Despite the Reverend Mr. Sayres's efforts to discourage drinking on such occasions, the custom had persisted, and King's funeral was no exception. It was a warm day, and waiters circulated indoors and out with silver trays loaded with decanters, glasses, and cigars. John A. King to Edward King, May 5, 1827, James G. King to Edward King, Apr. 30, 1827, King Papers, Cincinnati Hist. Soc.; James G. King to William King, Apr. 30, 1827, William King Papers, Maine Hist. Soc.; unidentified clipping mounted in Henry Onderdonk, Jr., *Jamaica Centennial, July 4th 1876. Also Recollections of School and College Life* (Jamaica, N. Y., 1876), 41, in the N. Y. Pub. Lib.; King's MS dated Oct. 11 [1826], now owned by James G. King; *Minutes of the Common Council of the City of New York, 1784–1831* (N. Y., 1917), XVI (1827–28), 259.

55. Rufus King's will, probated May 4, 1827, Record of Wills, Surrogate's Court, Hall of Records, New York City; John A. King to Edward King, May 5, 1827, King Papers, Cincinnati Hist. Soc.

CHAPTER XXI

RUFUS KING: AN APPRAISAL

THE CAREER OF RUFUS KING SPANNED THE FORMATIVE PERIOD OF THE United States. As a young statesman he evinced the vitality, ambition, and widely recognized ability that pointed to a bright political future. He effectively served Massachusetts and the still imperfect union under the Confederation, laboring on innumerable committees of the old Congress and becoming involved in nearly every aspect of its work. He played a constructive part in the forging of the Constitution of the United States and was highly influential in securing the ratification of Massachusetts. After taking up residence in New York, he was elected as one of that state's first two senators. With Ellsworth, Cabot, and Strong, he became a bulwark of Washington's administration in the Senate, and he fought valiantly for Jay's Treaty. His personal friendship with and loyalty to Alexander Hamilton, his powerful support of Hamiltonian fiscal measures, and their later collaboration in writing the "Camillus" papers marked King, with the possible exception of Jay, as the leading Hamiltonian Federalist.

His first mission to England removed him from the intra-party warfare that flared between President Adams and Hamilton's partisans. A moderate in politics as in everything else, he avoided the extremism of other Hamiltonians, and he remained on good terms with Adams. Unlike the High Federalists at home, he continued to serve the administration loyally when he disapproved of the President's policies. As a diplomat, his ability and initiative contributed enormously to what has been called the "first rapprochement" between Great Britain and the United States, and President Jefferson acknowledged his effectiveness by retaining him at London until he asked to be recalled. Seven years of difficult diplomacy, however, left the envoy less buoyant than in his Senate days, and upon his return to America at the age of forty-eight, he yearned for a quiet life on a country estate.

If, in the years after his London mission, King was remiss, it was in preferring retirement to active leadership. After Hamilton's death, he was the logical heir to the brilliant Federalist's political influence, but he was cautious, too little the initiator of measures, too lacking in popularity and personal magnetism to fill that void. He insisted, however, on maintaining his party's integrity and resisted all attempts to subordinate it to sectional or personal ambitions. He discouraged Pickering's disunionism and later unsuccessfully opposed Federalist endorsement of DeWitt Clinton for the presidency.

King's return to public life in 1813, occasioned by the War of 1812, was the beginning of his longest period of service in the Senate; unlike most Federalists, he was so aroused by American reverses, and particularly by the British attack on Washington, that he gave his support unreservedly to Madison's war effort. One of a small Federalist minority in the Senate, his efforts to shape fiscal and commercial policy were largely unavailing, except for his collaborative work on the Senate's finance and foreign relations committees. His hopeless candidacy for the presidency in 1816 is noteworthy mainly because he was the last Federalist to make the race. As his party disintegrated nationally, he continued to work in the Senate with new and younger Republican colleagues with whom he had little in common. Though wrongly accused of personal ambition in his later years, he crusaded against the admission of Missouri as a slave state and worked against the caucus system in state and national politics. Finally, after two periods totaling nineteen years in the upper house, he undertook another mission to England at the insistence of President John Quincy Adams—hoping, like Adams himself, that he might contribute to the calming of party animosities at home and apply his experience to the negotiation of key diplomatic and commercial questions. Illness, however, destroyed his customary equilibrium, and he failed to create with Canning the kind of rapport he had enjoyed with Grenville thirty years earlier. The mission was an utter failure, a sad anticlimax to a long and useful public life.

King's irritability in his later years was uncharacteristic, but throughout his life he had been proud, and both his appearance and manner seemed somewhat austere, especially to those who did not know him. He generally shunned controversy, and tried–not always successfully–to avoid giving offense. His natural reserve suggested a coldness which was more apparent than real. Lacking the common touch, he could not trim his sails to capture the popular breeze, nor did his aristocratic bearing and habit of wearing smallclothes in public long after they had gone out of fashion recommend him to a rising generation devoted to political democracy. As one contemporary put it, he no doubt had "something of pride and hauteur in his manner, offensive to the spirit of republicanism, and inconsistent with the nature of equality."[1]

In public life King was known as a leader of measures, not of men. After his return to the Senate in 1813 his minority voice soon identified him as a champion of the lost cause which Federalism had become. Harrison G. Otis expressed to him in 1823 the wish that "whoever writes your epitaph . . . may be able to say that you continued many years at your post, the last of the Romans."[2] If the only major legislation for which King bore full responsibility as principal author and sponsor was the Navigation Act of 1818, his work on key committees was both conscientious and productive. His determined struggle to prevent the extension of slavery and his final proposal that funds from the public lands be used to aid the emancipation of slaves show him deeply concerned about northern power in the Union and increasingly interested in an equitable and humane solution to the problem of slavery.

In an era when eloquence was admired for its own sake, King's oratorical prowess was early and widely recognized. His "graceful attitude" and "fine flow of words," together with his factual knowledge, were said in 1785 to have given him an unrivaled influence in the old Congress, and soon thereafter he was reputed to be the most eloquent man in the United States.[3] Webster considered King in 1814

1. William Faux, *Memorable Days in America: Being a Journal of a Tour to the United States . . .* (London, 1823), 136–37.

2. Harrison G. Otis to King, Jan. 1, 1823, "It is also certain that you prevent a great deal of mischief, and keep in check the framers of crude projects and cunning devices." King Papers, N.-Y. Hist. Soc.

3. Burnett, ed., *Letters of the Continental Congress*, VIII, 267; Brissot de Warville, *Nouveau Voyage*, I, 170.

unequalled in dignity, force, and effectiveness as a speaker.[4] As time passed, his style became more sedate, his effectiveness depending upon comprehensiveness and logic rather than fervor.

King's basic values were those held by all leading Federalists. He believed in social distinctions, and in general he opposed the lowering of property qualifications for voting, though in 1821 he voted for the democratic revisions of the New York state constitution. He held an exalted opinion of the judiciary and a scrupulous respect for legal and constitutional niceties. Like other Federalists, he rejected ideology as a guide to public policy. Human experience, not reason, was in his view the best test of what was enduring and what was not:

> There is an endless ebb and flood in human affairs; and the great secret of Life is to know when and where we are to cease in our Efforts to mend or improve our Condition. I do not make the observation with the vain purpose of repining at what has become irrevocable, but to confirm a truth which it is useful to establish, and which should convince us that Experience and its lessons are safer Guides than the deductions of our Reason, which after the utmost caution, are much influenced by the prevailing course of things, and the success of measures undertaken without prudence.[5]

The study of history, to which King was devoted, offered the best clues to policy-making. Like Madison and others in the Philadelphia Convention of 1787, he did not hesitate to bring historical knowledge to bear upon problems at hand. He was fortunate in possessing an extraordinary memory, which served him well in public life, and, as a careful observer of men and events in his own time, he often surprised listeners with his precise knowledge of details, so that his statements, particularly in his later years, were usually taken for granted.[6]

Few men, perhaps, were better equipped to write a history of their time, and it is unfortunate that he kept no sustained journal and wrote no memoirs, for he was exact and painstaking. His occa-

4. Daniel Webster to Ezekiel Webster, Feb. 5, 1814, J. W. McIntyre, ed., *The Writings and Speeches of Daniel Webster*, National ed., 18 vols. (Boston, 1903), XVII, 241. Jeremiah Mason considered King as the ablest man and the greatest orator he had ever known. Clark, ed., *Memoirs of Jeremiah Mason*, 57n.

5. King to Edward King, June 13, 1820, King Papers, Cincinnati Hist. Soc.

6. A contemporary appraisal which stresses the point is Faux, *Memorable Days in America*, 364.

sional memoranda were factual, usually objective in tone, and expressed few judgments on men and motives comparable to the pungent thrusts found, for example, in the memoirs of the Adamses.

Above all, King was a constitutionalist. Temperament, classical education at Harvard, and legal training under the conservative Theophilus Parsons made him an advocate of balanced government. As a Massachusetts delegate to the Congress of the Confederation, he had taken a provincial view of his state's interests, but he was shocked by Shays's Rebellion as well as deeply influenced by Hamilton and in the Philadelphia Convention threw his weight toward a strong central government. He shared responsibility for the clause in the United States Constitution forbidding the states to impair the obligation of contracts. Though he personally disapproved of parts of it, he defended the Constitution as promising a practical adjustment of conflicting interests and as affording a means of raising the stature of the United States in the eyes of Europe. Intrigued with constitutional questions, he raised them many times in Senate debates, notably on the Missouri issue and as an elder statesman in the New York state constitutional convention of 1821.

An ardent patriot but at the same time a northern sectionalist, King was never as extreme a nationalist as Hamilton or Marshall. He was concerned about the sovereign rights of the states, but after the adoption of the federal Constitution he never flirted with disunion as many New England Federalists did, though he was erroneously suspected of it. As a New Yorker he maintained New England friendships, and his lifelong interest in shipping and finance reveals ties that were essentially northern. As far as is known, he traveled no farther west than Harrisburg, Pennsylvania, and no farther south than Washington. None of his intimate friends were southerners, but although repelled by the views of some southerners, he held others in great respect, notably Washington, Marshall, and Charles Cotesworth Pinckney. From first to last, however, he hoped that northern and antislavery interests would prevail in the Union.

King invariably assigned the ambitious and unprincipled politician to the lowest circle of his political hell. Burr,[7] Crawford, and DeWitt Clinton he consigned to this category. Ignoring Clinton's genuine ability, King saw him through a narrow angle of vision as a Machia-

7. King was said to have remarked of Burr, "Nothing will satisfy that man but the throne of God!" William Plumer, Memorandum, entry for Dec. 24, 1806, Lib. Cong.

vellian who would exploit any means to gain and keep power. When the Federalists were climbing on the Clinton bandwagon in 1812, he warned them to keep their party pure and lose the election rather than support Clinton and lose their party. Because he lacked the gift of the political organizer, he never fully understood Clinton's *modus operandi*, and if he saw in Clinton no sincere ideological commitment, the latter presumably considered him a stickler for outmoded Federalist principles. Yet despite their differences, these two well-educated lawyers shared aristocratic tastes, and—to a degree—conservative connections. Their letters to each other on public issues were so friendly in tone that one cannot discern from them any political antagonism.[8]

King was clearly prejudiced against foreigners with the exception of the British, though he claimed to have no specific dislike of the Irish who hated him for his effort to prevent the banishment to the United States of the Irish rebel leaders of 1798. He was blind to Gallatin's great ability and, while briefly in Geneva in 1802, took pains to inquire into his family background. The alien laws of 1798 were enacted during his absence in London, but he approved them and all his life retained an anti-French bias.

Francophiles like Jefferson and Franklin were not appreciated by King, who regarded the former as a visionary and the latter as untrustworthy, not for his libertinism but for his diplomacy. He ignored Franklin's contribution to the harmony of Franco-American relations during the Revolutionary War. "Franklin has been an Old Rogue throughout," he was said to have remarked many years after the war, and when Franklin died, King was among those who defeated a motion in the Senate to wear mourning.[9]

Ambitious and determined as a young man to make something of himself, King took on the fashions of society, married well, and acquired riches. Wealth, however, remained for him but a means to a cultivated life: to buy and enjoy books, to maintain a country seat, and to secure the best education for his children. In the United

8. See, for example, Clinton to King, Dec. 13, 1817, Vol. 19, and King to Clinton, Jan. 4, 1818, Vol. 8, Clinton Papers, Columbia Univ. Lib., revealing their common interest in the progress of the Erie Canal.

9. Timothy Pickering to William Coleman, July 1, 1825, Pickering Papers, Vol. 38, Mass. Hist. Soc.; King to John Adams, Oct. 27, 1787, King, ed., *King Correspondence*, I, 261–62; King to Benjamin Franklin, Sept. 9, 1786, Franklin Papers, XXXIV, 141, American Philosophical Society, Phila.; Maclay, *Journal*, 240.

States, wealth was a convenient but "ignoble" distinction, he wrote his son Edward in 1820; "there is no other Country, not England even, in which by integrity, Diligence, perseverence and economy a man of Education can more instantly attain to Distinction than in the U. S.,—not that which acres and Dollars confer, but a distinction which wealth cannot buy, and to which it must pay Homage."[10]

At heart, King was an individualist, a believer in freedom of enterprise. His steady and strong bias in favor of merchants and propertied men marked his system of politics. "National wealth does not consist in *Gold and Silver*," he noted in 1820, "but in the productive powers of Land and Labour."[11] As a gentleman farmer he respected in agriculture and pasturage the cooperation of nature's energy and the industry of man, which produced qualities of strength and contentment and which discouraged laziness, intemperance, and avarice.[12] Friends speculated in lands, but he disliked speculation of any kind and scrupulously avoided it, and his insistence that lands should be sold only for cash had its effect upon public land policy.

Except for Marshall, King was the last of the original Federalists who, without joining the Republicans, enjoyed a continuing national reputation. It was unfortunate for him that when he had reached a position of leadership, his party was in its long twilight. Had he lived at an earlier or a later time, his political talents might have led to high executive office. As a diplomat or as a senator, he served during the administrations of the first six presidents, a record matched only by the sixth President himself, John Quincy Adams. The embodiment of political moderation, the conscience of his party, King was not marked for popular leadership, and he would not cooperate with a younger generation of Federalists who tried to master Republican organizational techniques and appeals to the people. As elder statesman, he stood on the rocks of Federalism, watching the democratic

10. King to Edward King, June 5, 1820, King Papers, Lilly Lib., Indiana Univ. King's income was derived from careful investments, mortgages, and rents. Some indication of his New York City real estate is afforded by Charles Osborne's Account Book, 1814–1828, N. Y. Pub. Lib., which shows rents collected and taxes paid for King from Sept. 1820 to May 1822. The bankruptcy in 1823 of Archibald Gracie & Sons, a firm in which King had a personal and financial interest, caused him considerable loss and much worry in his old age.

11. King's notebook, 1820, owned by James G. King.

12. *Ibid.* Forgetting his alarm at Shays's Rebellion in 1786–87, he asserted that husbandmen were "the best materials for a good form of Government and the least disposed to distrust the Government under which they live." *Ibid.*

tide roll in. The swirling waters surrounded him, but he remained firm, recognizing that history had passed him by.

Rufus King had the solid qualities of character that distinguished moderate Federalism. He embodied Christian and classical virtues in almost equal measure. His often intense partisanship was anchored in principle, and his firm political integrity and deep patriotism were a credit to his party, to his country, and to his age.

NOTE ON SOURCES

NOTE ON SOURCES

THE MAJOR COLLECTION OF RUFUS KING MANUSCRIPTS IS IN THE NEW-York Historical Society, where King's private library is also housed. The King Papers are a rich storehouse of information about not only King but also his many correspondents. Of the twenty-five boxes (mostly arranged in chronological order), fifty-two bound volumes, and four envelopes, much is of special interest, such as Box A (folders relating to the mobbing of Richard King, and letters relating to Francisco de Miranda), Box 1 (notes of the Constitutional Convention of 1787), Box 80 (King's correspondence with John Trumbull, 1809–22), Box "82–83–85" (King's letters to Henry Clay and George Canning's to King, 1825–26), and Box 87 (King's letters to John Laurance, 1793–99).

The bound volumes in this collection include letterbooks of private and official diplomatic correspondence, most written during King's first mission to England, 1796–1803. Especially important is Volume 28, with twenty-seven letters from Alexander Hamilton to King, and copies of five letters from King to Hamilton, 1787–99. Notebooks kept by King include memoranda of diplomatic discussions, excerpts from books read, and a brief account of a journey on the Continent in 1802. Volume 69 contains letters to and from John Alsop, King's father-in-law. Volume 73 lists books in King's library when it was appraised after his death. An unusually systematic person, King kept copies of all his diplomatic correspondence; in addition his papers include copies of official correspondence relating to Jay's negotiations in London in 1794 and three letterbooks of the diplomatic correspondence of King's predecessor in England, Thomas Pinckney, 1792–96.

Mr. James Gore King of New York has private letters, notebooks, and account books of his great-great-grandfather, and also volumes of copied materials related to Rufus King and his family. These afford greater insight into the personality of King than can be derived from most of the other collections.

Important repositories of King papers are the Henry E. Huntington Library (for correspondence while King was Minister to England, 1796–1803), the Cincinnati Historical Society (particularly for King's letters to his son Edward), the Lilly Library of Indiana University (also for letters to Edward), and the Library of the University of Texas. In the Columbia University Libraries are early letters of Rufus King to Daniel Kilham and letters to or from King in several collections, as well as papers of King's half-brother Cyrus. The Goodhue Papers in the New York Society Library include a folder of King manuscripts, and other small collections of King papers are in the Boston Public Library, the Queens Borough Public Library, New York, and the New York Public Library (which in addition has Charles Osborn's record of New York City property rents collected for clients, 1814–28, of whom King was one). The Free Library of Philadelphia has a remarkable early letter from King to Samuel Sewall, March 22, 1782, and numerous letters to King relating to his mission abroad, 1796–1802. The William King Papers in the Maine Historical Society contain letters of Rufus King to his half-brother William. In the Essex County Court House, Salem, Massachusetts, are dockets of King's law cases.

There appears to be no large group of King letters in England, other than those in the collection of Grenville papers at Boconnoc, Lostwithiel, Cornwall; these are almost entirely political and reveal little of the personality or philosophy of Rufus King. The King-Grenville correspondence and other documents in the Public Record Office likewise afford little appreciation of King's individuality.

Of the various additional manuscript collections consulted for this biography, a few deserve special comment. The Harvard University Archives afforded clues to King's activities in college. The papers of Caleb Davis, Henry Knox, Harrison G. Otis, and particularly Theodore Sedgwick and Timothy Pickering in the Massachusetts Historical Society delineated King's relations with New England Federalists. The Hamilton, Washington, Jefferson, Madison, Gallatin, Monroe, and Van Buren Papers in the Library of Congress proved essential to this study, as did the Jay, Gouverneur Morris, and DeWitt Clinton Papers in the Columbia University Libraries, and the Robert R. Livingston Papers at the New-York Historical Society. Also useful were the Jeremiah Wadsworth Papers and the Oliver Wolcott Papers at the Connecticut Historical Society, particularly the latter for Wolcott's fascinating correspondence with King during the War of 1812. Several collections of the

Historical Society of Pennsylvania contain important King letters, and the Society's Jonathan Roberts Papers illuminate King's crusade against slavery in Missouri. The Henry Wheaton Papers in the Pierpont Morgan Library reveal King's exertions for electoral reform in New York state in 1823–24.

INDEX

INDEX

C

H

I

Q

R

X

Y